At the Far Reaches of Empire

C·DE·N
QUADRA

At the Far Reaches of Empire

The Life of Juan Francisco de la Bodega y Quadra

FREEMAN M. TOVELL

UBC Press • Vancouver • Toronto

17 16 15 14 13 12 11 10 09 08   5 4 3 2 1

Printed in Canada with vegetable-based inks on ancient-forest-free paper (100% post-consumer recycled) that is processed chlorine- and acid-free.

Library and Archives Canada Cataloguing in Publication Data

Tovell, Freeman
At the far reaches of empire : the life of Juan Francisco de la Bodega y Quadra / Freeman M. Tovell.

Includes bibliographical references and index.
ISBN 978-0-7748-1366-2

1. Bodega y Cuadra, Juan de la, 1743-1794. 2. Bodega y Cuadra, Juan de la, 1743-1794 – Travel – Pacific Coast (North America). 3. Pacific Coast (North America) – Discovery and exploration – Spanish. 4. Pacific Coast (North America) – Description and travel. 5. Explorers – Spain – Biography. 6. Explorers – Pacific Coast (North America) – Biography. I. Title.

F851.5.T678 2008   917.904′1092   C2007-907481-2

Canada

UBC Press gratefully acknowledges the financial support for our publishing program of the Government of Canada through the Book Publishing Industry Development Program (BPIDP), and of the Canada Council for the Arts, and the British Columbia Arts Council.

This book has been published with the help of a grant from the Canadian Federation for the Humanities and Social Sciences, through the Aid to Scholarly Publications Programme, using funds provided by the Social Sciences and Humanities Research Council of Canada.

UBC Press
The University of British Columbia
2029 West Mall
Vancouver, BC V6T 1Z2
604-822-5959 / Fax: 604-822-6083
www.ubcpress.ca

Frontispiece: Medallion depicting Juan Francisco de la Bodega y Quadra. No portraits of Bodega made during his lifetime have survived, but this image by Juan Avalos captures his determined and intrepid spirit. The government of Spain presented this plaque to the Canadian Coast Guard in 1966 on the occasion of the launching of CGS *Quadra*. When the vessel was decommissioned, the plaque went to the Canadian Coast Guard offices in Victoria, British Columbia.
Photograph by Freeman Tovell.

To my wife,
Rosita,
for her constant encouragement and care

Contents

Appendixes

Illustrations

Maps

Plates

Following page 186

Preface and Acknowledgments

Capitán de Navío Juan Francisco de la Bodega y Quadra was the pre-eminent Spanish naval officer in the period 1774 to 1794 on the Pacific coast of North America. Today, the services that Bodega y Quadra rendered are honoured in his native Peru as well as in Mexico, Spain, and Canada. The name Quadra adorns an island and a thoroughfare in Victoria, British Columbia. In California, his name lives on in Bodega Bay, where he stopped in 1775 at the end of his first perilous voyage into northern waters.

The Spanish surnames that dot the natural features and waterways of the Pacific coast, such as Valdes, Haro, Malaspina, Galiano, and Quadra, recall the voyagers who substantially advanced, each in his own way, knowledge of the geography, ethnography, and natural history of this rugged and mist-shrouded region. Collectively, these Spanish explorers were a diverse and uniquely skilled assembly of talents and abilities. Unlike most of the Russian, British, French, and American voyagers in the region at this time, they were not interested in trade. All were career naval officers; many would later rise to senior positions; five would achieve flag rank; and two are buried in Spain's Pantheon of Illustrious Mariners at Cádiz. Juan Francisco de la Bodega y Quadra Mollinedo stands foremost among this accomplished group.

Bodega y Quadra was a success as a maritime explorer. He reached 58°N on the Pacific Northwest Coast in 1775 while commanding a twenty-four-foot schooner, and he was the first to chart the coast as far north as Prince William Sound. In 1779 he returned to explore and chart the entrance to Prince William Sound, Alaska. Twice he was commandant of the Naval Department of San Blas, Nayarit, Mexico, during its busiest period. It was the home port from which northerly explorations were launched as well as the base that supplied the infant Spanish settlements and presidios or garrisons of today's California. Under Bodega's direction, Spanish ships searched for the fabled Northwest Passage and surveyed and charted the continent's coast. Bodega also distinguished himself as a diplomat in an attempt, with Captain George Vancouver, to arrange the transfer to Britain of the Spanish establishment at Yuquot – today's Friendly Cove on Nootka Sound, Vancouver Island – under the terms of the 1790 Nootka Convention, which narrowly averted a war between Spain and Great Britain.

Bodega y Quadra was typical of the new class of naval officers who were the core of the Enlightened Navy of King Carlos III. Born in Peru into a distinguished family, Bodega graduated from the Naval Academy in Cádiz, Spain. Viewed by his superiors as a potential maritime explorer, he was given special training in the newest methods of navigation and cartography. Intelligent, observant, and literate, he received high praise from the two viceroys of New Spain he served, Antonio Bucareli and the second Conde de Revillagigedo. He was lauded by all who came in contact with him for his charm, generosity, and consideration in matters large and small. His enlightened policy toward the Nootkan people and his close association with Chief Maquinna are a matter of record, and his cordial hospitality to all, including his British rival George Vancouver, has been universally admired.

Such praise is deserved, but Bodega had his imperfections. He incurred enormous debts when his overarching ambition to make a name for himself in his chosen career exceeded his financial circumstances. Serving on the outer edge of the empire, he lacked the support of an influential patron at the Spanish royal court. Furthermore, as a colonial-born subject from Peru, he was hampered by the governmental prejudice that hindered colonial subjects seeking high rank in the church and government. Despite his constant efforts to be promoted from four-ring captain to flag rank, he was never able to gain full recognition for his achievements from his naval superiors and political masters.

A number of friends have asked me what led to my research on Bodega y Quadra's life and times. It was a natural evolution: an early interest in maritime exploration became a lifelong one, having been shaped and sharpened considerably at the age of fourteen, when my parents augmented my boyhood library with the Anderson (1784) edition of *Cook's Voyages* and, later, with the two very large 1764 volumes of *Harris's Voyages.*

The second element of my interest emerged when, while serving in

Canada's foreign service, I held two diplomatic postings in Peru. This enabled me to gain some insights into the character of Spain's colonial society and history; at the same time it allowed me to develop a working knowledge of Spanish, which made research into primary documents possible.

Third and finally, as Foreign Service Visitor at the University of Victoria, I realized that in Canada, the record of Spanish exploration of the Pacific coast of the North American continent is scarcely known or appreciated. I hope this new material will help Bodega find his rightful place among better-known maritime explorers of the Pacific Ocean and show the extent of the Spanish presence in these regions.

In undertaking this study, which stretched over more than fifteen years, I must first thank the Social Sciences and Humanities Research Council for a grant that enabled me to undertake the necessary research in Mexico and Spain, in the Huntington Library in San Marino near Los Angeles, and in the Bancroft Library at the University of California, Berkeley.

This research rested primarily on official reports and correspondence and on other documents found in the vast archival institutions of Spain – in particular, the Archivo Histórico Nacional and the Museo Naval in Madrid, the Archivo General de Indias in Seville, and the Archivo General de Simancas in Valladolid – and in Mexico at the Archivo General de la Nación in Mexico City. To a lesser extent, supplementary materials were found in the diaries and ships' logs of the Spanish, English, and American seamen with whom Bodega came into contact.

Because Spanish naval officers seldom if ever commented on one another, very little of consequence is to be learned from those closely associated with Bodega. The most regrettable gap, however, is the absence of any personal papers, such as correspondence with relatives or friends, which would provide insights into his personal and private life. One longs for the discovery of a box of such material in some attic or archive.

In the course of researching and writing this work, I have received much assistance from a number of people. Some are mentioned in the footnotes and some are not, but to all I am most grateful.

Of those who have contributed significantly to my task, I would mention Dr. Christon I. Archer, professor of history at the University of Calgary, who first aroused my interest in the Spanish presence in the Pacific Northwest. I would couple his name with that of Dr. Donald C. Cutter, professor emeritus at the University of New Mexico, an acknowledged authority on the history of the Spanish era in the American Southwest and in California. Their counsel was frequently sought and freely given.

I owe a special debt of gratitude to the late Dr. W. Kaye Lamb for his constant interest and encouragement. I derived much benefit from his deep knowledge of the exploration of the Canadian West and, in particular, of the career of Captain George Vancouver.

A number of people have been of incalculable assistance as the manuscript evolved and finally emerged. The late Vivian C. Fisher, head of the Microforms Division of the Bancroft Library, University of California, Berkeley, gave unstinting help both while at the library, retrieving documents on microfilm in the Bancroft's collections, and later in retirement, by locating documents I required and volunteering others she thought would be of interest. Dr. W. Michael Mathes, formerly of the University of San Francisco and a recognized authority on the early Spanish voyages, has given me constant advice on matters pertaining to the Catholic Church in New Spain. His familiarity with the Mexican archives both in Mexico City and in Guadalajara has been most useful. I must acknowledge the assistance of two senior members of the staff of the Museo Naval, Madrid, for without María Luisa Martín-Merás and María Dolores Higueras, I would have become lost in the museum's rich holdings.

Ethnologist Richard Inglis's first-hand knowledge of the Mowachaht-Muchalaht First Nations has guided me around the dangers that await a stranger venturing into their history and culture. Our conversations have been absorbing and wide-ranging. His support has been invaluable.

Camilla Turner refined the manuscript in the later stages of its development. Her skills as an experienced editor have been well honed in working with other authors and organizations, and she has been a joy to work with. Robin Inglis, president of the Vancouver Spanish Pacific Historical Society, who has an extensive knowledge of the history of this last great period of maritime exploration, greatly encouraged me and spent untold hours in an attempt to reduce the bulky draft to manageable proportions. My daughter Susan has been particularly expert and indefatigable in streamlining and reshaping what was a stubbornly lengthy manuscript. With her husband, Professor Peter Moogk, she accomplished a feat of clear-mindedness, professionalism, and tact. I appreciate their work enormously. Finally, I wish to thank Jean Wilson at UBC Press for her support and enterprise that brought this endeavour to final publication, and Anna Eberhard Friedlander and Matthew Kudelka, who copyedited the manuscript.

Let me add three editorial notes. Throughout this work, I do not refer to our subject as "Quadra," as he is generally and incorrectly known in Canada, but as "Bodega" or "Bodega y Quadra," by which names he is known in

Spain, the United States, Mexico, and Peru. Unless noted specifically in the text, "Peru" refers to the Viceroyalty of Perú, which in Bodega's time included large parts of what is now Ecuador, Chile, and Bolivia. Also, unless otherwise credited, all translations from the Spanish are mine.

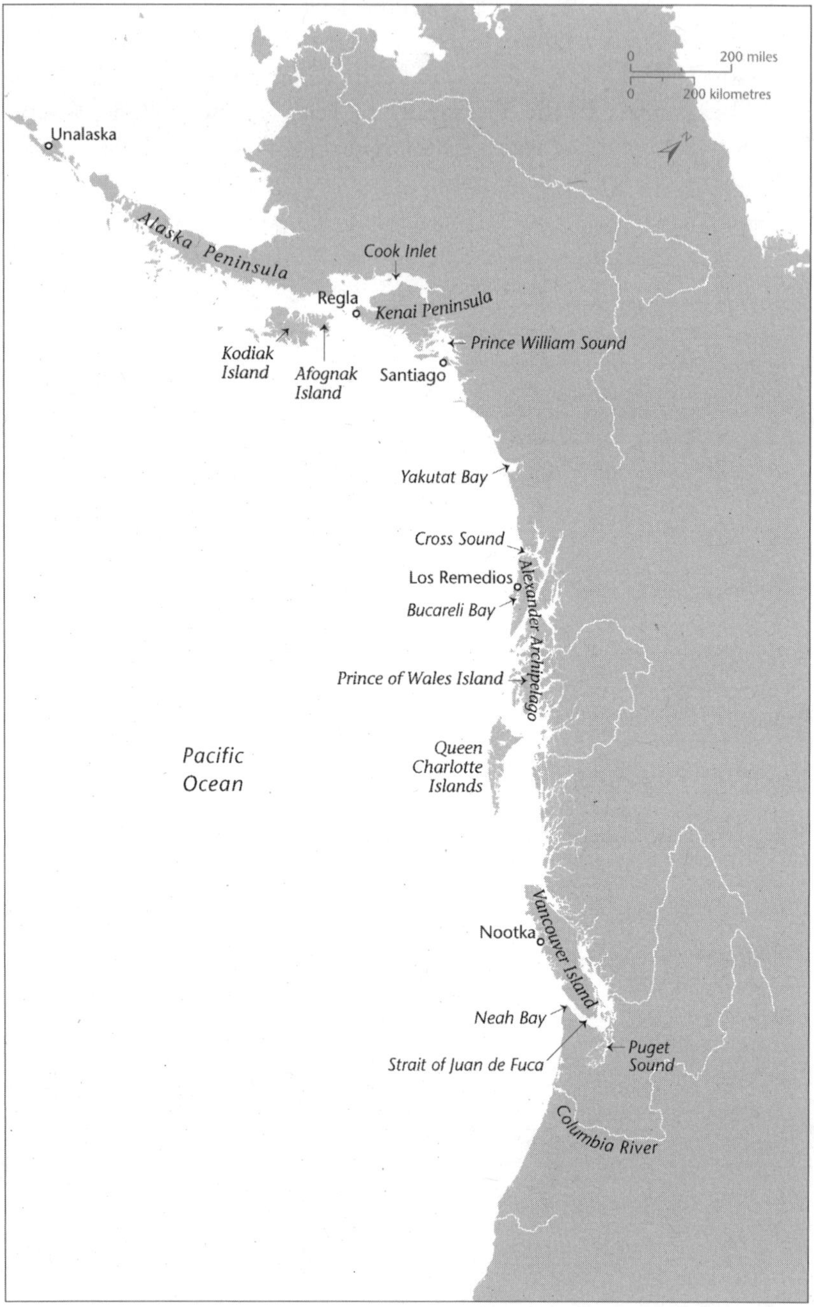

The northern section of the West Coast of North America, showing the places in Washington State, British Columbia, and Alaska visited by Bodega on his 1775, 1779, and 1792 voyages.
Map by Eric Leinberger

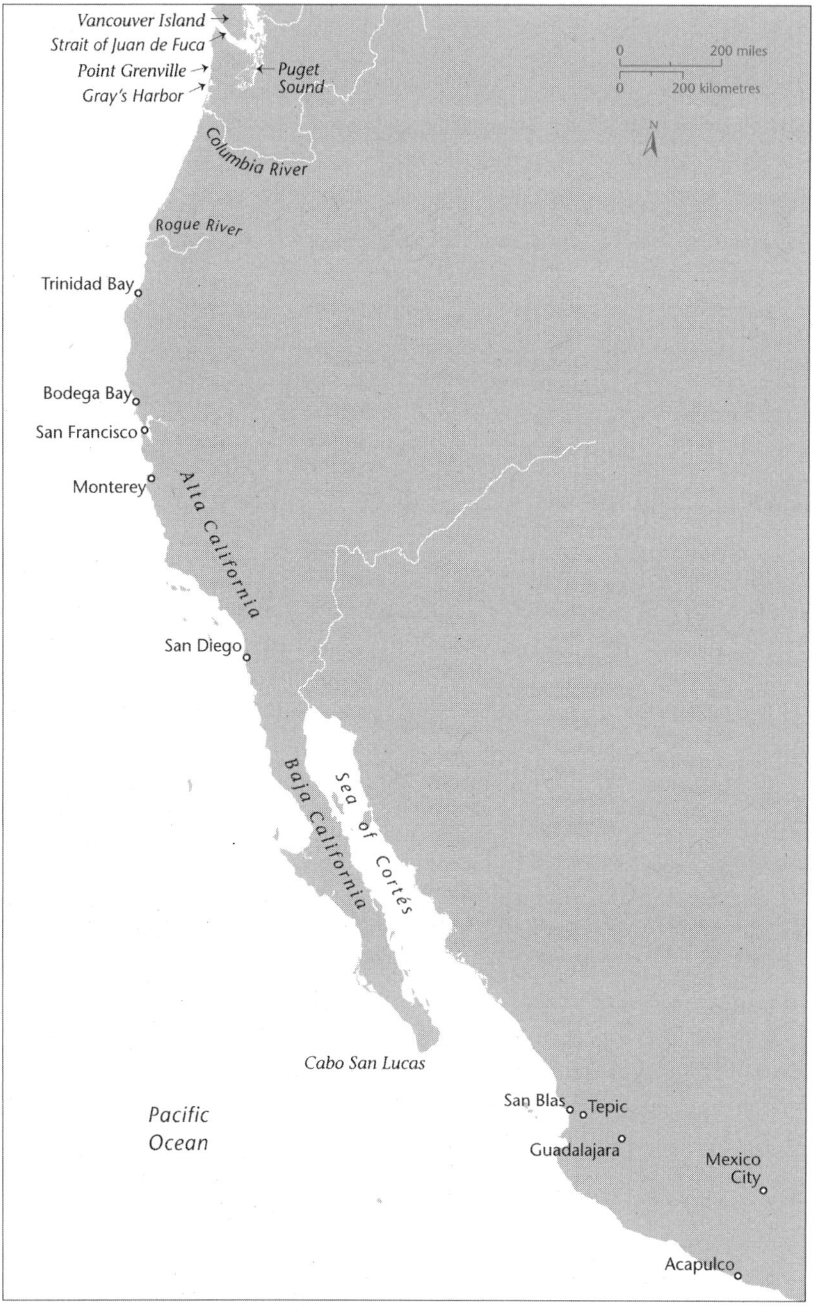

The southern section of the West Coast of North America, showing the Naval Department of San Blas in relation to the California missions and presidios, and other harbours on the coast north to the Strait of Juan de Fuca.
Map by Eric Leinberger

At the Far Reaches of Empire

1

Beginnings

Spain and the Americas

When Juan Francisco de la Bodega y Quadra was born in Lima, Peru, on May 22, 1744, Spain's American empire consisted of three viceroyalties: Peru (modern-day Peru, Chile, and Bolivia), New Spain (Mexico), and New Granada (Ecuador, Colombia, and Venezuela). In 1766, Buenos Aires, later named La Plata, was added as a fourth imperial division.

In 1775, the population of this enormous territory was more than fifteen million.[1] In 1780, this figure included about seven million Indians, four to five million *mestizos*, one million blacks, and three million whites. Of the whites, about 150,000 were *peninsulares* who had come from Spain to serve in the army, the church, and the imperial administration. The remaining whites, including Bodega's family, were *criollos,* or creoles. Most of the creoles owned and managed mines, landed estates, and large commercial ventures.

After its conquest by Francisco Pizarro in the 1530s, Peru became the treasure house of the Spanish Crown. Its gold and silver not only provided financial support for the wars and foreign ventures of King Charles I of Spain (Charles V of the Holy Roman Empire) and King Philip II but also stimulated Spain's domestic economic and cultural life. This wealth gave rise to the popular expression *vale un Perú* (it's worth a Peru), a phrase referring to wealth and opulence.

Peru's primary source of wealth was silver mining. Forced Indian labour extracted the silver ore from the mine in the cone-shaped mountain of Potosí.[2] Once cast into ingots and bars, the silver was carried by mule to the coast at Arica, where it was loaded onto ships bound for Callao, the port of

Lima. Here, other exports to Spain would be added, especially gold and mercury ("quicksilver"). The cargo was shipped on merchant vessels to Panama, where Indians transported it across the isthmus to the docks of Portobello on the Caribbean coast. There, it would await the convoy from Spain, called the Galeones a Tierra Firme y Perú, which left Cádiz every August. Peru's thriving maritime trade was vulnerable to foreign attack, and Peruvians never forgot the late-sixteenth-century depredations of Sir Francis Drake and Thomas Cavendish.[3] The Spanish navy maintained a base at Callao to protect the transport vessels.

When Bodega was born, Lima was home to a variety of social groups: a European elite of administrators, clergy, and merchants; *mestizo* craftsmen (*mestizos* were people of mixed European and indigenous ancestry); black household slaves; and Indian workers, who did most of the manual labour. Lima had a high percentage of non-Indian residents because it was the commercial and political capital of the viceroyalty. A census taken in mid-century gave Lima a population of 26,241. About one-tenth of Limeños were priests and nuns serving the many churches, convents, hospitals, and schools. The white population was sharply divided into *peninsulares,* who were born in Spain, and *criollos,* who were born in the Americas. There was scarcely any middle class, and the city's geography reflected its social hierarchy. Around the Plaza de Armas in the city centre were the viceroy's residence, the municipal offices, the cathedral, and the principal commercial establishments. On this square or near it, the leading families had their homes.

These families' houses had windows protected with iron grilles and shuttered balconies in the style of southern Spain. As a mark of sophistication and elegance, some *criollo* women wore the traditional Andalusian *tapada,* which covered the face except for the eyes. Eighteenth-century visitors to Lima, such as the Frenchman Amédée-François Frézier, admired the regularity of its streets, the grandeur of the churches, and the vivacity of the city's well-dressed inhabitants. Outside Lima, wrote Frézier, "the dwellings of the Spanish in Peru do not match the magnificence of their clothes."[4]

Living standards fell in Lima during the 1700s. Production from the silver mine at Potosí and the mercury mine at Huancavelica declined, and an earthquake in 1746 – the second in sixty years – was calamitous. Matters worsened in 1776 after the decision was made to transfer jurisdiction over Alto Peru (Bolivia) and its silver mine at Potosí to the recently created Viceroyalty of La Plata. Lima's growth slowed, although its intellectual life flourished. The University of San Marcos continued to be the leading institution of learning in the Americas, and the way of life of the resilient aristocracy underwent little change.[5]

While Peru was declining during the eighteenth century, the Spanish Empire was experiencing a renaissance. Thirty years before Bodega's birth, the Hapsburg kings of Spain had been replaced by the Bourbon dynasty from France and Navarre. The Bourbons, especially Carlos III, who came to the throne in 1759, modernized Spain and its empire with the goal of restoring Spanish prestige to the levels it had reached in the sixteenth century. Carlos III actively promoted reforms in the administration and the economy, as well as in the arts and sciences to free Spain from its intellectual isolation.[6]

Carlos III also reorganized and vastly expanded the navy, considering it vital to his foreign policy objectives.[7] Spanish naval historians refer to the navy during this period as La Marina Ilustrada, "the Enlightened Navy," because under Carlos III the Spanish navy was modernized to rival those of France and England. The ministers of the navy supervised three departments with the support of a very small staff. The *comandante* of the first department, which had its headquarters in Cádiz, was also the Capitán y Director General de la Armada, the technical commandant of the navy. The centres of the other two naval departments were at El Ferrol on the northern coast and at Cartagena in the Mediterranean.

Bodega's thirty-two years of service, from 1762 to 1794, coincided with the apogee of the Spanish navy. During his naval career there were three ministers of the navy. When he graduated from the naval academy, Julián de Arriaga y Rivero was in office. After Arriaga's death in 1776, responsibility for the navy went to Pedro González de Castejón. After he died in 1783, Antonio Valdés y Bazán became the minister. During Valdés's twelve-year watch, the Spanish navy reached its greatest strength ever.[8] With the death of Carlos III in 1788 and the resignation of Valdés in 1795, the navy went into decline, and Spain soon ceased to be a major maritime power.

Under Carlos III, the Spanish government also took a more active role in the Americas. From 1754 to 1776, the Minister for the Indies (as the Spanish-American kingdoms were called) and the Minister of the Navy were the same man, Julián de Arriaga y Rivero. The two portfolios had been united because the American empire depended heavily on the Marina de Guerra – the War Navy – both for defence of the American kingdoms and for security of the merchant fleet and its trade routes. When Arriaga died, the portfolio was divided and the Indies went to the highly experienced and effective José de Gálvez. Between 1765 and 1771, before he became Minister for the Indies, Gálvez had been *visitador general* to New Spain. His appointment marked the beginning of a new, more active period of Spanish policy making, for the Americas in general and for New

Spain in particular. As a result of Gálvez's investigatory mission, the *intendencias,* the local administrative jurisdictions, and the *audiencias,* the regional governing councils, were restructured. He introduced major changes in Spain's commercial policy by relaxing the tight controls that had prohibited trade between the viceroyalties. This was done when Madrid promulgated the Reglamento de Libre Comercio in October 1778. This title was misleading, since the new policy only allowed commercial contacts between twelve ports on the Iberian Peninsula and twenty-four ports in "the Indies." Only two of these were in New Spain: Acapulco on the Pacific coast, and Veracruz on the Caribbean. Commerce between ports in the Americas was still reserved for Spanish ships.

After 1776, Peru's seniority as viceroyalty passed to New Spain, which, with a population exceeding one million, became the most important political and economic segment of the empire.[9] Most of this population increase was homegrown, as there was little immigration. In 1790, Mexico City, with a population of 112,000, became the second-largest city of the empire after Madrid. Guanajuato, Puebla, Valladollid, and Guadalajara were other important Mexican centres.

Until the arrival of José de Gálvez in 1765, New Spain's northern region (later called Alta California) was viewed as marginal to Spanish interests. Gálvez soon came to fear that the thinly occupied west coast of New Spain, with its undefined northern border, would endanger the viceroyalty's security. As *visitador general,* he initiated the development of San Blas as a port to support military and naval operations for the colonization of Alta California, which began with the founding of San Diego in 1769. Bodega eventually became the commandant of the Naval Department of San Blas.

When the Spanish government in Madrid received reports from its ambassador in St. Petersburg about Russian activities in the North Pacific in 1774, Gálvez's expansionist views were given the highest priority. After the papal bull that divided the globe between Spain and Portugal was issued in 1493, Spain had claimed sovereignty over these seas. Yet it had never explored the Gulf of Alaska, which was within its portion. Moreover, by 1774, Spain's claim to sovereignty over the *mar del sur,* or Pacific Ocean, was being challenged by the Dutch, the English, and the French, whose navigators and traders were exploring and developing their respective commercial empires. By the latter part of the eighteenth century, the North Pacific had become a cockpit of rival imperial ambitions. This contested region was the setting for the life and career of Juan Francisco de la Bodega y Quadra Mollinedo.

The Bodega and Quadra Families

As his name indicates, Juan Francisco de la Bodega y Quadra was descended through his father from both the Bodega and Quadra families of Spain.[10] They were Basques of the minor, landed nobility and had lived for several generations in the valley of Somorrostro near Bilbao.[11]

The Quadras, to whom the Bodegas were connected by more than one marriage, were well established in the region. In 1476, Iñigo López de la Quadra, who served as page to King Ferdinand the Catholic when he visited Guernica, was severely wounded defending the king from an assassination attempt in Barcelona. He and his heirs were awarded a special annual income of four thousand ducats for his fidelity. Iñigo retired and died in Somorrostro. A later Quadra, Alvaro de la Quadra, was the Spanish ambassador in London who arranged Philip II's marriage to Mary Tudor. Pedro de la Quadra, as Archbishop of Burgos at the beginning of the eighteenth century, ordered the construction of the parish church of San Juan Bautista de Somorrostro, adjacent to the Quadra ancestral home. Finally, among his illustrious kin, Sebastián de la Quadra served as Secretary of State under Felipe V.[12]

The Bodegas owned land adjoining that of the Quadras. They, too, were well established in the region. In 1638, Pedro de la Bodega was alderman for the district known as Oyancas, now San Julián de Muskiz. The family resided near the village of La Poveña, where they managed a small estate.[13] His son Pedro became mayor of Somorrostro in 1651. In 1721, Juan de la Bodega y de la Quadra, Juan Francisco's grandfather, was an alderman of Muskiz.[14] From his first marriage, he had two sons, Juan and Tomás, both of whom became mayors of the valley of Somorrostro. The second, Tomás de la Bodega y de las Llanas, Juan Francisco's father, was elected mayor of the valley in 1761.[15]

Tomás left Spain for Peru in 1720 and Juan followed him in 1722, probably because their father had left the family holdings to the three children of his second wife. Members of the Quadra family had immigrated to Peru earlier and had done well; they held influential posts in the church and in the commercial world of Peru and Chile. The two young men had an uncle in Lima, José de la Quadra y Sandoval Rojas, who taught law at the University of San Marcos and who served on the viceroy's staff. He agreed to look after them.

Eight years after leaving Spain, Tomás Bodega married Francisca de Mollinedo de Losada, the daughter of a long-established, aristocratic colonial family in the Chancay region on the northern coast of Peru. They were married in Lima's cathedral on November 20, 1728, where Francisca herself had been baptized on April 27, 1713. Presiding over the ceremony was her brother, the Franciscan priest Manuel Mollinedo, who later became the Bishop of Cuzco. Tomás and Francisca seem to have had children between 1731 and 1754, seven boys and five girls. Four of the children died before reaching adulthood. Of the surviving children, three of the older boys and the two girls pursued careers in the Church. The three youngest surviving children pursued secular careers. Their youngest son, Manuel Antonio, studied law and became an administrator and politician. The second youngest, Alberto, took over the family business and was given the family house in 1774. In sharp contrast to his siblings, the ninth child, Juan Francisco, chose a life of action and became an officer in the Spanish navy.[16]

Bodega's Early Years

Juan Francisco, Tomás and Francisca's fifth son, was born in Lima on May 22, 1744, and was named for his paternal grandfather and his mother. The cathedral's baptism register for June 3 records the following:

> Juan Francisco de la Vodega y la Quadra: In the City of the Kings on the third of June of seventeen forty-four, I, Don Francisco Javier de Tapia, *teniente* of the priests of this holy metropolitan church, in the sacrarium placed oil and holy water on Juan Francisco, twelve days old. He was baptized [earlier] in case of need by Father Pedro Carillo of the Order of St. Francis. [He is] the legitimate son of Don Thomás de la Vodega and de la Cuadra and of Dña. Francisca Moyinedo.[17]

Tomás's mercantile affairs in Peru prospered, and he quickly acquired a small fortune through agriculture, shipping, and, possibly, shipbuilding. He became a full member of the Tribunal del Consulado, a merchant's guild that adjudicated commercial disputes, and he served as second consul from 1762 to 1764 and as first consul from 1765 to 1766. He held a number of properties in the Chancay Valley, some of which may have come from his wife's family.

In 1748, Tomás bought two houses, one near the San Augustín convent on Calle San Sebastián and the second one on the Jirón Ancash. The second one had been destroyed by the 1746 earthquake. Tomás built a new, spacious house on this site.[18] Close to the viceroy's residence, it was built on the standard plan of residences of the day, the pattern of family houses in Seville. The family crest was usually carved over the wide door that led to a large courtyard.[19] Two sets of apartments for the children were built along the sides. Across the end was the parents' apartment, consisting of a large salon, a dining room, and bedrooms. At the back was an enclosed garden planted with fruit trees, which reached down to the Rimac River (which gave "The City of the Kings" its other name, "Lima"). Off the courtyard was a shed for the carriages and horses, and to one side of the house, in a lane, were the kitchen and servants' quarters. The house would have been filled with furniture made with wood from Guayaquil, with occasional luxuries imported from China, the Philippines, or Guatemala. Because silver was readily available in Peru, all the tableware for daily use would have been silver, along with the chandeliers, flower vases, and hot-water heaters for counteracting the damp chill of the winter months.

Although Lima had a population of little more than 25,000, it was home to more educational institutions than any other city in the Americas, as well as the most famous ones. They were run almost exclusively by the Jesuits until their expulsion in 1767. The University of San Marcos offered courses in the humanities and law, the Colegio de San Martín offered courses in law and theology. The Colegio del Príncipe provided education for indigenous nobles, or *caciques*. We know nothing of Juan Francisco's early education. It is probable that when he was seven, he attended an elementary school in one of the convents. As for his secondary schooling, it is possible that he attended courses in navigation, geography, and mathematics at the Colegio del Espíritu Santo between 1756 and 1760. The lectures would have fostered an interest in a maritime career, rather than a life in the Church, as had been his siblings' vocation.

Juan Francisco enrolled in the Colegio de San Martín on March 16, 1761, to begin his post-secondary education, but he remained there for only one year. The success of his application to the Real Colegio de Guardiamarinas, the naval academy in Cádiz, was probably due to his father's connections in maritime shipping. At the age of eighteen, he began his preparations for a career as an officer in the revitalized Spanish navy, La Marina Ilustrada.

The Beginning of a Naval Career

Juan Francisco de la Bodega y Quadra was a midshipman at the Real Colegio de Guardiamarinas from September 27, 1762, to October 12, 1767. The Real Colegio was the most important of several institutions offering technical training for officers in the War Navy that had been established in Cádiz in the eighteenth century.[20] Most of the officers who served on the American Northwest Coast at the end of the eighteenth century were graduates of these institutions. At the time Bodega was a student at the Real Colegio, it was becoming an important centre for naval education in Europe. Jorge Juan y Santacilla, who had been appointed director in 1751, oversaw the building of an observatory, which complemented the academy's courses in navigation. While in England in 1748, he had made a careful – and secret – study of the training methods of the Royal Navy, acquiring British books and navigational instruments. A similar mission took Antonio de Ulloa to France, Sweden, Denmark, Holland, and Germany. Juan y Santacilla also brought to Spain various foreign makers of scientific instruments.

The academy's regime was set out by a statute enacted by Felipe V in 1748. Its principal purpose was to "educate and endow the noble youth of my kingdoms in the sciences most useful to the navy." Each cadet had to prove that he was legitimate and a "gentleman of notable nobility" as defined in law – that is, of pure blood and not a *converso* (i.e., a Jew or Muslim who had converted to Christianity). The candidate had to be between fourteen and eighteen years old, able to write, and of clean habits in mind and body. Excluded were those with any condition that would "prevent the cadet from taking advantage of his studies" or be "inappropriate for his duties in the service." The total enrolment of the academy at any one time was not to exceed 150, and preference was given to the sons of serving army and navy officers.

The statute did not determine the length of time a cadet would attend before graduating, We know, however, that Bodega was a cadet for five years. Nor did the statute prescribe which courses were to be offered, although the needs were clear: a graduating officer had to be well grounded in all aspects of navigation, gunnery, and seamanship, in theory as well as practice. He also had to be well versed in the new and more sophisticated disciplines of naval science. Accordingly, the curriculum would have included mathematics, geometry, cosmography, trigonometry, cartography, manoeuvres and fortifications, artillery, and naval construction. The observatory would have offered courses in calculus, astronomy, geography, and navigation. Training in the academy would have entailed an interdisciplinary approach that avoided traditional professional rivalries. While no documentation has yet been found on Bodega's record as a student at the naval academy, he evidently displayed ability as well as an ambition to make a name for himself. He attracted the attention of his seniors, including the influential director, Juan y Santacilla, who taught navigation and ship handling, and Vicente Tofiño, who taught astronomy and cartography.

On graduation, the cadets were given the lowest commissioned officer's rank, *alférez de fragata*.[21] Further promotions depended on performance and experience. Inevitably, promotion was faster in the lower ranks and slower as an officer climbed the ladder. There were no promotion boards and performance assessment was perfunctory, so rapid advancement depended on having an influential patron.

Graduating as an *alférez de fragata* on September 21, 1765, Bodega began his career with a series of junior postings in the Mediterranean. He was assigned to the seventy-gun frigate *Terrible* for a cruise to Cape St. Vincent and Corsica. This was followed by other voyages in the Mediterranean, first on the *Princesa,* of the same class, size, and firepower, and then on the frigate *Garzota,* transporting expelled Jesuits from Spain to Civitavecchia and Genoa in Italy.

In 1767, fearing British occupation of Las Malvinas, or the Falkland Islands, the government in Madrid decided to reinforce the squadron based at Callao, Lima's seaport. Bodega returned to Peru on board the *Septentrion.* At Callao, the crews of the *Septentrion* and the two other ships of the squadron attempted a mutiny after the viceregal treasury failed to pay them for two months. Although the mutineers won their case, the punishment meted out to them was harsh. On Bodega's ship, of twenty-seven seamen chosen by lot, seven were shot and the rest were flogged. It was an experience the young Bodega would not forget.

By 1773, Juan Francisco was back in Spain, where he received two quick promotions, to *alférez de navío* in 1773 and then to *teniente de fragata* in 1774.[22] His next assignment, to the Naval Department of San Blas, was a key moment in his career. It introduced him to the Northwest Coast, where he would earn his high reputation as an explorer and a diplomat.

Part I

The Explorer: New Spain and the Northwest Coast

2

The 1775 Voyage on the *Sonora*

IN 1774, A YEAR BEFORE BODEGA ARRIVED at the Naval Department of San Blas on the Pacific coast of New Spain, the Spanish court had received vague reports from the Spanish ambassador in St. Petersburg that the Russians were active in the territories and seas north of Alta California. Spain's immediate response was to send an expedition from San Blas to explore the Northwest Coast of the Pacific Ocean and to investigate the situation. This would be one of only two explorations of the coast in which Bodega was not involved.

Early in 1774, Juan Antonio Pérez was the only experienced officer in San Blas available to lead the expedition. A Majorcan who had recently been given the rank of *alférez graduado de fragata*, Pérez was a veteran of the Californian supply ships and had served aboard the Manila Galleon.[1] His ship, the frigate *Santiago*, had been built in San Blas in 1773.[2] The viceroy governing New Spain, Antonio María Bucareli y Ursúa, provided Pérez with detailed, secret instructions – a document that would become the model for instructions issued to the commandants of subsequent explorations.[3] Without explicitly citing concern over the Russian encroachments, he ordered Pérez to ascend to 60°N and return to Monterey. Should he meet any foreign ship, he was not to divulge the reason for his expedition. Nor was he to make any settlement on land; he should simply mark with a wooden cross and take formal possession of any site deemed suitable for occupation. Should any foreign settlements be encountered, he was to avoid them and sail farther north, where the ceremony of taking formal possession should be performed according to his instructions.

Pérez sailed on January 25, 1774, with supplies for the Alta California Christian missions and provisions for one year of exploration. Estéban José Martínez was the second-in-command.[4] Father Junípero Serra, the Father Superior of the California mission, who was returning to Monterey, and two chaplains, the Franciscan fathers Fray Tomás de la Peña and Fray Juan Crespi, whose journals record many details of the voyage, sailed with him.[5] The *Santiago* also carried some twenty-four passengers and a crew of sixty-two, including fourteen gunners.[6]

Pérez sailed out of San Blas far to the west to catch the prevailing northwesterly winds, which would carry him back to the more northern reaches of the coast – a practice that would be followed by all subsequent explorers. After a delay of one month in San Diego to repair the ship and another month spent at Monterey unloading supplies, the northerly voyage of exploration began. On July 18, Pérez first sighted land; it was the west coast of Langara Island in the Queen Charlotte Islands. He remained offshore for four days, with the weather and winds preventing him from finding an anchorage and making a landing. He and his people, however, did meet Haida Indians and traded with them. Sailing farther north, Pérez reached the Dixon Entrance at latitude 54°40′N, far short of the 60°N that his instructions had called for.

Turning south, Pérez sighted Vancouver Island, the first European to do so, and dropped anchor off the entrance to Nootka Sound near a point he named Punta San Estéban – today's Estevan Point. Again the weather prevented him from going ashore, but he traded with the Indians and named the entrance the Surgidero de San Lorenzo. He did not enter the sound or lay claim to it for Spain.[7] However, in the course of trading abalone shells with the Indians, two silver spoons were apparently left behind. These spoons, seen by later English visitors, were cited by the Spanish as evidence of their prior discovery of the area. Martínez would claim that they had been stolen from him. Another failure, if true, was Pérez's refusal to investigate the wide entrance to the Strait of Juan de Fuca, which Martínez declared he had seen while coasting Vancouver Island en route home.[8]

Pérez's voyage produced only slight immediate results. No sign of Russian activity had been observed. Nowhere had possession been taken, nor were any charts drawn up to increase Spanish knowledge of the coast. Little new geographic information had been obtained to add to what had been charted by Vitus Bering and Alexei Chirikov some thirty years earlier, in 1741. These early results had been recorded on a map full of conjecture issued by the Russian Academy of Sciences in 1758.

Pérez's voyage is more important for what followed than for what it achieved. Clearly, further exploration would be necessary to banish all anxiety about a Russian threat from the minds of Spanish officials. Even so, the voyage had established a basis for Spain's historic claim to sovereignty over the Pacific Northwest; there would be many references to Pérez's voyage in the crisis that would later develop with Britain over Nootka Sound.

For the moment, the native artifacts that Pérez obtained in trade – the first of many acquired by maritime explorers – caused a minor stir in the Spanish royal court. When Carlos III displayed the Chilkat cloaks and other objects collected by Pérez before members of the court and foreign ambassadors, they were universally admired for their artistry and technical quality. "If these cloaks are woven by Indians of the country," the minister Arriaga wrote effusively to Viceroy Bucareli, "that nation is more cultivated and civilized than all the others discovered up to now in America."[9] As Christon Archer has commented, the Spanish were now aware that the native cultures of the Pacific Northwest were superior to those with which they were familiar in Alta California and that "the numerous differences they revealed might hinder attempts at meaningful Spanish sovereignty."

The 1775 Voyage

Bodega, along with five other officers, was sent to San Blas because New Spain's Viceroy Antonio María Bucareli y Ursúa wanted to increase its complement of officers. The Pérez expedition of 1774 had made it clear that the department's dual obligation to supply the growing number of Alta California settlements and to meet the perceived Russian threat to Spanish sovereignty was more onerous than had been anticipated.[10] The government in Spain had already reached the same conclusion. As early as April 1773, Minister of State Grimaldi told Bucareli that he had already informed the king "it would be necessary to select able and expert youths who could, with the ships at your disposal in San Blas, frequent those seas as far as Monterey and even higher if possible."[11] The king approved the proposal to strengthen San Blas with six officers, and steps were taken to appoint them.[12]

On May 18, 1773, Minister of the Navy (and for the Indies) Arriaga wrote to the *capitán general* of the Spanish navy, the *capitán general* at Cartagena, and the *capitán general* at El Ferrol. He asked each to nominate six or eight officers of the rank of *teniente de fragata* and *alférez de navío* for service in New Spain.[13] By August 3 the king had chosen Bruno de Hezeta y Dudagoita and Agustín de Moncada, both of whom were on duty in

Cartagena.[14] They were ordered to go to New Spain by the first available transport and to place themselves under the orders of the viceroy, "who would assign to them their command of the ships employed on the Californian coast for exploration."[15] On August 7, Arriaga learned that while Hezeta had accepted this posting, Moncada had already been assigned to another position. In his stead, *alférez de navío* Diego de Choquet and *alférez de navío* Juan Francisco de la Bodega y Quadra were nominated. Of the two, Bodega came with the better recommendation; he had agreed to go to New Spain, and his commandant at Cartegena thought him "to have a quiet and gentle disposition, good application and other suitable requirements for the purpose."[16] Bodega and Choquet were joined in Cádiz by Miguel Manrique, Fernando Bernardo Quirós y Miranda, and Juan de Ayala.

Bodega's joy at his selection is evident from the letter he wrote immediately to the minister in the formal, highly affected style he used throughout his career:

> Your Excellency, Sir. I recognize my obligation to inform Your Excellency of my arrival in this city on the 24th of this month by virtue of His Majesty's order, communicated to me by the commandant general of the Department of Cartagena (where I was posted), after to be assigned to the Californias, where, if Your Excellency wishes to send me, I hope to merit repeated orders in your service which guarantee my special acquiescence. May God keep you many years.
>
> I kiss Your Excellency's hands [and remain] your most humble subject.
>
> Cádiz, 28 September, 1773.[17]

"The Six," as these hand-picked officers have become known to historians, undertook further training in navigation and chart making at the Real Colegio de Guardiamarinas before they left Spain. Although their primary task was to verify the accuracy of the reports from St. Petersburg about Russian penetration into Alaska, it was recognized that this investigation could only be accomplished through a detailed exploration of the uncharted coast north of Alta California.

The discipline of navigation was changing rapidly in 1773. The Spanish navy was adopting new instruments such as the chronometer, as well as new methods such as the determination of compass variation by azimuth readings. When Vicente Tofiño, the great hydrographer who taught Bodega at the Real Colegio, became the academy's director, he had introduced a special program of advanced studies to help serving officers meet the new requirements for astronomical navigation and mapmaking.[18] On learning that Bodega and his companions had been selected to go to New Spain to take part in exploration, he arranged for them to return to the Real Colegio for a special course on "the new navigation" and to spend "three or four months in our academy and Observatory where they [could] practice the technicalities of astronomy and the use of the instruments."[19]

Tofiño also urged Andrés Reggio, the *capitán general* of the navy, to make certain that the six officers were provided with good instruments to achieve the greatest possible accuracy in their navigation and charting assignments. Assuming that each expedition would consist of two ships, he suggested that each vessel be issued "two good azimuth needles to record accurately their course, observe the variation, and indicate land; and three sextants to observe the latitude and to make longitudinal observations." To make charts of a small section of coast or a port, metal protractors and small tables on tripods would be necessary. To lay down features on a chart covering a longer section of coastline, the officers would be provided with astronomical clocks, quadrants having a radius of thirty inches, azimuth compasses to measure variation, and telescopes of a focal length of twenty-four inches. Tofiño's recommendations for more training and the provision of up-to-date instruments were met. The group not only delayed their departure for New Spain on the store ship *Santa Rita* until the following June 13, 1774, but also took with them seven cases of instruments. They also were given five hundred pesos each for travel expenses.

Trials

The journey to San Blas took nearly six months. The six officers arrived in Veracruz on August 26, 1774. They paused in Mexico City from October 25 to December 15 to meet with Bucareli, who briefed them on Pérez's voyage. The viceroy was disappointed that Pérez had not attempted even one landing or any serious cartography. Bucareli had already begun preparations for the next expedition to the north. In this, he gave the new officers from Spain a leading role. As the senior member of the six, *teniente de navío* Bruno de Hezeta, in the *Santiago,* was placed in command; Pérez, the experienced old hand, was appointed his second-in-command. They were to be accompanied by Juan Manuel de Ayala on the schooner *Sonora,* whose shallow draft would make her useful for inshore surveying and for taking possession on land. A third ship, the packet boat *San Carlos,*[20] commanded by Miguel Manrique, was to make a thorough survey of San Francisco Bay. Quirós was given command of *El Príncipe*[21] and was to take her on resupply missions to Alta California. Diego de Choquet and Bodega were to report to the commanding officer at San Blas, *teniente de navío* Ignacio de Arteaga y Bazán, while they awaited an assignment to another expedition.

It is not evident why Bucareli selected Ayala over Bodega to command the *Sonora*. Both were of the same rank, and although Ayala was older, Bodega was his senior in the service. Was this a case of the well-known preference for *peninsulares* over *criollos*? If so, it would not be the last time Bodega was passed over. Bodega himself was disappointed. He noted tersely, "I thought that on account of my seniority, some position was due me."[22]

The six travelled on to San Blas with their seven cases of astronomical instruments. A pendulum clock had been damaged en route and was left with a clockmaker in Guadalajara to be repaired. As soon as he arrived in San Blas, Bodega rode down to the harbour on horseback. Undaunted by the small size of the schooner *Sonora,* he was determined that he would serve on her even though

> [I] realized that its lack of any capability for such a lengthy and dangerous voyage could delay the expedition and that it would be carrying only one officer, I decided for the sake of the success of the commission to ask permission to embark on the schooner as second-in-command, not considering it to be an obstacle of having to serve under an officer of the same rank as myself or [failing to] recognize that I was exposing myself to infinite risks for my own satisfaction.[23]

As there was no time to consult the viceroy, Bodega made a formal request to Hezeta to be allowed to embark on the schooner, assuring him he would be pleased to serve under an officer of the same rank. His petition was granted on March 8, 1775.

Piloto Francisco Antonio Mourelle de la Rua, who had been assigned to the *Santiago*, asked to be transferred to the *Sonora*. Hezeta granted this request as well. It was the beginning of a fruitful association and solid friendship between Bodega and Mourelle; they were among the most intelligent and able Spanish naval officers who served on the Northwest Coast. In addition to being a superb cartographer, Mourelle was interested in natural history and ethnology.

The *Sonora* had been built for short trips from San Blas to Loreto in Baja California.[24] Bodega thought her to be no longer than a launch belonging to a ship of the line. Mourelle described the *Sonora*'s inadequacies:

> A deck and a tiny cabin were all it had for security or living quarters, with no chests or other baggage than the bunk and what could be contained in a box underneath; the height and width of the space for the crew [was so small that] they had to remain in a sitting position; the meagre deck did not allow the convenience of a walk; and in this inactive manner, we lived for ten months.[25]
>
> We could not help but be sorry to observe the horror which the crew conceived of the bad condition of the schooner, which afforded miserable quarters for the sick. The seamen could not go about their business without getting thoroughly wet, except when it was calm.[26]

With the *Sonora* being so small, some of her stores for the voyage had to be carried on the larger *Santiago*, a frigate.[27] Of the *Sonora*'s crew of fourteen, only four had previously been to sea; the remainder were newly recruited farmhands (*vaqueros*) from ranches around San Blas. The *Santiago* and *Sonora* were each provisioned for a year and carried water for four months.

Bucareli gave much the same instructions to Bruno de Hezeta as he had given to Pérez.[28] The viceroy wanted him to attempt to reach 65°N (the latitude of Fairbanks, Alaska) or higher. While examining the coast, he was to stay close to shore, avoid contact with any foreign establishments, and report on the native peoples, their customs, their form of government, and their trade patterns. Most important, he was to assert possession by Spain in as many places as he could get ashore.

The expedition departed on March 16, after a delay to allow some of the new crew to finish harvesting the fruit crops on the *haciendas*. A second delay occurred when, three days out from San Blas, Miguel Manrique on the *Sonora* became delusional. Ayala was accidentally wounded in the right foot by one of the pistols Manrique brandished. An assembled *junta* agreed unanimously that Manrique should be sent back and that the injured Ayala should take over the *San Carlos*, which was bound for the California missions. Hezeta appointed Bodega to command the schooner *Sonora*. Bodega's providential act of volunteering to serve on the *Sonora* not only saved the expedition from failure but also launched his career as an explorer.

In the open sea a third serious problem arose. The *Sonora* was found to be a very poor sailor. Bodega felt that he had been grossly misled. "The information we had was that she was swift," he wrote, and "her qualities had been praised to the skies." She could make only two knots in a medium breeze, three with all possible sail. He replaced the foresail with a spare mainsail, which "stretched from bow to stern," and he added two small sails in the mastheads. He tried shifting the cargo to alter her drag and loosened the stays and hemp lines. All his efforts made little difference to her speed. On one occasion the *Santiago* took in sail so as not to get too far ahead. At another point the *Santiago* was even obliged to tow the *Sonora.*[29]

To test the spirit of his crew, Bodega put on as much sail as he dared, but "such was the fear they felt ... that they pretended to have some ailment in order to be transferred to the frigate." They were even more dismayed when they saw the command ship's topsails reefed when their schooner was under full sail. The same fear of *Sonora*'s inadequacies, he noted, was shared by the crew of the *Santiago*; Hezeta threatened them with transfer to the *Sonora* as a "rigorous punishment." On the smaller ship, the sailors' condition

> would have become insufferable, had not [Bodega] behaved with the greatest kindness to the crew ... He encouraged them to persist also, by giving them small presents frequently, and reminded them of the glory they would obtain on their return, if they reached the proper latitude.[30]

During one heavy windstorm at night, when both Bodega and Mourelle had gone below to get some rest and the boatswain was on watch, one of the cabin boys informed them that the mainsail had been lowered and reefed, just as the *Santiago*'s had been. Bodega rushed up on deck and ordered the reef removed and the sail hoisted. Very annoyed, he gave orders that no sail was ever to be lowered without his permission. He told his men he

> was ashamed to see them ... such cowards ... I asked what confidence could I have and what could I expect from them in higher latitudes, where it is certain that the seas and winds will have greater strength, if now, when the weather was clear, they feign so much timidity ... Finally, I told them of the glory they would have ... and the esteem they would merit from all and especially from me, who was their companion in their labours.

This exhortation apparently did some good, for Bodega saw a new spirit in them, a desire to please him and a resolve "to participate in my own fate and even to follow me to any destiny whatever."

After a month of very slow progress, Hezeta convened a *junta* of officers to decide whether or not to put in at Monterey. In his lengthy written opinion, Bodega argued strongly against stopping at Monterey. He wanted to continue sailing until they reached the supposed Río de Martín de Aguilar.[31] Bodega wrote:

> I am of the opinion that on no account should we put into Monterey. The reasons which compel me to hold this view are solely dictated by service to the

King and the better fulfillment of our mission. It cannot be denied that in the latitude in which we find ourselves, it will be less difficult to anchor in 43° (the inlet discovered by Martín de Aguilar) than to go to Monterey. This being granted, what doubts can we have when the advantages are so well known?[32]

Francisco Mourelle concurred:

According to reports, water is not lacking there, and the few sick we have will improve as soon as they step ashore. The damage to the topmast and the bowsprit can last out with the lashings we have made, and if not, we can fix them as much as possible. One cannot always navigate with everything in order ...

If we put into Monterey, we must realize that as the season is well advanced, we risk making no further advances this year and will have to wait until next year to continue. This will result in a serious delay in the service of His Majesty and his interests and we will not fulfill the orders of His Excellency the Viceroy. To decide to make a new topmast and bowsprit is the same as deciding to spend the winter there.

As to what is said of the condition of the schooner with all its futtocks split and totally useless, unable to hold a nail, and that this damage can have disastrous results because of the continuous and strong winds, none of this appears to me to be a sufficient reason to delay the expedition.

Bodega then added with a touch of bravado:

The command has been given to me and I must carry out my orders, I say, with the honour corresponding to my birth. I know the advantages which can result from the mission if, as I hope, I am able to reach 61° or higher in company with the frigate. I am fully aware of the consequences of what I have said and the arduous nature of the undertaking because of the small size [of the schooner], its poor handling, slow speed, and because it is essential for me to carry more sail than normal.

All these reasons, and those now being added, should have been put before His Excellency [the viceroy] by those persons who informed him maliciously of its [good] characteristics. It is now too late to change opinions. This fear, however, must not be an obstacle since those who are gladly willing to sacrifice themselves with me are my *piloto* and my small crew, who are resigned to their fate.

This should not be interpreted as rashness since up to now not the slightest amount of water has been found [in the hold] and we have not stopped working. Although the speed is low and the amount of sail is too much, they

> are remedied by the continual care the *piloto* and I show to avoid accidents.
>
> In the final analysis, God encourages and aids great actions and when fortune is so adverse that nothing can be done about it, it is glory for posterity for each one to die doing his duty and [to die] for the King.[33]

Although all the other officers favoured going into Monterey, Hezeta deferred to Bodega's opinion, and the slow voyage northward continued.

The weather was poor, the winds were variable, the sea was rough, and the temperature turned colder as they sailed on. On June 1, the routine was broken by the death of one of the *Sonora*'s cabin boys. He had gained access to the brandy barrel and drunk himself into a blind stupor. Bodega transferred him to the *Santiago* for medical attention, but the boy did not recover. Father de la Serra, the *Santiago*'s chaplain, noted wryly, "He went blind drunk into Eternity."[34]

Trinidad

The first signs that the ships were approaching land appeared shortly after. Bodega estimated that they were thirty leagues from Cape Blanco and twenty-seven from Cape Mendocino, if the Bellin map they carried could be believed.[35] On June 7, the coast was sighted clearly, stretching from north to south. The following day, Hezeta signalled to Bodega to sail ahead and seek a good harbour. This was the task for which the *Sonora* had been added to the expedition, and Bodega complied. A reconnaissance over the next two days and careful navigation between the large rocks, which extended as much as a mile out to sea, were rewarded: the *Sonora* found an inlet that seemed to offer the haven they were seeking.[36] Bodega signalled the *Santiago* to follow him in. Once safely inside, both ships anchored "a stone's throw from the beach." This was Trinidad Bay, home of the Yurok.

Even before the ships entered the bay, canoes full of natives came out to greet them.[37] Once the vessels anchored, more came alongside and "with the greatest affability mixed with the crews and began in a friendly manner to exchange deer skins and sea otter pelts for knives, beads, and other trifles the sailors bartered with them." The next day, June 10, both captains, accompanied by some of their officers, the two chaplains, and forty armed men, went ashore to visit the natives' village. The Spaniards found the people suspicious but not obstructive. Trading continued as they walked around the village, but the villagers showed no interest in bartering for European clothing.

The commandant decided to take formal possession of the region "on the top of a high hill which stood at the entrance to harbour" on the following day, the day of the "ineffable mystery of the Most Blessed Holy Trinity." All the journals recorded the proceedings. The cross was first set up on the beach, where the first adoration was recited.[38] Fathers Miguel de la Campa and Junípero de la Serra wrote that they chanted the hymn of gratitude, *Te Deum Laudamus*. The formal act of possession, the text of which had been prepared beforehand in Mexico City, required only the addition of the names of the ships, their commandants, the date, and the name to be given to the place. The document recorded that there was "no hostile resistance." Hezeta assured the Yurok people, in response to their "desire to establish perpetual friendship with us," that they could do so "as long as they maintained the cross." In his account, Bodega omitted many details recorded by the chaplains, but his general description concurs with those by others.

The following day, both ships took on wood and water. There was plenty of "delicious water" in the ravines, and collecting water and wood on the beach was easily accomplished. The *Sonora* was boot-topped[39] in the hope of increasing her speed. Bodega also cut trees for two masts and yardarms as well as caps for the masthead. The Indians made no objection to the crews' cutting trees for the purpose. On the contrary, they assisted the sailors' work details.

Bodega made a careful chart of the bay with Mourelle. Bodega also wrote a report on the harbour. Any ship, he thought, should be able to anchor safely in the small bay protected by Trinidad Head, provided the cables were sheathed, but care needed to be taken to avoid the many protruding rocks in the bay. After repeated observations, its position was determined to be 41°07′N and 19°04′W of San Blas.[40]

The viceroy's standing instructions to all captains on exploration missions included a directive to report on the customs, characteristics, religion, and political organization of the natives.[41] Despite the difficulties of communication and the limitations of time, Bodega, with the help of Mourelle and undoubtedly that of the officers and chaplains of the *Santiago*, was able to compile a good deal of information, which was based, he says, on visits to the ships from more than 250 Indians and on Spanish excursions to some of the villages.[42] While his account is not as full as those of the chaplains, who had more time for the task, Bodega went beyond simple observations on material goods and economic patterns. He also recorded that he had seen iron used in the Yuroks' weapons, and that they liked tobacco and had a small garden plot of it.

Bodega failed to record some events that occurred during the ships' stay, perhaps because he was not personally involved. First, the *Santiago* grounded because of the very low tide. Then two of the *Santiago*'s apprentice seamen, José Antonio Rodrigues and Pedro Lorenzo, deserted. Hezeta, suspecting at first that the Indians had kidnapped them, seized two Yuroks as hostages, but they were released when Lorenzo returned voluntarily. He received two hundred lashes for his offence. Rodrígues was never found and became California's first illegal immigrant. Neither did Bodega mention Hezeta's exploration of Little River, which the Spaniards called Río de las Tortolas (Turtle Doves). On June 12, the day after the possession ceremony on Trinidad Head, the officers of both ships had a picnic ashore, which the chaplains had organized.

After spending nine days in Trinidad Bay, the two ships sailed away, apparently amid tearful farewells from some of the Indians who had boarded the ships before their departure. After presenting the sailors with shellfish, they embraced the Spanish, throwing their arms around everyone and saying, "Adios, amigo." They made signs that Bodega interpreted to mean that "they would weep when they saw the Holy Cross."

On June 28, the vessels set a northerly course and sailed to a point south of Vancouver Island, where the winds and currents drove them west and south. By the end of June, the ships were more than a hundred leagues from the coast.

The trying weather conditions did not, however, prevent a celebration on June 24, the feast of St. John the Baptist, Bodega's patron saint. Bodega invited the officers and chaplains of the command ship to celebrate the day with him. The ships lay to from one p.m. to four p.m. for the occasion. Father Serra tells us that "the officers went, and the occasion was celebrated with great rejoicing, including speeches, and both ships were dressed with flags, and salvos of musketry were discharged as the crews vied with each other in acclamations of 'Long live the King.'"[43]

Using the new spars made in Trinidad Bay, Bodega put on extra sail and ended what he regarded as the embarrassment of being towed. It was still necessary to exercise great care. On July 9, when they were in the latitude of the strait of Juan de Fuca, the *Sonora* nearly foundered. A squall snapped the main topmast and caused the tiny ship to turn on her beam ends, whereupon the heavy seas prevented her return to an even keel. The water barrels broke loose from their chocks and rolled around, and water entered the hold, damaging some of the stores. Bodega was able to turn into the wind to make temporary repairs.

Tragedy at Grenville Bay[44]

The coast of what is today Washington State was sighted on July 11. Turning south to seek a safe anchorage, the *Sonora* sailed close to shore while the *Santiago* stood off to await her signals. On his chart, Hezeta identified the location as the Rada de Bucareli. Perhaps anticipating criticism for the tragedy that followed, Bodega recounted in some detail the careful manoeuvres he was compelled to make to avoid the shoals in the waters less than a mile offshore. Coming in under the lee of nearby Cape Elizabeth at high tide, he sailed over the shoals, or sand banks, protecting the beach, without realizing they were there.

> At this time the frigate was about a league away; I signaled it to come and anchor and I came in sounding 8 *brazas,* for which reason I immediately signaled "low water" to the frigate.[45] Although I attempted to get out, it was not possible to do so because of a great series of sand banks, which stretched outside all along the coast. To get outside was not possible because the wind was coming from the opposite direction to the way we came in, so I had to anchor. I sent the launch [with Mourelle] to inform the Commandant where I was, of the impossibility of my getting out at low tide, and the impossibility of his using the place as a safe anchorage for the night. I also asked him to let me know if there was a sheltered harbour by the point which was about a league to leeward.

Mourelle returned at midnight with the news that there was no shelter at the point to leeward and that the frigate had anchored a league from the *Sonora.*

The schooner's presence quickly attracted the attention of people from the nearby Quinault village. They were the first residents of the area to encounter European visitors. They tempted the sailors with "offerings and flattery," and by signs seemed to invite them to go ashore to visit their houses. Bodega noticed that they were soon joined by about sixty others. As the Spaniards were outnumbered, he ordered his people to arm themselves discreetly.[46] The Indians seemed to appreciate the glass beads, pendants, and kerchiefs presented to them. They returned with more fish without showing any fear. They approached the ship and exchanged pelts for glass beads and knives. With signs taken to show "gratitude and friendship," they endeavoured to persuade the Spaniards to spend the night in their village. The Indians approached the anchor cable, which Bodega interpreted as meaning that if they accepted the invitation, they would be towed in. The Indians finally left "with the same signs of friendship and making a great noise and demonstrating by their actions and their arms that we were friends." Later that evening, nine canoes approached the schooner, their occupants shouting. As the hour was late, Bodega armed his men so as to be ready for any treachery. As matters turned out, the Indians were so pleased with the presents made to them earlier that they had come to offer a large amount of food, including salmon and smelt, whale meat, meat of other land animals, and sweet onions, as well as some fresh water. To show his appreciation and once more to assure the Indians of his peaceful intentions, Bodega gave kerchiefs and glass beads to the men and rings and earrings to the women. After this, "they then returned happily to their villages, and I marvelled at how they behaved."

The next day, June 14, Hezeta, whose ship was a short distance to the south, decided to perform the possession ceremony where he had anchored and without the *Sonora*'s officers. Because he feared that his own ship's exposed position would worsen when the wind and sea came up, he conducted the ceremony hastily at 6 a.m., "following the instructions strictly in every detail [and] giving it the name Rada de Bucareli. As the situation did not admit any delay, Mass was omitted."[47] Apart from Hezeta, Pérez, the surgeon Juan González, twenty armed men, and the chaplains themselves, the only witnesses were six unarmed Quinault "grown boys," who were gathering and eating shellfish on the beach.

Meanwhile, Bodega made ready to sail to the *Santiago*. While he waited for high tide, he decided to take on wood and water, as well as cut a much-needed cap for the masthead, since a lengthy voyage "of four months' continuous hardship" lay ahead. He thought the job could be accomplished easily, for he could see "running streams of water and an infinite number of logs" on the beach. Moreover, the Indians who had returned again to trade were "showing the same sincerity and friendship as on the previous day and night." A detail of six men was organized under the boatswain, Pedro Santana, who was "known for his good conduct and bravery by all." Each was armed with a musket and sword, and some with two pistols. They were also given "some articles of little value" to offer for trade if approached by Indians. As the launch was too small to carry everyone, Bodega instructed it to return as soon as they had disembarked to take Mourelle and himself ashore with some barrels.

His journal then records the subsequent tragedy:

> As there was some swell to the sea, they were not able to get ashore with all stability and so as soon as they began to step ashore, all of a sudden 300 Indians

> came out of the woods and finding the men defenceless assassinated them treacherously. As I was without any means to help them, I ordered a few shots fired to see if they would frighten [the Indians], but they paid not the slightest attention since the shots could not hurt them. Just as useless were the various signals for help I sent the frigate, as the distance was too great for them to be seen. Thus I found myself isolated, without a launch, [and] without people to go to their defence.

On the schooner with his telescope, Mourelle saw the Indians come out of the woods, which were only twenty-five to thirty yards from the shoreline. He saw only a single flash from either a musket or a pistol, and he heard no shot. Aboard the *Santiago,* the shots were interpreted as a signal that the *Sonora* was in trouble among the shoals. Hezeta dispatched his launch with a kedge anchor and a cable. Bodega scanned the shore for any one of his people who might have escaped the massacre. He saw two men swimming toward his ship, but they were defeated by the cold water. He did not know "if when they retreated [to the shore] they died at the hands of the barbarians or escaped in the thickness of the woods."

At noon, he weighed anchor in the hope of getting free with the high tide. Besides Mourelle, Bodega had on board only five men and a boy who were healthy and another four who were ill. There was very little wind as he manoeuvred his ship to get out to sea, when nine large canoes came out, each carrying more than thirty Indians. As the canoes closed, Bodega recognized in one, which had only nine men aboard, the "most robust youths" who the day before had each commanded one of the other canoes. They coasted up beside the schooner, bows at the ready and shielded by "some beautiful hides of great thickness." The Indians made the same signs of friendship and, as before, appeared to invite the men of the *Sonora* to visit their village.

Rejecting these entreaties, Bodega noted sarcastically: "This was a contemptible reward for the noble treatment we had accorded them." The Indians then began to approach the schooner from the stern. Bodega stationed his tiny group to repel any attack – one at the helm, another sounding the water's depth, another looking out for shoals, another making cartridges, and the last carrying them to where they would be needed. He, Mourelle, and the cabin boy were the only ones left to fire the muskets and man the swivel guns.

At first the Indians kept the same distance from the *Sonora,* but when the nine natives saw that no one was manning the prow, they decided to board. Once they came within range, Bodega

> opened fire with two swivel guns and three muskets, peppering them in such a way that we gave them no time between volleys. They paddled to escape with great swiftness. However, their skill was to no avail, as the first shots killed the greater number of them and the others quickly covered themselves with their leather skins.[48]

He thought he could have killed more had he not been compelled to keep watch as the *Sonora* picked her way between the shoals to open water. The Indians hastily withdrew out of the range of the muskets and swivel guns to hold a conference and then decided to return to their village. Bodega did not record an ethnographic description of the Quinault. What little Mourelle recorded was clearly what he learned from the two chaplains, Fathers Campa and Serra.[49]

Bodega rejoined the *Santiago* as soon as he could get free and immediately boarded it with Mourelle to report to Hezeta. Distraught and angry, he asked for thirty men to go ashore to "seek the most severe satisfaction for such an abominable atrocity and to be sure of the fate of the two unfortunate ones." He and Mourelle argued their case strenuously, but the *Santiago*'s officers were all opposed to their plan. Hezeta did not criticize Bodega for having allowed himself to be trapped inside the shoals, nor did he blame him for the tragic incident that followed. He concurred that the Indians had "shown great gentleness," and he noted that they "had brought their women on board" and had exchanged meat and fish for glass beads – all signs of "true and sincere friendship." He no doubt sympathized with Bodega's desire to seek revenge; nevertheless, he counselled prudence. Hezeta had good reason for opposing Bodega's request. His instructions permitted him to resort to force only in self-defence, and because he had so many on board affected by scurvy, the "least loss of manpower would have forced us to give up the mission." Bodega and Mourelle accepted Hezeta's ruling reluctantly. "Even though it did not conform to my opinion," Bodega noted, "the Commandant decided to let such audacity go unpunished."

A possible explanation of the sudden change in the natives' attitude has been suggested by Quinault ethnologist David H. Chance:

> Perhaps the land-claiming ceremony by twenty-four men, twenty of them heavily armed, had been perceived for what it was. The Quinaults would have surely known that erecting a pole with a cross-bar on it, while a medicine man in robes chanted, meant that something of great religious power was being done to their land. Some who doubtless watched from hiding in the woods half-circling the cove may have wondered if these were the Black

> Klokwalle spirits from out in the ocean, a perfectly reasonable deduction from the Quinault perspective. This may be why the current Quinault tradition of the *Sonora/Santiago* affair recalls events only at Point Grenville; the land claim may have been the most significant and galling part of it.
>
> The people of this coast were territorial even if in a slightly different way than that of the Europeans. They were very much accustomed to the communication of important facts through symbols like poles stuck in the sand. This may have been the first awakening, after a mere twenty-four hours of honeymoon with the presumptuous Europeans. The second may have been when the Spaniards evened the score with their guns.[50]

Another possible explanation has been suggested by Delbert J. McBride, former curator of the Washington State Capitol Museum in Olympia and a scholar of Cowlitz-Quinault extraction. He believes that the expedition would not have been aware that the beach where Bodega's people went ashore was a sacred place connected with the coming into puberty of female members of the tribe, promising death to anyone who profaned it.[51]

The Spanish had charted the roadstead and named it after Viceroy Bucareli. Point Grenville was named Punta de los Mártires to commemorate their murdered companions. The shoal that had trapped Bodega's ship still appears on today's maps, appropriately, as Sonora Reef.

Opportunity

By mid-July, Bruno de Hezeta was deeply concerned about the *Sonora*'s ability to continue in company. The evening before the massacre, Bodega had received word that Hezeta wanted him to attend an officers' *junta* to decide whether "the schooner should continue the voyage to a higher latitude since at every moment he [Hezeta] feared we would perish with seas and winds such as we had experienced on the 9th and 11th." Reflecting on this order, Bodega wrote:

> This news did not surprise me, as from the beginning after leaving San Blas they have taken great pains to dissuade me from such an undertaking and urge me to return to port, trying to make me believe that it was impossible to reach a latitude higher than Monterey. I consider it to be of greater merit that I have not paid any more attention to such mournful predictions of the inconveniences and exertions I have undergone and await me in such a lengthy voyage.

During the *junta* that discussed the massacre, Hezeta voiced his concern that the schooner had twice been close to foundering.

Bodega and Mourelle were adamant about wanting to continue. On returning to his ship, Bodega put his reasons in writing for Hezeta:

> On 21 May when we were in latitude 37° and longitude 27°46′ west of San Blas, bearing in mind the slow speed of this schooner and finding all the futtocks useless as the carpenters attested and, finally, its resistance poor, we held a *junta* to determine whether it should return to the Department [of San Blas] or put into Monterey to examine the damage.
>
> As it seemed to me, this was insufficient reason for me to return as to do so would completely delay the expedition. I felt this would not be acceptable under any circumstances, bearing in mind the service of the King and the reasons I expressed in writing.
>
> The *piloto* of the schooner, Don Francisco Maurelle [sic], was of the same opinion. You decided that we should proceed [as planned] and I have reached latitude 49° without having had any reason to oblige me to put into harbour. Now on this occasion and with greater reason, I must be of the same opinion, having experienced such severe seas and winds, and I am certain that I can lie to without suffering the least damage. Even though [the schooner] heels over and water is shipped excessively, the former will always occur with every small ship and the second is not all that consequential as *ser de punta a la oreja* [the deck is completely covered].[52]
>
> Its speed with the sails I have had added does not differ much from that of the frigate. And finally, I am obliged to reach 65° as I have reached 49°. The labours I have experienced and expect are fundamental to every navigation, especially to explorers, and must be accepted with resignation and fortitude as they are for the King's service and the honour of the nation.
>
> As I wish to fulfill, as required, the commission entrusted to me, considering that it would more difficult for the frigate to accomplish the task without the schooner, of reconnoitering the coast and its harbours, I expressed the opinion at the *junta* that we should continue [the voyage] and do so now in writing, adding that it would be an unbecoming affront to my nature to abandon the mission without serious reason.[53]

Juan Pérez sided with Bodega. Hezeta agreed and acceded to the request that he replace from his own crew the six seamen the *Sonora* had lost.

With light winds and sailing west, the ships left the coast early in the morning of July 14. Five days later, Hezeta sent Bodega a letter enclosing a representation by Pérez, his second-in-command, as well as a certificate from the *Santiago*'s surgeon to the effect that the frigate could not reach a higher latitude because of the advanced season and the number of crew suffering from scurvy. Bodega replied, Mourelle agreeing, in his usual resolute tone:

> I am of the opinion that, notwithstanding their strong and powerful reasons, we should continue for a while longer to see whether, in the meantime, we can gain more favourable winds to help us and not discontinue a voyage which has cost us so much discomfort. Although I recognize that few of my crew are well and that the greater part are in wretched health and tired after four months of navigation to which they are not accustomed, it seems to me appropriate to carry on in some way until it is obvious that the sick will not recover greater strength. If that should be the case, we could withdraw, reconnoitering the coast with the northwest winds we have experienced in the vicinity.

Reluctantly, Hezeta accepted Bodega's view, and they sailed on. The season was far advanced, and they had a long way to go to reach 65°N. The *Sonora* was in a wretched state, and her slowness only exacerbated difficulties. Bodega and Mourelle were certain that Hezeta had decided to abort the expedition.

On July 29, when the two ships were near the latitude of the Strait of Juan de Fuca but well out of sight of land, the weather turned nasty. Strong winds and high waves forced both ships to lay to. The night was so dark that the *Santiago*'s lantern was scarcely visible. Several rockets and the swivel guns were fired to signal the *Santiago*'s position, but on the *Sonora,* only one rocket could be seen dimly. Bodega attempted to move closer to what he thought was the *Santiago*'s position, but as the wind and waves frustrated his efforts, he decided to stay where he was by heading up into the wind.

That night, he and Mourelle resolved to carry on the expedition alone. Both failed to record that decision in their journals. On July 31 Bodega noted only that the horizon was very cloudy, with visibility less than two leagues, and that the frigate was nowhere to be seen. As the weather deteriorated and forced him to maintain his position, he wrote that he had assumed the command ship would do the same. The following day, August 1, the weather was worse, with visibility only half a league. When the weather improved at noon, the *Santiago* had disappeared. Bodega began a search on a westerly course, assuming, he said, that the winds would have forced Hezeta to do the same. On August 4 he claimed that squalls, fog, and varying winds had persuaded him to alter his course to the north:

> Now that the winds began to be more favourable and the frigate was nowhere to be seen, I decided to continue the exploration in accordance with instructions in spite of realizing that the consequences could be disastrous, so advanced was the season, if we attempted to reach a higher latitude in a ship so small, lacking medicines and surgeons and even water. I pressed on, taking fresh trouble for granted.

Somewhat disingenuously, he added:

> All in all, it was necessary to put up with these inconveniences as it would be distressing having to incur again further expense for the Royal Treasury for succeeding expeditions that perhaps would suffer their own misadventures and not produce results unless we seek to overcome them with determination.

Some years later, Mourelle, whose journal repeated the same yarn even more cryptically, would confess that their separation from the command ship had indeed been premeditated and was not accidental. Their "official" version of what happened was not entirely false, for the night truly was unusually dark and overcast. They did steer westward to look for the *Santiago,* but, as Mourelle later admitted, they "slowly drifted away to the west ... [as] masters of their action."[54]

Mourelle described at some length how, for three hours between seven and ten that night (July 29), they had discussed what they should do, admitting that it was he and not Bodega who urged abandoning their senior officer. "As [we] both had the same thought, it was not difficult," he later wrote, "to convince him to separate in spite of superior orders to travel in consort." They were well aware of the risks involved. They would be sailing into unknown seas, and they could be trapped in archipelagos. They faced a shortage of food. Their meat, all seventy-two *arrobas,* about 1,800 pounds in weight, was stored on the *Santiago.* All they had left on the *Sonora* was rice, beans, soggy bread, lard, and water. Without medicines, they faced the certain loss of crew members through scurvy. There was also the possibility that they would be accused of insubordination were they to return to San Blas "without [any] progress worthy of consideration." None of these risks, however, could prevail over their anxieties: they could not face their fellow officers if they turned back after they had come as far as they had, and they had as yet achieved nothing that was worthy of their superiors' attention. Perhaps closer to the truth was Mourelle's later admission that he and Bodega y Quadra were "two youths eager for fame and reputation."[55] Thus began "one of the truly epic voyages in the coastal exploration of North America."[56]

Reaching North for the Arctic Circle

After altering course to almost due north, the *Sonora* sailed on without much difficulty until August 15. Bodega and Mourelle knew they were near land when the sea became darker and tree branches, seaweed, whales, and birds with red beaks, feet, and chests were sighted.[57] They calculated their position to be 56°08′N and 154 leagues from the supposed coast. The fog was so thick they could not see the bow of their ship. They believed they were near an archipelago of unknown islands and that their situation was dangerous.

At noon the next day they sighted land at a distance of six leagues. This was Kruzof Island, immediately west of modern-day Sitka, Alaska. Sailing in closer, the explorers noted the high mountains capped with snow, among them the distinctive Mount Edgecombe.[58] Navigating carefully along the west coast of Kruzof Island, they entered an inlet three leagues wide. Despite being exposed to winds from the south, Bodega decided to spend the night there at anchor on a sandbar. He called the place Guadalupe.[59] As the ship left the next day, the crew saw two canoes, each carrying two men and two women, who showed no desire to come alongside. The men and women made signs, which the Spaniards took to be an invitation to go ashore. The now distrustful Bodega declined their offer.

Three days later, the *Sonora* entered Sea Lion Cove at the northern end of Kruzof Island. Bodega described it

> as a harbour which was not as large as the previous one. It had a beautiful beach, a river four or five yards wide, a depth of water of eight *brazas*, sheltered from the winds on the first, second and fourth quadrants, and protected on the third by a chain of islands, linked one to the other, which go out to sea.

The *Sonora* anchored close to shore near a well-built house defended by a stockade of poles. Bodega decided to go ashore and take possession of the land at noon on the same day. Taking no chances against another surprise attack, he disembarked with fourteen well-armed men. To cover a possible retreat, he positioned two swivel guns and some men with muskets in the most defensible part of the cove while he planted a cross on a small hill, "taking possession of these lands with all the required formalities." Bodega named the place Puerto de Nuestra Señora de los Remedios, and situated it at latitude 57°20′N and 34°12′W of San Blas.[60] When the Spaniards returned to their ship, the Indians, who had remained behind their parapet, were seen to carry off the cross. They erected it in front of their house, which suggests that they considered it something akin to a totem pole. Puerto de Nuestra Señora de los Remedios would assume symbolic importance as the farthest point north that a Spanish explorer had taken possession to date.

Bodega inspected the river and beach to see how best much-needed water could be taken on board. Although the Indians continued to remain behind their stockade, Bodega decided it was too dangerous and returned to the ship. The following day, August 19, he disembarked with the same number of men on a beach closer to the entrance to the cove. As he had done the day before, he established a strongpoint and fortified it with swivel guns and men with muskets. Taking six men with him, he went first to cut a tree and gather wood. When they began to fill the water barrels from the river, while others fished near the river mouth, about twenty unarmed Indians carrying a white pennant on a pole came out of their house and took up a position across the river. For some time they harangued the Spaniards. In due course they fell silent, as if expecting a reply. Bodega attempted to explain that the Spaniards meant them no harm and that they should have no fear. He signed that they had come to get some water, whereupon one of the natives, who was thought to be the chief, ordered water to be brought to the Spanish. It was offered in a goblet made of grass and handed over in the middle of the river. In exchange, Bodega gave them some beads and kerchiefs, which were repaid with dried fish.

All seemed to be going well as the water casks were filled, until the Indians saw that the water was being carried away. "They endeavoured to make us pay for the water, giving us to understand that it was theirs." This was the first time the Spanish became aware of the highly developed sense of private property that was widespread on the Northwest Coast. When offered more beads, the Indians threw them on the ground and ran to their house, from which they returned carrying very long, flint-tipped spears. When they gestured their intention to attack, Bodega told his people to hold fire. Seizing his own musket, he approached the riverbank and warned the Indians that he would fire on them if they advanced one step closer. He added that the Spanish wished to be friends and that he would lay down his musket if they laid down their spears. The Indians apparently understood Bodega's proposal and retreated to their house. Without further incident, the Spaniards finished drawing water and gathering wood. They also cut a tree for the topmast.[61]

The *Sonora* remained at Los Remedios for three days. With the weather turning very much colder, with constant rain and fog, the lack of adequate shelter for the crew was becoming a matter of concern. Departing on August 21, Bodega sailed westward hoping to gain a northing breeze, but the winds conspired against him. His observations were proving the Bellin maps to be totally useless. Bodega did not know where and when he might find the mainland.

On August 22 the voyagers reached the farthest north they would achieve. Their observations gave the ship's position as 57°58′N.[62] Reluctantly, Bodega decided to turn back. The greater part of his people were sick – Mourelle noted that only two men could be mustered for each watch – and the season was too far advanced to allow him to sail sufficiently far west to find the winds he needed to take him to higher latitudes. He wrote: "I decided to return steering east-southeast, following the coast at a distance of one mile, and resigned myself to have sailed as high as 58°, especially in a ship which could not have been expected to obtain such success." He then added characteristically: "Having many times been urged to return and not to endanger myself, I never abandoned my purpose until compelled to do so."

Mourelle questioned Bodega's decision. He later recorded, writing as usual in the third person:

> The captain decided to turn back to reconnoitre the coast to the south, a determination with which the *piloto* did not agree. As a result, for a few days there was a small quarrel that differences of opinion can produce. But as both wished to contribute to the best success of the exploration, they became reconciled in the knowledge they had reached 58° of latitude, which has never been reached by other navigators who in our times have sailed north from California.[63]

The Return Journey

Bodega's purpose in hugging what he thought was the mainland coast as he sailed south was not just to correct the Bellin maps he had with him, but also to search for the entrance to the passage across North America that Admiral Bartolomeo de Fonte claimed to have discovered in the same general latitude in 1640. Bodega failed to find the "great archipelago of San Lázaro through which Fonte is said to have entered," but with considerable exaggeration, considering the highly complex geography of the region, he said it was not for lack of trying:

> Eagerly, I have examined the deepest and smallest inlets, going around whatever points presented themselves, refraining from any navigation at night so as not to lose a single indication, forcing myself to take special care as required by such an earnest task and so that the slightest doubt does not remain in my mind as to the direction and position of the coast.[64]

Bucareli Bay

The search for the mythical passage was not a total waste of effort. On August 24, the *Sonora* sailed into a large bay on the west side of Prince of Wales Island. It was so well protected from the winds that the ship was nearly becalmed almost immediately. Bodega anchored near the entrance. Feeling unwell, he sent Mourelle ashore to take formal possession "with the usual formalities." The bay was named the Entrada de Bucareli after the viceroy and today retains the name of Bucareli Bay. The spot on which the cross was raised was most likely a promontory overlooking the bay he called Puerto de la Santa Cruz, a name it still bears, on the west coast of Suemez Island.[65] Although the voyagers remained there only two days, they charted the bay and established its position as 55°17′N and 32°09′W of San Blas.[66]

Bucareli Bay was a discovery for which Bodega would always have a special regard. "The Entrada," he wrote,

> is worthy of esteem because of its mild climate, the tranquility of its waters ... the excellent bottom, and the fish. I would undoubtedly have stayed a few days longer were the season not so far advanced ... The soil is fertile, as is the entire coast. We saw no Indians, only some trails they use when hunting and fishing. The nights are exceptionally bright and mild because of seven volcanoes of snow and fire, which their vapours illuminate and temper.[67]

After the rough journey that the *Sonora* had endured and after the hardships sustained by all, finding such a haven was a welcome surprise. They could not stay long. Having provisioned their schooner with water and wood, they departed two days later, on the August 26.

Sailing due south, they encountered Forrester Island, which was "almost level with sea" and surrounded by reefs, and where the currents were so strong that the lead of the sounding line "could not descend to the depths."[68] He estimated that Forrester Island lay "four or five leagues" to the east of Cape Augustine on Dall Island.[69] Bodega fixed the position of Cape Augustine at 55°N, the same latitude on which Pérez had reported having seen an entrance.[70] Bodega was not convinced that Pérez was wrong, but two of his seamen who had sailed on the 1774 voyage told him they thought they had been farther south.[71]

As the *Sonora* sailed along the coast of Dall Island, the winds changed direction and made it impossible to continue on a southeasterly course. Bodega and Mourelle agreed they should attempt another northing in the hope of reaching 60°N, which they thought they could do "in a few days" provided the winds maintained the same direction, especially since most of their crew now showed signs of recovering their health from the fresh fish and warmer temperatures of Bucareli Bay. In his frank, unbuttoned style, Mourelle later wrote that he thought it "imprudent" to do so, as there was still much coast to reconnoitre, but he added that "no determination could be so agreeable as this one because the verve of the spirits of two youths was such as to fill them full of enthusiasm to find themselves at [the North] Pole."[72]

The weather turned much colder, and Bodega distributed to the crew four jackets, some flannel capes, and cloth that Hezeta had given him for trading with the Indians, as well as some shirts and overcoats belonging to Mourelle and to him. He did so because he realized that "the cold would frighten them and made them sick."

The winds did not keep up the steady direction he hoped, and the weather became stormy and the seas turbulent. Instead of proceeding northward, he found the ship being pushed nearly imperceptibly toward the deep, rough waters off Baranof Island. He was forced to tack until September 1, "when God was pleased to give us westerly winds, which enabled me to get away from the coast."

Seven seamen were found to have been struck with scurvy. Some were affected in their mouths, while others had pains that restricted the movement of their legs and joints. Only two were fit to stand watch: one at the helm, the other working the ship. Bodega and Mourelle took turns handling the sails and manning the pumps, even though they themselves were beginning to feel the first effects of the dreaded infirmity. Bodega was obliged to draw the only possible conclusion:

> Finding myself with people struck with this contagious illness, without medicines for them and exposed to having it spread to others, as it was impossible to keep them separated, I realized that, however much I might force myself, reaching a higher latitude would be out of the question. One could even doubt whether we could return should the winds grow stronger without people to work the ship.

Reluctantly, he and Mourelle abandoned their second attempt at reaching a more northerly latitude and, taking advantage of a favourable wind, headed southward. They carefully examined the shoreline whenever it was possible. They estimated their latitude – the highest they would reach on this second attempt – at 56°47′N, southwest of the entrance to Sitka Sound.

At midnight on September 6, the winds began to blow with such force that the mainsail had to be double-reefed. Even this was not sufficient, and the *Sonora* had to heave to. Knowing that he was very close to land, Bodega struggled for two hours to control the ship, with the crew becoming visibly alarmed. Their panic reached a peak when

> a sea of great strength broke over the ship, tearing out railings, stanchions, clamps, and the gunwales of the deck house. The water carried away everything over the deck. We believed we had foundered, because for four minutes nothing could be seen in the ship but a foaming sea. The cabin was flooded ... and we could not tell one from the other.
>
> When the water began to drain away through the scuppers and carry away things in the hold through the hatches, we began to hear moans and wailing, as the railing had smashed the boatswain against an anchor, leaving him senseless. Other sailors were also hurt, and although not seriously so, they could not help working the ship. In this critical moment, I found myself with only two seamen, the *piloto*, the boatswain's mate, and one of my servants.[73]

Manoeuvering with only a fore topmast staysail, Bodega managed to swing the tiny schooner about to put the wind behind him and steer northwest to avoid running ashore.

Although tarpaulins had been spread over the hatches, water was flooding into the hold faster than the pumps could cope with it, and up on deck the scuppers were unable to provide much relief. Despite the exertions of those manning the pumps, there was a sense that the ship would sink before the storm ended. Eventually, the pumps began to function properly, and by eight in the morning the ship was free of water. The gudgeon of the rudder was discovered to have split. A nail found in the broken tiller was inserted in one eye to secure the rudder. When the storm passed, only one seaman was well enough to man the helm, and Bodega and Mourelle had to handle the sails.

Following a generally southeasterly course, the *Sonora* passed Graham Island in the Queen Charlotte Islands without attempting a landing. Because of the debilitated condition of his crew, Bodega was compelled to abandon any attempt to sail close in along the shore to inspect every inlet.

When some of the men had recovered sufficiently to be of help and when he was certain of a steady wind, he did attempt to sail in closer, but generally, he had to be content with gaining a good idea of the general direction of the distant coast.[74]

By September 17, Bodega was off the entrance to the Strait of Juan de Fuca. He states in his journal that he was within one league of the coast and that he saw land but was compelled to turn out to sea when the winds shifted to the southeast. He thus missed being the first European to sight the fabled strait. By now, both Bodega and Mourelle were suffering from fever as well as scurvy pains. The crewmen were aware of their superiors' sickness and "became so dismayed that they thought themselves lost." To allay their fears, the two leaders "made every effort to show ourselves on deck and God was pleased to help us to this end."

Off the coast of Oregon, the vessel closed in at 45°27′N, never sailing more than one and a half miles from shore. Bodega's health was now improving, and he began to search carefully for the legendary Río de Martín de Aguilar.[75] Although he anchored every night at sunset so as to be sure not to miss the river, he found nothing. He wrote with assurance that "it does not exist between 45°27′ north and 42°50′ north," where he sighted Cape Blanco. The river was supposed to be at 43°N, but his search between 44°50′N and 42°50′N was so carefully done, he thought, that the fault must lie with the instruments that Sebastian Vizcaíno had used in his 1602-3 voyage, which were notoriously inaccurate.

Bodega Bay

Continuing south and still hugging the coast, Bodega began searching for San Francisco Bay. On October 3 he encountered a large bay, into which he sailed. Examining it, he spied a river to the southeast, one "of great volume, and entering it, I saw a large harbour." When the sea came up with "extraordinary violence" because the tide was coming in, he felt certain he was in San Francisco Bay. He was actually in Bodega Bay, a small harbour just north of San Francisco, having mistaken the entrance to Tomales Bay for a river. After he anchored off the tip of Tomales Bluff, a large number of Indians came in their canoes from all parts of the bay, gathering on a hill overlooking it. For a considerable time they shouted at the ship. Nothing was understood, but two Indians came out in their canoe to offer feathers, bone collars, a basket of seeds that tasted like hazelnuts, and other goods. Bodega gave them some of the little cloth, mirrors, and beads he had left.

The presence of the Indians caused Bodega to realize he was not in San Francisco Bay as he had thought. He described the newly found bay as "large and indeterminate to the southeast; it provides a perfect shelter as it is like an inner harbour." He made no attempt to explore it because all he wanted was "to land the sick, full of pity seeing them almost at their end without the slightest succour [possible]."[76] He anchored just inside Sand Point for the night. At two in the morning the incoming tide collided with the outgoing tide, creating a tidal bore that broke so violently against the schooner that breakers covered it from stem to stern. One such breaker carried off the launch that had been tied up alongside, "smashing it in a thousand pieces," and caused one of the anchors to fail. It could not be retrieved. Although the entry had been easy, leaving the bay without a southeast wind was another matter. It was necessary to wait for the ebb tide. Given this experience, he did not recommend Bodega Bay as a harbour, as the "currents enter and leave with such force that when the weather outside is bad, the seas break at the mouth." Nor did he give it a name.[77]

Monterey

Leaving Bodega Bay the following morning, he rounded Point Reyes. Bodega saw the entrance to San Francisco Bay and was tempted to go in, but discretion being the better part of valour – and having no launch or knowledge of the tricky waters of the entrance – he suppressed that desire. He headed for Monterey, which was sighted indistinctly through the fog at three in the afternoon of October 7. Mourelle confessed that they were not certain of their location until they entered the bay and found the *Santiago* and the *San Carlos* riding at anchor. According to one witness, the *Sonora*'s arrival was greeted with "extraordinary joy, as it was feared that it had been lost."[78] After firing welcoming shots with their cannon, to which the *Sonora* replied, Hezeta and Ayala came out in their launches to welcome the *Sonora* and her crew in person and to take her in tow to the anchorage.

Miraculously, Bodega had lost none of his crew since the massacre off Cape Elizabeth. Although the entire crew and both Mourelle and Bodega were weak with scurvy when they arrived in Monterey, none died of it.[79] As Bodega remarked:

> The ship had so few conveniences that it is a miracle we did not all arrive back crippled, because we were continuously almost inundated [with water], [had] no space at all to take more than two steps, and [were] obliged to remain standing or seated, which was the best rest possible.[80]

All were incapable of walking and had to be helped off the ship and into the launches.

Bodega and Mourelle recuperated in a house overlooking the harbour made available to them by the commandant, Fernando de Rivera y Moncada, while the crew of the *Sonora* was taken to the nearby mission of San Carlos Borromeo de Carmelo. Then

> the captains and pilots of the schooner accompanied by the members of the crew who could make the journey came to this mission of San Carlos ... to fulfill a vow they had made while performing their tasks in moments of danger to offer a solemn mass made to Our Lady of Bethlehem, the Conqueror, who is venerated in the church of this mission.[81]

Thanks to the excellent care they received from the Franciscan fathers, the vegetables from the mission garden, the fresh meat and milk, and the warmth of the Californian climate, all began a slow recovery. The *Sonora* was in such bad shape that she had to be careened and her planking tightened "because of the heavy blows received during the voyage." The process took longer than anticipated and delayed the two ships' departure.

After their reunion, both captains and their officers no doubt exchanged accounts of their respective adventures. After the ships separated, Hezeta had undertaken a search for the schooner until August 11. At that point, he was probably off either Esperanza Inlet or Kyuquot Sound, just north of Nootka Sound on Vancouver Island. He recorded seeing "some high mountains in the interior of this coast which have quite a lot of snow in their ravines."[82] Heading south for Monterey, Hezeta began to hug the coast as he had been instructed to do. On August 17 he encountered the entrance to the Columbia River, naming it the Bahía de la Asunción de Nuestra Señora (Bay of the Assumption of Our Lady), although it would later be known to the Spanish as the Entrada de Hezeta. He attempted to enter, but his crew members, weakened by scurvy, were in no condition to battle the swirling currents. He speculated that "these currents and the seething of the waters have led me to believe that it may be the mouth of some great river or some passage to another sea." After searching without success for the Strait of Juan de Fuca and convincing himself that "no such strait exists," Hezeta concluded that the turbulent "bay" might possibly be the strait.[83]

The officers and *pilotos* met to reconcile and perfect their charts, observations, and journals. Hezeta, Bodega, and Ayala each wrote short accounts of their respective voyages for the viceroy, which Ayala took with him when he left for San Blas on October 13 in the *San Carlos*. In his formal correspondence with Hezeta while at sea in 1775, Bodega had always showed respect for his commandant, and when it came to assessing Bodega's performance, Hezeta seems to have chosen to pass over the decision by Bodega and Mourelle to steal away under cover of darkness and continue north, alone in their inadequate vessel. Bodega y Quadra closed his report with a tribute to Mourelle:

> I would fail in my duty to Your Excellency if I did not inform you of the honour with which Don Francisco Mourelle, the *piloto* of this schooner, has served. Because of the great intelligence he has exhibited during the voyage, so much vigilance, and the continual care he has shown, I doubt that I would have been able to suffer so many miseries had I not had such a companion with whom to share the labours.[84]

Hezeta called a *junta* with the officers and *pilotos* to consider what the expedition should do next. He proposed that the ships spend the winter in San Diego and continue the explorations the next spring. While all agreed that that would be an "honourable determination," the *junta* decided against it. After the hardships of the summer, the ships were in no condition to undertake another lengthy voyage. New sails were required, and the crewmen, with their clothes in rags, were practically naked. There was no brandy left, no lard, oil, or vinegar. While corn might be found in San Diego, the amount would not be sufficient to feed them all. A formal statement was drawn up recording their decision and was signed by all present.[85]

On November 1, twenty-two days after the *Sonora*'s arrival, the health of most of the crew having greatly improved, Hezeta and Bodega departed for San Blas. The voyage was uneventful, except that two days out the veteran mariner Juan Pérez succumbed to typhoid fever. He was buried at sea "with salutes of musketry and cannon."[86]

The vessels arrived at San Blas on November 20, 246 days after their departure. Bodega concluded his journal with the laconic remark: "In spite of the labours expended in the course of the voyage, I count myself fortunate to have carried out that part of the orders of His Excellency Don Antonio Bucareli which fell to me." Bodega was forced to take to his bed for three months to recover his health.

Achievements and Disappointments of the 1775 Voyage

The remarkable saga of the *Sonora* tends to obscure the expedition's achievements and disappointments.[87] Although no Russian settlements were found, their existence remained a possibility. In the realm of discoveries,

Hezeta had sailed too far out to sea to see the Strait of Juan de Fuca or other significant straits and bays that make up the complex geography of the Northwest Coast, and Bodega had had no better luck.

Hezeta's sighting of the entrance to the Columbia River was a major discovery. He was the first European in the historical record to do so. Unfortunately, he was unable to confirm whether it was indeed "the mouth of some great river or some passage to another sea" because he was unable to cross the bar at the entrance.[88] Bodega missed the river completely after encountering contrary winds when he reached that latitude.[89]

Although Bucareli Bay was not a major discovery, it was a natural jumping-off point for exploration farther north that could be used to avoid the three-month voyage from San Blas.[90] Hezeta recommended that a shipyard be established at Trinidad Bay in northern California. He saw this as "a virtual necessity" both for practical reasons and for another that was always present in Spanish strategic thinking – namely, the fear that leaving the bay unoccupied would make it accessible to any foreigner wishing to occupy it or to use it as a port for illegal trade.[91] Bucareli admitted that he was attracted to the idea of a northern base, but he was not prepared to recommend it until the number of navy ships on the coast had been increased. Nothing ever came of the proposal.[92]

Bodega's discovery of the bay that today bears his name was followed up almost two decades later, when he was naval commandant at San Blas. In spite of his earlier unfavourable report, in 1793 he recommended it as an outpost to protect the coast north of San Francisco. This was after Bodega Bay had been visited by George Vancouver and some English fur traders, including James Colnett. Viceroy Revillagigedo, always worried about possible English encroachment, decided to occupy the area, but the effort came to naught.[93]

Viceroy Bucareli was highly pleased with the expedition's accomplishments. He wrote eight letters to Minister Arriaga, each devoted to a particular aspect of the expedition.[94] Overlooking their insubordination, he praised Bodega and Mourelle in the warmest terms. Of Bodega, he wrote:

> The schooner in which he embarked and carried out this expedition would have destroyed the spirit of anyone else considering the enterprise. To Lieutenant Quadra [sic] neither this consideration nor the fact that he first embarked as second officer to one of the same rank could not dissuade him from going to sea, and, with the gallant zeal with which he has dedicated himself to the service, he has carried it out happily and with good fortune.[95]

Bodega, he thought, would have journeyed even farther north had his "heroic constancy and disdain of risks" not been defeated by the number of his people afflicted with scurvy, by the contrary winds, and by the lateness of the season. Francisco Mourelle, Bucareli wrote,

> has demonstrated honour, prudence and intelligence in his career, as all reports given me testify ... Bodega y Quadra praises him highly and recommends that his work warrants his transfer to the Royal Navy as an officer, for which he is well qualified.[96]

A memorandum containing the main points of the viceroy's eight letters was prepared for the king.[97] Carlos III was so delighted that he took the unusual step of ordering that the expedition be announced in the *Gaceta Oficial* for March 14, 1776. After a brief reference to the Pérez expedition of 1774, the notice went on:

> As a consequence of these valuable events, the king ordered officers sent to the port of San Blas to extend these navigations and discoveries as much as possible. To this end at the beginning of 1775 *Teniente de Navío* Bruno de Hezeta in the frigate *Santiago* and *Teniente de Fragata* Juan Francisco de la Bodega y Quadra in the schooner *Sonora* and for the same purpose *Teniente de Fragata* Juan de Ayala in the packetboat *San Carlos* sailed to Monterey.
>
> The first reached 50° of latitude, the second 58° and the third 37°42′. They reconnoitered the coast in between, which is populated by savage Indians. The harbour of San Francisco was charted carefully, and the Indians in the neighbourhood were especially docile and tractable.
>
> His Majesty, in consideration of the special and distinguished service which these naval officers and *pilotos* have rendered and to encourage others, has promoted Bruno de Eceta [sic] to *capitán de fragata*, Juan de Ayala and Juan Francisco de la Bodega y Quadra to *teniente de navío*, and Juan Pérez to *teniente de fragata*. The *pilotos* José de Cañizares and Francisco Maurelle [sic] have been promoted to *alférez de fragata*.[98]

Finally, the newly appointed Minister of the Indies José de Gálvez sent a letter conveying the king's approval of the promotions for all the officers and *pilotos*. In the same letter, Gálvez confirmed the king's desire that another expedition be organized, and he specifically ordered that Bodega be given command of one of the ships.

The Hezeta-Bodega voyage launched Bodega's career. He was justly proud of what he and Mourelle had achieved. Mourelle's pride is especially obvious in the candid and blunt *notas del redactor* he inserted here and there in the synopsis of the voyage he wrote later while he was compiling the compendium of all Spanish voyages north for Viceroy Revillagigedo of New Spain. A *nota* that appears at the very end of his summary of the 1775 voyage, is revealing:

> It will never be denied that those who sailed in the *Sonora* were the first to gain that latitude of a vast continent and, more or less, establish its coastline and harbours to the extent possible with so many sick and in the [short] time available. They will always retain the satisfaction that his [Mourelle's] journal gave Cook sufficient information to navigate with a knowledge of those seas, since he carried a copy of it on his ship.[99]

As for Bodega, from the moment he made his offer to sail on the *Sonora* rather than remain in San Blas, his strong desire to actively serve the King and his own appetite for adventure were plain for all to see. It was entirely by chance that command of the small schooner fell to him, and he immediately determined, with no apparent lack of confidence or courage, to make the most of his good fortune and to exploit it to his advantage. Shortly after returning to San Blas, he ensured that his efforts would be noticed in Spain. He not only forwarded his formal report, the *Navegación*, to Viceroy Bucareli, as was customary, but also sent a copy directly to Arriaga, the Minister of the Indies.[100] In the covering letter, he was not afraid to write:

> I have no doubt that I will merit Your Excellency's respect and attention when you are informed of this particular achievement. The principal reward I desire, one which acknowledges my performance, is to be given only the most hazardous assignments which would fulfill my wishes.

Cartography and Navigation

In his papers, Bodega said nothing about his navigational procedures or what instruments he used to determine his position at sea during the 1775 expedition. We know that when he and his companions left Cádiz in 1774, they brought with them the instruments recommended by Vicente Tofiño, but we do not know whether Bodega had any of them aboard the tiny *Sonora*. Tofiño considered that for charting small bays the only requirements were a metal protractor to measure angles on paper and a small table on a tripod; however, he contended, the exploration of vast spaces required an astronomical clock, a quadrant of two-and-a-half-foot radius, telescopes of a focal length of twenty-four inches, azimuth compasses to measure variation, and sextants.[101] From the number of sightings Bodega and Mourelle recorded and the tables in which they listed daily their position and the variation of the compass, it is evident that they had, besides the indispensable lead line, a magnetic compass, a sextant, and an azimuth compass. But they did not record what type of instruments they were or who had made them. Mourelle in his journals suggests that when returning from the north, hugging the coast as much as possible from 49°N down to Monterey, weather permitting, he and Bodega located prominent features by triangulation. They were making a running survey. But that is all they tell us.[102]

In the area of cartography, the expedition produced a full harvest of plans and charts.[103] Especially important was Ayala's first comprehensive chart of the San Francisco Bay, drawn by his *piloto,* José de Cañizares, who made the survey. Bodega produced two *cartas reducidas.*[104] The archipelago of the Alaska Panhandle was shown as a single line as if it were the mainland. Only the bays, the *ensenadas* (coves and inlets), and the rivers actually seen were indicated. Mount Edgecombe was shown as San Jacinto, the name Bodega gave it. There was, naturally enough, no indication on either chart of the Strait of Juan de Fuca or of the Queen Charlotte Islands. Bodega's two charts were the first to delineate North America's Pacific coastline north of San Francisco with any degree of realism.[105]

Bodega recorded a wealth of knowledge about the weather, winds, tides, and currents, and also about the natural signs he observed at various distances from the coast that would guide a mariner, such as the darkening colour of the water as the coast was approached and the sighting of birds, sea otters, whales, sea lions, and jellyfish when the coast was very near. These observations would be put to good use by later voyagers, including Bodega himself.

The maps the expedition produced were accorded special attention in Spain. Carlos III directed that one set of the maps, charts, and courses be conveyed on a confidential basis to the Ministry of Marine for study by the *pilotos.* Two months later he authorized a second notice about the Hezeta voyage, which appeared in the *Gaceta Oficial* for May 19:

> [The viceroy] has also reported that the officers and *pilotos* have made very accurate maps and charts of the coast and seas of northern California, which His Majesty has decided to have engraved and so publicize the results of the aforementioned navigation from Monterey.

This announcement and the publication of the maps were the first exception to Spain's short-sighted policy of keeping secret the activities and findings of her explorers. Although the British ambassador in Madrid at this time did not report the first notice of March 19 in the *Gaceta Oficial*, several English newspapers printed what purported to be a translation of the Spanish account.

Political Implications

Viceroy Bucareli outlined the political implications of the voyage for Julián de Arriaga, the Minister of the Indies and the Navy. He began with the most immediate task of the voyage, which had been to discover whether the reports of Russian activity on the Northwest Coast of America were true. He assured the minister that up to 58°N,

> there need be no fear of any foreign establishment; that between that latitude and Monterey there are twenty-two degrees [of land] inhabited by Indians more or less tractable; that they have no commerce with outsiders; that the bow and arrow is common up to 56° where the Indians arm themselves with spears; that the knowledge obtained of the coast and harbours and the problems of navigation are such that there is no need to take special measures, as nothing is urgent.[106]

He also pointed out that by performing four acts of formal possession between Trinidad Bay and 57°18′N, the expedition had extended the king's dominions northward by almost five hundred Spanish leagues, as shown on the charts they had produced.[107]

Bucareli was overly optimistic in assuring his government that there was no immediate threat to Spanish sovereignty. In fact, Russian fur traders had established themselves in the Aleutians as well as in Cook Inlet and were about to move into Prince William Sound and the Alexander Archipelago. Bucareli failed to appreciate that, having claimed the entire area the expedition had charted, Spain was increasing its vulnerability to foreign threats. Spanish efforts to sustain a claim over this area would produce nothing but problems over the next two decades. The Northwest was about to become a scene of international rivalry over the trade in sea otter furs.

More Exploration

Viceroy Bucareli said nothing specific about the possibility of subsequent northern expeditions in his letters to Madrid. However, he prepared the ground by pointing out that the expedition had found several valuable harbours with safe anchorages as well as abundant forests that promised ample timber for shipbuilding. As further enticement, he reported that as a whole, the native people seemed docile and open to trading as well as proselytization. In a letter forwarding copies of the expedition journals and charts, he also praised them as a source of information:

> You will find in these [documents] new intelligence acquired at the cost of much hardship, continual risks and heroic steadfastness, highly useful information we [formerly] did not have, suspicions [are] dispelled of such a magnitude that exploration can be promoted as the King wishes and necessity demands.[108]

Bucareli would realize his ambition for more exploratory expeditions. An important consequence of the Hezeta-Bodega expedition of 1775 was that Spain became irrevocably committed to a search for the Northwest Passage. At first, Viceroy Bucareli struggled with inadequate funds as there seemed to be no inclination to indulge in pre-emptive efforts. This changed dramatically after 1776, the year when Arriaga died and was replaced as Minister of the Indies by José de Gálvez. When news reached Madrid that James Cook would be making an attempt to find the Pacific entrance to the legendary Northwest Passage, the Spanish government felt that it could not ignore a British venture that might threaten the security of the Spanish Americas. Yet when the king immediately ordered Bucareli to prepare another expedition to sail north the following year, 1777, employing the same officers, the viceroy kept this royal directive to himself.

3

Preparations for the 1779 Voyage

Even before Bruno de Hezeta's 1775 expedition returned to New Spain – indeed, as early as August of that year – the viceroy of New Spain, Antonio Bucareli y Ursúa, anticipated Madrid's continued interest in exploring the coast north of the Alta California settlements. He ordered the commandant at San Blas, Ignacio de Arteaga y Bazán, to make plans with *comisario* Francisco Hijosa y Rodríguez for another voyage, even though there was some doubt as to whether Hezeta, Bodega, and Mourelle would be healthy enough to undertake another arduous voyage so soon.[1]

Bucareli's Dilemmas

Bucareli was well aware of the obstacles he faced. The Naval Department of San Blas had some purely administrative problems that made it difficult to mount another expedition to the north. The department was undergoing one of its periodic financial crises, the Pérez and Hezeta-Bodega expeditions having left a debt of nearly 8,000 pesos. Bucareli covered this departmental deficit by providing an additional 20,000 pesos.[2] More serious was the shortage of ships. Apart from one or two small ships, there were only the frigates *Santiago* and *Concepción*, the schooner *Sonora,* and the packet boats *San Carlos* and *El Príncipe.* They were seldom all available at the same time, for each had to be careened or laid up for repairs periodically. Related to the shortage of vessels was the constant shortage of trained personnel of all ranks. To mount a third expedition to the North Pacific, the viceroy would have to augment the meagre resources at his disposal. To make matters worse, famine had struck the missions and presidios of Alta California. This was the priority of the San Blas department, and it meant that resupply ships would need to be sent to the region.

After March 1776 the San Blas Naval Department assumed further importance when James Cook's third voyage became the subject of many letters between Bucareli and Gálvez, who was now a dominant force in the administration. In a confidential message, Gálvez told Bucareli that "the king has received very certain information from London" that two "frigates" [sic] under Cook's command, the *Resolution* and the *Discovery*, were being readied for a voyage to the South Seas under the pretext of returning to Tahiti "the Indian he had taken from there on a previous voyage." Cook's real purpose, however, seemed to be to "examine the route of our next fleet"; to explore the Ladrones Islands; to continue on to the Californias to investigate trade with "New Mexico"; and to search for the Northwest Passage and thus win the £20,000 prize offered by the British Parliament. Gálvez noted that as the expedition had so many different objectives, the news might be "doubtful." But, he concluded, it was nevertheless necessary to exercise the greatest vigilance.[3]

Gálvez directed Bucareli to hamper Cook's exploration. He was to instruct the commandants on the California coast

> to be vigilant and cause [Cook] to fail in every way possible without using force but by taking measures to restrict assistance and supplies ... Your Excellency should warn them that if they encounter either of [Cook's] frigates, they should examine their intentions and the instructions and orders they carry, and practice all the formalities required in such cases.

Bucareli replied by letter on June 26 that San Blas did not have the resources to carry out this order, nor did the Alta California missions. He was troubled by the new, more bellicose tone of the instructions regarding the reception of foreign ships calling at Spanish settlements and by the order that those instructions be applied rigorously to Cook's expedition. Lobbing the responsibility back to Gálvez, he pointed out that the use of force raised a delicate point, meaning the possibility of war, which only the king himself could declare. Bucareli said that pending further instructions, he would be sparing when giving Cook any supplies.

Gálvez's reply to this letter bluntly rejected Bucareli's arguments. The minister was in a foul mood. Clearly, he said, Bucareli had written his letter before receiving the the Royal Order of July 14, 1776. According to the

Royal Order, Cook had already left England and Bucareli was to instruct the authorities in Alta California to watch for him and to refuse him entry into Spanish ports. Bucareli obeyed. In a further Royal Order, this one dated October 18, Gálvez told Bucareli that his instructions had been issued in full knowledge of the weak maritime and land defences of San Blas and Alta California. Nevertheless, Cook was to be detained, imprisoned, and tried in accordance with the Spanish Laws of the Indies. Bucareli was ordered to stop procrastinating: "I expect you to comply."[4] Reluctantly, Bucareli passed on these instructions to those in charge of the ports of San Blas and Acapulco and to the army commandant of the viceroyalty's *Provincias Internas.*

When Gálvez also asked the viceroy to transport the newly appointed *visitador general* José de Areche from New Spain to Peru, the lack of shipping on the west coast compelled Bucareli to establish priorities. He declared the resupply of missions in Alta California to be his "first and most important objective."[5] He solved the transportation of the *visitador general* to Peru when, by chance, a merchantman, the *Fénix,* arrived in Acapulco to discharge a cargo of cacao beans from Guayaquil. It was scheduled to return to Peru in January 1777. Bucareli immediately ordered that arrangements be made with its captain to transport Areche and his party. Most likely with Bodega in mind, he told Gálvez that the *visitador general* would be accompanied by a "naval officer."[6] The shortage of vessels compelled Bucareli to postpone the new northern expedition until 1778.

A Quick Voyage to Peru, 1777-78 – the *Favorita*

Bucareli had decided that San Blas needed two more frigates before the department could undertake a new northern expedition. One was to be built in San Blas, the other was to come from Peru.[7] Bucareli ordered Bodega to go to Peru to secure the second frigate. He was to ask Peru's viceroy, Manuel de Guirior, for help in purchasing a frigate suitable for northern exploration, with sufficient equipment and armament, and additional cannon, for the other San Blas ships. Guirior had been forewarned of the purpose of Bodega's visit. One suspects that Bodega lobbied for this mission to Peru for personal reasons. He had not visited his birthplace since 1772.

Bodega and the *piloto* José de Cañizares[8] arrived in Acapulco on March 16, 1777. There they were joined by José Antonio de Areche, the newly appointed *visitador general,* who was on his way to investigate serious administrative problems in the Viceroyalty of Perú. As the *Fénix* had not yet completed wooding and watering and because Bodega was interested in Acapulco's harbour as a possible alternative to San Blas, he and Cañizares joined Francisco Cañaveral, the port's commandant, to sound the harbour and to draft a comprehensive chart of the bay depicting all the features of the port as they existed at the time.[9] Bodega thought the harbour "should be among the best" but found it in a "deplorable state." He noted that the town had no protection from the wind and that there were no defences for the entrance or the anchorage.

When the *Fénix* sailed from Acapulco, she carried as passengers Bodega, Cañizares, and Areche, as well as the latter's *oficial mayor,* a *fiscal,* and nine other officials.[10] For the most part, the voyage was pleasant. The weather was good, but progress, Bodega thought, was much too slow. His mission was urgent since the next northern voyage was scheduled to depart San Blas in February 1778, in less than a year. Like a doctor who makes a poor patient, Bodega the navigator was a poor passenger. He and Cañizares chafed at the seemingly indifferent manner in which the ship was handled. Bodega gave vent to his frustrations, both in his journal and in his reports to Viceroy Bucareli.

He criticized the captain of the *Fénix* for following the traditional course between Acapulco and Peru: "They never attempt any [new] route and nothing dangerous so as not to risk the trade in which the ships are engaged or burden [their owners] with greater expenses that they suspect will result." Bodega was not much kinder when commenting on the *pilotos,* who showed "little experience and knowledge" of their responsibilities or of how to exploit changing weather conditions. They would routinely and unnecessarily shorten sail when the winds strengthened, the only result being to cause the ship to roll and make everyone seasick. "I am convinced," he wrote in his report, "that the *pilotos* in this career will never make any progress in their seamanship." He went so far as to call them together and show them "the advantages to be obtained if they steered southeast," which they then did, but when the winds changed the following day, they were incapable of responding properly.[11] Bodega and Cañizares eventually assumed an active role in sailing the ship.

The Silla de Paita, on the northern coast of today's Peru, was finally sighted on May 5. The *Fénix* entered the inner harbour the following morning after a voyage of forty-six days. Bodega and Cañizares estimated that if they had sailed west of the Galápagos Islands, the trip could have been accomplished in one-third of that time. Instead of proceeding on the *Fénix* to Callao, Lima's port, the passengers decided it would be faster if they travelled the rest of the way overland, a distance of more than a thousand kilometres down the narrow coastal desert. The group arrived in Lima in mid-June "in spite of the distance and the desolate road." This road went past the ancestral home of Bodega's mother in the Chancay Valley.

In Lima, Bodega's first duty was to call on the viceroy, Guirior, to seek his support and goodwill.[12] Guirior assured Bodega that he would assist him in every possible way and obtained the cooperation of the naval squadron based in Callao. Bodega and Cañizares were allowed to examine all the navy ships in the harbour, but they did not find a vessel that was sturdy enough for the merciless waters of the North Pacific. Bodega considered ordering such a ship to be built, but a lack of appropriate timber ruled out that option. He decided to await the arrival of the merchant ship *Favorita* from Chile – a potential purchase. "In this," he wrote, "I placed all my hopes, as I had seen her although incidentally [when in Lima] in 1772." He waited three months for the merchantman to arrive. To pass the time, he and Cañizares charted the harbour and reconnoitred other harbours nearby, as they had done in Acapulco and Paita. Bodega concluded by recording what his trained eye told him was an unsatisfactory situation:

> In the light of all these openings and the ease with which [our] enemies could enter Lima, it must be recognized that the fort of Callao has no purpose other than the defence of the ships anchored there and the supplies in them.

As soon as the *Favorita* arrived, probably on September 5, Bodega examined her carefully. He was certain that, with changes, she could be a suitable frigate for his purposes. Her dimensions were right, and he was satisfied with her speed and resistance in the water and with the number of feet she drew. She had been built in Guayaquil and weighed 197 tons.[13] He formally asked the viceroy to attend a naval board to determine her condition and make an exact evaluation of her worth. At first, the owner was unwilling to sell. After the usual offers and counteroffers, a price of 25,000 pesos, free of sales tax, was agreed upon and the deed of sale and necessary documents were drawn up.[14] This was all accomplished by September 9, four days after the ship's arrival.

Bodega lost no time taking charge of his purchase and preparing her for conversion. First, he drew up a plan of the work to be done

> to put the vessel in condition to resist the winds and seas which, in the high altitudes, are considerable and [to] fit her out with armament that, while not perfect for war, would be sufficient to gain the respect of the natives.

As he did not wish to proceed alone, he asked Cayetano de Langara, a local *capitán de fragata* and a man of "sound intelligence," to attend a meeting with the squadron's shipwrights to determine the extent of the work required and the means available to do it.

Once the rebuilding plan had been formulated, he wrote to the viceroy to request that the entire naval dockyard and all tools in the royal stores be placed at his disposal and that an accountant be provided to keep proper and detailed records of payments. He also requested an advance of 30,000 pesos, which he had calculated would be indispensable for the conversion and arming of the *Favorita,* plus another 30,000 pesos to pay workers' wages and to purchase timber and supplies that were not in the naval stores. He assured Guirior that Viceroy Bucareli had given him a free hand and that all the expenses incurred, once audited, would be repaid by the treasury of New Spain. Guirior gave Bodega's request prompt approval. The commandant of the local naval squadron was instructed to give any assistance requested, and an advance of 15,000 pesos was paid so that work could begin immediately. The viceroy directed the treasurer of the port to make all the required payments.

The ship's conversion began on September 15. Bodega and Cañizares shared the administrative duties: the former undertook direct supervision of the work "to make certain there was not the slightest waste in the consumption of wood, nails and other materials"; the latter kept lists of everything provided. The navy yard lent them 182 men to work on the ship and provided twenty-five day labourers to carry the wood. The conversion was done as quickly as possible and, Bodega claimed, due care was taken to make certain that everything was done to his satisfaction. The work was finished on November 30. In accordance with the custom of the Spanish navy at this time, the *Favorita* acquired a religious alias, *Nuestra Señora de los Remedios.* Although Bodega does not say as much, it seems likely that he gave her this name since, as he venerated Our Lady of the Remedies.[15]

At the time of purchase, the *Favorita* had been a simple two-decked vessel with no cabin, forecastle deck, or separate quarterdeck, with no poop of any sort, and, probably, with only tiller steering.[16] Conversion turned her into a frigate, which was only slightly less Spartan. The most visible change was the addition of a decorative quarter-gallery extending over two deck levels, with windows opening onto the gallery from the second deck cabin and main deck. This was probably done to provide sleeping quarters for officers on the main deck level. The ship's sides were raised, and 170 bulwark stanchions were added that provided additional storage space besides improving ventilation between decks. The main deck was replanked, the second deck partly replanked. The entire underwater body was rebuilt to rid it of marine worms and to provide more space for stowing sails and rigging. Other improvements were made to strengthen the hull and to improve her sailing capabilities.[17] Finally, a lion, emblematic of the ship's new role in the king's service, replaced the mermaid figurehead. Bodega felt that all these changes meant that "without the least doubt [the vessel will] be capable of sailing up to the highest latitudes."[18] In the future, whenever the vessel developed a problem, Bodega would never lose an opportunity to reassure the viceroy that the *Favorita* was one of the best ships in the Naval Department of San Blas.

Before he left the dockyard at Callao, Bodega obtained eight cannon and eight swivel guns for the *Favorita.* He also purchased a number of additional items – anchors and kedge anchors, cables, sails, more swivel guns, munitions, rockets, and miscellaneous accessories – for the other San Blas ships. And he purchased wine and a number of food items, which would later cause him considerable grief.

Although Bodega spent several months in Lima, nowhere does he mention his family or imply that he took time off to visit them. Although Bodega claimed that he "was continuously present at the careening" and that the work went on "even on most holidays," it is inconceivable that he did not see some members of his family while in the city. His father had died three years before, in 1774, and his mother had died earlier, in the 1760s. Of his immediate family still alive, his youngest brother, Manuel Antonio, was absent in Spain teaching law at the University of Salamanca. The oldest, Tomás Joseph Aniceto, was serving as a priest at Lima's cathedral. The third oldest brother, Joseph Antonio, was also in Lima in 1777. It is possible that Bodega was able to visit his two sisters in their convent. He certainly saw Alberto Magno, his younger brother who had inherited the family home and who would board the *Favorita* as a passenger to San Blas en route to Spain.

When the careening was completed, preparations began for the journey to San Blas. The *Favorita*'s passengers, besides Bodega's brother Alberto, included two junior *pilotos,* Joseph Tobar y Tamariz and Juan Pantoja Arriaga, and a Franciscan chaplain, Cristóbal Antonio Díaz. The *Favorita* sailed with a crew of fifty-two, including two petty officers, a surgeon–blood letter, a carpenter, a caulker, eleven gunners, thirteen ordinary seamen, fifteen novices, and five servants for the officers.[19] The complement was probably recruited with the assistance of the commandant of the naval squadron based at Callao. Bodega himself would certainly have selected the chaplain and the two junior *pilotos.*

The paperwork, which had to be completed before the ship could sail, was substantial. It included the vessel's manifest. The demands of Spanish bureaucracy and treasury regulations also required a detailed inventory of every piece of equipment purchased or otherwise provided to enable the ship to function. An affidavit certifying the inventory's accuracy had to be signed by all the officers concerned. Then an equally detailed account of the costs of the civilian labour employed had to be prepared, signed, witnessed, and certified.

Although the ship was ready to sail on December 17, a good portion of the paperwork remained incomplete. Bodega enlisted the assistance of the viceroy himself. By official letter, he requested a ruling as to whether he should further delay his departure or sail immediately, reminding Guirior that the North Pacific expedition had to leave San Blas in February. The viceroy replied that he should sail immediately and undertook to forward the accounts to Mexico.[20] After Bodega took his leave of Guirior, having personally delivered the ship's manifest to him, the *Favorita* was allowed to sail on the evening of December 19.

Since the northern expedition was scheduled to leave San Blas in a matter of months, Bodega abandoned any hope of sailing west of the Galápagos Islands on his journey from Callao to San Blas. The heavy winds and currents encountered off the coast of what is now Ecuador provided a good test for his new ship's sailing qualities. Bodega found that she could exceed five knots in a light wind and that the steering was excellent and "in no way boisterous." Then a violent storm blew up, producing conditions he thought were similar to those he would have to face in the high northern latitudes. Experimenting, he found that speeds of six, seven, and eight knots could be obtained by increasing the draft astern. Unfortunately, the pumps were not as efficient as they should have been. After the storm came further frustrating periods of calm. The ship reached San Blas on the evening of February 8, 1778, sixty-five days after leaving Callao.

In the covering letter for his report, Bodega assured Bucareli he had "returned with a frigate [for] which it would be difficult to find another of equal properties" and that he had "not the slightest reservation that she will be able to sail to the highest latitudes."[21] Bodega hinted strongly that he hoped to be selected to command one of the ships. The only reward he desired, he said, was to be included in the expedition, for which purpose, he wrote, "I will place myself in readiness."[22] Bucareli approved all that Bodega had done and gave him authority to carry out some additional work on the ship, but he said nothing about his participation in the forthcoming expedition.[23]

At the same time, Bodega sent a letter on another matter that would cause him some distress.[24] He reported that Peru's Viceroy Guirior had given him permission to export cacao beans and "other small items" for the mess on the return voyage as well as for the expedition. He hoped that Bucareli would grant these goods an exemption from customs duties. Replying quickly, the Viceroy of New Spain asked for details. Explaining that he had asked Guirior to permit the export of the foodstuffs free of tax because of the "absolute scarcity and great expense of supplies in San Blas," Bodega attached a list of the exports: 141 sacks of cacao beans, ninety-six *arrobas* of olive oil, twenty-five jugs of olives, 140 jugs of brandy,[25] twenty-six *quarterolas* of wine, four jugs of vinegar, various amounts of sugar, flour, rice, lentils, sausages, salami, ham, almonds, and spices, and two flasks of an unidentified antiscorbutic medicine. Overlooking the extraordinary amount of cacao beans, Bucareli granted an exemption for all the equipment and foodstuffs Bodega had purchased, and then turned Bodega's letters over to the tax authorities. They agreed that all the equipment and armaments brought into New Spain could be imported free of customs duty; however, the food and wines would be subject to tax. As no tariff had been drawn up for goods brought from Peru, the tax men decided to apply the tariff applicable on goods arriving at Veracruz.

When Bucareli was suceeded as viceroy by Martín de Mayorga, the latter decided to refer the whole matter to Madrid. In May 1780, the reply came back in the form of a confidential Royal Order. It told Mayorga that Guirior had had no authority to grant any exemption at all and that in doing so he had violated the royal *cédula,* or decree, governing commerce between the dominions in the "South Sea," as the Pacific Ocean was called. Moreover, as Acapulco was the only port authorized to receive imports, Bodega should have unloaded everything there.[26] Because the three-way correspondence was producing no clear answer, Mayorga took the initiative to decide the matter himself. He decreed that while the armament and equipment for the ships would be exempt from any import tax, Bodega should pay duty of 3 percent on the foodstuffs, or 6 percent should any of these goods be resold in Mexico. It was some time before Bodega learned of the viceroy's ruling. After delaying his reply, he agreed to pay the duties. Then there was a disagreement over what the total amount owing should be. The accountant in San Blas claimed it should be 1,483 pesos, of which Bodega was credited with having already paid 736 pesos. Bodega protested that he had paid 1,182 pesos. Finally, although it is not clear whether Bodega had appealed to the king or Mayorga had appealed to José de Gálvez, a Royal Order arrived – four and a half years after Bodega had left Peru. Signed by

Gálvez, it said that the king "has been informed of the cargo of fruits and effects which Lieutenant Dn. Francisco de la Bodega y Quadra brought from Perú to the port of San Blas with the permission of the Viceroy of Perú and has approved (but not to be considered a precedent under any circumstances whatsoever) the moderate tax he was made to pay on his arrival at the port."[27] How much Bodega had to pay in the end is not recorded, but presumably the "moderate" tax was 3 percent. This was still a substantial amount, considering that Bodega's salary as a *teniente de navío* at the time was only 160 pesos a month.

Bodega did not learn of the final decision until he returned from the 1779 expedition. This financial burden added to the heavy personal expenses he claimed to have undertaken while in Lima, which had obliged him to draw on his inheritance.[28] Given Bodega's poor record for managing his personal and official finances, one may ask whether he was an unwitting victim of rigid commercial laws or guilty of attempting to circumvent controls of which he almost certainly would have known – or was he just naive? Being human, he may have decided to see what he could get away with. He had good reasons to bring back to San Blas the foods and wines, but to believe he was not aware of Spain's strict mercantile laws strains one's credulity. The trouble he ran into on this occasion, however, pales in comparison with what he experienced on his return from his second trip to Perú in 1783.

Planning the Third Northern Expedition

The expedition had to be postponed, once more, until 1779. Despite Bodega's best efforts, he had arrived back from Peru too late for the expedition to complete the necessary preparations to leave in early 1778. Moreover, the construction of the *Princesa,* the expedition's second frigate, had not been completed.[29] Because the ships would be venturing farther into northern waters than those of any other nation except the Russians, the expedition had great political and strategic significance. The construction of the *Princesa* and Bodega's voyage to Peru to acquire the *Favorita* made it evident the cost of this venture would be very high.

The delay gave Bodega an unforeseen opportunity: the chance to plan carefully, unlike the casual preparations for the two previous voyages. It was an opportunity for him to ensure that if, as he expected, he were assigned command of one of the frigates, he would be in a better position to earn a promotion. But Bodega's position as second-in-command in the expedition was not a certainty. Apparently, Bucareli was unhappy with Gálvez's choice of officers for the expedition, as outlined in the Royal Order of May 20, 1776. The king was so pleased with the results of the 1775 expedition and the saga of the *Sonora* that he ordered the third expedition to use the same officers and ships, meaning that Bodega would be given command of the second ship. Probably playing for time, Bucareli delayed acknowledging the receipt of this order until December 1778.[30]

The problem may have been that Bodega, although he held the same rank as Arteaga and Quirós, had less seniority in that rank.[31] Strictly speaking, it would be very difficult to appoint Bodega to a position of command over either of these men. Yet Bucareli could not disappoint Bodega, who may well have regarded the king's order as a fiat that he be second-in-command of the expedition. Bucareli needed Bodega's enthusiasm, experience, and administrative skills to plan the expedition. This may account for the Byzantine process Bucarali followed when informing the officers of their roles in the expedition.

His appointment of Ignacio de Arteaga y Bazán to command the expedition was determined by undisputable seniority, not experience. One of the oldest officers based in San Blas, Arteaga was inferior to Bodega in ability. He had spent three years in naval prison before being exiled to San Blas. After twenty-three years in the navy, he was only a *teniente de navío* when Bucareli appointed him to this new responsibility. In what appears to be an amazing lack of communication between the viceroy and his naval officers, Bodega learned only indirectly through Fernando Quirós's appointment to the *Princesa* that, although he would be captain of the *Favorita*, he would not be second-in-command of the expedition. Quirós, one of the six officers who had come to New Spain with Bodega in 1774, had written to the viceroy in November that he hoped "to be assigned in any way whatever to the expedition."[32] The viceroy's reply to Quirós confirmed his dilemma and Bodega's role:

> I have already appointed you second-in-command of either the frigate *Princesa,* or the ship which *teniente de navío* Ignacio de Arteaga will command. It was not possible to choose you as first commandant of the frigate *Favorita* because the king has ordered that this assignment be given to *teniente de navío* Juan Francisco de la Bodega y Quadra.[33]

As far as is known, Bucareli never told Bodega about his appointment. Bodega probably heard it in person from Arteaga when he officially informed Bodega that the viceroy had approved all the appointments that he, as commandant, had requested.

In the spring of 1778, Bucareli convened a meeting in Mexico City to initiate detailed planning for the voyage. Arteaga had already been told he would command the expedition, but the officer who was to be his second-in-command had not yet been announced. At the meeting, Bucareli asked Arteaga and Bodega to formulate a plan for the expedition. On returning to San Blas, they wrote a joint letter after "reflecting together with the maturity which so important a project demands."[34]

They proposed that the expedition depart no later than mid-January 1779. Depending on the weather and the health of the crews, the ships should sail to Bucareli Bay in the Alexander Archipelago without stopping to resupply any of the California missions. In 1774, when Pérez had been ordered to carry supplies to Monterey en route north, it had been a twofold error: precious summer weather required for exploring in the far north had been lost, and insufficient cargo space had been devoted to stores needed by the expedition. Bucareli Bay was proposed as the point of reunion should the ships become separated. From there, they would follow the coast until they reached "65° or higher" and formally take possession "as high as possible." Returning, they would "carefully examine all the bays and inlets of the coast" as far south as San Diego, which would also be a port of rendezvous, and from there they would sail directly to San Blas. There, all the charts and journals would be prepared. Since these were to include what they had observed of the Indians, as required by standing orders, they required some "gifts of glass beads, rings, mirrors, blankets and rolls of cloth" to obtain this information about the native people.

The captains asked for permission to select their own ships, the armament they should carry, and their officers and crew, and to determine the additional work the ships might require. They also recommended that each ship be supplied with stores for fifteen months and water for eight. The chaplains and the surgeons, they said, should enjoy the same rations as the officers. Moreover, they added, "it is indispensable, especially on voyages to very high latitudes, that to combat scurvy and other illnesses to issue a *quartillo* of wine ... and allow each member of the crew the same from San Francisco north until we return there."

Bucareli agreed to the plan in principle but withheld his formal instructions because he needed more information. He wanted to know which ships would be selected, what armament they would carry, what additional work had to be done, how the crews were to be selected, what stores were to be supplied, and what medicines and trade goods were required from Mexico City.

Responding to the viceroy's request for these details, Arteaga and Bodega considered what they needed. As to his ship, Bodega confirmed what Bucareli must have already known – namely, which one he had chosen: "the [frigate] I brought from Perú to the department." He attached a list of the crewmen and the troops he wanted and requested approval for some additional work that was required on the *Favorita.*[35] In all, his frigate would have a complement of 105.[36]

Bucareli cautioned Bodega that securing soldiers to serve as marines would be a problem, as there were none available in the department. He was certain Veracruz would be unable to help:

> Up to now, people have never been brought from Veracruz for ships of the department. Those from the country [colony][37] who sail on ships can never be useful unless they are supported and work beside Europeans, and they do not train them unless out of necessity.

He suggested that the two corporals and the twelve soldiers Bodega requested be selected from among the prospective seamen. Bodega found this disheartening, because the number of seamen he was planning on would be materially reduced. He appealed to the viceroy, saying that he had little confidence in sailors acting as soldiers. The experience in the navy in this regard had not been good, he said. Then he dropped a more telling point: trained soldiers were needed to guard parties being sent ashore for wood and water and to protect those carrying out possession ceremonies.[38]

When Bucareli received Bodega's crew list, he was surprised that Bodega had not requested Francisco Mourelle as his second-in-command, so he added Mourelle to the list of officers for the *Favorita.* Perhaps, being junior to Arteaga, Bodega felt that he could not request a *segundo capitán* as well as a master gunner, a sergeant, two corporals, and twelve soldiers.[39] He may have been reluctant to suggest an officer capable of commanding his own ship on another important mission. Whatever the reason, he replied to Bucareli's query on this matter by saying he was merely following the practice of ships coming from Spain. Then, in an atypical burst of emotion, he expressed his delight at the idea of having his erstwhile companion as second-in-command. He recalled a particularly poignant moment they had shared on the *Sonora* when he and Mourelle were so ill with a "fever" that they could not show themselves to the crew, who were "making exclamations to the heavens, as quite justifiably, they considered themselves lost." Bodega was confident that Mourelle, with his experience on a voyage similar to the one on which they were embarking, would serve well as *segundo capitán.*[40] Although Quirós's appointment to the *Princesa* gave that ship a heavier complement of senior ranks, Bodega had no reason to complain of the quality of the support and assistance he would receive from his people, especially Mourelle.

As for armament, Bodega asked to keep what he had brought from Lima: eight cannon and eight hundred shot for these, eight swivel guns with 180 shot, and ten quintals of powder[41] and 150 rockets for signalling. He requested additional powder to replace what he had brought from Peru that had been either used up or damaged by the humid climate of San Blas.

Bucareli replied, not too promptly, saying that the interim *comisario*, Faustino Ruiz, had been informed of his approval of the necessary expenditures for the additional work to be done on the *Favorita* and, as well, for any additional work Arteaga wanted done on the *Princesa*.[42] As for the powder and rockets, Bucareli assured Bodega that the appropriate official had been instructed to supply what was needed to "arrive a little before the ship's departure to avoid deterioration by the climate."

In the end, the command structure for the 1779 expedition was settled as follows:[43]

The *Princesa*
Ignacio de Arteaga, in command of the ship and the expedition
Fernando Quirós, second-in-command of the ship and the expedition
José Camacho, senior *piloto*
Juan Pantoja Arriaga, junior *piloto*
Father Juan Antonio García Riobo, chaplain
Father Matías de Santa Catalina Noriega, chaplain
Juan García, surgeon[44]

The *Favorita*
Juan Francisco de la Bodega y Quadra, in command of the ship
Francisco Mourelle, *segundo capitán* of the ship and senior *piloto.*
José de Cañizares, *primer piloto* and route pilot[45]
Juan Bautista Aguirre, junior *piloto*
Cristóbal Díaz, chaplain
Mariano Núñez Esquivel, surgeon

In July 1778, along with the list of crew members, Bodega sent three lists of requisitions for approval: one of medicines to be prepared by the "surgeons of the department"; one of supplies and stores required for the ship; and one of trade goods, including blue Mexican baize cloth. He also submitted requests for greatcoats for the soldiers, extra clothing for the seamen, and additional rations of bacon.[46] He did not forget to ask for six barrels of brandy as well as wax candles for the chapels.

Shortly after informing Arteaga that he approved the officers proposed by him and by Bodega, Bucareli sent similar letters to each officer to confirm their respective appointments. These appear to be the only written instructions they received.

The letter to Arteaga read in part:

> On this campaign, you will remain in company to the greatest extent possible and observe the instructions of which I informed you under date of 18 November last.[47] You are to make a copy of them. As the last expedition reached 58°, you should do better [*adelantar*] and [attempt to] reach 70° and from that point on reconnoitre the coast. I am persuaded that nothing will prevent the early departure of the ships and that you will sail as soon as the chaplains reach the port ... and take advantage of the first good weather.[48]

The letter to Bodega contained a similar passage

> For this campaign, you will remain in company to the greatest extent possible and follow the instructions of which I informed you on 18 November last. You are to make a copy of them. [The expedition] is to reach 70° of latitude, as I have advised Arteaga, whose orders you are to obey. I am persuaded that nothing will prevent the early departure of the ships ... as soon as the three chaplains I have appointed to the expedition have reached the port. You will carry one of them so that, with Cristóbal Díaz, you will have two on your ship.[49]

Ignoring the veiled reference to his deliberate separation from Hezeta in 1775, Bodega acknowledged receipt of this letter and pointed out that he "had not been informed up to now" of any detailed instructions. He could only assume they were the "same as for the previous expedition of which Hezeta had given [him] a copy ... which I still have."[50] As for carrying two chaplains, Bodega declined Viceroy Bucareli's offer of a second priest from the Franciscan college, explaining that while it was always useful to have two in case of the "remote likelihood of an accident," Father Díaz had always carried out his duties reliably and did not need an assistant. Moreover, chaplains had to be given "decent quarters," and his ship could not accommodate more than the six officers already assigned to it.

Just before their departure, Arteaga ordered Camacho and Bodega, with Mourelle, to separately plot a course for the expedition from San Blas to

65°N "to include all necessary details, warnings and precautions to enable us to make a complete survey of the entire northern coast of the Californias." He would compare their proposals and then decide the one to be followed.[51] In reply, Bodega pointed out that "it is not possible for the first *piloto* of my ship, even less for anyone under your command, to plot a course for such an expedition, because we do not have the necessary knowledge of these coasts and the seas [of the region]." Obviously exasperated with the pointlessness of the task, he expanded on the problem at the beginning of his journal of the expedition:

> We had no information to which we could give the slightest credence. The hydrographers differ so much. Some would have the coast from 62° [north] take a southeasterly direction and others a northeasterly direction ... This very considerable variation scarcely made it possible to form an idea of the course to be followed, and should it perhaps be found not to be the right one, a fruitless voyage might have been undertaken.[52]

Bodega's voyage in the *Sonora* had provided some knowledge of the direction of the coast only as far as 56°N, and the map published by the Russian Academy of Sciences, dated 1758, showed the routes followed by Bering and Chirikov in 1741-42 and the points of land they had sighted on the Alaskan coast.[53] Everything north of 56° was the subject of myths and speculation.

In an attempt to overcome the difficulty, and ignoring Arteaga's orders that each officer work independently, Bodega held a *junta* with Mourelle, to which he invited all the officers and *pilotos* assigned to the expedition. Besides the maps mentioned above, they examined the information obtained on the 1775 expedition. Bodega described the result of this effort in his journal: "I encountered insuperable difficulties in describing the method for laying down the course because of the dissimilarities of the maps north of 58°." The detailed work of drafting the composite chart, Bodega says, was done by Mourelle, Cañizares, and himself: "Both assisted me not only in drawing the chart with the greatest clarity in a few days, but also in making copies for use on the voyage."[54]

Considering his chart of his voyage in the *Sonora* to be "absolutely correct," Bodega placed it

> on the entire map of Monsieur Bellin in red so that it can easily be identified. In the same way, I indicated in black dots from the same point[55] [the coast] as shown on the map in [Burriel's] *Noticia de la California,* and finally, I showed in yellow the map of the Imperial Academy of Saint Petersburg. In

> this way, with this variety on the same chart, it would be easy to bear in mind all assumptions so that, at first sight, the slightest deflection [from which we might observe during our exploration] would not be considered.

Bodega also described the next phase of the process, the drafting of the actual routing instructions:

> I traced the route in accordance with my practice of taking the seasons into account. I included as an indispensable port of call the entrance to Bucareli [Bay] ... so that here we could take on fresh water, procure firewood, refresh the crews and take on ballast for greater security since, on arrival, we will have consumed some part of our stores.
>
> By laying down the route in this way, I had not only watering and wooding in mind but also reconnoitering this entrance while the ships were being made ready to begin the navigation in the mildest months of June and July from a latitude in which, should the coast be found to be as in the map of the Imperial Academy, the most arduous part of the voyage would be undertaken, bearing in mind the tenacity of the winds of the first and fourth quadrants which are encountered from San Blas to higher than 40°, principally at a distance of one hundred leagues from the land.
>
> And even if the coast shown on the map in the *Noticia de la California* should be correct, it would be equally possible to fulfill our orders. If by some misfortune both were incorrect, and only the French map were the most accurate, we could at least attempt to make some reconnaissance of the direction of the coast and extend the discoveries as far as the weather permits in order to be free once and for all from such doubts.[56]

The route thus worked out "in the most understandable terms" and laid down on the colour-coded map was presented to another *junta* on January 22. Some of those present pointed out certain difficulties – Bodega does not say what they were – but in the end, all were "fully satisfied and the route was ordered to be followed." As an integral part of the planning process, Bodega also drafted a *Método de la navegación*, and a *derrota,* or course, that he proposed.

The *Método* was a treatise on how to cope with the problems of navigating in the waters off the Alta California coast and the Northwest Coast. It was based not only on his own experience but also on that of others who frequented the routes to Baja California and who had commanded resupply missions to Alta California. At the outset, Bodega stated that departures for northern waters should take place between the middle of January and the first of February. Ships leaving San Blas should take advantage of the gentle northeast trade winds, which blew as far as the Tres Marías Islands; then, instead of following the coast north and risking embayment, they should strike boldly westward as far as necessary, then to gain a northing or northerly latitude they should catch the prevailing westerly trade winds. Care should be taken to avoid luffing or tacking, which could cost any latitude already gained. The higher the latitude desired, in short, the greater longitude west should be sought. Thus, if a ship hoped to reach 60°N, the commandant should sail north-northwest to reach 45° of longitude west of San Blas. If variable winds were encountered as vessels proceeded farther north, the landfall to be met, be it 55°N, 60°N, or higher, would be found only by gaining sufficient longitude west, where southerly winds might be encountered. The treatise goes on to point out that the winds two hundred leagues from the coast may be more favourable, whereas those closer to shore – say, 150 leagues – are likely to be inconstant and may veer to the northwest.

Bodega also emphasized that the weather was a further aid to saving time. Up to 40°N, it would probably be favourable, but farther north, squalls and fogs and periods of calm could be experienced. From 40°N to 50°N, great caution had to be exercised, since the winds from the northwest were generally strong. Sudden gusts could be expected from the southeast, and it was therefore advisable to proceed with very little sail to avoid dismasting.

Above 50°N, because the winds blew very strongly and could come from the northeast as well as the west but never constantly, it was advisable to lay to and watch all signs carefully. In the vicinity of the coast, from 54°N northward, strong northwesterly winds could be expected, but these were never destructive, since they came from aft and were followed by a clear sky that made it possible to survey the coast. Similarly, seas up to 40°N could be choppy, but from 40°N to 50°N, if a ship was more than one hundred leagues offshore, seas could instead be "heavy." In this situation, laying-to was advisable.

Bodega's treatise next dealt with problems of navigation when the coast was sighted. As this was the "most critical part of the voyage," special care had to be taken to observe the signs presented so that landmarks could be accurately charted. When eighty or ninety leagues offshore, bull kelp – described this time as a "grass with the head of orange similar to those grown from the seeds of garlic" – would be seen first, and closer to the coast, long green leaves would be observed stemming from the head. Between forty and fifty leagues from the coast, the sea would appear a "faint leaden grey," and between twenty and thirty leagues, it would be very clear but too deep to take soundings. At this distance, seals, sea otters, whales, various birds, and some sea grass would be visible, as would, quite close to shore, jellyfish and some black birds with red on their breasts, feet, and beaks. The shore could be approached to within a league without fear of running onto sandbars, as there were none.

Finally, if the expedition hoped to reach 62°N, Bodega advised the commandant to make his landfall at 55°17′N,[57] where a passage to the north could be found. The coast could be followed at a distance of three leagues (ten nautical miles) with favourable, although sometimes variable, winds. When a good harbour was encountered for watering and wooding and for resting the crew before sailing to higher latitudes, it should be easy to get away when the winds were favourable. The cold would always be the main concern. Bodega concluded: "With these precautions, it will be impossible to fail in your discoveries, and you will fulfill everything you desire."

The point of the *Método* was to free expedition commanders from having to record in their logs and journals the details of normal winds, currents, weather, and other matters affecting their progress when sailing in well-travelled waters.[58] Such records would not be necessary until unexplored waters were entered. The *Método* was also meant to help the expedition reach its goals more expeditiously.

The companion document, the *derrota*, was based on the Bodega-Mourelle composite chart. It began with a general statement about the difficulties posed by the variety of opinions about the longitude position of the coast between 58°N and 68°N, the former being approximately Bodega's farthest north in 1775 and the latter the goal of the expedition stipulated in Bucareli's instructions. Because of the many possibilities that lay north of 58°N, Bodega favoured making a landfall at 58°18′N and, from there, reconnoitring the coast to ascertain whether it trended to the southwest, the west, or, "more likely," the northeast. Because of the uncertainty, if the navigation were to begin at San Blas and to continue as far as Bering Island, it would be wisest to begin the reconnaissance at Bucareli Bay (55°N).[59] If the Russian map could be relied on – and it probably could be – this seemed the wisest course to follow. Moreover, it was certain that wood and water could be obtained at Bucareli Bay. For these reasons, he recommended no route other than that making a landfall at 55°18′N.

Bodega then spelled out his routing proposal. From San Blas, the coast should be followed to the northwest, taking advantage of the offshore winds that blow at night. This would mean tacking until the Tres Marías were reached. If no time were wasted there, the ships should proceed to windward of them. If delayed, it would be preferable to sail south of the islands. In either case, the ships should then proceed west-southwest or west, winds permitting. They should continue on this course until they reached 30°W of San Blas, or some 258 leagues from the coast.[60] From that point, they should steer a northwest-north course until they reached 55°18′N, at which position they should be about sixty leagues from the coast. At this latitude, they should steer toward the entrance of Bucareli Bay and anchor off Cape San Bartolomé, where the water was twelve to fourteen *brazas* deep and had a bottom of mud. The route from Bucareli Bay onward was conjectural, and this last leg of his proposed route was based on speculation.[61]

The two frigates sailed out of San Blas during the night of February 11-12, 1779, almost a month later than their captains had promised the viceroy but still in good time for a northern voyage. For this expedition, the *Favorita* and the *Princesa* proved to be excellent and well-matched ships. Their speeds were comparable.[62] Although the *Favorita* was slightly faster, there would be no problem of station keeping such as had plagued the mismatched vessels of the 1775 expedition. The manifests for the *Favorita* and the *Princesa* give no figures for their displacement, but their tonnages are generally estimated to have been similar: 193 and 189 tons respectively. As to their dimensions, Malcolm Kenyon notes that the frigates were identical in beam and depth of hold. The *Princesa* was a little shorter at both the lower deck and the keel as well as a little broader at the bottom.[63] The *Princesa* carried six four-pounder cannon and four three-pounders. The *Favorita* was armed with eight four-pounders and eight swivel guns of two and three pounds calibre.[64]

Three years had passed since José de Gálvez had ordered the expedition. The Spaniards had no idea where Cook was, nor were they aware that, once they reached the Alaskan coast, they would in large part be retracing his voyage as far as Kodiak Island. Arresting Cook was one of the purposes of their expedition, so it is somewhat ironic that the great English navigator would be killed, far away in Kealakekua Bay on the island of Hawaii, on February 14, 1779, two days after the Spanish expedition finally departed from San Blas.

4

The 1779 Voyage

North to Bucareli Bay

The two frigates were ready to leave San Blas on the night of February 11, but persistent weak winds prevented them from doing so until the following afternoon.[1] Progress was very slow, and by noon on the fourteenth they had advanced only five miles.[2] The weather was so hot and humid that after only eleven days at sea the *Favorita*'s crew had already consumed seventeen barrels of water.[3] Bodega was in high spirits and eager to sail straight to Bucareli Bay, the starting point for exploration. He seized on the least advantage the varying winds afforded. The commandant, Ignacio de Arteaga, took a more cautious tack. The *Favorita* was proving to be the faster vessel, but she had a strong tendency to drift to leeward, which made station keeping difficult. The feeble offshore winds from the northeast caused the ship to drift two or three leagues away from the *Princesa*, and Arteaga signalled periodically to Bodega to keep close company.

As they approached the Tres Marías about ninety nautical miles northwest of San Blas, Bodega was concerned that Arteaga seemed to want to pass them to the north rather than to the south.[4] When one reads between the lines of his journal (which is often necessary), it becomes clear that he was relieved when, on February 25, Arteaga ordered the course to be altered to pass the islands to the south. "At last," Bodega wrote,

> the commandant, tired of seeing the delay which his ship and the winds caused him to experience and that it was impossible to pass to windward of

> the Marías, decided (sacrificing the few leagues he had advanced) to follow the opinion I expressed in the *Derrota* in which he was warned that, when the winds are not favourable for going north of these islands, time should not be wasted in the effort unless it can be done quickly ... Only rarely will the winds be favourable.[5]

Francisco Mourelle, who never missed an opportunity to criticize Arteaga, expressed himself more bluntly:

> The weak winds from windward did not contribute to the advance of the navigation ... Experience has shown that for the most part, those who attempt to pass to the north [of the islands] experience longer voyages than those who pass to the south ... The commandant of the mission, being of the opinion that one day or another he would accomplish this task, maintained his practice of tacking until the slow progress made him despair and decide to take our advice.[6]

Arteaga wrote only that the winds were insufficient to permit passage either between or to the north of the islands.[7]

As Bodega had predicted, the winds strengthened almost immediately beyond the islands. Concerned that the *Princesa*'s new yardarms and topmasts had not yet been tested, Arteaga took down the topgallant sails and yards and sailed with only his four principal sails. Bodega fretted that sailing with so little canvas would cause a further unnecessary delay. The *Princesa*'s slower speed, he wrote impatiently,

> and the distance I had to fall to leeward to keep in company not only forced me to haul down my frigate's topgallant masts and yards but also, having to navigate continually with the sails on the main mast only half set, being unable to luff as much as the wind permitted.[8]

Later, seeing that Arteaga was altering course to north too soon, Bodega took advantage of a calmer sea to approach the *Princesa* and advise him to continue sailing farther westward. Although Arteaga had no previous experience navigating the difficult waters off Mexico, he rejected this advice on the grounds that if they sailed farther westward, "much latitude would be lost and little longitude gained." Bodega obeyed reluctantly. But Arteaga must have given Bodega's advice further thought, for on April 1 he altered course back to the northwest.[9] Bodega wrote tersely that "the commandant agreed to follow the course I had proposed."[10] A few days later and farther out to sea, the two ships began to settle on a northerly course to make their landfall at Bucareli Bay.

Generally, the weather was good and the winds favourable and moderate. The daily run varied between fifty and seventy nautical miles, sometimes more. Some days it was possible to send launches across from one frigate to the other. On one such visit, Bodega asked for a couple of seamen capable of steering his ship, as he had only two. Arteaga agreed, and in exchange Bodega gave him two gunners.[11] On another occasion, off San Diego, Bodega invited Arteaga and his officers to Easter lunch. Arteaga declined because, as Quirós recorded, "we were embarrassed to say that we had already eaten."[12] The visits were also used to exchange observations and sightings, to estimate the ships' position, and to discuss changes in course.

The good weather did not last. The winds steadily increased in strength and shifted to the northeast. Heavy swells flooded the decks, and a gathering storm reached gale force. On the night of April 4, when the northeast wind blew "with great fury," Father Riobo recorded that the *Princesa* was "tossed about [so] violently [that] nothing remained in place. Even the medicine chest, notwithstanding its great weight, was thrown about and the greater part of its syrups, essential oils and medicines were lost."[13] For several days the *Favorita* had to shorten sail continually in order to remain in company and not get beyond signalling distance. On April 17 the Tropic of Cancer was crossed, and the first signs of land were seen. With the temperature falling steadily, Bodega distributed to his men

> the two changes of clothing, which His Excellency the Viceroy had ordered supplied, a move which was greatly appreciated, especially at this time as the unhappy ones were without anything to change into or unable to wash their clothes.[14]

On April 19, a second storm struck the expedition off northern California. When the command ship disappeared from view, Bodega decided to continue on the same course, believing that the *Princesa* would be sighted as soon as there was a break in the clouds. This was not to be. The winds did not abate – all the journals use the word "hurricane" – and the seas grew ever higher. Although the lanterns on the poop decks of both ships were lit and rockets fired, the seamen could see nothing of the other vessel. When dawn broke on April 20, the command ship could not find the *Favorita.* Father Riobo on the *Princesa* recorded that "on the morning of the same day, I went with the commandant to the quarterdeck, and in the name of all the crew on the frigate, he made a vow to Our Lady of the

Rosary, the patroness of the frigate."[15] Arteaga vowed to give the foresail as an offering at her shrine and that he would carry the mast in procession, barefoot, to the church at San Blas "if the Blessed Virgin would obtain our delivery from this and other dangers we might encounter and should we return safely to harbour."[16] Adding that "Our Lady favoured us with her powerful protection," Father Riobo recorded that "henceforth the winds continued as favourably as we could wish, although the rain and cold were annoying." This apparent benediction of gentle winds proved to be more a pious hope than a realistic prediction.

With the *Princesa* nowhere to be seen, Bodega convened a *junta* to obtain his officers' opinions on what should be done. All agreed that their best chance for a reunion with the command ship would be to continue on the same course with a small amount of sail. In fact, neither captain spent any time looking for the other, which would certainly have proven futile in the terrible weather. Independently, each decided to continue directly to Bucareli Bay, their agreed rendezvous in the event of separation.

Bucareli Bay

On April 24, having calculated that he had reached latitude 55°N, Bodega readied his ship to enter Bucareli Bay, which Mourelle estimated lay some distance to the east. The shifting winds frustrated the sailors' desire to reach their destination quickly. The number of ducks, sea lions, whales, sea otter, and jellyfish they observed, as well as the changing kelp – all the signs mentioned in Bodega's *Método* – meant that they were indeed close to land. Finally, early on the morning of May 1, land covered with "snow from the top of the hills to the foothills" was spotted. Bodega claimed that the "mountain ranges I saw at noon were the same which formed the Príncipe and del Susto bays, which I had discovered in 1775."[17] A cold wind was blowing from the west, and it began to snow heavily.

Escorted by a pod of whales,[18] the *Favorita* rounded Cape San Bartolomé, entered Bucareli Bay during the night of May 2, and anchored early the next morning after a voyage of eighty-two days.[19] The *Princesa* entered the bay in the early afternoon of the same day. Considering the weather, that neither ship had a chronometer, and that heavy reliance had been placed on dead reckoning, it was a tribute to the navigating skills of the two captains and their *pilotos* that the expedition's ships both had reached Bucareli Bay so readily. Bodega was justified in pointing out that the voyage had been "felicitous" and not much longer than the time of a normal voyage from San Blas to San Diego, Monterey, and San Francisco. They had travelled almost double that distance in sixty-five days.[20] With just a touch of vanity, Bodega and Mourelle added that the present voyage had been greatly facilitated by their knowledge of the weather, the winds, and the trend of the coast gained on their earlier voyage.

When the *Princesa* was observed entering the bay, Bodega sent Mourelle off in a launch to "pay his respects" and to help Arteaga anchor next to the *Favorita.* However, gusty winds compelled the *Princesa* to continue to an anchorage six miles away to the east, in a small bay of Suemez Island.[21] Discovering that it was an unsatisfactory spot, Arteaga warped his ship into a nearby bay, which would become known as Port Santa Cruz because it was the feast day of the Holy Cross.[22] When he reached the *Princesa,* Mourelle told Arteaga that on the way in he had found a port in "a gorge formed by the mountains in which, he could assure him, we could conveniently [anchor] and remain for as long as we might wish without the slightest worry, as it was a beautiful basin."[23] Arteaga replied that he was well satisfied with his new position and gave Mourelle a written order for Bodega to join him there. Bodega was not content with his own anchorage, and he warped the *Favorita* into Santa Cruz and anchored slightly ahead of the *Princesa.* After he had saluted Arteaga's pennant with a single cannon shot, the two captains each fired a salute of five guns to the Virgin Mary. The Indians hovering around the two ships were so startled by the echoing noise that they fled immediately, vacating the bay so quickly that they left three dogs on the beach.[24]

Arteaga's second anchorage was perfect. Mourelle wrote enthusiastically: "The best harbours in Europe could not provide the same advantageous conveniences as this one offered us."[25] Pantoja said that Port Santa Cruz could easily accommodate "thirty or forty" ships of the line.[26] All were impressed by the steep walls of the bay and the tall forests that covered them from water's edge to the snow-topped ridges. The anchorage was well sheltered from all winds; the depth was nineteen fathoms; stones for ballast to replace stores consumed were readily available; and, because a large freshwater stream flowed down from the hills across a beach to the shore, replenishing water was straightforward. Also, the inlet's openness would provide protection against a surprise attack by the Indians.

Satisfied that Port Santa Cruz offered a safe anchorage, Arteaga and Bodega considered how best to carry out their instructions. Bodega, Arteaga, and Quirós agreed

> that considering the promise which at first sight this bay offered with its extension, panoramas and variety of headlands, they should undertake an examination of its bays and inlets with as much exactness as could be expected in the short space of fifteen or twenty days without delaying our principal goal.

Although Bodega had planned for this possibility in his *Método,* the implementation of Arteaga's and Bodega's decision was mishandled.[27] While the captains agreed it would be undesirable to delay their departure for unknown parts, they also agreed that the exploration of the bay could not be undertaken until the weather improved. Unfortunately, during their stay of almost two months, the weather was terrible. The wind was cold, and heavy fogs allowed for only a few clear days. It rained almost every day, and sometimes the rain was mixed with snow and even hail. In the end, their departure to the northern latitudes was delayed less by the weather than by their determination not to leave Bucareli Bay until they had completed charting it.

Despite the inclement weather, some essential tasks had to be undertaken. The carpenters of both ships were sent to examine trees nearby to judge whether they would serve for spars and to repair the weak sections of the frigates' masts. Bodega ordered that the *Favorita*'s hold be cleared and prepared to take in wood, water, and ballast. Then the carpenters and some of the men went ashore to build a trench of stones and a wooden conduit, constructed in such a way as to take water on board without the crew needing to fill barrels. They also built a gangway to carry the wood aboard. Bodega welcomed the days it did not rain, for, as he noted in his journal, not only

> could the task be carried out with the desired rapidity, but also my principal purpose would be accomplished, which was to make certain no one got wet, thus preserving them from scurvy and other accidents to which they would be exposed [in] the cold and dampness they would experience.[28]

At no time did the Indians interfere. Although fully armed, they watched silently. In contrast to Bodega's experience in Sea Lion Cove in 1775, when the Indians compelled him to pay for water, they sought nothing on this occasion.

On May 13 the Spaniards celebrated Ascension Day with a mass on the south shore of the port.[29] It was carried out with all the ceremony and pomp that the expedition's circumstances allowed.[30] Wrote Pantoja, the junior *piloto* on Arteaga's ship:

> On this day, the commandant decided to celebrate on land with all possible solemnity the Holy Sacrifice of the Mass as an act of thanks to the Most Holy Mary of the Rosary, the patroness of our ship.
>
> As soon as [her image] was taken out from on board, she was saluted by the artillery and, when passing the *Favorita*, her captain honoured this Divine Lady by calling out "long live the Virgin," followed by an artillery salute. When she arrived on the shore, our commandant saluted her, singing the "Salve," followed by a salute from the swivel guns, fired by those who had formed a small battery to defend us against the Indians should they have wished to insult us.
>
> When Mass was over, having been sung by Licenciado Cristóbal Díaz, assisted by the Reverend Missionary Fathers Matías Noriega and Juan Riobo, the latter preached a short sermon and all sang the "Vigilia Regis." Then a Cross was nailed to the trunk of a large tree, which for the purpose had been cut down the day before. It was fifteen feet across and had been carried in procession on the shoulders of the commandant and the officers. The [ceremony] ended with another salvo [of the cannon].
>
> The ceremony was attended by some Indians, who paid much attention to the rituals they witnessed. They were impressed by our silence and formality as well as by the ornaments and the tidiness [*descencia*] of the altar. At six we withdrew to return on board, and the Indians returned to their habitation.

Cañizares mentioned that the Indians present seemed particularly impressed by the Spanish worshipping on their knees. Aguirre recorded that, before returning to their respective ships, the crews enjoyed a feast on the beach and that when all were back on board, another salute was fired. Arteaga noted that the altar was erected underneath a large tent and estimated that the Indians present, having come in nine canoes, totalled "some seventy" men, women, and children.

During the bad weather, Bodega, presumably with Mourelle, drew up a detailed plan to ensure the safety and security of their ship as well as of the officers and men when they were ashore or when they had ventured away from the ship in small boats.[31] Bodega's experience on his previous voyage suggested that, when threatened by aggression from the Indians, the Spaniards should display their strength. The thunder of the cannon, especially when fired in a salvo, made the natives more respectful and less inclined to attack the ships and their personnel. To ensure that the boat parties were adequately prepared to meet hostile natives, the crew and the soldiers had practised firing the ships' guns and their muskets; also, they had been trained in the use of knives and swords while en route to Bucareli Bay.

Mourelle's Survey of Bucareli Bay

Once the weather improved, Arteaga and Bodega decided it was time to survey Bucareli Bay. Mourelle was put in command of the mission. He was advised not to conduct the survey with "excessive detail nor the greatest accuracy" because the bay was so large.[32] Juan Bautista de Aguirre accompanied him in the *Favorita*'s launch. José Camacho took Juan Pantoja of the *Princesa* in the other launch. The *Princessa*'s surgeon, Juan García, joined the group. They were given five soldiers and the master gunner as protection as well as some of the best seamen from their ships. All told, there were eleven people in Mourelle's boat and fourteen in Camacho's. Provisioned for eighteen days and with a supply of glass beads, baize cloth, and some coins to be given out "as faithful testimony of the dominion of our August Sovereign," the two launches departed from their ships at seven in the morning of May 18. With their lateen sails hoisted and the seamen rowing, the boats towed a canoe that had been purchased from the Indians to carry some of the voyagers' equipment. Immediately the *pilotos* began taking careful soundings and noting the bearings of the land's prominent features.

The surveyors crossed the bay to the west point and proceeded up the coast on the northeast side of Baker Island until they came across a deserted Indian village atop a steep hill.[33] On the crest they found houses built with large wooden beams six *varas* long and a quarter of a *vara* in diameter. The houses were open on all four sides. Catwalks had been built to connect one house with another over the uneven ground. Mourelle called the village an "inaccessible, impregnable fortress."

Establishing a daily routine and taking advantage of the long northern summer day, survey work continued as long as there was sufficient light. The boats were so crowded that it was necessary to look for a small, protected inlet to prepare meals on land. When camp was pitched for the night, the boats' sails were spread overhead to serve as shelter.

On May 20 they entered Port Real Marina.[34] The extent of the port made Mourelle

> realize that it would not be possible to continue [our mission] in the same detailed fashion, not only because of the short time in which we had been ordered [to complete the survey] but also because it would require several months. This reflection obliged us to adjust our methods and conduct the reconnaissance to fit the time we had been given.

While they were at Port Real Marina, they were approached by Indian fishermen in two canoes, who readily traded some of their catch, including salmon, for the usual trinkets and bits of iron; they would not accept the Spaniards' biscuits. On May 21, a group that included Pantoja went ashore to take bearings at the mouth of the bay. They came across a mortuary platform supporting a wooden box holding a body wrapped in a sea otter pelt. The platform had been placed in a tall tree and was held up by posts. A short distance away, they came across a small house, inside which they found "four or five boxes, old and new, with their lids of various colours. They measured one *vara* high and half a *vara* wide ... We left them in their places."[35]

The next day the launches sighted Arriaga Passage,[36] which led to the Pacific Ocean and adjacent islands. As these islands were numerous, "we did not wish to engage ourselves [in their examination] with the exception of those which could be examined without too much delay." Pressed for time, Mourelle turned south to examine the east shore of San Fernando Island. On May 25, all work had to be abandoned because of rain and strong winds. The launches anchored in a bay on a cape's west side, where they remained for five days. The *pilotos* took advantage of the delay to "perfect what had been surveyed to date and to depict everything in understandable terms." When they were finally able to travel again on May 30, they sailed east until another large, and apparently deserted, Indian village was spotted atop an island. The next day, June 1, they climbed the steep hill to explore and found a number of houses. The roofs were constructed with good wood, recently cut, and the posts holding them up were painted black and blood-red. Arteaga named the island on which this village was found La Ranchería "because it had no trees and a large stockade like an Indian village."

Continuing southward, the survey party reached the entrance of Trocadero Bay, which "extended a considerable distance, as it was not possible to see its end. Its size obliged us to renounce the task of surveying it." Mourelle decided to retrace his steps and proceed southward. On June 2 they reached Port Dolores on the north side of Suemez Island. Delayed by more bad weather, he decided to take five or six more days to complete his mission rather than return directly to Port Santa Cruz. He sent Pantoja in one of the boats "with [two] letters for the captains to inform them of the progress we had made and to request sufficient supplies to conclude [the survey]."

Arriving on board the *Favorita* and finding the two captains together, Pantoja related that

> the commandants, the chaplains and remaining persons were greatly concerned when they saw me coming [alone] in one launch, presuming that as

> on previous days they had seen a large gathering of Indians with their canoes and many more at the entrance to Bucareli [Bay], the other [launch] had been captured ... However great the worry, much greater was the joy.[37]

After explaining that the survey had been held up by persistent rain and contrary winds, Pantoja reported to Arteaga and Bodega that there was little that remained to be done to complete the chart. Pantoja left the next day with enough provisions for eight more days.[38]

Returning to Port Dolores at four a.m. on June 5, Pantoja was met by eight large canoes of Indians, who came out as he passed their village and followed him until he rejoined Mourelle and his party. While he had been away, the Indians had hindered the other launch and prevented the *pilotos* from doing their work. A number of thefts had been committed, and the Indians had shown contempt both for the Spaniards and for their weapons. Following orders, Mourelle had refrained from ordering his people to fire on the Indians. The two launches left immediately for Point Arboleda, a short distance away on the northwestern tip of Suemez Island, but they could not enter the inlet there "or conduct any operation because of an immense crowd of Indians in it."[39] Late that day, they found a defendable beach where they could camp for the night. Mourelle sent an armed party of five soldiers and four seamen ashore to make certain no Indians were about. Those who remained in the launches waited with the swivel guns and *esmeriles* manned and muskets loaded.

While the meal was being prepared, a large group of Indians entered the inlet in their canoes. They landed, making the usual signs of peaceful intentions. As soon as the small beach was full of natives, some made mocking signs to the effect that Spanish weapons only made noise and did not frighten them. Others made threatening gestures with their spears, while still others put on their wooden breastplates and their hide armour. They let out a "horrible yell" and gestured that their daggers and spears "wounded the heart and killed." The Spaniards stood firm. They had been given a clear demonstration not so much of hostility as of the fact that the beach was not their property, that they were intruders and should leave. Camacho thought that the demonstration they had witnessed could have been ended by a single volley from the swivel guns. Having killed one or two Indians, this would have caused the others to flee. Anything more than that would have caused too much "destruction." Instead, "as it was never our intention to do them any harm, in spite of having suffered so many impertinences and taunts ... we all withdrew quickly and with stealth to the launches, together with our big cooking pot and half-cooked supper."[40]

Mourelle crossed the bay to Port Mayoral on Baker Island, which had been visited at the beginning of the survey, a place where, according to Camacho, they had found some "precious objects" he did not identify. Some three hundred Indians followed in their canoes, continuing the taunts and insults. Mourelle counted twenty-three canoes, one of which he estimated measured between twenty and twenty-five *codos* and carried twenty-three Indians. They showed no inclination to be appeased by gifts of glass beads, coins, or other trinkets. Fed up, Mourelle ordered the canoe they were towing punctured by musket fire, and one of the swivel guns was fired into the trees to show the damage they could inflict. The noise frightened the Indians but did not deter them, for that night they stole into the camp and took the sails over the shelter where the *pilotos* worked on their charts.

A party sent out to the nearby village captured an Indian as a hostage.[41] Acting as go-between, this man persuaded his companions not only to give up the launch's sails, which by that point had been torn to pieces, but also to return some other items that had been stolen. Nothing made of iron was recovered. The hostage was given forty lashes in front of his companions and then set free. The swivel guns fired shots into the woods, where other Indians had taken refuge, and into their canoes with the "intention of teaching them a lesson." The Indians returned to their village, and the *pilotos* resumed their work. The next morning, some of those who had taken part in the thieving returned with a supply of fish, for which they would accept nothing in return.

This was the worst encounter the survey party experienced with the native people. Otherwise, except for constant thievery and the need to maintain careful watch, the trip was trouble free. Mourelle's frequent references in his journal to the Indians' "insufferable arrogance" and their "demonstration of pretended peace when they used the expression *coacan*, with their arms open," confirmed the extent of his forbearance. Only once did he allow his exasperation to get the better of his usual calm judgment. Generally, he was philosophical about the situation – writing, for instance, that the Indians valued iron as the Spanish valued gold and silver.

After another two wet days of surveying, Mourelle ordered the launches to return to Port Santa Cruz, which they reached early in the afternoon of June 12. Expressing the feelings of those who had accompanied him, he recorded that "we were received with noticeable pleasure by all, both for the work we had accomplished as for the joy of our arrival." Reporting to the two captains, Mourelle placed in their hands the "general plan of the bay and the particulars of the ports [examined] and an account of his [mission]."[42] He had been absent twenty-six days.

Expressing the sentiments of those who had remained behind in Port Santa Cruz, Father Riobo noted:

> Their return was a great relief to us, as we feared that some mishap had befallen them. Indeed, everything was to be feared, as a very great number of Indians, in more than one hundred canoes, had come to establish themselves in a cove of this harbour.[43]

In his usual matter-of-fact manner, Bodega reported:

> At 2:30 in the afternoon, we had the satisfaction of seeing the launches returning from their commission and, when they arrived, the officer in command [Mourelle] handed us the general plan of the bay whose harbours evidenced by their appearance the greatest security which could be obtained ... We were greatly pleased to see that so remarkable a reconnaissance had been accomplished without difficulty. It can be said with assurance that [this bay] contains within it the greatest ports which have been discovered up to now.[44]

The experienced cartographer Camacho summed up the reason why:

> The chart we have made will show at first sight how spacious this harbour is. I doubt if in the entire universe there is another to equal it. Besides containing eleven capacious, sheltered harbours which are clear of obstacles [*limpio*], there are an infinite number of places to anchor and be sheltered with the greatest security. It is especially to be noted how unobstructed [*limpio*] everything is ... In short, I say that this harbour is capable of safely containing within it all the ships which today ply the seas in the four parts of the world without inconveniencing one another.[45]

Indeed, these general charts were titled either the "Famoso," from the term used by Camacho to indicate how spacious a bay it was, or "Insigne Entrada y Puerto de Bucareli." Note, however, that none of the chroniclers suggested that the bay might be the entrance to the Northwest Passage.

At Puerto de Santa Cruz

While Mourelle was carrying out his survey, the Spaniards completed the wooding and watering in spite of almost incessant rain. The task was slowed because only the small boats were available. They also made charcoal for the ovens and repaired the sails and the rigging. The crews cleaned between decks and washed their clothes, health measures on which Bodega insisted. Cañizares sounded Port Santa Cruz, measured the rise and fall of the tides, and completed the plan "to insert it in the general chart."

So far there had been no outbreak of the dreaded scurvy, but almost as soon as the survey party departed, a strange sickness, which may have been food poisoning, broke out on the *Princesa*.[46] To deal with the malady, surgeon Núñez Esquivel had the most seriously affected removed from the ship to the shore, in the hope that fresh air and greater space might provide some natural remedy. The invalids were housed in a small temporary hospital made from ships' sails and erected on the beach near the cross, with the encampment protected by a small detail of the soldiers. Of the seventeen seamen taken ashore, two died. Remarkably, these were only the third and fourth recorded fatalities suffered to that date by the expedition. The men were buried at the foot of the cross, where a seaman who died suddenly had been interred earlier. The rest of the men became "well and robust," as Bodega wrote, "ending that epidemic, which we feared was a plague."

The two frigates attracted the natives of the Prince of Wales archipelago, who were either Tlingit or Kaigani Haida. As soon as the ships anchored in Port Santa Cruz, two canoes full of Indians approached; however, they would not come alongside. They gestured with their arms open while chanting in unison. They also carried a "dead bird" in their hands and removed the small feathers, which they sprinkled in the air and on their heads. The Spaniards, correctly, took these to be signs of "seeking peace and a desire to be our friends." In response, they called to the Indians and offered them "a few things," but the Indians still refused to come alongside, departing after viewing the ships.

The next day saw the native people's first attempts at trade. The Indians offered fish in exchange for trinkets and small pieces of old barrel hoops. These visits were an almost daily occurrence thereafter. Often, the men were accompanied in their canoes by their wives and sometimes their children. They offered fish, sea otter and seal pelts, bear and deer skins, and, sometimes, seagull eggs, which were judged to be "large and tasty."[47] On one occasion, a deer was offered. In exchange, they wanted the usual trade items, especially iron. Bodega rather deprecated some of the objects that were offered, such as mats, dismissing them as "having no value."[48] As word spread around Bucareli Bay, Indians appeared in ever greater numbers, to such an extent as to cause concern. Despite early native protestations of peaceful intentions and the Spaniards' efforts to assure them of their own goodwill, the Kaigani Haida consistently showed not merely a lack of "respect" but also an aggressive hostility. The Spaniards' patience was not inexhaustible, but all they could do was increase their watchfulness. The growing numbers of visiting Indians heightened concern not only for the safety of the survey party but also for that of the frigates themselves.[49] The commandants ordered increased vigilance; meanwhile, Bodega feared that their tolerance was only encouraging the Indians to be bolder in their now open hostility. The Indians desired to trade, yet they also made signs that Bodega interpreted to mean that the Spaniards were not welcome guests and that they "should leave the port of which they [the natives] were the owners."

An additional source of anxiety, again according to Bodega, was a warning that several villages had assembled some hundred canoes to carry out a night attack on the frigates. Seeking confirmation, Arteaga, Bodega, and Quirós set out in one of the boats to reconnoitre the inlet where the Indians were camped. The Indians came down to the beach to greet them with the usual signs of peace, to which the three officers responded in kind, then withdrew "after having informed ourselves of the state of their strength." Bodega does not say what they estimated that to be, but that night, the watch was doubled and sentinels on each frigate were ordered to call out to each other periodically to show any Indians approaching in the dark that the ship was not asleep. They also fired a musket shot every half-hour to make certain the Indians did not approach until daylight.[50]

Then on the morning of June 11, some Indians pulled down the cross to remove the iron nails. This act horrified the Spanish onlookers. "It was," wrote Bodega, "an act of insufferable arrogance." He surmised that the Indians knew how much it was esteemed by the Europeans and that they were aware that to remove the cross "would be the greatest hurt they could cause us." The *Princesa* fired a cannon shot, and Quirós went with the small boats to gather up the pieces of the cross and take them on board. In the afternoon a single canoe holding two Indians came alongside the *Favorita.* They indicated that they understood how deeply the Spaniards regretted that the cross had been torn down. One of them said that the perpetrators had been punished and added that if the Spaniards wished, they could raise another in the same place. The offer was accepted, and a new cross was made on board, carried ashore, and raised where the first one had been. The Indians involved in this exchange then came on board Bodega's ship. Having been given coats of cloth, they left happily.[51] The next day, Mourelle returned from his survey with the longboats.

Trade was generally conducted without conflict, but extra care was taken when the Indians were alongside or permitted to come on board. Iron objects were always a special target for thieves, and despite the precautions taken, metal items were deftly pilfered: ramrods; carpenters' tools, axes, and nails; and cooking pots, spoons, and ladles. Even the pintles of the *Princesa*'s rudder, the same ship's waist band, the hitching rings on the *Favorita*'s sides, and the rings of her main ladder disappeared. Although both ships kept bits of old barrel hoops on hand for exchange, there was never enough iron to meet the demand.[52]

According to Quirós, the only items recovered were the pintles of the *Princesa*'s rudder, two chisels from the *Favorita,* and the *Favorita*'s large cooking ladle.[53] To retrieve the chisels, Bodega, who was "tired of tolerating" such thefts,

> sent the boats of both ships after [the thieves] and, when they jumped ashore abandoning their canoe, it was captured and brought aboard ... Indians in another canoe nearby were told that they could have the canoe of those who stole the chisels if they brought them back. One of them accepted the proposal, went to see his companions and quickly returned with [the chisels] ... In spite of their impudence, I forgave the aggressors and handed over the canoe.[54]

The constant pilfering altered Bodega's opinion of the natives. At first he talked about their "gentle behaviour," then of their "audacity," and finally of their "shamelessness," which stretched "our limit of endurance."[55]

A significant feature of the trading relationship was the acquisition of native children by the Spaniards. At first, the commandants were reluctant to give their consent. The chaplains thought otherwise, believing that to acquire them would save them from "an unhappy fate" of living with their heathen parents. The trade began almost immediately after the ships anchored in Port Santa Cruz. The first purchase occurred on May 7: a girl of eight or nine was acquired for a "coat of rough cloth and two barrel hoops." She was turned over to the chaplains for them to teach her catechism and to "baptize her when she was ready."[56] Bodega said she was "very ugly," thinking perhaps it was for that reason her parents did not value her. Mourelle at first thought the offer of children stemmed from the strong desire for iron and cloth; later, though, he realized that healthy children were not being offered for sale.[57] On May 19, a four-year-old boy was given to the soldier on watch on the *Favorita,* without anything being asked in return. He was not accepted or kept, because he was not included in the total of three boys and two girls mentioned by Father Riobo. On another day, a very sick young girl was presented to Father Noriega, who tried to care for her. When it was certain she was dying, Father Noriega baptized her, with Arteaga acting as godfather. One girl was accepted and baptized, but "because she was so young," she was returned to her mother. Bodega reported that the boatswains of his ship purchased two boys, one aged five or six and the other aged four. He agreed to this, as they were "offered voluntarily, and because the purpose was to Christianize them and free them from the unhappy state into which their wretched fate had consigned them."

Bodega himself acquired a boy of between

> nine and ten ... whose vivacity endeared him to the entire crew. It seemed to me to be an act of piety to receive him. He would also be useful in the days ahead to learn of [the Indians'] life style, of the conditions in which they live and other such intelligence. I therefore decided to take him under my protection [and] to instruct him to the extent his application would permit.

Bodega named the boy Juan Francisco after himself. He remained in Bodega's care for some time and accompanied him to Peru in 1783.[58] A priest, Juan Francisco Domínguez, took charge of his education, but we do not know what happened to the boy after Bodega left Mexico to return to Spain in 1784. The other children were not so fortunate. The two girls on the *Princesa* died at sea, and Manuel and Antonio, the boys who had been purchased by the two boatswains of the *Favorita,* died shortly after returning to San Blas, but not before being baptized.

On June 13, the day after the launches returned from their survey of Bucareli Bay, there began a chain of events that culminated in a serious incident. A number of men from both frigates had gone ashore to wash their clothes. Although they were guarded by eight soldiers, a sergeant, and one of the boatswains, two of the *Favorita*'s seamen were missing when the party returned on board. The launches sent out to look for them found no trace of them, and it was assumed that they had been captured by the Indians who had been seen in the vicinity. The launches gave chase and captured two canoes. One was full of fish; the other contained a lone fisherman, who was taken hostage and brought on board the *Favorita.* Bodega, who described him as "robust and well proportioned," told him that if he persuaded his countrymen to bring the sailors back to the ship, he would be set free. The Indian accordingly called out, and three other natives arrived in a canoe. One was an old man, sitting in the middle and not paddling but giving orders to the others. He had been seen before on one of the frigates. He informed Bodega that the two men were indeed in the village, that they were very happy, and that they were being well treated. They would spend the night there, while he would remain on board. He promised they would be brought back at sunrise.

All night long, the old man remained content, being given presents of beads and baize cloth and being entertained with music played on flute, guitar, and violin. The elder took the violin in his hands and, with some success, attempted to play it. After he ate at Bodega's table, a bed was made for him in the great cabin, where he slept peacefully. At four in the morning, the elder rose and spoke to the occupants of one of the canoes near the *Favorita.* Four hours later, more canoes approached, but the two seamen were not aboard. The Indians assured Bodega that the men were still sleeping. The elder pleaded with those in the canoes, but they shouted at him derisively. When Bodega repeated that the old man would be released as soon as the seamen were brought back, he was greeted with a "mocking laugh." At 9:30 a.m. a large number of canoes neared the frigates, one of which was seen to keep apart from the others, at the distance of a musket shot. When Bodega asked whether the missing men were in the canoe, the Indians replied that they were still sleeping. Then one of the seamen was spotted hidden under a mat. When he was ordered to come on board, he replied that the Indians would not allow it. He grabbed a paddle in an attempt to escape but was overpowered. With a great shout of glee, the natives carried him off again to their village.

The Spaniards considered taking one or two canoes of people hostage, but the idea was rejected as too risky, as the Europeans were greatly outnumbered. On the *Princesa,* an attempt was made to entice another old man aboard with promises. The Indians countered with a demand that one of the ship's people become a hostage. One seaman, most likely not a volunteer, jumped – or was pushed – into one of the canoes, but the effort to make the exchange ended and the situation began to turn ugly. It is difficult to determine exactly what happened next, because the journals reflect the confusion that followed. The beach began to fill with men wearing leather breastplates, gorgets, and helmets, which covered them from head to toe. They began to hurl their long spears and shoot their arrows, although without any effect. Quirós took the launches to block the entrance to the inlet. When the seaman who had jumped into the canoe was seen being hustled ashore, Arteaga ordered one of the swivel guns to fire several bursts as warning shots and a cannon to be fired without ball. Taking the gunfire to mean that the *Princesa* was being attacked, the *Favorita* opened fire with muskets, swivel guns, and cannon. In the melee that ensued, the Indians scattered, terrified by the noise, and several canoes capsized. One Indian was killed and another drowned. Quirós, with the launches and small boats, proceeded to pick up twenty-one Indians, including some women and children. They were brought on board the *Favorita* and given presents of baize, beads, and shawls.

With around twenty-two Indians as hostages and a large armed escort from the two ships, Mourelle took four small boats to the nearby inlet to attempt to negotiate the return of the seamen. He was met by the armed group on the beach. Each side hesitated to make the first move, but eventually it was agreed that both sides would put down their arms and discuss the next steps. Since the Indians refused to go on board one of the frigates and the Spaniards could not advance farther up the beach, it was agreed that the negotiation for the seamen's release should take place on neutral ground: a nearby point of land. The Spanish sent two or three men in one boat. Once they sorted out which Indians came from which village and to which village the seamen had been taken, the elder who had spent the night in the *Favorita*'s great cabin was exchanged for one of the seamen, and twenty-one Indians for the other two.[59] The entire drama, concluded with the usual exchange of presents, had lasted two hours.

And so it all ended peacefully, although not for the two original deserters. As soon as they arrived back on board, they were interrogated. At first they claimed to have been forced by the Indians to go with them, but when bound to a cannon for punishment, they admitted that their "separation from their companions had been voluntary, as they deliberately wanted to go with the Indians. Seeing a canoe close by, they asked to be taken to their village."[60] By the time they realized their mistake, it was too late to get away. They had spent the night in the village with considerable anxiety; the Indians had kept them awake with cries and shouts, to some unclear purpose. Nevertheless, Bodega ordered that they be punished with one hundred lashes each and with imprisonment because their desertion had delayed the expedition's departure from Bucareli Bay.[61]

The Arteaga-Bodega expedition of 1779 provided particularly good information about Bucareli Bay, on the society and culture of the native peoples encountered, and on the geography and natural history of the lands discovered. The explorers' journals are limited by the circumstances of the observations and vary with the personalities of the authors. Both Bodega and Mourelle had much to say, and Pantoja revealed a keen interest in everything he saw. Since almost all trading took place in the southern portion of Bucareli Bay, and especially in Port Santa Cruz, what was recorded applies mainly to the Kaigani Haida. Lacking all knowledge of the language, and unable to distinguish syllables or words because of the nature of the sounds, the Spaniards resorted to signs and gestures, which were easily misinterpreted. Bodega describes the problem:

> The difficulty of pronouncing words of their language has been a great inconvenience, as we have been unable to record the many words they used to answer our questions. They form [their words] from the throat with the tongue against the palate in such a way that to express them, a large number of diphthongs would be needed. This was noticeable in the little use the women can make of their lips, which hardly ever come together. We nevertheless [understood] when they counted to ten and started again. One gave us the word for "twenty."[62]

Despite such difficulties, much useful information was recorded.

Bodega described the Kaigani Haida as "having ... an arrogant spirit, and generally inclined to warfare." Mourelle added that they were "well built" and "full of verve." After noting the animal skins they used for clothing, Bodega recorded that some also wore "well-woven woolen blankets, a *vara* and one-half long and one [*vara*] wide with a fringe about a one-quarter [*vara*] wide." These, Mourelle reported – perhaps at the suggestion of his Peruvian commandant – were sewn in the same manner as the Peruvian shawls called *pellones*. Bodega noted that some natives wore boots of doubled skin, open in the front, which they closed by running a cord through them. The men, he said, wore finely woven hats made of the inner bark of a tree and shaped like a funnel. On their wrists they wore bracelets of copper, iron, or whale whiskers; around the neck, various strands of beads made of bone and "very fine" necklaces of copper, two fingers thick. They wore earrings of twisted copper wire holding bits of shells and tiny gourds.

As for the women, wrote Bodega, "to whom the manner of dress shows the honesty with which they behave, [they] have most agreeable faces, fairly clear complexion and very rosy cheeks." Father Riobo did not disagree with this assessment but noted that "the women are very warlike and full of scars due, according to their own report, to injuries from knives."[63] Like all other European explorers and traders, Bodega was repelled by the women's characteristic labrets, which made their lower lips protrude. Pantoja was the only Spanish observer to comment on how the women were employed. They spun wool and made mats and various kinds of blankets and undershirts. Only two blankets were obtained by barter, and these for a high price. Very few of them were seen, and these were heavily worn. He added: "Besides being very well woven, they have woven into them yellow and white flowers which make them more attractive."[64]

Bodega remarked on the Indians' ingenuity in making their weapons, which stemmed, he thought, from their martial nature. For armour, they had a breastplate and a back piece

> made of small narrow slats, woven together with many threads which they knit together, leaving them flexible in such a way as to fit the body and leave the movements of the arms free ... Around the neck they wear a wide and thick piece of wood like a collar which covers the throat to the eyes and above the head a helmet which normally represents some ferocious animal. From the belt down they wear an apron of wood and on the back a beautiful piece of hide which covers them down to the ankles.

Regarding their weapons, Bodega noted that their long spears were tipped with iron blades and that they had iron knives "longer than our bayonets." He also mentioned small flint axes and "some other stone which is green and so hard that after splitting any wood, no nicks can be seen." According to Pantoja, all weapons and armour were manufactured by the men, as were their knives and stone axes and "all the tools necessary for war such as helmets ... and for hunting sea wolves [i.e., seals], sea otter, deer, bear, leopards and mountain lions."[65]

Bodega next dealt with items the Indians offered to trade:

> Given their vivacious nature and fondness for trading, it must be concluded that [the Indians] are rather industrious. They continually brought mats of various colours, skins of land and sea wolves, sea otter, deer and bears, and woolen blankets of mixed colours, white, dark grey and yellow, beautifully woven and well spun,[66] sashes, skeins of thread, well-carved wooden bowls, small canoes painted in various colours, always shaped with drawings of heads with all their features, well-imitated frogs made of wood which open in the same manner as snuff boxes, well-drawn boxes of three cubic quarters, carved figures of men with heads on their feet, the helmets on their heads, lines and nets for fishing, copper necklaces, bracelets and rings, iron in all kinds of weapons, so much so that these two metals are never traded unless for an excessive price, and whistles which they play like a flute sideways.

Father Riobo added that some of the carving was done by women, especially what he described as "wooden trays of different shapes." Without elaborating, Mourelle added that the "commandants only took what they judged to be special, leaving the rest to the dealings of our people."

Bodega admired the canoes:

> The canoes they generally use are of pine [sic] and have no more capacity than needed to carry one family. Nevertheless they have some very large ones. They are constructed in three pieces, one of which is the bottom which serves as the keel, has the two sides and is hollowed out by fire. On top of it are placed two upper pieces, one on each side, each joined to the other and to the base as if sewn to the sides with thread. Most are narrow and have at each end a large sharp point which rises up noticeably. They are very light and when [the Indians] jump out of them onto land, they carry them onto the beach to a position where the tide will not reach them. They take great care to preserve them even though they had no difficulty trading one with me, which has been very useful.

Finally, Bodega noted that because the inhabitants of the villages near the ships' anchorage realized that the Spanish greatly appreciated fish, not a day passed when they were not out fishing and catching large amounts to bring to trade. They offered several kinds, especially salmon, in abundance, as well as a kind of *lenguado* (halibut) that they called *azetla* or *chatla.* They also brought "hake, herring and other fish similar to *cabrilla* [perch]." From their abundance, Bodega assumed that these fish could be found throughout the bay. The shellfish found on all the shores included mussels, clams, and *persebes* (barnacles) as well as a herb of which the Indians were very fond, which in Peru was called *cochayuyo.* Fish was the Indians' principal food, whether boiled or roasted on a spit, fresh or dried. Various herbs and roots, and the meat of deer, whale, bear, ducks, and even of the abundant dogs, which were similar to *collotes* (coyotes), were also eaten. The surgeon Juan García found medicinal herbs such as sorrel, alder, celandine, nettles, wormwood, and fennel, as well as two varieties of wild celery.[67]

Bodega thought that the Indians' houses were of "little value." None were found complete and furnished because, he observed, whenever the Indians moved, which was frequently, they took everything with them. On the other hand, the houses seen on Mourelle's survey were "well made with well carved thick beams, all with corridors, open on all four sides and the floor perfectly level."

Because of their inability to communicate fully, little could be learned about the "rites of the Indians' religion," although "at times they showed an inclination to worship the sun." As for their government, "we thought at most, seeing the manner in which they obey some older men, it might be oligarchic." The two deserters had told him that in the bay to which they had been taken, there was a "majestic person" thirty or forty years of age, whose

> particular dress, aloofness and manner of dealing with the others and the respect shown him, led them to believe he was superior to the rest ... Although he did not have the title of king, his power was shared with various chiefs and captains.

In a final note on this sojourn during his second visit to Bucareli Bay, and as if to summarize his thoughts on departure, Bodega described its geography as follows:

> The mountains on the *entrada* as well as at the ports of San Antonio, Santa Cruz, Asumpción and Mayoral are fairly high and slope down to the shore of the water with the exception of a few small ravines in the interior of each port in which small plains are to be found. Their crests are unproductive and for the greater part of the year are covered with snow. It cannot be doubted that this considerably influences the climate, which is cold and humid as we experienced appreciably during our sojourn. Although it was June, we noted great inconsistency in the weather and we suffered from frequent strong rains and thick fogs.
>
> The core of the mountains consists of bare rock over which nature has created an impenetrable thickness of pine trees, very tall, very straight and stout. Their quality would make them of the greatest value if they could be cultivated. In the course of time they grow so tall that their roots provide no resistance and they are blown down by the winds.
>
> After they rot, a very light soil is formed over the crags, in which a thick underbrush grows abundantly, within which are to be found nettles, chamomile, wild celery, anise, plaintain, common celandine, elder bush, wormwood and sorrel. It would not be surprising if the soil of this country were examined carefully some useful discoveries would be made by way of minerals and vegetables.

There is little doubt that the two months spent in Bucareli Bay were a high point of the voyage for most people on the expedition, despite the cold, wet weather. All the journals devote more space to it than to any other location. Despite this enthusiasm, the exploration of Bucareli Bay and the events that occurred there were not nearly as important from a political and geographical point of view as what lay ahead for the intrepid explorers.

North to 60°

Before leaving Port Santa Cruz, a *junta* had agreed to sail north to Alaska's Cape St. Elias (later, Cape Suckling) and then to follow the coast for a few days, keeping land in sight, to learn its direction so that they could determine whether the Russian map or Bellin's map should be followed.

The expedition's departure from Bucareli Bay was delayed. When the mariners attempted to get away on June 18, strong winds "blowing with such tenacity and strength" from the south-southwest compelled them to return to Port Santa Cruz. They had to wait for another twelve frustrating days. Not until July 1 did the weather and winds improve enough to allow them to depart. Bodega feared that the best part of the navigation season had been lost.

As soon as they rounded Cape San Bartolomé, light winds slowed their progress. Periodic banks of fog obscured the land and were so thick that the ships lost sight of each other even when they sailed close together. At times the ships were becalmed. It took them nineteen days to sail from Bucareli Bay to the port they would call Santiago, at the entrance to Prince William Sound. For the greater part of this leg, an overcast sky made it impossible to obtain celestial sightings, and the captains had to navigate by dead reckoning and conjecture about the variation of the compass. The situation required exchanges between the two ships to compare calculations and to decide on any changes of course. These periods of calm also enabled the surgeons to visit each other's ships to compare notes on those reporting sick and for the chaplains to hear confession from those requesting their services.[68]

As the ships proceeded north, the sky at midnight was almost as bright as during the day; Bodega was able to see an offshore shoal from half a league away.[69] On July 9, land stretching east-northeast was sighted, and the *Favorita* signalled the news to the *Princesa*.[70] The peaks and slopes could be seen clearly, and were entirely covered in snow, but because the mountains were so close together, it was difficult to obtain any reliable bearings.

On nearing Bering's Cape St. Elias, Arteaga signalled Bodega to close up with him.[71] He conferred with his colleague about their distance from the cape and about which course they should follow to reach it. Bodega estimated the distance as "twenty-one and two-thirds leagues" and recommended staying on the same course. When Arteaga sought his advice on whether they should continue to follow the coast, Bodega replied in the affirmative, until reliable bearings could be obtained. On the same day, the surgeon of the *Princesa* reported that twenty-five of the crew were showing signs of scurvy. This was decidedly unwelcome news, coming as it did at the point when the expedition was entering unknown waters and the Russian and French maps were beginning to diverge both as to the direction of the coast and the latitude of its key points.

The usual signs of the nearness of land, such as birds and kelp, appeared, and at dawn on July 16, Bodega recorded sighting "a very high mountain," which we took to be Mount St. Elias, whose peak could be equal in height to that of Orozava."[72] Mount St. Elias, a good sixty miles inland, towers above the others. Seeing the mountain's four distinctive peaks, Camacho rhapsodized:

> They, like the entire coast which can be seen, are covered with snow, making such a beautiful sight, especially when the sun's rays strike them. I doubt whether it is possible to find anything so agreeable to the sight. As most of the time the tops of these mountains are covered with clouds, we saw them clearly for only a short time.[73]

Closing in to the shore, Bodega could make out trees, beaches, and lowland fields. Mount St. Elias lay to the southwest at the western end of Kayak Island, which they named Isla del Carmen.[74] The cape was found to be a good two degrees farther north than shown on the Russian map. Bodega thought the difference was "due to the few observations made by those who discovered them at this altitude, since the sun is rarely seen."[75] To the north of the northeastern end of Kayak Island, small islands could be seen but not clearly enough to obtain a satisfactory bearing.[76] Bodega noted that as he approached them, beaches could be seen as well as small trees sticking out through the snow, which covered everything. Only the islands' highest peak, on the eastern end, was bare of snow.

Skirting along the south coast of Kayak Island to the southwest, as close as advisable, Bodega saw a shoal. As he had the faster ship, he approached Arteaga for permission to go ahead to reconnoitre. This was granted – provided, the commandant cautioned, he returned in time for evening prayers. Rejoining Arteaga, Bodega fell into the *Princesa*'s wake and continued to sail toward the flat southwestern end of the island, avoiding small rock outcropings. The *Princesa*'s lookout also reported seeing shoals ahead.[77] Since the currents were proving treacherous, Bodega kept an anchor ready to be dropped.[78]

Prince William Sound

The following day, July 18, Bodega recorded seeing a "large *ensenada* [inlet] very similar to that shown on the French map extending from the northwest one-quarter to the north." This was Prince William Sound, and he and Mourelle were "in no doubt whatsoever about the Russian reconnaissance in these parts, the only differences being found in the latitudes and extent of objects [laid down]."[79] At the same time, the Spaniards also sighted Hinchinbrook Island, earlier named by Cook for the country seat of his patron, the Earl of Sandwich.

At a moment when they were becalmed, they were met by two native men, each in his own "canoe." This was a surprise, as they had not expected to see people so far out to sea. Arteaga and Cañizares estimated that they were at least five leagues from shore. The men first visited the command ship, singing in a high and harmonious voice and making demonstrations of peaceful intentions. In their honour, the *Princesa* unfurled the Spanish flag and Arteaga's pennant. When the visitors showed particular interest in their kayaks, a type of craft these Europeans had never seen before, one of the Indians proposed an exchange: if a crewman of the *Princesa* wished get into his kayak, he would climb on board the frigate. The proposal was accepted.[80] The natives next visited the *Favorita,* and Bodega described their visit:

> They showed not the slightest fear. After going around the frigate, they came near [us] and, removing the copper point of their arrows, handed them to us. I took this as a demonstration of peace they make among themselves. I presented them with pieces of cloth, baize and trinkets, which they much esteemed. They then withdrew, making it sufficiently clear by signs which we should enter [the coast] by an opening to the west of us.

The natives presented the Spaniards with pieces of salmon and animal skins. One of them made a gift to Bodega of "a tunic or shirt made of the skin of various animals, very neatly sewn together."[81]

The natives' directions persuaded Arteaga, Bodega wrote, that the opening to which they were pointing could be the one shown on the Russian map. Arteaga made this intriguing point: "By hand signals they indicated that to the north were many, which we understood to mean ships like ours and people with clothes like us, and they had eaten bread like we had given them." They also indicated that the Spanish ships were "not the only frigates they had seen." Arteaga and Cañizares, alone among the diarists, mentioned this episode, but they did not speculate about whose ships they might have been.[82]

Arteaga decided that the expedition should investigate the natives' directions to see whether there were a passage to the northwest or, more precisely, whether "the inlet, judging from its large extent, might be the bay indicated by the Russians."[83] Accordingly, the ships sailed toward it. Rounding Cape Hinchinbrook and sailing north along the west coast in search of an anchorage, the frigates found an opening that, according to Mourelle, they thought was the one the natives had pointed out. Bodega did not find it satisfactory:

> The force of the currents experienced in this inlet, and some rocks which were suddenly seen on the surface of the water half a cable away, placed us in jeopardy. But Providence, which up to now had favoured us, did not abandon us on this occasion and preserved us from imminent danger.

Although in only three fathoms of water, he had time to lower the launch and get into a position to let go a kedge anchor. When the location proved to be dangerous, made even more so by the freshening winds, Arteaga decided to search for a better place despite the foggy weather. The ships sailed round the northern end of the peninsula.

Santiago: 61°17′N

Where they anchored is not well recorded. The *Favorita* dropped her anchor first. It was July 23. Once the fog had dissipated, Bodega commented on the extraordinary view: "The entire coast [to the north] could be seen for a distance of some fourteen leagues. It formed a huge gulf with the southern portion of the inlet [in which we were anchored]." They named the island they were on Isla Santa María Magdalena, and the bay where they were anchored Apostol Santiago el Mayor.[84] In his account of the expedition, Father Riobo noted that "we called it St. James the Apostle because at that time we were celebrating the novena of the Saint, and also because, as the patron of Spain, he would be our help during this voyage."[85]

Arteaga immediately called a *junta.* The officers agreed, first, that Camacho should examine and chart the extensive bay to the east of their anchorage, and second, that one *piloto* from each frigate – Cañizares of the *Favorita* and Pantoja of the *Princesa,* accompanied by a small protective force of five soldiers – should head out in the *Favorita*'s launch to learn whether there was a clear passage to the north.

The *junta* also decided to perform the formal possession ceremony with the usual solemnity. All the officers, Fathers Riobo and Noriega, the soldiers, and as many crew members as possible went ashore in procession, carrying a cross. Arteaga raised his sword and proceeded to cut small trees, branches, and some grass. He then moved some stones into place, all "without any opposition and, asking all those present to act as witnesses," solemnly declared on behalf of

> His Majesty the King, don Carlos III ... [that] he was taking possession of this land where at present they were disembarked, and which he had discovered ... by reason of the gift and bull of the Most Holy Father Alexander the Sixth to their Catholic Majesties Ferdinand the Fifth and Doña Isabel, his wife ... in Rome the 4th of May 1493.

Arteaga raised the cross to the accompaniment of volleys of musket fire and a small cannon discharged by the soldiers drawn up in battle order. The cross was worshipped for the first time; the two chaplains led the singing of the "Te Deum"; this was followed by a litany in which all joined. The cross was venerated again, with all kneeling, and prayers were offered that the word of the Holy Gospel would be "announced and spread among these barbarous nations who up to now have been deprived of any knowledge of it." One chaplain preached a sermon and led the incantation of the "Vigilla Regis." After Arteaga had made and erected another smaller cross from the limbs of two trees, the formal deed of possession was drawn up and signed by the officers and the chaplains. Title to Puerto de Santiago was of particular importance to Spain. It was the northernmost point where her explorers had performed this ceremony, and it became the basis for the Spanish government's later claim to sovereignty in the North Pacific up to 61°17′N.[86]

When Cañizares and Pantoja returned from their northerly survey early in the morning of July 24, Arteaga immediately called a second *junta* to consider what they had found. Cañizares recounted how, propelled by oar and sail, the launch had crossed the bay and travelled north to Bear Cape. They had followed the coast, trending northeast as far as the top, Johnstone Point, and a little beyond. On this leg, the mountain range to the east and northeast was constantly visible and entirely covered with snow, as they had seen from Cape St. Elias. The whole landscape to the north gave the appearance of "a wall," and sightings of prominent features led them to conclude that, "as shown on the Russian map, there is no passage [to the north] since from Cape St. Elias to the southwest the coast forms one large bay."[87] Cañizares's conclusion meant that the expedition might be unable to reach 70°N as directed. More important, it provided the Spaniards with another reason for doubting there was a passage across North America to the Atlantic. Bodega reflected

> We were about ten leagues distant from the land to the north and this evidence made us realize to our great pain that it was an obstacle which prevented us from gaining the higher latitudes. As it agreed with the French map, we decided that we would follow this map in all situations. As a consequence we doubted the [existence] of the passage shown on the Russian map and in their reports.

There was more bad news. The surgeon reported that ten men on Arteaga's ship were sick, five with scurvy in a "more or less dangerous condition," the other five with other illnesses. All, however, were expected to recover. Bodega reported that on the *Favorita,* he had eight medical cases:

two were men afflicted with scurvy. The officers feared that scurvy would rapidly lessen the number of seamen fit to work the ships. Arteaga asked each officer to give him an opinion in writing; this was a sign that a momentous decision was about to be made. He then recorded that it was agreed unanimously that

> we should sail and steer a westerly course, reconnoitering the coast at a normal distance to see whether a passage north could be found. In the event it were found, it would be followed up to 70° of latitude as provided for in the superior orders I have. The coast westwards would not be followed if the season at the time or another urgent reason should prevent it.[88]

Arteaga was well aware that the summer – the only season when exploration was possible – would soon end in these northern latitudes, and he assumed sole authority to make any further decisions. Bodega justified the *junta*'s agreement by citing the cases of scurvy, but did not mention Mourelle's strong objections. In the early 1790s, when Mourelle was compiling a compendium of the Spanish voyages to the Northwest Coast for Viceroy Revillagigedo, he inserted an "editorial note" of his own, writing in the third person:

> The *junta* was directed to agree on the return [route] supposing that the coast running at that altitude afforded no passage. But the second captain of the *Favorita* [Mourelle himself] was adamant in the opinion he expressed in six hours of deliberation, after which he was asked to give way. In the end, he said that day was the end of the gains made in that expensive exploration. Although all signed the above opinion, they returned [to San Blas] without any further consultation.[89]

These two different records of the *junta*'s conclusion were important, because later, when Arteaga decided unilaterally to abort the expedition and return to San Blas, he justified himself by saying that his decision was implicit in the consensus reached at Puerto de Santiago and that no further consultation was necessary. This decision became a source of irritation in Bodega's relations with Arteaga, which so far had been formal and even respectful, although not noticeably warm.

Beside the testimony of the two kayakers at the mouth of Prince William Sound, there were two more clues that the Arteaga expedition was not the only European party in the area at the time. First, during the survey, the launch party had been intrigued to see three pennants – one red, one blue, and one white. Some natives in a boat unfurled these when they saw the

Spaniards. The explorers urged them to come closer, which they did, but only close enough to accept some cheese and biscuit in exchange for pieces of salmon. Because the pennants had been put away by the natives, it was not possible to determine of what material they had been made or to find out how they had been acquired. Second, while describing the clothing of the native men, Bodega noted casually that

> around their necks they wear a collar of large glass beads, and although we urged them to tell us how they obtained them, it was impossible to make out their reply, but they told us by sufficiently clear signs that they had seen other, larger ships enter by the part where we were.[90]

More likely, the beads were presents, and the pennants were trading markers from the Russians. Cook did not mention presenting such gifts, in trade or otherwise. In their official reports, the Spanish officers seem to have deliberately omitted their suspicions that other Europeans were in the area.

Bodega's description focused on the natives' kayaks, which he said, "particularly attracted the greatest attention."[91] He described these as built like a harp:

> They are so light that any man can lift them with one hand, for which reason they appear to fly when they navigate ... To make them they prepare thin rods for the futtocks, which serve as the inside of the boat. These are fastened one to another with spars of medium thickness, leaving sufficient space between each one. The skeleton of the canoe being constructed in this way, they line the outside with skins of animals in such a way as to leave only an opening in the upper part, the same shape as the mouth of an earthen jar. Only the waist of the person managing it is visible. No water whatever can get in if they wear shirts made from bladders, closely sewn together, which they join to the edge of the opening.

Then he reported having seen one capable of carrying two people. Also, he had learned from the Cañizares party that they had seen five very large boats with forty people on board. Without questioning the source of the copper, Bodega recorded:

> For fishing they carry arrows whose manufacture is the greatest curiosity. The points of some of them were of copper, others of flint in the shape of a harpoon, the point cut with such delicacy that the ablest lapidary might have fashioned it ... Their language seemed to us to be a confused jargon with no

> mixture with any other tongue. They are gentle in character and live peacefully among themselves.[92]

The observant Pantoja added details to Bodega's description. He portrayed the natives as more peaceable than those of Bucareli Bay. He also noted that some painted their faces.[93] He thought that their shirts were made of deerskin, although he also saw large shirts that he thought were made from the lining of the belly of some fish. They did not shoot their arrows with a bow; rather, they used a "stick in the shape of a barrel stave."[94]

On July 25, the day after the second *junta,* Arteaga gave the order to prepare for departure. Rain and strong contrary winds forced another serious delay until the July 28. On that day they discovered that the cables of the *Princesa*'s kedge anchors had become entangled with those of the *Favorita.* After a number of futile attempts to free them, and because the winds were coming up again, it was agreed they had no alternative but to cut the cables and abandon the kedges. So far from port, this loss was a serious matter. Bodega was philosophical:

> The wind kept blowing continually with the same strength and the same heavy showers, with the result that the sick grew worse, more on the command ship [than on mine]. The departure would have been [even more] difficult and delayed if we had decided not to sail and keep at anchor. Each decided to cut loose a kedge anchor.[95]

No blame was attached to this shambles. All were content to say that the unpredictable winds and currents were the cause.

The two frigates got away from Puerto de Santiago on the afternoon of July 29. Arteaga ordered the course set to keep the north shore of the southern peninsula of Hinchinbrook Island in view.

Cook Inlet, Regla [Elizabeth Island]; 59°08′N

The voyage from Puerto de Santiago to the next anchorage, Nuestra Señora de Regla near the entrance of today's Cook Inlet, was rough. On July 30, the winds became so strong and the seas so turbulent that both frigates were forced to double-reef their foresails, single-reef their topsails, and clew their mainsails. The next day there was such a violent storm that the ships were compelled to take down all sail but their mizzens and foresails and lay to. Miraculously, the frigates were able to remain in company. The sky was invariably overcast, which was especially troublesome because it prevented the officers from taking the crucial noon sightings. Again, navigation was entirely by dead reckoning, and only the occasional break in the clouds permitted glimpses of land. In these trying conditions, it was futile to attempt to correct or reconcile the Russian and French maps, whose inaccuracy was already manifest.

In the early afternoon of August 1, the storm abated and the clouds broke to reveal land to the southwest.[96] Later that afternoon, as more islands became visible, Bodega realized that he had sailed too far ahead and was in danger of becoming separated from the command ship. He needed to fall in astern of Arteaga, who was now threading his way, constantly tacking, through the narrow channels opening up to view.[97] It was a dangerous manoeuvre requiring great seamanship. At one point, the seaman on the lookout in the *Princesa*'s foremast reported seeing a large rock with seas crashing against it, two or three leagues away. Its presence was signalled to the *Favorita,* and both ships quickly altered course.

Although the storm was waning, it was by no means over, and the expedition urgently needed to find shelter in a cove or inlet. As Bodega put it:

> We saw that we were close to some islands and trapped with the coast to the northwest; it was imperative to look for some shelter where we could anchor and remain there until the winds from the fourth quadrant could take us out ... At nine that night, we anchored on the south side of an island which had a number of channels. Seen from the outside, though only a short distance away, the land appeared to be continuous. To obtain information, my frigate's launch was sent out with one of the officers to a nearby channel from which it was possible to see the communication between them. He also reconnoitered an inlet northwest of where we were anchored, where there was shelter and a sufficient depth of water for both frigates to anchor with greater safety [than where we were], being protected from the winds of the 1st, 2nd and 4th quarter and with a smooth bottom of seventeen fathoms.[98]

Shifting their mooring to the second location on the northwest side of what they would discover was an island, the *Princesa* and the *Favorita* anchored two cable lengths offshore. The shores were sheltered by high hills covered with small pine trees and an abundance of wild herbage. This was today's Elizabeth Island, a short distance south-southeast of Cape Elizabeth at the southern end of the Kenai Peninsula and the entrance to Cook Inlet.

At noon the next day the sky was clear and the *pilotos* were able to obtain their first sightings since leaving Hinchinbrook Island four days earlier. Bodega calculated their position as 59°08′N and 48°26′W of San Blas.[99] This, he noted, was where the Bellin map placed the southernmost point of Vitus Bering's Cape St. Hermogenes.[100] He did not think Bering could have made such a precise sighting, because "when the discoverers were in the vicinity, they were at a great distance from the land and concluded that the coast ran consecutively from one peak to another."[101]

Arteaga did not wish to remain in the inlet any longer than necessary; nevertheless, he decided to perform the act of possession at this second location. Being unwell, he ordered Fernando Quirós to preside. As at Puerto de Santiago, a cross was raised, the "Te Deum" sung, and a sermon preached by one of the chaplains. The deed of possession was drawn up and signed by the officers and chaplains, and the small bay was named Ensenada de Nuestra Señora de la Regla after the patroness of monastic orders. The chart made of the inlet by Juan Pantoja indicates the ceremony's location on the west side of the island, which they named Isla de San Aniceto.[102]

After the ceremony, Bodega studied Pantoja's chart of the bay and realized that they were not on the mainland. Patches of pine trees could be seen here and there, and the coast, all bare rock with no snow, rose steeply. The only signs of native settlement Pantoja found were three unoccupied huts, inside of which he found four "sea wolves" (perhaps sea lions), which were already skinned and one of which was roasted, as well as some dried fish. On returning from his excursion, he reported that one "canoe" had sailed by. Its occupants had not responded to his invitation to come alongside. Three days went by before any natives came near the frigates, and none were seen when shore parties landed for wood and water.

August 3 was another rare, clear day. Bodega wrote in his journal:

> On the horizon [to the northwest] we could see from the anchorage a very high mountain, covered with snow, doubtless no lower than the peak of Tenerife. After sunset we saw in the clarity of the twilight that on its eastern side, it emitted a torrent of thick smoke which seemed like a cloud falling down its slope. Sometimes it burst out with greater violence without stopping in such a way that we were in no doubt that it was a large volcano.[103]

Mount Iliamna was not named in any of the *diarios,* but on the expedition's general charts it was called Volcán de Miranda.[104] So clear was the weather that Bodega estimated the volcano to be from fifteen to thirty leagues distant. He could see the entire Chugach range, most of its peaks covered in snow. To the south he could also see snow-capped peaks some twenty leagues distant; these were the mountains on the northwestern tip of Afognak Island.

At midnight on August 6 the heavy rains returned, accompanied by very strong winds. The anchorage, which had been selected hurriedly, proved to be hazardous. Bodega described what happened:

> The winds on the first and second quarters blew with such violence that, had they caught us while under sail, we would undoubtedly have had to lay to. We were now in danger of being lost ... for the wind veered to the south, from which we had no shelter. After a few hours, one of my [anchor] cables gave way and, thinking that some rocks on the bottom might be the cause, I immediately ordered the other [cable] hauled up. I found it completely ruined and in no condition to bear the strain.

Bodega signalled Arteaga to inspect his cables, which he did, only to find them in almost the same condition. They decided quickly to depart before more damage was done. Despite sudden changes in both the direction and strength of the winds, the *Princesa* managed to get off with slight damage. The *Favorita* was not so fortunate. The shifting winds made towing by the small boats difficult; they also complicated the work of the crew on board, which had to adjust the sails constantly. Bodega tried to recover the buoy of the anchor he had lost, but it did not even float to the surface because of the downward drag of the strong currents.[105] Early in the morning of August 8, once the winds had greatly diminished, both frigates got underway with full canvas, sailing on a generally southeasterly course.

Conclusion of the 1779 Expedition

It was then, as they were passing a number of small islands west of their route and without convening a *junta*, that Arteaga took the controversial decision to conclude their northern mission and head south for Cape Mendocino. Arteaga believed he had valid reasons for doing so:

> [I considered] the weather and the intense rains which never let up, the constant storm clouds, that we were lodged in an archipelago of islands, and that as instructed, we had reconnoitered to longitude 57°30′ [west] from San Blas and followed the coast of California to the west without encountering any passage to the north in order to climb to latitude 70°. We [also] found ourselves with a great part of the crew sick, and every day more were falling ill because of the unremitting rains and excessive cold.[106]

Arteaga had another reason for his decision, which he revealed much later, when he was writing his report to Gálvez after the end of the voyage. Only then did he suggest what was perhaps the true cause of his difficulties and of his decision to end the voyage:

> I found myself [suffering] from a paralysis ... caused by the very cold weather and powerful storms we experienced, and each day it was impossible to do anything. Thanks to God, I was able to reach this port of San Blas.[107]

Fernando Quirós sought to support Arteaga's decision. He reasoned that the survey made by Mourelle and Aguirre in Puerto de Santiago had established "indisputably" that the coast they saw ran north from Cape Suckling and had no passage. Moreover, the expedition's route from Puerto de Santiago to Regla had established that the coast trended westward. Thus the Russian map showing a passage to the north was completely false. In addition, Quirós wrote, the condition of the *Princesa*'s crew was such that

> we found ourselves with seven less, because of those who died on the voyage, and ten sick, some with scurvy. As a consequence, considering the illness is so contagious, there was a great danger that others would quickly be stricken, as was almost always the case on lengthy voyages such as ours. We had been sailing for six months continuously without reaching a port where we could obtain any assistance ... Realizing this and, in addition, seeing there was no passage to the north, it would be very difficult to carry on with our reconnaissance of the coast, finding our way between islands and coping with strong currents. There were many days of heavy, overcast skies before they cleared. Above all, we conjectured that our return voyage would be lengthy."[108]

Bodega and Mourelle objected to this abrupt end of the expedition. Bodega wrote:

> The commandant ... contemplated the miserable state of his crew because of scurvy, from which contagious sickness eight had died already. Although this situation was not to be found on my frigate, I agreed, of course, that we should retire (in spite of my desire to continue our navigation for a few more days). He was no doubt aware that, even if he wanted to accomplish his mission, he was in no condition to follow [his instructions] ... At the time I had no opportunity to give him my opinion or to propose any other course of action, because I was under orders to remain in company and remain [alert] for any evidence that he might need assistance.[109]

This carefully worded statement reflected respect for his commandant; perhaps it also tacitly acknowledged the state of Arteaga's health. That said, it was certainly formulated to declare for the record that he did not agree with the decision. Quite in character, Bodega was eager to continue the exploration. It was an echo of the bravura he had shown on his 1775 voyage.

What he and Francisco Mourelle really thought is to be found in the latter's summary of the voyage prepared at a later time:

> The reasons expressed by the commandant have little substance. It is normal to find many islands on a voyage of exploration. The illnesses scarcely existed, since on the *Favorita* only one seaman had died [and that] owing to his advanced age. Such hardships [as were experienced] are usual in such navigations. We had stores in abundance. His desire to return in accordance with the opinion of others was evident in the *junta* he held in Santiago. He did not hold a consultation this time, as he had foreseen, and had heard the opinion of the second captain of the *Favorita* [meaning Mourelle] who, in a meeting in Regla, expressed all the above reasons.[110]

There had been no formal agreement on the return route to San Blas, although Bodega had proposed in his original routing that the coast be followed as far as San Diego. The expedition sailed south, past the islands at the eastern end of Afognak Island and onward into the open ocean. Because of overcast skies and mist on most days, no sightings were made until August 15, eight days out of Regla. When the ships were twenty-five leagues west of Cape San Bartolomé at the entrance to Bucareli Bay, Mourelle once more criticized Arteaga in a later editorial note:

> In this position the commandant should have taken advantage of the best part of the season which remained to reconnoitre the coast to the south, inasmuch as the previous expeditions [of Pérez and Bodega] had not been able to do so. This [expedition] was equipped with two beautiful ships for the purpose, ample stores, well supplied and well manned, and the most propitious season [to undertake it]. But [the commandant's] determination to return rendered fruitless the terrible costs incurred by the Royal Treasury and the most notable care taken by His Excellency Viceroy Bucareli to ensure that nothing required was lacking.[111]

Mourelle was expressing an opinion that Bodega would certainly have shared. At a later time, Bodega would twice propose expeditions to this part of the coast to fill in this gap in the Spanish charts: the first time when he was back in Spain in 1783, and the second when he was concluding his command of the 1792 Expedition of the Limits.

San Francisco

Near Trinidad Head in Alta California, the frigates became separated. They did not meet again until they both anchored in San Francisco Bay on September 14. Bodega navigated the tricky waters into the bay without any apparent difficulty, and the *Favorita* anchored shortly after noon in front of the presidio. The *Princesa* had a harder time entering the bay because she was pushing forward against the outgoing tide, but Arteaga finally made it in, "flying our flag and pennant and firing salutes to the Virgin [del Rosario]." He anchored two-thirds of a cable from the shore, a short distance from the *Favorita.*

On arrival, lodgings and shelter were secured for everyone. The most urgent task was to attend to the seventeen sick men, most of them from the *Princesa.* The *pilotos* moved into the house of the commandant to harmonize the data they had recorded separately. They used the mean between any differences in their sightings, compass variations, and estimates of longitude and latitude. The purpose of doing this, Bodega wrote, was to "avoid any differences which would cause confusion." Mourelle noted, however, that the differences were few. The *diarios* were also worked on ensure that these journals, including those of Arteaga and Bodega, did not differ radically from one another. This resulted in a good deal of similarity between them, as even identical paragraphs were incorporated into more than one account.

In spite of the duplicated passages, each journal writer revealed something of his own character. Bodega took the occasion to add to his 1775 reputation as an ambitious maritime explorer anxious to make his name far from the centre of power and determined to carry out his instructions, regardless of the difficulties. In 1779 he added an important dimension to his reputation – that of a careful planner who left as little as possible to chance. Arteaga revealed himself to be very much the professional sailor. His writing was impersonal, dry and devoid of emotion, and he said what a commandant would be expected to say. Mourelle, always interesting, was concerned less with making a complete record of the voyage – he left some important gaps, especially in navigational matters – than with writing fully about moments where he played an important role, such as during the survey of Bucareli Bay or in the *junta* at Regla. Also, he was more garrulous when he had a special interest, such as when it came to ethnological details, in which he displayed admirable discernment.

Of the *pilotos*, the veterans Cañizares and Camacho often offered quite full descriptions, and they exhibited the assiduity that the expedition required and that Bodega admired. Pantoja was a keen observer and wrote intelligently and fully. He was young, and it is clear that for him the expedition was a great adventure. Aguirre's account reflected his inexperience but also that he matured as the expedition progressed. The writings of Father Riobo are especially valuable. He not only related incidents that other chroniclers did not mention but also contributed a more human dimension to the expedition by recording his own activities and those of the other chaplains.

Work on the *diarios* and charts was completed on October 24, and Bodega and his companions put them aside to enjoy

> all the delights we could desire after such a long voyage. The happy outcome of the expedition, the abundance of vegetables and fresh meat with which we were immediately supplied by the presidio and the mission, together with the kindnesses and welcome of the Reverend Father Lector Fray Francisco Palau [sic] the minister of the mission, sustained the cheerfulness and endeavours of everyone.

In his *Historical Memoirs*, Father Palou recounted an event that Bodega did not mention even though it concerned him. It has been suggested that Nuestra Señora de los Remedios, the name given to his first stop in Alaska in 1775 and the alias given to the *Favorita,* was the object of Bodega's personal devotion. According to Palou, Bodega had left San Blas with a "sacred image of Nuestra Señora de los Remedios" as he wanted to "deliver it in person" and see it installed in the church of one of the missions.[112] Arteaga had intended to stop at San Diego, not San Francisco, but when the frigates became separated in the fog, Bodega had slipped into the bay with the intention of anchoring briefly and leaving the image at the mission before continuing on to San Diego. When the expedition lingered in San Francisco to cure the sick and to work on the maps and the *diarios,*

> it was possible to celebrate with all ceremony the installation of Nuestra Señora de los Remedios. They carried her in procession on a frame, which they made for the purpose, and placed her on the main altar after a solemn ceremony, in which all the men, the officers as well as the crews, took part, only the most necessary men being left to guard the ships.

Father Riobo was the only one of the expedition's journal keepers who wrote about the ceremony. He added that a High Mass was sung with all solemnity. An artillery salute was fired, and there was general rejoicing at the success of the expedition. The day ended with a musical concert in the plaza.[113]

Father Palou arranged two more religious ceremonies for the visitors. On October 3 there was a solemn celebration of the feast of Nuestra Señora del Rosario, the patron saint of both the *Princesa* and the expedition. Mass was sung by three priests, and a sermon was preached. This was followed by "many salutes, to the great pleasure of everybody."[114] The next day,

> the feast of Our Seraphic Father San Francisco, patron of the port, presidio and mission was celebrated with the same solemn ceremony of Mass, sermon, procession and salutes in the presence of all the people, those of the sea as well as of the presidio.

By October 25 the welcomed period of rest and recuperation was near its end. There had been only three days of rain since the expedition had arrived in San Francisco. The health of all the sick, including those affected by scurvy, had been fully restored by the mild California climate and fresh food. The explorers heard news of the world outside the North Pacific when Arteaga received a message from Bruno de Hezeta in San Blas informing him that Viceroy Bucareli had died.[115] Even greater news was that Spain had joined France in the war against Britain, which was attempting to put down the revolt of thirteen of her American colonies. Arteaga was ordered to return to San Blas "as soon as possible." Bodega's reaction to the latter news was casual: "we had not the slightest apprehension, but nevertheless I prepared myself for any occurrence." He did not seem to comprehend the impact these two events would have on the future of Spanish exploration in the North Pacific.

Weak offshore winds and fog made it impossible to get away from San Francisco until October 30. As soon as the frigates sailed into the Pacific Ocean, they were enveloped in the thick fog that often blankets the area in the morning hours. They lost sight of each other and set their separate courses for San Blas. For the most part, the weather was good, the sky clear, and the sea smooth; but the winds faltered now and again or fell entirely into periods of calm. The *Favorita* sailed into her home port on November 21. The *Princesa* came in four days later, flying her large flag astern with Arteaga's command pennant on the mainmast. Bodega sent his launch to greet her.

Fernando Quirós calculated that the expedition had traversed 3,116 leagues or 9,348 nautical miles. Broken down by segments, the distance sailed from San Blas to Bucareli Bay was 1,420 leagues (4,260 nautical miles); from Bucareli Bay to Puerto de Santiago, 277 leagues (831 nautical miles); from Puerto de Santiago to Puerto de Nuestra Señora de la Regla, 94 leagues (282 nautical miles); from Puerto de Señora de la Regla to San Francisco, 762 leagues (2,287 nautical miles); and from San Francisco to San Blas, 562 leagues (1,687 nautical miles).[116]

Reports on the 1779 Expedition

Francisco Hijosa, the ever-efficient *comisario*, promptly informed the new viceroy, Martín de Mayorga, of the ships' safe arrival in San Blas. This initiated a blizzard of reports from the captains of the expedition to their superiors in Mexico City and Spain.

Bodega was the first off the mark. Within a week of their arrival he had forwarded his *Navegación*, a journal of the voyage, to the viceroy, together with a long letter.[117] In the letter he began by describing his actions during the expedition in the best light. Referring to his disagreement with Arteaga's decision to terminate the mission, he wrote with hyperbole:

> With this manifest disappointment, we could no longer hope to climb to 70° of latitude, much as my officers and crew approved the ardent spirit which naturally accompanied my desire to see the success of this unique enterprise.[118]

Bodega softened his criticism of Arteaga by referring to, as "no less of an obstacle," the number of sick on the *Princesa* and the certainty that the eight who had died of scurvy were not the only ones who would have eventually succumbed. He was equally deferential yet critical of his commandant in his *Navegación* when he wrote:

> By the express orders of [Viceroy Bucareli], I was charged insistently with the duty to remain in company, especially in the event of some unfortunate occurrence. As it was imperative that I never disregard them for any reason whatsoever, I saw myself having to issue the order to return to one of the presidios in our new establishments ... without being able to [present my opinion]. That some of my crew were also suffering from [scurvy] did not discourage me as to my purpose, but it would have been impossible to advance the expedition in the condition in which we found ourselves.

Bodega concluded the first portion of his letter with this thought:

> I have no doubt that Your Excellency will recognize that throughout my commission I have spared nothing to fulfill the royal orders and have undertaken with constant perseverance to satisfy the needs of the royal service.

As for himself, Bodega said he felt "satisfied" with what he had accomplished as commandant of his ship and with the "glory" of having participated in the two voyages sent out from San Blas since his arrival. Both expeditions had advanced knowledge of the Northwest Coast, he said. He concluded by asking the viceroy, in the florid phrases of those times, to allow him to devote himself to fulfilling his obligations and "to not allow me any rest other than continued duty in the king's service in whatever missions may offer greater risk."[119]

He then paid tribute to his officers and men, all of whom had "sacrificed themselves with the greatest honour, energy and zeal," and recommended them for appropriate recognition and "remuneration for which I consider them worthy."

Bodega's already close relations with Francisco Mourelle were strengthened by their association on the 1779 expedition. Commenting on his performance, he gave Mourelle a glowing recommendation for promotion:

> Qualified [*graduado*] *alférez de fragata* and *primer piloto* Don Francisco Antonio Mourelle, while attending to the execution of his duties throughout the voyage as second captain, always carried out my orders with the greatest exactitude, sacrificing himself on all occasions with greatest honour and zeal, especially in the conduct of the commission with which the commandant and I entrusted him [in charting] Bucareli Bay. He accomplished it with the brilliance we expected and with the same exceptional distinction he performed under my orders in the schooner *Sonora* on the expedition of 1775. [Because of] the energy with which he carried out his duties on the packet *Príncipe* and many commissions entrusted to him by the commandant of the department, not to mention his services in Europe, I consider him deserving the rank of *teniente de fragata*.[120]

In later life, Mourelle showed himself to be worthy of Bodega's high praise. He eventually rose in the commissioned ranks to *jefe de escuadra*, or rear admiral, and was buried in the Pantheon in Cádiz as one of Spain's naval heroes.

Bodega had equally high words of praise for Cañizares, who had served as senior route pilot with "intelligence," and who during the entire voyage had "shown special devotion for the royal service." He, too, had fulfilled all the tasks given him with "notable success," and his conduct on the voyage had added

> to the distinction with which he carried out my orders on the voyage to Perú [to purchase the *Favorita*] and when in command of the packet *Principe* to the presidio of Monterey as well as on two voyages in which he charted San Francisco Bay, all to the satisfaction of his superior officers, as well as many other commissions entrusted him in the ten years he has served in the department such as in the careful surveys he has carried out of the Gulf of California and of the presidios on the coast. All these have earned him well-deserved promotions and I consider him worthy of the same rank [as Mourelle] of *teniente de fragata.*[121]

In the same vein, Bodega wrote warmly of Juan Bautista de Aguirre, his junior *piloto,* who had performed his duties throughout the entire voyage "to my entire satisfaction, performing all the tasks given him with great energy." He recommended that Aguirre be promoted to *primer piloto.*

Of his chaplain, Father Cristóbal Diaz, Bodega wrote of the care with which he had carried out his duties and the "devotion and solicitude he had shown for all the sick during the voyage, leaving me with nothing to desire." He recommended, "as a reward for his excellence and Christian zeal," that Diaz, whom he had brought back with him from Peru on the *Favorita,* be promoted to Chaplain of the Navy. Bodega also praised his surgeon Mariano Núñez Esquivel for his "vigilance and knowledge, which enabled him, in spite of all the accidents which befell the crew," to cure "the contagious ones [disorders] which threatened dire results." He recommended him for promotion from second to first surgeon.

Bodega was equally pleased with the non-commissioned officers. Singled out for special mention were Antonio Medina, the first boatswain, and Manuel Quirós, the second boatswain, for their "unalterable spirit, which matched their competence and vigilance." He wanted to see Medina confirmed in his rank and Quirós promoted to first boatswain. He recommended that Alonzo Moreno, the coxswain, be promoted to the rank of *guardián,* effectively a third boatswain, and that Rafael Rodríguez, the *cabo de guardia,* be promoted as his replacement.

Bodega concluded by pointing out that of all the crew, these men deserved to be rewarded for the "superior ability they had evidenced at all times." Their promotions, he added,

> will cause others to emulate them and make them endeavour to excel each other. In this way the Department would have skilled trained mariners of which up to now there has not been a sufficient number. At the same time they will not attempt to gain exemption from serving on voyages of exploration, knowing that [it is by participating in such voyages] future promotions will be obtained.

Viceroy Mayorga forwarded Bodega's letter with its enclosures to the home government with his support for Bodega's recommendations for the promotion of his officers.[122] Mayorga also ordered the commandant at San Blas to implement Bodega's recommendations for the promotion of his non-commissioned officers. Having so recently assumed his viceregal office, Mayorga was in no position to add any meaningful comments, so he limited himself to presenting a summary of the events of the expedition.[123] He did not comment on Arteaga's decision to terminate the expedition, although he did venture the opinion that, by their zeal, the commandants had justified the confidence that Bucareli had placed in them.

Arteaga took a week longer than Bodega to write to Gálvez to forward his *diario,* his charts, and his reports on his officers. His tone was very different from Bodega's. He praised both Quirós and Bodega, especially the latter, for having taken control of matters "in relieving me when I was suffering many indispositions, especially when assisting in conducting reconnaissances and by remaining in company."[124]

Arteaga did not seek a promotion for himself, but in a submission to the king that he enclosed with his letter to Gálvez, he asked for a special favour. As he had married without permission, he hoped that in the event of his death, his widow, two sons, and two daughters would not be deprived of his pension. He was moved to make his request so that they would not "perish in misery, and because the situation in which I find myself is such that only by a miracle of the Most Holy Virgin will I achieve the restoration of my health."

As Bodega prepared to send his report and its covering letter to the viceroy, his thoughts also turned to his private affairs. He wrote a personal letter to the viceroy enclosing a submission to Minister Gálvez, suggesting that he would welcome a promotion in rank that would bring an increase in his salary and thereby relieve his financial woes.[125] He listed several honourable reasons for his financial difficulties. On his voyage to Peru to purchase the *Favorita,* he had incurred "considerable expenses, which, to meet them, had wiped out a part of my inheritance." Moreover, his expenses since arriving in San Blas five years earlier had been "exorbitant." If his requests were granted, they would be the first royal favour "that up to now I have not enjoyed and would cover my debts." Bodega's submission to Gálvez was in the same vein. After summing up what this most recent voyage had accomplished and his role in it, he expressed the hope that he would be promoted. He expressed his fear that since the new viceroy was not as familiar with the "talents, enterprise, and performance" of each individual as was Viceroy Bucareli, their merits would not be conveyed to Gálvez with "strength." He concluded by requesting that Gálvez "make use of me in any function in which the risks are greatest in the service to the king."

Viceroy Mayorga's covering letter to Gálvez, despite Bodega's plea, was quite perfunctory and totally lacking in warmth.[126] However, the home government was pleased with the outcome of the expedition. In his capacity as Minister for the Indies, Gálvez replied to Mayorga's various communications by saying that Carlos III had been "informed with particular pleasure and approval of the happy outcome of this voyage and of the zeal with which the officers and crews had discharged their obligations."[127] He said nothing about the expedition's failure to find and arrest James Cook.[128] The king approved the viceroy's recommendations for promotions – Bodega and Quirós from *teniente de navío* to *capitán de fragata*, and Mourelle and Cañizares from first *piloto* and *alférez de fragata* to *alférez de navío*. The king also asked that the Cámara de las Iglesias de Nueva España [the Council for New Spain's Churches] be consulted about obtaining a sinecure for Father Diaz. Although no other promotions were approved, Arteaga was granted his request to have his pension continued in the event of his death.[129]

The 1779 voyage had not advanced Bodega's career as much as he had hoped. The 1775 voyage had shown him to be an audacious explorer and an able navigator and commander. His performance during the 1779 voyage neither added nor detracted from his reputation. Like other participants, he was rewarded with a promotion. This new promotion, while welcome, was not the only recognition he sought. Viceroy Bucareli's strict orders to Bodega to remain in company with Arteaga at all times had clearly limited Bodega's initiative. Bucareli had issued that instruction to reinforce Arteaga's authority over the mission; however, his directives had also prevented Arteaga from letting Bodega make any independent investigations as part of the expedition. For example, although Arteaga's ship was in no condition to carry out a more detailed survey of the Pacific coast on the return journey southward, Bodega could have done so. The crew of the *Favorita* was in better shape and had the time to do it, and the expedition would have achieved more results. At the same time, the foresight and meticulousness that Bodega had shown in the planning of the expedition marked him as an organizer who was able to coordinate all the elements of a complex operation to ensure the greatest success within the limitations imposed by the department's available facilities. This talent for organization may have been a key reason why the government accepted his offer to return to San Blas as commandant in 1789, after a number of years of relative inactivity in Spain.

Achievements of the 1779 Expedition

The achievements of the Arteaga-Bodega voyage of 1779 were disappointing, considering the preparations and resources put into it. Mourelle blamed Arteaga. "The fruit of this most expensive exploration," wrote Mourelle, in concluding his "Tercera Exploracíon,"

> ... bore no relationship to the great hopes expected of it. The two previous ones [of 1774 and 1775] were small experimental attempts to gain knowledge of the lands, seas, winds, and what preparations would be required. This one was undertaken with the experience gained from the first two. The helpfulness of His Excellency the Viceroy was notable, as he supplied everything asked of him. The two frigates were suitable for the task, the crews were good, the stores ample and appropriate, and finally, [we had] a collection of officers and *pilotos* who in their individual tasks were more than equal to the execution of the commission. It is scarcely possible to imagine anything which could have hampered its progress.
>
> On August 7, when the weather began to improve, the commandant decided to return to the port of San Francisco without taking advantage at least on the voyage south [of the opportunity] to reconnoitre and course [obtain sailing information for] the vast continent which extends from California to the north. For such a purpose he avoided hearing the opinions of all in order not to have an argument he was certain he would have to face.[130]

Is this too harsh a judgment? It is clear that the expedition's achievements were not commensurate with the extensive and careful preparations and that it fell short of the expectations of its planners, Bodega in particular. No subsequent Spanish voyage to the Pacific Northwest would be so carefully prepared, so well equipped, or so costly. Henry Wagner's comment that the "discoveries made by the expedition were of no particular importance" is substantially true.[131]

It is fair to ask whether the time taken to survey Bucareli Bay would have been better spent exploring northward. Bodega had tentatively suggested the survey in his first routing proposal but had left it out of his *derrota.* Bucareli Bay was designated only as the point of rendezvous in the event of separation. The decision to examine it carefully was made on the spot. The only reason given in Bodega's *diario* was that the voyage from San Blas had been quicker than expected. Even so, the time taken to make a careful reconnaissance cut significantly into the amount of summer weather that the leg north to 70° required. Perhaps Bodega's motive was personal: his desire to explore more carefully the bay that he himself had discovered.

The Arteaga-Bodega voyage suffers from a comparison with those of Cook and Vancouver, who explored the same region. Cook sailed well past Cape Elizabeth into Cook Inlet and then through the Aleutians into the Bering Sea, where he succeeded in reaching Point Barrow on the northernmost tip of Alaska. Vancouver made much more extensive surveys of both Cook Inlet and Prince William Sound.

The expedition also failed to fully appreciate the evidence of a European presence in the North Pacific. Although the Spanish were aware that Cook was in the Pacific, they did not learn that he had been on the Northwest Coast the year before them until his journal and maps were published in 1784. Arteaga's and Bodega's ships came very close to a tiny Russian trading post at Cape Elizabeth, yet they failed to detect its presence. The failure to inquire into the origins of the tricoloured cloth seen by Camacho's party when it was exploring the north shore of Hinchinbrook Island could be explained by the problem of language. Even so, it would have been well worth learning whether the cloth had been obtained from Europeans and, if so, whether it came from Cook's men or from Russian traders. The Spaniards also failed to ask whether the glass beads and the copper for the arrows' tips had been acquired in trade with other native groups in the region or from elsewhere.

It has been suggested that Arteaga's failure to report such evidence gave the Spanish government a false sense of security that allowed Carlos III and his ministers to assume that Madrid had acquired uncontested dominion over that coastline, by virtue of previous discovery and symbolic acts of possession.[132] But it must be pointed out that the decision to defer any further voyages of exploration was taken because the war against England had to be given priority, not because of Spanish complacency or indifference.

A major failure of the 1779 voyage was that it did not investigate thoroughly the waters inside Prince William Sound. Instead, the explorers accepted – apparently with little discussion – Cañizares's opinion that the view from Johnstone Point at the northern tip of Hinchinbrook Island indicated that the route north was blocked by a range of snow-capped mountains. Had Prince William Sound been charted carefully so that it was proven to be an enclosed body of water, this could have justified the failure to reach 70°N. But it wasn't, and this oversight made it necessary for the subsequent Fidalgo expedition to reconnoitre the sound more completely. We can only assume that Arteaga's health, which was beginning to break down, influenced his decision not to survey the sound.

The expedition was not a total failure. From a political point of view, the most important action taken by the 1779 expedition was the ceremony of possession performed at Santiago at the entrance to Prince William Sound, the northernmost latitude at which the Spanish would ever carry out such a ceremony. This would be important when Spain's claim to sovereignty as far north as 61° was contested later on. Regarding cartography, Camacho's *carta reducida* added substantially to Bodega's chart of 1775. It provided details of the coast from Mount St. Elias around the entrance to Prince William Sound to as far southwest as the entrance to Cook Inlet.[133] The charts corrected the Russian and French maps then in use. Considering the infrequency with which reliable sightings could be obtained and the fact that much of the charting had to be based on dead reckoning, it is remarkable that so few errors were made.[134]

The records the expedition produced are valuable to modern historians and ethnologists. The *diarios* kept by all the officers, *pilotos,* and chaplains meant that the Arteaga-Bodega expedition was one of the best-documented Spanish voyages to the Northwest Coast. The considerable amount of important ethnological information and the artifacts gathered were evidence of native life and culture at the time, even though the objects had been collected as "curiosities." Viceroy Mayorga forwarded three cases of items collected by the expedition for the royal cabinet or museum, together with the commandant's reports.[135] As happened when Carlos III displayed the Chilkat cloaks and other artifacts collected in 1775 to members of the court and foreign ambassadors, the artifacts collected on the Arteaga-Bodega voyage were universally admired for their originality, technical quality, and artistry.[136]

5

Away from the North Pacific

A Second Voyage to Peru, 1781-83

In September 1780, Minister of the Indies José de Gálvez sent a Royal Order to Viceroy Mayorga informing him that all further expeditions were in abeyance until the war with Britain was concluded. Hezeta, Quirós, and Bodega were to report to Havana for wartime duty.[1] Bodega was not pleased with this assignment. Reminding Mayorga that much of the Northwest Coast remained to be explored and charted and that he had a strong desire to complete what he had undertaken, he reiterated his desire for further work as a maritime explorer.[2] Bodega's transfer to Havana was postponed for four years.

The viceroy replaced Bruno de Hezeta, the commandant of San Blas, with Arteaga, who would serve in that post until his death in 1783. After the rigours of the 1779 voyage, Arteaga was not well enough to assume command immediately. Bodega, who recovered more quickly, filled the position until November 1780.

Sometime between mid-November 1780 and February 1781, Bodega was summoned to Mexico City and appointed to a mission to Peru. The assignment was important enough that the viceroy set aside the Royal Order transferring him to Havana. Because of the war with Britain, the supply of quicksilver, or mercury, which was required by the Mexican silver mining industry, had fallen off sharply, since the ships that would normally have delivered it had been diverted elsewhere. Bodega was instructed to sail to Peru to acquire as much mercury as possible from the mine at Huancavelica.[3]

Bodega would not have hesitated to accept the assignment. One even suspects that he sought it. The war seemed to be winding down, and it offered little scope for advancement – certainly nothing like his voyages of exploration had gained for him. A voyage to Peru could both delay his transfer to Havana and allow him to see those members of his immediate family who were still alive and whom he had not visited since 1776-77.

Bodega's instructions, dated February 13, 1781, were simple: he was to sail for Callao, pick up any surplus quicksilver the viceroy and the *visitador general* could place at his disposal, and deliver it to Acapulco.[4] For this mission, he chose the *Favorita* and the same officers who had served him well on the 1779 expedition.

Officers for the Voyage to Peru, 1781 to 1783
Juan Francisco Bodega y Quadra, in command
José de Cañizares, now *alférez de navío*, second-in-command
José Camacho, now *alférez de fragata*, first *piloto*
Father Cristóbal Antonio Díaz, a Peruvian, chaplain
Mariano Núñez Esquivel, surgeon

From the outset, the voyage seemed jinxed. Although Bodega had planned to get away in two weeks, he had to wait almost thirteen for the delivery of some hourglasses from Mexico City before he could sail on May 8, 1781.[5] The weather was perfect, but on May 15 the ship inexplicably began to "turn forward" and luff excessively.[6] After various ineffective adjustments were made to the sails and to the cargo, Bodega convened a *junta*. Realizing that it was impossible to continue the voyage under such conditions, the officers decided to return to San Blas.[7] After a complete waste of eleven days, they arrived back on May 19. Bodega appealed to Arteaga, the commandant of San Blas, for the use of the *Santiago*, even though she was partially loaded and ready to sail for Alta California. Arteaga agreed, and Mayorga approved.[8] Bodega expected that it would take eight or ten days to transfer the *Favorita*'s cargo to the new frigate.[9] It took two weeks. On June 5, two days after the reloading was completed, the veteran frigate sailed.

The southerly winds that prevailed that time of year meant that progress was slow. From the outset the old frigate began to take on water.[10] Bodega thought that with luck the *Santiago* might be able to reach Guayaquil, where she could be careened so that the senior caulker could properly examine the hull and mend it. At noon on August 17, while the crew was struggling to cope with the water in the hold, Cape San Francisco, south of the present Colombia-Ecuador border, was sighted about seven leagues off. A local coastal pilot, or *práctico,* whom they met by chance, informed Bodega that given the seasonal winds, it might take thirty to forty days to reach Guayaquil; furthermore, finding water and wood would not be easy anywhere along the coast except at Atacame. With water for only "a little more than a month" and "somewhat short of wood," Bodega decided to sail back to Atacame, even though this meant a further delay.[11]

In the afternoon of August 18, seventy-four days out of San Blas, the *Santiago* anchored some six miles east of the town of Atacame. Since there was no immediate prospect of careening the vessel, the starboard and port pumps were taken out and repaired. Wooding and watering took far longer than Bodega had expected. By August 24, everything was ready for departure; however, unfavourable winds delayed the *Santiago*'s departure until the next day, when she was able to continue her voyage to Guayaquil.

After two or three days of fine weather, heavy rains returned and the winds became contrary. Cape San Francisco was in sight, yet they could make no headway toward it for thirty-six days.[12] Bodega convened another *junta* of the officers,[13] and they decided to return north to Panama.[14] On September 16, ninety-nine days after leaving San Blas, the *Santiago* anchored four miles out within sight of what is now Panama City. Bodega planned to resupply and repair the ship in time to sail again in November, when the winds normally favoured a ship sailing south. However, he was unable to get away before late February of 1782.

As there was now no need to stop at Guayaquil, Bodega set sail for Paita, farther down the coast. The ship crossed the equator on March 14, and on April 16 the conspicuous Silla [Saddle] de Paita was spotted looming above the slight haze of the coastal desert. Soon afterward, Paita's houses were visible. The following day, fifty-four days after leaving Panama City, the *Santiago* anchored three cable lengths from the town. In Paita, Bodega replenished his wood and water and augmented the limited stores he had obtained in Panama City. While in port, the *Santiago* was joined by a small frigate, *Nuestra Señora del Pilar*, also called the *Princesa de Aragón*, under the command of *teniente de navío* Miguel de Orosco, en route to Callao. Bodega suggested that they sail in company. Both vessels sailed during the night of May 17. The *Pilar* remained in company until the night of July 1, when the ships became separated in a sudden storm. Bodega's vessel continued the voyage alone.

The storm forced the *Santiago* to sail southwest for some distance, and they overshot Callao. Bodega found himself off Nazca, roughly three hundred miles south of Lima and their destination. Finally, on July 16, 1782,

Bodega sighted the large, familiar island of San Lorenzo, which guards the entrance to Callao. At sunrise on July 17, the wind returned strongly enough to carry the frigate around the north side of the island and into the outer harbour, and that night Bodega was able to anchor two leagues out from the port. At dawn on July 18, he streamed the Spanish flag and his own pennant. Under sail with the rising wind, the *Santiago* reached her moorage late that afternoon.

It had been a miserable and frustrating voyage. Thirteen months had been needed to reach Callao from San Blas; the voyage from Panama City to Callao alone had taken sixty-three days. The problems and disappointments continued, and worse was yet to come.

Before leaving Panama City, Bodega had written to the viceroy of Peru, Agustín de Jauregui, to advise him of the purpose of his voyage.[15] When he finally called on him in Lima, he got a nasty surprise; there was no surplus quicksilver in Peru. On learning of Bodega's mission before his arrival, the viceroy had expedited matters and sent all the quicksilver he could spare to Acapulco on a merchant ship, the *San Pablo*.

Seeking the support of a higher authority, Bodega called on Jorge Escobedo, the new *visitador general*, who informed him there was no possibility of making any more mercury available.[16] Escobedo replied with a counteroffer. Certain supplies and munitions had to be transported to Guatemala and El Realejo (on the Pacific coast of today's Nicaragua) in the Viceroyalty of New Spain, for the "defences of that kingdom against any invasion by the enemies of the Crown." As it was urgent to deliver these, he and the viceroy had chartered a merchant ship. Although the transportation charges would earn at least twelve thousand pesos, the merchantman's owner was more interested in taking four hundred jars of brandy to Panama City. The savings to the treasury would be obvious if Bodega agreed to take the military stores. There was a catch: Bodega had to sail immediately. Furthermore, Escobedo wanted an immediate answer, because he had to obtain the viceroy's agreement and release the merchant ship. With that flattering turn of phrase at which the Spanish are so masterful, he added:

> I am persuaded that your sense of honour, enterprise and zeal will incline you to facilitate this saving to the Royal Treasury in the circumstances in which both the savings to be obtained and the urgency not to delay the assistance of those ports will ennoble your merit in the pursuit of your worthy services.

Perhaps seduced by such stirring prose, Bodega agreed. The *Santiago*, he said, was capable of fulfilling the task. However, he did not mention the need to fix her leaking hull.

This plan began to fall apart when the warship *Santa Paula* arrived from Cádiz for the same purpose. Her captain advised the viceroy that because of seasonal storms and gales, which typically lasted until the end of October, this was not the opportune time for a ship to sail north along the coast. Bodega accepted the captain's "sound" advice and asked to be released from his commitment to leave immediately. The artillery, muskets, and ammunition could await his own departure or be shipped on a merchant ship, whichever the viceroy wished. Juaregui's reply was surprisingly curt. It was now October and the negotiations with the viceroy and the *visitador general* had gone on for more than two months. The viceroy "suggested" that as there was no purpose to be served by remaining in Callao, Bodega "should prepare for your return immediately as your ship is not required here but is so on the coasts of your kingdom [New Spain]." The *visitador general* replied in the same vein.

Bodega persisted in seeking a cargo. He was grateful for the viceroy's permission to leave, but he was concerned about returning with an empty ship. Even if he took the brandy to Panama City and the cannon and munitions to El Realejo, the high cost of his voyage would still not be adequately covered. He repeated his willingness to also transport cannon and other war supplies to San Blas. It would help, he suggested, if he could also take some "fruits of the country" – in particular, cocoa. He would be prepared to order the necessary amounts from local merchants both in Lima and in Guayaquil. He assured the viceroy that to import them into New Spain would not be contrary to Spain's commercial laws, since those had been relaxed in the latest *reglamento*. Jauregui did not alter his decision. It would take too long, he said, to assemble "fruits" because it was not harvest time; and in any event the duties payable for taking them into Guayaquil would hardly cover the shipping costs. But if Bodega was prepared to leave immediately, he would order the cannon and other arms he had requested to be assembled.

Now, for the first time – at least in writing – Bodega pointed out that the repairs required by the *Santiago* could not be completed before the end of December. When the frigate was careened, it had been discovered that many of the planks next to her keel were rotten, so much so that oakum could no longer fill the gaps. As the viceroy and Escobedo were anxious that Bodega leave as soon as possible, it would be helpful (Bodega said) if they could order the dockyard to expedite the repair work. He also asked that the stores depot hasten the assembling of the supplies to be taken to San Blas. All of this was agreed to, although some of the items Bodega wanted, such as sextants, were not available.[17]

The *Santiago* was in Callao for thirty-four weeks. When she sailed for San Blas at the end of March 1783, she carried twenty-nine passengers. These included the departing *visitador general*, José Antonio de Areche, his chaplain and a dependant, nine other gentlemen, some with their wives and dependants, and thirteen servants. Considering the size of the ship, the volume of the cargo, and the number of officers, crew, and passengers, the frigate was must have been packed. Compared to the journey south from San Blas to Callao, the voyage back was peaceful and uninterrupted. Whereas 212 days had been spent at sea on the journey south, only 92 were required for the return voyage. The weather this time was much better, and the prevailing winds from the south obviated the need to tack or to sail close hauled. In the early afternoon of June 20, 1783, the *Santiago*, flying her flag and Bodega's pennant, anchored two cable lengths off the entrance to San Blas harbour to await a tow. He had been absent for almost twenty-five months.

As a matter of course, Bodega forwarded his report to Mayorga, who was concluding his term of office.[18] The report was formally acknowledged without comment. If Bodega had hoped to receive approval of the manner in which he had conducted his mission, despite its obvious disappointments, none was forthcoming. Instead, he received two unexpected shocks.

First, the Real Tribunal y Audiencia de Cuentas (a fiscal body) had forwarded to the new viceroy, Matías de Gálvez,[19] a scathing report on the manner in which Bodega's accounts of the voyage had been kept and submitted.[20] This long document provides an illuminating example of the extent to which the Royal Treasury's bureaucracy scrutinized accounts of expenses. In all his life, Bodega would never learn to manage either his official or his personal financial affairs. The tribunal's report criticized Bodega on a number of points. The costs incurred in Panama City for careening the *Santiago* and for other assistance (such as the provision of wood and water) were to be charged to the treasury of New Spain, but they had not been properly justified, acknowledged as received, or certified as satisfactory. As for Bodega's expenses in Peru, the tribunal generally found "very serious and substantial defects" in the documents submitted. Some flaws were minor omissions, such as his failure in one document to name himself as the *Santiago*'s commandant and to state that the ship "belonged to His Majesty." But important differences were found in the reimbursable costs of items in the cargo brought back, and in the accounts for repairs carried out at the Callao dockyard, amounting to some thirty-nine thousand pesos. Bodega's accounts did not make clear what had been done for the *Santiago* and what was undertaken for some other ship; and no evidence was found that the normal 5 percent duty had been paid on goods that had not been brought in specifically for the Crown. The report concluded:

> This Royal Tribunal has reviewed with much sadness [the documents relating to the voyage] of the king's frigate commanded by Don J. Franco. de la Bodega y Quadra ... The expenses incurred by the frigate on behalf of the Royal Treasury in so much time are great, and this Real Audiencia de Cuentas finds itself full of perplexities and doubts.

The tribunal recommended that the entire project be examined again, back to the original decision to send Bodega to Peru, and that Bodega be requested to give a fuller explanation of why he stopped in Panama City and provide "any other pertinent information in the possession of the Your Excellency's secretariat for review by the *fiscal*."

Bodega must have been startled by the severity of these criticisms, but more serious to him personally were charges brought against him by Antonio José López de Toledo, a disgruntled warehouse guard at San Blas. Writing directly to Viceroy Matías de Gálvez, he accused Bodega of defrauding the government by taking "illegal supplies" out of the viceroyalty, of compromising the resupply missions to California by taking the *Santiago* to Peru, and, as his accuser strongly hinted, of bringing back to New Spain prohibited items as he had done on his earlier voyage to Peru.[21] Gálvez ordered the matter investigated, and Bodega was summoned to Mexico City. He departed from San Blas on July 2 on three days' notice, while Trillo y Bermúdez, the acting *comisario,* conducted a survey of the *Santiago*'s cargo. Once in Mexico City, Bodega wrote a long letter to the Fiscal de Hacienda to defend himself as an "officer of honour" against the charges of malfeasance and negligence. Beginning by saying that he had learned of López de Toledo's charges "by accident," he characterized the accusations as "unjust and false slander" and dealt with each at some length. He concluded with a recital of his own achievements – his voyages of 1775 and 1779 and his accomplishments during 1780, when he was acting as naval commandant of the department – and noted the high regard in which two viceroys had held him. He was concerned about how López de Toledo's accusations might be viewed by his superiors. Bodega ended his defence with the following reflection:

> This, Sir, is the reward for the nine years which I have been employed in the service of His Majesty in these parts. I do not ask for any favour other than to clear my name. If Your Excellency considers this request just, I hope you will satisfy me by enlightening [your brother] José de Gálvez and others of similar importance.[22]

Eventually, Bodega was cleared of all charges. The *fiscal* informed the viceroy that Bodega was neither responsible for the high cost of the voyage nor guilty of the charges that the disgruntled employee had brought against him. Later that year, Bodega was officially informed of his exoneration.[23]

Still anxious for advancement, Bodega wrote to Minister for the Indies José de Gálvez seeking promotion to *capitán de navío.* After reciting the measures he had taken to increase the usefulness of the port and defences of San Blas during the brief time he had been commandant there, he went on to emphasize that he had "completed the most difficult of the San Blas maritime explorations." Without revealing his source, he claimed that "it is painful to learn that the Ministry of Marine is not aware of my arduous exertions over the last nine years."[24] Bodega's fear that this imbroglio would damage his chances for promotion were justified. Viceroy Matías de Gálvez had recommended him for promotion to *capitán de navío,* but this would not be granted until November 1786.

Havana and Spain, 1784-89

Shortly after arriving back in San Blas, Bodega received new instructions, in a Royal Order dated June 25, 1783, to proceed to Havana. Bodega left San Blas for Havana by way of Veracruz on December 2, 1783. He travelled with *capitán de fragata* Juan Manuel de Ayala, one of his associates on the 1775 expedition. The journey to Veracruz, roughly nine hundred land miles over primitive roads and with miserable overnight accommodations, took them almost three weeks. When they arrived in Havana on December 20, they wasted no time in submitting a joint request to Francisco de la Borja, commandant of the Havana squadron, to seek reimbursement for their expenses: eight hundred pesos and back pay.[25] Not until September 1787, four years after his initial request, was Bodega granted his salary as well as 622 pesos for all his travel expenses.[26]

Three days after arriving in Havana, Bodega was ordered on board the *Dichoso,* a vessel used as temporary quarters for supernumerary officers. With nothing to do and disheartened about his experiences of the past three years, Bodega composed a nine-page petition to the king.[27] He harboured a strong belief that his superiors in the Ministry of Marine were unaware of what he had achieved in New Spain. The purpose of this appeal was not so much to seek once again his promotion to *capitán de navío*, as to be granted permission to return to Spain, where he wanted to solicit a high appointment in person. To support his case in the petition, Bodega summarized his entire career to date, from his entry into the navy in 1762 to the moment he was informed he was to proceed to Havana because all exploration had ceased. Finally, he came to the nub of his appeal: that he had arrived in Havana "with a view to continuing my voyage to Europe and to inform Your Majesty of my inadequate services, especially now that ... I am required to reside in a department where I am not needed and that is very harmful to my health."

On March 15, 1784, after two-and-a-half months of idleness, he was appointed second captain of the *San Cristóbal*, alias *El Bahama*, escorting a convoy to Panama City. Within a year, his petition was answered, for *comandante de marina* Borja of the Havana squadron eventually received a Royal Order stating that the king had authorized Bodega's return to Spain. It said nothing about a promotion, however. Almost fifteen months after arriving in Havana, Bodega was on his way to Spain. On January 14, 1785, the *San Cristóbal* sailed for Cádiz.

As soon as Bodega reached Cádiz on March 2, 1785, he wrote to Antonio Valdés, Minister of the Navy, to request an audience.[28] When this was refused, he forwarded a formal request for leave to go to meet his brother to settle their father's estate.[29] He enclosed with it a letter from his youngest brother, Manuel, who had just been appointed *oidor* in Guatemala.[30] On the eve of catching the ship that would take him to New Spain, Manuel was anxious to meet with Juan Francisco, possibly at the University of Alcalá de Henares, where he was teaching law. Valdés granted the necessary leave for Bodega to meet his brother.

Bodega spent the next four years in Spain. It proved to be a frustrating and discouraging time for such an ambitious officer.[31] Having exhausted his inheritance and with no particular employment, he was in straitened financial circumstances. The little documentary evidence of his activities from the time of his arrival in Spain in 1785 until his return to New Spain in 1789 attests to his efforts to further his career and to obtain the rank and distinctions that his accomplishments on the Pacific and at San Blas merited.

The first matter that Bodega attended to while in Spain, was to lobby for his promotion to *capitán de navío*. He began his campaign with an appeal to the minister, José de Gálvez, to intervene with Valdés on his behalf.[32] Gálvez supported the plea and passed it on to Valdés, who decided to take no action until the accusations made by López de Toledo had been settled.[33] The king finally approved Bodega's promotion to *capitán de navío*, a rank normally held by the commandant of at least a second-level naval department or a large warship, on November 15, 1786.

Bodega also succeeded with another objective – membership in the Order of Santiago, the most prestigious of Spain's four orders of chivalry. The cost of earning a commission in the Order of Santiago was very high. Bodega had first sought admission to the order after returning from his 1775 voyage of exploration.[34] It is possible that part of the twelve thousand pesos of his inheritance that Bodega spent in Lima in 1776 went to legal fees for the preparation of the genealogy for his application to the order. After depositing the required two hundred silver ducats, Bodega submitted to the process known as the *pruebas*. Evidence was given that he had performed the necessary valorous deeds during his 1775 voyage. It was established that he was of noble lineage, that he possessed *limpieza de sangre* (purity of blood), and that no one in his parents' families was a *converso*.[35] The head of the order gave his approval in principle on November 13, 1776. Bodega had to remain in the navy for at least one more year or else forfeit his deposit. Since the king also had given his approval, Bodega was declared a *caballero novicio*.[36] On February 10, 1777, he swore formally that he wished to be named to the order in the convent church of the sisters of San Augustín in Mexico City. Because the induction procedure could not be completed in the Americas, Bodega asked his brother, José Antonio, who was studying for the priesthood, to serve as his proxy in Spain for the next stage.

But no further steps could be taken until he was in Spain in person. On his arrival in 1785, he revived the induction procedure by submitting a document to the order's governing *junta* stating that he was still serving in the navy and had remained in the king's service. He was promoted to *caballero profeso* and took the oath to become a full-fledged knight in the Order of Santiago. The king issued the final *real cédula* conferring the knighthood in the palace of Aranjuez on April 8, 1788.

In February 1788, Bodega requested and was granted six months' leave with pay to travel to the province of Galicia. His close friend and companion on his two great voyages, Francisco Antonio Mourelle, had asked him to act as his *testigo* in the *pruebas* for his own candidacy for admission to the Order of Santiago. Mourelle did indeed duly receive his knighthood.[37] And soon after, Mourelle left for a short stint as commander of the naval department at San Blas, where explorations in the North Pacific were being resumed with an expedition to the Aleutians led by Estéban José Martínes and Gonzalo López de Haro. After a voyage to the Philippines, Mourelle returned to Spain in 1789.[38]

It seems that in October 1788, Bodega had an audience with Minister Antonio Valdés. No doubt Bodega intended to press his case for another assignment as an explorer in the Americas.[39] Bodega was aware of Vicente Tofiño's project to make an accurate atlas of all of Spain's overseas possessions as a companion to his atlas of the Iberian coasts.[40] Realizing that a detailed survey of the coast between Nootka and Prince William Sound would be a major contribution to such a project, Bodega proposed an expedition to chart the entire Pacific coast from Tierra del Fuego to Prince William Sound, with particular attention to the coast north of Alta California.[41] But it seems that Valdés was more interested in appointing a commandant at San Blas.

Bodega travelled thirty miles northwest of Madrid to Philip II's austere, monastic palace, San Lorenzo del Escorial, where the court was in residence. Well aware that senior administrators had little knowledge of what he had accomplished in the Americas, he used the occasion to present the minister with the special leather-bound copy of the journals of his two voyages (the *Comento*) to the North Pacific, which is now in the Museo Naval in Madrid. Bodega probably also took the opportunity to seek a response to the letter he had written to the minister twenty-one months earlier in Cádiz, shortly after his promotion to *capitán de navío.* In that letter he had sought permission to marry, proposed another voyage of exploration in the northwest Pacific, and, as an afterthought, volunteered for the post of commandant of San Blas. He also revealed his public ambitions and private aspirations.

> Most Excellent Sir,
> During the lengthy period of my career devoted to the exploration of the northern coast of California, I attempted to marry a young lady [*niña*] of one of the principal families of the town of Tepic, the daughter of Lieutenant Colonel Don Miguel Marín del Valle, Commandant of the militia which garrisons the Port [of San Blas] and the ships. But the difficulty in obtaining permission at that distance and my constant voyages at the time stood in the way of my desires.
>
> With this in view, I came to Europe and, although I brought the papers attesting to her birth and circumstances, my few financial resources obliged me to postpone [the marriage] until time would allow me some independence.

Perhaps in view of the charts and journals I have delivered to Your Excellency, it might be possible to undertake a voyage to the South Seas via Cape Horn or the Strait of Magellan, as useful and worthy of eternal memory. Since such an expedition would increase knowledge of this passage, it would also be possible at the same time to reconnoitre the Galápagos Islands and the Cocos situated in the Pacific Ocean near the Equator to determine if these islands offered some shelter and an adequate supply of water and firewood.

Also, exploration might be extended to the north coast of California, or New Albion, making a detailed examination of Bucareli Bay, situated in latitude 55°17′N and longitude 32°9′W of San Blas, until it is evident that it is impossible to penetrate through any of its large openings, rivers and channels to Hudson's [sic] or Baffin Bay.

Such a splendid expedition could continue between the coast and the archipelago, which is to be found above 70°N, or higher until blocked by ice. It could return to Europe by the Cape of Good Hope or Cape Horn, after having taken possession at the highest latitude reached, observed the exact position in longitude and latitude of the harbours, the declination of the compass, the direction of the capes and headlands, the strength of the tides and currents, the produce of the land, the character of the natives, searching to see if there are any establishments of other powers, and, in short, drawing up precise charts and leaving nothing to be desired.

The voyage could be carried out in two frigates well supplied with sails, well armed and [staffed] with select officers, carrying two small boats in sections and appropriate instructions for the viceroys, captains-general and presidents of the kingdoms of Buenos Aires, Chile, Perú, Santa Fe, New Spain, the Interior Provinces and the Philippines.

Because of the knowledge I have of these areas, I believe the expedition could be accomplished in three years to the satisfaction of the Sovereign, the honour of [Spain's Royal] Navy and the nation.

However, on reflection, I recognize that as I have been inactive for nearly two years [and] my financial obligations have increased, the chances of being given this command are remote, as is being favoured by the grant of a commission for which I appealed to the benevolence of His Majesty in August of last year. In short, without the resources to ask for leave of absence for one year, I have had in mind applying for the command of the Department of San Blas, should this be the pleasure of Your Excellency and not prejudice my promotions in the navy.

Accordingly, Most Excellent Sir, it only remains for me to assure Your Excellency before you make any decision that I would warmly welcome any commission or position whatsoever in the service. I draw this to Your Excellency's

> attention in the desire to gain some relief through your kindness in which I place my hope, and that you will see fit to honour me with whatever suits you. Please forgive me for troubling you. My situation compels me to do so.
> May Our Lord keep Your Excellency for many years.
> Cádiz, the 23rd January 1787
> Juan Franc[isc]o. de la Bodega y Quadra [rubric][42]

There is no record of Valdés's reply, but he neither rejected the petition nor took any immediate action. There is no response to Bodega's request for permission to marry María, the daughter of Lieutenant Colonel Don Miguel Marín del Valle. There is evidence that Bodega's performance in New Spain was not rated as highly as he thought it should be. A confidential assessment of his abilities made about this time was reserved. "Known worth, good conduct, moderate talent, has had success fulfilling his commissions, satisfactory intelligence, has exercised command and shown aptitude for it."[43] More to the point, perhaps the government thought that the Californias did not warrant special priority over concerns that were closer to home. The administration was becoming increasingly preoccupied with European and Mediterranean affairs as well as with the war against North African tribes and pirates. In spite of the rapid expansion of the navy under Carlos III, all available trained officers were needed for these more essential responsibilities.

Whatever other factors entered the picture at this particular time, Valdés was not attracted to the specific hydrographic and cartographic expedition Bodega proposed. He had another proposal in mind – a more attractive one. In Spain as elsewhere, the publication of the journal of James Cook's third voyage in 1784 had aroused tremendous interest in the scientific community. Cook's three voyages, followed by that of the Comte de La Pérouse (1785-88), were in the spirit of the Scientific Enlightenment embraced by Carlos III.[44] The idea of a Spanish expedition with a similar scope was already on Valdés's desk. A month before Bodega's audience, the minister had received from Alejandro Malaspina and José Bustamante their "Plan de un Viaje científico y político alreador del Mundo," dated September 10, and this globe-circling voyage obviously appealed to him. Indeed, he probably encouraged its presentation.[45] Valdés quickly sought royal approval, which was granted with unprecedented speed on October 14.[46] Clearly, Bodega's proposed expedition, with its more limited focus, would not have brought Spain the prestige of a major expedition; Malaspina's ambitious plan promised just that.

With nothing coming his way, Bodega must have wondered whether his career, which had earlier shown such promise, had reached a dead end. It certainly appeared to be at its lowest point. The competition for positions in the navy was fierce. The naval schools and the Real Colegio de Guardiamarinas were producing talented officers. As Lowell Newton has noted, there was "an officer corps whose composition was that of men eager for promotion and advancement, men anxious to distinguish themselves in each assignment."[47]

Was Bodega a victim of the well-known bias against "colonials" or *criollos,* those of pure Spanish blood but born in the colonies?[48] He would have been quite aware that he had no friends at court to champion his cause, having served for ten years in one of the empire's remotest naval stations, far from the centre where decisions on senior appointments were made. A strong argument can be made for the importance of patronage; he had been in Spain when each of his previous promotions was granted. Among the officers who did know Bodega well and to whom he might have turned to for support were Hezeta, his chief on the expedition of 1775, and Mourelle – but they were overseas for most of the time that Bodega was in Spain. Hezeta was in Havana and would not return to Spain until mid-1788. Even then, the help he could have offered would have been slight, because he was under a cloud for his scandalous behaviour "savouring the renowned good life of Havana."[49]

Bodega decided to escape the dead end in which he found himself by volunteering to return to San Blas. It is evident that Bodega's offer was an act of desperation when we consider that at the time he wrote his letter, the post of commandant there was a minor one. There were no immediate plans for further exploration; the only naval activities were occasional voyages across the Pacific to the Philippines, the regular resupply missions to California, and the policing against the smugglers and pirates harassing Spain's trans-Pacific and coastal trade.

But as fate would have it, this picture was about to change dramatically, and once it did Bodega would have another chance to sail to the Northwest Coast and to advance his career at the same time. In retrospect, then, Bodega's decision to send his letter was the best choice he could have made. As commandant of San Blas, he would soon find himself at the centre of an international crisis, the Nootka Controversy. Even so, he had to wait another two years, until 1789, before his offer was formally accepted.

Part 2

The Commandant

6

The Nootka Crisis and the Spanish Response

THE ORIGINS OF THE NOOTKA CRISIS LAY in the 1788 voyage to the Aleutians led by Esteban José Martínez and Gonzalo López de Haro. The lessons learned by the Arteaga-Bodega expedition of 1779 prepared the way for its success. The detailed information recorded by the earlier expedition's *pilotos* regarding winds, currents, compass variations, and weather patterns, as well as more general descriptions of the weather, enabled Martínez and López de Haro to sail as far west as Unalaska Island, where they found the first clear evidence of Russian commercial activity in the North Pacific and heard rumours of Russian intentions to occupy Nootka.

When he received their reports of Russians in the North Pacific, Manuel Antonio Flores, the Viceroy of New Spain, took immediate action.[1] On November 24, 1788, he warned his minister, Antonio Valdés, that he was "preparing ... another reconnaissance of the port of Nootka and the rest of the coast."[2] On December 23, 1788, without waiting for a response from Spain, the viceroy informed Martínez that he was to command the expedition in the *Princesa,* accompanied by López de Haro in the *San Carlos.*[3] The frigate *Aránzazu* would follow under José de Cañizares. Martínez was to show Spain's intentions by occupying Nootka with a "humble shed." Russian and English vessels were to be "received with tact and civility." Martínez was to make it clear to them that there were "just grounds" for Spain to establish a settlement at Nootka "without precipitating a harsh expression which might cause serious ill feeling and create a rift." The viceroy directed Martínez to be firmer with any American ships that might appear, as none of them had ever explored the area.[4]

On the same day that Flores gave Martínez his instructions, he wrote to Valdés to explain that "the essential object of this new expedition is none other ... than we take possession of the port of San Lorenzo or Nootka before the Russians do, and, should they or any other foreigners arrive, make it appear that we have already occupied it formally."[5] He added, however, that "to insure our situation, there will be sent a commandant and a respectable body of troops, priests, missionaries, settlers, livestock and other auxiliaries appropriate to the enterprise." Although this latter statement may have given Valdés cause to hesitate, he could not have failed to notice that Flores had repeated the word *fingir* – to feign or simulate – three times. Flores's bold action rapidly received royal approval.[6]

As events unfolded, Martínez would face a much more difficult situation at Nootka than either he or Flores had foreseen. Setting up an establishment that would challenge all foreigners called for some astute diplomacy, for which he was not equipped psychologically. The bluff would call for steady nerves and self-control. Instead of these qualities, Martínez, a superb seaman, had an exaggerated sense of his own importance, which was far beyond his rank of *piloto primero* and *alférez de navío.*

Martínez and López de Haro left San Blas on February 17, 1789. As they neared the entrance to Nootka Sound on May 2 and May 12, respectively, Martínez met the American fur trader Robert Gray on the sloop *Lady Washington* out of Boston, heading for the same destination.[7] After a wary exchange of courtesies, gifts, and salutes, Gray left to continue his cruise. Martínez entered the sound the following day, where he found the *Columbia Rediviva,* under John Kendrick, and John Meares's *Ifigenia Nubiana,* under a Portuguese captain, Viana, flying the Portuguese flag but manned by English-speaking officers and crew. Having been assured that the natives were friendly, Martínez went ashore, where the Indians welcomed him with the traditional greeting, "Wakash, wakash." The following day, Martínez and Kendrick exchanged visits. Martínez' men began to build a small multipurpose house, plant the first vegetable garden, construct a fort, and restore a wrecked schooner they found on the shore.[8]

Martínez took several steps to assert Spanish sovereignty.[9] On May 13 he seized the *Ifigenia Nubiana,* had her hoist the Spanish flag, and transferred all her artillery, arms, and powder to his ship. Then, changing his demeanour, he allowed the *Ifigenia* to sail away with a promise that she would not return to Nootka nor trade on the coast. When Meares's *North West America* arrived on June 8, Martínez seized her. She was followed in by Meares's *Princess Royal* under Thomas Hudson on June 15, but that ship was allowed to go free on the grounds that she had entered Nootka Sound in distress.

Hudson departed on July 2 after telling Martínez he was sailing for China. While Hudson was still in port, Martínez decided that further action was required. On June 24 he conducted an extraordinarily elaborate ceremony to take formal possession of the sound for the Spanish king.[10] Later that summer, to reinforce Spain's claim to Nootka, he performed the possession ceremony a second time, on August 23, this time planting a cross that would be visible from the sea.[11]

The real trouble began on July 2, when the *Argonaut* under James Colnett arrived in the sound. He told Martínez that his ship belonged to the "United Company of Merchants" of England and that he had been appointed governor of the port by order of the King of England. The ensuing debate over who owned the sound ended on July 3 when Martínez ordered Colnett and the *Argonaut* arrested.[12] On July 13 – the eve of the *Argonaut*'s departure for San Blas under *piloto* Tobar y Tamáriz with a Spanish crew, Colnett, and some of the prisoners – Meares's *Princess Royal* returned from her short cruise. Hudson and his crew were promptly taken prisoner and in turn dispatched to San Blas.

Later the same day, Martínez succeeded in alienating the native people.[13] Many of the English prisoners were able to get ashore after they had been stripped of their valuables. They complained to Maquinna, the chief of the village, and to his relative Callicum. Callicum went to see López de Haro on the packet boat *San Carlos.* López de Haro calmed him with presents and protests of friendship. When Martínez, on the *Princesa,* saw Callicum leaving the *San Carlos*, he urged him to come aboard for a similar meeting. Callicum refused, calling Martínez, among other things, a *pisec*, a wicked man. In his journal, Martínez wrote: "Irritated by such slanderous words, I took a musket ... and aiming it, I misfired. One of my sailors who saw this took another and fired it, from which shot Callicum died." Maquinna quickly fled the village to seek refuge to the south in Clayoquot Sound with his relative and fellow chief, Wickininnish.

On July 29 the frigate *Nuestra Señora del Aránzazu* under Cañizares arrived at Nootka. Along with the news that Carlos III had died, Cañizares brought an order from Flores to abandon the establishment before the end of October. Martínez prepared to do so. The fort was dismantled and the house was torn down. The enlargement of the small schooner *Santa Gertrudis la Magna* (soon the *Santa Gertrudis*) was completed. He hoped to return to San Blas with it as a gift to the king. In anticipation that the establishment would be reopened, he buried the crates of bricks and lime he had brought to Nootka.

On October 20 the twenty-six-ton *Fair American,* which had come from

Macao and had been trading for furs around Unalaska, sailed into Nootka Sound. Martínez seized the tiny ship and then departed Nootka with her, reaching San Blas on December 6. The *Fair American* was released immediately on arrival there. The *Santa Gertrudis*, under José Verdia, arrived shortly afterward.

In a reassessment of Spanish policy in the aftermath of the Nootka crisis, the Spanish government decided to pursue its own program of discovery to counter English explorations in the Pacific. The government wanted to protect Spanish economic interests in the international rivalry generated by the sea otter fur trade and to provide for the well-being and defence of the California missions and settlements. In the five years of his tenure, from 1789 to 1794, the new viceroy to New Spain, the Conde de Revillagigedo, re-energized Spanish activity along the Northwest Coast. As the viceroy's naval right arm on the Pacific coast, Bodega y Quadra became deeply involved in these political, scientific, and commercial issues. As the new commandant of San Blas, Bodega's first tasks were to arrange for the release of Colnett and his ships, to reoccupy the fort at Nootka, to restore the relations with the native people and the English traders that Martínez had broken, and to renew Spanish exploration. While pursuing this agenda, he exercised his administrative skills while working from a desk on land rather than from the deck of a ship at sea.[14]

The Appointment to San Blas

The official minute of March 24, 1789, that informed Bodega of his appointment to San Blas read as follows:

> In consideration of your understanding of the conditions of San Blas in California and experience in those regions, the king has appointed you to its command. You are being informed of his Royal Order for your information at this time, pending communication of your instructions.[15]

It is not clear who in the Spanish government first suggested that Bodega return to New Spain to command the department. He himself thought it was Flores, who was concerned about the management of that department.[16] The harried viceroy would certainly have been aware of Bodega's qualifications for the position. Madrid had received Flores's latest plea for assistance in the governance of San Blas early in 1789.[17] The news of Flores's momentous decision to occupy Nootka Sound would have reached Madrid a month later. The Spanish government had already taken steps to recover control of the situation. On December 23, 1788, the king had approved the appointment of Juan Vicente de Güemes Pacheco y Horcacitas, the second Conde de Revillagigedo, as Flores's successor.[18] When Valdés met with Revillagigedo to assess the situation created by the old viceroy's bold action, they would have agreed that it was urgent to appoint a naval commandant of proven ability. Bodega's name would have surfaced if, as seems likely, the minister was now more aware of his accomplishments. His meeting with Bodega the previous October might well have been fresh in his mind along with Bodega's offer to return to New Spain.

Three weeks after Bodega's appointment, the *capitán general de la armada* Luis de Córdoba was instructed by the king to select "in consultation with Bodega six junior officers between the ranks of *teniente de navío* and *alférez de fragata* ... to serve under his orders."[19] Bodega's first choice was *alférez de navío* Manuel Quimper Benítez del Pino, who had been born in Peru. It is possible that the two met in Lima in 1777 when Bodega was purchasing and reconfiguring the *Favorita*; Quimper was serving in the merchant marine and wanted a commission in the Spanish Royal Navy. Bodega selected *alférez de navío* Ramón Saavedra Guiráldez y Ordóñez out of friendship, after the young man's uncle, a highly placed naval officer, wrote to Bodega in support of his nephew's desire to serve with him in the Americas. Although reports on Saavedra's character had been generally satisfactory, Bodega noted that there "was a violent streak in his character." Bodega found three other officers in Spain: *teniente de navío* Francisco de Eliza y Revenga, *teniente de navío* Salvador Fidalgo y Lopegarcía, and *teniente de fragata* Jacinto Caamaño Moraleja. The last officer Bodega selected for service at San Blas, *primer piloto* Salvador Menéndez Valdés, was already in New Spain. Juan Bautista Matute may have been assigned to San Blas at this time. Each of these men would make his mark in the maritime history of the Northwest Coast.

Return to the Americas, 1789

After a voyage of sixty-three days from Cádiz on the *San Ramón*, Bodega and his companions arrived in Veracruz on August 8, 1789. Conde de Revillagigedo, the new viceroy, was on the same voyage; the two men probably used their two months at sea to take each other's measure. Over the next five years Bodega would enjoy an exceptionally close and productive association with the count. Revillagigedo was a demanding and "hands-on" administrator who left no doubt as to who was the master, but he was generally willing to accept Bodega's advice on purely naval matters. On those occasions when Bodega was unable to persuade his superior to accept his recommendations, he never failed to be respectful. This mutual trust and confidence would survive the problems that often arose owing to the long time it took for messengers to travel between San Blas and Mexico City, and Mexico City and Madrid.

As soon as Bodega arrived in Veracruz, Flores wrote to urge him to travel to Mexico City as quickly as possible.[20] Considering his painful experience with the Spanish financial bureaucracy, Bodega lost no time in asking Flores to authorize travel expenses for his group.[21] When Bodega insisted that the amount offered was insufficient, Flores replied that Bodega and his officers should come to Mexico City; meanwhile their travel expenses would be looked into.[22] The new commandant agreed, informing the viceroy that four of the officers would leave right away and that he would follow as soon as he had "recovered from a slight indisposition from which I am suffering."[23]

Before his departure from Spain, Revillagigedo had received copies of Flores's dispatches, including those which dealt with Martínez's voyage of 1788. He studied Martínez's reports on the Russian establishments he had encountered, and he noted the mariner's belief that the Russians were planning to occupy Nootka. He also read Flores's report on his decision to order its pre-emptive occupation.[24] On landing in Veracruz on August 8, Revillagigedo quickly found himself immersed in New Spain's foreign affairs. The first letter he received from Flores informed him that Martínez had seized an English packet boat (the *Argonaut*), as well as a bilander[25] (the *Princess Royal*) that had sailed from Macao to "take possession of Nuca [Nootka] for the king of England." In the same letter, Flores added that the two ships and their men were on their way to San Blas.[26] Flores had no desire to deal with this imbroglio and urged Revillagigedo to relieve him as quickly as possible.[27]

Revillagigedo was not as certain as Flores that the Nootka incident was destined to end in war. In a polite but unambiguous reply, he argued that a peaceful end to the crisis was likely. The situation was sure to be discussed by the two governments before any action was taken, as was normal. To calm the viceroy, Revillagigedo added that most of the officers who had come with Bodega would leave immediately for the capital, with the others following shortly. He himself would remain in Veracruz to familiarize himself with the port's activities and defences.[28] Flores was not reassured by Revillagigedo's calm approach to the crisis. He asked Revillagigedo to meet him as soon as possible in Guadalupe to discuss, with Bodega, what further measures should be taken – in particular, whether the *Argonaut* and the *Princess Royal* should be further detained.[29]

Revillagigedo replied with a letter that foreshadowed the approach he would be taking on assuming office: to avoid complicating the discussions between the ministry and Britain's government, nothing further should be done until instructions were received from Madrid.[30] Flores backed away from debating the broader issue but did not give up his position. He informed Revillagigedo that the *Argonaut* would be made ready, that the medicines and other supplies Martínez had requested were being assembled, and that the First Company of the Catalonian Volunteers, comprising eighty men stationed in Guadalajara, had been told to prepare to move to San Blas for onward transportation to Nootka. Martínez had requested a detachment of two hundred infantry, but it seemed preferable to await a discussion of the subject, when he "would have the pleasure of giving you an *abrazo.*"[31] Exasperated by Flores's persistence, Revillagigedo replied that it would indeed be useful to discuss these points when, he added sarcastically, "you will have the pleasure of giving me an *abrazo!*"[32] The rather strained correspondence ended with Flores informing his successor that on August 27 the *Princess Royal*, commanded by José María Narváez, had arrived in San Blas. He did not say anything about his order to Martínez to abandon Nootka and return to San Blas, an order that Martínez had received at the end of July 1789. The two viceroys finally met in Guadalupe for the *transmisión de mando* (transfer of authority) ceremony.

Once Revillagigedo had assumed control in Mexico City, he found himself faced with two pressing matters arising from Martínez's actions at Nootka: the release of Colnett along with his men and his ships; and the Royal Order of April 14, 1789, to maintain the Nootka establishment with "honour and firmness."[33] As commandant in San Blas, Bodega would be charged with carrying out Revillagigedo's orders.

The Release of Colnett and His Ships

Both Bodega's courtesy and his natural ability to manage difficult people were severely tested by James Colnett, who was a troublesome prisoner.[34] During his ten-and-a-half-months detention at San Blas, the prisoner became suspicious to the point of paranoia, and complained constantly about the Spanish officials who dealt with him. Bodega and Revillagigedo were the exceptions to this.

Colnett was taken from Nootka on July 14, 1789, as a prisoner on the *Argonaut* under the command of José Tobar. The *Princess Royal* followed. After the ships reached San Blas on August 27, well before Bodega's arrival late in December, the *piloto* José Camacho took control of the situation. In response to the viceroy's request for a statement of his complaints against Martínez, Colnett wrote a long letter that concluded with a request to be allowed to "reside a few miles in the country or some distance from hence for a few days, part of us [my crew] at a time." The viceroy gave his immediate consent to the move on October 21; Colnett then complained that the English prisoners did not leave San Blas until November 14. He admitted, though, that once in Tepic their situation "became tolerable, and we were not sorry for shifting from San Blas."[35] The prisoners lived among the naval officers and senior civilian personnel and were allowed to roam freely around the town and the countryside, riding, walking, and hunting on a "parole of honour."

Shortly after his transfer to Tepic, Colnett wrote about his first meeting with Bodega, who had arrived in San Blas within a day or two of December 28:

> The new commandant arrived, named Don Francisco [de la] Bodega, Captain in the Royal Navy, with several other officers ... He and his officers paid me a visit, during which he promised through the interpreter that I should soon go away with my vessel, and lose nothing, and in a few days he would order our declaration to be taken against Martínez for capturing and robbing us.

Their initial meeting appears to have been cordial. Indeed, Colnett wrote the viceroy:

> I have the pleasing satisfaction to add that we were received by Don Quadra [sic] with that distinguished politeness and attention which has ever shone [sic] in his behaviour since our first knowledge of him on which we rest our whole content[ment], well assured that not an item wished but that he will comply with and that we shall be dispatched with the greatest expedition.[36]

Their next encounter, however, signalled trouble ahead. Sometime in December, Colnett had heard that Martínez had said he "would hang me and all my crew" and that "to revenge himself on me, he [had] appealed to the commandant for myself, officers and people when they saw him if they were coming one way, and he the other, to run away from him, and by no means to pass his door." According to Colnett, Martínez had prevailed on

Bodega to issue this imprecise order and Bodega himself had showed it to Colnett.[37] As a protest to the "no contact" order, Colnett refused to attend Bodega's levee, causing the latter to send one of the priests to inquire into Colnett's absence. Bodega accepted Colnett's reply that the order was "too derogatory for me to comply." "It was not common," he added, "for an Englishman to turn his back to any single man." Bodega claimed to have intended no offence. In a conciliatory gesture, he accepted Colnett's explanation and assured him that he could continue to enjoy the freedom of the town.

Their next contact came when Colnett learned that the *Princess Royal* would not be returned to him as he had come to believe; rather, she was to sail back to Nootka on a resupply mission. On January 14, 1790, in a sharp letter written in that irascible style Colnett used when he believed someone was double-crossing him, he protested Bodega's

> resolution to send the sloop *Princess Royal* to Nootka, without any restitution for damages already sustained, [as] being so opposite to the laws of Great Britain, her colonies and settlements, in justice to the company of Merchants to which the vessel belongs and by whom I have the honour to be entrusted with the sole direction of their affairs on the North West coast of America, to acquit myself to them and my country, [that] I cannot forbear to declare to you my disapprobation of the sloop *Princess Royal* being employed by you till condemned by the laws of civilized nations and capture.[38]

Bodega replied briefly that he was acting on orders from the viceroy. He promised that "should it [the ship] have suffered any damage on its return, and the King orders that it be returned to you, it will be careened to your satisfaction."[39]

Bodega invited Colnett to accompany him to San Blas to "collect" the *Argonaut,* which had been damaged returning from a short trip to Acapulco to pick up some cannon. Bodega found it difficult to communicate his good intentions to a suspicious and truculent Colnett. Colnett said nothing about any damage to the *Argonaut,* but regarding their visit to the *Princess Royal* he wrote:

> The Commandant took me on board the *Princess Royal* and was so rude as to tease me about what a fine vessel she was, and what a repair they had given her, new[ly] sheathed, etc. I said as little as possible without being uncivil.

The trip to San Blas was not a happy one for another reason. Colnett wrote:

> At last what he [Bodega] had long been labouring to tell me came out: that I could not possibly leave this country. I made answer I would have thanked him to have told me that before, and not promised on his first arrival I should go away in a few days. He now denied it and laid the blame on the interpreter, but some of my own officers who by [then] understood too much Spanish to be deceived, and he also took much pains to explain it to them.

Meanwhile, one of the Franciscan fathers had taken pity on Colnett and urged him to go to Mexico City to present his case to the viceroy. Revillagigedo received Colnett cordially in a formal audience. Acting under the authority he had received in a Royal Order of April 27, 1790, he gave Colnett permission to repossess the *Argonaut* "with all the individuals of your nation and everything else which belongs to you, [and] withdraw to Macao." Revillagigedo released Colnett on the sole condition that he was not to "trade in establishments or coasts of the Spanish nation." Otherwise, the viceroy was generous to his prisoner. Colnett was promised that the *Princess Royal* would be delivered "in useful and good condition of service" to her captain, Thomas Hudson, in Nootka. In addition, Colnett was to be given "provisions equivalent to those taken from your vessels, and the crews will be taken care of by paying them the salaries and rations which the King of Spain pays his subjects according to the rules and regulations [*reglamento*] for the South Seas." On Bodega's advice, Colnett asked for and obtained Revillagigedo's agreement to have his people provided with funds to replace their worn-out clothing. He was also promised reimbursement for his own travel and other expenses for the time he was in New Spain. He was even given some pocket money for expenses in the capital.

Colnett was not totally appeased. He objected to the restrictions that had been placed on his Hawaiian servant, who had been turned over to the Dominicans. He was told that the man would be returned only if he voluntarily wished to follow his English master, because being a heathen and free, he had to be allowed to choose of his own free will the place and religion he desired. Colnett's protest led to a flurry of angry letters and charges of bad faith. Revillagigedo, a man known for his temper, must have been exasperated. Colnett recorded that the viceroy was invariably courteous on those occasions when they met, even though his written communications were brief and sharp.

On July 8, 1790, Bodega gave Colnett the necessary written permission to repossess the *Argonaut,* telling him he could leave whenever he wished and was "completely satisfied" with the condition of his ship.[40] Colnett went to San Blas to inspect his stores and provisions. Taking advantage of

Francisco Hijosa's assurances that everything would be made good, Colnett claimed that there was much that was spoilt, ruined, stolen, or missing. The next day, Bodega wrote to the viceroy to assure him that he had directed "more than enough" stores be placed on board.[41]

It seemed that at last, Bodega had mollified the irascible Englishman. In his journal, Colnett complained about delays in readying the *Argonaut* for departure, "notwithstanding the activity, rectitude and good will" of the commandant of the Naval Department of San Blas. When the *Argonaut* was reloaded and ready to sail, Colnett returned to Tepic at the "request of the commandant to celebrate his birthday."[42] Bodega had always been fond of "occasions," and the festivity at Tepic was no doubt well celebrated.

Bodega assured the viceroy that Colnett departed "full of gratitude for the good treatment" he had received, but this was not quite true. As Colnett was about to take his leave, Bodega had to inform him – so Colnett's journal states – that "a complaint had been lodged against me in the Court of Inquisition for having in my possession indecent pictures and of showing them to the inhabitants of the town." Bodega had "called a general meeting of officers, principal inhabitants and clergy and all had unanimously declared it was a malicious accusation." Bodega suggested to Colnett as a friend that "if I had any, [I would want] to destroy them." Colnett thanked him for his advice and assured him that someone had planted them in his house – "if there were any." The only prints in his possession, he said, were "prints in the Dictionary of Arts and Sciences."

A final dispute caused Bodega to lose his temper. It occurred over what Colnett called "my accounts," or what has since been termed the Spanish Balance. Handing them to Colnett at the last moment without giving him an opportunity to study them carefully was asking for trouble. What they showed, in meticulous detail, was that Colnett had a credit for approximately twenty-two thousand pesos for the use of his two ships, reimbursement for provisions taken from the vessels at Nootka, and tools purchased from him, as well as for a "schooner in pieces." Against this total were charges amounting to thirteen thousand pesos for provisions and goods to enable him to reach Macao, for medicines and hospital charges relating to those sick in Tepic, and for the decking of his longboat, as well as, the largest amount of all, for cash advances to his men for food and clothes in San Blas and Tepic. Colnett was left with a balance of slightly more than nine thousand pesos in his favour. "There were," he wrote, "few articles but I found fault with." Colnett retreated to his lodgings and, with Hudson, compiled a list of "complaints." On delivering these to Bodega,

> the commandant ... returned them to me ... flew into a violent passion with the interpreter, forbade him to explain anything further for me of my accounts ... [He said] that he had already done more for me than he could answer for and what I did not like I must write to the viceroy ... [or] abide by them as now settled.

One item to which Colnett strongly objected was a "credit given me for my boat in frame 92 Dollars which was 70 feet keel." His exasperation growing, Bodega agreed to increase the value of the "schooner in pieces" to five hundred pesos, but nothing more. Colnett capitulated; an appeal to the viceroy would have delayed his departure another month.

To confirm the agreement, Bodega asked Colnett to sign a letter he had drafted and addressed to himself. It read as follows:

> I will always gratefully acknowledge the good sojourn [*buen pasaje*] and the civility with which I have been treated in this country where I have been a prisoner in name only. With the prerogatives which your kindness has granted me, my officers and I have had the regard of the commissary and of the whole department; in a word, I am leaving entirely satisfied with the kindness and favour of His Excellency the Viceroy, with your attentions and of the whole kingdom, but I must ask you, and do not be surprised, to permit me upon my arrival [in Macao], after manifesting my gratitude, to clear myself of all responsibility for the damages and delays which the company has suffered because of Martínez and the bad faith with which he seized me, which action I shall never be able to forget.

Most likely Bodega wanted something "for the record" to make Colnett understand that Bodega had been limited in what he had been able to do to make his detention more bearable. Forcing Colnett to sign a letter with which he clearly could not have agreed, under the threat that his departure would be further delayed, was not characteristic of Bodega, who would later show great tact as commander of the Expedition of the Limits.

Colnett and Hudson, the captain of the *Princess Royal*, left Tepic to board the *Argonaut* on the afternoon of July 5, accompanied by Bodega and Hijosa. On his departure, Colnett recorded that "we manned the yards and saluted them with three cheers coming and going." Formal naval protocol did not assuage Colnett's bitterness. After twelve months and four days of imprisonment, he recorded in his journal, "I took what money they chose to give me, took leave of them ... and sailed immediately and released myself from the tyranny, cruelty, [and] robbery of the inhabitants of New Spain."

Despite his altercation with Bodega over the Spanish Balance and the letter he was forced to sign, Colnett managed a few words of praise for Bodega and Hijosa. On leaving San Blas, Colnett assured Viceroy Revillagigedo that he had "every reason to be satisfied with the behaviour of the commandant and commissary of this department." But he could not resist one final shot, adding that the "money I have received here is but little more than my own private damages and not a fifth part of my whole damages upon the most moderate calculation."[43] True to form, he complained about the shoddy repair work done on his ship and the inferior stores with which he was provided. Only then did he deliver a backhanded compliment to Bodega. He wrote to the viceroy:

> I have the highest veneration for Your Excellency, but am sorry to say I found none at S[an] Blas, C[ommander] Quadra excepted, who in the most distant manner imitated the noble and disinterested disposition you showed me and my concerns.[44]

Colnett sailed along the coast as far as Bodega Bay. There he agreed to Hudson's suggestion that Hudson take the jollyboat and head out with his mate, Thomas Temple, and five seamen to trade for furs. This was a direct contravention of the sole condition that Revillagigedo had placed on their release.[45] Colnett traded for furs along the coast before arriving in Nootka on January 4, 1791. He was well received there by Francisco de Eliza, who arranged for prompt repair of the damage the *Argonaut* had suffered en route and who provided him with sufficient stores to reach the Sandwich Islands.

The Reoccupation of Nootka

While they were dealing with Colnett, Revillagigedo and Bodega proceeded to deal with the second element in the Royal Order of April 14, 1789: the maintenance of the Nootka establishment with "honour and firmness."[46] At the Naval Department of San Blas, Bodega set about implementing the viceroy's plans in cooperation with the commissary, Hijosa.

When he first assumed his post early in 1789, neither Revillagigedo nor anyone else in Spain had anticipated either Martínez's actions during the summer of 1789 or Flores's order for the abandonment of Nootka. In an October 1789 letter to Valdés, Revillagigedo – understandably perturbed because he had finally found out about Martínez's performance – criticized Flores for not having informed him of all the problems at Nootka:

> When my predecessor, Don Manuel Antonio Flores, handed over to me the command of this kingdom in Guadalupe, we had repeated and lengthy discussions, but perhaps because of natural oversight, or a preference for other serious matters, he did not touch upon the matter of the English packet boat and bilander seized in Nuca. He should have done so.[47]

Turning his attention to the Nootka establishment and still unaware that Martínez had actually left Nootka, the viceroy proposed to resupply it using the two captured English ships.[48] On December 7 and 8, 1789, he initiated a stream of orders and detailed instructions to San Blas, which advised Bodega that the king "desired Nootka sustained" and for this purpose had "selected you and your companions to accomplish this under my orders."[49] To this he added a hortative message as an expression of confidence that, no doubt, was crafted to appeal to Bodega's best instincts:

> I confidently promise myself success no less brilliant, since I am relying on some officers of honour, whose profession and character make them crave a favourable indication of their good fortune as they will be exposed to dangers and the opportunity to guarantee their good credit with the church, the king and the state.

Stressing the urgent need to relieve Martínez, Revillagigedo ordered that the 300-ton frigate *Concepción* as well as the packet boat *Argonauta* (the *Argonaut*) and the bilander *Princesa Real* (the *Princess Royal*) set sail from San Blas "in January without fail," well equipped, crewed, and armed for war with cannon and munitions. The choice of the port commandant was left to Bodega, but Revillagigedo stipulated that he "must be of the highest rank or one who because of his spirit, disposition and talent will best be able to satisfy your confidence. I particularly charge you to make the choice from among your subordinates." At the time Martínez handed over his command of the Nootka establishment to the new officer, he was to draft a detailed report on his 1788 expedition and another on the state in which he left Nootka, with details on the relations he had established with the natives and other visitors and the measures he had taken to ensure the port's security.

In accordance with the briefings he had received in Madrid, Revillagigedo attached a very high priority to exploration throughout his administration, and this mission was no different. Revillagigedo reminded Bodega that he had five ships at his disposal: the frigate *Aránzazu* and the packet boat *San Carlos*, as well as the *Concepción*, *Argonauta*, and *Princesa Real*. Bodega was instructed to use each vessel to "survey the coast and islands which have been charted in a confused way or those which have been discovered between the port of San Lorenzo [Nootka] and north to Prince William Sound." In particular, the ships were to investigate José María Narváez's sighting of a "certain opening south of Nootka in [latitude] 48°25′ stretching seven leagues from shore to shore," which Martínez believed to be the Strait of Juan de Fuca." Unwilling to rely on Martínez's judgment, the viceroy wanted it investigated "to enable a more concise idea of this discovery to be formed."[50]

Revillagigedo's lengthy instructions concluded with a characteristic exhortation to Bodega to

> devote your zeal to seeing that your subordinates and those dependent on you carry out the obligations of your office and assure them that in so doing they will advance their careers and [with] the expectation that I will recommend them to the King that they be rewarded with his generosity.

When he learned about Martínez's unexpected return to San Blas on December 6, Revillagigedo did not alter the substance of his instructions to Bodega for the planned expedition, except to remark that "this news makes even more urgent the early departure of the three ships."[51]

Bodega was quick to assure the viceroy that the re-establishment of the outpost at Nootka "is today the principal object of attention." Despite the inherent weaknesses of the department, he promised that he would proceed to arm the *Concepción*, the *San Carlos,* and the *Princesa Real,* and would also load the "schooner in pieces" that had come to San Blas with Colnett so that it could be assembled at Nootka. They would probably be ready to sail in January.[52]

Eager to revive his career as an explorer, Bodega expanded on Revillagigedo's plans for further exploration. He believed he might be ready by March to leave on an ambitious expedition that would reconnoitre the Hawaiian Islands, carry on to Bucareli Bay, from there explore the coast to the south, call in at Nootka, and visit the California presidios to see to their proper defence. Once he was satisfied that Nootka was adequately resupplied and fortified, he would explore the Strait of Juan de Fuca. Should the viceroy approve this idea, Bodega eagerly offered his services to carry it out. While not rejecting the proposal out of hand – there would always be time for "distant reconnaissances" – the viceroy reminded Bodega that there were more urgent matters to be considered. After Nootka was reoccupied, he and Bodega would be called on to handle the reaction from London that would inevitably arise once the seizure of Colnett's ships became known.[53]

Bodega and Revillagigedo had another divergence of opinion. Bodega had selected three officers for the expedition to Nootka: Francisco de Eliza, the senior of the three, to command the expedition; Salvador Fidalgo to command the *San Carlos;* and Manuel Quimper to command the *Princesa Real.* Revillagigedo approved Bodega's choice of Eliza as commandant of the expedition but thought he could benefit from Martínez's knowledge and experience at Nootka. For this reason he had "decided," and had so informed Martínez, that Bodega would send Martínez on the *Argonauta* to serve as second-in-command of the expedition. This quasi-order flew in the face of the sacred convention of seniority – having served briefly in the army, Revillagigedo should have realized the naval officers' sensitivity over the matter. As was to be expected, Bodega reacted strongly. In a letter dispatched by special courier, he told the viceroy:

> I cannot look upon this [decision] with indifference and fail to inform you of the problems I can foresee. Martínez is a *piloto graduado.*[54] If I appoint him second-in-command of the expedition, I will be unable to appoint any officer alive, nor even *pilotos* of greater seniority, with the result that those who should command because of their character and [other] circumstances will remain on land without acquiring any knowledge of the coast.

He felt certain the viceroy had been moved by no other desire than to ensure success, but even if

> no other person has Martínez's knowledge, I must implore you to embark him as *piloto de derrotas* as this appointment will grant him sufficient honour and favour.[55] Moreover, he is not unaware that in the department there are persons of ability, experience and solid principles who could discharge this role [of second-in-command] without the commandant wishing it were so.
>
> I trust that this representation will not surprise you, nor that you will think ill of me if I await your final decision. I am compelled to reflect the opinion of those who serve under my orders and avoid any motive for trouble.[56]

Faced with Bodega's strong reaction, Revillagigedo retracted his commitment to Martínez, an act that brought forth an angry, even violent, response from Martínez:

> I have had an interesting career in the service of the king, my master. And I have fulfilled my duties as I must as his servant and subject. I can only cry when Your Excellency orders measures which are not carried out ... Believe

> me, Your Excellency, I am of illustrious birth and cannot commit a disgraceful act [*bastardia*] which is not honourable.[57]

After reviewing the reports of Martínez's calamitous actions at Nootka the previous summer, Revillagigedo sent three more directives for the expedition to Nootka. First, there was to be no repetition of the events of the summer of 1789. Should any foreign ships call in at Nootka, the commandant was to "proceed with the greatest prudence and discretion and not insist on a careful search, and under no circumstances apprehend them unless they show disrespect for our flag, in which case he will have to use force to contain and punish the insult." Second, Martínez had suggested that to meet part of the costs of the new establishment, the commandant should be provided with five or six thousand sheets of copper. These could be used to barter for sea otter skins, which would be shipped to Acapulco for sale in Canton by the Royal Philippines Company. Revillagigedo did not order that this be done, but the copper sheets were forwarded.[58] Third, he appointed Father José Alejandro López and Father Alejandro Jordán to act as chaplains to the expedition.

At this point in his association with Revillagigedo, Bodega began to take the initiative in drafting instructions himself. With the viceroy's comprehensive instructions in hand, he wrote a detailed set of instructions for Eliza. They were classified "secret" and dated February 4, 1790, the day of his departure from San Blas.[59] Because they provided the framework within which the settlement at Nootka would be manned and governed, the key articles are reproduced in Appendix B.

Bodega's instructions to Eliza included the standard admonition to report on the nature of the land, and its natural life and minerals, as well as on the "spirit, character, temperament and number of Indians, and foreigners who inhabit those lands, who are to be treated politely and with courtesy." Sea otter skins were to be acquired in exchange for the copper plates, and possession was to be taken in the name of the king, with the consent of the natives and where it would be advantageous to do so. In dealing with naval regulations, Bodega cautioned Eliza that "as not all members of the crews have served the king, and as a consequence, are not accustomed to follow [naval] ordinances exactly, you will attempt to soften the required punishment until such time as they become aware they have the obligation to suffer sensibly the prescribed punishment." Finally, Eliza was advised that he was to remain in Nootka until such time as the viceroy determined he should return.

Getting the First Company of Catalonian Volunteers ready to sail to Nootka proved to be very difficult.[60] Stationed in Guadalajara and commanded by Pedro de Alberni, they were a company of some eighty men when up to full strength. Earlier in 1789, the outgoing viceroy had ordered them placed on alert to transfer to San Blas; but when Revillagigedo ordered them moved on December 7, Alberni painted a sad tale of their unreadiness. No new weapons had been supplied to him since 1776, and those he had on hand were worn out by extensive use over twenty years of marches in northern New Spain.[61] As soon as Alberni arrived in San Blas, Bodega allowed him to select sufficient arms from what he had on hand in Tepic and in the naval department: seventy-eight muskets, bayonets, and pistols, "new, clean, useful and well-crated."[62] Alberni asked for warm clothing to "protect [my people] against the cold of the higher latitudes." Alberni also needed more men; he wanted to wait until he could fill the ranks by further recruitment, by rounding up deserters, and by the eventual return to health of his sick men. Not one to tolerate delay, Revillagigedo peremptorily ordered Alberni to do as he was told.

There was a final matter that threatened Alberni's participation in the enterprise.[63] As a good commanding officer concerned for the well-being of his men, he confronted Antonio Villa Urrútia, the *intendente de comisario* in Guadalajara, about the two months' back pay owed to the Catalonian Volunteers. The shouting match that ensued culminated with the *intendente* ordering Alberni to consider himself under arrest. On the grounds that Villa Urrútia was not his superior officer, Alberni refused. Villa Urrútia complained to the viceroy, who in turn ordered Bodega to place Alberni under arrest as soon as he arrived in San Blas for having "repeatedly shown insubordination and disrespect." He was to remain under arrest until he arrived in Nootka; and Eliza, as commandant of the expedition, was to be advised that he (Revillagigedo) would expect to receive reports that Alberni had not only "mended his ways" but also "performed useful tasks" before being granted his freedom.[64]

At this point, a difference of opinion regarding Alberni's reprimand arose between Bodega and Revillagigedo. In acknowledging the viceroy's order, Bodega said he would comply and would inform Eliza in confidence of Alberni's arrest.[65] Revillagigedo assured him that this was not at all what he meant. Alberni was to be formally arrested, and Bodega was to inform the viceroy when this had been done.[66] Finally, on New Year's Day of 1790, the Catalonian Volunteers began their march from Guadalajara to San Blas. Alberni himself left on January 4 without formally informing Villa Urrútia, thus adding insult to injury.

Bodega summed up the difficulties under which he had laboured to get Eliza's expedition away in a letter he wrote to the viceroy on the eve of its departure:

> The resources of the department are so few that, even with forewarning, it would have been difficult to carry out my present responsibilities ... I am obliged [once again] to ask for *pilotos*, surgeons and seamen [to replace those which are ill] to man the frigates *Princesa* and *Aránzazu*, for rope for cables, of which only four hundred and eight *varas* are on hand, canvas and powder of which there is not a grain.[67]

On February 26, Revillagigedo reported to Valdés that Eliza and his three ships had left San Blas on February 3. It was, he wrote, with "pleasure that I have seen the ships leave San Blas."[68] Bodega had overrun the viceroy's January 31 deadline by three days. Bodega and Hijosa had accomplished a huge feat of organization and surmounted numerous obstacles in their determination to get the large expedition under way in such a short time.

Never one to be silent on the subject of his own accomplishments, Bodega also wrote to Valdés, with justifiable satisfaction, that

> after overcoming all the obstacles which hampered the preparation of the expedition to Nuca [sic], I have managed in the short time of thirty-six days since I arrived in this port to see sail yesterday the frigate *Concepción*, the packet boat *San Carlos* and the bilander *Princesa Real*. I communicate this information to Your Excellency for your satisfaction.[69]

The three ships reached Nootka in early April 1790, all having suffered extensive storm damage along the way. Their captains found the port unoccupied, with no evidence that any other ship had been there since Martínez's departure on October 20, 1789, five months earlier.

Eliza had four main tasks to accomplish: to reassert Spanish sovereignty by restoring the establishment; to reconfirm Chief Maquinna's donation of the site to Martínez; to re-establish good relations with the Indians after the murder of Callicum; and to renew the exploration of the coast north of San Francisco. To accomplish these tasks efficiently in an isolated post such as Nootka, cooperation among the naval commandant, the army captain, and the clergy was essential. Unfortunately, while they were still at sea, a dispute arose between Alberni and Eliza. Alberni wrote to Revillagigedo to tell him he was not happy that although he, Alberni, was to be in command of the fort and of his own troops, Eliza was to be in overall command.[70]

Alberni pointed out that he was senior to Eliza in rank (he was a senior army captain, whereas Eliza was a *teniente de navío*) and had served longer (he had thirty years and Eliza only seventeen).[71] The viceroy settled the dispute by appointing Alberni as Governador del Castillo de Nutka, a meaningless title. While this was accepted by Alberni with a fulsome expression of thanks and his assurances that he would defend Nootka "to my death," it meant that the establishment as a whole would remain a naval command.[72]

Eliza's first task was to build up the harbour defences of Yuquot, the site chosen for the Nootka establishment. He seems to have planned three lines of defence: the *Concepción,* the troops on land and on the ship, and the battery on San Miguel Island.[73] The construction of the battery proved an onerous task for his officers and men. Bodega's instructions called for it to be able to "contain any insult and command respect."[74] Embrasures had to be built to support the guns, and Eliza reported that four days were required to emplace eight of the sixteen larger cannon. Because of the terrain – the top of a rocky island on the outer edge of the San Miguel group – he doubted that it would be possible to place any more.[75] Six smaller cannon were also emplaced; the remaining eight large ones were stored ashore. Eliza was confident that no hostile vessel would be able to enter Nootka Sound "without being sunk."[76]

At the same time, Alberni threw himself into the tasks assigned to his Catalonian Volunteers. Besides constructing corrals for the animals and building an oven for baking bread, he undertook the planting of a large vegetable garden. Five houses and a hospital were built under his supervision. He had the soldiers dig wells and irrigation ditches to ensure a good supply of potable water. More houses would be added as the land was cleared, as would a barracks and storehouses.[77]

Two years later, in July 1792, when Alberni departed Nootka, Bodega paid him the warmest of tributes:

> I wish to inform Your Excellency that the development of this establishment and the subsistence of those who have spent the winter here is due to the activity of this officer. He has not only contributed to the cultivation of the land and the construction of some large houses but has also made himself loved by all the natives. Because of these services, I am obliged to recommend him to Your Excellency in order that [His Majesty] might grant him a just reward.[78]

The viceroy supported Bodega's recommendation, adding that Alberni had just been promoted to lieutenant colonel, or *teniente coronel.* "The captain of the Volunteers has given the best proofs of his activity and zeal in the port of Nuca," he wrote to the minister of state, Pedro Pablo y Bolea, Count of Aranda.[79] Alberni's subsequent career in New Spain took him far from Nootka.

One of Bodega's key instructions to Eliza, on the reopening of the establishment in 1790, was to restore good relations with the Indians, relations that had been poisoned by Martínez's murder of Callicum in the previous year.

> As one of the most essential points [of your mission] is to maintain harmony with the natives, you will endeavour to treat them with kindness and understanding. This is what prudence demands and what the king orders.[80]

Eliza welcomed the chiefs to his house and presented them with a number of gifts. He persuaded Maquinna to return to Nootka from Clayoquot, where he had taken refuge with Chief Wickininnish. The ever resourceful Alberni taught his troops to sing a song in the native language in praise of the chief:

> *Macuina, Macuina, Macuina,*
> *Asco Tais hua-cás;*
> *España, España, España*
> *Hua-cás Macuina Nutka.*[81]

When the natives heard the song, they reported it to Maquinna, who was greatly flattered. When he visited the cove, he asked that it be sung to him and requested that it be repeated several times until he was able to sing it himself. He sang it to Alejandro Malaspina when he was visiting Nootka the following year.

Despite Eliza's efforts to restore amicable relations, native hostility toward the Spaniards did not abate. Matters were not improved by a series of outrages: a night attack on Eliza's ship that resulted in the death of five Indians who were trying to steal metal barrel hoops; an attempt to kidnap a Spanish sailor; and the killing of an Indian who arrived at the establishment seeking to murder Martínez. To some extent, the animosity generated by these clashes could be patched up with generous gifts to the chiefs and elders – textiles, sheets of copper, and the prized abalone shells from Monterey – but gifts did not prevent recurrences. The "plank issue" in particular was an ongoing source of tension.[82] One serious clash occurred when people from Chief Tlupanalaug's village at Owis at the entrance to Tlupana Inlet tried to prevent Spanish sailors from stealing wall planks from native houses for the construction of their own houses and barracks. The confrontation left one native dead. Eliza took steps to prevent similar raids on temporarily vacated villages.

During the winter of 1790-91, the situation worsened after the troubled state of Spanish-Indian relations made it dangerous for the Spanish to hunt wild game.[83] To make up for the shortage of fresh foods, the Spanish depended heavily on fish caught by the natives, who in turn drew on neighbouring groups for more fish and other foods to trade with the Europeans. The Spanish presence was putting a strain on the native economy and local natural resources.

The Spanish establishment's occupation of the site of Maquinna's summer village was another major irritant in Spanish-Indian relations. Yuquot gave access to the ocean for whaling, an activity that was vital to the native population, especially to the chiefs. The Spanish establishment in the cove protected Maquinna against his more powerful neighbours, but it was also an impediment to the annual cycle of Indian life and to Maquinna's exercise of his authority over villages within Nootka Sound. Not surprisingly, the Indians often asked the Spanish when they would be leaving. *Primer piloto* Juan Pantoja recorded that "they are continually asking when we are going to leave, the eagerness with which they solicit this being noteworthy."[84] When he was temporary acting commandant, Ramón Saavedra reported that

> on the 14th [of June], Maquinna came to see me to ask when we would be leaving the port so that he could return to establish himself with his people ... as it was the best site in the entire sound. He was very sick as there was not enough to eat. As he was so thin, I asked him to come here [from Tahsis], to which he replied that he would not do so as my people would violate his women, even though the senior chiefs were not distrustful.[85]

In spite of the continuing discord, Eliza believed that he was gradually overcoming Martínez' legacy; he was confident that his more liberal attitude would in time produce favourable results. He assured the viceroy that the natives

> have been accorded good treatment by me and everyone under my orders in the establishment. They come to eat and sleep in my house with too much frequency, not only the chiefs or captains of the villages of Nuca but also those who come from Clayoquot to visit those of this port. This has happened not once but on different occasions. From this, it is evident that the inhabitants of Nuca are happy and grateful for the manner with which they are treated.

Eliza had grounds for his optimism. During that first winter, when heavy rains almost destroyed Alberni's vegetable gardens, Maquinna provided the garrison with gifts of deer meat and fresh fish.

As 1790 progressed, with threats of war between Spain and England over Nootka, the Spanish Minister of State José Moñino Redondo, Conde de Floridablanca, informed Revillagigedo that negotiations were underway with England to "resolve the question" of the arrest of Colnett and the seizure of his ships. He also instructed the viceroy that English traders arriving at Nootka were not to be molested, hindered, or opposed by force should they attempt to "locate in another part than where our establishment is situated."[86] Clearly believing that any "crisis" was over, Revillagigedo told Bodega that, because it was no longer necessary to retain such strong forces at Nootka, some of the Catalonian Volunteers could be withdrawn and that only one frigate would be needed for periodic resupply missions. Revillagigedo transferred the responsibility for decisions about the mission at Nootka to Bodega and Eliza. Eliza was informed that he was to remain in Nootka until further notice. Bodega concurred that only one company of the Volunteers need be retained; but he suggested that the naval force not be reduced until exploration of the northern coast had been completed.[87]

Expansion of Exploration, 1790-91

By 1789, Spanish foreign policy was focused on the North Pacific coast of North America. For many years, dreams of glory had been inspiring explorers to investigate every corner of the Pacific. The principal aim of these explorers had been to discover the long-rumoured Northwest Passage, the *paso del noroeste*, between the Pacific and Atlantic Oceans. Like the English, the Spanish had long been fascinated with this mythical northern route, initially referred to as the Strait of Anían.[88] Over time, four possible waterways through the continent had been identified. From south to north, these were the Río de Martín de Aguilar, the Strait of Juan de Fuca, the passage of Admiral de Fonte, and the passage of Lorenzo Ferrer Maldonaldo. The governments that sponsored these expeditions had recognized the international political implications: control of the Northwest Passage, if one was to be found, would bring untold economic benefits to the nation that found and secured it.

With the arrival of other nations' ships at Nootka, it was vital for the Spanish to determine whether such a passage existed.[89] If it did, the Spanish establishments in Alta California would no longer enjoy the protection provided by their isolation. This explains why, during Bodega's term as commandant of San Blas, the search for the passage shaped the expeditions he oversaw. The four years of Bodega's command, from 1790 to 1793, were the most intense period of Spanish maritime exploration in the region; he sent out seven maritime expeditions from San Blas.

1790

- Manuel Quimper explored the Strait of Juan de Fuca.
- Salvador Fidalgo surveyed Prince William Sound and Cook Inlet.

1791

- Francisco de Eliza and José María Narváez sailed through the Strait of Juan de Fuca, explored the San Juan Islands, and penetrated the Strait of Georgia between Vancouver Island and the mainland.
- Alejandro Malaspina and his scientific expedition destroyed the myth of the passage of Lorenzo Ferrer Maldonaldo at 60ºN.

1792

- Alcalá Galiano and Valdés's circumnavigation of Vancouver Island disproved the legendary transcontinental passage of Juan de Fuca.
- Jacinto Caamaño explored the waters north and east of the Queen Charlotte Islands in search of the supposed passage of Admiral de Fonte.

1793

- An expedition by Eliza and Martínez y Zayas charted the coast south from the Strait of Juan Fuca to San Francisco and explored the mouth of the Columbia River.

Because the season for exploration in northern seas was very short, Eliza took steps to continue "the discoveries with the other ships of [his] command" well before he had restored the fort of San Miguel at Nootka.[90] The following section deals with the 1790 and 1791 expeditions. The Malaspina expedition was the only one not under Bodega's direct command.

Fidalgo in Alaska in 1790

The first exploration Eliza sent out from Nootka during the summer of 1790 was led by *teniente de navío* Salvador Fidalgo, who sailed into Alaskan waters. It was his first test as a navigator in the North Pacific. He was given the *San Carlos*, which he had commanded on the voyage to Nootka. Fidalgo wrote in his *diario* that his instructions were to inspect the

> anchorage of Regla, known as the Rio de Cook, with precision to find out whether the Russians have fortifications, as reported by Captain Colnett,

> and, when certain, to continue his navigation in order to reconnoitre the Entrada de Santiago, known to the English as Prince William [Sound] ... from which point he will not lose sight of the coast until he reaches the entrance to [the Strait of Juan de] Fuca.[91]

Fidalgo was expected to meet Russian fur traders (*promyshlenniki*). For that reason, Eliza ordered *segundo piloto* Estéban Mondofia, who was reputed to speak Russian, to sail with the expedition. Fidalgo also took with him *pilotos* Antonio Serantes and Salvador Menéndez, as well as fourteen soldiers of the Catalonian Volunteers.

The *San Carlos* left on May 4, shortly after arriving at Nootka. Fidalgo's quite inadequate *diario* makes it difficult to follow his course or to determine where he anchored and took possession.[92] After sailing directly north from Nootka, he explored Prince William Sound's eastern shore. He then anchored in Cook's Snug Corner Cove, today's Port Fidalgo. He also entered Port Gravina, Orca Inlet, and Cordoba Bay and visited Valdez Arm, named after the Spanish minister. He found no evidence of Russian settlements. After leaving the sound, he sailed west for Cook Inlet; within it he found two Russian forts, which he described in detail.[93] After sailing west to Kodiak Island and briefly visiting the Russian settlement at Three Saints, he made no effort to explore the coast between Prince William Sound and Juan de Fuca. Instead he attempted to return to Nootka; however, winds forced him to head directly to Monterey.

Fidalgo had discovered little or nothing not already known or suspected; but his three ceremonies of possession in Prince William Sound served to trump any English claims to the area visited by James Cook in 1778.[94] Fidalgo was also able to confirm what Arteaga and Bodega had strongly suspected in 1779: that Prince William Sound was closed and did not lead to a navigable passage across the continent. His survey of Cook Inlet led him to the same conclusion. More important, he found no settlements or trading posts in Prince William Sound and thereby established that, contrary to rumours, the Russians had not yet penetrated east of Cook Inlet. According to Fidalgo, the threat to Nootka reported by Martínez in 1788 had not arisen.

Quimper in the Strait of Juan de Fuca in 1790

The second expedition that left Nootka that summer was led by *teniente de fragata* Manuel Quimper, commanding the *Princess Royal*. Before Colnett departed San Blas in the *Argonaut*, it had been agreed that his other ship, the *Princess Royal*, would be returned to him at Nootka. When she arrived, commanded by Quimper, Colnett was away with the *Argonaut* on a fur-trading voyage. Eliza therefore decided to use the sloop for an expedition into the Strait of Juan de Fuca. For his second-in-command, Quimper was assigned the experienced *piloto* and admirable cartographer, Gonzalo López de Haro; also sailing with him would be the *pilotín* Juan Carrasco, another veteran of northern waters. Eliza's instructions to Quimper were straightforward.[95] He was to sail south from Nootka and explore the coast of what is now Vancouver Island as far as the entrance to the strait. He was to "reconnoitre well the Strait of Fuca, which is what most interests us as we do not know where it leads." Finally, he was to return to Nootka by mid-August at the latest. No doubt, Eliza assumed that Colnett would be back in Nootka by then to reclaim the ship for Thomas Hudson.[96]

Quimper left Nootka on May 31, 1790.[97] He spent two weeks in Clayoquot Sound, where he unexpectedly encountered Chief Maquinna, who had taken refuge with his relative, Wickininnish, after the murder of Callicum the previous summer. Quimper persuaded Maquinna to return to Nootka, having assured him that the feared and hated Martínez, although present, was no longer in command.

After exploring Barkley Sound, Quimper entered the Strait of Juan de Fuca and skirted its northern shore as far as Royal Roads, near the site of present-day Victoria. He then crossed the strait to Dungeness in what is now Washington State. He entered Port Discovery, which he named after Bodega.[98] Continuing eastward, he missed Puget Sound's entrance; but while approaching the San Juan Islands, he sighted the entrance to Haro Strait, trending north, as well as other passages at the end of the strait.[99] In the belief that these were merely passages through the San Juan archipelago, he concluded (incorrectly) that the strait was closed.

Quimper then turned back westward, sailing along the north shore as far as Esquimalt Harbour before crossing the strait once again. Bucking the currents and strong contrary winds coming off the Pacific Ocean, he navigated along what is now the coast of Washington until he reached Neah Bay. He performed the possession ceremony on August 1, 1790, calling the place Núñez Gaona after the Spanish admiral Mariano Núñez Gaona. His favourable description of what actually turned out to be a poor anchorage would lead to it being selected as the preferred alternative site for an establishment should Nootka have to be turned over to the British. As the onshore winds made it impossible for him to reach Nootka in time for his assigned deadline, and with his stores almost exhausted, he turned Colnett's ship, the *Princess Royal*, south toward San Blas, where his unexpected arrival caused great surprise.

Although he had not achieved as much as the authorities might have wished, Quimper's effort was not wasted. He was the first to disclose the full extent of the Strait of Juan de Fuca, and he had taken possession at four locations to ensure Spanish sovereignty over the waterway.[100] The ceremonies at these sites would be of importance later on during Bodega's 1792 meeting with the British at Nootka.

When they were received in Madrid, Quimper's *diario* and charts and what they revealed of the Strait of Juan de Fuca also aroused much interest.[101] Minister of State Floridablanca sent the viceroy a Royal Order on instructions from the king, saying it was very important to explore the opening that Quimper had sighted at the eastern end of Fuca and that he had marked on his general chart as Haro Strait. It was necessary, he wrote, "at all costs to ascertain whether ... the Canal de López de Haro leads to Hudson or Baffin Bay, or whether it turns to empty into the Pacific Ocean, or if it ends without leading anywhere."[102]

Eliza's Exploration in 1791

As soon as he received the reports from Quimper and Fidalgo, both of whom had returned to San Blas earlier than expected, Bodega informed the viceroy. He expressed his regret that owing to the "rigours of the season," neither Quimper nor Fidalgo had been able to "meet the expectations" of their instructions, but he hoped the viceroy would agree they had done their best.[103] He urged the viceroy to order Eliza to conduct a further expedition the following summer, this time to thoroughly explore the coast from Mount St. Elias south to Trinidad Bay in California. This would complement what other expeditions had already charted and, he hoped, would fill in some gaps.[104] While agreeing to Bodega's proposal, Revillagigedo was particularly concerned that the interior of the Strait of Juan de Fuca be given special attention. Although it was normal practice for the commandant of the Naval Department to select the officers for an expedition, Revillagigedo requested that *segundo piloto* José María Narváez and *pilotín* Juan Carrasco be included.[105]

This news delighted Bodega. His written communications with the viceroy were usually formal, but in this instance he adopted a rare effusive tone:

> I am fully persuaded that Your Excellency's trust in the worth of these officers will not be misplaced and that they will respond to your goodness and honour by willingly sacrificing themselves in the most arduous commissions they are given. Moreover, I have no doubt that this year Commandant Francisco

> Eliza will complete the discoveries we lack, including those points to which Your Excellency was pleased to alert me.

He said he felt certain that, when the expedition returned, he would be able to send the king an "exact and perfect general plan of the entire coast" and to "see concluded what little remains to reconnoitre of the Estrecho de Fuca; in his late voyage, the commandant of the bilander, Manuel Quimper, examined this strait with so much care and many times exposed his ship to assure himself of the nature of its depth and harbours."[106]

With unwarranted optimism, Bodega issued new directions to Eliza. These specified where the next stage of exploration should be carried out.[107] Bodega seems to have ignored Revillagigedo's emphasis on the Strait of Juan de Fuca; the key paragraphs of the further instructions gave the strait very low priority, and read as follows:

> The object of this expedition is to inspect those points which have not yet been well examined, with a view to form an exact general plan of the whole coast. As the principal ones are the Entrada de Bucareli, the Estrecho de Fonte, Ezeta, Bahia de San Rafael and Carrasco, Puerto de Clauycuat and the inside of Fuca, you will take your course to strike land at the Monte de San Elias.[108]
>
> From this place you will follow the coast down to the Puerto de Trinidad, without ever losing sight of it or neglecting to sound these inlets.[109]
>
> In order that you may fulfill your obligations with more attention to detail and with less risk, you will take with you the schooner which you carried in pieces since, by this time, I think she is in a state to sail.

Just prior to his departure, Eliza received another instruction from Bodega, one that added to his already weighty task. This last-minute addition was to inform him that the viceroy also wanted him to look for the Río de Martín de Aguilar.[110] Bodega enclosed a copy of a general map of the coast that he had prepared for Alejandro Malaspina, who had been ordered by the Spanish government to go north in search of the passage of Ferrer Maldonaldo.

Eliza left Nootka on May 4, 1791, in the *San Carlos*, which had just arrived with supplies for the establishment. At the last minute he had decided to take her instead of the much larger *Concepción*, which was left in port as guard ship.[111] As officers, Eliza had *primer piloto* Juan Pantoja y Arriaga[112] and *segundo piloto* José Antonio Verdia. They were accompanied by José Maria Narváez commanding the *Santa Saturnina*, "the schooner in pieces."[113] The experienced *pilotín* [pilot's mate] Juan Carrasco was with Narváez.[114] Between them, the two ships carried ten of Pedro de Alberni's Catalonian Volunteers.

Sailing north out of Nootka, the two vessels soon encountered strong, contrary northwest winds that greatly impeded the *Santa Saturnina*'s progress. Fearing it was too late in the season to attempt to reach Bucareli Bay or higher, the overly cautious Eliza decided to abandon the plans to explore anything north of Nootka after only three days. He turned south and headed for Clayoquot Sound. After Pantoja and Narváez had charted it carefully, the two vessels proceeded south along the coast. Narváez next surveyed Barkley Sound before entering the Strait of Juan de Fuca and sailing to its eastern end. Approaching Haro Strait, Eliza saw the passages in the San Juan archipelago. He sent Narváez in the *Santa Saturnina* and Pantoja in the longboat of the *San Carlos* to carry out the exploration between the islands. Pantoja went through Haro Strait, and Narváez went up Rosario Strait to the east of it. After the ships circled back and reunited off the south shore around New Dungeness and Port Discovery, Eliza himself went off exploring; but like Quimper before him and like Narváez on the return journey to Nootka, he missed sighting Puget Sound.

Meeting at the southern end of the Strait of Georgia, Narváez and Pantoja proceeded up the eastern coast of Vancouver Island. Narváez sailed as far north as today's Nanaimo. Crossing the strait, he anchored off the headland of today's Point Grey at the entrance to English Bay; thus he was the first European to view the future site of the city of Vancouver.

The results of the expedition were vividly represented in a large chart, which is generally referred to today as the "Narváez Map" or the "Eliza Map."[115] The chart provides information that cannot be found in the participants' written accounts. Although Eliza was not the most resolute of the Spanish mariners on the Northwest Coast, the importance of this chart for determining future policy and action cannot be overstated. Nor can Eliza's own conclusion:

> The [Gran Canal de Nuestra Señora del Rosario la Marinera] continued much further on.[116] I believe that if there is anything of particular importance or consideration to be explored on this coast it is this large channel, as according to my method of thinking, and that of my pilot, it promises much ... I assure Your Excellency that the passage to the Atlantic Ocean, which foreign nations search for with such diligence on this coast, cannot in my opinion, if there be one, be found in any other part; it is either, I think, by this great channel, or it is continent.[117]

The following year, Alcalá Galiano and Valdés would prove that Eliza was right.

Malaspina to 60°N in 1791

Because Cook, Arteaga and Bodega, and Fidalgo had all failed to discover any opening that led to a navigable passage through Prince William Sound or Cook Inlet, the Spanish authorities were prepared to dismiss the idea of any passage in the far north as illusory. But one more possibility remained. In 1788 a memoir, apparently written around 1609, had been found that described how a Spanish captain, Lorenzo Ferrer Maldonaldo, had sailed from Spain north toward Iceland to reach 60°N and then west along the line of latitude to find the entrance to the Strait of Anían, which, he said, was "more than thirty leagues wide." The strait itself was described as fifteen leagues long and easily navigable at high tide. It required six hours to traverse. At the point where it entered the Pacific was a port capable of holding five hundred ships. Maldonaldo was said to have then returned to Spain the way he had come.

The Spanish authorities reconsidered the idea of a northern passage after the highly regarded French cartographer and geographer Jean Nicolas Buache de Neuville published the text of a paper he had read before the French Academy of Sciences in Paris in November 1790, expressing his belief that Maldonaldo's memoir was genuine. Urgent orders were sent to Mexico to reach the scientific expedition of Alejandro Malaspina in Acapulco. He was ordered to postpone his plans to sail to the Sandwich Islands in favour of going north to examine the coast between 59°N and 60°N.

The Malaspina expedition was under the direct operational control of the Spanish naval minister, Antonio Valdés, and Revillagigedo had been told to ensure that Malaspina's corvettes *Descubierta* and *Atrevida* received all the support they required. The viceroy informed Bodega that the base at Acapulco was to provide any repair services, stores, and crew replacements that Malaspina might request.

On his own initiative, Bodega provided Malaspina with a chart he had drawn especially for the expedition. On the chart he had included the most recent information available on the North Pacific coast as well as a listing of all the Spanish discoveries since 1602 in order to avoid unnecessary duplication of place names.[118] Bodega also prepared for Malaspina a lengthy and detailed document titled "Course which I conjecture would be proper for the commandants to observe on the Northern Coast of California to eliminate the doubts which we have up to the present time."[119]

Despite his own skepticism about the genuineness of the Maldonaldo account, Malaspina obeyed the Royal Order. The corvettes left Acapulco for the Northwest Coast on June 1, 1791. Twenty-five days later they sighted land just south of Cook's Cape Fairweather.[120] The snow-capped peaks of the St. Elias Mountains were plainly visible. The ships ran along the coast at a distance of one to two leagues, searching for an opening. They eventually reached Yakutat Bay, where they found an anchorage in Port Mulgrave, a small bay in the southwest corner of the sound, which had been visited and named by the English fur trader George Dixon in 1787. One of Malaspina's artists, Tomás de Suría, was lyrical when he recorded what was seen in his journal:

> A small inlet presented itself to our view. Great was the joy of the commandant and of all the officers as they believed, and with some foundation, that this might be the so-much-desired and sought-for strait, which would form the passage to the North Sea of Europe and which has cost so much trouble to all the nations in various expeditions they have made for simply this end ... They now took out the manuscript of Ferrer Maldonaldo who marks this strait in the same latitude of 59°30′ of which we are talking ... and even the figures and the perspective agree with the one which he gives.[121]

The "great joy" quickly evaporated when, proceeding farther into the bay, the huge Hubbard Glacier was found to block any further access to the interior.[122] Aptly, Malaspina named the interior of the inlet Puerto de Desengaño (Port Deception).[123] Before departing, he erected a cairn as a symbol of possession on the south shore within sight of an island he named after his naturalist, Tadeo Haenke. He substantially shortened the elaborate ceremony that had been prescribed by Viceroy Bucareli in 1774 for Juan Pérez and followed by all Spanish explorers up to that time.

Malaspina skirted the coast between Yakutat Bay and Prince William Sound to see whether some other bay might offer a passage. Unable to find one, he abandoned the search and sailed south for Nootka and from there to Monterey and Acapulco, before resuming his planned course across the Pacific. From Mexico, he wrote to Antonio Valdés:

> By 28 July when we found ourselves off Monte Buen Tiempo [Mount Fairweather] we could consider the orders of His Majesty as having been complied with since we knew that between that mountain and the Entrada del Principe Guillermo [Prince William Sound] there is no intervening river along the shore, nor does the unbroken line of the coastal cordillera leave the least hope of the existence of an inlet.[124]

Like Arteaga and Bodega in 1779 and like Fidalgo in 1790, Malaspina had seen a 180-degree horizon of snow-capped mountains.[125]

From a Spanish perspective, the explorations carried out in 1790 and 1791 provided clear evidence that neither Prince William Sound nor Cook Inlet nor Yakutat Bay led to the fabled Northwest Passage. A final two-part effort was required, however: first, to establish absolutely that the Strait of Juan de Fuca was not the desired passage, a task undertaken in 1792 by Dionisio Alcalá Galiano and Cayetano Valdés; and second, to prove that the story of Admiral de Fonte was also a fiction. That task would fall to Jacinto Caamaño, in the same year. These two efforts were undertaken as part of Bodega's Expedition of the Limits.

7

The Administration of San Blas de Nayarit

DURING HIS CAREER, Bodega served two terms at the Naval Department of San Blas: from 1774 to 1780, and from 1789 to 1794. When he first arrived, he was a young officer awaiting the command of his first ship. He rose in rank until 1780, when he served as acting post commandant while Ignacio de Arteaga y Bazán recovered from the rigours of their 1779 expedition to the north. When he returned to San Blas in 1789, he was commandant in his own right. He held the post until his death in March 1794.

Even as a young officer, Bodega made efforts to solve the department's administrative problems. His experience in planning would contribute to the success of his later explorations.

History and Geography of San Blas de Nayarit before 1774

The naval base of San Blas de Nayarit was founded on the west coast of New Spain in May 1768 by Viceroy Marqués de Croix and José de Gálvez when he was *visitador general*.[1] Prior to this, the region had not received much attention from the Spanish government. The expeditions of Hernando Cortés (1524-25) and Nuño de Guzmán (1531-32) had marched across it, and as early as 1644 the Jesuits had constructed some elementary port facilities three miles south of San Blas, at Matanchén and Chacala, where they had built launches to support their operations in Baja California and to ship out the important revenue-producing salt obtained from the salt flats of Zapatillo to the north.[2] San Blas was founded for military, not naval, purposes when the campaign of 1767-68 to subdue the Seri Indians of Sonora required a port on the west coast to transport soldiers, ammunition, and supplies by sea rather than over the long and dangerous land routes from inland settlements such as Guadalajara.

At first, the base staff consisted of a civilian, Manuel Rivero, who was *comandante de marina* of the department; a commissary, Francisco Hijosa y Rodríguez; and an accountant. At the time, only two ships were assigned to the port: the 193-ton packets *San Carlos,* commanded by Juan Pérez, and *El Príncipe,* commanded by Vicente Vila. The previous year, Gálvez had ordered four new vessels to be built in order to meet the requirements of the Sonora campaign. One of these was the thirty-ton schooner *Sonora.* Because San Blas lacked a shipyard, it was built on the Río Santiago farther up the coast.

Within a year of its founding, San Blas had assumed the role of a naval base providing logistical support for the line of Franciscan missions being established in Alta California.[3] The missions were slow to become self-sufficient in food and other necessities.[4] As the number of missions increased and their population grew, more frequent supply voyages were required. The farther north the settlements stretched, the greater the strain on the base's perpetually inadequate resources of men and ships. These shortages persisted.

From 1774 until the 1795 abandonment of the establishment in Nootka Sound, the development of San Blas was shaped by the requirements for the exploration of the Northwest Coast. After a period of stagnation between 1782 and 1789, there was a great increase in the department's activity, owing to the vigorous direction of Revillagigedo and Bodega. This was the beginning of what Enrique Cárdenas de la Peña has called the "zenith" of San Blas's history.[5] The port strained to support the expanding Alta California settlements, the further exploration of the Northwest Coast, and the new establishment at Nootka. For twenty-one years in the late eighteenth century, San Blas would be one of the busiest ports and shipbuilding centres on the Pacific coast of the Americas. In New Spain it even rivalled Acapulco, the eastern terminus of the annual trans-Pacific convoy from Asia, the Manila Galleon.

San Blas de Nayarit was 200 miles south of Mazatlán and 160 north of Puerto Vallarta. It was 300 miles from Mexico City – at least three days' journey by horseback over what was a road in name only – and 900 from Veracruz. Spreading down the landward slope of a steep hill, the town itself was about three-quarters of a mile from the ocean. As the port developed, the town came to include administrative offices, a hospital, and a church, as well as stone houses for departmental staff, naval officers, and private individuals. In the final decades of the eighteenth century, the port's arsenal, careening wharf, and storehouses and workshops were built on the lowlands alongside the harbour. The Indians and native workers employed by the navy built their miserable palm-thatched houses around these facilities.

San Blas was a poor choice for a deep sea harbour. It was so small it could never hold more than four ships at a time. Also, the Río Santiago empties into the Pacific thirty-six miles to the northwest, and its annual flooding brought down so much mud and debris that the sandbars at the harbour entrance were constantly shifting. This meant the harbour needed to be dredged constantly.

San Blas was also a poor choice for a settlement. No land in the vicinity was suitable for agriculture. Instead, the site was backed by almost impenetrable mangrove swamps. The climate was dreadful: stifling humidity slowed work in all seasons, and from May to August torrential rains brought all work to a standstill as clouds of gnats and voracious mosquitoes descended on the town from the brackish water of nearby lakes and ponds. Dysentery, typhoid, malaria, and other fevers were endemic. At one point, Bodega referred to the San Blas climate as the "terror of humanity."[6] Life improved marginally for senior naval and civilian personnel at the base after their quarters were moved to Tepic, some forty miles away in the hills behind the port. The drier, cooler air provided welcome relief.

Despite these inherent disadvantages, there were good reasons for the selection of San Blas. As Edward Inskip has written:

> This region lies relatively near Guadalajara, the chief city in western Mexico, and on a direct line between Guadalajara and Baja California or the water route around Baja California to Alta California. This general area was a logical location for a port because it minimized time-consuming travel without increasing the total distance to the Californias.[7]

The high ridge called Cerro del Vigía provided some defence against outside attack for the narrow entrance to the harbour. It also provided shelter from the ocean winds for the anchorage in the inner harbour and the careening area. The region possessed plentiful hardwoods such as rosewood, mahogany, and lignum vitae for making blocks, tackles, and bearings. In particular, it had the cedar the Spanish required for shipbuilding. This wood was preferred over oak because "it was easily worked, durable, light (less than half the specific weight of oak) and had little disposition to crack."[8] Fresh water was readily available year round. Even so, in 1774 the naval personnel and man-made facilities at San Blas were inadequate for the port's role as a base for exploratory voyages.

Bodega's First Report on San Blas: 1774

Bodega and his five companions were shocked at what they found at San Blas when they arrived in 1774. There were only six *pilotos* available for sea duty – Estéban José Martínez, Juan Pérez, José de Cañizares, Juan Bautista de Aguirre, Cristóval de Revilla, and Francisco Alvarez de Castro – and the base staff consisted of the commissary Hijosa, four treasury officials who served as paymasters and bookkeepers, and one warehouse worker. There were only two stone houses in the settlement; 752 inhabitants lived in 113 wooden shacks, while the Indian population lived in hovels along the riverbank. There was one barracks for the seamen and one casemate. The commissary building was still under construction, and the church begun in 1768 was still not finished. The harbour had retained only half the depth recorded in 1768, and silting was becoming worse each year.[9] The dockyard was only big enough to build two or three small ships or one frigate. In all, 194 people worked there, mostly maintaining naval vessels. There were only two master shipbuilders, one master and fifty caulkers, one master and twenty-one carpenters, thirty-three blacksmiths, and eighty nonspecialized workers for ship construction and repair.[10]

Bodega and Diego de Choquet, anxious to prove themselves as naval officers, wasted no time writing directly to Andrés Reggio, the Director General of the Navy in Cádiz, to inform him about the condition of the port. On the eve of the departure of the Hezeta-Bodega expedition of 1775, they had found assigned to the "alleged department" only six ships: the 225-ton frigate *Santiago* and the 32-ton schooner *Sonora*, the packets *El Príncipe* and *San Carlos* (alias the *Toisón de Oro*), and two more packets, the *Concepción* and the *Rosario*, which were then en route to California.

Bodega and Choquet were sharply critical of the personnel assigned to San Blas. The dockyard workers were inferior. They were "European," native, and Chinese: the first lot tolerable, the second unenthusiastic and slow, the third very quick. All lacked discipline. There was "a sorry carpenter" who called himself a shipbuilder and who built "monsters, not vessels, which are steered by planks instead of rudders." The two officers were particularly concerned about the lack of surgeons. There were only three in the whole department; two were at sea and the third was incapable of helping the sick in San Blas, where people died by the dozen, usually after three days of a fever. The lack of priests was deemed "notable and painful," as there was no one to minister to "these poor people." The two officers were concerned that crews on the ships had no charity to turn to in the event of distress, accident, or lack of food. As none of the ships carried "even one soldier," they suggested that a few of the army and militia veterans in the viceroyalty be assigned to them. There were ordinances and general laws, but they were neither published nor obeyed – nor were naval officers shown any respect. "We are like the captains of merchant ships, exposed to the slights of the citizens," they sniffed.

As to the facilities, they were dismayed that the warehouse, the accountant's office, and the treasury were all housed in one building. They pointed out that although there were a few blacksmith shops, the workshop to manufacture rope was "imaginary." The harbour was completely inadequate. The bar at the entrance was so high that frigates had to be taken out over the bar before being loaded, thus risking their cargo in windy conditions. These and other difficulties, they understood, inclined the viceroy to favour moving the port to Chacala, ten leagues to the south, where the bay was ample, safe, and of sufficient depth and the weather less "vigorous."

After requesting that their report be forwarded to Minister Julián de Arriaga, Bodega and Choquet assured the director general that, although "we lack an infinite number of things we have requested and have been told are not to be had, we will fulfill our duty, come what may, in spite of all that we have expressed to Your Excellency and do not doubt that you will contribute to making everything now deficient good."[11]

San Blas was a horrible place for anyone who served there. For Bodega, seeking to prove himself in the first land posting of his career, it was a rude awakening.

Bodega's 1776 Memorandum

In the wake of the 1775 voyage to the Northwest Coast led by Hezeta, Viceroy Bucareli acted to strengthen the missions of Alta California and to make further voyages of exploration to the north. He asked Bruno de Hezeta and Bodega to provide him with specific advice on how to improve San Blas's ability to support these initiatives.[12] Early in 1776, Bodega and Choquet jointly penned a twenty-two-page memorandum. It was a wide-ranging critique of the chaotic state of the department's affairs that identified many of the problems he would face when he was its commandant.[13]

Bodega and Choquet began by addressing problems in the ships' captains' role that had come to Bodega's attention as the third-in-command on the 1775 voyage of exploration. He recommended that to ensure the success of such endeavours, the officers selected for voyages of exploration be men of "honour, experience and character [who] will carry out orders, follow manoeuvres, be able to overcome the ship's defects and cope with unexpected difficulties." The ships should be manned with large, experienced crews and with enough properly trained troops for their defence. Bodega was particularly interested in expanding the authority of ship captains. He wanted each one to have the power to choose his crew, as well as a say in the selection of his officers. The captain should be able to specify and inspect the stores that went into his ship. In the event of a vacancy at sea, he should have the power to promote an officer temporarily. He should also be able to recommend for promotion not only the officers, but also the soldiers and crew serving on his ship. Finally, the captain ought to be able to monitor and control the payment of salaries.

After considering the heavy demands placed on a commandant of a voyage of exploration, Bodega and Choquet turned to the problems they had observed in the administration of San Blas. That department was a unique political unit in New Spain. Although part of the province of Nueva Galicia within the larger *audiencia* of Guadalajara, San Blas was directly answerable to the viceroy in his capacity as *capitán general* of the viceroyalty.[14] Although San Blas was a naval port and employed naval personnel, it was also home to civilians employed by the navy. Local administrative responsibilities were shared between the naval commandant and the civilian commissary. Both reported to the viceroy rather than to provincial officials. Regarding the administration of justice, cases that concerned anyone not employed by the navy fell under the jurisdiction of the *audiencia* of Guadalajara. Similarly, church matters, except for the appointment of chaplains and priests to serve on ships, were overseen by the Bishop of Guadalajara.

Bodega and Choquet's basic premise was that the department's administration needed to be restructured so that its personnel would be able to support a program of exploration while supplying the missions in Alta California. The officers called for a clear division of responsibilities between the department's civilian and naval arms. Matters that concerned both positions would be decided by the war council (*junta de guerra*). That council would comprise all available naval officers, the commissary, and the master shipwright. Issues would be decided by majority vote and be immediately put into effect. To ensure that the final authority in the war council would lie with the naval commandant, the most senior naval officer present would preside over the meetings; in the event of a tie vote, he would have the deciding voice.

Finally, Bodega and Choquet dealt with the office of the *constructor,* or master shipwright, the third essential departmental position. This man had to be able to provide the commandant with all the information about the wood required for careening and repairs and for the construction of new ships. If necessary, the master shipbuilder's estimates could be reviewed by the war council.

The longest part of Bodega and Choquet's memorandum dealt with the ships and their crews.[15] Preparing the ground for Bodega's trip to Peru to purchase the *Favorita,* they recommended that a spare ship be built to ensure that the department would be able to respond to emergencies; this ship should be strong enough to serve as an expedition ship. Such vessels, Bodega remarked casually, were being built in Peru and China.

Bodega and Choquet devoted three paragraphs to the welfare of lower-deck personnel. Their salaries needed to be increased to reduce desertions and to improve the quality of crews for ships sailing into high latitudes. Rations should be increased and improved to provide sailors with the strength and energy they needed to do their work. A large ration of meat, fresh or dried, should be provided.

Arguing in their own self-interest, Bodega and Choquet recommended that the pay scales for officers and *pilotos* be raised.[16] Their pay must be appropriate to the "condition of the country, to enable them to maintain themselves with the honour corresponding to their corps." Salary scales needed to reflect the differences in climate, the repeated illnesses, the rigours of the voyages, and the "increased amount of labour."[17] For the same reason, the messing allowance should be increased to two pesos a day, and officers and *pilotos* should not have the costs of maintaining their houses deducted from their pay on top of other expenses – a practice that could only compel them to "seek superior piety," meaning some viceregal favour.

The last part of Bodega and Choquet's memorandum was a detailed inventory of the personnel and armaments they thought necessary for each vessel.

Over time, many of Bodega and Choquet's proposals were adopted in practice or implemented provisionally by Bucareli and his successor, Revillagigedo.[18] During the two periods when Bodega was naval commandant, the division of responsibilities between the commandant and the commissary was essentially what he had recommended to Bucareli. The recommendations for the treatment of the department's personnel were not enough to improve the living conditions of most of the men serving on land or at sea. Throughout Bodega's years, the only substantial relief provided for officers, *pilotos,* and senior administrators was to permit them to establish their residences in Tepic, where they could escape the steamy climate and ever-hungry mosquitoes down on the coast.

There was little change at San Blas while Bodega was absent in the 1780s. When Malaspina's expedition arrived in the spring of 1791, José Bustamante y Guerra, commandant of the *Atrevida,* wrote:

> The climate is not healthy. The town has few buildings and is made up of huts covered with straw, giving it the look of poverty and misery. The best are those built by the Crown ... The natives are listless and sad in their appearance, which they use as justification to abandon the place and move to Tepic. As a result, the population varies between 2,000 and 4,500.[19]

Francisco Xavier de Viana, one of the *Descubierta*'s officers, wrote that the town was full of misery and "induced horror." There was no public order, and the inhabitants were "not very agreeable, crude and ugly troublemakers, dirty [and] given to idleness."[20]

When Bodega returned from Spain in 1789, he noted that the community on the Cerro de Basilio had grown. It had been founded in 1773 after the original town by the harbour was relocated to escape the summer floods of the Río Santiago. A few private homes had been built by some of the staff. The church was still unfinished. The stone accountant's office (*contaduría*) at the top of the hill, which had been near completion when he left for Havana and Spain in December 1783, was now serving as a storehouse for supplies and as headquarters for the administrative staff.[21] While living in the department, Bodega did most of his work at home in Tepic. When he did travel down to San Blas on one of the two horses he maintained for the purpose, he used one of the *contaduría*'s administrative offices.

Bodega's Governance of the Department

In the 1776 memorandum, Bodega had chafed at the idea of having the commandant share the department's governance with the commissary. He felt that the naval commandant should be solely in charge. Hijosa, the first and long-serving commissary, had tactfully avoided challenging Bodega's authority during his first posting as commandant in 1780.[22] Because of his abilities and long familiarity with the department's problems, Hijosa was virtually coequal to the naval commandant.

The surviving documentation reveals no instance in which this divided authority was a problem while Bodega was naval commandant.[23] The war council, which included all available *pilotos* and the shipbuilder, was effective at settling differences of opinion. There was only one known instance when Bodega and Hijosa had a sharp disagreement. It arose very early on in their association, during the deliberations of the special commission appointed by Bucareli to consider moving the San Blas department to Chacala. Hijosa, as chairman of the commission, despite the wishes of all its members, did not support the move. It was a rare instance in which Bodega commented unfavourably on an associate to a higher authority.[24]

In later years, Hijosa and Bodega became accustomed to working together, dealing with the many problems affecting an active department. When Revillagigedo investigated complaints over delays in the payment of salaries – which had been withheld to deter desertions – Bodega assured him that they worked well together:

> My operations have never had any object other than the best service. Even when there might have been the occasional difference with the commissary ... there never has been between us any matter which interferes with the good harmony which Your Excellency wants us to observe.[25]

Hijosa wrote in a similar vein, making it clear that both men had developed a mutual trust and that they shared a desire to make their governance work.

Civilian and Naval Personnel

Many of Bodega's 1776 recommendations were incorporated in Revillagigedo's *Reglamento Provisional*, which was introduced in December 1789 when Bodega took command of the department. According to Cárdenas, the new order "signified, first, an increase in salaries, then a security of labour and an influx of useful elements."[26] The rules covered both civilians and all ranks of commissioned and non-commissioned naval personnel and brought some order to a confused situation. The viceroy's *Reglamento* simplified the tasks of those who had to implement the government's policies – in particular, Hijosa and Bodega.

Its forty articles abolished differences in naval and military pay arising from where an individual had been recruited, such as in Veracruz or Callao. Pay for all ranks coming from Spain would now begin at rates set for the South Seas as soon as the individual arrived in Veracruz. Special pay scales were established for those taking part in supply voyages to Alta California, and incentive pay was introduced for those engaged in trans-Pacific voyages and exploration. Provision was made for messing allowances, sick pay, officers' servants, and "double salaries" for military and naval officers, as well as for salaries and fees for surgeons and blood letters, pilots, chaplains, masters' mates, and boatswains' mates.[27]

During Bodega's first term at San Blas, only essential maintenance was undertaken in the dockyard. In 1780, when exploration was suspended because of wartime economies, the number of dockyard workers fell to six. Things changed quickly with the arrival of Revillagigedo and the return of Bodega in 1789. With the decision to strengthen Spain's presence in the North Pacific, there was a dramatic increase in the number of civilian and naval personnel. In his budget for 1790, Bodega called for a further increase in the department's naval and military strength.

Between 1789 and 1792, the dockyard was overseen by the master shipwright (*constructor*), Manuel Bastarrachea. He was replaced, over Bodega's objections, by Ignacio Arteaga.[28] The actual number of dockyard workers for which the master shipbuilder was responsible – carpenters, caulkers, coopers, sawyers, blacksmiths, rope makers, painters, armourers, lantern makers, and a large number of unskilled workers (*peones*) – increased from 286 in 1790 to 374 in 1792. Another seventy-four labourers were engaged in cutting timber and transporting it to the dockyard.[29]

There was no corresponding increase in the civilian administration. The commissary, Hijosa, worked with a small staff and two treasury officials. As naval commandant, Bodega found only a few occasions when he had to ensure that funds for the payroll were not delayed and that vital supplies for the arsenal arrived in time. Generally, Hijosa did what he could to ensure the smooth functioning of the dockyard.

Bodega was particularly active in administering the naval personnel. When he resumed command of the department in December 1789, he recorded that he was short two *segundo pilotos*, three *pilotines*, eleven surgeons, and eighty seamen of various ranks.[30] The shortage of sailors was especially serious, since despite the punishments authorized by naval regulations, desertions continued and vacancies could not always be easily filled.[31] In his revised budget of 1790, Bodega called for one *capitán de navío* and ten other seagoing officers, thirteen *pilotos*, 340 seamen of different ranks and trades, six stores guards, and seven chaplains of the fleet in addition to vicars and sacristans. He also requested one infantry company of eighty-four men.

San Blas was chronically short of *pilotos*. When Bodega requested four additional *pilotos* from Havana, only two were sent: José María Narváez and Juan Martínez y Zayas. As late as February 1793, Bodega was again seeking, unsuccessfully, the appointment of several more experienced *pilotos*. He had only seven available for sea duty because José Camacho was too old to go back to sea.[32] Bodega was particularly concerned with the exhaustion from which all the *pilotos* suffered as a result of constant overwork and the lack of time to rest between routine voyages.

Personnel shortages were a constant worry. Much more serious, though, were living conditions in the department and their effect on people's health. The corps of *pilotos*, shipwrights, and senior civilian staff petitioned repeatedly to move to Tepic in the hills. The principal reason for rejecting such requests was the time it took to travel back and forth from Tepic to the coast. Nevertheless, some made the move. The fact that military personnel had always been allowed to live there was a constant source of resentment among civil administrators.

Bodega proposed that all tours of duty at San Blas be limited to five years, a measure intended to avoid breakdowns of health, which were frequent. Just before Bodega's death in 1794, Revillagigedo accepted the idea of a periodic rotation of officers and *pilotos*. He justified it as a matter of discipline. The horrible San Blas climate, the high cost of living, the distance from any large town, and the small population, "which consisted for the most part of unhappy people who offer a crude and irritating relationship to support the desires of human nature," caused men to "lose or consider remote the hope of a better fate or destiny" and therefore "they will usually prostitute themselves in abominable vices or abandon their obligations." One consequence of this sorry situation, the viceroy went on, was the large number of requests for leave or for a transfer. People asked to live in Tepic or pretended to be ill in order to go to Guadalajara for "interminable cures."[33]

The Defences of San Blas

When Bodega had assumed command of the department for the first time in 1780, Spain, supporting the rebelling American colonists, was at war with England, and the long coast of the Californias lay defenceless. Seeking to improve the defences of the regions around the viceroyalty's two principal ports, Veracruz on the east coast and San Blas on the west, Viceroy Martín de Mayorga requested that Bodega send him a report on the military forces at San Blas.[34] He asked specifically whether militia units could be formed by drawing men from the shipyard and the neighbouring communities. Without any help from the acting military commandant in Tepic and his superior, the regent in Guadalajara, Bodega answered Mayorga directly.

Without listing the armaments on hand, Bodega outlined what was required for defence in time of war. Two batteries of eight cannon of twenty-four pounds calibre were needed on the top of the two hills to defend the harbour entrance, the arsenal, and the ships in the harbour. Also, 32 six-pounder guns were needed to arm the frigates *Favorita* and *Santiago.* As for small arms, he wanted 225 muskets, 350 pistols, 175 sabres, 22 swivel guns, and 175 bayonets, as well as gun powder and ammunition – including cannonballs, grenades, and musket balls.

Turning to the question of the militia, Bodega noted that Tepic already had a regular army unit.[35] He suggested that seven militia companies be formed in the wider region and two others in the shipyard and in the surrounding settlements. He felt that to lead and train these nine companies, he would need at least three but preferably nine veteran officers. Each of these officers should have a sergeant, a corporal, and a drummer to assist him. The troops would have to be supplied with a thousand muskets, bayonets, and swords, as well as ball and powder from the factory in Guadalajara. Their uniforms should be provided by the state and designed by the viceroy. Serving for a full month at a time, militia men would be expected to turn out for drill on holidays and special ceremonial occasions.[36]

Reporting to José de Gálvez in Spain, Mayorga supported Bodega's proposal for a battalion of nine companies of militia. He estimated that the expenditure for the nine units and their arms and equipment would amount to thirteen or fourteen thousand pesos.[37] He instructed Bodega to proceed with the new militia organization using all the means at his disposal. Command of the battalion went to Lieutenant Colonel Miguel Marín del Valle, the father of the young woman Bodega wished to marry. When it came to tangible assistance, the viceroy offered little. The army could not supply any officers or non-commissioned officers to train the men, and there was no money available to pay them. This did not prevent him from instructing the commissary on the design of their uniform, assuring him that the cost would be met by the treasury. He also promised that the muskets, bayonets, and ball and powder would be provided.

Without substantial aid, Bodega proceeded with the formation of one militia company and equipped it as best he could with uniforms and weapons. He never said exactly how many men had been recruited, but in August 1780 Hijosa requested their help to "contain the disorders" in the town. Bodega employed two corporals and twelve soldiers to maintain the peace. When this news reached the ears of the viceroy, Bodega was told that the militia were not to be used as police![38]

As for the port's defence, Mayorga told Bodega it would not be possible to provide cannon for the two batteries and the ships. Cannon of that calibre were too heavy to transport overland by mule, Acapulco did not have enough for its own needs, and he needed the king's authority to secure some from either Manila or Peru. Undeterred, Bodega began construction of a battery on the Cerro del Vigía at the entrance to the harbour.[39] The project was completed in June 1781 by his successor, Ignacio Arteaga. Lacking heavier cannon, he installed ten small-calibre guns.

Bodega's third initiative for the defence of San Blas was the formation of two companies of Indian bowmen (*flecheros*) for the frontiers and coastlines where there were insufficient men or resources to organize formal militia companies of infantry and cavalry. The archers were unpaid but were rewarded by gaining a certain status.[40]

It was nearly a year before the Minister for the Indies, José de Gálvez, sent word to Mayorga that he approved the measures Bodega had taken.[41] Finally, in March 1781, the viceroy was instructed to order Bodega to "take the most effective measures to vigorously oppose any strike against Acapulco and the other southern coasts of [New Spain]." Gálvez had learned that the British admiral Sir Edward Hughes had left England in March 1779 for the Bay of Bengal with a force of ten ships of the line and three thousand men. It was said that he had been ordered to leave half his force there and to use the remainder to "destroy Spanish commerce" and "attack our southern dominions." The viceroy ordered Bodega to do what he could to defend San Blas and to call on the captain general of Guadalajara for any assistance he might need. If "any sails were seen," Bodega was to order the ships to sail to warn Felipe Neve, the governor of Alta California, so that he, in turn, could warn the presidios and missions.[42] There was little else he could do.

When Bodega returned to San Blas nine years later in 1789, the situation had improved slightly. When he left, the permanent garrison had numbered only seventy-six men; by July 1789, an increase to 162 had been approved. Also, measures had been taken to integrate San Blas into the militia division protecting the south coast.[43] No real improvement had been made to the permanent defences of San Blas. The ships lacked swivel guns and had only twenty of the sixty cannon they were supposed to be carrying.[44] Reluctantly, Bodega improved the defences of the Alta California presidios. Some of the cannon in San Blas and Acapulco were sent to Monterey, Santa Barbara, and San Diego. Bodega expressed his concern to Revillagigedo that these measures were inadequate, even misdirected. He believed that the ships should be given priority.[45]

In 1793, when war with revolutionary France was threatening, Bodega reminded the viceroy that San Blas's floating defence consisted of just two ships, neither of which had been built for war: the 300-ton frigate *Concepción* and the 200-ton schooner *Activa*. He repeated his request for war frigates "which would command respect."[46] When war was declared, on the assumption that French forces would attempt to interfere with the resupply missions to California, Bodega requested that the army unit in San Blas be strengthened by an additional company and that a second battery be placed on the beach at the harbour entrance.[47] This request was not granted.

The Budget

During both terms as commandant at San Blas, Bodega constantly received viceregal and even ministerial exhortations to reduce costs. Typically, when Bodega wrote enthusiastically in 1780 to Minister Valdés to inform him of the activity in the department, he was cautioned "to economize as much as possible, and to bear in mind when incurring expenses that, at the present time, we are at war and [be mindful of] the delicate condition of royal resources." They were so delicate, in fact, that all salaries had been frozen by Royal Order.[48] One small attempt to economize involved Bodega's proposal to the mayors of six neighbouring towns – Jalapa, Tecualtichillo, Ganusco, Tabasco, Tallagua, and Valle de Guajucar – that supplied the navy with *pita* fibre.[49] He urged them to sell directly to the navy without going through any intermediary and to enter into supply contracts based on a fair price. His proposal was ignored. The intermediaries found a number of excuses to protect their profit margins, such as the suppliers' inability to furnish the supplies on a regular basis.[50]

In 1790, Revillagigedo asked Bodega to justify the amounts outlined in a budget that Hijosa had submitted to Viceroy Flores. The new viceroy was attempting to bring some order to the chaotic state of the department's finances, a consequence of conflicting instructions from the home government and confusion in their application by the local administration.[51] Bodega replied:

> It is so difficult to establish adequately and economically the expenses of this dockyard which I doubt I can succeed, in spite of the pain it causes me to see the treasury having to meet such greatly increased expenditures required to support four small, defenceless ships.[52]

Bodega reviewed each section, especially the dockyard operations, the labourers' and seamen's salaries, and the shipbuilding projects.[53] Without mentioning names, he was sharply critical of those responsible for assembling the previous budgets. He submitted some revisions to Hijosa's budget, reducing the number of dockyard workers by discharging 198 woodcutters who were not needed as well as letting go thirty-five lower-deck seamen who had no fixed assignment. He also told the viceroy he had initiated a plan to close the dockyard during times when there was no work in hand, estimating that this would save between nine to ten thousand pesos annually. On the other side of the ledger, Bodega provided salary increases for certain non-commissioned and lower-deck naval personnel and for civilian labourers, using the substantially higher pay scales authorized by Revillagigedo's *Reglamento Provisional* of December 7, 1789.

Bodega submitted his proposed revisions to the war council, which approved them unanimously.[54] The revised budget called for a total annual expenditure of 365,087 pesos, more than double the budget for 1782 (157,822 pesos) and considerably higher than Hijosa's original budget of 287,412 pesos. New provisions included monies to build a warehouse and to manufacture anchors. Expenditures were expected to be offset by anticipated revenues of 40,670 pesos, mainly from the salt and mescal monopolies and from the rental of state properties and tin mines. As always, however, the customs duties went directly to Mexico City.

In an extensive minute written on the margin, Revillagigedo told Bodega that his revisions were approved, that the proposals to increase the allotments for the department's manpower were justified, and that the *intendente* in Guadalajara would be instructed to advance the needed extra funds in four quarterly instalments. Surprisingly, Revillagigedo did not take the opportunity to again remind Bodega and Hijosa to make every effort to keep expenses to a minimum. In the current circumstances, the costs were justified. The cost of living in San Blas was steadily increasing, leading to constant demands from workers for higher salaries. Many necessities, such as food, as well as the basic supplies for the navy, such as gun powder, oakum, sailcloth, nails, and iron for anchors and artillery, had to be brought in from outside. Overland transportation by mule was difficult and expensive. The high cost of ship construction and repair – especially of labour and materials – led to repeated suggestions that this work be done in the shipyards of Spain, Peru, or the Philippines. Bodega himself advocated such a measure. These difficulties stemmed from Madrid's failure to foresee the financial consequences of its decision to develop a presence on the American Northwest Coast – in particular, to maintain an establishment at Nootka Sound. The total cost of sailing ships back and forth between Nootka and San Blas – that is, exclusive of the costs of the establishment itself and of assisting visiting Spanish and foreign vessels – amounted to 351,370 pesos between January 1789 and November 1792.[55]

The Relocation Question

San Blas's shortcomings as a harbour and town site were evident from the earliest days of its history. During his second term as commandant, Bodega was faced with the issue of whether to relocate the base.

In 1774, a special commission under Francisco de Hijosa was formed to look into the possibility of relocation.[56] Hijosa travelled to Chacala, six leagues south of San Blas, where he concluded that the bay was too small unless a quay some twenty to twenty-five *brazas* long were built at considerable expense. Although the roadstead was more exposed than at San Blas, the air was fresher, good drinking water was available nearby, fruit trees seemed to abound, the region had good cedar for ship construction – and there were no mosquitoes.[57] All of the commission's members except Hijosa favoured relocation. He considered the cost of establishing a new port too high and was reluctant to abandon the existing installations in San Blas. The commission next examined the bay of Matanchén, one league south of San Blas. It possessed many of the same advantages as Chacala. Arteaga and Choquet favoured the move, but again, Hijosa was firmly opposed for the same reasons.[58] Arteaga submitted the commission's detailed report to Bucareli.[59]

Because their opinions were so sharply divided, the viceroy consulted Miguel Costanzó, an engineer who had been a member of the expedition that had selected San Blas. Costanzó recommended a fourth possibility, a move to Acapulco.[60] A further detailed assessment from Miguel del Corral, another military engineer, still produced no consensus. Meetings held over the next few months, attended by naval officers, *pilotos*, and civilians, resolved nothing.[61] The same arguments for and against were endlessly rehearsed: San Blas was unhealthy; the facilities could not be expanded to build and maintain larger vessels; the port itself was silting up at an alarming rate; and the flow of debris from the Río Santiago was filling up the Estero del Pozo, its estuary. Acapulco, although closer to Mexico City, with a healthier climate and a naturally safe harbour, did not provide easy access to the lumber essential for shipbuilding, and furthermore, it was farther from Alta California.

At that point, relocation was shelved, since despite all its disadvantages, San Blas was able to handle its responsibilities for the time being. Bucareli brought matters to a temporary end when he recommended to José de Gálvez that nothing be done until San Blas's "total uselessness be confirmed." When that happened, he said, a "provisional" move might be made to Acapulco, which he agreed was "more secure and healthier."[62] The last phrase of the viceroy's final decision made a slight bow to an earlier opinion of the Marqués de Grimaldi, the Minister of State; even so, Bucareli had gone against Grimaldi's judgment.[63] Whatever the reason, the government approved the viceroy's decision, effectively putting off any further debate. Instead, plans to implement a number of urgently needed improvements at San Blas, such as the construction of storage sheds and barracks, were authorized and undertaken.

In 1789, with the arrival of the energetic Revillagigedo and the experienced Bodega, the relocation issue was opened once again. Revillagigedo had studied the file on San Blas before leaving Spain; he was well aware of its problems and of the debates under his predecessors. As soon as he took office, he began to urge Antonio Valdés to relocate the San Blas facilities to Acapulco.[64] He favoured Acapulco because it would require very little additional expenditure. It already had a hospital, a church, soldiers, and cavalry as well as a small militia to protect it. Most important, it was closer to the capital. Supplies for San Blas had to be brought eighty leagues from Guadalajara, whereas everything was closer to hand in Acapulco, reducing shipping costs. Finally, Acapulco's climate was healthier, which meant there would be less sickness and absenteeism and better opportunities to recruit and retain naval and civilian personnel. Revillagigedo did not advocate a complete shutting down of San Blas. The woodcutting operations there could be continued and the timber transported by raft.

Early in 1790, after taking over as commandant, Bodega reported that San Blas was no longer capable of responding to current needs.[65] He pointed out that it could now repair only small ships. These small vessels could not defend and sustain the Alta California establishments, nor could they exclude foreign nations from the lucrative contraband trade. Two large frigates had become "indispensable." As the cost of a frigate built in San Blas or Realejo, useful only for carrying supplies, had risen to at least 100,000 pesos, Bodega suggested that the two large ships be built in Spain at much less expense. Anticipating a move to Acapulco, Bodega went on to suggest that as the port's "deterioration was obvious and its total ruin very probable," it would be unwise to undertake any more work on the works, the arsenal, or the harbour itself. He pointed out that Acapulco had trade links with Peru and the Philippines, from which many items needed at San Blas could be obtained: necessities such as canvas, needles for compasses, iron, and the nails required by the arsenal. He concluded that

> the King would lose nothing by abandoning a useless port, four unserviceable storage sheds, a warehouse on top of a hill, a coach house which serves as a hospital, a single barracks in name only, the small *contaduría* and a church, the construction of which is just beginning.

Without a clear response from Madrid, Revillagigedo sought the opinion of the two officers in whom he had the most confidence – Francisco Mourelle, who was now serving on his staff, and Bodega. Their detailed replies merely repeated their earlier opinions and well-worn arguments.

In his twenty-five-page report, Mourelle listed the advantages of San Blas. He emphasized the shorter distance to the California settlements and Manila from San Blas compared to other contenders.[66] In rebuttal, Bodega questioned Mourelle's statement that the coast offered good anchorages. As for Acapulco, he pointed out that couriers travelling to and from Mexico City with dispatches for the department and the presidios would arrive in half the time and that goods coming from Europe would not be so expensive.[67] Finally, he did not think that ships sailing north from Acapulco would require more than ten or twelve days' additional sailing time.

Forwarding these conflicting views to Madrid, Revillagigedo remarked philosophically that opinions about relocating San Blas were as unchanged as they had been since the time of Bucareli. He firmly believed that further debate would not advance matters.[68]

Revillagigedo never wavered in his support for Acapulco, and he returned to the question several times.[69] The most effective sally was in his briefing of Manuel Godoy, Duque de la Alcudia, when he replaced Floridablanca as Minister of State:

> Although there are some who are opposed to the relocation of the department, they are very few and less worthy of credence when the measure is supported by the *capitanes de navío* Alejandro Malaspina and José Bustamante y Guerra, who visited both ports in their corvettes; the commandant of the department, Juan Francisco de la Bodega; the *capitanes de fragata* Dionisio Galiano and Cayetano Valdés; and by all the intelligent officers who sailed in the same corvettes and who serve in the department.[70]

Finally, by Royal Order of September 24, 1794, Carlos IV approved the relocation of the department to Acapulco. There is an unsigned note in Bodega's service file in the El Viso archive implying that, had he lived, Bodega would have been appointed commandant of the relocated department.

Refitting and Overhauling the Ships

In spite of Bodega's insistence in 1776 that San Blas needed more ships, no vessels were built there during his first administration. In 1780, he revived his proposal for the construction of a large frigate, but when his *constructor*, Francisco Segurola, estimated that the cost would be 100,000 pesos, the idea was rejected as too expensive, especially since the department was already facing the high cost of the *Favorita*'s first refit.[71] Nevertheless, ways were found to enlarge and improve San Blas's fleet. In 1781 the Manila-built frigate *Aránzazu* was exchanged for the San Blas–built packet *San Carlos;* and in 1783, before Bodega's return to Spain, the second *San Carlos*, another packet built in Manila, replaced the *Príncipe.*

When Bodega returned to San Blas in 1789, some of the vessels from his first term as commandant were still in service. The three frigates *Favorita, Princesa,* and *Aránzazu,* and the packet boat *San Carlos* remained useful as did the launches used for coastal traffic. To meet the Nootka crisis, Bodega augmented the San Blas fleet by building four more ships: the schooners *Valdés* and *Activa* and the twin schooners *Sutil* and *Mexicana.* The *Valdés* was completed in the summer of 1790 and immediately sent to Manila carrying news of the war with Britain. Little is known of her except that she did not return to San Blas until September 1794.

Construction of the *Mexicana* was begun on March 27, 1791, under the direction of the new *constructor*, Manuel Bastarrachea, who followed Bodega's specifications. Her command was assigned to Francisco Mourelle. She was launched on May 21. The *Mexicana* weighed 46 tons and cost 10,513 pesos. Then, "in order to avoid the disagreements which regularly occur when the builder does not take part in [a new ship's] sea trials," Bodega had Bastarrachea put her through her paces.[72] After nine days at sea in variable winds, the *constructor* declared himself generally satisfied; she was sturdier than expected and steered well. Not being on board, Bodega did not assess her sailing qualities personally.[73]

In 1791, when Alejandro Malaspina returned from his search for the mythical passage of Ferrer Maldonaldo, he was asked to undertake the exploration of the Strait of Juan de Fuca. Malaspina said that his corvettes would be neither suitable nor available, adding the mission could be carried out by the *Mexicana* and a second schooner that ought to be built.[74] Construction began on the *Sutil* on September 23, 1791, also under Bastarrachea. She was completed on November 15. Although identical to the *Mexicana* except for a slight difference in her rigging, she cost only 8,967 pesos.[75] In late December the two vessels arrived in Acapulco under the command of Malaspina's two young officers, Dionisio Alcalá Galiano and Cayetano Valdés, to be fitted out for exploration. The ships handled poorly, and much of their construction was defective and needed strengthening. Carpenters made alterations to increase the space for stowing water and supplies. Although the ships were still defective and further alterations would have to be made later at Nootka, the *Sutil* and *Mexicana* finally left Acapulco on

March 8, 1792. Revillagigedo was angry about their poor workmanship, faulty design, and extensive cost overruns.

George Vancouver visited the schooners in June 1792 off the shore of what is now Vancouver. His comments on them were damning. He was

> astonished at the vessels in which [Alcalá Galiano and Valdés] were employed to execute a service of such a nature. They were each of about forty-five tons burthen, mounted two brass guns and were navigated by twenty-four men, bearing one lieutenant, without a single inferior officer. Their apartments just allowed room for sleeping places on each side, with a table in the intermediate place, at which four persons, with some difficulty, could sit, and were, in all other respects, the most ill calculated and unfit vessels which could possibly be imagined for such an expedition.[76]

The *Activa* was built after Bodega persuaded Revillagigedo that he would require a special ship for his 1792 mission to determine the limits or boundary between the Spanish and English interests on the North Pacific coast. Her keel was laid on December 9, 1791, and she was completed in sixty days at a cost of 29,854 pesos.[77] Displacing 195 tons, she carried twelve three-pounders and two three-pounder swivel guns. When she departed, she had not undergone sea trials and lacked such basic equipment as a main capstan and pumps. As she sailed out of San Blas on February 29, 1792, en route to Nootka, the *Activa*'s main topmast broke off. Then her main yards snapped in a light wind just after she passed the Tres Marías islands. She had to return to port. Reporting this setback to Antonio Valdés, Revillagigedo admitted she had been built too quickly.[78] Yet as soon as he arrived in Nootka, Bodega assured the viceroy that in spite of the terrible weather and strong winds encountered during the journey, the *Activa* had come through well. In high spirits, he was confident she would prove herself to be "the best vessel of her kind the king possesses." The *Activa* did indeed prove her worth and remained in active service until at least 1808, when she was still listed in the inventory of San Blas ships.

Repairs accounted for most of the work done in the San Blas shipyards. The vessels of the San Blas fleet were in constant use in the Pacific Ocean, and the wear on the ships was considerable. The master shipwright's continuing problems included workers' absenteeism, time lost through illness, a lack of good shipwrights, tardy delivery of materials, high humidity that rotted stored wood and sails, and funds that ran out before costs were covered or before workers were paid.

The career of two ships closely connected with Bodega, the *Favorita* and the *Princesa*, illustrates these difficulties. The *Favorita* became a problem ship even though Bodega had had extensive modifications, costing 62,000 pesos, made to her in Callao. The changes were to make her suitable for exploration amid the brutal storms in the Gulf of Alaska. Bodega praised her sailing qualities during the 1779 expedition. In his journal he wrote: "It would be difficult to find a frigate with equal properties for [northern exploration] such as the one I have brought back."[79] Her problems began during the same expedition, when she took a terrible beating.

On her return to San Blas she had to undergo the first of a series of overhauls. Rebuilding started in April 1780. *Constructor* Francisco Segurola proposed lowering her main and second decks, replanking much of the hold, building a new quarterdeck, and adding a forecastle deck. The estimated cost was seventeen thousand pesos. On August 5 of that year, the ship was struck by lightning, which split her mainmast, destroyed one of the pumps and two beams, and blew out a number of side planks.[80] When repair costs began to exceed the budget, the shipyard had to stop work and await an infusion of money. On September 26, Bodega reported that there was a shortage of workers because many had fallen ill, possibly from dysentery or the San Blas fevers. Furthermore, the heavy seasonal rains made it impossible to continue work until the weather improved. When more of the *Favorita*'s defects came to light, Bodega and Segurola agreed that she needed a new keel among a long list of other repairs. To compound their problems, there was a shortage of vital materials.[81] The viceroy agreed that work should go ahead as soon as possible, but the overhaul was not completed until the following May, and the total bill came to 42,321 pesos. The following year, 1781, when he went Peru to obtain quicksilver for the Mexican mining industry, Bodega had been forced to abandon his plans to take the *Favorita* because her steering was defective. That problem was rectified eventually, and the *Favorita* was able to undertake her share of resupply trips to California.

A serious problem developed on a supply run to Loreto in 1788 that ended the *Favorita*'s working life.[82] Under *piloto* Joseph Tobar y Tamariz, she returned to home port after taking in eight inches of water in twenty-four hours. Acting commandant José Camacho discovered on inspection that all her frames were worm-eaten and her hull rotten. He estimated that the cost of a second refitting would match the expense of the one carried out in 1780-81. He doubted that the twenty-year-old *Favorita* was worth the heavy expense; she "did not possess the best properties" and had a very limited capacity for carrying cargo. Viceroy Flores's instinct was to scrap her, and he recommended that course to Antonio Valdés, suggesting that it would cost little more to build a new vessel. Under the viceroy's orders, Camacho had a detailed repairs estimate drawn up that amounted to 26,402 pesos. He warned the viceroy that the *Favorita*'s hull was so rotten she might sink at any moment. She was only protected by her copper sheathing. He had her moved closer to shore so that she would not block the harbour if she sank. When the war council in San Blas recommended that the ship be scrapped, Viceroy Flores sought the opinion of the treasury of New Spain, the Junta Superior de Real Hacienda.

At this point, Bodega returned to San Blas from Spain to resume command of the department. When he learned of the possible fate of a ship that meant so much to him, he asked permission to have master carpenter Arteaga carry out a further inspection and to provide him with an "impartial inspection, without deception and free of any preconceptions." Arteaga estimated the costs at 32,000 pesos, slightly higher than the previous statement. He said the ship would "emerge useful for the services of the department and could end up becoming one of the best among those on hand." Pleased with this opinion, Bodega forwarded Arteaga's report to Revillagigedo with the plea that he himself had "sailed in her, was aware of her good qualities and aware of the care and ability with which Arteaga had carried out his task."[83]

By then, the viceroy was in receipt of the treasury's report that recommended the breaking of the ship. The viceroy ordered the *Favorita* "destroyed." Anything useful, such as sails, cables, rigging, and futtocks were to be salvaged and made available to the *Activa,* which was then being built.[84]

Bodega did not give up the fight to save his *Favorita.* He told Revillagigedo that

> it will not have escaped Your Excellency's superior discernment [*penetración*] that my thinking has only been guided [by the thought] that the expense to the king is small for a vessel so useful to this department or any other to which she might be transferred for whatever service purpose. But supposing that Your Excellency has ordered [her destruction] for this reason, it is incumbent on me to point out that the timbers to be removed from the frigate for the schooner [*Activa*] will be little less than useless, that they can only be used in a ship of the same burthen, that the pieces are rotten, too thick ... and could not hold nails ... All that can be salvaged is the ironwork. It would cost too much to remove it as was found when the *Santiago* was written off.[85]

He consulted the San Blas war council once more. The report with the response to Bodega's final plea is not in the *expediente*. It must have gone against him and the *Favorita*, for on May 20, Bodega wrote a bitter letter that must have been the shortest he ever addressed to his chief: "I have witnessed the burning of the frigate *Favorita*. Anything useful to the service and the ironwork found in the ashes has been placed in the stores and an account given to the *contaduría*."[86]

The *Princesa* underwent a brief overhaul in 1791, while the *Activa* was under construction. Although Revillagigedo thought the cost, at 27,009 pesos, was too high, the repairs were undertaken without sufficient care to prepare her for the arduous conditions that would face Bodega's squadron on the Expedition of the Limits.[87] She was hardly outside the harbour than she began to take on four inches of water an hour and had to be sent back. Once she was unloaded and her ballast removed, it was discovered that rats had made holes in the hull in three places on the port side by devouring the oakum in the seams. They had also tunnelled into the sternpost as far as the rudder hinges. Her entire hull had to be unplanked from the keel to the gunwales.[88] At a later time, owing to other urgent work being done in the shipyard, the *Princesa* had to be careened in the Estero del Pozo. The enormous number of mosquitoes made work there difficult, because the time taken swatting the insatiable insects slowed the work.[89]

Never a patient man, Revillagigedo was incensed by these delays. Each of the officers involved – Ramón Saavedra, who had been left behind as acting commandant of the department, and Fidalgo, who had been in charge of the careening – offered their excuses, such as poor wood and "hidden accidents," but it was not just the inadequate careening of the *Princesa* and the errors in the construction of the *Activa* that fuelled Revillagigedo's anger. It was also a matter of the poor workmanship on the *Mexicana* and the *Sutil*, which had necessitated the further work in Acapulco and entailed huge cost overruns. Casting around for someone to blame, he told Bodega he was "highly displeased" with the semiliterate *constructor* Manuel Bastarrachea; he doubted the builder's competence.[90] The viceroy had requested replacement of the shipwright before this.[91]

Coming to the poor fellow's defence, Bodega wrote in a long letter that he was

> aware that Bastarrachea does not have sufficient intelligence to be the perfect master shipbuilder, but he does not lack experience and has carried out the functions of his job with care ... I must inform you, to honour the truth, that

> I do not blame him for the *Activa*'s defects, or for the careening of the *Princesa*, nor the costly repairs to the *Mexicana* and the *Sutil* in Acapulco.

The *Activa*, he explained, had been built as quickly as possible, and the additional work required could be done when time permitted. The *Princesa* was careened in a difficult place where it was not possible to discover the poor condition of the keel.[92] As for the twin schooners, Bodega described in some detail the misunderstanding among Malaspina, Bustamante, and himself regarding what was needed and the purpose for which the ships were being built. Bodega, in effect, was assuming some of the responsibility so that Bastarrachea would not be blamed for the costly defects.[93]

In the end, one must agree with Malcolm Kenyon's conclusion that

> in view of the conditions of life and work in San Blas, it is rather amazing that anything of value was accomplished there; but in spite of material shortages, disease, discomfort, insects, heat, humidity, squalid living accommodations and impermanent, inadequate facilities, the shipyard fulfilled its responsibilities. This achievement can be attributed to either staunch, heroic patriotism or to perverse stubbornness; and considering the protagonists were Spanish, probably to an ample combination of both.[94]

Plates

King Carlos III ascended the Spanish throne in 1760. Influenced by the ideas of the Enlightenment, he encouraged land reform and reduced the power of the Church and the aristocracy. A great supporter of the navy, he encouraged innovative methods for shipbuilding and the training of officers.
Courtesy of the Museo Naval, Madrid. Photograph by Freeman Tovell.

Vicente Tofiño de San Miguel was an influential teacher and hydrographer at the naval academy in Cádiz. He taught Bodega navigation, surveying, and chart making. Originally an army officer, Tofiño became one of the leading representatives of the mariner-scientists who dramatically changed the effectiveness of the Spanish navy in the last half of the eighteenth century. He trained many young officers in the 1780s by having them work on his *Atlas Marítimo de España,* published in 1789. *Courtesy of the Museo Naval, Madrid.*

Antonio María Bucareli y Ursúa was the viceroy of New Spain during the 1770s. A good administrator but not a visionary, he was concerned with the defence of New Spain's northern frontier and its western coast. He strengthened the settlements in Alta California, initiated the founding of San Francisco, and mandated the first Spanish expeditions to the Northwest Coast, in 1774, 1775, and 1779. After these voyages, he held Bodega in high regard for his skill and organizational abilities, courage, and tenacity.
Courtesy of the Art and Architecture Collection, Miriam and Ira D. Wallach Division of Art, Prints and Photographs, The New York Public Library, Astor, Lenox and Tilden Foundations.

Antonio Valdés y Bazán earned a solid reputation as a naval officer in both peace and war. He served as Minister of the Marine during the later years of the reign of King Carlos III. In these positions, he was central to the development and implementation of policies for the defence of Spain's interests on the Northwest Coast in the years of the Nootka crisis, 1790-95. In October 1788, he approved Bodega's return New Spain as commandant at San Blas.
Courtesy of the Museo Naval, Madrid.

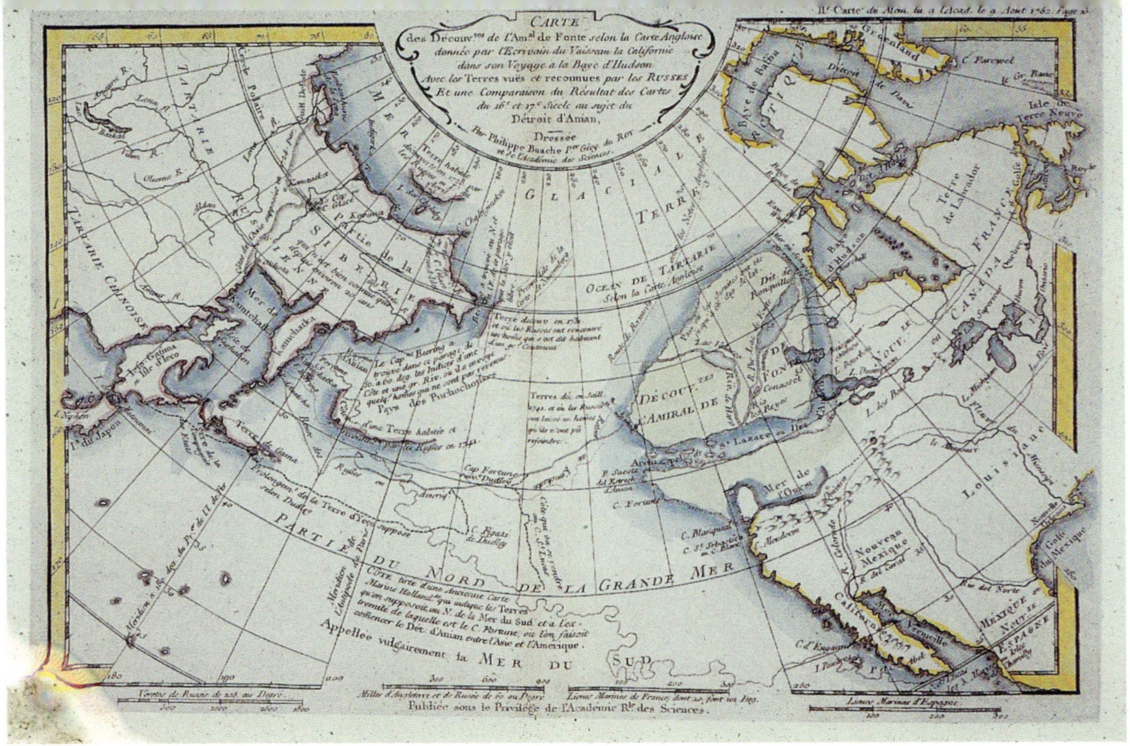

1752 map of the North Pacific Ocean, by Philippe Buache. The French cartographers Philippe Buache and Guillaume Delisle used their limited knowledge of Russian explorations to construct a series of highly speculative maps of the Northwest Coast, which purported to fill in the gaps between the known areas of Hudson Bay, Kamchatka, and California. They based their creation on the voyage of the fictitious Admiral Bartholomew de Fonte. This map was touted by cabinet geographers and others, especially in England, who wanted their nations to find and control the passage between the Atlantic and Pacific Oceans.
Courtesy of the Instituto de Historia del Pacífico Español, Vancouver.

Francisco Mourelle was a twenty-five-year-old *piloto* when he was assigned, along with Bodega, to the 1775 northern expedition commanded by Bruno de Hezeta. Fate gave him and Bodega the opportunity to make their remarkable voyage to southern Alaska. In 1779, they sailed north together once more. These two voyages determined the nature, extent, and trend of the coast for the Spanish government. Mourelle later made voyages to the Philippines and South Pacific and served with distinction as a wartime officer and administrator in Spanish waters. This portrait of Bodega's great friend was painted in 1819, many years after their heroic voyages of exploration of the Northwest Coast. At his death in 1820, Mourelle held the rank of rear admiral.
Courtesy of the Museo Naval, Madrid.

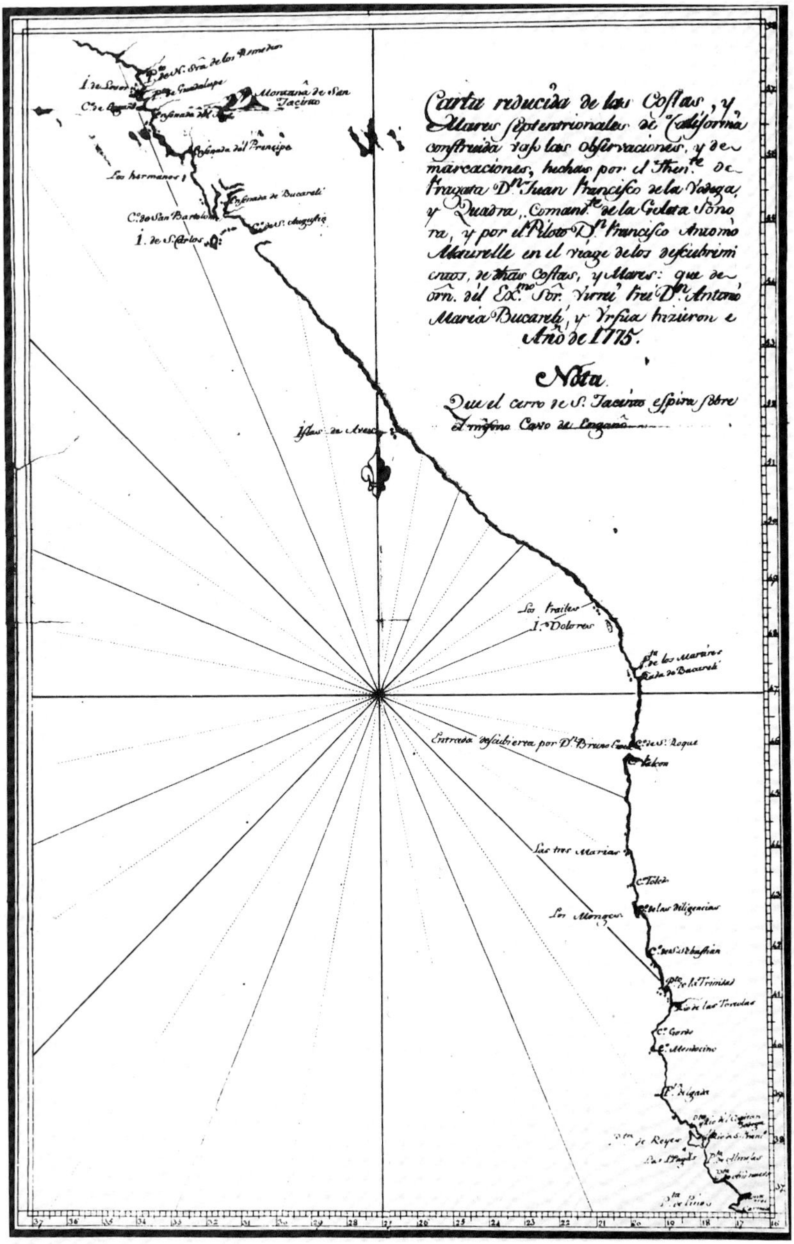

This chart of the American Northwest Coast is a record of the achievements of the 1775 Hezeta-Bodega voyage from San Francisco to southern Alaska aboard the *Sonora.* Bodega and Mourelle's discoveries in the north are rendered in detail. "Montaña de San Jacinto" is today's Mount Edgecombe. In the centre, the *entrada* (strait) discovered by Bruno de Hezeta is the mouth of the Columbia River. *Courtesy of the Museo Naval, Madrid.*

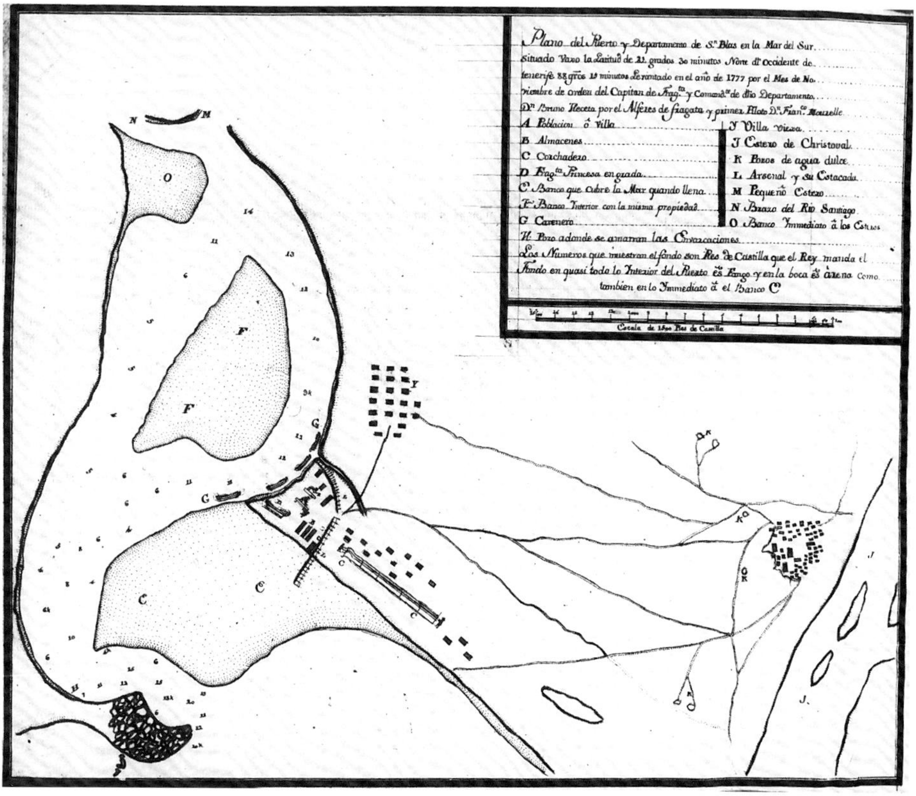

This 1777 plan of the port and naval department of San Blas was drawn by Francisco Mourelle. San Blas was established in 1768 to support exploration and settlement north of Baja California. Chosen for its fresh water, sheltered harbour, and abundant timber for shipbuilding, its summer rains brought mosquitoes and malaria, which made it a miserable place to live and work. Its harbour silted up annually. As its commandant, Bodega pushed to have the base moved to Acapulco. It was relocated soon after his death in 1794.
Courtesy of the Museo Naval, Madrid.

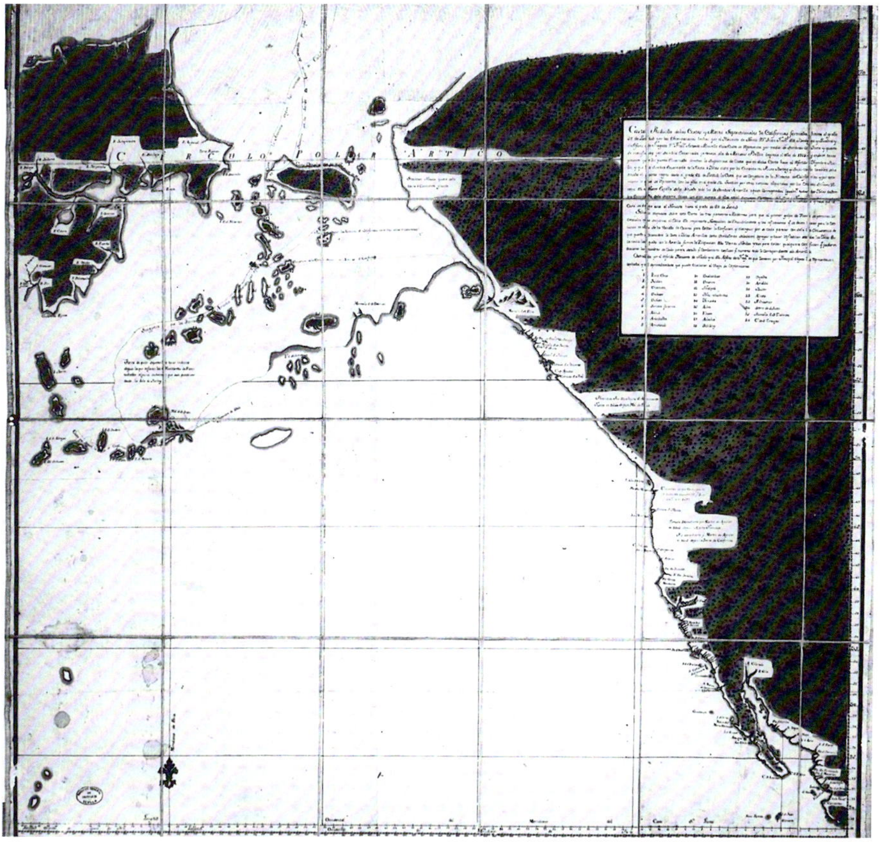

1778 planning chart of the Northwest Coast. Bodega's talent for detailed planning, together with the unexpected amount of time available for preparation, meant that the 1779 Northwest Coast voyage was much better organized and informed than the two previous expeditions. In constructing this composite chart, Bodega drew on the results of his earlier voyage in 1775, on maps from St. Petersburg that purported to reflect the results of Russian exploration in the North Pacific, and on Bellin's map. Unfortunately, the Russian maps were wildly inaccurate, as both the Spaniards in 1779 and James Cook in 1778 found out.
Courtesy of the Archivo General de Indias, Seville.

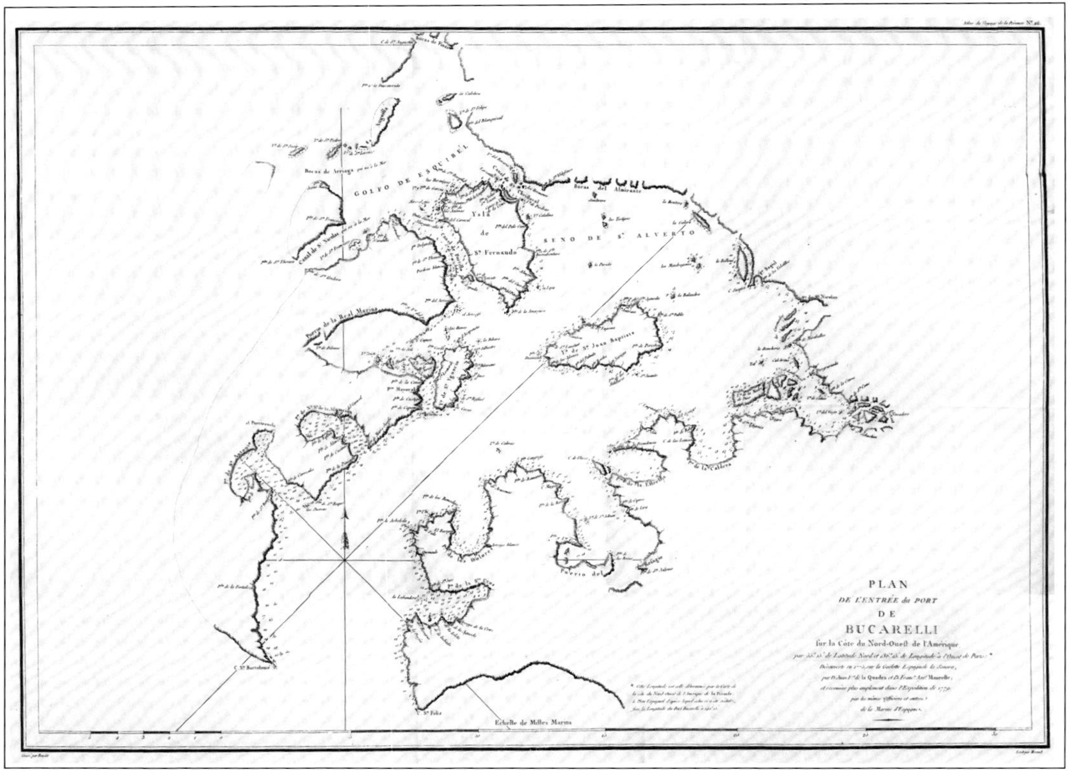

Bucareli Bay in southern Alaska was discovered by Bodega in 1775. When the 1779 expedition returned to it for an extended visit, Francisco Mourelle undertook a detailed survey of the immediate vicinity of the ships' anchorage off Suemez Island. José Camacho, a pilot on Ignacio de Arteaga's *Princesa*, assisted him, and drew this chart of the bay and port of Bucareli in 1780. Camacho's finished chart is particularly noteworthy for the drawing and description of a Tlingit canoe, the first documented Spanish image of ethnological interest from the Northwest Coast.
Courtesy of the Servicio Hidrográfico de la Marina, Cádiz.

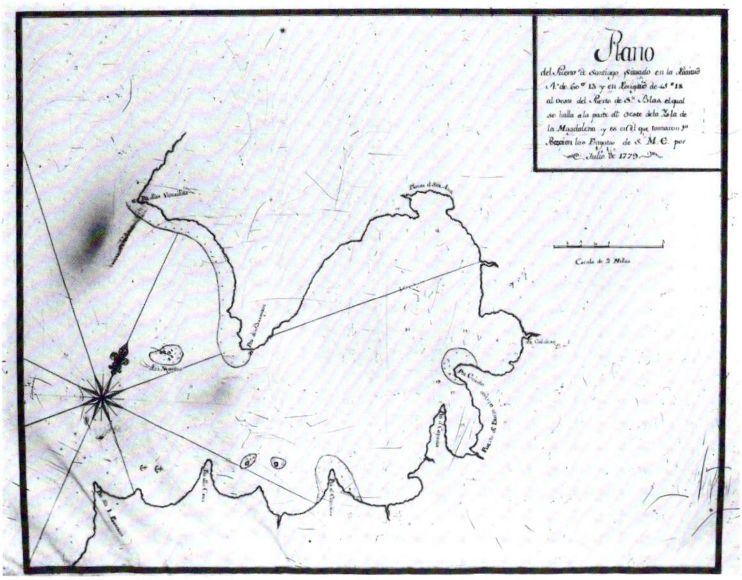

Chart of the Port of Santiago, drawn in 1780 by José Camacho. The 1779 expedition anchored in the "Puerto de Santiago," today Port Etches, on the west side of Hinchinbrook Island in Prince William Sound. This was the northernmost point on the Northwest Coast of America of which the Spanish took formal possession. A cross marks the spot where the possession ceremony took place; the anchors mark the ships' anchorages.
Courtesy of the Museo Naval, Madrid.

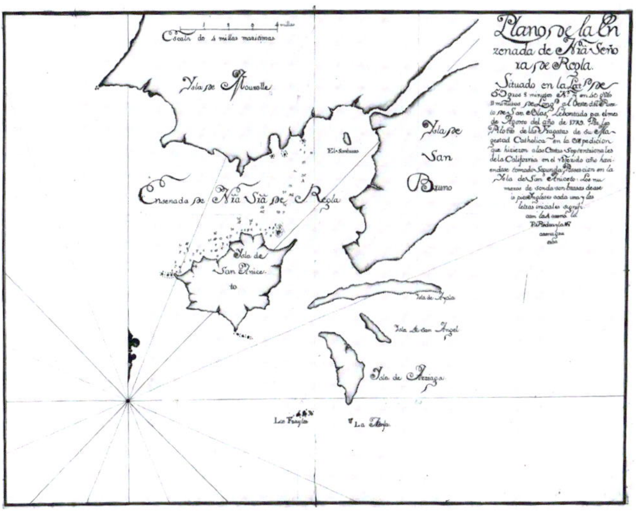

Juan Pantoja, a junior pilot on Arteaga's *Princesa*, drew this chart of the Bay of Nuestra Señora de la Regla in 1780. Regla, today's Port Chatham, is a bay off the southern tip of the Kenai Peninsula. When the 1779 expedition encountered poor weather after leaving Prince William Sound, the ships sought refuge in an anchorage inside the island labelled here as "San Aniceto" and now known as Elizabeth Island, near the mouth of Cook Inlet. A cross marks the spot where the cross was raised.
Courtesy of the Museo Naval, Madrid.

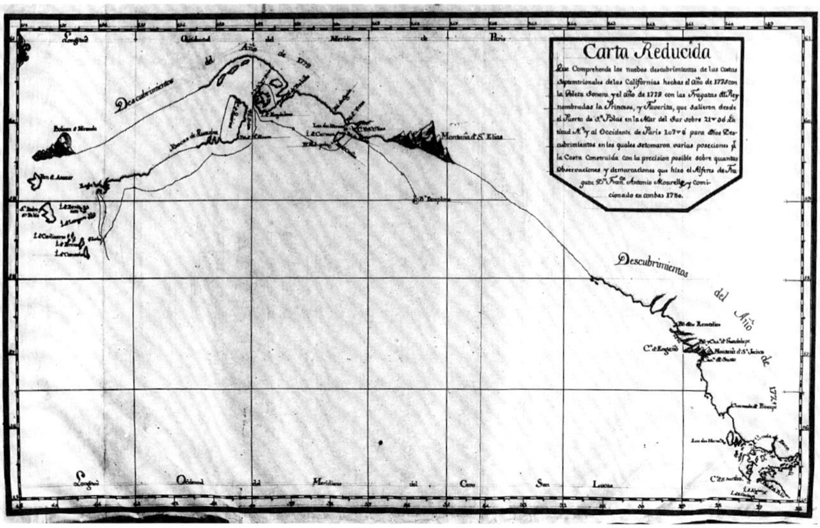

This 1779 comprehensive chart of the Northwest Coast includes a record of the results of the Arteaga-Bodega voyage north from San Francisco to the Gulf of Alaska. At the top of the chart one can find "Montaña de San Elias" and evidence of the expedition's visit to Prince William Sound. Poor weather resulted in the chart of the coast off the Kenai Peninsula being largely inaccurate.
Courtesy of the Museo Naval, Madrid.

A view of Friendly Cove (Yuquot), Nootka Sound. This drawing by Miguel Arias is a copy of the missing original sketch made in 1792 by Atanasio Echeverría. The establishment was two years old at the time of the sketch. Bodega's two-story commandant's house, where he entertained Chief Maquinna and George Vancouver, as well as other American, Spanish, English, and Nootkan men of rank, stands at centre-left. The letters "A-B" on the right delineate Meares' Cove, the only land at Yuquot of which Bodega was prepared to cede possession during his negotiations with Vancouver.
Courtesy of the Ministerio de Asuntos Exteriores, Madrid.

Juan Vicente de Güemes Pacheco de Padilla y Horcacitas, second Conde de Revillagigedo, served as viceroy of New Spain between 1789 and 1795, years of heightened Spanish activity on the Northwest Coast in the aftermath of the Nootka crisis. Able but demanding, Revillagigedo respected Bodega's knowledge, experience, and judgment and chose him to be the commissioner who met with George Vancouver at Nootka to determine the future of the Spanish establishment in accordance with the Nootka Convention.
Courtesy of the Art and Architecture Collection, Miriam and Ira D. Wallach Division of Art, Prints and Photographs, The New York Public Library, Astor, Lenox and Tilden Foundations.

The interior of Chief Maquinna's house, 1792. Maquinna is dancing before Juan Francisco de la Bodega y Quadra (seated second from the left end of the bench at centre-left) and George Vancouver (seated on the right end of the same bench) during their visit to his winter home at the head of Tahsis Inlet in Nootka Sound, September 4-6, 1792. Bodega had suggested to Vancouver that they make a formal visit to Maquinna's winter village. For Maquinna, the visit was an important sign of the respect accorded him by his European visitors; for Bodega, it was part of a plan to assure the chief that, in the event of an expected British takeover of the establishment at Friendly Cove, he could count on their willingness to recognize him as the ranking chief of the sound. The figure standing behind Bodega and Vancouver is either Moziño or Dobson, Vancouver's interpreter. The man standing to the right of the house post is wearing a wolf mask. The original drawing of this scene by Atanasio Echeverría has been lost; this is a copy made by José María Vasquez, a young artist at the Academy of San Carlos in Mexico City. *Courtesy of the Ministerio de Asuntos Exteriores, Madrid.*

The Bay of Nootka viewed from the beach of the Spanish establishment, 1792. This "finished copy" by Gabriel Gil, an artist at the Academy of San Carlos in Mexico City, is based on an original drawing, now lost, by Atanasio Echeverría. The small harbour of Friendly Cove was a busy scene in the summer of the Expedition of the Limits. It was visited by the expeditions of Malaspina, Vancouver, and Bodega, as well as by several American and English fur traders.
Courtesey of the Archivo del Ministerio de Asuntos Exteriores, Madrid: MS 146-5.

Mexican artist Tomás de Suria drew this portrait of Maquinna, chief of the Nootka, during the 1791 late-summer visit of the Malaspina expedition to the Spanish establishment at Nootka. Through his encounters with explorers and fur traders, this Maquinna (a name passed from one hereditary chief of the Mowachaht people to another) encouraged their visits to Nootka Sound, gaining great wealth and prestige. He acquiesced to the Spanish presence in Friendly Cove (Yuquot) and enjoyed mutually cordial and respectful relations with Bodega during the summer of 1792.
Courtesy of the Museo Naval, Madrid.

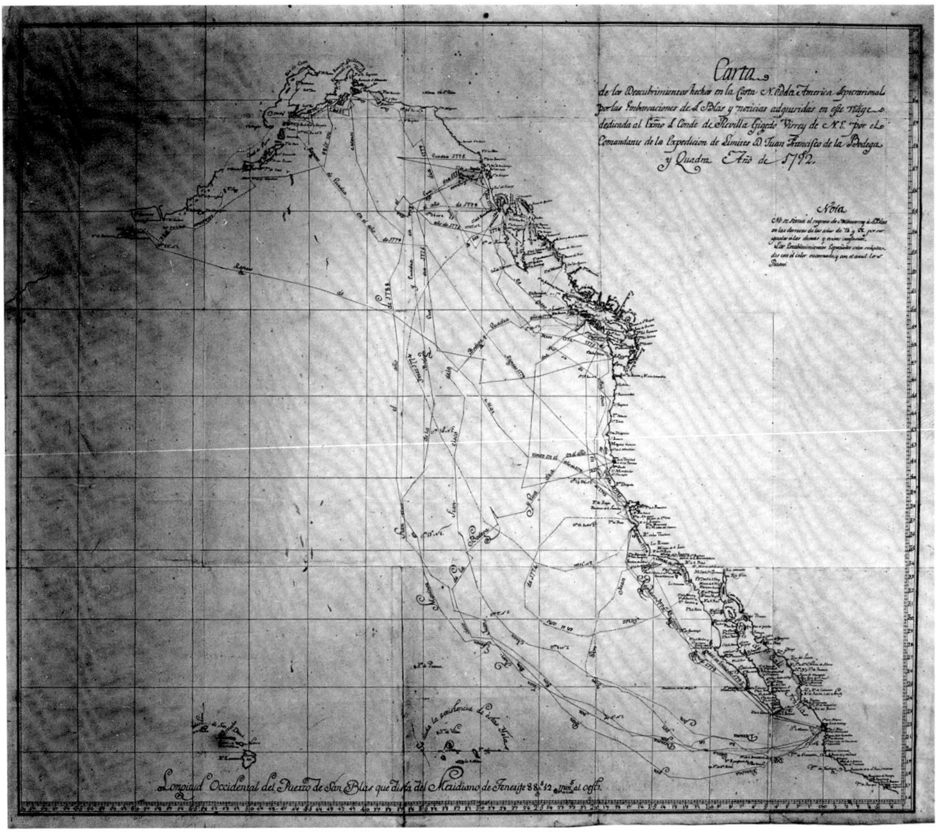

Chart of the discoveries made on the Northwest Coast by expeditions from San Blas. Bodega completed this "summary" chart in 1792 upon his return to San Blas from the Expedition of the Limits. It stands as a testament to Bodega's long association with the exploration of the coast – the best part of his career in the Spanish navy.
Courtesy of the Ministerio de Asuntos Exteriores, Madrid.

Part 3

The Diplomat

8

The Nootka Convention and the Expedition of the Limits

Bodega's next assignment as commandant of San Blas was to arrange the turnover of the Nootka establishment under the terms of the Nootka Convention with Captain George Vancouver. This diplomatic mission marked the high point of his career. The convention was intended to settle the quarrel between Spain and Britain that had erupted after Estéban Martinez's seizure of James Colnett's ships. Instead, the attempt to implement the convention exposed the conflicting imperial policies of the two governments. Spain's imperial policy was to protect her three-hundred-year-old claim to sovereignty over the waters off the Northwest Coast of America, citing her *Leyes de Indias* by which foreigners were "excluded from the commerce with our Indies."[1] In the 1770s and 1780s, Spain had enforced her claim through formal acts of possession performed during the recent voyages of exploration to the Northwest Coast. During the same period, British merchants had been moving into the "empty" North Pacific and challenging Spain's monopoly. Facing an election, Britain's prime minister, William Pitt, was pressed by the commercial community to assert the doctrine of freedom of the seas, which entitled British ships to visit and trade in all places not yet settled by a foreign power. Seizing the opportunity presented by Martínez's action, Pitt challenged Spain's claim to exclusive sovereignty over the Pacific. The two governments were on a collision course, and as Viceroy Revillagigedo had foreseen, the clash at Nootka became a matter for the governments of Spain and Great Britain to settle.

News of the seizure of the English ships reached Madrid sometime in November or early December 1789.[2] In January 1790, Antonio Valdés wrote to Viceroy Revillagigedo that, pending a peaceful solution, he was authorized to restore the *Argonaut* and the *Princess Royal* to Colnett on the condition that the ships return to Macao and trade no more on the American coast.[3]

The British chargé d'affaires in Madrid sent reports of rumours of the seizure to his Foreign Secretary, the Duke of Leeds, who received them by mid-January. The information was neither complete nor accurate. Taking the initiative, the Spanish Minister of State, Count Floridablanca, instructed the Spanish ambassador in London, the Marqués del Campo, to lodge a protest asking that the "trespassers" be punished and that Britain "restrain" her subjects from continuing such undertakings on "lands which have been occupied and frequented by the Spaniards for so many years." To this, the first English response was to "suspend all discussion ... until a just and adequate satisfaction shall have been made" for the seizures.

The tone of the negotiations worsened in mid-April 1790. Arriving in London, John Meares began to lobby ministers and members of Parliament with a mendacious "memorial" in which he sought their support for some grossly inflated claims of financial loss.[4] Meares was a superb pamphleteer who won public support and secured a meeting with Pitt's cabinet.[5] At first, his complaints were accepted at face value, and Pitt became more belligerent. Although the two governments claimed to be seeking an understanding, both prepared for war. As the crisis deepened, Pitt assumed personal responsibility for the negotiations and took the opportunity to assert two important principles of British imperial policy: freedom of the seas, and the right to trade anywhere. In May he appointed his most experienced diplomat, Alleyne Fitzherbert, as Ambassador to Madrid. The Spanish position began to weaken. By July, Spain could no longer rely on France, her premier ally, because the French were embroiled in an incipient revolution. In August, Madrid received Revillagigedo's extensive report on the deplorable state of the economy and defences of New Spain.[6]

Late that summer, Revillagigedo learned that the two courts, in London and Madrid, were engaged in secret negotiations in an attempt to resolve the "question of Nootka and trade between the two nations in those parts." He was reminded that English traders coming to Nootka were not to be molested, nor was "force to be used to prevent them from establishing any settlements in other parts of the world than where our establishments are to be found."[7]

British belligerence also waned. By October, Pitt found himself being criticized for failing to solve the dispute peacefully, and even though the mood for war was strong, there was concern over the high cost of keeping the navy at a full state of readiness. On October 12, 1790, under Pitt's instructions, Ambassador Fitzherbert handed Count Floridablanca an ultimatum demanding acceptance of all of Britain's principal demands. England wanted a determination of the northern limit of Spanish sovereignty on the Northwest Coast; freedom to trade in and occupy unsettled lands; restitution of the buildings and lands seized from Meares; definition of the distance from which vessels might approach Spanish-occupied land; freedom to engage in the southern fishery; and the loosening of control over whalers using unfrequented harbours on the coast.

In a stormy meeting of the Council of State, Floridablanca's recommendation that Pitt's ultimatum be negotiated was unanimously rejected. For the Spanish councillors, war was preferable to capitulation. Floridablanca decided to consult the king directly. He secured royal support before he called a second meeting of the Council of State, where he obtained unanimous approval for the draft treaty. The first Nootka Convention was signed on October 28, 1790, at San Lorenzo del Escorial near Madrid.

In the end, Floridablanca obtained two important concessions. First, Spain's exclusive rights would not be written into the text but would be covered in the preamble by the phrase "laying aside all retrospective discussion of the rights and claims of the two parties." Second, there would be no mention of a boundary. For him, this was the most important issue of all. Had a boundary been specified, Pitt would have insisted on the latitude of San Francisco, which would have made it impossible for Spain to create any more establishments farther north. From the Spanish point of view, Article V of the convention, which allowed English and Spanish subjects to trade in each other's settlements, was key because it was open to differing interpretations. It read:

> It is agreed that as well in the places which are to be restored ... by virtue of the first article as in all other parts of the Northwest Coast of North America or of the islands adjacent, situated to the north of the parts of the said coast already occupied by Spain, wherever the subjects of either of the two powers shall have made settlements since the month of April, 1789, or shall hereafter make any, the subjects of the other shall have free access and shall carry on their commerce without disturbance or molestation.

The First Nootka Convention was a blow to Spain's prestige. According to Lennox Mills, "Spain was compelled to give reparation for an insult she denied having committed without being allowed to discuss ... the Spanish claim to sovereignty on the coast."[8]

The Nootka Convention did not resolve the serious differences of imperial policy between Britain and Spain. The basic issue of sovereignty was ignored. Much of the essential information needed for negotiating a final settlement was lacking. For example, what constituted the "buildings and tracts of land" of which Meares claimed to have been dispossessed? Moreover, the key clauses, designed to reflect Britain's demands and to respect Spanish pride, could be interpreted in different ways. In 1792, these ambiguities became apparent once Revillagigedo began to prepare Bodega's instructions for his upcoming dual role: commandant of the Expedition of the Limits, and Spanish commissioner for negotiations at Nootka with his British counterpart, George Vancouver.

A month after the convention was signed, Floridablanca informed Revillagigedo that "at last" a settlement had been negotiated with England.[9] But not until March 1791 did Revillagigedo receive four Royal Orders (#221, #222, #223, #224), all dated December 25, 1790, which enabled him to implement the convention.[10] Royal Orders #222 and #223 formed the basis for the Expedition of the Limits.

Royal Order #222 included a written permit for the "governor or commandant of the port of Nootka" to turn over the port to the bearer of a duplicate permit that had been issued to a British commissioner appointed to take possession of Nootka. The same order suggested that the Spanish ambassador in London propose to the British government that a degree of latitude be agreed on, north of which both nations could establish settlements and engage in trade. This point could be established at 48°N – the entrance to the Strait of Juan de Fuca – which would give to England "all the districts purchased" by her traders. Second, the coast to the south of that point as far as San Francisco would be a "neutral interval." Finally, it was suggested that to forestall any British commercial expansion inland that would threaten the Alta California and New Mexico missions, an eastern boundary should be set that would stretch as far north as the entrance to Prince William Sound or Bucareli Bay.

Royal Order #223 informed Revillagigedo that both courts had agreed that an English ship would travel to the Pacific and, together with a Spanish vessel to be designated by the viceroy, would carry out a joint survey of the "coasts adjacent to Nootka." Having made an exact chart, it would agree on a "point to the north of those parts of the coast occupied by Spain below which English navigators and traders may not pass." North of that point, there would be shared use and commerce as permitted by Article V of the convention.

In his ensuing correspondence with Floridablanca, Revillagigedo suggested refinements to the interpretation of the convention that would improve the outcome of the negotiations for the Spanish. He was concerned about the implications of Article V, which allowed British and Spanish subjects to trade freely in each other's settlements as might be established at Nootka or to the north of it. To avert possible conflict over Article V, he proposed a radical solution: abandon Nootka altogether and relocate the Spanish outpost to one of "the best ports" in the Strait of Juan de Fuca. This new establishment would be in a position to monitor the "movements and designs" of the English and would become Spain's "last possession on the northern coasts of California." Revillagigedo also proposed that the eastern boundary proposed in Royal Order #222 be more clearly specified as a line drawn from the entrance of the Strait of Juan de Fuca extending due north to 60°, the latitude of Prince William Sound. Only the coast and islands west of that line would be governed by Article V. This line had an additional advantage for Spain; it would protect Spain's claim to the coast where the entrance to a Northwest Passage might be. Revillagigedo thought the idea would have some attraction for the English, as they would gain Clayoquot Sound (Port Cox) and the best waters for the sea otter hunt, but he recognized that they would make "some objection" to being prohibited from entering and trading with the Indians in the Strait of Juan de Fuca. He did not foresee that an even stronger objection would be that overland fur traders from Canada would be cut off from to the coast, toward which they were advancing steadily across the continent.

After hearing nothing for six months, Revillagigedo wrote again at even greater length to convey to the Minister of State "with the greatest possible clarity and brevity" how he understood the different Royal Orders he had received, as well as an outline of his approach to their implementation.[11] Accepting the loss of the establishment at Nootka as a fait accompli, he rationalized "that we lose nothing if we cede Nootka to the English." Instead, he had turned his attention to the future. He expanded on his plans to remove the Nootka establishment to a convenient location in the Strait of Juan de Fuca; he also considered the royal plans for further exploration. He suggested that the explorer's priorities be altered. While he acknowledged the king's desire to explore the Strait of Juan de Fuca, he felt it was more important to explore the entire coast from San Francisco north to Nootka and on to Bucareli Bay at 55°N because the Royal Order called for the English and Spanish to determine jointly a boundary somewhere along this coast. Before agreeing to a northern boundary, the Spaniards had to know where the entrance to the Northwest Passage, if it existed, was located.

Revillagigedo outlined the ambitious mission he had in mind: the Expedition of the Limits. First, the mission would make the "most scrupulous examination of the Strait of Juan de Fuca," after which it would continue on to Nootka and then examine the "rest of the coast as far as 56° of latitude."[12] It was a bold concept that contained the essence of what he expected from the exploration program later carried out under Bodega.

Soon after sending this letter to Floridablanca on October 21, 1791, Revillagigedo learned that there was a good reason for the minister's silence. Floridablanca had been replaced as minister of state in a palace coup by the Conde de Aranda. Turmoil in the home administration, the alarming course of the French Revolution, a weak king ruled by his wife, and Aranda's unfamiliarity with the Nootka file all meant that for six months and longer, Viceroy Revillagigedo had to work on without any reaction to his proposals or any clear indication – other than the general direction he had been given by Floridablanca – of how the government wanted to see the convention implemented.[13] Finally, on February 29, 1792, the court approved the viceroy's plans, but with one important proviso: Nootka was not to be given up.[14] By the time the viceroy received the authorization for his ambitious expedition and the final, crucial caveat, Bodega was already at sea, on his way north to meet the British commissioner, who was expected to arrive at Nootka Sound early in 1792.

Revillagigedo's Instructions to Bodega for Nootka

Once the broad lines of policy for the handover of the Nootka establishment had been developed, the Spanish court had to appoint a commissioner to meet with the English commissioner on the Northwest Coast. Bodega's name had been suggested early on, possibly by Antonio Valdés. Carlos IV did not reject the idea and was prepared to leave the choice to the viceroy, but he wanted assurance from Revillagigedo that Bodega's "experience and knowledge would ensure the greatest success."[15] The viceroy immediately assured Floridablanca that "Quadra's [sic] scrupulous observance of his instructions is guaranteed by the high regard I have for the zeal, talent, prudence and substantial character of this distinguished officer and his practical knowledge of everything."[16] Shortly after this, he reiterated this assurance to Valdés, writing that Bodega's "practical knowledge of the [northern] seas, experience and zeal give me hope for the best success."[17]

The viceroy's first set of formal instructions to Bodega for the Expedition of the Limits was forwarded to Madrid with his letter to Floridablanca of October 24, 1791, even before Bodega had an opportunity to see them or comment on them. After discussions with Bodega, the viceroy attached a memorandum to his instructions. It emphasized and expanded on three key matters: the turning over of the Nootka establishment and the immediate founding of a new establishment at Fuca; the organization and operations of the new establishment; and the urgent need to explore the coast between San Francisco and 56°N as well as the Strait of Juan de Fuca, as part of the process of determining the boundary between Spanish and English interests.[18] On receiving of a copy of Meares's memorial along with British press reports of Meares's activities in pursuit of his claims against Spain, Revillagigedo issued further instructions to Bodega regarding three issues generated by this new information: the devolution of the Nootka establishment, the reciprocal rights of Spain and England, and compensation for Meares's losses.[19] These further instructions included some extracts from Meares's memorial that Revillagigedo had translated. He forwarded these to Bodega so that he could "correct some of its errors and the weakness of his arguments." Revillagigedo's formal instructions to Bodega for the Expedition of the Limits are in Appendix B.)

During his briefing with Revillagigedo in Mexico City, it had become clear to Bodega that matters could not move as fast as the viceroy wished. Bodega objected to the viceroy's plan to combine the survey of the Strait of Juan de Fuca with the survey examination of the coast from San Francisco to 56°N. He knew from his own experience that this was more than could be accomplished in one summer.

Once again, the issue of ships came to the fore. Revillagigedo had underestimated the difficulties of assembling even a small fleet from the inadequate resources of San Blas. When Bodega pointed out to the viceroy that it would be necessary to build another ship to ensure that the expedition would have the number and size of ships it needed, the viceroy ordered the construction of the twelve-gun schooner *Activa* without waiting for authority from Spain.[20] Bodega's request that the veteran *Princesa* be included in the voyage was immediately granted, but first she had to be careened. When Francisco Mourelle, who was to explore north of Haro Strait with the *Mexicana,* fell ill, Alejandro Malaspina, commander of the scientific expedition, offered two of his officers, Dionisio Alcalá Galiano and Cayetano Valdés, both *capitanes de fragata.* When Malaspina recommended that their mission be carried out in two schooners rather than one, the *Mexicana*'s twin, the *Sutil,* was built.[21]

The general plan agreed on was that the *Mexicana* and the *Sutil* would undertake the exploration of the Strait of Juan de Fuca and the waters beyond to see if they opened into a navigable passage to Hudson Bay or James Bay. The *Princesa,* commanded by Salvador Fidalgo, would search for the best location for a new establishment on the Strait of Juan de Fuca. The exploration of the outer coast from San Francisco north to 56°N would be assigned to the *Activa*, along with the old frigate *Aránzazu* and the frigate *Santa Gertrudis* from Callao. These two ships would also be available to search, with Vancouver's ships, for the "dividing point" or "limit" if Vancouver agreed to that joint enterprise. Either way, the three ships would ensure an impressive Spanish presence at Nootka.

The inclusion of the thirty-four-gun *Santa Gertrudis* in the plan bought its own problems.[22] As soon as it became apparent that San Blas could supply neither the type nor the number of ships required to impress the English, a Royal Order dated December 11, 1790, was sent to the viceroy in Lima. He was asked to send a frigate belonging to the squadron based at Callao to New Spain for use "in the matter of determining the boundaries, subsequent to the convention entered into with Great Britain, regarding the settlements at San Lorenzo de Nocka [sic]." He was to choose a commandant who possessed "prudence and judgement."[23]

The viceroy selected *capitán de navío* Alonso Torres y Guerra, commandant of the *Santa Gertrudis*, who has been described as a "very junior four-striper, with the gold braid of his latest stripe not yet darkened by the effects of salt air."[24] When the young officer was informed that he was to be the second-in-command, he protested that the king had informed the viceroy in Lima that he would have command of the mission. To serve as Bodega's second-in-command would impugn his honour and would not correspond to the confidence the king had placed in him. In these circumstances, he would disembark and await the return of his ship or seek a transfer back to Spain.[25]

When Revillagigedo sought Bodega's advice, the latter suggested offering Torres three choices: he could command the *Princesa;* he could accept the post of *capitán de bandera* (flag captain) on the *Santa Gertrudis,* in which office he would retain responsibility for the ship's governance and assist Bodega with the chart work; or he could remain in the commandant's house in Tepic until the expedition returned.[26] Revillagigedo accepted this advice. Never one to mince words, and emphasizing that the king had left the selection of the commandant of the expedition to his judgment, he replied brusquely to Torres that he had appointed Bodega to command the mission because he considered him the

> best able to fulfill the king's legitimate intentions. Not only does this officer's knowledge of these seas assure the best prospect for success but [the command] is appropriate to his seniority, his position and his accomplishments.

He also noted that since all the ships would be travelling in convoy, it was important that command be given to someone who held the respect of his officers so that he could carry out the mission with familiarity and frankness. He assured the young captain that the role of *capitán de bandera* was appropriate for him because it would afford him the opportunity to give the commandant the advice needed to ensure the success of the mission.[27]

No doubt reflecting that command of the *Princesa*, normally commanded by a *teniente de navío*, was a demotion, and not wishing to wait uselessly for six months or more in Tepic or, worse, in the steamy climate of San Blas, Torres chose to serve under Bodega. Revillagigedo assured Valdés that Torres did not have the same qualifications as Bodega to command the mission, nor did he have the latter's "practical knowledge of the seas where his task was to be discharged." Moreover, he pointed out, Bodega was senior in rank.[28]

Another problem arose with the appointment of *alférez de navío* Félix de Cepeda as Bodega's adjutant to provide the diplomatic mission with an English/Spanish interpreter. Cepeda had come to New Spain on the *San Ramón* with Revillagigedo and Bodega. In formally advising Bodega of his choice, the viceroy described Cepeda as an officer of ability, talent, and zeal who could speak English and French.[29] Bodega, in reply, said he was "aware of his attitude and knew that this officer very much wants to use his talents," adding, in reference to his knowledge of languages, "and his uncommon education."[30] In using the term "attitude," Bodega was hinting that he was aware that Cepeda was said to possess "a large and unfounded pride." In his assignments, he had shown himself to be "no brighter than others, but treated everyone else as dunces and was involved in interminable disputes." Topping it off, "he was remiss in obedience."[31] One report, written before Cepeda came to New Spain, concluded that "he should correct his character and the rest of his defects."

Cepeda's knowledge of English was the determining factor in his appointment, but he would never have the opportunity to demonstrate it at Nootka. A month before Vancouver arrived, he was sent back to San Blas with Torres on the *Santa Gertrudis*. Later, in Monterey, Bodega assigned him to accompany across New Spain to Veracruz a stranded English merchant captain and Robert Broughton, the commander of the *Chatham*, who was returning to England with Vancouver's reports.[32] Bodega must have had a compelling reason to leave himself without an interpreter. He never wrote a detrimental report about Cepeda, and when he explained his decision to the viceroy, the decision seems to have had less to do with any personality defect than with a need to meet Torres's need for help surveying the coast of present-day Washington and Oregon en route to Monterey.

In fact, Bodega said it was with "real sorrow" that he was "obliged to separate myself from my adjutant ... in whose education and zeal I have the greatest confidence, [and who] is the only one capable of ... stimulating the others by example to assure the success of the mission."[33] Revillagigedo himself thought well enough of Cepeda to recommend his promotion from *alférez de navío* to *teniente de fragata* to both Valdés[34] and Minister of State Aranda.[35] Nothing came of this support, however, and after returning to Spain, Cepeda's career languished.

Bodega and Revillagigedo discussed the level of hospitality to be extended to Vancouver and his squadron. Bodega pointed out that none of the Royal Orders dealing with his mission made any mention of a "gift or reciprocal attentions, which, without being feasts or indiscreet displays, constitute correct acts in the intercourse of persons representing two nations who have to deal with important matters." He asked that his regular messing allowance be increased by four thousand pesos.[36] The viceroy agreed and ordered the treasury to make the money available.[37] With these funds, Bodega ordered delicacies and wines with which to fête Vancouver and his men, to be shipped to him in San Blas.[38] The costs must have been higher than Bodega had anticipated, for on departing San Blas, he informed the viceroy that besides the four thousand pesos above his usual messing allowance, he had obtained an advance on his salary for one year – that is, thirty-six hundred pesos. He justified his decision on the grounds that he

> wished to satisfy my desires and those of Your Excellency. In Article XVI of my instructions you not only caution me to maintain the best possible relations [with Vancouver] but also [show] openness in our dealings. At this distance, everything is very costly and I have spared no expense [to ensure success]. I have no resources other than my salary.[39]

He asked that the king be informed.

Revillagigedo delayed writing back. It is possible that he wanted the approval of the ever cautious watchdogs of the treasury. Not until the end of June, four months after Bodega departed for the north, did Revillagigedo write to Minister of State Aranda to explain the situation. Aranda agreed that the advances were justified but asked the viceroy to take the matter up with the Minister of Finance. Accordingly, Revillagigedo wrote a long letter to the minister, Diego de Gardoqui, and, for good measure, a shorter one to Valdés.

Preparations for the Expedition

Once the viceroy accepted the modifications to his original plans, the need to move as quickly as possible obliged Bodega to return directly to San Blas instead of joining Torres in Acapulco. The *Activa* and the *Sutil* had yet to be built, and the expedition had to be ready to depart by the beginning of March at the very latest in order to arrive in Nootka in time to receive Vancouver and to carry out the planned explorations.[40]

Back in San Blas, having had more time to review his instructions, Bodega thought it would be helpful to have as much information as possible on past maritime explorations of the Northwest Coast, not only from Spanish sources but from English and Russian ones as well. He asked Revillagigedo for Pérez's *diario* of 1774, his own journals of 1775 and 1779, Martínez's journals of 1788 and 1789, and those of Fidalgo and Quimper from 1790. In addition, he wanted copies of Cook's account of his third voyage and George Dixon's recent publication, as well as the reports of the Marqués de Almodóvar, who as the Spanish ambassador in St. Petersburg had secured a good deal of information about Russian activities, in particular about the 1741 voyage of Bering and Chirikov.[41] The only *diarios* the viceroy could find in his secretariat at that time were those of Pérez and Bodega from 1775. As it would take too much time to copy those and the others whenever they were located, he offered to send Francisco Mourelle's compendium of the reports of all the Spanish voyages.[42] This compendium, the viceroy thought, would provide Bodega with all the information required and "make it easier to understand [what is essential] without having to deal with a mass of detail and confusion of paper."[43]

When drafting his routing instructions, Bodega produced a general chart of the coast from San Blas to the island of Unalaska in the Aleutians. It was intended to complement his plan of operations and to demonstrate to the viceroy what exploration should be carried out during the Expedition of the Limits. It listed four parts of the coast that still had to be examined. These were the Canal de Flores, a small stretch of water between the Alaskan mainland and Kodiak Island; the coast between Bering's Bay[44] and the Puerto de los Remedios;[45] the coast from Bucareli Bay south (especially the intricate section of the Canal de Fonte[46] and the Punta de Boiset);[47] and the coast from Cape Flattery at the entrance to the Strait of Juan de Fuca south to San Francisco.[48] It seems most likely that while drafting this important chart, Bodega told the viceroy that he really saw no particular purpose in the joint survey Revillagigedo proposed in partnership with the

English, since much of the coast had already been well examined by Quimper, Eliza, Narvaéz, and Malaspina. Any remaining gaps, he forewarned Revillagigedo, he would like to explore himself in the *Activa*.[49]

Although the Expedition of the Limits was essentially a diplomatic mission, events conspired to give it an unexpected scientific component. Bodega's desire to add a scientific dimension to his mission was inspired by his meeting in San Blas with members of the Malaspina expedition, which was on its way north to search for the passage of Ferrer Maldonado. Having observed what able scientists and artists could do to support maritime exploration, he realized that they would enhance the lustre of his own mission. In this regard, Bodega would be well served by José Mariano Moziño, Atanasio Echeverría y Godoy, and José Maldonado.

Carlos III had offered his patronage and encouragement to a number of scientific expeditions to the Americas.[50] One had been the Royal Scientific Expedition to New Spain, directed by an Aragonese physician living in Cuba, Martín de Sessé. After three years' work, a shortage of funds forced Sessé to discharge two of his scientists. He replaced them with a young "botanist-naturalist," Moziño, whose work at the Royal Botanical Gardens in Mexico City had come to his attention; Moziño's assistant, Maldonado, an anatomist and botanist; and Echeverría, whom Moziño later praised as "one of the best artists" on the expedition. On his return to San Blas after meeting with the viceroy, Bodega learned that Sessé was expected in San Blas shortly and had on his staff "good professors." Moziño was specifically mentioned, as was Echeverría. Writing to Revillagigedo, Bodega suggested that a naturalist and an artist "would embellish [his journal] with illustrations of what was discovered." He hoped the viceroy would agree with his proposal to add a scientific component to the mission and suggested that the two men be assigned to his frigate. Bodega assured the cost-conscious Revillagigedo that the only extra expense would be their food allowance.[51] Agreeing to Bodega's request, the viceroy asked Sessé to make Moziño and Echeverría available. Although Sessé viewed the loss of Moziño and Echeverría as "irreparable," he agreed to let them go.

Bodega also had his eye on another of Sessé's men. In view of the difficulty of finding the two surgeons he had requested for the expedition in Mexico City, and realizing that those coming from Spain would not arrive in time, he told the viceroy that Sessé had offered to lend him Maldonado, whom Bodega described as a qualified surgeon and anatomist. Revillagigedo also agreed to this request. It was agreed that Moziño and Echeverría would each receive an annual salary of 1,000 pesos and that Maldonado would receive the salary of a second surgeon: 850 pesos a year.

A number of unforeseeable problems delayed the expedition's departure. The *Santa Gertrudis* required some minor repairs and also had to await a shipment of flour coming from Guadalajara. Furthermore, Bodega wanted to add twenty more "robust" Catalonian Volunteers to the mission; these men had to march all the way from Puebla.[52] During this delay, some thirty of the *Santa Gertrudis*'s crew came down with a fever.[53] Then, twelve days before sailing, Bodega decided that the *Aránzazu* should remain behind to take on the stores the other ships could not carry.[54] Commanded by the newly promoted *teniente de navío* Jacinto Caamaño, she remained in San Blas an additional three weeks. She sailed on March 20, stopping along the way to deliver supplies and papers for the California missions and presidios.[55]

With Bodega flying his pennant on the *Santa Gertrudis*, the three ships – *Santa Gertrudis, Princesa*, and *Activa* – left San Blas on February 29, 1792. On board with Bodega were Cepeda, Moziño, and Echeverría as well as forty-three Catalonian Volunteers. Moziño's assistant, Maldonado, travelled on the *Princesa*. The *Princesa* was hardly outside the harbour when she began to take on four inches of water an hour and had to be sent back to port. Then the *Activa* lost her main topmast and snapped her main yards in a light wind just ten leagues past the Islas Tres Marías. She, too, had to return to San Blas. Keen to reach Nootka before the English arrived and with a schedule that was already very tight, Bodega pressed on alone in the *Santa Gertrudis*.

He ordered Salvador Menéndez, in command of the *Activa*, and Fidalgo, in the *Princesa*, to follow as soon as their vessels were seaworthy again. Eventually, both ships departed San Blas on March 23, so late that the *Princesa* under Fidalgo never did go to Nootka, but instead sailed directly for the Strait of Juan de Fuca.

9

Bodega at Nootka

NOOTKA SOUND IS ONE OF SEVERAL large inlets on the west coast of Vancouver Island. Clayoquot and Barkley Sounds lie to the south of it.[1] Within the sounds, at the time of the expedition, several independent groups of native peoples lived in well-defined territories. Some were bound together in loose confederations. One confederacy was the Mowachaht, a group under Chief Maquinna, who lived at Yuquot, a village on a small cove right at the entrance to Nootka Sound.[2] The site has been occupied continuously as far back as 2000 BC.[3] When Estéban Martínez formally took possession of Nootka Sound for Spain in June 1789, he called it San Lorenzo de Nuca; the name he gave to the Spanish establishment at Yuquot was Santa Cruz de Nuca.[4] Ever since Captain Cook's visit in 1778, British navigators had called the village "Friendly Cove."

Santa Cruz de Nuca provided a safe harbour for the Spanish establishment. However, Yuquot was not the best site for a Spanish settlement. The climate was cool; the weather was changeable in summer, and cold and wet in winter. There was barely enough soil to grow food for the sailors and soldiers of the establishment. The Franciscan fathers assigned to Santa Cruz de Nuca, accustomed as they were to the milder climate of Alta California and the abundance of arable land there, were disappointed that Yuquot could never serve as a farming mission from which to "preach to the Indians."

The scientist José Mariano Moziño noted the facility with which the native peoples grasped matters when they were explained. This led him to comment that "[we should be] very sorry that the ministers of the Gospel have not taken advantage of such a fine opportunity to plant the Catholic faith among them." He was aware that the "cross-bearers," or friars, had reported that a mission could not be established at Nootka because there was insufficient land for cultivation and for settling the natives around a mission station, as was done in Alta California. But he was not convinced:

> Could not a doctrine which was taught by fishermen in the first place be communicated to those who out of necessity, ignorance and a lack of resources follow this profession? What results might have been achieved in four years, had the Spanish not abandoned Nootka or been without a chaplain?[5]

Moziño was confident that "agriculture could have been promoted, not by trying to find actual farmland on the beach or land which would be fertile without any work, but by exploring the interior of the island [and] clearing a large part of it."[6]

From its beginning in 1789 until it was abandoned by the Spanish in 1795, Santa Cruz de Nuca was essentially a military outpost that was maintained in order to deny the area to other nations. It was administered and commanded by the navy and was maintained with considerable human effort and at great cost to the treasury.

Bodega spent the summer of 1792 at Nootka Sound waiting for the arrival of the British commissioner. But George Vancouver, the commander of the English mission, was spending the precious summer months exploring and did not reach Nootka until the end of August. While Bodega waited at Nootka, he questioned visiting fur traders about the events of 1789 at Nootka. He also directed the development of the Spanish establishment at Nootka and the new establishment at Neah Bay. He dispatched Caamaño's exploration for the passage of Admiral de Fonte and worked to establish good relations with both visiting ships and the Mowachaht chief Maquinna.

Bodega's Arrival at Nootka

After an uneventful voyage of sixty days, on the afternoon of April 29, 1792, flying his pennant from the mainmast of the *Santa Gertrudis*, Bodega arrived at Nootka. Francisco de Eliza's frigate *Concepción* was riding at anchor in the cove and rigged down. Bodega made no mention in his *Viaje* of any honours extended to him by the Spanish forces on his arrival; he did, however, record that no sooner had his ship anchored than he was welcomed by the Mowachaht chief Maquinna and by other chiefs of the sound. They joined him on a tour of the Spanish establishment, and Maquinna offered to hold a potlatch in his honour.

The rest of Bodega's fleet appeared over the next two weeks. The schooner *Activa*, under Salvador Menéndez, arrived on May 4, the twin schooners *Sutil* and *Mexicana*, commanded by Alcalá Galiano and Cayetano Valdés, on May 11, and the frigate *Aránzazu*, under Caamaño, on May 13.[7] The sight of so many ships crowded into the small cove was likely the inspiration for the "Vista de la Bahia de Nutka desde la playa del establicimiento," drawn by José Cardero, which Bodega included in the atlas folio volume attached to his *Viaje*.

In his *Viaje*, Bodega says he was pleased with the "disposition of our houses, offices and kitchen garden," and he praised Eliza and Pedro de Alberni for the "efficiency, work and activity" with which they had developed the establishment. Bodega found the *Concepción*'s crew and the soldiers "healthy and robust and extremely contented." This report was only half true. The two years that Eliza had spent at Nootka since re-establishing the post in April 1790 had been difficult. Two winters of cold and heavy rain had taken their toll. The second winter in particular had seen a good deal of sickness. In his *Diario*, Caamaño recorded that it had been especially cold and had snowed almost constantly:

> The commonest illnesses we have experienced during our stay, are catarrh, colds, rheumatic pains, flatulent colics, diarrhoea, dysentery, bloody flux, and scurvy which spread the most rapidly among the crews with the constant threat of fatal consequences. It would have been worse when we were there [in Nootka] had our surgeons not prevented [this fatal outcome] with tea made from the shoots of green pine ... they mixed with their antiscorbutics.

When he was briefed by Eliza and Alberni, Bodega learned that what Eliza described as the "unbearable climate" and the humidity of the region had caused nine deaths among the garrison and ships' crews and that he had been obliged to send thirty-two sickly men back to Monterey in the *Princesa*, under Caamaño.[8]

On his arrival, Bodega set about refurbishing and enlarging the Spanish settlement at Yuquot in order "to receive and entertain the English more fittingly." When he first saw it, the house Eliza had built for the commandant was in poor condition, having been built "in great haste and with green wood." Later that summer, Archibald Menzies, the botanist accompanying Vancouver, described the result of Bodega's renovations as a

> decent house two stories high, built of planks with a balcony in the front of the upper story after the manner of the Spanish houses. One end of the

> ground floor was occupied as a guard room and the other as a kitchen and servants' hall, while the upper story was divided into small apartments and occupied by the governor and his officers, who were separated by a large hall in the middle where they commonly dined.[9]

Accounts differ as to how many buildings Bodega erected at Yuquot that summer. Joseph Ingraham, the captain of the American fur trader *Hope*, stated that "the village consists of 16 houses."[10] John Boit, the fifth mate of Robert Gray's ship *Columbia Rediviva*, estimated that there were "about 200 Inhabitants, consisting of Spaniards and Peru Indians, but no females."[11]

For the new arrivals, the establishment seemed a beehive of activity. With a hint of skepticism, Menzies noted

> the well-stocked poultry yard and the goats, sheep and black cattle feeding around the so-called village. Blacksmiths were seen busily engaged in one place and carpenters in another so that the different occupations of building and repairing vessels and houses were at once going forward. In short, the Spaniards seem to go on here with greater activity and industry than we are led to believe of them at any of their other remote settlements.[12]

Only Bodega's *Santa Gertrudis* had arrived in good condition. The other Spanish ships needed repairs. The *Activa*'s topmost mast had sprung, and she was leaking so badly she had to be careened. The sturdy *Aránzazu*, the workhorse of many Alta California resupply missions, had suffered so much storm damage that she, too, had to be careened, and an entire month was required to complete her repairs. The voyage north had also been hard on Malaspina's twin schooners, in part owing to the hastiness and shoddiness of their construction. The *Mexicana* had lost her mainmast off Baja California. The *Sutil* had struck a rock while entering the sound. On top of all that, the work that had not been finished in Acapulco in the rush to sail on schedule had to be completed. As Bodega had strict orders to ensure that the explorations by Malaspina's men were not delayed, and because the results of their voyage were vital to his impending meeting with Vancouver, he ordered that work on the schooners be done first.

The *Sutil* and *Mexicana* were hauled into the small cove on the north side of the beach, which the Spanish called Caleta de Santa Cruz or Campo Santo.[13] Alcalá Galiano observed that although Bodega had orders to provide them with "any assistance which was required, the small resources at his disposal and his many preoccupations made him unable to refit the *goletas* with the speed we wished."[14] As a consequence, their "needs were drastically reduced." Bodega freely acknowledged in his *Viaje* that the required repairs were extensive; even so, he took the unusual step of writing Alcalá Galiano a formal letter, with a copy to the viceroy, asking him to confirm that, in spite of the urgent needs of his own ships, he had fulfilled his orders.[15] Graciously expressing his indebtedness to all concerned for what had been accomplished in a fortnight with such limited resources, Alcalá Galiano wrote that he was particularly grateful because the work had been carried out in constantly bad weather and endless rain. He had hoped it would be possible to make other repairs, but none of these were essential.[16] After he and Valdés departed on June 5, the same small workforce began repairs on the *Aránzazu* and *Activa.* These were the first of a series of careenings and repairs carried out on ships visiting Nootka during the five months of Bodega's stay. Sixteen fur-trading vessels of English, French, Portuguese, and American origin were also refitted.

Investigating the Events of 1789

Before Vancouver arrived at the end of August, Bodega interviewed three men who were eyewitnesses to the affair of 1789 and who by chance had returned to Nootka. He wanted to confirm the facts that Viceroy Revillagigedo wished to use to build the Spanish case against British pretensions. Bodega was gathering ammunition not only to refute Meares's memorial regarding the extent of his losses, but also to expose his trickery – that he had had the vessels of his English syndicate masquerade as Portuguese ships.

On June 11, Francisco José Viana, the Portuguese who was putative captain of John Meares's *Iphigenia Nubiana* in 1788-89 and who was now the nominal master of his *Feliz Aventureira,* returned to Nootka. Bodega seized the opportunity to investigate Viana's role in the 1789 affair. On June 18, in a blunt official letter to Viana, he demanded to be told the grounds on which Meares had based his complaints regarding Martínez's actions.[17] Viana's reply was brief and simple. He stuck to Meares's version of the events where his own interests were concerned: the *Iphigenia* was Portuguese, as were the forty sea otter furs and the fur traders on board. Martínez had treated them generously. But when it came to the house that Meares had built, Viana's loyalty to Meares evaporated. He told Bodega it was very small, that it had been built from a few boards got from the Indians, and that it had been pulled down as soon as they sailed away. Thus, when Martínez "entered this port of Nootka, there was not the least remains of a house &ca."[18]

On July 22 the American fur traders Robert Gray and Joseph Ingraham sailed into the harbour at Nootka. Gray was captain of the *Columbia Rediviva;* Ingraham had been the second mate of the *Columbia* in 1789 and was now in command of the *Hope.* Bodega was more courteous in his dealings with Gray and Ingraham than he had been with Viana. On August 2, he wrote:

> In order to address, as is just, the injuries, prejudices and usurpations the court of England believes it suffered in the year 1789 in this port, would you be kind enough to inform me with the sincerity you possess and corresponding to the honour of truth what caused Don Estéban Martínez to detain or seize the ships of Captain Colnett, the *Iphigenia* and the *N.W. America*? What establishment or house did Meares have when the Spanish arrived? What territories are those which he says he purchased from Maquinna, Yuquinanni[19] or any other chief of these villages? For what reason was the crew of the *Northwest* [*America*] transferred to the *Columbia* and 96 skins placed on board that ship? And, finally, what was the total number [of pelts] taken to China and to whom did they belong?[20]

Ingraham answered Bodega's letter because "as I knew every circumstance, Captain Gray desired I would answer and he would sign it jointly."

Ingraham began with the seizure of the *Iphigenia.* When Martínez arrived in Friendly Cove on May 5, 1789, he found the *Iphigenia* already there. Challenging her right to be in Spanish waters, he examined her papers. Ingraham's pro-Spanish, even anti-English bias now began to reveal itself. He referred to Viana as the "so-called commander" of the *Iphigenia.* He said that Viana had referred to the *Iphigenia* as a Portuguese ship in distress. According to Viana at that time, they expected Captain Meares to arrive soon with help. Satisfied, Martínez helped them with their repairs. Then on the morning of the May 11, Martínez seized the *Iphigenia,* saying that he had read in their Portuguese instructions that they had orders to capture any English, Spanish, or Russian subjects they met on the Northwest Coast. Ingraham explained that this reading was afterward found to have been a mistake, owing to a poor translation. However, after the vessel was taken, the officers and seamen were well treated.

While in Spanish hands, the *Iphigenia* was repaired and reprovisioned. Captain Douglas, whom Ingraham described as the real captain, paid Martínez for this work with bills on a Macao merchant's account. On May 31 the *Iphigenia* sailed away, free. When Martínez seized the *North West America* in 1789, he explained to Ingraham that there had been an agreement between Captain Douglas and himself that he should hold on to her as security for the bills of exchange drawn on the Portuguese merchant's credit, not because of any threat to Spanish sovereignty. When Meares's sloop *Princess Royal* arrived from Macao, commanded by Thomas Hudson, she was not detained and was allowed to sail out of port. When Ingraham turned to the question of Meares's house, he declared that there had been a rough hut in 1788, but that Captain Douglas had pulled it down before sailing that same year; so on Martínez's arrival, "there was no vestige of any house remaining." Neither had he heard of any land purchase by Meares during the nine months he had spent at Yuquot. "Captain Kendrick was the only man to whom they [the native people] had ever sold any land."[21] No tempers flared until Martínez had to deal with James Colnett of the *Argonaut.* According to Ingraham, after talking to Colnett.

> [Martínez] understood that Captain Meares, with some Englishmen at Macao, had agreed to erect a fort and settle a colony in Nootka Sound. Ingraham and Grey heard Captain Colnett inform the Spanish commodore he had come for that purpose, and to hoist the British flag, take formal possession, etc.; to which the commodore [Martínez] answered that he had taken possession already in the name of his Catholic majesty; on which Captain Colnett asked if he would be prevented from building a house in the port.
>
> The commodore, mistaking his meaning, answered him, he was at liberty to erect a tent, get wood and water, etc., after which he was at liberty to depart as he pleased; but Captain Colnett said that was not what he wanted, but to build a blockhouse, erect a fort, and settle a colony for the crown of Great Britain. Don Martínez answered no, it would be relinquishing the Spaniards' claim to the coast. Besides, Don Martínez observed, the ships did not belong to the British King, nor was he [Colnett] invested with proper powers to transact such public business. To that Captain Colnett answered that he was a King's officer, but Don Estevan [sic] replied, his being in the service was of no consequence in the business.
>
> In conversing on the subject after the arrival of the vessel in port, it seems that Captain Colnett insulted the commodore by threatening him and drawing his sword in the *Princesa*'s cabin; on which Don Martínez ordered the vessel to be seized. We did not see him draw his sword but were informed of the circumstances by those whose veracity we had no reason to doubt.
>
> After the seizure of the *Argonaut*, the sloop *Princess Royal* arrived a second time and as she belonged to the same company, the commodore took possession her also.

Gray and Ingraham were certain that the English prisoners were well treated. They concluded their account with a paragraph that revealed where their sympathies lay:

> We sincerely hope, sir, when things are represented with truth, it will rescue our friend Don Estevan J. Martínez from censure; at least that he may not be deemed an imposter and a pirate, which many, from only hearing part of the story, suppose he was. As to the treatment of the Americans by Don Estevan [sic], we have ever testified to it in terms due to such hospitality, and we are again happy to have it in our power to do what we deem justice to his conduct.

It is evident from his journal that Bodega was pleased to receive such a favourable account. He had found Ingraham "an active young man, very talented," who gave him "full information about his extensive explorations," confirming that he "possessed a great knowledge of the coast."[22]

The Arrival of the *Daedalus*

On July 4, while Bodega was conducting his investigations, Vancouver's 350-ton stores ship *Daedalus* arrived with supplies for Vancouver. Bodega had been waiting about ten weeks for Vancouver, and he was becoming increasingly concerned because the garrison and his three ships were consuming an enormous quantity of stores, more than the establishment's gardens and livestock could replace. Furthermore, the short season for exploration was approaching its end.

The *Daedalus* had left Portsmouth on August 18, 1791, under the command of Richard Hergest. After Hergest was killed on the Sandwich Islands (Hawaii), the ship's command was taken by Thomas New, described as "very clever" and "a jocose old gentleman."[23] New informed Bodega that Vancouver had left England in March 1791. New believed that Vancouver had wintered in the Sandwich Islands , but had sailed from there before the *Daedalus*'s arrival. New had been told to wait for Vancouver at Nootka until the end of the summer. This was the first firm news the Spanish had received about the movements of Vancouver's expedition. Bodega's aide-de-camp, Félix de Cepeda, recorded a tart opinion that he implies was shared by other Spaniards: that by not proceeding directly to Nootka, Vancouver "had made us wait and lose three or four months of the best season which we could have used for other purposes."[24]

New handed Bodega a note and a copy of a Spanish Royal Order. The first was an undated directive that Hergest had given New. It ordered him, in the event of Hergest's death, and if

> Captain Vancouver should not be anchored in Nootka or you do not encounter him before arriving there, you are to hand the letter [the Royal Order] to the [Spanish] commandant at Nootka, and request on behalf of His Britannic Majesty its restitution as provided in the orders which you must read and follow to the full extent of your ability.[25]

The Royal Order was signed by Minister of State Floridablanca and addressed to the "Governor or Commandant of the Port of San Lorenzo de Nootka," authorizing him to turn over the establishment to the English commissioner in accordance with the terms of the Nootka Convention.[26]

Bodega was caught by surprise, since the viceroy had not given him a copy of this crucial document. There had been no mention of it in his instructions, nor had it been discussed during their meetings in Mexico City. Perhaps it reached the capital after Bodega left for San Blas. Bodega interpreted the presentation of this order as New's request that the Spanish turn the establishment over to him. In a long and cordial letter to New, Bodega declined to do this, on the basis of the information he had gathered from Viana in June. He said that before he could comply with Floridablanca's Royal Order, he would have to learn what kind of buildings constituted Meares's establishment and where they were located, since nothing about them had come to his attention.[27] As these were "highly delicate" matters, and as there was insufficient information about them "in Europe" – that is, in both Spain and England – at the time of concluding the "preliminaries" (meaning the convention), he thought it best to "suspend" any discussion until the arrival of Captain Vancouver, who had been officially charged with the mission. On the other hand, should Vancouver be delayed, Bodega was to be prepared to

> demonstrate with unequivocal proofs our legitimate right to this port, that here the subjects of His Britannic Majesty had suffered no act of violence or hostility and that what had been reported up to now had been done frivolously. [Even so], I am prepared to cede to you [the British] our houses, gardens and offices and everything which has been developed in order to ratify the friendship and good harmony my Sovereign desires to maintain and carry out all the points of the Convention.[28]

New's reply was brief and to the point: "My ideas coincide with yours and I deem it best to await Vancouver's arrival."

For some reason, Bodega interpreted Vancouver's delay in reaching Nootka as an indication that Vancouver might not be aware of the second facet of his mission, which was to negotiate with him the northern limits of Alta California and all that entailed. Bodega also concluded that it was now too late to carry out his remaining instructions. On the same day that he replied to New, he wrote to both Floridablanca and Revillagigedo to alert them that he was contemplating adjusting his instructions to meet this unforeseen situation.[29] In an earlier letter dispatched the previous month, he had expressed his concern that the season was already far advanced, and should Vancouver be delayed, the exploration program would be affected, and the need to abandon the establishment would have to be considered because his stores were not sufficient to feed his personnel and to resupply all the ships in harbour.[30] In the second letter, Bodega wrote:

> It remains only for me to inform Your Excellency that the only way I see to fulfill the Royal Order (of December 25), not to waste the past expenditures which have been made, incur even greater ones, and observe the instructions which have been given me, is to leave the port open.

Knowing that Revillagigedo was already questioning the need for an unproductive and expensive establishment, Bodega added that he thought nothing would be lost by abandoning Nootka altogether:

> Even though the shelter it provides and its situation makes it valuable, we have others of equal quality and greater commerce if we were to think of establishing ourselves there at some time. But it will be very costly to the king and no advantages will ever be obtained by undertaking it.[31]

Raising the possibility of negotiating with New, he concluded:

> So as not to stir up old worries, I have resolved to turn over the establishment to New should Vancouver not come. Before doing so I would make him see our legitimate right, the frivolousness with which Meares represented his case and how important and necessary it is to conserve the most perfect friendship with Great Britain without prejudice to our sovereign and his interests.[32]

Bodega set about reducing the size of the Spanish establishment at Yuquot. The *Aránzazu* had already left with Caamaño to search for the imaginary passage of Admiral de Fonte. Eliza was ordered to depart with the *Concepción.* Torres was given command of the *Santa Gertrudis* to deliver Bodega's dispatches to Monterey for transmission to Mexico City. He was to take Alberni and a substantial number of the Catalonian Volunteers along with six of the eight cannon from the battery on the island at the entrance to the cove. Two were left for saluting. With the departure of the *Santa Gertrudis,* Bodega would transfer his pennant to the *Activa.*

Knowing from experience that Torres had a prickly personality, Bodega gave him instructions that were considerably more extensive than those he usually gave his associates.[33] On the way to San Blas, Torres was to stop at Neah Bay at the mouth of the Strait of Juan de Fuca, where he would find a frigate, the *Princesa,* supporting the expedition of the *Sutil* and the *Mexicana.*[34] While at Neah Bay, he was to examine carefully the land, the harbour, the edible foods, and the availability of sea otter skins for trade and of wood for construction; he was also to observe the character of the natives and their numbers, customs, and alliances. Torres was to use this information to help Fidalgo and the other Spanish officers ascertain Neah Bay's suitability as an alternative to Nootka. After completing his duties at Neah Bay, he was to explore the coast from the mouth of the Strait of Juan de Fuca south to Cape Mendocino "with such exactness that no river or inlet will be left uninvestigated." To assist him in making charts, Bodega assigned two people – Cepeda and Cañizares – both of whom he described as "persons of education, talent and good will."[35]

Torres left Nootka on July 19, followed five days later by Eliza in the *Concepción.* The departure of these two large ships meant that, of the imposing fleet assembled for the Expedition of the Limits, Bodega had only the *Activa* with him to await Vancouver.

Salvador Fidalgo and the Establishment at Neah Bay

The village of Neah Bay lies on the south coast of the Strait of Juan de Fuca near the western end of the Olympic Peninsula. The fur traders Charles Barkley in the *Imperial Eagle* in July 1787, John Meares in the *Feliz Aventureira* in June 1788, Charles Duncan in the *Princess Royal* in August of the same year, and Robert Gray in the *Lady Washington* in April 1789 were among its first non-native visitors. The first Spanish visitor was José María Narváez in July 1789 in the *Santa Gertrudis la Magna.*[36]

The Makah were the native inhabitants who met these early European visitors. In the 1780s the Makah numbered perhaps around two thousand. Early visitors, such as Alcalá Galiano, noted that their language and culture were similar to those of the Nootka of Vancouver Island. Like the Nootka, the Makah were whale hunters. They were also bellicose, constantly raiding their neighbours both for slaves and to protect their role as middlemen in the indigenous coastal trade between the Columbia River and Nootka Sound.

In 1790, as part of his exploration of the area, Manuel Quimper had entered Neah Bay and found a safe anchorage in the lee of Waddah Island, which protected the village from the strait. Active trading began with native men and women. The Makah bartered "bear skins, exquisite fish, among which were salmon weighing over one hundred pounds, and fruits," as well as sixteen sea otter skins for some of the "king's copper." When half the ship's crew were ashore washing their clothes, they were attacked by Indians. One soldier had strayed into the woods in search of berries; he was surrounded by a group of natives, disarmed, wounded by several blows to his head with his own sword, and struck by an arrow in the face before he was able to flee. Other natives attempted to make off with two canoes tied to the ship, but fire from a swivel gun drove them off. When their chief, Tutusi, learned of this attempt on the life of the soldier, he sent a messenger to say that the man who had wounded him had been punished.[37] Quimper concluded that "all these natives are warlike, intrepid, thievish and treacherous."

Notwithstanding the skirmish with the Indians, Quimper was sanguine about the site in his reports. Although the winds were tricky and the currents ran with great strength, the broad bay was sheltered on all sides except on the northwest. The bay abounded in fish, the land seemed fertile, and there were deer, rabbits, foxes, and dogs. As the area was especially rich in sea otter, the Spanish obtained a large number of pelts, and trading continued throughout the visit.

Revillagigedo always studied the journals of his maritime explorers thoroughly. Quimper's detailed report must have been of particular interest not only for its revelation about how far inland the strait extended, but also for its description of Neah Bay's potential as an alternative establishment should Nootka have to be given up. Quimper believed that Neah Bay was the only adequate harbour on either side of the strait. It was on the outer coast but free of strong tidal currents; also, the strait at that point was narrow enough to allow any ships stationed there to intercept foreign ships coming through the passage. The location would serve admirably as a visible symbol of Spanish sovereignty to seaborne passersby.

In a letter to Floridablanca in March 1791, Revillagigedo proposed "removing our present presidio [sic] at Nuca to one of the best ports in the Strait of Juan de Fuca on its north [sic] shore."[38] Six months later, not having received a reply, he repeated the proposal. This time, having thought about it for some time, he included many details on how he conceived the new settlement.[39]

In October, still without a substantial reply from Floridablanca, Revillagigedo decided to wait no longer. On his own authority, he issued the following instructions to Bodega with regard to Neah Bay:

> There is no doubt that we can keep our present establishment of Nootka without hindrance or interference from anything the English might also erect and build on the opposite northern shore. But considering the just reason for removing any obstacle which would cause discord, disagreement or trouble, the best course seems to me that you abandon Nootka and remove the settlement to the north [sic] shore of the Strait of Juan de Fuca. In this way the complete transfer to the English of the lands they claim to have acquired and purchased from Port Cox or Cayuclat [sic] to Nootka and from which it is supposed they were dispossessed by the Spanish will be accomplished.

Following Bodega's recommendation of November 2, 1791, the viceroy ordered Salvador Fidalgo to make ready the 189-ton frigate *Princesa* to establish a provisional post at Neah Bay. Provisioned for fifteen months, Fidalgo took with him eighty-nine men, including thirteen soldiers. His second-in-command was acting *primer piloto* Antonio Serantes, who had served with him in the *San Carlos* on his expedition north in 1790. Fidalgo was provided with maps, course directions, and the information about the strait known at the time.

Bodega gave Fidalgo his instructions on the eve of his departure from San Blas on February 29, 1792. He was to proceed directly to Neah Bay and erect a small battery. From this base, he was to make a careful survey of all the bays in the strait where a settlement might be located. Once the best site had been found, he was to select a sheltered spot, one that had a smooth bottom for safe anchorage, space for growing crops, and sufficient water and wood. Formal possession was to be taken in accordance with the prescribed formalities. He was to fortify the site and erect temporary structures to house the sick and to store supplies and ammunition. Bodega cautioned Fidalgo that there was to be no repetition of Martínez's imprudent conduct in 1789. Any trader venturing into the strait should be asked "with all due courtesy" not to trade south of the settlement. Fidalgo was particularly enjoined "to show every mark of kindness" to the Indians "even when their ignorance makes them commit some offence." With the experience of the Franciscans at the California missions in mind, Bodega suggested that, if treated well, the natives would have no reason to attack the settlement and might even be willing to share in the cultivation of the land.[40]

Sending Revillagigedo a copy of these instructions, Bodega informed him that inasmuch as "nothing in his instructions opposed the setting up of the establishment of Fuca" and being "certain of its importance and usefulness," he had decided not "to delay one moment the prompt occupation of the Strait." Should it be shown that the base would not be needed, it could be abandoned when he returned from Nootka.[41]

Although Bodega had been respectful of his superior's position and authority in the past, the assertive wording of Bodega's plans brought an immediate sharp reaction. Without clear authority from Spain, Revillagigedo was obviously having second thoughts about even a temporary settlement. As one who kept his political ear close to the ground, perhaps he had also decided that discretion was advisable because of the new administration in Spain.[42] The viceroy could not halt the machinery he had set in motion, but he could advise great restraint. In a pithy letter to Bodega written after Bodega had left San Blas for Nootka, the viceroy "requested strict fulfillment and immediate observance" of his instructions. No settlement, he added with emphasis, should be established "except in case of grave necessity or a very obvious advantage obliges you to undertake it."[43] Thus began an unfortunate disagreement that did not end until after the Spanish had abandoned Neah Bay.

Bodega could not have received the March letter until June; he was already halfway to Nootka while it was being written. To underscore his concern, Revillagigedo also wrote to Fidalgo. He was to "occupy the Strait as ordered and not attempt to establish yourself formally, but to survey the entrance [to the strait], select a good shelter and there await" Bodega's arrival from Nootka. It is not known whether Fidalgo received this letter. We do know that by the time Bodega received his admonition, Fidalgo had already begun construction of the new fort. He never ventured out to find another possible site, and the Neah Bay settlement was more than "provisional."

Bodega stuck to his position when he replied from Nootka to Revillagigedo's letter. He confirmed that he had always understood that the settlement in the strait should not be established without very good reason. He reminded the viceroy that he himself had instructed Fidalgo to go directly to Neah Bay.[44] Since he was mindful of the link the viceroy had made between giving up Nootka and establishing a post at Neah Bay, and since he was expecting Vancouver to reach Nootka at any moment, action had to be taken quickly. Neah Bay was the only harbour in the area of which the Spanish had any practical knowledge. Bodega thought it would be best, before searching elsewhere, to find out whether Neah Bay was suitable for settlement. It was for this reason, he informed the viceroy, that he had asked Alcalá Galiano and Valdés to stop at Neah Bay and to report to him about its advantages, or shortcomings, as a site for a permanent establishment.

Fidalgo had been unable to get away from San Blas until March 24. After an uneventful voyage of sixty-seven days, he dropped anchor in Neah Bay on the morning of May 29, as close inshore as the shallow bay permitted. He selected a spot close to the beach in the southwest corner where the stream noted by Quimper flowed into the bay. He set his people to work clearing a circular field with a radius of one musket shot. Logs were used to build a barracks for his men, a blacksmith's shop, a bakery, an oven, and a kiln. The roofs were made from grass. A palisade was erected and four cannon mounted for defence. Corrals were built for the cows, sheep, hogs, and goats brought from San Blas, and a vegetable garden was begun with seedlings transported in containers ready for planting.[45] As the *Princesa* had to anchor some distance from the shore, a longboat was kept on the beach for emergency purposes. Fidalgo issued strict orders that no one was to go any distance beyond the enclosure and that a cannon shot was to be fired every evening at sunset as a signal to the natives not to approach the settlement or the ship until dawn.

No plan of Fidalgo's little post has ever been found. Visitors' accounts do not agree on how many buildings it had or how they were disposed. In September 1792, just before Fidalgo's departure, Ingraham visited Neah Bay and recorded that "the settlement consisted only of a few huts and a tolerably good garden."[46] Boit, on the *Columbia*, recorded that "the Spaniards had erected a Cross upon the beach, and had about 10 Houses and several good gardens."[47] On June 6 the infant settlement received a two-day visit from Alcalá Galiano and Cayetano Valdés. Alcalá Galiano recorded that although Fidalgo had been at Neah Bay for "one month" and had achieved much to "prepare for wintering if the establishment was decided on," he was still awaiting "orders from Commandant Quadra, either for the formation of an establishment, or the abandonment of the harbour." Alcalá Galiano also found the natives "most friendly, [having been] honoured by Fidalgo," but added that Fidalgo did "not place much faith in them."

On July 2, Fidalgo received his second visitor, the English fur trader Henry Shepherd, out of Bengal en route to Nootka in the brigantine *Venus*. Seeing her entering the bay and believing her to be the *Activa* bringing instructions,

Fidalgo went out to the vessel. Returning to his own ship after the *Venus* had anchored, Fidalgo learned that Serantes had gone ashore and not returned. He immediately went ashore, where he learned that Serantes had left with his musket and an Indian to go hunting. Fearing the worst, the next day Fidalgo sent out a party of twenty armed men with dogs to search the thick woods. When they returned empty-handed, he sent them out again. Back on board, he learned that an Indian had come to say that Tutusi's people had killed a Spanish sailor. Taking no chances, Fidalgo kept his men under arms "awaiting the moment [Tutusi] attacks me on shore with his people." He could do nothing more; the shallowness of the bay made it impossible for him to bring his ship within gunshot range of the beach. "The barrack house," Fidalgo reported to Bodega in a letter delivered by Shepherd,

> is well fortified, well provided with men, cannon, flintlocks, and ammunition, and in an advantageous position, connected with the sea by a river which passes through [the settlement]. A boat is kept there permanently so that if not able to resist an attack, we could board it while firing, leaving the land and abandoning everything.[48]

Eventually, Serantes's decomposed body was found and was buried within the compound. Back on board ship, in a blind rage over Serrantes's murder, and seeing two canoes full of natives approaching, Fidalgo assumed he was being attacked. He ordered the gunners to open fire, which they did with deadly accuracy. All except two were killed. He told Bodega that he had been "forced to fire on the two canoes, of whose occupants I hold a boy of about fifteen and a girl of six, the others having been victims of Serantes's transgression."

The news travelled quickly to Nootka. Understanding the seriousness of the situation, Bodega quickly wrote a letter to Fidalgo to calm him down. First, expressing his sorrow at Serantes's death and his concern for Fidalgo's own plight, he pointedly wrote that he was anxious to avoid Tutusi's death and the shedding of any blood for a deed whose cause was not known. "It does not seem right to me," he continued, "that you should have taken vengeance on persons who might have been quite innocent and when the assassin is not known." He bluntly told Fidalgo to protect only himself and to follow his official instructions to maintain good relations with the Indians.[49] The matter did not end there for Fidalgo. Bodega sent copies of Fidalgo's letter and of his answer to the viceroy, who in his reply commended Bodega for the "prudent counsel the situation demanded" and approved the manner in which he had proceeded.[50] Revillagigedo, in turn, informed the new minister of state, Manuel Godoy, Duque de la Alcudia, who responded that Fidalgo's "severity was all out of proportion," that it "could turn the natives against the Spanish," and that the king had "found it just that the Commandant [of the Limits Expedition] condemn the Captain's severe act."[51]

Bodega had ordered Torres in the *Santa Gertrudis* to stop at Neah Bay and preside over a *junta* with all the officers to assess its suitability for a permanent settlement. Their opinion, and the report expected from Alcalá Galiano and Valdés, would help decide the future of the post when Bodega met Vancouver. As the senior officer, Torres presided. Fidalgo spoke first. He pointed out the advantages of the harbour, the bay, and the land, and he added that the site fulfilled the requirements regarding water, wood, and good soil. Furthermore, the bay was well located for keeping track of traffic entering and leaving the strait. Neah Bay had some drawbacks, however; the rocky bottom made it impossible for ships to anchor closer than "one cannon shot" from the settlement, nor could any ship remain there during the winter months because there was no shelter from the northeast and northwest winds. Torres agreed, also noting the disadvantages Fidalgo had pointed out. The only one who commented on the natives, he wrote that "heathen populations are difficult to civilize and [the settlement] could never be without the presence of a ship that would command respect." He concluded by saying that a decision to develop a more permanent settlement would have to be made by civil authorities. Cepeda also stressed the disadvantages, yet he suggested that a longer stay might lead to a more definite opinion. Meanwhile, he was prepared to accept Fidalgo's judgment that the site would have to be abandoned in the winter months. The two junior officers of the *Santa Gertrudis* were circumspect in offering their opinions, partly because they were seeing Neah Bay for the first time and partly out of deference to their seniors. The *junta*'s report was forwarded to the viceroy without any recommendation. In their later opinions, Alcalá Galiano and Valdés were brief and to the point: a permanent settlement would bring no advantages, only more expense and responsibilities.[52]

By the end of that summer, just as Bodega was realizing that Nootka would remain Spanish for the foreseeable future, it had become clear to him that Neah Bay could no longer serve any real purpose. Via Ingraham, he sent word to Fidalgo to dismantle everything and to prepare himself to take over command at Nootka from Caamaño, who would be left in charge there temporarily. Bodega arrived at Neah Bay on September 26; Fidalgo left the same day for Nootka. Four months to the day after his arrival,

Fidalgo took with him everything, including animals, stores, feed, and crops, that could be removed in the very short time he had been given. He reached Nootka three days later.

In his difference with Bodega over Neah Bay, Revillagigedo had the last word. Unaware of Bodega's decision to abandon Neah Bay, in reply to Bodega's June letter as late as November 12, he repeated once again that no formal establishment was to be created.[53] The viceroy forwarded the negative report of the *junta* to Madrid and was told in reply to await the government's "final decision" before issuing any further instructions. By this time, however, the site had been abandoned, and Bodega was sailing for Monterey on his way home to San Blas.

It seems that no final decision was ever made regarding whether Neah Bay should be retained or abandoned. Instead, its effective end was marked by Fidalgo's departure and by the removal to Nootka of all personnel, animals, cannon, and ammunition.[54] After the brief flurry of Spanish activity, the site reverted to the Makah Indians, who occupy it to this day.

Caamaño's Search for the Passage of Admiral de Fonte

In his plans for the Expedition of the Limits, Revillagigedo viewed as essential the need to confirm or disprove the existence of the Passage of Admiral de Fonte – as essential, in fact, as the exploration of Haro Strait. Revillagigedo had a compelling reason to seek verification of the Fonte account. In 1787, as a mark of appreciation for the assistance given to repair his ship, the *Argonaut*, at San Blas, James Colnett had allowed Eliza to copy his chart of his exploration of the region. From the chart, the viceroy gained the impression that Colnett had perhaps found Fonte's passage. Colnett made no such claim, but Revillagigedo's study of the chart made him realize that the coast between Nootka and 55°N, the latitude of Bucareli Bay, had yet to be carefully examined. The mysterious passage was believed to lie at latitude 53°N.

In fact, the passage was a hoax that had been launched in 1708 in an obscure and short-lived London publication, the *Monthly Miscellany or Memoirs for the Curious*. An anonymous letter, believed to have been written by the editor, James Petiver, stated that in 1639 the Spanish authorities had commanded Bartholemew de Fonte, an "Admiral of New Spain and Perú and Prince of Chile," to "find out if there was any North West Passage from the Atlantick Ocean into the South Tartinian Sea." Ostensibly, Fonte had sailed with four ships in April 1640 from Callao, the port of Lima, and at latitude 53°N (roughly the southern portion of the Alaska Panhandle) reached a river he called Río de los Reyes in an archipelago he named San Lazaro. One of his ships, under a Captain Bernardo, was ordered to follow a river that flowed in an east-northeast direction. Fonte himself followed the Río de los Reyes, farther to the east. He reached a lake he called Belle and then, by way of other rivers and lakes, reached close to Hudson Bay. There he met a Captain Shapley from Boston and, after an exchange of courtesies, purchased from him with his diamond ring, "1000 Pieces of Eight," and Shapely's "fine Charts and Journals." The Admiral concluded that because he had met a maritime traveller from Boston coming the other way, there was obviously a passage across the continent. He then returned to Peru by the same route as he had come.

In 1744, the influential Arthur Dobbs, a severe critic of the Hudson's Bay Company for its diffident efforts at exploration, revived the tale as part of his campaign to promote British interests in the search for the Northwest Passage. Dobbs's book brought the story to the attention of two of France's most highly respected geographers, Guillaume Delisle and Philippe Buache. Their writings and maps lent the Fonte story a strong measure of credibility, and their reputations served to arouse the interest of other, equally respected geographers.[55]

The Spanish Jesuit Padre Andrés Marcos Burriel, director of the Spanish royal archives and libraries, conducted a search of the archives in Madrid, Seville, and Cádiz but found nothing about Fonte or his voyage. In his publication in 1757 of the important Venegas manuscript, *Noticia de la California,* he made a detailed critique of the letter, demonstrating its absurdities and concluding that the whole episode was false. However, the publication of the *Noticia* in French, German, Dutch, and English did not include the all-important appendix on the subject of Fonte. Given the great secrecy with which the Spanish government cloaked its geographical discoveries and overseas ventures, the apparent absence of any contribution by a Spanish scholar to the extensive international debate was seen as proof of the authenticity of Petiver's letter. So stood matters in subsequent decades, certainly into the 1790s.

Bodega assigned Caamaño to search for the passage in the *Aránzazu.* Although the veteran of many resupply missions, the *Aránzazu,* a 205-ton frigate, was unsuitable for coastal exploration. Drawing fourteen and a half feet – a substantial depth of keel – she was described unflatteringly by Cepeda as "a defective vessel in every respect, too large for the task, and possessing no good qualities. In short, she is a monstrous cargo ship."[56] En route to Nootka, the *Aránzazu* suffered such extensive storm damage that she had to be careened for a month. The delay meant the loss of precious summer weather.

Caamaño received his instructions from Bodega at Nootka on June 5, immediately after the departure of the *Sutil* and the *Mexicana*.[57] He was to sail directly to Bucareli Bay, explore its various arms, and then examine the coast between it and Nootka, making every effort to discover and chart the principal channels, gulfs, and harbours. He was specifically instructed to determine the actual position of the Estrecho del Almirante Fonte, although, as Caamaño observed in his *diario*, it "is considered by recent opinion as doubtful, or even imaginary."[58] Caamaño was assigned the *primer piloto* Juan Pantoja, who had accompanied Francisco Mourelle on his 1779 survey of Bucareli Bay. He was also given *segundo piloto* Juan Martínez y Zayas; Josef María Maldonado, José Moziño's naturalist; a chaplain; a blood-letter [surgeon]; thirteen soldiers from the Catalonian Volunteers; and stores for two months.[59]

Departing Nootka on June 13, Caamaño arrived in Bucareli Bay eleven days later and anchored near the entrance of Port San Antonio on Baker Island. Two survey parties were sent out immediately: the pinnace commanded by Pantoja, and the cutter under Zayas. Pantoja accomplished his task in eleven days, compared to Mourelle's twenty-six. One suspects that he took some shortcuts or, with the exception of one or two points, was prepared to accept Mourelle's earlier determinations. Nevertheless, some corrections were made to the latter's chart.[60]

Satisfied that Fonte's passage could not be reached through Bucareli Bay, Caamaño sailed down the west coast of Dall Island to Cape Muzon at its southern tip. From there, he crossed the Dixon Entrance to the Queen Charlotte Islands, anchoring between Langara Island and Graham Island. He found nothing to fit the description in the Fonte letter. Even so, he charted the passage between the two islands and carried out the possession ceremony. He then sailed back across Dixon Entrance to Cape Muzon and found, to the northeast, a "large bay as capacious as that of Bucareli." Pressed for time, he could not explore Cordova Bay. Instead, he crossed its entrance to the southeasternmost point of Prince of Wales Island. There he sighted the broad expanse of Clarence Strait, running north and south. He sailed into it until fog set in, followed by rain, squalls, and contrary winds that forced him to retreat to the Queen Charlottes, where his earlier examination of the waters off the north shore of Graham Island had been hampered by fog.

Still finding nothing, he crossed Hecate Strait, sailing southeast in search of the narrow Principe Channel between Banks and Pitt Islands, which Colnett's chart suggested would lead into the Estrecho de Fonte. Caamaño entered that channel, even though its narrowness was risky for a ship as broad as the *Aránzazu.* Still following Colnett's chart, he entered Nepean Sound; having done so, he sighted the wide entrance to Douglas Channel. Feeling "confident that we would soon sight the Estrecho de Fonte," he then entered a large harbour near the southern tip of Pitt Island, which he charted. For the second time, he formally took possession of the region.[61]

Again taking Colnett's chart as his guide, Caamaño sent Zayas in the longboat to explore Douglas Channel. Refusing to be deterred by Indians' tales of "huge sea animals that thrust their whole bodies out of the water, attack and overturn the natives' canoes and devour their victims," Zayas proceeded with his task. He reported to Caamaño that, having penetrated up the northeast arm of Douglas Channel for eighteen leagues,[62] and having observed the tidal action in it, he certain that the channel was a dead end of "little importance."

If, as seems to be the case, Caamaño assumed that Colnett's chart was credible, it should have struck him that Douglas Channel might be the river up which Fonte had sent Captain Bernardo, since it ran in the same direction: east-northeast. But Zayas's report of the channel's sluggish tide did not correspond with the description in the Fonte account, nor did he encounter the reported tides of twenty-two and twenty-four feet. Caamaño wrote that the report from Zayas "led me to deprive this region of its name of the Estrecho de Fonte and replace it by that of Bocas y Brazos de Moñino."[63]

It was now late in the season. Frequent rains, squally weather, and intermittent fogs were impeding the survey work and making navigation in these unfamiliar waters dangerous. Although he understood from the Indians that there was a passage that would take him back to the Queen Charlottes, Caamaño doggedly searched the area for some other passage that might be Fonte's. His investigations eventually led him into the open waters of Hecate Strait, and he arrived back in Nootka Sound on September 7 after an absence of eighty-six days.[64]

The results of his exploration were definitive. None of the passages Caamaño encountered bore any resemblance to any waterway on Fonte's supposed route: not the broad Entrada de Juan Pérez, now called Dixon Entrance at 53°N; not Clarence Strait; and not Hecate Strait between the Queen Charlottes and the mainland. He did not encounter any of the giant cataracts, rivers, or lakes flowing into Hudson Bay, nor did he find highly civilized Indians inhabiting large cities. A glance at a contemporary map today shows that Caamaño missed no other opening that could have been Fonte's Passage.

Caamaño had, however, settled the controversy over Admiral Fonte. And in his *diario* he had recorded a great deal of information on the Tlingit, Tsimshian, and Haida he encountered. The ethnographic information was probably gathered by Maldonado, his naturalist, although Caamaño gave him no credit for it. Maldonado also compiled a detailed list of land and water animals, birds, fish, plants, and fruit. Included in Caamaño's *diario* are descriptions of the region's geography, its trees and vegetation, its climate, and its dearth of arable land. Caamaño was much more interested in the cartographic information he had collected. He concluded correctly, first, that the coast from Bucareli Bay to Nootka was all one archipelago formed of a vast number of large and small islands; and, second, that the mainland lay much farther to the east than had been thought.

Caamaño appended to his *diario* a lengthy discourse titled "Opinion concerning the Estrecho del Almirante Fonte," in which he stated firmly that no such passage existed, at least not in the waters around 53°N, where it was supposed to be. He believed that Fonte's

> expedition said to have sailed from Callao on April 3, 1640 ... never took place. For, to me, it seems to have no foundation other than the ravings and ignorance of someone who, devoid of all knowledge of either navigation or geography, who, wishing to stimulate the search for a N[orth] E[ast] passage leading to the North Atlantic Ocean, invented (so I venture to suggest) this story of channels, great rivers, cataracts twenty feet high over which he ascended with his ship, fertile islands, large towns inhabited by very civilized people, and a passage extending even so far as 80° of north latitude wherein he met a vessel from Boston, and other absurdities.[65]

He concluded that "should the idea of a passage to the North [Atlantic] not prove, as I fear [that it is], an illusion, then there can be no hope of finding it in the archipelago between the parallels of 51° and 54°46′ of latitude."

On his general map, Caamaño restored the name Entrada de Juan Pérez to the Dixon Entrance, replacing that of the Estrecho del Almirante Fonte, which had appeared on some Spanish maps, including Bodega's general chart of 1791. But then, curiously, he gave Fonte's name to Hecate Strait, not because he thought it might be the route Fonte had taken but because of the "veneration with which I regard the fame of early Spanish explorers." For this, he was roundly chastised by Cepeda in his *Memoria* for "preserving the imaginary memory of this admiral ... His name should be removed [from all charts]. Any idea that can lead to error or cause the least confusion should be committed to oblivion."[66] Unlike Cepeda, Bodega accepted Caamaño's appellation and used it on his fourth general chart of 1792, which he included in the folio volume of his *Viaje*.[67] Bodega praised Caamaño for his work: "His reconnaissance warranted the greatest appreciation from me and from Vancouver as well, to whom I gave a set [of charts] in return for what he gave me."

In the account of his own voyage, Vancouver mentions that before Caamaño left Nootka to return to San Blas, they dined together on board the *Discovery*. We may be certain they went over the charts together very carefully. Exploring some of the same waters the following year, Vancouver made some minor corrections, which he was able to do with his better instruments, but he retained or modified most of Caamaño's place names – a fact that undoubtedly explains why so many still appear on contemporary charts today.

Bodega repeated his appreciation of Caamaño's efforts when forwarding the documents to Revillagigedo, but the viceroy acknowledged their receipt without comment.[68] At a later time, he remarked that Caamaño's journal "adds nothing of particular importance to the explorations carried out in 1779; and, although certain points are corrected on his chart, he does not satisfy [me] whether or not there is a passage between the Pacific and the Atlantic."[69] This was a strange comment from one who took more than normal interest in the journals of his maritime explorers. Perhaps he had not read Camaaño's discourse, or perhaps he was not convinced by it.

Although pleased with what Caamaño had accomplished, Bodega was well aware that much of the coastal archipelago remained to be examined. In his *Viaje*, he wrote:

> Even apart from other considerations, it is necessary to undertake an expedition with the frigate *Concepción*, the schooner *Activa* and the sloop *Orcacitas*, which, from different points, should survey the continent from 50° to 60°.[70] Its direction is unknown and it is probable that all the land discovered, that up to now has been considered to be firm coast, may be an archipelago.

One could conclude from this that Bodega still suspected that Fonte's passage might not be a complete fabrication. What would be the purpose of such a major expedition except to make certain that the Estrecho del Almirante Fonte, or some other passage, did not lie somewhere beyond that mass of islands or elsewhere on that partially charted coast? Further exploration would indeed be carried out, but after Caamaño's report, no one volunteered to prove that the Estrecho del Almirante Fonte existed. Caamaño had put to rest the myth of Admiral Fonte's passage, thus effectively ending the need for any further Spanish exploration north of the Strait of Juan de Fuca.

The Genial Host

The viceroy's instructions for Bodega had included a general statement about his approach to the British envoy during the negotiations at Nootka: "It is not necessary for me to suggest to you [the importance] of seeking complete harmony and the most cordial relationship with the commander, officers and crews of the ships of His Britannic Majesty, [and] to be open and decorous in your dealings with each other."[71] Bodega had been assigned a new role, that of a diplomat. Before leaving Mexico City for San Blas, Bodega had ordered delicacies suitable for entertaining guests, such as "barrels of brandy, table wines, cases of bottled vintage wines, wine skins of cider, and beer; Flemish [fine] lard and hams; pickled greens, vegetables in oil, jars of oil, Castillian vinegar and olives; parboiled fowl and marinated meats; flours, cookies, chocolate, coffee, sugar, and sweetmeats."[72] Further purchases of cattle, hens, potages, cheese, preserves, dried fruit, and other items were made in Tepic and Ahucatlán.

All the purchases were made for the "greater honour of the nation extended to the foreigners who touched at our establishments" – that is, not just Vancouver and his people but others encountered at Nootka, San Francisco, and Monterey.[73] Well before Vancouver arrived at Nootka on August 27, Bodega had entertained the officers of the 600-ton French merchant ship *La Flavie*.[74] He had also wined and dined the starving officers of the "Portuguese" ship *Felíz Aventureira*, which had arrived from the north after exhausting her provisions.[75] Ingraham recorded that on August 1, the day of his arrival at Nootka, Bodega "gave us an excellent dinner, and as usual with the Spaniards of any rank, everything was served on silver ... The commodore gave me a general invitation to dine with him during our stay. This he did to all masters and supercargoes of vessels that arrived in the port."[76] Around the same time, Robert Gray put into Nootka to repair some damage to the *Columbia*, and he, too, was entertained by Bodega at dinner in the commandant's house. John Boit described with astonishment what was possibly the same occasion. Bodega, he wrote,

> gave a grand entertainment at his house, at which all the Officers of the Fleet partook. Fifty-four persons sat down to Dinner, and the plates, which was

> [sic] *solid silver*, was [sic] shifted five times, which made 270 plates. The Dishes, Knives and forks, and indeed everything else, was of Silver and always replaced with spare ones. There could be no mistake in this as they never carried the dirty plates or Dishes from the Hall where we dined, as *I thought*, on purpose to let us see the quantity of plate used by Spaniards in South America.[77]

All visitors remarked on both the variety of dishes offered and the number of courses served, but it was his personal silver plate that Bodega had brought with him that most impressed visitors. Boit's comment about the use of silver was not very far from the truth. Then, as now in Peru, silver was commonly used by well-to-do families for all manner of domestic objects, including table service. It was not only elegant but more durable and, in Peru, less expensive than imported porcelain.

Bodega's hospitality did not falter with Captain George Vancouver's arrival. On his second evening at Nootka, Edward Bell, clerk on Vancouver's *Chatham,* described the "grand dinner Seigr. [Señor] Quadra gave at his house on shore to the two Commanders [Vancouver and Broughton] ... in a style but little expected in such a place as Nootka."[78] Vancouver, for his part, commented:

> As many officers as could be spared from the vessels with myself dined with Senr. Quadra, and were gratified with a repast we had lately been little accustomed to, or had the most distant idea of meeting with at this place ... A dinner of five courses, consisting of a superfluity of his best provisions, was served with great elegance.[79]

At a later time, Salvador Menéndez, who served as both *primer piloto* and purser of the *Activa*, recalled that Bodega

> maintained at Nutca a splendid open house of twenty-four places daily, and the same number in Monterey for all of Captain Vancouver's officers and supplied his crews for a month and a half [with] fresh meat, milk and vegetables. On his return [south at Monterey] he offered them a most abundant supply of food without permitting their repayment ... He made himself loved by all the foreigners and natives of the country in such terms that they did not know how to express their gratitude for such generous conduct and kind treatment.[80]

Bodega not only entertained lavishly at dinner but also supplied visiting ships with fresh produce while they were in port. Every day, each ship in port was sent hot rolls from the oven, vegetables from the gardens, and fresh milk from the goats and cows. Bell recounts that on the evening of Vancouver's arrival, Bodega "sent a couple of fine sheep with a large stock of Cabbages &c., on board each of the vessels and also a cask of Rum to the Ship's Company."[81] He also provided fresh food for ships leaving Nootka. The exhausted stores of the allegedly Portuguese *Féliz Aventureira* were replaced with foodstuffs from the establishment's warehouse and fresh produce from the Nootka gardens. When Ingraham informed Bodega that he would be leaving for the Strait of Juan de Fuca with dispatches for Fidalgo at Neah Bay, he was sent "forty fresh salmon, some fresh pork, eggs, butter, fifty loaves of new bread, some wine, brandy, and a great supply of cabbages, salad, etc." To which Ingraham added: "Considering the part of the world we were in, I thought this a very handsome present. Not a day passed during our stay in this port, but every ship – without respect to nation or person – received marks of Don Juan's hospitality."[82]

Bodega also provided a building in the establishment as a guest house. One guest was the stranded English fur trader Matthew Weatherhead. Bodega supplied Captain Robert Gray with a small house near his own to "lodge in."[83] The disreputable Captain James Magee, claiming to be too ill to cruise with his Boston ship, the *Margaret*, moved in when Captain Gray left and proceeded to abuse Bodega's hospitality by indulging in the profitable business of selling diluted New England rum at greatly inflated prices to thirsty sailors, Spanish and otherwise. According to Edward Bell, Magee

> was generously charging only four Dollars a gallon [that] cost him most probably about 2 shillings or half a crown per gallon ... The ill effects of this shameful trade was soon too great to pass without [Vancouver] taking notice of it, and endeavouring to put a stop to it. Our seamen were continually drunk which from the badness of the liquor threw them into fits of sickness; and Captain Vancouver was at last oblig'd to take measures that prevented any further trade of that nature with our people.[84]

Bodega's hospitality extended to less glamorous but nonetheless practical matters. When the French trader *La Flavie* arrived at Nootka in July, her captain, known only as Monsieur Magon, was unfamiliar with the waters of the coast, and Bodega supplied him with a set of charts. Any vessels requiring repairs, such as Gray's *Columbia* and Vancouver's *Discovery* and *Chatham*, were immediately taken in hand by the port's caulkers, blacksmiths, carpenters, and shipwrights, and careened if necessary.

When, on September 21,Bodega left Nootka, Edward Bell was moved to comment:

> Never was the departure of a man more regretted than that of Mr. Quadra's. He was universally beloved and admired and the only consolation we had was that we should see him again in Monterey ... There he said he wou'd wait for us and make it his business to receive us. In such a place as remote as Nootka, so remote from all civilized places ... and after having been so long there, he lived in a style that I should suppose is rarely seen in such circumstances, and supported the dignity of his Court in a very becoming manner. His house was open to every gentleman, he gave few particular invitations, they were general. He was fond of society and of social amusements and the Evening parties at his house were among the pleasantest I have spent since leaving England.[85]

The hospitality Bodega offered to Vancouver created a congenial atmosphere for what soon became a difficult negotiation for both commissioners. To the culinary delights he offered at his table, he added his Latin charm. Vancouver's journal and report to the Admiralty and the journals of his officers all attest to their gratitude to Bodega and the pleasure they took in his company. Vancouver responded as fully as his more limited resources could provide, but he did not succumb to Bodega's blandishments.

While Bodega's generosity might seem somewhat exaggerated, it was not without purpose. The fellowship he displayed in the commandant's house was not exclusively for Vancouver's benefit. In his instructions to Bodega, Revillagigedo had indicated that Bodega was to conduct himself with the greatest courtesy and attention and that he should take special care to sustain the honour of the Spanish monarchy and of Spain's Royal Navy.

At another level, Bodega's conduct had two discernible purposes. In the first place, he saw his mission as a diplomatic means to restore the prestige and stature that Spain had lost in England and elsewhere as a result of Prime Minister William Pitt's skill in negotiating the Nootka Convention. Bodega wrote in his *Viaje:* "[Vancouver] and all the captains of the sixteen French, English, Portuguese and American ships that called in to the port during my residence will publicize the assistance they owe to me."[86] Second, he must have felt that a successful mission was his last opportunity to obtain promotion to flag rank. With a good record behind him, he was well qualified for a major assignment that called for an officer of the rank of rear admiral. Nearing his fifties and in declining health, he could never hope to get back to sea in command of a major expedition. He was already beginning to contemplate an easier assignment, such as the governorship of Callao. His lavish spending and generosity can thus also be viewed as a personal investment in his own future.

Bodega was practising correct diplomacy. Being served a beautifully prepared meal on silver plate in Lima in the eighteenth century would not have caused the astonishment that Bodega's silver service created at Nootka, but it was quite in character for a person of his class to believe that life on the west coast of Vancouver Island should be lived without compromising standards. Bodega's hospitality was not a mere façade. These courtesies would have been a matter of personal importance to him, for his approach sprang quite naturally from his upbringing. The elite of Peruvian colonial society – of European stock, proud, aristocratic, and isolated – had developed a way of life that was extravagant by today's standards, and memorable social occasions were made possible by easy wealth and large houses. Bodega saw no contradiction between the enjoyment of life in the capital and the same pursuit in the wilds of Vancouver Island. As a *criollo* gentleman in Spanish colonial society, he had all the characteristics of his class. His courtesy, charm, and fondness for company reflected his origins and can still be found in upper-class Lima society, especially in families of Spanish ancestry. His general invitation to visiting officers, mates, and super-cargoes brings to mind the traditional Peruvian expression of welcome to visitors: "Aqui tiene su casa" (literally, "Here you have your own house"). In Lima today, one finds not only ostentation but also warm and discreet friendship, generosity in matters large and small, and consideration for the happiness of others. Those who encountered Bodega at Nootka would attest later to his magnetism, his outgoing nature, his willingness to help with ships' repairs and to provide daily supplies of fresh foodstuffs, and his insistence that they consider the commandant's house a home away from home.

Enlightened Policy

Another role Bodega played at Nootka during the summer of 1792 was as a friend to the native people. It was one that came easily to him, despite his anger over the tragic events off Point Grenville in 1775.[87] The Spanish never viewed the people of Nootka Sound as subjects. After Martínez's blunders in 1789, no attempt was made to use them as allies against other nationalities. The Spanish presence was based solely on the Mowachaht chief's verbal consent, and it was limited to the period of occupation.[88]

Bodega's attitude toward relations with Chief Maquinna differed dramatically from past Spanish policy toward the native peoples of Alta California and from the even earlier "Black Legend" of cruel oppression in Mexico and Peru. The "new" Enlightenment policy of Carlos III toward native peoples was set out in the instructions that Revillagigedo laid down for the expedition exploring the Strait of Juan de Fuca:

> I expect that presents, kindness, possible toleration of such offences as they may commit, and your vigilance over your men to see that they do not insult the Indians, even in the most trifling matter, will prove the bonds to unite you with those natives and thus leave behind a cemented friendship with them which may in the future be very useful for religion and to the king, never using your arms to attack them unless some stringent necessity obliges you to do so ...
>
> You will neither take from the Indians nor permit to be taken from them anything belonging to them unless it has been agreed to and offered by their hand.
>
> It is of interest to observe this point so they may always comprehend that we profess good faith and are truthful, thus removing from their imagination that we are capable of deceiving them. You will therefore punish any member of your crew committing any infraction of this rule. You yourself will bear and make them endure whatever treason the natives commit.[89]

The viceroy continued:

> Good treatment and harmony with the Indians is of the first importance to establish in this way a solid friendship with them so that our visits should not be as distressing as those of other voyages to the detriment of humanity and the national credit ... [The] use of the superiority of ... arms ... is a last resort to [do anything] directly opposed to humanity, and it can only be justified by the need of self-preservation.[90]

Although these benevolent injunctions were to some extent a repetition of the orders that Viceroy Bucareli had issued to Juan Pérez in 1774, there is a notable difference in the tone, substance, and purpose. After the Nootka crisis, there was an obvious need to win native support for Spanish sovereignty. To maintain a presence on the Northwest Coast, Spain would need to foster stability. Without good relations with the native peoples, any exploration or future settlement would be much more difficult to sustain.

In the beginning, relations between the Spanish and the Mowachaht had been harmonious. Maquinna, the Mowachaht chief, had gone out from Yuquot in 1789 to greet the two ships in his large canoe, and Martínez, in turn, had paid Maquinna a visit and was given an elaborate welcome. He was permitted to construct some houses for his stores, as well as a hospital and an oven to make bread. He was further allowed to clear land for a garden to grow vegetables and permitted to erect a battery on one of the San Miguel Islands. It was not long, however, before conflict caused the peaceful atmosphere to vanish.

The most egregious incident was the 1789 murder of Callicum, a high-ranking chief who had sided with the English. In his efforts to recover the natives' trust, Bodega would have to overcome this serious liability. Eliza had made some progress toward conciliation in 1790 and 1791.

In August 1791, Alejandro Malaspina's expedition had called in at Nootka.[91] For the first week of their two-week stay, Maquinna resisted invitations to visit the ships, ostensibly because it was fishing season. In light of Callicum's murder, it is possible that he feared for his own safety. Maquinna changed his mind when he learned that his rival for primacy in the sound, Tlupananulg, had visited the two ships and been given gifts. A week after the arrival of the corvettes, Maquinna came down the inlet in his large war canoe with a full retinue, including three of his four wives. He did not permit his wives to go aboard either of the ships, although he was presented with some copper sheets and more gifts were promised. As many as five more visits followed, yet Malaspina's officers recorded that the great chief never seemed at ease. On the last day of the expedition's visit, and with apparent facility, Malaspina was able to obtain the chief's confirmation of his temporary cession of Yuquot to Martínez in 1789 and to Eliza in 1790.[92] In return, Malaspina promised Maquinna that the settlement would be returned to him and his people should the Spanish finally leave the region, that the commandant's house would go to him, and that the other buildings would be divided among the other chiefs.[93] Malaspina and his officers made sufficient progress in reconciling the Nootka and the Spanish that Maquinna was confident he had nothing to fear from Bodega.[94]

Immediately on his arrival, Bodega told the captains and officers of the ships of his command and the garrison ashore that he "would view with displeasure the conduct of anyone who did not show the greatest friendship and harmony towards the natives."[95] Unlike his predecessors, Bodega made regular visits to the chiefs in their villages. He also gave them gifts of blue cloth, abalone shells, and, especially, copper plate. A special present made to Maquinna was a metal coat, made of leaves of tin plate beautifully cut into the shape of scales, which the chief would wear on special occasions.

Bodega's openness was met with invitations from the Nootkan chiefs. When Bodega arrived on April 29, 1792, Maquinna and some of his chiefs lost no time in coming to Yuquot to welcome him. Bodega assured them of his desire to establish the best possible relations, and Maquinna invited Bodega to a feast in his honour. Bodega was also a guest at a celebration hosted by Maquinna at Kupti for his daughter, Apenas, who had reached puberty and was now ready to receive suitors for marriage.[96] Another feast was given by Maquinna's rival, Tlupananulg, the chief of Tlupana Inlet, who set up his camp on the beach opposite Yuquot. A frequent guest at the commandant's house, as he had been on Malaspina's ships, he constantly sought Bodega's support for his claim to higher status. His feasts were followed by dances and often by ceremonial displays on the water in his large war canoe. Quiocomasia, chief of the Ehattesaht group, also sought to challenge Maquinna's superiority and vied for Bodega's favours.[97]

Thanks to José Mariano Moziño's facility with languages, especially that of the Nootka, Bodega was able to understand the Nootkan people better. With Moziño as interpreter, he was able to establish friendlier relations with Maquinna in particular. Of special importance was Moziño's knowledge of Mowachaht and Nootkan history, their political and social structure, their religion and intertribal trading patterns, and their relationships with the other groups in the region. Bodega used all of this information to carry out Spanish policy on the Northwest Coast. Because Moziño resided ashore in the commandant's house and participated in the festivities, there were many opportunities for the two men to discuss the botanist's findings.[98]

Bodega made it a point to recognize and respect the ranked order of the chiefs around the sound in such a way as to reinforce Maquinna's supremacy. He "constantly treat[ed] Maquinna as a friend, singling him out among all with the clearest demonstrations of esteem." Bodega's courtesies had various aspects:

> He always occupies the place of honour at my table, and I myself take the trouble to serve him. I favour him with anything that might give him pleasure; he boasts of my friendship and very much appreciates my visits to his villages.[99]

Bodega was not swayed by the other chiefs' attentions and was able to discern the game they were playing. He proved himself as adept a politician as any chief. Summing up the success he had achieved in one of the self-serving phrases he was wont to use, he wrote in his *Viaje:*

> I can say with assurance that it is not possible to mistake the confidence they have in me and the affection that not only the common people declare they have for me, but the chiefs as well, since they frequently sleep at night [here] with the satisfaction that perhaps they would not have in the houses of their most intimate relatives. Thus I have no difficulty in establishing with them a human relationship towards which my nature inclines.[100]

Because festivities and ceremonies, exchanges of gifts, and reciprocated hospitality were as fundamental to Spanish colonial society as they were to the native culture, Bodega had no difficulty adjusting to Nootkan customs.[101]

George Vancouver confirmed that Bodega's liberal policy toward the Nootka had done much to improve relations with the people at Yuquot: "I could not help observing," he wrote, "with a mixture of surprise and pleasure how much the Spaniards had succeeded in gaining the good opinion and confidence of the people, together with their very orderly behaviour, so conspicuously evident in their conduct toward the Spaniards on all occasions."[102]

Bodega's approach to native relations had beneficial results, but at no time was the relationship free of stresses and strains.[103] Bodega acknowledged that he did not always succeed in maintaining harmony, and he was quick to punish any of his people who committed what he called "excesses," both "to serve as a warning and to give the Indians an idea of our justice." In his view, it was important politically for visitors of other nationalities to observe the extent to which the Spanish had succeeded in integrating themselves into the native community and to see the support that the Nootkan people offered to Spanish sovereignty.

Bodega's sincerity about restraining the conduct of his personnel is evident from his prompt reaction to Salvador Fidalgo's report of the shocking conflict that summer at Neah Bay. After drafting a letter of reprimand to Fidalgo, he asked Maquinna for the use of a canoe to deliver the letter directly to Fidalgo. Because of his esteem for the commandant, the chief undertook to take it himself.

Bodega's trust in Maquinna's friendship was rewarded. En route to Neah Bay, Maquinna stopped at Clayoquot to see Wickininnish and found him together with Tutusi and "Captain Hanna" (Cleaskinah).[104] Tutusi, angered by the brutality and capriciousness of Fidalgo's response to the murder of Serrantes, had come to Ahousat in Clayoquot Sound to seek the support of Wickininnish and Captain Hanna for a combined assault on the Spanish settlement at Santa Cruz de Nuca. They asked Maquinna not to deliver Bodega's letter. To turn him against all Europeans, the three chiefs also told him about a violent incident that had just taken place in Clayoquot Sound. Some of the sailors of the English fur trader *Butterworth* under William Brown had entered a village to steal skins off the backs of the Indians. When the villagers fought to keep their clothes, four of them were killed. Wickininnish's warriors gave chase, but the retreating English sailors were saved by a cannon shot from the American fur trader *Margaret*, under Captain Magee, which was also trading in the sound. In retaliation, Brown fell on some Indians who were fishing nearby and had them whipped and thrown into the water, after which an English trading ship, the *Jenny*, which was lying astern, fired on them and killed them all.[105] The three chiefs – all interrelated by blood and marriage, as was Maquinna – attempted to enlist Maquinna's support for a joint attack against all Europeans and Americans.[106] Maquinna argued so vigorously that the Spanish were his friends that the chiefs told him to leave.

Two days later, "very upset" about what he had learned at Wickininnish's village, Maquinna arrived back at Nootka, where he immediately sought out Bodega to warn him that the chiefs were plotting revenge for Brown's actions and, presumably, for Fidalgo's as well. A joint attack on the Spanish establishment at that time would have been devastating, since Bodega had only one vessel, the *Activa*, on hand to defend the port. The few remaining Catalonian Volunteers were only a corporal's guard to defend against a land attack. At that point, unexpectedly, Captain Hanna came alone to Yuquot, ostensibly to inquire about his children. Maquinna took the opportunity to convince Captain Hanna that the Spanish were friendly. He persuaded him to talk to Bodega, who heard him out and gave him a few presents. In his *Viaje*, Bodega records how Captain Hanna "became so reconciled and satisfied that, after having been two days in my house, he took the letter [to Fidalgo] and ... pacified the restlessness of the other chiefs."[107] A crisis was averted.

A tense situation that could have had tragic consequences had been defused by Bodega's tact, by his charm and prompt action, and by Maquinna's support at a critical moment. This incident shows the extent to which Maquinna and Bodega depended on each other politically. Bodega relied on Maquinna for the safety and security of the settlement and for his support of Spanish sovereignty; Maquinna relied on Bodega for support in upholding his ascendancy over other powerful neighbouring chiefs.

In a more general sense, however, the episode illustrates the brittleness of relations between the natives and the European and American fur traders and the tension that was never far from the surface. Because the Spanish were only minor participants in the fur trade, they were largely spared such violent encounters, but they could not entirely escape the results because the native peoples did not always differentiate between the Spaniards and the other white strangers. An offence by one European might bring a collective reprisal against all of them.

On the eve of Bodega's departure from Nootka, a gruesome incident occurred that illustrates the respect he had for Maquinna's jurisdiction over his people. On September 14 the mutilated body of the fourteen-year-old cabin boy on the *Activa*, José Navarro, was found in the woods.[108] Bodega tersely recorded: "On the 14th I was informed that a seaman was missing and that a cabin boy from the *goleta* [*Activa*] had been found in the hills with his throat cut, but as it was not possible to ascertain the whereabouts of the [boy's body] or the killers, I sent for Maquinna to ask him to undertake the task."[109] When the Indians in the cove heard what had happened, they feared an instant Spanish retaliation. They "took instantly to their canoes ... and in a few minutes not a canoe was to be seen."[110] There was general agreement that the cabin boy had been murdered by the Indians, but no agreement on what to do about it. Bodega declared that such a matter should be dealt with by the natives themselves; shrewdly, he was leaving the matter in Maquinna's hands.

A rumour circulated that blamed Maquinna himself. When Maquinna heard it, he came to see Bodega and berated the Spanish commandant at great length. In this speech, recorded by Moziño – who served as interpreter and described it as "as exciting as it was poetic" – Maquinna said he did not believe that Bodega actually thought him responsible. He asked him to realize that

> Maquinna has a thousand obligations to be your friend. You have given me much copper; because of you I had many [abalone] shells to distribute at the celebration of the first menstruation of Apenas. Yours are the cloth, beads, coat of metal, instruments of iron, glass window panes, and many other things with which I am provided. Our mutual trust has reached the point of our both sleeping alone [sic] in the same room, a place in which you find yourself without arms or people to defend you. I could have taken your life if my friendship were capable of betrayal. One thinks very lowly of me and of my dignity if he imagines that, seeking to break a friendship, I would order the murder of a boy less able to defend himself than if he were a woman ... You would be the first whose life would be in great danger if we were enemies ... Have not you yourself gone accompanied by few of your men and found only that the multitude of my subjects surrounded you with the purpose of making the liveliest demonstrations of friendship? ... Make all [your

> men] know that Maquinna is a true friend, that he is far from harming the Spanish ... Maquinna is the same as Quadra and Quadra is the same as Maquinna.[111]

As further proof of his innocence and of his great respect for the commandant, Maquinna asked Bodega for a launch with four or six swivel guns, manned by Spanish sailors and his own people, to punish the "treacherous ones of Itz-coac,"[112] whom he surmised were responsible for the boy's death. Doubtless, Bodega was taken aback by the vehemence of the chief's disclaimer; however, true to his policy of refusing to arm the Indians and avoiding involvement in intertribal disputes and jealousies, he wisely declined Maquinna's request.

Bodega's refusal to take any action except to turn the matter over to Maquinna puzzled those present. Even Ingraham, whose admiration for Bodega was boundless, doubted that Bodega's decision to "choose to look over it than to risk punishing the innocent" was the right one.[113] In his view, Bodega should have "detained Maquinna." Peter Puget, first lieutenant of the *Chatham,* believed that some of the chiefs should have been taken hostage: "I would on all occasions do justice to Mr. Quadra's humanity but here I must say [there] appeared a want of exertion, which I am afraid will rather encourage such barbarous and atrocious acts."[114] Edward Bell left no doubt as to his feelings: "It is surely to be regretted that Mr. Quadra's mildness and lenity would not suffer him proceeding further ... Mr. Quadra was *too good* a man; he even treated the Indians more like companions than people that should be taught subjection."[115]

Yet Bogeda's refusal to take reprisals was supported by Revillagigedo. The viceroy reported the affair to Aranda, the Minister of State, because he had been "assured that the Indians of the region had always behaved well and maintained the best harmony with the Spanish." In the circumstances, he thought, Bodega's decision to leave it to them to discover and punish the aggressors seemed the wisest course.[116] The Duque de la Alcudia, Manuel Godoy, having succeeded Aranda as Minister of State, replied in a Royal Order of February 23, 1793, that the king had been informed of Bodega's judgment and approved of it.[117] The home government's reaction to this incident and to Fidalgo's cannon blast at Neah Bay are further evidence that the Spanish administration had incorporated the Enlightenment's humanistic principles into its policies for dealing with native peoples, and that it was aware that native populations needed to be treated well.

Whatever his true feelings, Bodega's policy was not entirely altruistic; he did have an ulterior purpose. Historian Christon Archer observed that

> Bodega made seduction and good treatment of the Natives ... into key elements in building Spanish claims to sovereignty ... [But] if Quadra manipulated Maquinna to bolster Spanish claims to sovereignty, the Nootka chief proved himself equally adept at using the Spanish to strengthen his own diplomatic position.[118]

The Spanish had a strong impact, both good and ill, on the people of Nootka Sound. Some of the ills, such as the rapid depletion of the sound's fish and game, were recognized at the time; others not so much. The obligation to act as hosts to the Spanish and other European visitors and to neighbouring tribes led to more feasting than had occurred in pre-Contact times, and this placed a great strain on the economic and political resources of the Mowachaht. With the Europeans encamped at Yuquot, the gateway to their whaling grounds, the Mowachaht temporarily lost their easy access to the ocean. There was constant fear of attack by covetous neighbours to the east and south. Most damaging were the depredations of the Spanish sailors on the native commoners, the memory of which is still strong in indigenous oral history. In his *Noticias de Nutka*, Moziño was sharply critical of the conduct of the Spanish sailors:

> Either as a result of their almost brutal upbringing or because they envied the humane treatment the commandant and other officers always gave the natives, [they] insulted them at various times, crippled some and wounded others, and did not fail to kill several.[119]

Some benefits did accrue to the local people. The Spanish presence greatly increased Maquinna's prestige over that of his rivals, and his wealth was augmented by his control of the sea otter fur trade and by the receipt of many gifts of copper sheets. There was also an improvement in Nuu-chah-nulth material culture as a result of the introduction of iron tools acquired in trade. Less tangible, but no less significant, is the fact that Chief Maquinna is today a source of pride to his people; in this regard, Bodega's special relationship with him was the high-water mark of his chieftaincy.

After Bodega's departure and the abandonment of the Spanish establishment in 1795, Maquinna's standing declined. Yuquot ceased to be a centre of international diplomacy, and the wealth generated by the fur trade dwindled as the local sea otter herds were destroyed and the traders moved north. Maquinna's seizure of the trading ship *Boston* in 1803, and the murder of all but two of its crew, was a desperate attempt to recover his prestige in the power struggle with his local rivals.[120]

10

The Commissioners' Negotiations at Nootka

THE ROYAL NAVY'S MASTER AND COMMANDER George Vancouver came to Nootka as the British commissioner appointed to implement the Nootka Convention. He did this while undertaking two larger tasks: the detailed survey of the coast to latitude 60°N, and a search for the fabled Northwest Passage.[1] Captain James Cook had revealed a coast that lay so far north that only short seasons were available for surveying. Vancouver was instructed to bear this in mind and not to waste time along the southern portions of this coast. He was, however, to pay particular attention to the "supposed straits of Juan de Fuca," the waterway that seemed most likely to give access to the great passage. Bodega's Expedition of the Limits had the same two objectives: exploration of the coast, especially inside the Strait of Juan de Fuca, and the implementation of the Nootka Convention, but in reverse priority.

Vancouver had not been the Admiralty's first choice to lead the expedition. Henry Roberts was initially appointed to its command, but at the last moment he was given another assignment. Vancouver was to have been his first lieutenant and Richard Hergest his second lieutenant. When Vancouver was appointed to lead the mission, Hergest was named captain of the *Daedalus*, the expedition's stores ship. Vancouver had gained considerable experience while serving with Cook. He had visited Nootka Sound in March 1778 as a midshipman on the *Discovery*, Cook's second ship. Although he had shown himself to be a diligent officer, this particular experience does not seem to have been a determining factor in his selection. After serving with Cook, nothing in his career before the appointment to command this expedition foreshadowed the courage and skill with which he was to complete one of the great voyages of exploration and surveying. The *Discovery* was Vancouver's first and only command, although he would ultimately have three ships under his authority: the 330-ton *Discovery*, the 131-ton tender *Chatham*, and the 350-ton *Daedalus*, which met him at Nootka with supplies. Departing from England in April 1791, Vancouver rounded the Cape of Good Hope and in the spring of 1792 made his North American landfall at 39°20′N, near Cape Mendocino.

Vancouver's Arrival at Nootka

On April 29, the day before Bodega arrived in Nootka, Vancouver was nearing the entrance to the Strait of Juan de Fuca. Knowing that Vancouver would likely be in the area but unaware of his precise plans, Bodega took advantage of the departure of Alcalá Galiano and Valdés from Yuquot on May 12 to ask them to inform Vancouver, should they encounter him, that Bodega was awaiting him at Nootka. Vancouver received the message on June 22 when the two expeditions met off Point Grey at the entrance to what is now Vancouver Harbour. Vancouver acknowledged receiving the message, adding that he experienced "no small degree of mortification" on learning that Spanish explorers had been on the same mission and that José María Narváez, Francisco de Eliza, and Manuel Quimper had thoroughly explored the strait in 1790 and 1791. This would not be the only surprise the Spanish gave Vancouver before he left the region.

Vancouver's ships reached Nootka on August 28. The *Chatham* was the first to arrive. Edward Bell, her clerk, recounted in his lively journal that

> as we approached the Cove we observed a Boat coming out to us with the Spanish colours flying. She came on board us and proved to be the Guard Boat. The officer in her, on hearing who we were and that we were coming out in company with the *Discovery* to receive this place of them, discovered much satisfaction and the people in the Boat were ready to leap onboard for joy, for it seems we were so long expected that they had now given up all hopes of seeing us at all this season.[2]

Guided by launches, and after saluting the fort with thirteen guns, which were answered with an equal number by the *Activa*, the *Chatham* dropped anchor at noon. When her commander, Lieutenant Broughton, went ashore to thank Bodega for the assistance he had been given, he was invited to remain for dinner.

Later that afternoon, the *Discovery*, momentarily delayed by fog, appeared at the entrance to Yuquot, and Bodega sent out an officer with a pilot to welcome her. At three in the afternoon she hove into view through the fog; at four, she dropped anchor next to the *Chatham*, whereupon Vancouver sent his first lieutenant, Peter Puget, ashore to formally acquaint the commander of his arrival. Reflecting his uncertainty as to how Bodega would receive him, Vancouver instructed Puget to say that he "would salute his flag if he would return an equal number of guns." On receiving an affirmative reply, Vancouver saluted with thirteen guns, a gesture that was duly returned.[3]

Bodega had drawn up a guard of honour on the beach and personally received Vancouver and his officers at the door of his renovated residence. They were taken upstairs to the "Great Hall," where they engaged in some "general conversation concerning our voyage and the route we had hitherto pursued."[4] Bodega told his visitors that "every refreshment and accommodation which the settlement could afford" was at their disposal. His house was their home, he told them, and the more often they came, the greater the pleasure they would give him. In the early evening, Bodega took Vancouver on a tour of the establishment to show him the houses, barracks, workshops, storehouses, hospital, and vegetable gardens. The Englishman was impressed by how much had been accomplished in such a short time.

Bodega returned Vancouver's formal call the next morning, bringing with him "several of his officers," who were welcomed by a guard of honour and saluted with thirteen guns. Vancouver served them breakfast, after which he showed Bodega his charts and took him on a tour of the ship. Bodega stated in his *Viaje* that he took Maquinna with him to present him to Vancouver; he neglected, however, to say that earlier that day, Maquinna had tried to board the *Discovery* but had been rebuffed by the sentinels and the officer on deck "as there was not in his appearance the smallest indication of his superior rank." Maquinna complained angrily to Bodega about this insult. The Spanish commandant was able to smooth things over, allowing Vancouver to report that

> at breakfast time [Maquinna] appeared to be satisfied of our friendly intentions; but no sooner had he drunk a few glasses of wine, than he renewed the subject, regretted the Spanish were about to quit the place and asserted that we should presently give it up to some other nation; by which means himself and his people would be constantly disturbed and harassed by new masters.

Bodega assured Maquinna that he and his people would be "as kindly treated by the English as they had been by the Spanish." After this exercise in diplomacy, Bodega was again saluted with thirteen guns as he left the *Discovery.* He then visited the *Chatham,* where the same salute was renewed.

This practice of almost continuous saluting caused Menzies to remark somewhat sarcastically that

> saluting was so common among the trading vessels which visited the Cove that there was scarcely a day past without puffings of this kind from some Vessel or other, & we too followed the example, & puffed it away as well as any of them, till at last we were become so scarce of ammunition to defend ourselves from the treacherous Indians that we were obliged to get supplies of Powder from both the Spaniards & Traders before we left the Coast.[5]

That night, Bodega entertained Vancouver at a banquet, the first of many demonstrations of his diplomatic hospitality, and Maquinna was among the guests. The dinner was very formal. Bodega gave the first toast to the sovereigns of England and Spain, accompanied by a twenty-one-gun salute from the *Activa,* and a second toast, accompanied by a seventeen-gun salute from the *Activa,* to the success of the voyage of the *Discovery* and the *Chatham.* The *Discovery*'s guns boomed out in reply to both toasts.

None present described the menu, although wild fruits as well as vegetables from Pedro de Alberni's gardens and some of the delicacies that Bodega had brought with him would have been available. Nor do any of the accounts of this particular evening mention that the elaborate dinner was served on Bodega's own silver plate. Menzies, however, described the evening as a "very sumptuous entertainment ... spent with that unreserved conviviality which made us forget we were strangers, in the mutual pleasure which each individual seemed to enjoy."[6]

The commissioners had made a good impression on each other. Vancouver was pleased with "the greatest cordiality and attention from the commandant," and Bodega told Vancouver that "he derived the greatest satisfaction from finding a person of my character, with whom he was to transact the business of delivering up Nootka." Bodega, Vancouver added, offered to

> accompany us in our researches to the southward, and to conduct us to any of the Spanish ports I might wish to visit; or he would sail, and wait my arrival at any place I should think proper to appoint, recommending San Francisco or Monterey for that purpose.[7]

That two such different personalities should have established such obvious rapport from the outset and maintained it for the time they were together in Nootka and later in Monterey boded well for their association.[8] Despite the differences in age and rank,[9] they had much in common. They were wholly dedicated to the mariner's life. Each had begun his career as a midshipman, and both were veterans of Pacific exploration, especially that of the Pacific Northwest. There were, however, important differences in their backgrounds and character. Bodega belonged to the lesser nobility and had first learned his seamanship, gunnery, navigation, and other maritime arts in the classroom. Vancouver came from a prominent middle-class family, had entered the navy as a midshipman at the age of fourteen, and had learned his trade at sea – fortunately for him, under the eye of the greatest maritime explorer of that century, James Cook.

With the ceremonies concluded, Vancouver turned to practical matters. On August 30 his tents, chronometers, and other instruments were sent ashore. Under the direction of Joseph Whidbey, the master of the *Discovery*, a "markee" (marquee) and a large tent were erected for the observatory. The site chosen was a "spot near the beach behind the village," possibly on the present site of Yuquot's church. Having run aground in Queen Charlotte Sound, both English ships required repairs. Also, the rigging had to be overhauled and the sails aired. The ships were given a thorough caulking by the Spanish craftsmen. The *Chatham* was hauled onto the beach at high tide, as it was suspected that she had suffered the more severe damage. When the tide ebbed, she was indeed found to need much work. Despite the limited facilities of the cove, the vessel was made fully seaworthy.

On Sunday, September 2, having assumed that the territories would be turned over to Vancouver, Bodega asked him who would be left in possession of the territories. Although he had no instructions on the matter, Vancouver replied that it would be Broughton and that the supplies the *Daedalus* had brought would be placed in his care and charge. Bodega then invited Vancouver to take a walk with him around the establishment to decide "how to direct the depositing of the different stores." Vancouver "found the different places sufficiently secure, and more extensive than was necessary to answer all the purposes we could possibly want." He also observed that a large oven had been built for his use and that most of the houses had been repaired.

An especially noteworthy event occurred shortly after Vancouver's arrival during a break in the negotiations. This was the formal visit by the two commissioners to Maquinna in his winter village at the head of the Tahsis Inlet. According to Vancouver, the idea of such a "visit of ceremony," as he called it, originated with Bodega over breakfast on board the *Discovery* on Monday, September 3. Bodega considered it "essentially requisite" to miss "no opportunity of impressing on the minds of the natives the highest and most favourable opinion of our little squadron; and the more effectually to insure a good understanding in future."

Menzies ascribed a more precise purpose to the visit:

> Don Quadra proposed as the weather was favourable to take a jaunt up the Sound to visit the chief of Nootka at his own habitation, that he might have the pleasure of recommending the English commanders and their officers to the particular notice of the chief and his tribe, and thereby do away any alarm they might prepossess about our quarrelling, by convincing them of the friendship that subsisted between the two nations, and likewise, as the place was soon to be given up to the English, he wished for their own happiness to do away with any bias they might have formed in favour of the Spaniards from their residing so long amongst them.[10]

Vancouver readily agreed to the idea. Word was sent ahead to Maquinna at Tahsis, and the party set out the following morning, on September 4.[11] Bodega and Vancouver, Broughton, Menzies, Puget, and some of the Spanish officers travelled together in the *Discovery*'s yawl, the largest boat.[12] The rest, Spanish and English, divided themselves among the *Discovery*'s pinnace, the *Chatham*'s cutter, and a large launch belonging to the Spanish. A guard of soldiers accompanied the group, making about ninety people in all.[13] The small fleet travelled first along the shore of Nootka Island and then, after stopping for a late breakfast in Marvinas Bay, sailed into Tahsis Inlet. Menzies noted that the weather remained

> uncommonally [sic] favourable and, as the water was smooth, the vessels proceeded at an easy rate with drums beating and fifes playing to the no small entertainment of the Natives, as it gave a martial solemnity to our visit, highly gratifying to their feelings in thus imitating their own customs on similar occasions, for in their friendly visits their approach is always announced by vociferous songs and plaintive airs.[14]

As they rounded a bend near the head of the inlet, Maquinna's village came into sight. Since the visitors had arrived late in the day, it was decided to camp in a meadow a little short of the village. While the tents were being pitched and dinner prepared, some of the officers walked along the beach to pay their respects to the chief at his own house, whereupon Maquinna with some of his attendants returned with the officers to the encampment and dined with them. When darkness fell, Maquinna and his people "retired to their own habitations, leaving us to spend the evening with our new friends in social hilarity and mirth."[15]

Not only was this visit important for political reasons, but also the detailed accounts of the event in the journals of Vancouver's people provide what may be the first description of a potlatch. Menzies described their formal arrival the following morning:

> After breakfast the next morning we all embarked in the boats and made a kind of martial parade with our little musical band before the village of Tashees where we landed amidst the noisy acclamations of the Natives.[16] Maquinna together with his brother and attendants received us on the beach, and we were conducted to the chief's house, which was large and spacious and occupied by himself, his brother and other families of distinction.[17]

After commenting that "it was evident that [Maquinna's] pride was not a little indulged by our shewing him this attention" – an understatement, as will be seen – Vancouver recorded that before entering Maquinna's house, all were taken around the village by the chief, visiting most of the houses and distributing presents to the inhabitants, "who all conducted themselves in a most civil and orderly manner."[18] He judged that the Europeans "appeared to be welcomed guests."

Puget thought Maquinna's welcome was "friendly to a degree." Then, in a more positive vein, he added that Maquinna

> appeared highly flattered at such a mark of attention, nor could he conceal that inward satisfaction which the countenance will always proclaim, when it springs from an undisguised & honest heart, for such I believe Maquinna's to be. He wished to shew his hospitality, his friendship and his obligation to us.[19]

Entering Maquinna's house, the visitors found "the women seated on mats spread on little risings on each side of the house and benches were placed at one end covered over with rich furs and clean mats for the party to sit down on."[20] They paid their respects to the wives of the chiefs and to Maquinna's daughter, Apenas, whom Vancouver described as "of low stature, very plump, with a round face, and small features; her skin was clean, and being nearly white, her person altogether, though without any pretensions to beauty, could not be considered as disagreeable." Menzies estimated that she was "about thirteen years of age." Nearby were seated three of Maquinna's wives. Gifts that Vancouver considered "suitable to the occasion" were presented to the "princess," to Maquinna, and to his brothers and other relations.

At this point in his journal, Menzies recorded an occurrence, mentioned by no one else, that suggests that Maquinna's reception of the two commissioners took the form of a potlatch:

> When the Natives were assembled ... a throne was erected on which the young princess was seated by her father, and from thence copper, iron, beads, etc. and every other article of any value the chief possessed was thrown down and scattered in the most profuse manner amongst the people, who scrambled for it and expressed their approbation by continual plaudits. After this ceremony they continued their rejoicing by feasting, singing and dancing for some days, till the chief with respect to riches was brought almost upon a level with the poorest of his tribe.

As soon as all were seated, Bodega addressed Maquinna to explain the purpose of the commissioners' visit. Bodega, Menzies relates,

> said everything in recommending Captain Vancouver, Mr. Broughton together with their officers and the English nation in general to his kind attention and to a friendly intercourse with all his tribe; he assured him [of] the friendship and good understanding which subsisted between the English and [the] Spaniards, and that the latter were only to quit his territories by a mutual agreement between the two nations, but that they would ever continue steadily their friendship and respect for him and his tribe.

Maquinna, in reply, expressed his regret that so soon he would be losing Bodega "to whom he seemed attached by the most sacred ties of friendship."

At the appropriate time, Vancouver and Broughton, to cement their friendship, presented Maquinna, his brother, their wives, and Apenas with sheets of copper, cloth, blankets, beads, and "other ornamental articles." In return, Maquinna presented the Spanish and English officers with "some rich furs."

Two different menus had been prepared for the dinner that followed. Menzies relates that

> the Natives entertained themselves at a Mess ... of a large tunny and a porpoise cut up in small pieces, entrails and all, into a large trough with a mixture of water, blood and fish oil, and the whole stewed by throwing heated stones into it. When thus cooked, they seated themselves round the trough, some with spoons, others with large shells, scooping it up and devouring it with relishing appetites."[21]

The second menu was for the visitors. It had been agreed "on setting out that Don Quadra should furnish the eatables and Captain [Vancouver] the drinkables." Bell added that "one would have imagined that Seigr. Quadra's whole household had been there ... We were served up two courses, on [his silver] plate, in a style little inferior to what we met with at the Governor's own house."[22] Menzies and Puget both confirmed the lavish nature of this dinner, noting that

> everything else that could contribute luxury and comfort was profusely provided by Sr. Quadra who had brought along with him on this occasion not only his steward, cooks and culinary utensils, but even his [silver] plate, so that our dinner was served up in a manner that made us forget we were in such a remote corner, under the humble roof of a Nootka chief."[23]

One of the planks from the roof served as their table. Placed in the middle of the house, it was large enough to accommodate the visitors. Smaller planks extending on either side served as seats. They ate apart from Maquinna, his wives, and the other chiefs, no doubt in strict order of precedence. After each group had finished, Maquinna joined the visitors "for a convivial glass of wine."

The dinner concluded, the visitors moved back to their seats at the end of the house and, at a sign from Maquinna, the dancing began.[24] The English were clearly intrigued. Vancouver, Menzies, Puget, and Bell all give detailed descriptions of the performance, and each was fascinated by different aspects of it. Vancouver wrote:

> Maquinna entertained us with a representation of their warlike achievements. A dozen men first appeared, armed with muskets and equipped with all their appendages, who took their post in a very orderly manner within the entrance to the house, where they remained stationary, and were followed by eighteen very stout men, each bearing a spear or lance sixteen or eighteen feet in length, proportionately strong, and pointed with a long flat piece of iron, which seemed be sharp on both edges, and was highly polished; the whole however appeared to form an awkward and unwieldy weapon. These men made several movements in imitation of attack and defence, singing at the same time several war songs, in which they were joined by those with the muskets.[25]

Menzies provided more detail:

> The Natives ... assembled at the chief's door in a group of the most grotesque

> figures that can possibly be imagined, dressed, armed, and masked in imitation of various characters of different countries. Some represented Europeans armed with muskets and bayonets, others dressed as Chinese and others as Sandwich Islanders armed with clubs and spears. The rest were equipped either as warriors or hunters of their own nation.
>
> After a party of them armed with long spears entered and were drawn up at the further end of the House, the actors came in one at a time and traversed the area before us, with the most antic gestures. If a warrior, he shewed the different evolutions of attacking an enemy, sometimes crouching down, sometimes retreating, at other times advancing with firm steps and eyes firmly fixed on the Commanders who were seated in the middle of our group, and to whom all their feigned aims and motions were directed, sometimes with much pointed archness as to occasion some alarm of their intentions being real.
>
> The hunters equipped with various marks and implements, shewed all the wiles and stratagems usual in taking or chasing different animals as deer, bears, etc., while those armed with muskets represented sentinels or went through various motions of the manual exercise. And those representing the Sandwich Islanders traversed the area in different attitudes of wielding their clubs or darting their spears, and as each finished his part he retreated back and took his station among the masked group at the further end of the house.[26]

Edward Bell adds details that show how much the fur trade with Europeans was beginning to change Indian ways and culture. The dancers, he wrote, "were most fantastically dressed and I suppose in their best and most showy apparel, which was for the most part all of English manufacture, such as woolens, blankets, helmets and a number of other different wearable articles."[27] He added that "indeed Maquinna's brother was habited in a complete suit of stage armour which very likely was often the property of Hamlet's Ghost." This may well have been the "handsome helmet and coat of mail of tin plate worked in scales" that Bodega had given Maquinna.[28]

Bell observed that the faces of the dancers "were ludicrously painted in all the colours among which red and black were the predominant and their hair was richly perfumed with fish oil, powdered with red ochre and profusely adorned with the down of birds' feathers ... They entered running furiously, making horrid gestures, hallooing and dancing."[29] When each dance was concluded, he went on, the "performer was summoned by a signal given by a number of men who sat near the door and who with small bits of sticks smartly struck a long plank of wood."

Regarding the conclusion of this phase of the entertainment, Bell noted that

> after each man had made a circuit before the place where we were seated, they retired to the opposite end of the house and being now assembled there they joined in a song which they executed with great exactness in keeping tune and beating the ground together with their different weapons. Some of their songs were not devoid of harmony. They were all of the fierce and warlike style and subject and one or two of them ended with a frightful yell that to a strangers' ear was truly terrific.

Maquinna joined Bodega and Vancouver for this "representation," as Vancouver called it, and then stole away to prepare himself for the next part of the evening. He returned to dance "with great agility ... much to the satisfaction of the whole group, who testified their approbation by repeated and universal plaudits."[30] Bell recorded that the chief was dressed in "a very rich garment of [sea] otter skins with a round black hat, and a mask on, and with a fanciful petticoat or apron, around which was suspended hollow tubes of copper and brass and which as he danced by striking against each other made a wonderful tangling noise."[31] Maquinna "played some dexterous pantomimical tricks with his hat and mask." In the illustration of the chief's dance, based on the wash drawing by Atanasio Echeverría, Maquinna's long sea otter cloak and tunic are drawn as described by Bell, but he is shown as bare-headed.[32] With the dancing concluded, "a man then came forward holding up a sea otter skin and after most pompously and vociferously proclaiming that it was a present from the King Maquinna to Captain Vancouver, laid it at his feet, then retiring and, producing another skin, went through the same form [to present one to Bodega]."

According to Menzies, Captain Vancouver, "anxious to shew [the Natives] a specimen of our English capering, got some of the sailors to dance a reel or two to the fife." Vancouver recorded that the "natives seemed ... to admire their songs."

Vancouver observed that, just as the guests were ready to take their leave, Maquinna "was scarcely able to express the satisfaction he had experienced in the honour we had done him, saying, that neither Wickininnish, nor any other chief, had ever received such a mark of respect and attention from any visitors." The visit was also of significance to Vancouver and Bodega. To the former, it was confirmation of Bodega's good standing with the Nootka chief and an appropriate preparation for the turnover of the settlement to the English. For Bodega, it was yet another opportunity to promote Maquinna's status and influence over his rivals.[33]

Maquinna told Vancouver, and presumably Bodega as well, that he wanted to return their visit, and Vancouver promised him he would be "entertained in the European fashion," meaning with a display of fireworks. Although the hour was late, the party decided not to spend the night at Tahsis. They embarked in their boats, and "amid repeated acclamations of 'wacash, wacash' from the whole village,"[34] rowed for about two miles down the inlet to seek shelter in a small cove, where they spent the night.[35] Tents were pitched, and with "an excellent supper, and much conviviality and pleasantry [we] concluded the day."[36] They were not disturbed by "nightly visitors," for Maquinna had been given "strong injunctions" not "to suffer any of his people to come near the boats at those unseasonal hours."[37]

The English and Spaniards set out again after breakfast the following morning. Although the weather was pleasant, a contrary wind slowed their passage and made it advisable to stop for lunch "on a very pleasant point of an Island,"[38] possibly today's Bodega Island. They also stopped for tea at Marvinas and, after experiencing some rain, thunder, and lightning, arrived back in Yuquot at dusk, to dine once more at the commandant's house.

For Vancouver and Bodega, the excursion back to what was truly Cala de los Amigos (Friendly Cove) was to have special meaning. At some stage on their journey back to Yuquot, according to Vancouver, Bodega

> very earnestly requested that I would name some port or island after us both, to commemorate our meeting and the very friendly intercourse that had taken place and subsisted between us. Conceiving no spot so proper for this denomination as the place where we had first met, which was nearly in the centre of a tract of land that had first been circumnavigated by us, forming the southwestern sides of the gulf of Georgia, and the southern sides of Johnstone Straits and Queen Charlotte Sound, I named that country the island of QUADRA and VANCOUVER; with which complement [sic] he seemed highly pleased.[39]

Bodega would record, however, that it was Vancouver who made this suggestion of combining their names to designate some geographic feature, and that he did so much later, on September 19, on the eve of his own departure for Neah Bay. He mentioned it almost casually, in the same sentence in which he noted that Vancouver had sent him the charts of his discoveries and invited him to dinner. Vancouver apparently asked Bodega to allow him "to do me the honour of perpetuating our friendship by giving the 'Gran Isla de Fuca' my name and his."[40]

Maquinna wasted no time in returning Vancouver's visit, arriving without ceremony the following evening in a small canoe with two of his wives and several other relations. He was especially anxious to see the promised fireworks. When he learned that darkness was necessary and that he would have to wait until after sunset, Vancouver recorded that "his impatience was almost unrestrainable ... [and he] accused us of a breach of promise and telling falsities." Bodega intervened to assure Maquinna that what Vancouver said was true. To smooth the waters, he invited the chief and his party to spend the night in the commandant's house.

The fireworks went ahead as planned. Because the devices had been on board for a long time, Vancouver was concerned that they might be damp, but each one detonated as he had hoped. He even persuaded Maquinna and his brother to light a few rockets, later reporting that the display of "rockets, balloons and other fireworks ... were regarded by the Indian spectators with wonder and admiration, mixed with a considerable share of apprehension."

Menzies thought that the natives were more restrained:

> The display was followed by a party in the commandant's residence at which the Indians gave a specimen of their singing, dancing and capering till they were perfectly tired, consisting of such uncouth attitudes and gestures as are not easily described but which they performed with great glee and good humour till late in the evening and then retired very orderly to rest.[41]

The Bodega-Vancouver Negotiations

The formalities and social events did not interfere with the primary purpose of the commissioners' meeting. The negotiations began on August 29, the day after Vancouver's arrival. Each commissioner had similar instructions to guide his actions during these parleys.

Both Bodega and Vancouver had been instructed to be civil in their dealings. Vancouver had been told to be "particularly careful ... to avoid, with the utmost caution, the giving of any ground of jealousy or complaint to the subjects of His Catholic Majesty." He was directed to extend "every possible degree of assistance and information" to any Spanish ship "employed on any service similar to that which is hereby committed to you." There was to be "reciprocally a free and unreserved communication of all plans and charts of discoveries." Viceroy Revillagigedo had written his instructions to Bodega in the same vein: "It is not necessary for me to suggest to you that you should seek complete harmony and the most cordial relationship with the commander, officers, and crews of the ships of his Britannic Majesty, to use frankness in your dealings, to be decorous in everything you do."[42]

Before leaving Britain, Vancouver had advised Evan Nepean, the Undersecretary of State, that he would be making his landfall on the North American continent south of the Strait of Juan de Fuca, and that instead of proceeding directly to Nootka he would first survey the strait to ascertain where it led.[43] He did not know when Bodega would be arriving at Nootka, and he did not want to waste valuable time waiting for him. He needed as much summer weather as possible for his survey, and knowledge of the waters of the strait would be as important to him as to the Spanish in the forthcoming negotiations. As well, he wanted to be certain that the *Daedalus* would have time to reach Nootka with the stores and his instructions for the talks.

The delay favoured Bodega's position in the negotiations. Had Vancouver sailed directly to Nootka, Bodega might have turned the establishment over to him without demurring, in accordance with his instructions. Bodega would not have known that Neah Bay was an unsatisfactory alternative to Nootka, and he would not have had the answers of Viana, Gray, and Ingraham to his questions about the true nationality of Colnett's ships and the real extent of Meares's losses. Vancouver's delay gave Bodega time to gather this critical information.

Unfortunately for Vancouver, his general instructions from the Board of Admiralty regarding the settlement were incomplete and based on false information.[44] Vancouver would later complain to Nepean that "the only orders I received on that subject [were contained] in the duplicate of a letter of the Count Florida Blanca to the Spanish Officer commanding at Nootka."[45] Information on key issues – in particular, which "buildings and tracts of lands" were to be restored – was inaccurate and inadequate. Vancouver had received oral briefings from officials of the Secretary of State's department, but these had been based on garbled reports from the British Embassy in Madrid, Meares's mendacious memorial to Lord Grenville, and the close questioning of Meares by Pitt's cabinet. All that Vancouver could be given before leaving England was a copy of the Nootka Convention and a promise that full instructions would be sent out by a stores ship, the *Daedalus*. But when the *Daedalus* arrived at Nootka on July 4, the promised instructions were not on board; nor, it seems, had they even been drafted.

Bodega opened the negotiations by placing Vancouver on the defensive. He sent him a lengthy letter that he had drafted over the summer. Viana's and Gray's and Ingraham's replies to his various inquiries were attached to the letter. The whole package of materials was delivered to Vancouver by Gonzalo López de Haro.[46]

Bodega's letter set out his basic position.[47] He firmly asserted Spain's historic rights not only to Nootka but also to the entire "coast north of California" by virtue of "solemn treaties, discoveries and possession from time immemorial" that were recognized by "all nations." A number of different expeditions had been carried out over land and sea at great expense, and the goodwill of the natives had been secured without violence. As for Nootka, the Spaniards had "seen" it in 1774 – before Cook arrived in 1778 – and formal possession had been taken twice in 1775 both to the north and to the south of Nootka. On the instructions of the viceroy, Estéban José Martínez had taken possession of the site in 1789 and fortified it without any objections from either the Indians or the Portuguese and American visitors. No European establishment of any kind had existed there at the time.

Bodega then described the various actions that Martínez had taken to defend Spanish sovereignty, as well as his open-handed reception of Portuguese and American ships. After reciting the reasons why Colnett, his ships, and his crews had been arrested, Bodega declared unequivocally that the "injuries, prejudices and illegal seizures Captain Meares represents [in his memorial] are groundless." The *Argonaut* and the *Princess Royal* and their captains had been released. Their cargoes had been returned, and the wages of their officers and crews had been paid handsomely. Viana, Gray, and Ingraham had all assured him that Meares had never purchased any land from Maquinna and that the large house he claimed to have built was nothing more than a shack and had been torn down as soon as he left. Certainly, the building no longer existed when Martínez arrived the following year. In short, there was "nothing to hand over, nor the smallest damage to make good."

Even so, the letter went on, since the Spanish king wished to establish a solid and permanent peace with all nations, and in order to remove any obstacle that might cause discord, "far from thinking of continuing in this port, I am ready, without prejudice to our legitimate right, nor to what our courts, better informed, may decide, generously to cede to England the houses, workshops and vegetable gardens, which have been cultivated with so much labour, and remove myself to Fuca."[48]

As Fuca would be Spain's northernmost settlement on the Pacific coast, Bodega proposed that the strait be declared a dividing line. To the north of it, in accordance with Article V of the convention, Spain and England would enjoy "common use, entry and commerce"; no other nation, however, would have that right except by joint agreement between Spain and Britain. South of Neah Bay, the British would not "pass."

Bodega did not mention Floridablanca's proposal of another dividing line – one that would have run north from Neah Bay to latitude 60°, and that would have prevented the English from penetrating the interior of the continent. Had they the right to do so, they would be in a position to threaten the California missions and to exploit the region's (suspected) mineral wealth. Nor did Bodega propose a joint survey to establish the boundary, thinking perhaps that it was unnecessary to do so in view of the amount of leeway the viceroy had allowed him.[49] Perhaps, as well, he thought it best to hold these two proposals in abeyance and await Vancouver's reaction to his first letter.

In his reply, Vancouver insisted that since the substance of the attachments to Bodega's letter "do not come within the limits of my commission," he could not enter into "any retrospective discussion." Also, he considered long passages of Bodega's letter "a discussion of rights and pretensions" of Spain and Britain north of California, a subject that "I consider equally foreign to our present business," since the subject had been dealt with in the preamble to the convention.

Vancouver wisely declined to discuss historic rights and the drawing of boundaries. He would have been at a considerable disadvantage here, since the British authorities were unaware that Spanish mariners had explored the coast north of San Francisco and had taken formal possession of the lands as far north as 60°N. He had to insist on confining the negotiations to the strict fulfillment of Article I of the convention: that the establishment at Nootka and all its facilities as well as Clayoquot Sound be turned over to him.[50] Vancouver refused to "enter into any negotiation further than that which is contained in the substance of Count Floridablanca's letter, which authorizes you to restore, and me to receive, the buildings, districts, and parcels of land, which were occupied by subjects of His Britannic Majesty, as well as the Port of Nootka or St. Lawrence, as in the other said to be called Port Cox."

Vancouver also questioned Bodega's interpretation of Article V. Britain, he said, had the right of unmolested access to any spot on the coast beyond the northernmost Spanish settlement made prior to April 1789. After quoting the article and underlining the words "already occupied by Spain," Vancouver said he

> should suppose the establishment His Catholic Majesty has made in the mouth of Fuca to come under the denomination of a port of free access, as well as such as may have been, or may hereafter be made from thence south to Port St. Francisco, conceiving that port to be the northernmost part of the said coast then occupied by Spain.

Vancouver's refusal to recognize Neah Bay as an established Spanish settlement placed Bodega on his guard. Unwittingly, the Englishman had confirmed what Bodega suspected – an apprehension shared by Revillagigedo, and indeed by the home government – namely, that England's purpose in this whole affair was to limit Spain's northward expansion to the latitude of San Francisco. It also reminded Bodega of an English map he had seen just before leaving San Blas that showed a line on the Pacific coast, just north of San Francisco, dividing the area into British and Spanish dominions. It had been published in London, dated June 20, 1790, and had been obtained by one of the *pilotos* of the *Santa Gertrudis.*[51] On the eve of his departure for the north, Bodega had sent this map to the viceroy. Believing that Article V of the Nootka Convention might govern this point, and referring to Articles XIII and XIV of his instructions, Bodega had asked that the viceroy's direction on how to deal with the matter be sent to him via the *Aránzazu.*[52] The viceroy's reply was blunt and to the point: "It does not matter in the least where the English arbitrarily fix boundary lines, whether at the port of San Francisco or any other location on the California coast, as they must be ratified by our court as well as that of London. [Bodega y Quadra] should therefore continue to be guided by Royal Orders and his official instructions."[53]

Bodega had another reason to be wary. The day before receiving Vancouver's reply, Alcalá Galiano and Valdés had returned to Nootka from their circumnavigation of Vancouver Island to report that Neah Bay was unsuitable for permanent settlement. The bay was too exposed, they told him, and the Indians were hostile.[54] Bodega immediately became more cautious, as well as less willing to hand over the cove on Nootka Sound.

In his second letter to Vancouver, dated September 2, Bodega did not retreat from his position; instead, he gave Article I of the convention a narrower interpretation.[55] He said he was authorized to restore only the buildings and portions of land "enjoyed" by the English. Furthermore, Meares's shack did not exist when Martínez arrived, and it was clear that the Spanish establishment was not located where Meares had set up his "factory." He suggested that since Vancouver did not agree with him, the two of them ought to "lay before our respective courts what we think most just" and allow them to resolve the matter. Meanwhile, he would consider "withdrawing" from Nootka until the decision, based on "clear and accurate information," was made.

Vancouver must have carefully considered how to deal with this clear sign that the Spanish commissioner would not be turning over the establishment as simply and unconditionally as he had expected. He did not reply until September 10.[56] The day after receiving the message of September 2, he and Bodega had set out for Tahsis to pay their "visit of ceremony" to Maquinna; they did not return to Yuquot (Friendly Cove) until September 5. Vancouver did not give this three-day interruption as the reason for his tardy reply; however, in a post scriptum he apologized for not doing so sooner because of "Mr. Dobson's arm not allowing him to write."[57] As Dobson could easily have dictated a translation to someone, Vancouver obviously wanted time to ponder his next move. When he eventually did reply, he excused himself by saying that the oral translation given him on receipt had led him to believe that only a simple and courteous reply was required. Having studied Dobson's translation, and having thought more about the matter, he could only repeat himself: Bodega's letter amounted to a retrospective discussion of rights that, as he had noted earlier, did "not belong to our present business." His only possible reply was that he was "ready to be put into possession" of what was set out in Article I, "as soon as it may, in every respect, be compatible with your situation and convenience."

In his reply, which he dated September 11, Bodega retreated even further from his initial position. He gave a yet more restrictive interpretation of Article I of the convention, stating that it "extends only to the delivery of the territories which British subjects occupied in April 1789" – meaning the small cove where Meares had built his hut and the *North West America*.[58] This he was prepared to hand over, together with what the Spanish possessed, until their respective courts could finally decide the matter.

Their negotiations were fast approaching an impasse, which the two men attempted to avoid with a face-to-face session. Who took the initiative here is unclear. Bodega would write that Vancouver "came to my house earlier than usual to inform me that he could not receive [the establishment] with the slightest restriction." For his own part, Vancouver would state in his report that after their usual dinner, Bodega "requested some personal discussion." Vancouver recorded that "besides ourselves, Mr. Dobson the interpreter, a Sr. Moziño, and Mr. Broughton, these two gentlemen speaking french [sic] very well made a greater certainty of our perfectly understanding each other."

The accounts of the meeting of the two commissioners differ. Bodega recorded that it was held in two sessions, one before dinner and one after. Bodega would write that at the first session, Vancouver told him that

> the preamble to the Convention, Article I, and the letter of Count Floridablanca authorized me to deliver everything to him, and if this were not done, he would leave and so advise his Court. Because of this, I explained to him

> that he was in error, making him see that none of these documents gave me the authority to transfer ownership nor abandon the establishment. [I added that] I was resolved to leave, believing that it was the best means of avoiding further unpleasantness and being convinced that his court would not be opposed to fixing the dividing line at [the Strait of Juan de] Fuca nor even for us to return to [re]establish ourselves if some day this should be considered necessary ... I said to him that if our sovereigns had in mind to determine that [the establishment] should be handed over without any further investigation other than the terms he sought, the commissioners had nothing further to do.

As dinner was ready, they decided to continue the discussion afterward. At the second session, Bodega would write, they "went over the same points and in agreement at last [Vancouver] decided to give way, replying [to my previous communication] at my own table." Vancouver's account is fuller:[59]

> Sr. Quadra principally vindicated the conduct of Martínez, and laid considerable stress on the donations of Maquinna, in putting them in possession of the lands they now occupy; and on these grounds, he seemed to establish the rights of the Spanish Crown, and to have adopted that opinion in consequence of the information he had acquired, and a certain part thereof communicated to me, since his arrival in this Port. He also pointed out the small place Mr. Meares' house occupied, which identical spot was not occupied by Spain. I might take possession of those few yards when I pleased. These being subjects entirely foreign to my business, he was informed that I could not enter into any argument or discussion to that effect ... This being finally understood, it was agreed we should respectively represent our transactions to our different courts, who possessing such information should decide on the subject of right &ca. In the meantime he would leave me in full possession of these territories, which he would quit as soon as his Vessel was ready to receive him.

According to Bodega, Vancouver wrote the following while seated at Bodega's dining room table and later dated it on board the *Discovery*, September 12:

> I have received your favour of the 11th and in reply have only to say, when it is convenient to you to put me in possession of the territories [sic] on the north west coast of America in accordance with Article I of the Convention,

or of the adjacent islands, which I conceive to be the territories [sic] with which we are concerned, I am ready to receive them.

Bodega understood from Dobson's translation that Vancouver had accepted his terms. Thus, in reply while seated at the table, he wrote that he was "ready to deliver in accordance with Article I the territory [singular] which British subjects occupied in April, 1789, and to leave [you] ours[60] until the courts have decided. This is as far as my powers extend."

Bodega signed his letter and handed it to Dobson. When it was translated to him orally, Vancouver believed it meant that Bodega agreed with his position. Likewise, Bodega took Dobson's translation to convey Vancouver's acquiescence in what he had affirmed from the outset. In apparent agreement, the two commissioners congratulated themselves on the successful outcome of their negotiation; however, their satisfaction was premature. It is clear from the texts of each letter that Vancouver wrote "territories," meaning the whole of Yuquot, whereas Bodega wrote "territory," meaning only the small cove where Meares had built his hut and the *North West America*.[61] Dobson translated both letters correctly, but because the meeting had been conducted in three languages, it is possible that, when pronounced, the difference in French between *territoires* and *territoire*, "territories" and "territory," would have been impossible to detect. It is also possible that, having had an excellent dinner and having enjoying a bottle or two of Bodega's wine, neither commissioner detected the difference between the two key words.

When he was back on board the *Discovery*, Vancouver realized that his optimism had been misplaced and that, although Bodega had not included his important caveat about not relinquishing Spanish sovereignty, his letter referred only to the small cove. Vancouver felt it necessary to reply in a further epistle, which not only took the negotiation back to the beginning but also injected an emotion that until now had been conspicuously absent. In a mood of exasperation he had not previously exhibited, he said in his reply dated September 13 that he was "excessively astonished" that after their "explanatory conversation" of the previous evening, translation of Bodega's letter made it necessary to correspond further.

This time he spelled out at great length his understanding of what he meant by territories:

What I understand to be the territories of which His Britannic Majesty's subjects were dispossessed and that are to be restored to them by Article I of the Convention and Count Florida Blanca's letter, is this place *in toto*, and Port

> Cox. If it is not in your power to put me in full possession, I can have no idea of hoisting the British flag in the place you have indicated in that cove,[62] which is of little more than one hundred *varas* wide in extent in any direction.[63] Nevertheless, if such are the circumstances in which you find yourself, I shall decline receiving any restitution on the part of His Britannic Majesty, and as soon as the ships of His Britannic Majesty under my command are ready, I shall proceed to sea if in the meantime I do not receive further instructions from the British court on this subject.

Vancouver went on to say that he could not avoid observing the "material difference" between Bodega's last two letters and his first, the key part of which he quoted;[64] he then added that in his view, the houses and gardens were located on the "territories of which the British subjects were dispossessed in April 1789." He was, of course, pointing out Bodega's increasingly narrow interpretation of Article I.

This change had also been noted by Vancouver's people. In one of his periodic letters to Sir Joseph Banks, president of the Royal Society, Archibald Menzies referred to Bodega's altered position as "wonderfully prevaricated."[65] Bell remarked: "Now Mr. Quadra says that, as this was the only place occupied by Meares, *this spot* of ground, and *this spot only* was all the tracts of land of which the subjects of His Britannic Majesty were dispossessed ... and to no more than which they have any right or claim."[66]

Although Vancouver is silent on the matter, some of his officers suspected that Bodega had been influenced by the Americans, in particular by Joseph Ingraham, captain of the *Hope*. In another letter to Banks, Menzies wrote that Bodega had at first been willing to hand over "all the houses, gardens, &c as they stood" but had been persuaded by Ingraham not to do so.[67] Thomas Manby, a midshipman on the *Discovery* and later master of the *Chatham*, wrote in his journal: "The arrival of an American brig stopped the intended plan [to turn Nootka over to the British], the master of her having sufficient influence with the Spaniards, persuaded them that the treaty between the two nations only gave the English the spot of which they were dispossessed by Senr. Martinez."[68]

In his journal, Ingraham also noted this change of position in a detailed account of the negotiation given to him by John Howell of the American fur trader *Margaret*, who was enjoying Bodega's hospitality ashore in one of the houses.[69] Ingraham implies that he offered Bodega advice: "In my opinion, agreeable to the 1st article of the convention if our information was his guide, he was to cede nothing as no subject of His Britannic Majesty was ever dispossessed of any lands or buildings – but of ships only.

The land when the Spanish arrived was occupied by the Indians only and buildings there were none, but had been long disposed of."[70]

It is worth examining whether Ingraham or other Americans influenced Bodega, as the British suspected. Recall that in the summer of 1789, Martínez had shown a marked friendliness toward the two Americans, Gray and Ingraham, who had witnessed his seizure of Meares's ships. Their vessels were not molested, and on the Fourth of July Martínez even shared in their celebration of Independence Day. Furthermore, Ingraham's letter to Bodega recounting the events of 1789 had been biased: favourable toward Spanish interests and hostile toward those of the Englishman Meares, their rival in the fur trade.

It is doubtful that Bodega was swayed by the Americans; it is also clear that he was pleased with the letters of Viana, Gray, and Ingraham, which suited the Spanish case – they had told him what he wanted to hear. More important, though, was that they confirmed essentially what the viceroy had concluded from his own inquiries. In the final analysis, Spain needed support for her position, and the American captains were fully willing to lend that support. In turn, their anomalous situation – they were foreigners infringing on Spanish sovereignty by trading on the Northwest Coast – was conveniently overlooked by the Spaniards. Whatever doubts he harboured about their objectivity, Bodega did not hesitate to use their testimony and support when negotiating with Vancouver.[71]

Spanish historian Luis Mariñas Ortero has written that, because the "Americans had no pretensions of any kind over the territory of Nootka, there was no need to take any measures against them."[72] Nor were they seeking any special concessions from Maquinna. There is no doubt that Bodega and Ingraham liked each other, and Ingraham's feelings for Bodega were shared by all the American visitors, both for his person and for the consideration he demonstrated for their welfare. But there is no evidence that Martínez and Gray conspired to refute Meares's claims.

Another factor united the American and Spanish interests against Britain. Spain shared with the infant United States an animosity and distrust of England. The American traders would not have viewed with equanimity the prospect of British merchants settling into Nootka and establishing a position that excluded all other traders. With Spain in possession, American access was virtually unrestricted.

Bodega expressed surprise at Vancouver's reaction; he, too, believed that their business had been successfully concluded. Replying immediately and at some length, he repeated his offer to leave Vancouver in possession not only of the territories (plural) that British subjects enjoyed in April 1789 but also of those lands that were formerly occupied by the natives of the country and now taken up by the Spaniards as a consequence of the cession made to them by Maquinna. He then referred back to the point of "legitimate right" he had mentioned in his first letter and amplified it: "Neither do you have the authority to dispute nor I to cede the ownership of this land ... Our [difference] consists solely over the rights of possession and of property. You say you are authorized to receive the whole. I am not authorized to deliver on those terms."

In other words, he was prepared to yield occupancy but not sovereignty. He repeated that he was willing to turn over to Vancouver the small cove "as something belonging to Great Britain" since "the English occupied it at that time." He would, in addition, leave the English in possession of the whole site while "reserving only the right of ownership which I have no authority to transfer." Joint possession, he thought, would "comply with the sense of the treaty." Bodega did not concede that he had changed his mind or that he had retreated from his first position, as his "first expressions" were always limited by the words "without prejudice to our legitimate right" – that is to say, "without renouncing the right of ownership which I understand must remain with the king, my master."

Bodega had introduced into the negotiation the distinction between occupation and ownership. Vancouver had failed to grasp the significance of the phrase "without prejudice to our legitimate right," by which Bodega meant that he was not empowered to surrender Spanish sovereignty over Nootka and that he could not agree to anything that might weaken Spain's claim to the coast north of San Francisco.

Vancouver was struggling with the circumstance that he had no formal instructions, which compelled him to rely on Article I of the convention and Floridablanca's Royal Order. He was also handicapped by the fact before reaching Nootka he had taken formal possession for Britain of land near the entrance to today's Puget Sound,[73] of the entire coast from Cape Mendicino northward to Cape Flattery, and of the Strait of Juan de Fuca, Puget Sound, Georgia Strait, and all the islands in between. Even had he been tempted to accept Bodega's offer to share Yuquot, either the whole of it or just that small cove on the northwest corner, to have done so would have meant weakening his own claim of title. His only recourse at this point was to dig in his heels and avoid any acknowledgment of Spain's sovereignty north of Cape Mendocino. Bodega had forced him into a stalemate.

The following morning, September 15, Vancouver replied at length, expanding his thinking but changing nothing of the substance of his previous letters. He did, however, insist on the cessation of any further correspondence on this matter other than a positive reply from Bodega indicating whether he wished "to restore through me ... the said territories."

Bodega, for his part, felt that an equally full reply was in order.[74] In a firm but patient tone, he reviewed their entire correspondence. He assured Vancouver "in categorical terms" that he was prepared to carry out everything required by Floridablanca's letter. In his first letter, he had demonstrated that when Martínez arrived, none of Meares's buildings were standing and that the Spanish established themselves without violence. In his next letter, that of September 2, he had pointed out that the Spanish establishment was located on land donated by Maquinna and not on the land Meares had occupied without purchasing it from Maquinna. The only stipulation he was placing on his agreement was to let their respective governments resolve the question of sovereignty over that portion of the cove which Spain had developed.

At this point, Bodega made a second offer. He proposed a division of the entire cove into two equal parts, one English and the other Spanish. In the event the Spanish court should decide that Spain should have "some establishment, it could count on the site as its property"; by the same token, the British could consider the other half as theirs. Meanwhile, the houses and the gardens would remain "at the disposal of British subjects." If this was not acceptable, he, too, while regretting their failure to reach agreement, would have to leave "in two or three days."

This second offer was not very practical, and Bodega must have been confident that Vancouver would reject it. He gave no reason for proposing it, and it is possible that he wanted to test the strength of Vancouver's determination to stick to his "all or nothing" stance.

Just before Vancouver received Bodega's letter, the *San José el Fénix*, a Portuguese brig, arrived in Yuquot with the Englishman Robert Duffin on board as supercargo. Duffin had been at Nootka with Meares in 1788 and again with Colnett in 1789. He had been arrested along with Colnett and sent to San Blas. Vancouver promptly asked Duffin for a sworn statement of his recollections of the events of 1789. Duffin flatly contradicted the testimony of Gray and Ingraham, asserting that Meares had indeed purchased from Maquinna and his near relative, Callicum, "the whole of the Land that forms Friendly Cove." Other buildings had been erected, and the house he had erected was substantial and was in good condition when Meares departed.

Vancouver did not mention Duffin's statement in his formal report, but he dealt with it at length in his *Voyage*. His editor and biographer Kaye Lamb believes that since he made no comment on Duffin's story, Vancouver himself probably doubted its veracity.[75] Nevertheless, Vancouver confronted Bodega with this new account. Bodega assured him that Duffin could not be objective in the matter and "that one should not make any judgement from a simple expression, especially when it was discovered how frivolous Meares's account had been when he compromised two friendly nations, thinking perhaps that without another report the fantastic amount [of damages] he was claiming from Spain would be satisfied."

Knowing that Vancouver would use Duffin's statement, Bodega sought a formal statement from Maquinna about any arrangement he might have made with Meares – something, he said, he had not previously thought necessary. He asked Maquinna to meet him in the house occupied by James Magee, commander of the *Margaret.* "All those who were able to attend" were asked to serve as witnesses for an affidavit. These included Barros Andrade, the commandant of the *San José el Fénix;* John Howell, a British passenger on the *Margaret;* José Jiménez, the chaplain of the *Activa*; and Salvador Menéndez, the *piloto* of the *Activa.* The naturalist José Moziño served as interpreter for Maquinna.

When cross-examined, Maquinna flatly denied that he had sold Meares any land. Asked what he had sold to Meares, he replied – using the word *huic* ("no") – that he had done no such thing. All he had sold him were "sea otter pelts at the rate of ten for each sheet of copper."[76] He had sold John Kendrick a bit of land in Marbuina [Marvinas Bay] for ten muskets and a little powder,[77] and he had "donated" to Eliza the site of the Spanish settlement on the condition that it be returned to him whenever the Spanish withdrew.[78]

The negotiations had now reached complete deadlock, and both commissioners announced their intention to depart. After studying Bodega's letter, Vancouver decided on September 19 to "request in person a moment's conversation to know if [Bodega] was firmly determined in adhering to the principle of his last letter." When Bodega replied that he was, "I informed him I should henceforward consider it a Spanish port, and requested his permission to carry on our necessary avocations." Vancouver thought it desirable to send one more letter. The Spanish commissioner's letter of September 15, he wrote, "instead of drawing (us) closer to a conclusion ... appears positively tending to make the execution of our instructions more and more remote."

Clearly annoyed that three weeks of valuable surveying time had been wasted in fruitless exchanges, Vancouver added in a final paragraph that he

> could not avoid mentioning the delay that the present mode of proceeding will occasion, so different from the sentiments you expressed in writing and

> in conversation on our arrival. [These] induced me to clear the store-ship and deposit her cargo in the warehouses, which at that time I conceived were to be ceded to His Britannic Majesty. The alteration that has since taken place obliges me to reload this ship. Thus my stay in this place will be prolonged infinitely longer than my desires or intentions.

To this unexpected barb of ill will, Bodega caustically commented in his *Viaje* that

> although I might have replied at greater length to the trivial reason he gives to attribute his delay to me, when he was forced to remove the cargo from the frigate *Daedalus* to examine the supplies, and neither the overhaul of the brig *Chatham* nor his [celestial] observations had been completed, I thought it better to take no notice [of it].

He confined his last letter to a simple expression of regret that Vancouver had been unable to "appreciate the expressions" of his first letter.

So ended the negotiations. The two commissioners could agree only to refer the entire matter to their respective governments for a final decision in light of the more accurate information their meeting had brought to light. They also agreed to meet again in Monterey in the hope that Vancouver's promised formal instructions would reach him there.

The strong sentiments in Vancouver's final letter, if examined in isolation or quoted out of context, could be taken to mean that the commissioners had clashed. But there was no interruption in the exchange of charts called for in their respective instructions, and we have it from Vancouver himself that

> it was a matter of no small satisfaction, that although on this subject such manifest difference arose in our opinions, it had not the slightest effect on our personal intercourse with each other, or on the advantages we derived from our mutual offices; we continued to visit as usual, and this day Senrs. Quadra and Caamaño, with most of the Spanish officers, honoured me with their company at dinner.[79]

The good humour, which continued to prevail after it was clear that there would be no agreement, is well described by Bell. Alluding to Vancouver's farewell dinner, he wrote:

> On this day Mr. Quadra took his farewell dinner with Captn. Vancouver on

> board the *Discovery* as he intended sailing the next day ... The healths of the Spanish and English sovereigns were toasted with great loyalty, and accompanied by a salute of 21 guns from the *Discovery*, and Mr. Quadra's health and good passage to his next port was most cheerfully bumpered, and accompanied by a salute of 13 guns. In the evening he insisted on our all going on shore, and spending the last evening with him, which we did exceedingly pleasantly with singing, music, dancing and all kinds of amusements ... Captain Vancouver and Seigr. Quadra parted on as good terms as they met."[80]

This last sentiment was confirmed by Vancouver. "The day passed," he wrote, "with the utmost cheerfulness and hilarity."[81]

It is evident that, as the negotiations progressed, Vancouver came to realize he would not be able to obtain the complete cession of the Spanish establishment. He had become more and more frustrated with the failure of his superiors to provide him with adequate instructions and by their ignorance regarding the extent of Spanish activities on the Northwest Coast. In a lengthy private letter written to Undersecretary of State Nepean, Vancouver worried that he might be criticized for his refusal to agree to either of Bodega's proposals.[82] Had he accepted this "small pittance of rocks and sandy beach" without positive direction, "there can be little doubt that I should either [have] proven myself a most consummate fool or a traitor." In addition, Vancouver wrote, "had cession been made agreeable to what I had conceived to be honourable and just," he would have left the *Chatham* at Nootka "to protect the port," weakening his ability "to prosecute a voyage of investigation ... I was left totally in the dark what measures to pursue." Faced with this situation, he could only insist on the exact wording of the convention and what "my own common understanding dictated as most compatible with honour and the duty and allegiance I owe my sovereign and country."[83]

To some extent, Vancouver's fears were confirmed. Among the Colonial Office papers is an unsigned and undated minute attributed to Philip Stephens, the Secretary of the Admiralty. The author "regretted" that Vancouver had not accepted Bodega's proposal, as "we would have been in possession and under these circumstances would have been on a better footing for negotiating ... than when the Spaniards are in possession ... All that we are anxious about is ... the safety of our national honour, which renders a *restitution* necessary. The extent of that *restitution* is not of much moment."[84]

Historians who have studied the Nootka crisis have generally dismissed the Bodega–Vancouver negotiation as unimportant because no agreement emerged. This is true in the narrow sense, but to dismiss the commissioners' failure to agree is to ignore what the negotiations revealed. In the first place, the accounts of the commissioners not only describe how they carried out their delicate mission but tell us a good deal about the men themselves. Bodega was the consummate diplomat, secure in the knowledge that he enjoyed the viceroy's confidence. He had prepared himself carefully for the meeting, and his communications, although not always drafted in the clearest language, were always courteous. Bodega's ability to deal easily with people, clearly established on his voyages, was manifest on this occasion as well.

Understandably, Vancouver was weakened by the failure of his superiors to provide him with any guidance. He could do little more than adhere strictly to what he understood to be the essence of his mandate – to accept the surrender of the Nootka establishment. However, it is doubtful whether any instructions would have been much help. The problem was not so much the lack of precise information on the "buildings and lands," important as that was, but the almost total ignorance of his superiors about the strength of Spain's claim to the coast based on nearly two decades of extensive exploration and numerous formal acts of possession along the coast.

Other factors affected the outcome. Despite Vancouver's poor health, which was growing worse and beginning to affect his behaviour, we should not underestimate his strength of character and his absolute devotion to his mission, as well his almost manic determination to succeed.

It is easy to criticize Vancouver for the manner in which he conducted himself. He was the first to acknowledge his lack of experience in diplomacy, but he also lacked Bodega's patience and flexibility. His single-mindedness can be seen in the way he limited his focus to the text of the convention and Floridablanca's Royal Order and in his growing impatience with Bodega's insistence on discussing issues he considered outside the scope of their mission. He never considered compromise on the core issue, on an ad referendum basis, as did Bodega. In the final analysis, Vancouver was not prepared to give up what amounted to a substantial claim to British sovereignty on the Northwest Coast, from San Francisco northward at least as far as Nootka, in exchange for a "small pittance of rocks and sandy beach," without authority from his masters.

The commissioners were playing a high-stakes political game, one that touched on important questions of imperial policy: for Britain, freedom of trade and access to the Pacific coast; for Spain, the protection of her American empire. By astutely playing his weaker hand, Bodega denied England the fruits of Pitt's diplomatic success. By refusing to discuss the issue of sovereignty, Vancouver frustrated the Spanish hope that the Strait of Juan de Fuca would become the agreed-on limit of their respective interests.

With the Bodega-Vancouver negotiations at an impasse, both governments reassessed their positions, as Bodega expected they would. The British government did not attempt immediately to reopen the issue of the turnover of the Nootka establishment; first, they dealt with John Meares's claims for compensation for his syndicate's losses. After a protracted negotiation, the Second Nootka Convention was concluded. In it, 210,000 pesos *fuertes* was set as a complete indemnification for all of Meares's losses, including land and ships, although Meares and his associates, according to one author, "did not receive a dollar."[85] Then in 1794, by the terms of the Third Nootka Convention, Spain and England agreed to the Spanish establishment's "mutual abandonment."

Bodega realized that his success in defending Spanish interests in the North Pacific had enabled Spain to regain some of the prestige and stature she had lost through her humiliation by Pitt and her desertion by France. This result of Bodega's mission was reflected in a comment in his *Viaje* "that [Vancouver] and all sixteen French, English, Portuguese and American vessels touching [Nootka] during my residence will spread word of the assistance for which they are indebted to me." Finally, the two commissioners' failure to agree on the northern limits of Spanish sovereignty forced a re-examination of New Spain's strategic situation.

11

Leaving Nootka

WITH THE NEGOTIATIONS ENDED, Bodega prepared to leave Nootka. He made the rounds to all the communities at Yuquot to assure them that the new commandants, first Jacinto Caamaño and then Salvador Fidalgo, would continue his friendly relations with them. Early on the morning of September 20, 1792, Maquinna arrived at the commandant's house in response to Bodega's invitation.[1] The news that Bodega would be leaving the next day so upset the chief that he wished he had not been told. Bodega consoled him with the hope that he would return. He asked Maquinna to maintain the same harmonious relationship with Caamaño and "never to forget the affection with which I had always treated him." The chief's distress may have been due to his knowledge that Fidalgo would be replacing Caamaño. Maquinna would have felt some apprehension, remembering Fidalgo's brutal response to the murder of a Spaniard at Neah Bay. The same day, Bodega called on the captains of all the ships in port to say good-bye and to let them know he had instructed Caamaño to allow the entry and use of the port by ships of all nations.

That night, when Vancouver and Bodega dined on the *Discovery*, they discussed their plan to meet again before the year's end. Vancouver needed to remain at Nootka for another three weeks, so Bodega assured him that Caamaño had been instructed to permit him "the use of the stores, the hospital and the vegetable gardens with the same freedom he enjoyed from me" and to give him any assistance he might request.[2] By mutual agreement, "Monterey was appointed as the next rendezvous where next we should meet."[3] After exchanging thirteen-gun salutes with Vancouver's ships, Bodega departed on the *Activa* early on September 21 and sailed for Neah Bay.

Neah Bay

Shortly after leaving the sound, Bodega sighted Robert Gray in the *Columbia* with the sloop *Adventure* in company.[4] Bodega had by then explored with Gray the idea of purchasing the sloop, and when they spoke, they agreed to discuss it further at Neah Bay. The *Adventure* joined Bodega in convoy.

The short journey to Neah Bay was uneventful until the three vessels reached Tatoosh Island. There the strong current flowing out of the strait and the variable winds made it dangerous to attempt an entry in the dark. Bodega tacked off the island for two days, until the elements moderated sufficiently to allow him to enter the bay. In his *Viaje*, Bodega did not mention two events that occurred during this delay. One was recorded by John Boit of the *Columbia*: "I went with the Pinnace to the Assistance of the *Acteva* [sic], she having been oblig'd to anchor near Cape Flattery, in a dangerous situation. When I came on board, instead of using ev'ry effort to get clear of the threat'ning Danger, they was performing Mass."[5]

The second was recorded by Joseph Ingraham on the *Hope*.[6] He was more understanding than Boit. When Ingraham and John Hoskins, the *Columbia*'s supercargo, went out to meet Bodega after his ship had anchored for the night, some four leagues from the *Adventure*, they found him

> displeased we had not sent our longboats off to him the preceding evening. But we informed him the longboats of both vessels were hoisted in; besides that the distance was too great to risk our boats with few men where the savages were so numerous and by no means to be trusted, having not long before murdered the first lieutenant of the *Princesa* not far from the ship. These well grounded reasons apparently satisfied Don Juan that our not sending our boats did not proceed from inattention or neglect, which is certain his kind treatment of us did not merit.[7]

Ingraham continued:

> I told the commandant if the boats would be of any service to him at that time we would send them immediately. He desired we would, which we did, being chagrined on our part that inadvertently we should give the least cause

to suspect our want of attention to the man from whom we had received many marks of kindness and whom we had the greatest reasons to esteem.

The *Activa* was taken in tow, and Ingraham and Hoskins were rewarded with an invitation to stay for dinner. A mollified Bodega was "in remarkably good spirits, joking on the arrangements they had made agreeable to the convention by the two learned plenipotentiaries."[8]

On September 28, Bodega anchored near the *Princesa*, which saluted him, as did the American ships. Fidalgo hauled down his pennant in recognition of Bodega's higher rank and came over to the commandant to present his compliments. Bodega invited all the officers to dine with him on his ship, after which they toured the establishment.

Bodega had several administrative items to attend to. First, even before anchoring, he wrote out instructions for Fidalgo to proceed to Nootka to relieve Caamaño of the command of the establishment – which, he noted, would remain Spanish "for the moment." Fidalgo was particularly enjoined to ensure "good treatment, harmony with the British and all foreigners who might arrive at [Nootka], granting them free entry, use and [the right to] trade with the natives, and granting them whatever assistance you have in your power as I have done up to now."[9] The orders to Fidalgo did not mention the good relations he should maintain with Maquinna or the natives, but in view of Fidalgo's earlier attack on a native canoe, the subject was most likely discussed. Fidalgo's tenure at Nootka would see no recurrence of this brutal act of vengeance, and although he did not prove to be as genial a host as Bodega, he nevertheless enjoyed good relations with the Nootkan people during the time he served there, from October 2, 1792, to June 7, 1793.

Second, Bodega investigated the circumstances of *piloto* Antonio Serrantes's death. He called a number of Neah Bay's local chiefs, especially the most important two, Tutusi and Tatlacu, to a gathering. All agreed that the murder had been committed by Indians of a neighbouring village, and each stoutly maintained his people's innocence. Bodega was not persuaded by their protestations; he believed that "Tutusi and Tatlacu are themselves capable of doing as much again to anyone who may be careless about trusting them or the women who come to the ships."[10] He nevertheless gave them the gardens and the buildings that Fidalgo had not had time to dismantle.[11]

Third, Bodega reviewed the decision reached by the *junta* convened by Alonso de Torres y Guerra at Neah Bay. The *junta* had judged that the strait contained no other harbour or bay suitable for an establishment; however, Bodega added the observation that Discovery Bay near the entrance to

Puget Sound was an excellent harbour even though it was too far from the ocean for the surveillance of shipping proceeding along the Pacific coast.

Finally, Bodega concluded the purchase of the *Adventure* on September 28. Gray had decided to part with her because "she sails very dull, is so small and we want the men; we thought it the best we should part with her."[12] Although he did not need her, Bodega thought she "might be very useful to the [Naval] Department [of San Blas] in case it was necessary to expedite some dispatches," and she did indeed prove valuable in that role. Because the witnesses' methods of calculating the value of a sea otter pelt varied, there is uncertainty as to what Bodega paid for the sloop. The bill of sale signed by Gray and Bodega and witnessed by Hoskins and Matthew Weatherhead indicates that the sale was for "Fifteen hundred Dollars in kind."[13] The "kind," according to Captain Robert Haswell, consisted of "75 [otter] skins of superior quality," which Boit, the businessman, calculated as "72 prime Sea Otter Skins worth 55 Dollars each in Canton which is equall to 3960$, which at 50 per Cent advance at home is 7440 Spanish Piasters, which is a good price."[14] Ever the courtier, Bodega renamed his new ship the *Orcacitas*, one of the viceroy's family names.[15]

Flying the Spanish flag and under the command of Gonzalo López de Haro, the *Orcacitas* sailed in convoy with the *Activa* for Monterey to meet Vancouver. As Bodega left Neah Bay on the morning of September 29, Gray saluted him with thirteen guns, and the honour was returned. Thus came to an end Spain's brief presence in what is today the State of Washington.

The Commissioners in Monterey

Bodega arrived in Monterey on October 9.[16] Caamaño, in the slower *Aránzazu*, sailed in on the twenty-second of the month. The frigate *Santa Gertrudis* and the schooners *Sutil* and *Mexicana* were already anchored in the bay. Having sailed from San Blas, the *Santa Saturnina*, commanded by Juan Carrasco, was in San Francisco. Carrasco hastened to join Bodega in Monterey to hand him a Royal Order, dated February 29, 1792, which informed Bodega that the king had not approved Revillagigedo's instruction to Bodega to turn Nootka over to Captain Vancouver. The Spanish court wanted to wait until Britain's intentions became more fully known.[17] This must have been a great relief for Bodega, for it confirmed the wisdom of his conduct throughout the negotiations. The Royal Order also informed him that as the Nootka Convention did not give equal rights to any other country unless agreed to by Spain, ships of a third country (the United States, for instance) were to be warned not to return to Nootka until that power signed a similar convention. López de Haro left on October 21 to convey this information to Fidalgo at Nootka. He returned safely on December 23.

Bodega was cordially received by the authorities at Monterey. The day after his arrival, Brother Fermín Francisco de Lasuén, Junípero Serra's successor as Franciscan Father President of the province, came to call. The following day, Bodega and some of his officers dined with the fathers at their mission. When Bodega took up residence in the presidio with the acting governor, Lieutenant José Dario Argüello, he continued to fly his broad pennant on the *Activa.*

If we can believe the gossip of Edward Bell of the *Chatham,* there were some rumblings of discontent regarding the manner in which Bodega exercised his authority as the senior officer at Monterey. Without revealing his source, Bell wrote that Bodega

> took on him[self] the command of the province but this step I have since heard was an usurpation that he was by no means authorized to take on him[self] and for which he was blamed by his own officers at the time. His power extended not so far; he was Governor of San Blas and Tepic only and commandant-in-chief of the Naval forces of San Blas and on the coast of California.[18]

It is unlikely that this grumbling arose from Argüello, who was friendly, helpful, and hospitable. There is no other reference to this criticism. Whoever Bell's source may have been, as a navy captain in command of all Spanish vessels on the Pacific coast, Bodega clearly outranked Argüello. Moreover, Bodega considered his position in Monterey as integral to his responsibilities as commandant of the Expedition of the Limits and in no way different from his role at Nootka.[19]

Bodega was shocked to find that Monterey was virtually defenceless. While awaiting Vancouver's arrival and to disguise the "abandoned" state of the port, he installed the eight cannon he had brought from Nootka in front of the presidio on a wooden platform to make a small battery.[20] As the powder on hand in the presidio was "useless," he ordered fifty *quintals* of dry powder to be brought on shore from the *Sutil, Mexicana,* and *Santa Gertrudis.* For the time being, the small battery would serve for saluting.[21] Bodega ordered the emplacement of guns on Punta Quemada for the better defence of the harbour, the presidio, and the ships at anchor.[22] Vancouver's trained eye noted the cannon and recognized the inadequate and temporary nature of their installation: "These guns are planted on the open plain ground without any breast work or other screen for those employed in working them, or the least cover or protection from the winter."[23]

Bodega continued to improve the defences even while the two commissioners and their squadrons were in Monterey. Thomas Manby recorded that "a few brass guns have been lately sent from St. Blas and an engineer is daily expected to erect a battery near the entrance to the Bay."[24] Vancouver himself commented that "the four dismounted cannon [already seen at the presidio], together with those placed at the entrance into the presidio, are intended for a fort to be built on a small eminence which commands the anchorage. A large quantity of lumber is at present in readiness for carrying that design into execution."[25] Even so, Vancouver did not think the change would materially strengthen Monterey's defences:

> When completed [the fort] might certainly be capable of annoying vessels lying in that part of the bay which affords the greatest security, but could not be of any importance after landing was accomplished, as the hills behind it might easily be gained, from whence the assailing party would soon oblige the fort to surrender; nor do I consider Monterrey [sic] to be a very tenable port without an extensive line of works.[26]

Although Vancouver's ship *Discovery* got away from Nootka on October 12, he did not rejoin Bodega for six weeks. En route south, Joseph Whidbey examined Gray's Harbor, and William Robert Broughton explored the Columbia River for a hundred miles upstream.[27] Delayed by severe storms, Vancouver reached San Francisco on November 14. He spent ten days there, during which he was warmly received and entertained by the elderly ensign Hermenegildo Sal, the acting commandant of the presidio, whom Bodega had ordered to extend the British captain any help he might need.

On hearing that the *Daedalus* had reached Monterey on November 22, Vancouver left San Francisco on November 25 with the *Chatham.* Both ships arrived in Monterey on November 27. Entering the bay, he hoisted a recognition signal previously arranged with Bodega. After an exchange of salutes, the ships were directed to an anchorage below the presidio. That evening the six ships of the two commissioners' squadrons were riding at anchor together once again.

No sooner had the *Discovery* and the *Chatham* anchored than Bodega called on Vancouver, who showed him the fruits of his survey of the coast, including Whidbey's chart of Gray's Harbor and Broughton's chart of the Columbia. Bodega was pleased to see Bruno de Hezeta's 1775 discovery of the river's mouth confirmed. He also accepted as more accurate Vancouver's location of Gray's Harbor and the longitude of Cape Mendocino; later he would incorporate these corrections on the *Carta General* he was drafting of the entire Pacific coast north of San Blas. He noted, though, that Vancouver had failed to see Puerto Sidman (Winchester Bay) at the outlet of the Umpqua River, which Captain James Baker of the British fur trader *Jenny* reported having seen.[28]

As at Nootka, Bodega was the cordial host. Vancouver's ships all needed repairs, and the Spanish caulkers again helped with the task. Bodega's guests once more dined off his personal silver service, and again as at Nootka, at least twenty-four people would sit down to dinner at the presidio.[29] Bell commented: "Mr. Quadra and his Officers rendered the place extremely pleasant. He ... gave free permission to every person to take their recreation on shore where they pleased without any bounds and furnished the officers with horses whenever they were applied for so that scarce a day passed without some party being made to ride through the country."[30] Bodega also arranged for shooting parties to go out into the countryside to hunt quail, partridge, geese, duck, deer, hare, and rabbit. Manby, one of the *Discovery*'s midshipmen, relished these outings and vigorous activities. He wrote that "the foxes afforded us excellent sport, as in the extensive plains they gave us a chase of great length which sometimes terminated in their death by riding over them ... The Spaniards frequently pursue them on horseback and kill them with their lances."[31] There were also bear hunts. Visits on horseback to neighbouring villages and missions and even horse races were organized. As Archibald Menzies related, "parties were out daily traversing the country in almost every direction for ten or twelve miles round."[32] On some occasions, Bodega accompanied his visitors, and when he did so he took along his "plate and cooking equipage ... so that we had always the luxury of dining in those retreats off silver, and on the best of everything he could afford."[33]

Not every event organized for the benefit of the British was appreciated. A bullfight that Menzies mentioned without comment was viewed with horror by Manby. He was obviously unfamiliar with the classic ritual of the *corrida* when he wrote: "A Bull is dragged into the presidio square and there cruelly tormented for an hour, till the poor Animal becomes perfectly mad. All the Spaniards express a partiality for this barbarous sport. Men on horseback attack the outrageous [sic] Beast with Lances."[34]

Bodega described his visit, accompanied by Vancouver, to the Mission of Carmel in general terms; but both Vancouver and Menzies wrote about it in considerable detail. Menzies recounted how early in the morning of December 2, a week after their arrival,

> saddled horses were sent down to the beach ... Captain Vancouver, Mr. Broughton and a large party of the officers from both vessels together with the two Sandwich Island [Hawaiian] Women mounted them. Joining Sr. Quadra and several Spanish officers, together with the Governor and his lady at the presidio, the whole formed a large cavalcade which was escorted by a guard of soldiers.[35]

As the group approached the mission, the bells were ringing. They were welcomed by Brother Lasuén, two friars, and a number of Indians, men and women, who had been converted to Christianity. The visitors were taken on a tour of the complex, including the modest quarters of the Father President and the "small and neatly ornamented" church, which, Menzies noted, was being replaced by a much larger one. They admired the mission's "very large" garden of all kinds of vegetables, melons, pumpkins, chili peppers, and a variety of fruits, including pears and peaches. Some of the group went out to see the well-cultivated fields of wheat, corn, and barley as well as peas and beans, and to view some of the eight hundred Indians working there. They also saw a large number of cattle and horses "swarming" over the fields. On their return to the mission, all were served a picnic under an arbour in one of the gardens. After dinner, some of the Indians, one disguised as a deer, demonstrated how to lure and kill such an animal with bow and arrows.[36]

The long day taken up with the visit was to prove even longer. When the British mariners and their Spanish hosts returned that evening to the presidio, the governor invited everyone to a dance at his residence. The festivities were supposed to begin at seven, but, Menzies says, the "ladies had such unusual preparations to make that they could not be got together till near ten." They were variously dressed and wore their hair "in long queues reaching down to their waists, and tied with ribands." They performed various "country dances," including the "exhilarating dance, the fandango."[37] Caught up in the spirit of the moment, Vancouver requested the two Hawaiian women on the *Discovery* to "exhibit their manner of singing & dancing," in a performance that Menzies thought "did not appear to afford much entertainment to the Spanish Ladies." It was, in fact, a disaster. Deeming that "this crude performance" mocked their favourite dance, the Spanish ladies departed quickly.

The following day, December 3, Vancouver hosted a dinner on board the *Discovery* for Bodega, the governor and his wife, and some of the women of the presidio. Unfortunately, it too failed to produce the desired results. "The motion of the ship," Vancouver wrote, "though very inconsiderable, greatly to my disappointment obliged the ladies, and indeed some of the gentlemen, very soon to retire."[38] The next time Vancouver offered such an entertainment, he did so under a large tent on shore. When it was sufficiently dark, he offered a display of fireworks, which delighted his Spanish guests.[39] "Most of the sky rockets went off well," Menzies recorded, "and were much admired, but the water rockets, being exceedingly good, never failed of exciting [the] most wonder and applause from the gazing multitude."

Vancouver and Bodega did not take part in all the outdoor activities. Vancouver spent a great deal of time writing letters, preparing charts, and making copies of his reports covering the entire expedition to the end of 1792. Bodega was also busy with administrative paperwork. His most pressing task was to report on the conduct of his subordinates during the expedition and to recommend promotions for those who had performed their duties well. At the conclusion of the Expedition of the Limits in November 1792, Revillagigedo sent to Minister Antonio Valdés in Spain a list of the officers who had "demonstrated constant proof in the performance of their responsibilities of application, zeal and ability" and whom he considered warranted their "next regular promotion and whatever beneficence the king might wish to grant them." Those mentioned in the list were Fidalgo, Caamaño, Francisco de Eliza, Manuel Quimper, Cosme Bertodano, Juan Matute, and Ramon Saavedra.[40] Bodega's endorsement of Félix de Cepeda is a puzzle. Although Bodega had sent Félix de Cepeda home before Vancouver's arrival, this seems to have had nothing to do with his difficult personality.[41] In fact, he commended him in bland terms: "Cepeda is an officer of education, he is talented and has good will."[42] He thought so highly of Quimper that he selected him to be his assistant when he became too ill to carry out his duties as commandant at San Blas in 1794.

Bodega also worked on his formal report as commandant of the Expedition of the Limits. He put a lot of time and energy into assembling the charts for the atlas folio to be annexed to the report. One chart was especially important: a revision of the third general chart he had prepared for the expedition. This fourth general chart included the information from Caamaño's exploration of the waters around the Queen Charlotte Islands, Vancouver's exploration of Puget Sound, and the findings of the Alcalá Galiano–Valdés circumnavigation of the newly named Quadra and Vancouver's Island. At the same time, he made recommendations that he presented as "reflections": first, he recommended further exploration; and second, he made a case for Spanish participation in the fur trade. He also wrote at length on the need to retain the Nootka establishment.

Taking advantage of the imminent departure of Torres and the *Santa Gertrudis* for Peru, Bodega wrote an interim report to Revillagigedo. Knowing that the viceroy would be impatient to know whether the Royal Order of February 29, 1792, not to hand over the Nootka establishment, had been received in time, Bodega offered a general assessment of his negotiations with Vancouver.[43] He described the impasse that had developed once Vancouver rejected the idea of a dividing line at the Strait of Juan de Fuca, noting that the English commissioner had refused to agree to anything less than a complete handover of the establishment at Yuquot (Friendly Cove). It was clear to him, he wrote, that

> Britain not only aspires to sole dominion and the right to trade but also to sovereignty based on Article I of the [Nootka] convention and the Royal Order issued by Count Floridablanca, that the entire land be formally handed over without any restriction whatsoever, that the Spanish flag be hauled down, and that [the British] sovereign be recognized as the sole owner of that port.

Unable to convince Vancouver that this was a position beyond his authority to negotiate, that it was not in the spirit of either Article I or the Royal Order, and that it did not recognize "our legitimate right to the lands we had cultivated," Bodega had decided to depart, leaving behind a frigate as a token of Spanish sovereignty until such time as the sovereigns could be informed and could determine the area's fate.

Bodega's second conclusion was brief: "I do not think that Britain has any right to claim the ownership of the port of Nootka, nor has Spain any obligation to cede it, or to make good the slightest injury." Expanding on this point, he revisited the arguments he had made to Vancouver about prior Spanish rights and voyages, the situation Martínez had found in 1789, and the testimony of Maquinna that refuted Meares's claim to have bought property on Friendly Cove.

Third, Bodega let Revillagigedo know that he had changed his mind over the suitability of Nootka as a port. After five months' residence, having witnessed at first hand the volume of ship traffic into the cove, he now appreciated Nootka Sound's commercial importance as a port:

> I must tell you that the port of Nootka has the best proportions of any along the entire coast. You can winter in it without fear, it can be entered and left

> quickly at any time, its inhabitants are docile, the climate healthy, there is no lack of land for growing crops nor timber for construction, and fur trading grounds abound in the immediate area.[44]

Recalling his earlier unfavourable opinion, he added that "in a word ... I see today that, without excepting our presidios, it is the only [port] in which could be formed a valuable establishment, useful to commerce." Bodega's change of mind about the sound was based on three points that had been brought to his attention the previous summer: the unsuitability of Neah Bay as a replacement for Nootka, the British desire to eliminate Spanish sovereignty north of San Francisco, and Yuquot's strategic importance as the centre of the sea otter fur trade. Holding on to Nootka, for the moment at least, seemed essential; doing so would buy the Spanish court time to decide what action to take.[45]

While he attended to these matters, Bodega also assisted two Englishmen who wanted to return to Britain by travelling across New Spain to the Caribbean. They were the merchant ship captain, Weatherhead, and Lieutenant Broughton of the *Chatham*. Bodega's efforts on their behalf led to a sharp confrontation with the viceroy.

Weatherhead had been the master of the *Matilda,* which had sailed from Spithead on March 27, 1791, carrying convicts and provisions from Britain to Port Jackson in Australia.[46] With his thirteen-year-old nephew, John Brand, he later had joined the southern whale fishery. On one such voyage, he stopped in Tahiti to refresh his crew. On departure, his ship was wrecked on an uncharted reef. Weatherhead and his nephew were rescued by the fur trader *Jenny,* which was en route to the Northwest Coast. They were let off in Clayoquot Sound, after which they made their way to Nootka.[47] Bodega arranged for them to be billeted on the *Daedalus* and promised Weatherhead he would arrange passage for him to Britain through Mexico.[48] Taking the captain and his nephew with him on the *Activa* as far as Monterey, he sent them on to San Blas on the *Santa Gertrudis.* According to Menzies, Bodega gave Weatherhead two hundred pesos from his own pocket for expenses.[49] Explaining his action to the viceroy, Bodega wrote that he had "offered him return passage to his country" in the care of Cepeda, who was sailing to San Blas on the same ship. Bodega concluded his letter by trusting "that Your Excellency's kindness will consider it appropriate to issue him a passport in order to fulfill my desires and yours."[50] In a brief reply, the viceroy told Bodega that he approved of his kindness and that a passport would be issued.[51]

Three days later, having had second thoughts and now clearly annoyed, Revillagigedo wrote again to ask a series of questions. Who had rescued Weatherhead in Tahiti? How had he reached Nootka? Why did Bodega promise to give him passage to Britain? Why did he not send him home via China with Zachary Mudge (who was going back to England with dispatches), or with Broughton, or on some British ship?[52] The viceroy's letter was waiting for Bodega when he arrived back in San Blas on February 1, 1793, but he did not answer it until February 15. His relationship with the viceroy had long been marked by mutual respect, so perhaps he was surprised that Revillagegedo was questioning his judgment now. And perhaps, as well, he simply underestimated Revillagigedo's distrust of foreigners, especially of Englishmen travelling in New Spain.

Bodega's eventual reply was short and sharp: "Human kindness alone encouraged me ... After his shipwreck he found himself in the sad condition of pleading for protection from one merchant ship to another. The captains of these ships made matters worse by forcing him to make frequent transfers." Bodega went on to assure the viceroy that Weatherhead's memory was so poor that, even though he had been in Tahiti many times, "he can tell no more than the most ordinary visitor. He will be unable to tell more in Britain than he could in San Blas."[53] Whether satisfied or not, the viceroy issued Weatherhead and his nephew the necessary travel papers and provided them with an escort to Veracruz, where they embarked for Spain on the stores ship *Santa Paula*.

Revillagigedo was much angrier when Bodega granted the same favour to Broughton. Vancouver had not thought to send Broughton back to Britain until Bodega mentioned to him at Monterey that he had received orders that British ships were to be free of the "least interruption or molestation," although vessels from other nations engaged in commerce were to be "captured" if they were encountered north of the California presidios.[54] According to Vancouver, this news led the two commissioners to believe that "our respective sovereigns had adjusted, and finally concluded, every arrangement with respect to the territories of Nootka," and that further instructions might be on the way.[55] Although Vancouver had already sent Mudge home from Nootka via China with some dispatches, including the original text of his report on the Nootka negotiations, he now considered sending the *Chatham* home with Broughton; he was anxious that the Admiralty should have "all the charts of the Spanish discoveries" that Bodega had given him so that the new negotiations would not founder for the same lack of information that had scuttled the first round of discussions. Vancouver decided it would be unwise to send a ship as small as the *Chatham* around Cape Horn alone, so he asked Bodega "if it were compatible with his inclination and the disposition of the Spanish court" that Broughton be permitted to travel through New Spain en route to Britain.[56] Bodega readily agreed. Describing Broughton as one of Vancouver's "most distinguished and able officers," he wrote to Revillagigedo to ask him "to facilitate his transit through this kingdom [New Spain] to Veracruz with all possible speed and from there to Spain in order to continue his trip to London."[57]

This letter, which arrived on the viceroy's desk at the same time as the request concerning Weatherhead, triggered an apprehension that was nearly paranoid. The viceroy could not repudiate the actions of his own commissioner, yet clearly, he was unhappy with the prospect of revealing the weaknesses of New Spain's defences to a representative of Spain's traditional enemy, especially one so highly recommended for his intelligence.

Revillagigedo's solution was to send Bodega two letters, one unrestricted, brief, and to the point. It enclosed the passports and instructed Bodega to arrange for a suitable escort.[58] The second was classified confidential, much stronger in tone, and couched in language that Bodega found distressing. It covered the cases of both Weatherhead and Broughton because, from the viceroy's point of view, they presented the same threat even though he recognized that their circumstances were different. It read as follows:

> When you informed me that the British officer [sic] Matthew Weatherhead had been sent to this kingdom, I pointed out the inconveniences and the dangers which could result from a reconnaissance of the Department of San Blas and crossing the entire kingdom, and allowing a few men who ordinarily are able and keen-sighted to [see] our harbour of Veracruz. Their secret designs do not leave any doubt.
>
> The circumstances surrounding the shipwreck which influenced you to arrange for Weatherhead to be sent to San Blas for onward passage to Europe through this kingdom and his arrival were not so distasteful to me as they arise from the desire to demonstrate hospitality, harmony and good relations.
>
> The same or similar considerations do not apply to [William] Robert Broughton. Any information which Captain Vancouver might wish to communicate to his court could be sent in writing, which would travel safely from Veracruz. You should have declined [Vancouver's request] on the grounds that the journey through our establishments by a well-educated subject of a nation which covets them is not in the interests of the state, which has imposed legitimate prohibitions.
>
> Furthermore, I would have wished to have been informed when Captain

Vancouver was expected to arrive in Monterey for the sound reason that I would have been aware [of it] in time to formulate instructions to guide you. When this was not possible, at the very least [you should have ensured] that his stay in this port was very brief.

Softening the blow a little, Revillagigedo added a final paragraph:

I appreciate the circumstances [you faced] in both cases, but, as there is no alternative, it is most important that [William] Robert Broughton not be detained in San Blas. If you yourself cannot undertake as soon as possible a journey to this capital and bring him with you, [you are to] appoint a trustworthy person to accompany him and keep an eye on him and not consent to any voluntary delay en route ... Henceforth the transportation of British people through this kingdom is to be completely avoided except in cases of shipwreck when it is offered for compassionate reasons.[59]

Stung by the tone and substance of the viceroy's letter, Bodega replied immediately and at some length.[60] He did not retreat one iota from his position, nor did he show the slightest contrition:

The conspicuous talent and deep understanding of Royal Navy Lieutenant William Robert Broughton might have caused me some misgivings if I had not seen the number of maps of our harbours and coastline already in Great Britain's possession. I also had [in mind] the precedent of Captain Colnett, who, after residing many months in this Department [of San Blas], travelled to the capital and learned that there was no reason for his journey other than to appear before your court.

After this indelicate reminder that the viceroy himself had agreed to receive Colnett while he was a prisoner in San Blas, Bodega raised the argument to a higher plane:

I generously agreed to this officer's journey as I was anxious to uphold to the last an attitude of frankness corresponding to the respect due to my mission and the honour of the Crown. [Broughton's] oral report was extremely necessary to Captain Vancouver, he told me, both for what we transacted at Nutca and to dispel many doubts that have arisen in this connection. Indeed, by itself, this purpose was sufficient to have him decide to deprive himself [of Broughton's services], notwithstanding the fact that he had sent the *Discovery*'s first lieutenant [to Britain] via China.

Bodega concluded by assuring the viceroy that he "omitted no means, consistent with civility and harmonious relations, to hasten [Vancouver's] departure."[61]

In response to Revillagigedo's suggestion that he accompany Broughton to Mexico City, Bodega arranged for José Mariano Moziño, his scientist, to accompany Broughton.[62] Moziño was given the necessary instructions and provided with letters so that they "could be supplied with all possible conveniences throughout the journey, without stopping anywhere." Broughton did stop in Mexico City long enough to call on the viceroy to thank him for the arrangements made for his journey across New Spain.

Soon after arriving in Monterey, Vancouver asked Bodega about the prices of the different livestock and "refreshements" he required to resupply his ships. Vancouver reported that Bodega put him off with the assurance that "everything the country offered was at our service" and that the cost "could easily be settled on our departure." Taking Bodega at his word, Vancouver began to replenish his ships with fresh meat, vegetables, and other foods. The fathers of the mission at Carmel undertook to provide as much as they could, and did so at no small sacrifice. Bell related that a few days before they sailed, finding that the presidio and the mission at Carmel had been "pretty well drained of vegetables, poultry, etc.," Bodega sent the *Orcacitas* across the bay to the mission at Santa Cruz. It returned with "about ten dozen fowls [and] an abundance of all kinds of roots and vegetables."[63]

Vancouver also wished to send some livestock to the newly founded colony of New South Wales, on the *Daedalus,* which had been reassigned to take supplies there. There is some disagreement as to how much livestock was taken on board. Vancouver and Menzies agree there were twelve cows, six bulls, and "a like number of ewes and rams"; Manby says there were eighteen head of cattle and thirty sheep. Since Vancouver also wanted to take some livestock to Hawaii, he asked Bodega if he could be supplied with "some black cattle, and two rams." He was provided with four cows, two bulls, four ewes and two rams.

Vancouver repeatedly raised the question of payment, but Bodega put him off each time. On the eve of his departure, Vancouver became more insistent:

> On my requesting an account of the expenses incurred for the refreshments, with which the three vessels of my command had been so amply supplied, here and at San Francisco[64] ... [Bodega] not only revolted at the idea of recovering any payment, but gave strict orders that no account would ever be rendered; nor would he accept the most common voucher, or other

> acknowledgement. [Bodega] insisted ... that ... the only settlement in which he could possibly engage, was that of seeing we were accommodated to the extent of our wishes. [His repayment would be amply made] by the promised success attending every creature and production, that we had received either for our own use, or for other purposes.[65]

An awkward problem arose on the eve of Vancouver's departure from Monterey – the desertion of some members of what he called his "community." Earlier, in December, Able Seaman James Bailey had gone ashore to seek sanctuary at the mission at Carmel. He enlisted the help of the fathers to intercede with Vancouver to seek his forgiveness for desertion but succeeded only in obtaining a promise that he would not be punished until after the ships had left Monterey. Bailey was brought back to the ships and placed in irons.[66] Two days before departure, two men from the *Chatham* deserted: a marine private, James Landon, and an armourer's mate, James Etchinson. Two Portuguese, a sailmaker and a gunner, both Roman Catholic, and an apprentice seaman disappeared at the same time. Menzies, Manby, and Bell strongly suspected that Landon's flight had been aided by the Spanish, as he had done a number of jobs for them. Vancouver did not share his officers' views. A reward of twenty-five dollars for each deserter apprehended was offered to the soldiers, but the men were able to hide in the hills until Vancouver had departed. Hearing the salutes fired by the departing ships, they surrendered at the presidio the following day.[67] When interviewed by an army officer, the Portuguese sailmaker and gunner gave as their reason that the British had not permitted them to hear the Roman Catholic mass or make confession to a priest. Landon and Etchinson claimed that they had been overworked and underpaid.

The loss of James Etchinson was especially serious. Vancouver characterized him as "a most industrious and excellent workman."[68] Bodega "very obligingly offered to replace [Etchinson] by substituting the only smith in this establishment."[69] Vancouver accepted "with great reluctance." José de los Santos was "brought on board under Guard" and "was obliged to serve much against his inclination." Bodega also ordered three apprentice seamen to replace the other deserters.[70] He gave the governor standing orders to take every measure to have all the deserters returned to Vancouver for the sake of good relations with Britain.[71]

By the beginning of January 1793, Vancouver still had not received any fresh instructions from London, so he decided to resume his voyage, which had fallen behind schedule. He would call at Nootka Sound during the summer, when he would again be on the Northwest Coast. By that time, he believed, he could reasonably expect to have received information and instructions more precise than those he held. On January 6, Vancouver completed his dispatches, letters, drawings, and charts for Broughton to take to London.[72]

Bodega was also ready to leave Monterey. He had completed his fourth general chart and had "satisfied those persons responsible in the presidios at Monterey and San Francisco for all the expenses incurred on behalf of the British and for my table." With "no other reason to delay," he left his quarters in the governor's residence and reboarded the *Activa.*

On the evening of January 6, Vancouver offered a farewell dinner, present at which were Bodega, Caamaño, the commandant of the presidio with his lady, and "most of our Spanish friends." The two commissioners "agreed we should sail together, so long as our southern course answered the purpose of our respective routes, that we might continue as long as possible to benefit from each other's society."

The *Daedalus* had already left for Australia. The departure of the remaining ships was delayed by unfavourable winds. Finally, the *Discovery* weighed anchor at nine in the morning of January 14 and proceeded to Point Pinos, there to await the *Chatham* and the three Spanish ships, the *Activa*, the *Aránzazu,* and the *Orcacitas*, which did not get away until the following day. Bodega, with the *Chatham* sailing in his wake, slowly caught up with the *Discovery*, which was tacking to enable him to do so. The slow *Aránzazu* was left behind, because Bodega "did not wish to place [Vancouver] at a disadvantage since he had the courtesy to vary his course to accompany me." The *Orcacitas* was able to maintain the pace, and when the four ships were once more together, they were at times so close that "we spoke at all hours." The group sailed in this way for three days, but on January 17, as their intended courses began to diverge – Vancouver's to the Sandwich Islands and Bodega's to San Blas – Vancouver hosted a final banquet with Bodega, Broughton, and "such of our Spanish friends could be spared." "The serenity of the sky," wrote Vancouver,

> and the smoothness of the sea, prolonged my pleasure on this occasion until near midnight, when we exchanged our mutual good wishes, and bade our friends of the *Activa* farewell ... On reaching the *Activa* our friends took their leave; we saluted them with three cheers, which they cordially returned; and we each pursued our respective voyages with all sail set.[73]

Bodega briefly mentions the banquet – "the last banquet we had" – after which "we said goodbye with the finest demonstrations of the sincere friendship we professed." Then "[Vancouver] passed astern of my poop deck and saluted me with a cheer and all his crew in the rigging, to which I responded in the same manner."[74]

This parting salutation accorded with naval protocol; it also corresponded to the close relationship that had developed between the two mariners, and was a fitting conclusion to their association. It has been variously described by historians as "a strong personal friendship," as the "very strong friendship [which] sprang up between them," as a "warm personal friendship," and as "a most cordial and friendly relationship."

Bodega, perhaps, at first considered Vancouver stiff and formal, but he saw the British officer warm quickly to his patrician charm and outgoing personality. They were able to draw on the strong bond of the sea and their experiences as maritime explorers. It was easy, then, for the two to develop a working relationship based on mutual esteem and regard. The two men shared qualities they could admire in each other – both had a strong sense of duty, were devoted to their respective sovereigns, were direct of purpose, and had plenty of what any plenipotentiary worth his salt must have: courtesy, sincerity, and respect for the other man's integrity.

Vancouver could admire the consideration that Bodega showed others, no matter what their station or vocation; his many acts of generosity, large and small; his concern for the welfare of others, expressed in many ways; and his sensitivity to native customs and culture, which Vancouver himself had shown in Hawaii. And he had witnessed the respect for Bodega shown by the Nootkan people and their chief, Maquinna. Like the native people and like the fur traders who had called at Nootka that summer, Vancouver quickly placed his trust and confidence in the Spanish commandant – sentiments shared by all who came in contact with Bodega.

On the eve of his departure from Monterey, Vancouver wrote Revillagigedo a fulsome letter in which he expressed his thanks and indebtedness to the Spanish officials in San Francisco and Monterey, not forgetting the fathers at the missions of Santa Clara, Carmel, and San Francisco. Concluding, he referred to Bodega as "my most esteemed and brotherly friend, whose noble character has made an indelible impression on my mind that will not be erased in my lifetime."[75]

Vancouver's officers and crew also held Bodega in high esteem. A year later, they raised a special toast to him on Christmas Day 1794, as they were approaching the Mexican coast during their return to Britain. As Vancouver recorded it:

> We were here at no loss to provide a repast for this our fourth Christmas day since we had quitted the civilized world ... the people were served such an extra allowance of grog as was sufficient for the celebration of the day and to call to their recollection their friends and favorites at home; on which occasion, though perhaps the circumstance may appear too trivial here to be noticed, yet as the sentiment arose spontaneously from the gratitude of the crew, I am induced to mention it: the memory of Senr Quadra."[76]

We look in vain for corresponding sentiments in Bodega's official papers, in the expectation that he might have reciprocated Vancouver's feelings. All we find are two references in his *Viaje* to "our sincere friendship," a Spanish cliché. The only compliment he pays to Vancouver relates to his chart (actually Broughton's) of the Columbia River: that "he examined it with that meticulous care that characterizes ... this indefatigable navigator." Too much importance should not be attached to this absence of private sentiments, as only on rare occasions do we find a Spanish naval officer of the period openly expressing any feeling about his brethren, be they senior or junior. Bodega's reluctance to disclose any personal sentiments for Vancouver may well have arisen from an expectation that his masters would not welcome expressions of this nature.[77] It would be sufficient to show that he had carried out the viceroy's instructions "to seek complete harmony and the most cordial relationship" with Vancouver.

In this context, although one could attribute differing motives for Bodega and Vancouver agreeing to name Quadra and Vancouver's Island after themselves, the gesture itself should not be considered hypocritical. Rather, it showed that the two men were "highly pleased" that, so far from home, they had found mutual satisfaction in a relationship that was always cordial and respectful, even when they found themselves in diplomatic disagreement.

12

Results and Consequences of the Expedition of the Limits

The Expedition of the Limits was the high point of Juan Francisco de la Bodega y Quadra's career. His diplomatic success won him recognition from his government. In the wake of the Expedition of the Limits, several people in positions of authority, including Bodega, began to consider ways of maintaining Spain's foothold in the region.

Bodega's Diplomatic Success

Bodega received warm praise from both the viceroy and the home government for his defence of Spanish interests during the negotiations with Vancouver in the summer of 1792. Even before receiving Bodega's journal – complete with the drawings, charts, and papers recording the cartographic and scientific work accomplished – Viceroy Revillagigedo congratulated him on his diplomatic success:

> Everything shows the felicity, the zeal and skill with which you have carried out the principal point of your interesting and delicate commission. Not only did you prevail over the most important ideas and designs of the English regarding the dividing line but you were able to surmount and forestall them, maintaining our occupation of the port of Nuca.

The viceroy was especially relieved that Bodega had unwittingly fulfilled the Royal Order not to surrender Nootka "by the happy coincidence of not having agreed with Captain Vancouver" and by following the "recommendations based on other Royal Orders and my letters of instructions." And all of this, he was pleased to note, had been accomplished without provoking irritation or unpleasantness, which was in accord with what both courts desired. After saying he would forward to the king Bodega's "reflections" on the retention of Nootka and other points, the viceroy promised to recommend Bodega to the monarch, "as is just [for your] efforts, hardships and the considerable merit you have shown, should he consider rewarding by whatever honours and favours might be his sovereign pleasure to award you."[1]

This was high praise from a man who demanded a high standard of performance from his naval officers and who rarely complimented them when they achieved it. One is tempted to see Revillagigedo's uncharacteristic exuberance as the expression of genuine relief on hearing that Bodega had not turned over the Nootka establishment to the British. Bodega had saved him from acute embarrassment and possible censure. Having unbent to such an unusual degree, Revillagigedo said nothing more.

The Viceroy of New Spain kept his word. He repeated his recommendation to the Minister of the Navy, Antonio Valdés, that Bodega be granted an *encomienda* in the Order of Santiago "with greater reason [since Bodega has] carried out an important and delicate commission of the Limits and exploration of the California coasts with zeal, merit and success."[2] Expressing the warm respect he had for Bodega, Revillagigedo added that

> this new distinguished accomplishment adds to other achievements realized in over thirty years of services performed under difficult circumstances. He is worthy of the *encomienda* and should be rewarded to reduce the obligations he has incurred in disinterested and honourable generosity and unavoidable expenses in carrying out the duties of the king's service.

He also urged that Bodega be rewarded with a naval promotion so that he could continue with the same "love, zeal, usefulness and gratitude he has always shown." Here the viceroy was firing the opening shot in a salvo to obtain for Bodega a financial reward for his services.

The praise Bodega received from Madrid was equally effusive. An unusually lengthy Royal Order signed by the new minister of state, Manuel Godoy, the Duque de la Alcudia, not only approved of the manner in which Bodega had conducted negotiations with Vancouver but also agreed with Bodega's reasons for not acquiescing in Vancouver's proposal to take over Nootka with no restrictions and with no recognition of "the [Spanish] sovereign as the sole owner of that port." The Royal Order also underscored the correctness of Bodega's refusal to accept San Francisco as the northern limit of Spanish dominion.

Meanwhile, Alcudia went on, the government would consider carefully whether to retain the temporary settlement at Neah Bay and "even Nootka," or both; or to withdraw to San Francisco and fortify the establishment there, as well as those posts at Monterey and San Diego, which would provide better security for the Californias. The Royal Order ended by saying: "Of course I must tell you that the King had expressed his approval of the zeal and sound judgement our commandant demonstrated and the conscientiousness with which he reported on all his operations."[3]

Bodega replied to the minister's accolade:

> It is with great satisfaction that I have faithfully carried out the desires of His Majesty on the Commission of the Limits with which he entrusted me and with gratitude for the honours with which his Royal Piety has distinguished me that I reply to this much appreciated letter of 23 February in which Your Excellency communicates to me such agreeable news. I beg you to please give me further reasons to manifest in this or any other country whatsoever, however unpleasant, the love with which I serve and the zeal which animates me.[4]

Although Bodega had not achieved his main diplomatic objective of establishing the Strait of Juan de Fuca as the boundary between British and Spanish interests, he had forestalled Pitt's plan to obtain a port on the Pacific Ocean. Nootka had not been turned over to Vancouver. Its status was open to future consideration; nothing had been lost by postponing the issue. In the end, events in Europe determined the fate of the Nootka establishment. Spain and Britain, allied in a war against Republican France, signed the Third Nootka Convention in 1794, which provided for its mutual abandonment. Spain had decided that retaining Nootka Sound was no longer important for reasons either of prestige or of imperial strategy. Britain did not take advantage of Pitt's diplomatic victory and acquire a permanent settlement on the coast until 1813, when the North West Company of Montreal purchased Fort Astoria at the entrance to the Columbia River from the American-based Pacific Fur Company.

Meanwhile, Revillagigedo warned the home government that, because Spain was still sovereign of the coast north of San Francisco as a consequence of the deadlock in Bodega's negotiations with Vancouver, policies for the region's governance required urgent consideration.[5] The future of the Nootka establishment was the primary concern, but three other related issues had to be addressed: further exploration both north and south of

Nootka Sound; Spanish involvement in the sea otter fur trade; and the construction of defences for Alta California.

Spain's Position on the Northwest Coast after the Expedition of the Limits

Late in 1792, while he was recuperating in Monterey after a summer of exploration and negotiations at Nootka, Bodega wrote a preliminary report to the viceroy to acquaint him with certain "opinions" he had begun to formulate regarding the future of Spanish rule on the coast north of San Francisco.[6] Bodega's ideas sprang from his realization that Nootka Sound had assumed strategic importance owing to the maritime fur trade.

The number of foreign ships calling at Nootka Sound in the summer of 1792 had made it abundantly clear to him that Spain's claim to the North Pacific coast was weakly defended. Bodega saw the difficulties of protecting Spanish sovereignty so far north:

> My experience has made me realize that today our flag is endangered because the ships from San Blas are the only ones which sail with little or no artillery. All together they amount to one-third of the English ships which plough these waters; and if some day thought is given to dislodging them from ports north of San Francisco, our efforts would be useless. Perhaps they could even invade this port (Nootka Sound) and the others in New California, which I cannot fortify at present.
>
> All the measures called for in these circumstances, besides being very costly, I consider would be unprofitable because a regular squadron requires exorbitant costs and, after all [is said and done], it would not be possible to defend the enormous expanse [of coast] which the foreigners frequent.[7]

Recognizing that rivalry with Great Britain could lead to a "useless and expensive war," he wrote: "Even if we might be left with the advantage of a large number of victories, we would still be unable to prevent either navigation through such vast seas or entry into harbours which we cannot protect because of the great distances between them."

The Abandonment of Nootka

Shortly after becoming the commandant of San Blas in 1790, Bodega had raised the possibility of simply abandoning Nootka Sound.[8] At the time he had found it

> painful to see such an enormous expenditure of funds with no purpose other than the protection of the missions, now that the explorations have been concluded ... [Nootka] is an establishment which cannot be maintained without great cost and heavy loss of life because of its harsh climate, lack of space for growing crops, the bad character of the natives and inadequate landing and loading facilities. In a word, it is a harbour which produces nothing but water and firewood.[9]

Furthermore, he pointed out, Nootka Sound was no longer producing enough sea otter skins for profitable commerce. In the past eleven months, only 323 pelts had been collected. Instead of recommending that the establishment be relocated, he preferred to see the defences of the existing presidios in Alta California strengthened by giving them the protection of two frigates. These warships would "command respect" – a favourite term of Bodega's – and would be noticed by foreigners.

Viewing his newly assigned responsibilities from steamy, mosquito-ridden San Blas in 1790, Bodega could see only the problems of keeping Nootka resupplied. It was so far from San Blas that the return voyage took five months under the best conditions; furthermore, provisioning this outpost tied up precious shipping capacity at the expense of other tasks. It was already a struggle to resupply the Alta California missions and presidios each year.

On leaving San Blas for Nootka Sound in the spring of 1792, Bodega had accepted without a murmur Revillagigedo's opinion that Nootka need not be retained; nor did he question Article VIII of his instructions, which directed him to abandon Nootka for a harbour in the Strait of Juan de Fuca. He had every intention of giving up the establishment after obtaining Vancouver's acceptance of the Strait of Juan de Fuca as the boundary between the claims of the two nations.

Prior to Vancouver's arrival, Bodega had taken a number of steps to reduce the Nootka establishment. He had removed all but two of the guns from the San Miguel battery at the entrance to Friendly Cove. He had sent back to New Spain the *Santa Gertrudis* as well as the huge *Concepción* under Francisco de Eliza with her large crew, together with a good part of the Catalonian Volunteers and their commandant, Pedro de Alberni, in addition to the stores that would have sustained them. He had written a letter to the viceroy and to the minister of state, Floridablanca, to inform them of his intention to turn the establishment over to Thomas New should Vancouver be further delayed.

Even after Vancouver's arrival, Bodega had continued to prepare to abandon Nootka. He would later justify their quasi-state visit to Maquinna at Tahsis as an opportunity during which "he might have the pleasure of recommending the English commanders & their officers ... as the place was soon to be given up to the English."[10] Bodega had asked Vancouver whom he would be leaving in charge of the establishment, and Menzies noted in his journal that "even the mode of putting us in possession of the Territory was agreed upon."[11] The Spaniards' intention to abandon the post was known to other chroniclers aboard the ships in the cove. Edward Bell noted in his journal that "on our arrival at this place it was settled that we were to winter here, and Mr. Quadra intended to leave the Houses, Gardens &c in good order for us ... Mr. Quadra was making preparation for his departure with all dispatch, and considerable progress was made in unloading the *Daedalus*."[12] Ingraham similarly recorded that Bodega had told him "he was getting in readiness to give up the place to the English."[13]

But after nearly half a year's residence at Nootka, all the while observing the growing fur trade, Bodega changed his mind about the value of the place. In his *Viaje*, Bodega recorded his newly acquired enthusiasm. He was quite sanguine about the site's potential for agriculture:

> My lengthy stay in this port has enabled me to see the advantages of the land to sustain a regular establishment. The soil is fertile and the small portions which have been cultivated up to now produce delicious vegetables. Potatoes reach a considerable size and alone could provide an article of subsistence in case of necessity. To the west there is an extent of about a mile which could be made into wheatfields capable of producing bread for a thousand people for the present. To the north, above the small hills which surround it, there is an esplanade [terrace] which could be used to advantage to grow maize.
>
> It would be very useful [to do so] as vegetables which have been grown there ... have been abundant. When these grains fail to mature, there remains a strong recourse to the bulbous root of the Kamchatka white lily which grows spontaneously over the whole island on land which [otherwise] seems quite useless.[14] This could make tasty bread, cultivating a small amount at first and it could be enormously increased when colonizers undertake its cultivation. As well, livestock would prosper, especially goats and pigs, although pasturage is scarce in winter.

As for the possibility of minerals and other useful natural resources that could be exploited, he took pains to add:

> There are several indications which lead me to believe the mountains contain veins of minerals, but I was not able to verify what kind of metals they are as I did not have the means to have analyzed what we believe we can see in the rocks. Copper, lead, iron and some which mineralogists classify as semi-minerals have been extracted out of distinct outcroppings ...[15]
>
> The forests are covered with tall pines [cedar trees?], many cypresses and some oak, trees which serve well for construction and which have served one foreigner or another. Large oysters are to be found on the shores of the sea: they serve two purposes, the meat they contain and the lime obtained from burning the shells, which is what I used for whitewashing this house. It [the lime] can also be used to make an oven. Mixed with fine sand from Maquinna's river, it makes excellent mortar with which it is possible to erect more spacious and permanent houses than we have now.[16]

Bodega optimistically pointed out that the cove was suitable as a harbour because

> the entire anchorage has the best proportions. It is sheltered from the winds, which are devastating in this latitude. The bottom is sand. Its capacity is more than sufficient to hold 15 or 20 ships, and water, ballast and firewood can be obtained without difficulty because two permanent streams and pine trees are within musket shot of the water's edge.

Correcting his earlier negative assessment of the character of the natives, he now wrote that they

> are of a most peaceful nature and less disposed to revenge. I have never had to fear any one of them ... On the contrary, I can say with assurance that it is not possible to mistake the confidence they have in me and the affection which not only the common people declare they have for me but [that of] the chiefs as well, because they frequently sleep at night in my house, with the satisfaction perhaps they would not have in the houses of their most immediate relatives. Thus I have had no difficulty in establishing with them a human relationship towards which my disposition inclines.[17]

Bodega's proposal to retain Nootka, although addressing the same issues, ran totally counter to what Revillagigedo had consistently advocated. It was also contrary to his instructions and to Article I of the Nootka Convention. While Bodega was now exaggerating Nootka Sound's advantages, he had his reasons. Four factors led him to favour retention of the port. First, he had seen at first hand the site's value as a harbour. Second, just after sending his first letter to Vancouver, he had received the report of Dionisio Alcalá Galiano and Salvador Menéndez Valdés that Neah Bay was not a satisfactory alternative to Nootka. Third, he had come to believe that the British were using the Nootka controversy to further their long-term plans to limit further Spanish expansion north of San Francisco. Fourth, he saw with his own eyes that Nootka had an economic importance of its own, one that threatened to break Spain's trade monopoly in this area of the Pacific Ocean. He could see that it had become a source of valuable furs for Portuguese, American, and especially British traders. In his *Viaje,* he pointed out that the trade in sea otter pelts would continue to attract other nations' ships unless Spain quickly adopted measures to deter them. He noted that in 1792 alone, six frigates, six brigs, and four bilanders had entered Nootka. Each was "on a measure of war footing," even though none, even the smallest, had reason to fear that it would be attacked by the natives. But it was especially the English, he emphasized, who "each day give us many demonstrations of their desire to make the trade as profitable as possible." He believed they would build other establishments on the coast, including one in the Queen Charlotte Islands, "where the sea otters are particularly abundant and their furs among the best," even better than those of Clayoquot Sound, Cook Inlet, and the Strait of Juan de Fuca.

Bodega's about-face is not entirely convincing. Certainly, he saw Nootka more favourably than before – the weather that summer had been better than usual, and he had more agreeable company than hitherto – but by extolling the sound in such exaggerated terms, he may have been attempting to assure his superiors that Nootka possessed some positive advantages that ought to be taken into account in the event that the two courts agreed to renegotiate the convention after receiving their commissioners' reports. Or, in the absence of any such agreement, perhaps Bodega wished to offer the Spanish government information that would encourage it to retain Nootka and thereby maintain a presence in the North Pacific. In either case, it was a bid to buy more time before a decision was made about the fate of the establishment on which he had expended so much effort. Both possibilities are implicit in Bodega's observations both to Revillagigedo and to Minister of State Aranda:

> Should the king on his own authority or for some other reason wish to hand over [Nootka Sound], nothing has been lost by suspending such action.

Besides, Vancouver did not come to this coast only for this reason and has to return next year to conclude his reconnaissance.[18]

Revillagigedo, who had urged an immediate withdrawal southward, remained unconvinced. Historian Warren Cook, quoting from what he assumes to be a draft letter by the viceroy, surmises that he "had decided to force events in regard to the northwest coast." It reads, in part: "If our Crown tries to embrace settlements that distant, the treasury will be burdened anew with swollen expenses, without obtaining the benefits which Quadra thinks, because the port of Nuca is not as good as he states, to judge by the opinion of other practical and intelligent mariners."[19]

Nor was Bodega's naturalist, José Mariano Moziño, convinced of the port's merits. In his *Noticias de Nutka,* Moziño argued against the idea of retaining Nootka. Marshalling his arguments around the same issues as Bodega and Revillagigedo had covered, he wrote:

Up to now, this establishment had not produced any advantage to the Crown, but, on the contrary, the enormous expenses we have had to pay out are notorious. Even private individuals have achieved nothing more than a miserable trade in furs and the hopes of making it very lucrative, besides from being extremely remote, could be realized just as well, as the Boston men have done and are still doing, if the port were independent.

Nootka is a place where one finds very few furs, and [they] come from the Nuchimanes, Clayoquot and Tutusi ... Nootka attracts foreigners at present only because they can supply themselves with water and firewood at no risk.

The security of our possessions in New Spain and California is neither insured more or endangered less by our being owners of this island, since if our enemies should seek to establish a site next to our territories, in order to invade us with greater facility, there is a distance of two hundred leagues between Nootka and San Francisco which is left free for them. There are various coves such as Gray's Harbor, [the] Ensenada de los Mártires,[20] the Entrada de Heceta [sic],[21] Sidman,[22] [the Puerto de] la Bodega,[23] and so forth in which to shelter a considerable number of ships.

After citing the case of Tahiti, which the Spanish had attempted to settle but then abandoned after two years, and the fact that the English used both it and the Sandwich [Hawaiian] Islands as ports of call for supplies, Moziño continued:

The present circumstances do not permit us to fortify Nootka in such a way that it could in any eventuality put up a vigorous resistance which would compel respect for our flag. For this purpose at least a battalion of infantry would be necessary and it can be seen that its maintenance, if one recalls the mounting costs of the frigate [*Santa*] *Gertrudis* alone after a very few months,. would reach nearly one million [pesos] in each of the three or four years which would have to be invested in clearing the land and preparing it for cultivation ...

In addition to all this, it would be impossible to cut off the commerce engaged in by the foreigners with the natives. They can anchor in Esperanza Inlet,[24] at Nuchimanes,[25] and even come up to Maquinna's [villages] without our artillery being capable of hindering them.

But suppose we fortified all these entrances in such a manner that no one could approach them without our permission? Could this be done with [the] Queen Charlotte Island[s], from which it is possible to go to California with the same or greater facility, and in the same number of days, as from Nootka, and farther to the south would Clayquot, the Archipelago of Carrasco,[26] and others remain unguarded?

Any one can see six or eight thousand men would scarcely be enough to guard these points, and that, even if we took exclusive possession of the fur trade, it would probably not defray the enormous expenses which their defence would require.[27]

Like Revillagigedo, Moziño urged that Nootka be abandoned to protect California.

The first object of our attentions should be [Alta] California. There our conquest has taken root, our religion has propagated, and our hopes are greatest for obtaining obvious advantages to benefit all the monarchy ... Throughout most of New California, the landscape is beautiful, the soil fertile, the mountains wooded, and the climate benign. There is no European product which could not be successfully grown there ... In no other place could our enemies establish themselves more advantageously, and consequently [it] demands more attention of our diligent government ... Far from being a liability to the state, as it has been up to now, it could sustain itself and contribute to the needs of the Crown.[28]

The Convention for the Mutual Abandonment of Nootka

After he dismantled the Spanish establishment at Neah Bay late in 1792, Salvador Fidalgo sailed to Nootka, where he relieved Jacinto Caamaño. In command until 1793, Fidalgo strengthened the battery on San Miguel Island at the entrance to the sound and made some improvements to the barracks and other houses ashore. This kept his people busy until he was, in turn, relieved by Ramón Saavedra, who was left in charge with the *San Carlos* as his guard ship. It was a grim time for the few remaining Spanish residents. They were chronically short of food. Scurvy reappeared, and several died from it. Periodically, Maquinna would remind the commandant of Malaspina's promise that some day the Spanish would leave. He and his people were looking forward to reoccupying Yuquot. There were occasional visits of foreign ships. Vancouver returned in 1793 and again in 1794 in the forlorn hope of finding his negotiation instructions awaiting him. Revillagigedo paid scant attention to the welfare of the establishment and provided the bare minimum to sustain this remote outpost.

Once more the North Pacific had become marginal to the strategic interests of Spanish officials.[29] The renegotiation of the Nootka Convention was left in abeyance, and the establishment remained in Spanish hands while Madrid's attention was diverted by the turmoil in Europe precipitated by the French Revolution. Spain's war with Republican France, in which Spain briefly found herself an ally of Great Britain, finally provided an opportunity to bring "the Nootka Incident" to a close.

Early in 1794, Britain and Spain concluded a Convention for the Mutual Abandonment of Nootka by which both courts finally resolved the crisis precipitated by Estéban Martínez in 1789. The convention was negotiated and signed by Spain's Duque de la Alcudia and the British ambassador, Alleyne Fitzherbert, Baron St. Helens, on January 11, 1794.[30] The accord's purpose was "to remove and obviate all doubt and difficulty relative to the execution of Article I of the [first] convention."[31] It called for commissioners of each government to meet "in the same place, or near, where the buildings stood which were formerly occupied by the subjects of His Britannic Majesty" – that is, the small tract of land that Meares claimed Maquinna had sold him – and to sign a declaration and a counterdeclaration, the texts of which were prescribed in the convention, restoring the land to Britain. Nootka Sound could be used by both nations, but no permanent buildings could be erected there by Europeans.

Carlos IV authorized a commission of appointment, which was signed by Alcudia, for Bodega to serve as Spanish commissioner for the ceremony.[32] Summoned by Revillagigedo to Mexico City to receive his commission and instructions, Bodega begged off "because my broken health does not permit me at present to tire myself much, nor do my excessive expenses allow me to enter into new ones."[33] He was, in fact, within a month of dying.

The viceroy considered first Eliza and then Fidalgo for the mission, but in the end he sent Brigadier José Manuel Alava, the commandant of the Puebla Infantry Regiment, who also spoke fluent English.[34] The British government appointed Marine Lieutenant Thomas Pearce as his opposite number.

After some delays and some false starts – one occasioned by Vancouver's third visit to Nootka[35] – the two commissioners eventually arrived at Nootka Sound in the brigantine *Activo*, the reconfigured schooner *Activa*, which Bodega had built for the Expedition of the Limits.[36] They were received by Saavedra, and the ceremony of reading and signing the declaration and the counterdeclaration took place on March 28, 1795, in the small cove where Meares had built his *North West America*. The Spanish flag was lowered, and Pearce hoisted the Union Jack as a token of possession before handing the flag to Maquinna for safekeeping.[37]

Spain never attempted to reoccupy Nootka Sound. The Cala de los Amigos (Friendly Cove) became neutral territory, visited from time to time by ships of various nationalities. Maquinna and his people reoccupied the site immediately, and today it remains the historic home of the Mowachaht-Muchalaht people of the Nuu-chah-nulth First Nation. After 1795, Spain withdrew to her bastion of New Spain with its northern outposts in Alta California. Here was a colonial frontier that held more promise for the Spanish than Nootka, although it too had problems.

Spanish Participation in the Fur Trade

While awaiting George Vancouver's arrival at Monterey, Bodega had time to collect his ideas on the economy of Alta California. He drew a dismal picture:

> Being obliged in every respect not to lose sight of the true interests of the nation, I can do no less than to point out that I find [these people] far from prospering. This northern part of California is a colony which, instead of creating heavy outlays by the state, should be contributing considerable subsidies after harvesting great wealth what with the richness of the soil and abundance of livestock. Every day it falls into greater decay.[38]

The population of Alta California in 1792 lay somewhere between the 1764 estimate of about 233,000 and the figure of 559,600 in 1803. The great majority of inhabitants were Indians. They lived in their own villages and in and around the missions. There was also a growing mixed-blood population. Spanish immigration had remained small in spite of the efforts of previous viceroys. In 1790 the total number of Spaniards in the population amounted to no more than 970, an increase of 370 since 1780. This increase was due to the arrival of settlers who had escaped the Yuma massacre of 1781.[39] Most of the Spanish in the region belonged to the military, who at first constituted almost the entire adult population except for the missionaries. Over time there developed a group of retired veterans around the presidios and ranches and a body of civilians in the *pueblos*, who were subject to call for military service but who were not enrolled in the permanent garrison. A few small traders and vagabond sailors drifted in.[40]

Bodega cited the problem of integrating the retired soldiers into the local economy. Two small villages that had been built for the veterans had failed. They "live in greater servitude and oppression than before they retired," existing without pay even though they were obliged to do guard duty. He concluded that if it were not for the labour of the Indians and the converted, "not a grain of wheat would be found on the 500 leagues of the continent."

Bodega thought that if Alta California were to become an important producer of goods for the Asian trade, its future would be brighter:

> It could also count on the harvesting of a limitless number of sea otter pelts, sea wolves [seals], bears and lynx, hides of bulls, salt beds, etc. By opening a channel of communication in the way I proposed when speaking of Nutca, these establishments would in a few years become wealthy with the Asian trade and, as a consequence, their population in a very short time would grow in proportion to the greater advantages enjoyed by their neighbours.

To succeed, this policy would require a relaxation of the strict rules by which Spain regulated trade and commerce within her empire. "The principal [rule]," he wrote,

> ... should be a freedom similar to that which the successful subjects of the Catholic King [of Spain] enjoy in all his dominions ... Free commerce for all Spaniards in the fur trade is one means which appears to me to be the only one capable of attaining our complete security with real profit to us. We can pay the Indians a higher price for their sea otter pelts than other nations by taking advantage of the copper which abounds in New Spain, encouraging the textile factories of Querétaro, Puebla, [and] Cholula, and harvesting the [abalone] shells of Monterrey [sic].[41] In this way, employment would be given to many people in our interior provinces who [at the moment] have

> none. Thus other nations will not be able to make the profits they now obtain and, as a consequence, they will abandon this [coastal fur] trade, which, in time, will see their fortunes reduced.[42]

Unfortunately, legal and bureaucratic barriers to a relaxation of trade restrictions and to the exemption of colonial products from duties doomed this and other attempts to promote entrepreneurship and economic progress.

Seriously concerned that Spain's government was indifferent to the foreign ships trading openly and profitably in her territorial waters, Bodega argued that his proposal would not tax the national treasury because it would stimulate the economy in Alta California. It would also enable Spain to "complete the geographic reconnaissance of the unknown parts of the continent north of 55° which up to this point has been accurately charted."[43] Knowing that exploration was still one of Revillagigedo's priorities, Bodega concluded his last point by arguing that "it is of great interest to us not to leave to foreigners the glory of discovering unknown countries."

Bodega had probably heard of the other schemes already put forward for Spanish participation in the fur trade. As early as 1784, the government had approved a proposal by the entrepreneur Vicente Vasadre y Vega.[44] Since the Mexican gold-mining industry suffered from an irregular and insufficient supply of mercury, and since China was known to have large quantities of this indispensable metal, Vasadre had proposed that sea otter and seal skins, which were fancied by Chinese mandarins, be exchanged for Chinese quicksilver. This triangular trade was tried out in 1786 with only modest success.

In 1789, Estéban Martínez, in the midst of arresting and detaining the three English trading ships at Nootka, had put forward to Viceroy Flores an elaborate plan for Spanish participation in the fur trade.[45] He proposed that a company of Mexican merchants be formed and that they be given a monopoly of the pelt trade between the Alta California missions and China. The associates should be given certain tax exemptions for fifty years and, in return, must undertake to establish four presidios, having a garrison of one hundred men each, and to found seventeen missions on the open coast north of San Francisco, which he called Nueva Calabria, as well as a presidio in Hawaii. These establishments would be served by twelve fast sloops, half of them to protect the posts and missions and the other half to transport furs to China. It would be sufficient to maintain one ship at Nootka and two sixteen-gun packet boats and schooners to travel up and down the coast to collect the pelts caught in traps given to the Indians for that purpose. The sloops would then sail annually to Canton to sell the furs for mercury or clothing and other personal items for the Indians, soldiers, and sailors. The Hawaiian Islands would serve as a way station for food and ship repairs. Flores took no action on Martínez's ingenious and detailed proposal.

Having found Martínez's proposal among Flores's papers, Revillagigedo, his successor, forwarded it to Antonio Valdés, who was intrigued by the proposal despite some concerns of his own. He was afraid, for example, that the venture could harm the Manila Galleon trade, and he questioned the practicality of involving the Royal Philippine Company. He made some helpful suggestions and recommended that the proposal be carefully considered. The scheme languished for three years in the Spanish bureaucracy until October 1792, when Valdés raised the issue.[46] This time Revillagigedo was strongly opposed to the plan. He termed it "one of those many projects which have preoccupied Martínez's shallow imagination. He has no true knowledge of the situation and, as a result, has not considered the difficulties, the cost and the consequences ... [The plan] is inopportune, difficult, costly, badly conceived and not thought through."[47] Nothing ever came of Martínez's elaborate and imaginative proposal, which, moreover, excited no interest in the Mexican business community.

Alejandro Malaspina promoted a similar scheme after his visit to the Northwest Coast. He first presented his idea in an open letter to the Mexican merchants; he then expanded on it in a formal report to the government. Malaspina's proposal was more practical. According to James R. Gibson, he based it on the need

> to enhance colonial trade and the wealth of the monarchy and to avoid conflicts such as the Nootka Sound dispute ... He argued that if Spain were to engage in the coastal trade rather than in costly exploration, territorial claiming and political posturing, then the "frightful noise of cannon and war is [going to be] replaced by the pleasant ties of lucrative trade, peaceful navigation, and the reciprocal efforts of nations towards mutual prosperity."[48]

Malaspina foresaw a "large number of thorns and difficulties" on the way to reaching this goal, but he was highly optimistic. One advantage to his scheme was that it would reduce the strain on Spain's hard currency reserves by replacing the silver coins, which European traders had to carry to China, with fur pelts. Spain possessed so many advantages over her rivals – geography, ships, shorter distances to the hunting grounds, possession of the essential trade goods, and a monopoly of the most desirable of all, the abalone shell – that her ability to compete successfully could not be doubted.

But Malaspina's proposal, like Martínez's, failed to arouse any interest either in Mexico or in Spain.

Revillagigedo was never completely persuaded that Spanish participation in the sea otter fur trade would produce the benefits that its proponents believed it could furnish. Nevertheless, he wanted to keep foreign traders out of what he regarded as Spanish waters.[49] Although he did not support any projects whose sole purpose was to engage in the fur trade, he did authorize the naval vessels engaged in exploration along the coast to take along copper plates, abalone shells, cheap cloth, and trinkets as trade items.[50] When exploring the Strait of Juan de Fuca in 1790, for example, Manuel Quimper collected more than two hundred pelts under the viceroy's orders.

Revillagigedo hesitated to endorse any expensive ventures in the sea otter fur trade because that trade was very risky. He feared that the Chinese might close the Canton market for the skins.[51] Before long, the Chinese did just that. Also, Revillagigedo knew that Bodega suspected that the fierce rivalry between maritime fur traders was already reducing the number of sea otters and sharply increasing the prices the Indians were demanding – a situation that narrowed the fur traders' margin of profit.[52] Indeed, within a decade the intense activity of the early years of the sea otter trade had been followed by a sharp decline, and the coastal trade eventually petered out.

In spite of his doubts about Bodega's recommendations – the viceroy called them "reflections" – Revillagigedo forwarded them to Spain with the comment that it would not be easy to persuade the merchants of New Spain to engage in the fur trade. There was no follow-up, and Bodega's suggestion suffered the same fate as the other proposals.

Securing the Northern Frontier

Bodega's concern for the defences of Alta California can be traced back to the situation he encountered in Monterey. The relocation and strengthening of the battery at Monterey was the only measure Bodega was able to undertake while he was there. As soon as he was back in San Blas, he made plans to strengthen the empire's defences further. He made a strong case to the viceroy that, in order to meet the growing British threat to Spain's trans-Pacific trade and to the Alta California settlements, and to prevent piracy and smuggling, the armament of the ships under his authority would need to be increased.[53] Furthermore, San Blas would have to be provided with faster frigates that would command "some respect," and the ports themselves would have to be better fortified.[54]

Bodega's formal report, his *Viaje*, did not reach Mexico City until February 1793. By then, Revillagigedo had already taken action. Bodega's informal reports had rekindled his own long-held concern about protecting the entire California coast, especially those portions north of San Francisco which were not yet settled. This area had been his greatest worry, because Article V of the Nootka Convention gave Great Britain free access to this coast. In April 1793, the viceroy warned Madrid that British policy was motivated not so much by the profits to be obtained from the fur trade, as by a desire that

> San Francisco be the [northern] limit of Spanish expansion, to establish from this point [north] which would be common to each nation and freedom to fish a distance of ten leagues from our Pacific coasts. This [purpose] can be seen as conspiring to encourage illicit trade and destroying that of New Spain and the Philippines by the clandestine introduction of goods and merchandise from Asia and Europe.[55]

Revillagigedo had outlined his plans for the defences of Alta California in a lengthy letter to Minister of State Aranda on November 30, 1792.[56] To put matters in perspective, he began with the bold statement that the ports of San Diego, Monterey, and San Francisco had no defences with which to resist "invasions of foreign powers, other than the useless presidios." Recalling that the presidios had been established solely to pacify the Indians, he noted that it had been sufficient to surround them with simple adobe walls and to garrison them with troops of cavalry and *lanceros*.[57] Although colonial troops were suitable for dealing with hostile "barbarians," they lacked the training and discipline required for European warfare. The viceroy wanted the soldiers in Alta California to be placed under officers with military expertise; he also wanted to form new units of artillery, infantry, and cavalry to "defend the coasts and assure the preservation of the peninsula."

Turning to the state of the defensive works, he cited Bodega's scramble to install cannon at Monterey so that Vancouver might not be aware of the "defencelessness or abandonment" of that harbour. As for the settlements of San Diego and San Francisco, he thought that "we should not lose a moment to fortify them so as to enable them to repel any enemy invasion," especially by warships or by a landing of battle-hardened troops. Defences for all the harbours of the Californias must be built up in order to deny them to "European enemies [who], in control of the coasts and territories, can aspire if not to outright control of the rich provinces of Sonora and

Nueva Vizcaya,[58] then to the profits to be made from illicit commerce, which would destroy that of New Spain and surely that of the Philippines by intercepting the galleons which come annually from Manilla [sic] to Acapulco." To oversee construction of the new defensive works, he proposed sending north "one of the best military engineers in this Kingdom."

Revillagigedo also wanted to see an improvement in the quality of the men who ruled the Californias. He wanted to replace the governor with a new appointee, one who was "talented, intelligent, robust, brave, zealous and prudent."

Clearly alarmed by Bodega's request that Broughton be permitted to travel across New Spain, Revillagigedo was anxious for the home government to act on his proposals without delay. He asked to be informed when a new governor was appointed to Alta California. Regarding the strengthening of the defences of the three harbours – a project he considered urgent – he asked for the king's agreement in principle to proceed without the usual preliminary estimate of costs. However, the viceroy's resolve to act quickly was confounded by the inertia of the Spanish bureaucracy. Three months later, Revillagigedo received an unhelpful reply from Alcudia that did not convey the king's agreement in principle for any action, but merely commented that the viceroy's observations were "most opportune."[59]

A few days earlier, on November 25, Revillagigedo had asked Bodega, who was still in Monterey, for a "clear and precise" report with recommendations on what should be done to fortify the ports "to make their defences respectable in case of being invaded," as well as for a "sensible estimate of costs with the works being carried out with the greatest possible economy."[60] At the same time, he asked José Dario Argüello, the commandant at Monterey and acting governor of Alta California, for a list of what he thought he needed.

Bodega did not reply to the viceroy's request until he was back in San Blas. At that point he asked for the authority to complete the work begun on the esplanade at Monterey and to fortify San Francisco and San Diego. In the same vein, he asked that the next ship sailing north bring the necessary equipment, along with "an energetic and intelligent master gunner."[61] The viceroy replied promptly to this request: "You may proceed as you request and send your letters on the matter to the governor of the province as regards the esplanade or trenches in those places which you may have examined and believe to be most in need of defence."[62]

The old governor of Alta California, Argüello, took several months to collect the information requested by the viceroy because the distances between the three presidios made communication difficult. Bodega got

Argüello's report into the viceroy's hands in July 1793. The governor's very detailed response could only have caused more alarm. At Monterey there were only sixty soldiers of all ranks although seventy-nine were needed. Santa Barbara, with sixty-one soldiers, was only two short of its entitlement. At San Francisco there were thirty-nine soldiers although ninety-one were required. And at San Diego there were fifty-nine soldiers though seventy-five were needed.[63] The situation was even worse as far as weapons were concerned.[64] Argüello summarized the present situation as "deplorable."[65]

Despite the viceroy's support, remedial action was slow. On February 23, 1793, Bodega had submitted a preliminary estimate of costs. He thought that a battery of eight cannon for each of the three presidios would be sufficient to guard against any incursion. The cost for these would likely not exceed 7,484 pesos.[66] When Revillagigedo merely acknowledged receipt of the estimate without comment, Bodega wrote on March 9 to urge that the cannon and other munitions be forwarded with the master gunner as quickly as possible.[67] The viceroy agreed and issued the necessary orders. A year later, in the spring of 1794, as one of his final acts, when Revillagigedo forwarded these documents to Alcudia in Spain, he supported Bodega's and Argüello's recommendations.[68] It is not clear whether any further decisions were made, because the *expediente,* or file, ends at that point. It is highly likely that the file was set aside because Revillagigedo was about to be replaced as viceroy and Bodega was dying.

On March 7, 1793, France declared war on Spain. Revillagigedo sent Bodega a viceregal warning that instructed him to take the necessary defensive measures in the event of an attack.[69] Bodega's reply reflected his profound sense of futility:

> I am obliged to inform you that the Department [of San Blas] has no forces other than the frigate *Concepción* and the schooner *Activo.* We have no other ship which can make use of artillery nor has one been constructed with such a purpose in view. These [two ships] are not sufficient to avert any intended hostilities should a break [in diplomatic relations] occur. As regards the *Concepción*, in reality it is no more than a corvette with twenty-six small-calibre guns.
>
> Please let me have your instructions after reflecting on what I have said, [remembering that] the presidios on this coast possess no frigates which command respect, which we need today, and that no one has thought of undertaking the works required for their defence and for the custody of the equipment if it is decided to forward them.
>
> This is what I proposed after my arrival [in San Blas] and will always, always [sic] maintain in spite of those who are opposed to the advantages

> [the batteries] will render to the interests of the sovereign and the security of his Americas.[70]

There is evidence that some work was begun at Monterey as a response to the rising international tensions. When Vancouver returned there in November 1793, he was faced with a number of severe restrictions that the new governor, José Joaquín Arriaga, placed on the movement of his ships and his people. Vancouver was forbidden to go ashore; however, Archibald Menzies observed that work on a battery was about to begin. He saw a number of people working on the high ground at the harbour entrance's south side, preparing a battery that, he noted, "perfectly commands the entrance."[71]

The preparations for war petered out. When Vancouver returned to Monterey a year later, in November 1794, he recorded that

> in the whole province [of California] there is not a single fort; and the only thing resembling [a] fortification is a very rude Barbet Battery of eleven cannon, of different sizes, erected at Monterey since our former visit, on a hill near the shores of that bay which commands the anchorage; and something similar was just begun on the South East point of [the] entrance into Port Sn. Francisco; every other place on the coast being nearly defenceless against any foreign enemy.[72]

The construction that Menzies had reported as underway in 1793 had not been completed. It had not even advanced very far. Although the viceroy had found Bodega's estimate of 7,484 pesos "modest," he had not authorized him to go ahead. No master gunner had been sent north, as he thought it best to await the king's agreement in principle before sending someone, and this he had not received. Nevertheless, the viceroy reiterated his orders to the governor of Alta California – and presumably to Bodega – that at each presidio trenches should be dug or a platform built of logs and earth erected, "the same as Fidalgo had constructed at Nootka." Eight twelve-pounder cannon, their carriages, and other necessary equipment had been sent to Monterey, and the other weapons requested had been provided. The viceroy recognized that these measures weren't sufficient for a "formal defence," but he knew they would be an improvement. The beginning of El Castillo de Monterey was the only improvement to the defences of Alta California carried out during Bodega's administration, and this strongpoint certainly fell far short of what he had wanted and felt necessary.

The exploration of North America's Pacific Coast was another unfinished task.

The End of Spanish Exploration on the Pacific West Coast

Admiral Fonte's passage was the final question that preoccupied Bodega in the early months of 1793. Although Bodega had pronounced himself pleased with Caamaño's efforts to find Admiral Fonte's strait during the Expedition of the Limits, he realized that much of the Alaskan archipelago had yet to be examined. In his *Viaje*, he recommended that

> even apart from other considerations, it is necessary to undertake an expedition with the frigate *Concepción*, the schooner *Activa* and the sloop *Orcacitas*, which, from different points, should survey the continent from 50° to 60°.[73] Its direction is unknown and it is probable that all the land discovered up to now [that] is considered to be firm coast may be an archipelago.

Although it is doubtful that Bodega believed the fabled passage might be hidden by the archipelago, it is certain that he wanted to complete an accurate chart of that long coast.[74]

At the beginning of his tenure as viceroy of New Spain, Revillagigedo had favoured Bodega's cartographic ambitions. When drafting his instructions for the Expedition of the Limits, he had remarked that a survey of the coast from latitude 56°N southward along the Alaskan archipelago was "exceedingly more important" than the survey of the coast south from the Strait of Juan de Fuca.[75] After the Bodega-Vancouver negotiations, the viceroy changed his mind when it became clear that an accurate survey of the more southerly Washington-Oregon-California coast was urgently needed.[76] He was now convinced that neither of the famous passages, Ferrer Maldonaldo's or Juan de Fuca's, led into the continent's interior, and he was probably certain that the passage of Admiral Fonte did not exist. Revillagigedo's new concern was the uncharted coast south of Nootka Sound, where foreign trading posts or settlements might be located and where unknown inlets, bays, and rivers might serve as havens for pirates and smugglers.

Looking for support for his new priority, the viceroy consulted the officers of the *Sutil* and *Mexicana* regarding Bodega's desire for further exploration of the Northwest Coast. Specifically, he asked Alcalá Galiano and his companions whether it was necessary to "repeat" the explorations carried out between 50°N and 60°N now that Fidalgo and Caamaño and their own expeditions of 1792 had obtained "all the necessary nautical information."

Alcalá Galiano thought that further exploration should be undertaken north of the Goletas Channel, the passage between the north end of Vancouver

Island and the mainland. Juan Vernacci, who had served on the *Mexicana*, disagreed, contending that the expense would be great and the advantages doubtful. He suggested a less costly alternative: some exploration could be carried out by the resupply missions, provided the ships' officers were skilled in navigation, astronomy, and geography and were given chronometers. Cayetano Valdés and Secundino Salamanca opposed any further activity because Vancouver's charts would be published soon and the Spanish survey would have to exceed what the English were likely to do if any kudos were to be earned. The two officers thought this would be impossible, given Spain's limited resources and the few skilled officers available.[77] Their advice turned out to be sound after Vancouver's maps were published. The British maps were so detailed and meticulous that they substantiated Caamaño's conclusion that the passage of Admiral Fonte did not exist.

Revillagigedo let the matter rest, gently rejecting Bodega's offer to organize and carry out another northern expedition, telling him it should be "left for a later time." The viceroy informed the home government that although the Spanish and the British had yet to find any navigable link between the Pacific and Atlantic oceans,

> we are close to removing all doubts. If it is not accomplished this year [1793] by either one or the other, in 1794 I shall assign a frigate of the Department of San Blas, the brigantine *Activo* and some smaller ships to sail to the highest latitude, should His Majesty approve this new expedition and send me some officers of the Royal Navy, well versed in astronomy, with whom we can put an end to disappointments and a full stop to our costly expeditions.[78]

In other words, he would support Bodega's proposal should Vancouver fail.

By this time, Aranda had been removed as minister of state by a palace coup in Madrid. He was replaced by its engineer – the queen's favourite, Manuel Godoy – who was promptly elevated to the nobility as the Duque de la Alcudia. Learning this, Revillagigedo composed for the new and unversed minister a *difuso informe* (lengthy report) on the key issues concerning Spain and the Northwest Coast.[79] It included Revillagigedo's assessment of the strategic situation following the Nootka Convention and Bodega's inconclusive negotiations with Vancouver.

The viceroy explained that the Northwest Coast had been his chief concern since his arrival in New Spain. Although expeditions ordered by his predecessors as well as the occupation of Nootka had all entailed a heavy expenditure of public funds, he now believed that Spain could no longer defend her sovereignty over the region because she did not possess the men and ships to drive out the Russians or to prevent the British from occupying portions of the coast and engaging in trade there. The only possible course was to set aside any thought of maintaining a position north of the Strait of Juan de Fuca and to concentrate on protecting the coast from that passage south. A detailed survey of the coast between the Strait of Juan de Fuca and San Francisco was a necessary first step to this revised strategic objective. Revillagigedo went on to propose two expeditions: one to chart the coast between San Francisco and the Strait of Juan de Fuca, including exploration of the Columbia River, and the other to occupy Bodega Bay.[80] These expeditions would be organized and directed by Bodega, who would also choose the commandants. This enterprise became Bodega's last major assignment.

Bodega had just returned to San Blas from the north when he received Revillagigedo's instructions to prepare for this new expedition. Bodega's response was muted. He offered to have Bodega Bay examined and occupied; he was less enthusiastic about a further survey of the coast.[81] He pointed out that Vancouver's chart of that coast had been included in the general chart enclosed with his *Viaje*. Nevertheless, "to better reconnoitre the Puerto de la Bodega and other points this navigator [Vancouver] did not see," he was prepared to carry out the viceroy's order if Fidalgo was unable to investigate these locations when returning from Nootka with the *Aránzazu*.[82]

The viceroy accepted and embellished Bodega's plans for Bodega Bay. It should "certainly be occupied," he said, whether or not the English were already there. He thought the British were probably well aware of its advantages over Trinidad Bay, which was "exposed and poor." He also thought that the mission to occupy Bodega Bay should be assigned to a schooner with a launch and should be commanded by an officer in whom Bodega had the "greatest confidence," one who was "talented, zealous, intelligent and active." Should the English be found there, they were to be "asked in a friendly way to leave." If they refused, he was to register a protest and withdraw to San Francisco. The viceroy believed there would be no problem if Bodega acted promptly. Ignoring Bodega's advice, Revillagigedo persisted with his plan to survey the coast as far north as Juan de Fuca. He believed that it was equally important and urgent to "make a careful and early" survey of the coast as far north as that strait. The survey, he said, should concentrate on the coast north of Trinidad Bay because it was unlikely that any establishment could be made between it and Bodega Bay.[83] Because the situation was urgent, Revillagigedo took the unusual step of ordering the two expeditions to set out without waiting for approval from Madrid.

The viceroy's final instructions, dated March 17, 1793, confirmed the expedition's goal to chart the coast northward from San Francisco to 48°N (including examination of the Columbia River) and to occupy Bodega Bay.[84] Bodega had strong reservations about one aspect of the viceroy's plan. Because the prevailing winds blew from north to south, Bodega urged that the survey begin at the Strait of Juan de Fuca and proceed south. As a mariner familiar with the waters, he knew full well that charting close inshore along a treacherous coast against the prevailing winds would be dangerous, time-consuming, and perhaps impossible. On the eve of the ships' departure, Bodega told Revillagigedo he had taken it on himself to order this change.[85] "I have no objection [to the survey] beginning at Fuca, as you suggest," the viceroy later told him.

The Columbia River had come to preoccupy Revillagigedo, as he explained in a letter to Alcudia:

> The Columbia River requires a lengthy and detailed reconnaissance until its source is reached or the point where it follows into the opposite ocean is determined, in case it is this river which crosses the continent and is the door to communication between the two seas ... Until now neither we nor the English have been able to find the passage between the Atlantic and Pacific Oceans, but the time is fast approaching when all doubt will disappear.[86]

His directive to Bodega, written after Broughton's exploration of the river's first hundred miles, stressed the importance of a careful survey:

> One of the most interesting points on the coast is the Columbia River in 46°12′ of latitude. This demands a lengthy and minute examination. After the brigantine has anchored inside in the most convenient place, the sloop will go on, with appropriate instructions, as far as circumstances may allow, towing the launch of the brigantine. When she anchors she will dispatch the launch in the best condition possible to stem and cut the currents, manned by a chosen crew, and be provided with all the food she can carry and with arms and ammunition to continue the survey.
>
> It would be advisable for two *pilotos* to go in her, carrying two compasses for taking bearings. They should follow the river until they reach its source, but taking note of the state of their provisions in order to calculate the proper time to return so as to reach the sloop and receive food and continue their survey in case this has not been concluded with the first reserve of food. The making of the chart can be done by estimated bearings and distances in view of the fact that the current will not permit distances travelled to be measured by the log.[87]

One can guess how a naval officer such as Bodega felt about being told by a military man, in such detail, how to undertake a marine survey.

The expedition to explore the coast north of San Francisco was delayed because the two ships Bodega had originally assigned to chart the coast, the *Orcacitas* and the *Aránzazu*, were in need of extensive repairs. He therefore pressed the *Mexicana* and the *Activo* into service, but he could not dispatch them until their crews had rested. Bodega chose Eliza to captain the *Activo* (the reconfigured *Activa*) and Juan Martínez y Zayas for the *Mexicana*.[88]

The *Activo* and *Mexicana* sailed from San Blas early in the morning of April 30. Eliza's sorry performance can be described briefly. He set their course for the entrance of Fuca, but in light of the lateness of the season and the *Mexicana*'s slow speed relative to the *Activo*, he decided after twenty days of contrary winds to sail on alone to Neah Bay. He never reached it. With adverse winds from the north and northwest persisting, with his water supply running low, and with eleven of his crew suffering from scurvy, he "determined with the agreement of my *pilotos* to turn back and seek the coast wherever it could be found." After sailing for eighty-four days by dead reckoning, he had no firm idea where he was. Land was finally sighted slightly south of Cape Foulweather on the Oregon coast. He entered Trinidad Bay, which he found "quite small: no vessel can be moored so as to turn with the wind and the tide." After watering and wooding, he sailed for Bodega Bay, but when the *Activo* proved too large to explore it, he went on to San Francisco. There he left a message for Zayas to join him at San Diego. Eliza had discovered nothing new.

Zayas made up for his commander's failure. Completely fulfilling the viceroy's purpose, his success must rank as one of the greatest achievements of the Spanish explorers of the region. Zayas sailed directly toward the Strait of Juan de Fuca, but the winds took him farther – to Vancouver Island, just north of Barkley Sound – before the notorious currents and shifting winds brought him south again to Tatoosh Island and then in toward Neah Bay. Not finding Eliza there, he asked the natives whether they had seen him; they had not. Assuming that Eliza must be waiting for him in Gray's Harbor, the alternate rendezvous, Zayas decided to head south. Again, the winds and currents made it necessary to tack frequently "to maintain ourselves at a regular distance from the coast" and even to reverse course on occasion so as not to miss any important indentation along the coast. He succeeded in crossing the bar at the entrance to Gray's Harbor, which he charted with some difficulty.[89] After a group of Indians attempted to take his launch by force, he concluded that the place was not a satisfactory site for a settlement as it afforded neither shelter nor safety.

Continuing south and still battling the winds, Zayas sighted Hezeta's Cabo de San Roque – Meares's Cape Disappointment – which marked the entrance to the Columbia River. The natives there could give him no news of the *Activo*. Instead of searching for Eliza, he decided to go upriver to seek its source, as his instructions called for him to do. He proceeded to "go inside" and cross the bar on a hazardous excursion, which he described without heroic flourishes.

> This we did at eight o'clock in the morning, being followed by innumerable war canoes manned by corpulent, strong people of good appearance. At twelve o'clock when we had already gone fourteen miles from the Cabo de San Roque we ran aground in only four feet of water.[90] The Indians rejoiced at our misfortune and were so insolent that the more we asked them to go away so we could extract ourselves from this dangerous situation, the closer they came.

Once the natives had been driven off, Zayas waited for the tide to float the launch. Reflecting on the responsibility that had fallen to him alone, he worried that the *Activo* had either been wrecked or sailed home. He knew that his launch could not carry the supplies necessary for a long, uncertain voyage up the river, and he knew also that the *Mexicana* should not be left downriver with only twelve men, where the Indians could attempt some treachery. Wisely but "sadly," Zayas decided he had to turn back, "not finding any expedient consistent with my good intentions."

Continuing south and always hugging the coast, Zayas arrived off Trinidad Bay but could not enter it because of the winds.[91] The ship headed for Bodega Bay, where Zayas anchored on the north shore.[92] He then entered Tomales Bay farther south but withdrew when he noticed the beginning of a tidal bore. He reached San Francisco on September 17, 1793.

Zayas was justifiably proud of what he had accomplished. He had completed his mission in an inadequate vessel and without the aid of sophisticated navigational instruments. He had conducted a standard running survey under difficult circumstances: foul weather, adverse winds, and uncharted currents had often made it difficult to take daily sightings. From his large *carta esferica* of the coast from Punta de Tutusi to San Francisco,[93] it is clear how careful he was to ensure the greatest possible accuracy. That chart is amazingly precise and has few obvious errors.

I have found no record of appreciation for Zayas's efforts, but Bodega and Revillagigedo would certainly have been satisfied that he had filled a troubling void in the Spanish maps, and he would have dispelled their fear that the coast north of San Francisco contained unknown havens where a foreign settlement might be established.[94] Regarding the three possible sites for such an establishment – Bodega Bay (including Tomales Bay), Trinidad Bay, and Gray's Harbor – all were found to have unfavourable features. In addition, no Rio de Martín de Aguilar had been encountered.[95] It had not been ascertained whether the Columbia River traversed the continent; but it was now clear that the currents, strong winds, and shallow waters – not to mention the hostility of the Indians – made it highly unlikely that other Europeans would occupy its mouth in the near future.

Bodega had selected Juan Bautista Matute of the *Sutil* as the commander of the expedition to occupy Bodega Bay. Bodega cautioned him that he might find a "foreign ship" there and "some small recently established foreign settlement." If his crew were outnumbered, Matute was not to force the intruders to withdraw because doing so would risk "an insult to the flag." Instead, he should courteously explain that his orders were to occupy the place and that, under Article IV of the Nootka Convention, no other nation could allow its ships to navigate or fish within ten miles of the coast. Should the interlopers refuse to move, he was to make an official protest, withdraw to San Francisco, and make a full report so that an effective response could be agreed on.

Bodega's instructions to Matute included a paragraph on relations with the Indians. He "most strongly" recommended, indeed, it was "essential," that they "be treated with love and kindness":

> In spite of repeated orders that have been issued, I find it daily necessary to repeat this advice, because without remembering that these unfortunate people are ignorant, they are punished under our own laws for their innocent deeds, sometimes more severely than we punish our own people. I most earnestly request that you seek to attract the Indians by humane means and never take the life of one as there are other ways of showing them that they are in the wrong and reprimanding them. As is natural, they will be amazed and, when they are docile, you will make them some gifts of cloth and beads ... and you shall not take any remuneration for these gifts unless they appear to resent the fact that you refuse to accept the gifts they offer you.

Matute was advised that for the settlement, he was to select the point "which lends itself best to fortification, to sheltering the sick and the stores." Because his ship could not carry all the stores, troops, craftsmen, and cannon required for the safety and development of the establishment, he was to take with him what he could and advise Bodega of what more he needed. These items could be brought north to him by the *Aránzazu,* which would be taking dispatches to the presidios early in the new year. Matute was also to bear in mind that an overland expedition from Monterey to Bodega Bay, which was being dispatched by the governor of Alta California, would require his assistance since the route had not yet been explored. Finally, he was ordered to chart the bay.[96]

Despite his best efforts, Matute did not fulfill Bodega's expectations.[97] He sailed from San Blas and anchored off Bodega Bay sixty-four days later, on May 26, 1793. He found the bay unoccupied. He also discovered that there was no wood for construction near the shore. For these reasons, Matute believed "there never will be any [foreign establishment] there as the port is not capacious enough for any vessel larger than the *Sutil.*" Clearly, Bodega Bay was unsuitable for a settlement. Matute also explored nearby Tomales Bay but found it too shallow for a vessel of more than fifteen-foot draft. Combined with the evidence collected by Bodega in 1775, the new information from Zayas and Matute made it clear that the Bodega Bay area was not suitable for a permanent Spanish establishment and would not be of much value to any other nation. So no effort was ever made to build an establishment there as Bodega had proposed in his *Viaje.* The remarkable series of maritime expeditions undertaken by the Spanish to the Northwest Coast had come to an end.

13

Endings

After his return to San Blas in February 1793, Juan Francisco de la Bodega y Quadra was in low spirits. He must have feared Viceroy Revillagigedo's reaction to his interim report on the summer's events on the Northwest Coast. Although he had forestalled British designs on the coast immediately north of San Francisco, he had not achieved his principal objective: Vancouver's agreement to designate the Strait of Juan de Fuca as the southern limit of British expansion. But it was mainly his private affairs that preoccupied him. He was obviously unwell. Three months in the restorative climate of Alta California had not brought any relief from the illness he had endured before leaving for the north and while at Nootka. Now he was back in San Blas, in as unhealthy a climate as could be found anywhere in New Spain. Surviving records indicate that he was preoccupied with the state of his personal finances; this suggests that he was worried about the future of María Marín del Valle, his wife, and their son, an aspect of Bodega's life that was hidden from the official records.

Marriage

Recall that while in Spain in 1788, Bodega had written to the minister, Antonio Valdés, expressing a desire to marry María, the daughter of Lieutenant Colonel Miguel Marín del Valle, commandant of the troops in Tepic and of the militia in San Blas. We read nothing more about her until 1815, when she appeared before a notary in Guadalajara, where she was then living, to make her last will and testament.[1] In that document, she declared that she had a natural son, Juan Francisco Bodega y Quadra. Although nothing had come of his appeal to Valdés, Bodega, on his return to New Spain in 1789, pursued his relationship with *la niña*, as he referred to her. Sometime around 1790, according to her testament, a son named Juan Francisco Bodega y Quadra was born to María.

There is no record that Bodega had made any provision to support this woman and his son after his death, but in 1815, María was clearly not destitute. She declared that she owned her house in Guadalajara and was owed some seven thousand pesos by unnamed persons. She specified that her estate should spend one thousand pesos on her funeral, that "at least" one hundred pesos should be given to her cook, Clemencia Cortes, "for her good services over the years," and that anything left over should be given to her sister, Josefa.

María formally declared that the younger Juan Francisco de la Bodega y Quadra was her "only and universal heir," but added that

> even though my son is more than twenty-five years old, I most strictly charge my executors, because of his notorious bad character and uselessness, to take whatever steps seem opportune, including recourse to legal measures, to preserve his portion of his inheritance for his subsistence.[2] Otherwise, I have no doubt he will quickly fall into the bad company which surrounds him, spend lavishly and so remain unable to maintain himself. As a consequence, I earnestly ask my executors to supervise his person and conduct until he proves that he can manage his affairs.

Although a ne'er-do-well, Francisco Bodega y Marín, as he called himself, lived at least until February 5, 1830, when he appeared before a notary in Guadalajara to draw up his own will.[3] He testified that he was the natural son of "D. Francisco de la Bodega and Doña María Marín," and added that he was "sick in bed from accidents which Our Lord God has been pleased to mete out to me." He wished to be buried with the "greatest possible humility," and five hundred pesos from the sale of his personal effects were to be given in equal shares to six friends. Anything left over was to be distributed by his executors as they saw fit, except for three hundred pesos that he wanted given to "the girl whose name I don't know" by whom he had a daughter.

María's financial security, coupled with her comments on her son and the reference to a granddaughter, add an intriguing mystery to Bodega's story. His attachment to María Marín provides a possible key to several puzzles in Bodega's life: his unswerving support for the irascible Father Alejandro Jordán; his great anxiety to pay off his debts after the Expedition of the Limits; and the small size of his estate at his death, as well as the haze of half-truths that surrounded its settlement.

Jordán, a native of Naples,[4] had travelled to New Spain in 1789 with Bodega and the new viceroy, Revillagigedo. Bodega took an immediate liking to the young chaplain and chose him as his personal confessor. It may be that soon after their arrival in New Spain, Jordán, a cleric who was independent of any religious community, bestowed God's blessing on the relationship between Bodega and María without the obligatory royal permission. At the time, a formal church wedding was not the only recognized form of matrimony. In eighteenth-century Lima, marrying "behind the church" but before a priest was a means of regularizing concubinage. This union, however, placed Bodega in an awkward position.[5] To avoid damaging his naval career, he had to keep his unauthorized connection with María out of the official record. Furthermore, knowledge of his secret would have given Jordàn a means for ensuring Bodega's patronage and protection.[6]

Jordán's evident hold soon became an embarrassment for Bodega. The priest had a difficult and eccentric personality. In his journal, Captain James Colnett refers to his "bitter enemy the curate at Tepic," describing him as "void of every qualification to admit him into any society but [that of] brutes or savages." In January 1790, when Colnett was being detained at San Blas, he gave a picaresque description of the man who accused him of possessing banned and obscene pictures: "Constantly while in company he was momentarily discharging wind off his bowels without any reserve, meal times not excepted, getting up or down in the presence of the commandant, to the mortification of my smelling faculties." Probably he was referring to Jordán.[7] Bodega defused the awkward accusation about the pictures by calling "a general meeting of officers, principal inhabitants and clergy and all had unanimously declared it [the story about banned illustrations] was a malicious accusation." As a friend, Bodega suggested to Colnett that "if I had any, [I would want] to destroy them." Colnett thanked him for his advice and assured him that someone had planted them in his house – "if there were any." "The only prints in his possession," Colnett said, "were prints in the Dictionary of Arts and Sciences."

After the ruckus over Colnett's prints, Bodega took measures to remove Jordán from San Blas. He recommended his appointment as *capellán de buques,* or naval chaplain. Although Jordán was not a Franciscan, Revillagigedo approved his appointment by viceregal decree. Jordán was assigned to the *Concepción,* which sailed under Francisco de Eliza's command to Nootka on February 3, 1790. A nasty dispute that pitted Jordán against Eliza and his brother-in-law, Jacinto Caamaño, disrupted the Spanish settlement at

Nootka. Eliza considered Jordán not only extremely lax in his religious duties but also a quarrelsome man. The surgeons accused him of interfering with their work, and there were public disputes over when and where mass should be said. Jordán loudly refused to obey a direct order from Eliza to move from his quarters on shore to Caamaño's ship, the *Princesa.* The priest responded with insults and foul language to all attempts to find peaceful solutions to his complaints. After two months of discord and indignities, Eliza was exasperated with Jordán. Taking advantage of the *Princesa*'s voyage back south with dispatches and thirty-one sick Catalonian Volunteers, he asked Caamaño take Jordán as well. Just before leaving Nootka, Eliza begged both men to forget their differences. His plea was to no avail. Jordán acquired an even more robust dislike of his new commander and behaved so badly on the voyage that Caamaño put him ashore at Monterey to find his own way back to San Blas.

When he received the reports on Jordán by Eliza and Caamaño, Bodega forwarded them to the viceroy "with the greatest regret," suspecting that the information would be received with "displeasure." Revillagigedo's first reaction was that the matter amounted to little more than a family squabble. He pointed out that when the three men, Jordán, Eliza, and Caamaño, had been together on the *San Ramon* in 1789 on their way to New Spain, they had shown the greatest "familiarity and openness," and that Bodega was a particular friend of all three. The viceroy acknowledged Eliza's and Caamaño's complaints, but he also chided them for failing to resolve matters by themselves. The viceroy asked Bodega for his advice, since besides being a friend of all three men, he was their senior officer as the commandant at San Blas. At first, Bodega demurred, saying he could not give a balanced opinion without first hearing Jordán's side of the story. But then he said that, while he could not justify the foul language that Jordán was accused of using, he was not "very far believing that the two officers had failed to conduct themselves as they should have."[8]

Within three years, Bodega had turned against Eliza and Caamaño. A letter from Revillagigedo dated April 30, 1793, and addressed to Antonio Valdés enclosed a curious letter from Bodega asking for the officers' recall to Spain. However, he gave no reasons. The viceroy had forwarded Bodega's letter to Madrid with the sole comment that "Bodega does not explain himself well."[9] Bodega's disillusionment with Eliza is understandable. He commended Eliza for the leadership he had shown during the difficult months of his command at Nootka; but at the same time, he would certainly have been disappointed with his lack of initiative as an explorer. Why Bodega wanted Caamaño replaced is puzzling, since he had praised him highly for his command of the *Aránzazu* in 1792 while searching for the passage of Admiral Fonte. The fact that a year later Bodega appointed Jordán the executor of his estate suggests an explanation. There is no doubt that by then, Bodega had sided with Jordán, and this would have alienated him from the two brothers-in-law.

Bodega's disapproval damaged Eliza's and Caamaño's reputations. The viceroy referred the matter to the *auditor de guerra*, whose judgment went against the officers. Both were given heavy fines – Eliza of 250 pesos and Caamaño of 351 pesos – damages they were obliged to pay Jordán for his difficulties after being abandoned at Monterey. Jordán pleaded for more compensation, especially from Caamaño, to cover his expenses for food in Monterey and San Diego while he waited for a ship to San Blas. Bodega passed Jordán's appeal on to the viceroy, commenting that Jordán had a case. Revillagigedo did not agree. Eliza paid his fine immediately; Caamaño refused to do so on the grounds that the amount was "arbitrary." In the end, Revillagigedo's successor, the Marqués de Branciforte, ordered that the fine be taken out Caamaño's salary in three instalments.

Debts

When his health declined dramatically early in 1793, Bodega became deeply concerned about putting his financial affairs in order. Throughout his life, he had been neither frugal nor a prudent manager of his financial records. This was apparent even when he was a naval cadet in Spain. The pay book of the Real Colegio de Guardiamarinas records several advance payments against his future salary, even before he graduated. The pay book of the Naval Department of Cartagena for 1768-70 shows that before Bodega embarked on the *Septentrión* on October 29, 1768, as a new officer, he drew several advances against his pay.[10] These debits were not particularly large; still, they foretold a growing prodigality. In 1773 Andrés Reggio, the Capitán General de la Armada, in replying to a query from Julián de Arriaga, the Minister of the Navy and the Indies, wrote that Bodega was known for his *genio gastador* (extravagant ways).[11]

Bodega's father was a successful businessman who bequeathed, either before or on his death, between 6,000 and 12,000 pesos to each of his children. In 1763, Bodega received an unknown amount as an advance on his inheritance.[12] And again in 1772, this time 8000 pesos.[13] In 1779, Bodega claimed that his expenses on the voyage to Peru to purchase the *Favorita* had "compelled me to wipe out part of my inheritance."[14] In his 1783 petition to the king from Havana, he stated that he had "consumed his entire inheritance in the royal service." In his 1785 petition to José de Gálvez, he stated that on that voyage he had spent 12,000 pesos of his "personal funds."[15] In 1789 the addition of María Marín del Valle with her servants and some of her family to Bodega's household increased his domestic expenses sharply.

Early in 1793, when Bodega returned to San Blas from Nootka, he was faced with a crisis in his personal finances. The auditors of the Real Tribunal y Audiencia de Cuentas had discovered that from the time of his assumption of the command of the department in August 1789 until December 1791, he had claimed for the cost of employing eight servants at Tepic instead of the two allowed to him by the navy's regulations. At fifteen pesos a month for each of the six extra servants, the expenditure had amounted to 2,586 pesos – a sum he was being asked to reimburse to the treasury. Eight was a large retinue of servants for a bachelor officer, unless the "servants" were really the family dependants who were not acknowledged in the official records. We know that Bodega had two bona fide personal servants, Juan Mesía and José Antonio Navarrete, in his household at Tepic. The six additional dependants could well have included María, her son, and her cook, Clemencia. The three remaining "servants" might have been a maid and a nurse – or perhaps María's sister Josefa and their mother – and Father Jordán. It is probable that members of María's family lived with the couple, since her relatives had not shunned her for her liaison with Bodega. Her brother-in-law, a churchman, Canon José Antonio Dávalos joined Bodega's household during the last months of Bodega's life.

If he hoped to keep his domestic life a secret from the naval authorities in Spain, Bodega could not contest the finding that he had six extra people in his household. In August he asked Francisco Hijosa, the commissary for San Blas, to charge the excess cost to his messing allowance. He explained that otherwise it would be impossible for him to pay the debt, since he had "no assets or means other than my salary." Hijosa suggested that Bodega write to the viceroy to see whether he would authorize an ex gratia increase in his food allowance. This was bad advice. Bodega explained to Revillagigedo that the additional cost had been approved by the departmental *junta* and was included in the department's budget, which the viceroy had approved. Revillagigedo referred the matter back to the Real Tribunal, which, in a lengthy judgment, stated bluntly that Bodega was wrong: the six additional servants had not been included in the budget. The matter seems to have ended there, and the burden of debt remained. It is possible that after 1789, the strain of maintaining a household for María Marín and their son led Bodega on occasion to dip into the department's treasury. In the Mexican archives there are demands that Bodega refund amounts he had charged to official funds for personal expenditures – for example, when buying a chandelier for his house at Tepic.

To compound his financial woes, Bodega ran up some extraordinary personal debts on behalf of the Naval Department during the years he was commandant at San Blas. In 1792 he incurred four large obligations in order to ensure the success of the Expedition of the Limits. To purchase the stores he would require at Nootka to receive Vancouver and the officers of other ships in a grand manner, the viceroy had approved payment of 4,000 pesos as a special advance. It had been Bodega's understanding that this amount was an outright grant that he would not have to repay, not a charge against either his regular messing allowance or his salary. However, the *fiscal* ruled that the 4,000 pesos were an advance on Bodega's allowance for rations for which the royal treasury would have to be reimbursed.[16] Then, on the eve of his departure, Bodega had taken a 3,600 peso advance against his annual salary for the same purpose. Next, there was the debatable matter of the 1,500 pesos' worth of sea otter pelts he had used to purchase the *Adventure* from Robert Gray; it wasn't clear whether the pelts had been obtained with goods belonging to the king or to him. Finally, José Dario Argüello, the governor of Alta California, certified that he had disbursed on Bodega's behalf 1,680 pesos in San Francisco and 5,850 pesos in Monterey to pay for the hospitality Bodega had extended to Vancouver and for the supplies he had given to the British expedition. While he was in Mexico City, William Broughton heard that Bodega had given "the Governor of Monterey Bonds to the amount of 1,800 dollars for the refreshments our vessels had received."[17]

When the 2,586 pesos for the excess servants in his household are added to these amounts, the grand total comes to 19,216 pesos – slightly less than five years' salary. This was reduced somewhat when Bodega made occasional repayments to the treasury – some of these instalments, it seems, he had raised through loans from his friends. After his return from Nootka in 1793, the treasury began to withhold one-third of his monthly salary on Revillagigedo's instructions.[18]

The effort of finding a way to reimburse the treasury, or at least to reduce his debt, occupied much of Bodega's time when he resumed his duties at San Blas early in 1793. He had spent his inheritance, and his salary was barely sufficient for him to meet his "exorbitant expenses." Other sources of relief would have to be explored, beginning with a promotion – the classic hope of impecunious officers.

Bodega was never reticent about appealing to his superiors for a promotion. The first time he did so was in 1772, only five years after his graduation from the Real Colegio de Guardiamarinas.[19] Officers, especially those without influential patrons in Spain and who were serving in the more remote parts of the empire, had no recourse but to petition for advancement through their commanding officer or the viceroy himself. Since final authority in such matters lay with the naval hierarchy and the king, much depended on how highly placed one's friends were. The process was capricious. As soon as he received his promotion to *teniente de navío* in 1776, Bodega learned that several officers of his class with less seniority had actually been promoted ahead of him.[20]

In 1793 his promotion to flag rank was highly unlikely, not because he did not deserve it but because there were very few openings for such officers. The chances of preferment were even more remote for a colonial officer such as Bodega, who had been born in the Americas and had served there. At the time of his death, he was well placed for promotion. He was one of 110 four-ring captains aspiring to flag rank, and there were only 58 (out of 1,324) serving officers who were senior to him in the Spanish navy.[21] He also explored the possibility of being appointed governor of Callao, Lima's seaport. He put forward this option even though he knew it would offer only small assistance to his efforts to liquidate his debts.

Bodega's first request for reimbursement for the debts he had incurred during the purchase and refitting of the *Favorita* came in 1779.[22] In a letter to Viceroy Martín de Mayorga, he explained that he was making this request as a "compensation for the exorbitant expenses I have had to incur in the royal service in the space of the five years I have been in the department."[23] While in Monterey over the winter of 1792-93, Bodega raised the matter again with Revillagigedo, asking him to write an appeal to the king on his behalf. Bodega emphasized that his "misfortune is such that today I find myself after thirty years of service beyond the ordinary, in poor health, with no inheritance, in debt [to the treasury] and with only the influence which Your Excellency extends to me."[24]

Revillagigedo quickly took up Bodega's cause, knowing full well that his subordinate needed relief from the debts he had contracted in the king's service. Over the years, Bodega had sent letters to a number of ministers, including Floridablanca, Aranda, and Alcudia when they were Ministers of State; to Campo de Alange, the War Minister; and to Gardoqui, the Finance Minister; as well as several to Antonio Valdés, the Navy Minister. None of these communications had led to either reimbursement or promotion. Finally, on

February 23, 1793, Aranda, after conveying the king's appreciation for the manner in which Bodega had carried out the Expedition of the Limits, said he would "bear in mind" Bodega's desire to be on the next promotion list.[25]

On May 26, Bodega took matters into his own hands. In a formal five-page *instancia,* or petition, he made a desperate appeal to the king. In the flowery language of the day, he wrote that he had been admitted into the Real Cuerpo de Guardiamarinas in 1762 and had served the king in the assignments entrusted to him as befitted an officer of his noble birth and that his services had been acknowledged by his superiors with many expressions of approval. He had been particularly satisfied, he wrote to the king, to have been able to expand His Majesty's empire on the Northwest Coast of the Californias and later to have defended the Spanish king's claims against those of Britain. Finding himself with "no inheritance and in poor health" and having "sacrificed my life in the service of my country and its interests," he was compelled to seek the king's benevolence and beg for aid to relieve his situation. Specifically, he asked the king for

> the governorship of El Callao de Lima or some other post where I could better use my poor talents, live in a healthier climate, fulfill my desires and make up for the lack of means which compels me to seek Your Majesty's benevolence after thirty years of service, mostly in this miserable climate.[26]

When this petition brought no result, Revillagigedo decided to get more information about his subordinate's situation in order to advance his case. He asked the Real Tribunal for a detailed account of all of Bodega's expenses. In a lengthy reply, the tribunal pointed out that since there had been no authorization for the purchase of either the *Orcacitas* or the supplies provided gratis to Vancouver in Monterey, the amounts had been charged against Bodega's messing allowance. It was suggested that Bodega be asked for more complete information on these matters.[27] The viceroy accepted this advice and wrote to Bodega accordingly.

The viceroy's request reached Bodega in Guadalajara, when he was so ill that his Franciscan confessor, Dávalos, who was also María's brother-in-law, was on the point of administering the last rites. According to the person who wrote Bodega's response, Bodega had dictated the letter and asked Dávalos to sign it on his behalf "as Sr. Quadra is unable to do so." He agreed that the *Orcacitas* cost 1,500 pesos, as shown on the receipt signed by Robert Gray and John Hoskins and witnessed by Matthew Weatherhead.[28] He also conceded, as Argüello had certified, that he had agreed to make good 1,680 pesos for supplies given to Vancouver as well as the 2,860 pesos for hospitality at Monterey.[29] As for the Nootkan post, everything that had been spent – the 4,000 pesos and one year's salary – was for food not just for Vancouver but for officers of other ships as well. Bodega's letter concluded by stating that if "I am guaranteed the advance I took of one year's salary, I would be prepared to demand no other costs," namely, 3,600 pesos.[30]

When he made this proposal, he was unaware that a solution along the same lines was being developed by Alcudia, as Minister of State, with the concurrence of Gardoqui, the Finance Minister. They sought and obtained the king's approval of a grant of one year's salary, but at the rate for service in Europe of 1,800 pesos rather than at the rate for service in the Pacific. Approval was given in order to "satisfy" Bodega and at the same time to deny him the "right to make any further claim."[31]

When Revillagigedo received this news, he wrote immediately to Valdés to point out that in accordance with Viceroy Bucareli's *reglamento* of 1776, Bodega's annual salary as a seagoing full captain serving in the Pacific was 3,600 pesos, not 1,800. He requested that the king be asked to reconsider his decision.[32] Valdés took the matter up with Gardoqui but was told there had been no mistake: the 1,800 pesos was all the king would approve. Revillagigedo decided to go over Gardoqui's head and write directly to Alcudia, who had earlier shown sympathy for Bodega's position. It was a long letter, and one of the last he wrote before turning over the viceroyalty to his successor, Branciforte. Because Alcudia was new to the job and unfamiliar with the issue, the viceroy in his letter recounted the entire story for him from the beginning.[33] He pointed out that the treasury had not realized that the 4,000 pesos was a special grant for which Bodega had agreed to account, not an advance against his messing allowance. He, as viceroy, had had no hesitation in approving this grant or Bodega's advance of a year's salary. It had been essential for Bodega to have the means to establish good relations with Vancouver. The very creditable manner in which Bodega had carried out his mission, he concluded, fully warranted the award of a year's salary at the rate of 3,600 pesos and an appointment to the governorship of Callao, as he had recommended several times.[34]

Revillagigedo's strong argument seems to have had some effect, for it set off another round of discussions among the ministers concerned. Valdés assured Gardoqui that the viceroy was correct.[35] The minister agreed to speak to the king again, and he did so on November 5, 1793. At first the king held firmly to his earlier decision, but Gardoqui succeeded in overcoming his reluctance. A Royal Order was issued the next day, authorizing a one-time payment of 3,600 pesos and nothing more.[36]

Bodega's other debts to the Treasury were not mentioned. They either remained on the books or died with him. The issue was revived some time later by his older brother, Tomás Aniceto, who was then Rector of the University of San Marcos and Canonigo Doctoral at Lima's cathedral and who claimed to be Bodega's sole surviving heir.[37] He instructed his lawyer in Mexico City, José Maria Santelier, to ask the Fiscal de la Real Hacienda to release to him the *expediente* containing the papers about his brother's claims for expenses incurred on the Expedition of the Limits and, in particular, for the purchase of the *Orcacitas*, which, Tomás stated, "belonged to him."[38] After much delay, Santelier was told bluntly that there would be no refund for the schooner and that the matter had been settled some time ago, together with all of Bodega's other claims. The question was not pursued, no doubt because of Tomás's death. By then it was April 1801.

Declining Health

Bodega's financial distress could only have drained what little remained of his energy. While his pleas were being considered, his health deteriorated rapidly. He died on March 26, 1794, a little more than a year after his return from the Expedition of the Limits. Before his return to Nueva España in 1789, Bodega enjoyed reasonably good health. Certainly it was no worse than experienced by most of his companions at San Blas. The northern voyages were hard on the Spaniards, accustomed as they were to warmer climes.[39] A recurring phrase in accounts of veterans of these northern voyages is *salud quebrantada* – "broken health." Bodega had suffered severely from scurvy on his 1775 voyage. In February 1778, when he returned to San Blas from his voyage to Peru to purchase the *Favorita*, he immediately applied for sick leave to get away from San Blas during the months of heavy rain, from May to August, as "my health suffers constant indisposition."[40] He could have been suffering from any one of a variety of illnesses: malaria, dysentery, and typhoid fever were all endemic to the area. On the expedition of 1779, Bodega had eight men sick with scurvy aboard the *Favorita*. Although the expedition was well equipped with medicines and warm clothing, the strong winds, tempestuous seas, and constant cold, made worse by the ships' damp quarters and by almost daily showers of rain or snow, took their toll on officers and seamen alike.[41] After this voyage, Arteaga was never well enough to go to sea again, while Bodega had to spend three months "prostrate in bed, almost in the arms of death."[42]

The first indication that Bodega's constitution was beginning to fail is found in a letter he wrote to the viceroy in June 1791. When he wrote it, he was preparing for the Expedition of the Limits:

> As a result of some *sangrias* [either bleeding, bloodletting, or continuous loss of blood], I have been suffering for four months from a headache without any interruption. I have consulted some doctors, all of whom are of the opinion that I should leave this place for a less humid region. As the nearest [place] is Guadalajara, and, as at the moment there is no matter of consideration to prevent me from doing so, I am informing Your Excellency of the foregoing and request I be granted permission to [be absent] until October.[43]

Replying immediately in an uncommonly solicitous vein, the demanding Revillagigedo told him to "take whatever amount of time it takes to recover your health. I am confident you will use [your leave] to good advantage. Return to the Department when you can."[44]

Bodega did not avail himself of the viceroy's permission. He informed his superior that, while he had intended to leave after Eliza's departure for the north with the *Princesa*, he had decided not to go because "the moment, the distance [from San Blas to Guadalajara] and other reflections" – which he does not enumerate – had led him to remain in the department.[45] Shortly afterward, however, Revillagigedo summoned Bodega to Mexico City to review the plans for the expedition and to discuss his formal instructions. Bodega remained in the capital from mid-September until early December. Since consultations with the viceroy could not have occupied the whole time, perhaps he took advantage of the change of climate to recover from his ailments.

Whatever recuperation he was able to enjoy in the capital was not sufficient to restore him, for Bodega was a sick man when he arrived at Nootka the following April. Joseph Ingraham recorded in his journal that the "commodore [Bodega] was a little indisposed" and unable to take him on a personal tour of the establishment, as was his practice with newly arrived visitors.[46] Archibald Menzies in a letter to Sir Joseph Banks wrote that Bodega

> put himself under my care as a patient on our arrival here for a Severe Headache of which he complained, he said, for upwards of two years, & I was extremely happy that my endeavours proved serviceable in the reestablishment of his health before he went away.[47]

Menzies, unfortunately, does not say what he prescribed, whether it was bloodletting, blistering, purging, or some other brutal eighteenth-century medical treatment. Whatever his "endeavours" involved, they did nothing for his patient; while awaiting Vancouver's appearance in Monterey, without offering any details, Bodega wrote to the viceroy that he was in "poor health."[48] In his *Viaje*, Bodega recorded that it wasn't possible for him to return quickly to San Blas from Monterey late in 1792; however, he made no mention of his faltering health. Then the following February, after returning to San Blas, he declined the viceroy's request that he accompany Broughton to Mexico City, explaining that his failing condition did not permit him to become fatigued.[49]

A month later, he again felt compelled to request sick leave. In a letter similar to his previous solicitation, he wrote:

> For some time I have been living tormented by a pain I can no longer endure. The doctors assure me that I should separate myself from the business of the Department for a while. [Accordingly], I am seeking Your Excellency's permission to turn [the command] over to the appropriate officer while I obtain some relief.[50]

The viceroy gave his immediate consent and expressed the hope that the change would bring about a restoration of his health.[51]

Bodega's Death

Despite Revillagigedo's willingness to allow him all the time and change of scenery he needed to improve his health, Bodega was reluctant to abandon his responsibilities as commandant when he learned that war had been declared between France and Spain. On April 9, 1793, he wrote:

> In spite of my poor health, I find I cannot take advantage of the permission Your Excellency has kindly granted me ... Even though [a change] would contribute much to the restoration [of my health], other inescapable matters, of which I was not aware when I sought your approval, stand in the way. As soon as the danger of the war [with France] recedes, I will appoint Don Manuel Quimper as my *ayudante* when it is not possible for me to carry out my duties.[52]

The viceroy commended Bodega for the "zeal with which [he] put the concerns of war" ahead of his personal welfare, and he approved his designation of Quimper.[53] Even so, on April 16, the same day Revillagigedo replied, anticipating the viceroy's agreement, Bodega officially informed Francisco Hijosa that he was appointing Quimper as his adjutant because "for the moment my illnesses [sic] do not enable me to attend to the business of the department."[54]

Six months later, Bodega was obviously no better and found it necessary to write once again to Revillagigedo, this time to inform him that he was taking advantage of the leave he had been granted earlier and was leaving immediately for Guadalajara:

> I have been unable to obtain the slightest relief from the ailments which have broken my health. Since I informed Your Excellency of the need to take leave for a while from the matters for which I am responsible, I have suffered a strong *fluxo de sangre* [literally, blood loss or haemorrhage] and must take better care [of myself].
>
> In the last three months of my suffering, I have lost all hope of recovering my health in this place and am compelled to follow the advice of the doctors whose opinion I have sought.
>
> I am turning over the command of the Department to D[on] Salvador Meléndez ... and leaving today for Guadalajara to see if the change of climate and other assistance available there can bring about the improvement I am assured it can. If it does not, I trust Your Excellency will kindly allow me to continue on to the capital.[55]

Unaware of the gravity of the situation, Revillagigedo told him again to "do whatever seems best for yourself." Bodega left Tepic for Guadalajara that very day, October 11, accompanied by Juan Mesía and José Antonio Navarrete, the two servants from his household in Tepic, and with his confessor Father Dávalos, Maria's brother-in-law. The latter informed Revillagigedo that on his arrival in Guadalajara, Bodega "was very seriously ill," so much so that he was unable to sign some official papers he was enclosing. Bodega had asked him to tell the viceroy that he "finds himself totally unable to do so [himself] and has very little hope of living."[56] Revillagigedo replied that he was "very sensitive" to Dávalos's news and hoped that Bodega's "health would be restored as soon as possible."[57] On March 3, 1794, Bodega added a codicil to the will he had drawn up on November 13, 1793, which was to be registered in Guadalajara. The codicil named Jordán as his sole executor.[58]

The group remained in Guadalajara for several months.[59] A search of the records of four charitable institutions in Guadalajara financed by Bishop Francisco Alcalde failed to find any evidence that Bodega stayed in any of them.[60] According to Jordán, a woman (presumably María Marín), her sister, and her mother cooked and repaired Bodega's clothes for some two months and attended to him "day and night" until his death. Jordán testified that the woman's sister and mother owned the house where Bodega died. He also testified that the house was in Mexico City, although according to María Marín's will in 1815, she owned a house in Guadalajara, where she had grown up.

Accounts of events of March 1794 strain credulity. Inexplicably, considering his weakened condition, Bodega left Guadalajara with his two servants and Jordán. On the eight-day leg of the journey between Irapuato and Querétaro, some of Bodega's personal effects as well as more than 1,000 pesos in cash were stolen. In Querétaro, they were joined by Juan Carbajal, a retired naval surgeon living in Guanajuato. When Bodega asked to be taken on as his patient, Carbajal agreed and looked after Bodega from then on. The date of their arrival in the capital was not divulged. According to this version of Bodega's death, he was taken to the Convento de San Fernando, where he died on March 26. He was buried at the convent the following day.[61]

In an official letter to Antonio Valdés, Revillagigedo reported Bodega's death formally and rather tersely: "On the 26th of this month, Capitán de Navío Dn. Juan de la Bodega y Quadra, the commandant of the Naval Department of San Blas, died of natural causes in this city, where he had been given permission [to stay] to re-establish his health."[62] It may be that he was profoundly shocked. He seemed unaware of how ill Bodega had been. Or perhaps, for the official record, he was confining his statement to the barest details about the death.

Bodega had linked his physical health to the stress induced by his debts. Revillagigedo also sensed the connection, and he did not believe that Bodega's death justifed abandonment of the late officer's campaign for reimbursement, which he now made his own. In a letter to Alcudia regarding Alava's appointment to replace Bodega as Spanish commissioner for the ceremony at Nootka, he wrote:

> [Bodega's] death in this capital resulted perhaps from the fatigues of his voyages and from the very cold climate of Nootka, as well as from the despair of having seen himself overdrawn with the Treasury and with other persons who generously provided him with the necessary means to meet the excessive expenses of a commission which were essential to carry out with splendour, not for the honour of the person [Bodega] but because the interests of the nation demanded it.[63]

An English internist, Dr. John Naish, who has made extensive studies of the health of mariners in the eighteenth century, conjectured that Bodega's death, which came after a seizure, was probably due to the same medical condition that caused him severe headaches, regarding which he had consulted Menzies in 1792. Naish postulated that he died either from a brain tumour or from the severest form of hypertension.[64]

In a personal communication, Naish explained his diagnosis. He ruled out chronic malaria because, except during his two northern voyages, Bodega seemed healthy until his return to New Spain in 1789. There would not have been any long-term effect from scurvy, as it is instantly curable and headaches are not a particular symptom of that illness. Similarly, he ruled out migraine, as it is not fatal. Only malignant hypertension or a cerebral tumour could make for a long history of headaches. The former is a "vicious circle" syndrome in which a very high diastolic blood pressure, causing renal glomerular damage, releases substances into the blood, which further elevate the blood pressure. Untreated, death can follow within a year of diagnosis, often from a sudden cerebral haemorrhage, showing up, perhaps, as a stroke or as apoplexy. Naish, however, believed that Bodega's progressive weakness, and what is known of his illness leading up to death, better fits a cerebral tumour. It is quite possible, he wrote, for a patient with a cerebral tumour to suffer from headaches and other symptoms for two years before complete incapacity and death. Such a death can be preceded by an epileptic fit.[65] However, the imprecise contemporary diagnosis and description leave "natural causes" as the indisputable reason for Bodega's death at the age of forty-nine.

Settling the Estate

Six weeks after Bodega's death, Revillagigedo ordered the *sargento mayor de la plaza* in Mexico City to make a special inventory of Bodega's possessions in the strictest confidence.[66] He was to locate Bodega's personal effects and furniture as well as all objects of value. Except for one inquiry made in San Blas and another at Cádiz, the investigation was limited to what had been brought to Mexico City from Bodega's house in Tepic. The inquiry did not go to Guadalajara.

Three chests of effects were examined. One contained mostly clothing, including four well-used regular uniforms, complete with shirts, gold stripes, and shoes with buckles, a full dress uniform with red lapels, and Bodega's ceremonial sword with a gold hilt and tip. The second chest contained used bed and table linens along with a variety of personal garments such as underwear, shirts, and cravats. Among the items found in the third chest were a large number of papers: maps; letters and copies of letters; several manuals and technical books (including a compendium of elementary geometry); books on the theory and practice of seamanship; a manual on manoeuvring ships in bad weather; an instruction manual for ship manoeuvres; a treatise on artillery; a collection of ordinances for royal arsenals; a signals book; a book of astronomical observations; and nautical almanacs. All of these would have been standard for the personal library of a naval officer. There was also a Spanish dictionary. The only book of a nontechnical nature was intriguingly described as *Relación Histórico del Viaje* – possibly a copy of Bodega's journal of the Expedition of the Limits. The list contained nothing that could be described as light reading; nor did it contain any private documents, such as memorabilia or correspondence with members of his family.[67] There were none of the items that would have been required to maintain a household with eight "servants."

In his report to the viceroy, the *auditor de guerra* conducting the investigation, Miguel Bataller, was surprised by some of the omissions in the list of goods. He found only two silver candlesticks and "no knives, forks or spoons, no silver plates and no furniture of consequence that [Bodega] absolutely could never have done without." He was certain that these sorts of valuables had been hidden from him. So he asked for and received authority to interview the surgeon, Carbajal, and the two servants, Mesía and Navarrete.

Their testimony was brief, guarded, and sometimes vague. Carbajal testified that some pieces of Bodega's silver service had been used by him until the day he died. On being shown the list that had been made of Bodega's possessions, Carbajal said he believed that the greater part of the silver service had remained in Tepic. He noted that Bodega's shaving materials and snuff boxes had not been included, nor had his chronometer and telescope been listed. He hinted that one of the two servants now had the chronometer in his possession. Also, he understood that there was a second telescope, which Martín de Sessé had given Bodega for night observations.[68] He said that Bodega had kept a small *reloj de observación,* or clock, on the table by his bed in order to time his medicines, which had been removed by Jordán when he died, together with other items in the room such as a washbasin, candlesticks, snuffers, and a vessel for holding burning coals.[69]

Shown the same list, Mesía pointed out that it did not include the chronometer or telescopes, nor Bodega's two horses. The bulk of the silver service, he said, had been left in Tepic with Father Cristóbal Díaz, whom

Bodega had instructed in the event of his death to "cover the debt he owed him and two other individuals."[70] Navarrete, the second servant, testified, as had Mesía, that many items of clothing had not been included in the list. Bodega had given some to him and other items to Father Jordán, the executor.[71] Bodega had also given a watch and some personal items to Guillermo Aguirre, the *oidor* (magistrate) of the department. Navarette said he believed that Bodega wanted his chronometer and other personal items given to his youngest brother, Manuel, in Spain. He confirmed that the bulk of the silver service had been left behind in Tepic in the custody of Father Díaz. Four settings of the service had been brought from Tepic, but as almost everything had been stolen en route, they had only four plates when they had arrived in Mexico City.[72] He believed that Bodega had given one of his telescopes to the *piloto* López de Haro and the other "to the English" at Nootka. He did not know the fate of Bodega's two horses.

Bataller forwarded transcripts of these interviews, recommending to the viceroy that Jordán be asked for a further deposition about the items that had been in his possession but omitted from his first statement. Jordán should also be asked to state what he knew of the whereabouts of the other assets. Revillagigedo agreed, and a revised list of forty-eight items including the two horses, the chronometer, and two telescopes, but not including the silver service, was presented to Jordán for his comments.

Jordán's testimony is a muddle of half-truths and evasions. The priest stated that the missing items of clothing and furniture were very worn and were of no value and that, in accordance with Bodega's instructions, he had given them to those who had attended him "day and night" until his death. The recipients included the woman (María Marín?) whose mother and sisters ran the house in Mexico City (or was it Guadalajara?) where Bodega stayed for the two months before his death. The two horses, he said, were in a commercial stable in Mexico City. Bodega had asked that one be given to his servant Mesía, because he would need it to get to Veracruz en route home to Spain. The other was to be given to Navarrete, who would be returning to his home in Tepic.

Despite Bataller's efforts, it seems that these witnesses withheld the whole truth. There was general agreement about the fate of the silver service and the horses, but what happened to the chronometer and the telescopes is not clear. Obviously, Jordán had not carried out his duties as executor in an open manner. Bataller suspected that Jordán had hidden some things, and his report to the viceroy mentioned that "there are well-founded grounds for suspecting [him] as he did not include in the inventory all [of Bodega's] goods and valuables." On the other hand, he did not think there had been any "fraudulent concealment" inasmuch as Jordán was "ignorant whether or not he could give certain things away and at the same time conform exactly to the wishes of the testator."

As executor, Jordán made a list of the papers he had found in the third chest.[73] There were four kinds of documents: orders, correspondence (some draft letters), maps and charts, and reports. He forwarded the list to Eliza, who had become the acting commandant at San Blas.[74] The number of documents in Bodega's luggage was impressive. Later, the Marqués de Branciforte, who was now viceroy, asked that the 132 orders going back some years, a file of official communications, five books of drafts of 264 letters, and twenty-four boxes of letters be sent to Eliza in San Blas for the departmental archives. The letters were bundled together into two dockets. They were communications with Bodega's associates: Hijosa, Fidalgo, Eliza, Quimper, Alcalá Galiano, Torres y Guerra, Arteaga, Cepeda, Saavedra, Caamaño, and Matute. Some, Jordán noted, were in English, and since he did not understand that language, he was not certain whether they were confidential. Branciforte asked that they be sent to him to be translated. Possibly these letters were Bodega's correspondence at Nootka Sound with the Americans and with Vancouver, or with the latter at Monterey.

The maps and charts were also sent to San Blas to be deposited in the departmental archives. This precious legacy never seems to have been inventoried further at any time, and it will never be known which were drawn by Bodega himself and which were produced by other officers or his *pilotos.* Unfortunately, Jordán described the maps and charts only in general terms. All sixty-two items were originals. Fifteen were of the North Coast, five of the Californian coast, two of the Sandwich Islands (possibly of Quimper's survey, which Bodega included in the atlas volume of his *Viaje*), twenty-seven were drafts, and thirteen "on English paper" were of "various ports and coasts." These last, no doubt, were ones that Vancouver had given to Bodega either at Nootka or in Monterey. It is not clear what happened to the reports, although they may have been among the "considerable number of papers without arrangement or order" that the viceroy instructed Jordán to forward to the viceregal secretariat.

Jordán attended to one final detail of Bodega's estate. William Broughton, probably while he was a passenger on the *Activa* returning to England via San Blas, had agreed to purchase for Bodega in London four dozen shirts "of the finest trim," as well as a number of nautical instruments, including an Arnold chronometer, a small pocket chronometer, a Ramsden sextant "with three telescopes," a thermometer, a glass "to determine distances at sea," and an artificial horizon.[75] When he got home in July 1793, Broughton purchased everything Bodega had requested. Writing to enclose the bill, which came to £250, he assured Bodega that the "instruments were the finest in England."[76] As had been arranged, a cousin, Pedro de la Quadra, who was living in Cádiz, paid the bill with 2,640 pesos.[77]

Jordán had written to Broughton to ask him to call again at Monterey and leave the items there. The priest would have them forwarded to Bodega. Broughton arrived in Monterey on June 6, 1796, and left everything with Diego de Borica, then governor of California. Borico received the instruments and the shirts and sent them by the first available vessel to Hijosa, still the *comisario* in San Blas. The viceroy instructed Hijosa to store the instruments in the royal warehouse. As the file ends there, it will never be known what happened to either these elegant shirts or the nautical instruments, but it takes no stretch of the imagination to assume that the Spanish navy appropriated them for its own use.

In September 1794, Vancouver returned to Nootka Sound once again, hoping to find his instructions and to continue the negotiations.[78] Instead, he was distressed to hear of the death of his friend, Juan Francisco de la Bodega y Quadra, six months earlier. He turned to his journal and wrote:

> The death of our highly valuable and much esteemed friend Senr Quadra, who in the month of March had died at St. Blas, universally lamented. Having endeavoured, on a former occasion, to point out the degree of admiration and respect with which the conduct of Sen'r Quadra towards our little community had impressed us during his life, I cannot refrain, now that he is no more, from rendering that justice to his memory to which it is so amply intitled, by stating, that the unexpected melancholey event of his decease operated on the minds of us all, in a way more easily to be imagined than described; and whilst it excited our most grateful acknowledgements, it produced the deepest regret for the loss of a character so amiable, and so truly ornamental to civil society.[79]

Bodega's career in the Americas spanned almost the entire twenty years, from 1774 to 1795, when this remote corner of the world was the focus of Spanish concern. Directly and indirectly, Bodega was responsible for the greater part of the Spanish exploration and mapping of the North Pacific coast. He gave outstanding service in three distinct roles; first, as an explorer on two expeditions that investigated the Pacific coast north from Mexico to as far as Cook Inlet; second, as commandant of the Naval Department of San Blas for two terms; and third, as a diplomat negotiating with George Vancouver. As an explorer, he experienced the transition from ad hoc exploratory ventures to carefully mounted, methodical expeditions. As an organizer, he transformed a remote, ill-suited, and poorly supplied naval harbour in Mexico into a more effective base of operations for sustaining Spain's outposts in Alta California. As a diplomat, he upheld the honour of Spain.

In the mid-eighteenth century, the Northwest Coast of North America was the last large blank on the map of the temperate zones. The effort to chart that coast produced giants in the history of maritime exploration: Bering and Cherikov, Cook and Vancouver, Lapérouse and Malaspina. English and American fur traders, who were working among the native peoples of the area, sometimes exchanged navigational information with the naval explorers. A group of Spanish naval officers, whose names have appeared in this biography, also contributed to this effort: Pérez, Hezeta, Mourelle, Arteaga, Martínez, López de Haro, Fidalgo, Quimper, Caamaño, Eliza, Narváez, Alcalá Galiano, and Valdés. Pre-eminent among them was Juan Francisco de la Bodega y Quadra Mollinedo, a Spanish naval officer of the eighteenth-century Enlightenment.

Appendix A

Bodega's Secret Instructions to Eliza for the Reoccupation of Nootka, January 28, 1790

As His Excellency the Conde de Revillagigedo, Viceroy of New Spain, has decided to fortify Nutka, reconnoitre harbours which have not as yet been adequately examined, and prevent foreign nations from continuing their commerce on the northern coast of California, I have ordered armed the frigate *Concepción*, the packet boat *San Carlos* and the bilander *Princesa Real.* In accordance with this order, I have appointed you because of your seniority and [good] conduct to command the frigate. *Teniente de Navío* don Salvador Fidalgo and *Alférez de Navío* don Manuel Quimper have been charged to follow your orders in the other ships of your command.

With such a just and worthy object, His Excellency has asked me to communicate to you certain admonitions he has conveyed to me, and those which I believe would be useful to the discharge of the commission I am entrusting to you.

1. Departure from this port must take place on the 31st of this month [January] without fail, unless some irremediable accident should prevent it. As the first object is to fortify Nutka before some other power does so, you will make every effort to arrive at that port; but if during this short period someone might have taken advantage of the absence of our arms, you will inform him of our right and precedence and of the orders you have to dislodge anyone who vainly tries to oppose you. Only in such a case or of disrespect to our flag can you use force to contain and punish the insult. Our Sovereign wishes to maintain peace and harmony and for this reason you will treat with the greatest prudence,

friendship and discretion any foreign ships you might meet or who arrive in the port; you will not insist on examining them scrupulously, nor apprehend them but assist them to leave, without permitting any commerce whatsoever with the natives.

2. To avoid any such intrusive attempt and to induce respect, you will establish at the point of your landing an appropriate fortification with the twenty cannon you are carrying ... in the most advantageous location with a competent guard. You will do this without leaving the ships of your command poorly manned.
3. This fortification is to be commanded by the Captain of the Catalonian Volunteers you are carrying on board, who in the same way as the entire garrison, will for now be under your command or whoever succeeds you.
4. When the frigate [*Concepción*] and the fort have been so arranged to resist whatever invasion, you will think of continuing the discoveries with the other ships of your command and the schooner you are carrying in pieces; those will begin at latitude 59° and 47°45′ west of San Blas in which is located the anchorage of Regla, known as Cook River,[1] which must be examined with precision to determine whether they are fortified by the Russians as stated by Captain Colnett, and having found out, the navigation will be continued to reconnoitre the entrance of Santiago called by the English Prince William [Sound], situated in latitude 60°21′ and 42°30′ west of San Blas, from which point the coast should be not be lost sight of until the entrance to [the Strait of] Fuca is reached. Its latitude is 48°30′ and 20°30′ west of San Blas ....[2]
5. For this task you will commission the most senior officer, to whom you will give a copy of the instructions, charts and signals which I have had prepared to provide the clearest knowledge.

AGN *Historia* 67, printed as document 13 in Cárdenas, *San Blas.*

Appendix B

Revillagigedo's Instructions to Bodega for the Expedition of the Limits

1. When the frigate [*Santa Gertrudis*] arrives in Acapulco, you are to take command of her. If junior to you, her captain will be your second-in-command, but should he be senior and not willing to serve under your orders, he is to remain in New Spain until the commission is concluded, when he may resume his command.
2. Instructions have been given to provide the frigate with stores and other items it will need. If these are insufficient or anything is lacking, you are to inform me without delay.
3. As soon as the frigate is ready, you will sail immediately to San Blas, where you will take on board *piloto* Gonzalo López de Haro and the clerk of the *contaduría* of the Department, whom you have requested [to accompany you]. You are to sail to Nootka when the weather permits.
4. There you will meet three English frigates, or smaller ships, two of which are directed to reconnoitre the coast and the other to receive and be delivered in accordance with Article I of the convention the buildings and tracts of land which are supposed to have been established and purchased in the port of Nootka, and the one called Port Cox, situated some seventeen leagues to the south and known to us as Cayuclat.
5. The English have claimed and endeavoured to prove that in April 1789, they were dispossessed by the Spanish of the above-mentioned buildings and tracts of land. But it is certain that in 1774 the Spanish discovered the port of Nootka and took possession of it, that in 1778 the English captain James Cook arrived in the same port, that subsequently it was frequented by many ships of different nations and that

no one formally occupied it until 1789. At that time, as our establishment was created legitimately, James Colnett, the captain of the *Argonaut,* could not do so for England.

6. Nevertheless, in advising you to proceed with caution, the genuine desire which animates our august sovereign is to establish the most perfect friendly harmony and good relations with the King of Great Britain. Accordingly, you will relinquish and surrender to the English everything they can prove in any way belongs to them in the harbours and along the coast of Nootka and Port Cox, either by purchase or occupation prior to ours, settling the matter provisionally and in a friendly manner, [and] declaring that it is without prejudice to our rights nor to what both courts may agree on the matter. You will bear in mind at all times that the English do not claim sovereignty but special authority and the right to trade with the Indians, who do not recognize nor are obliged to recognize Spanish authority.
7. Once the transfer and surrender has been made in accordance with the convention, the English cannot and should not prevent us from [establishing another] post in the harbour of Nootka or in another part of the continent, nor from trading for furs, even though the English will be to the north and the Spanish to the south at a reasonable distance apart so as not to harm or interfere with each other.
8. There is no doubt that we can keep our Nootka establishment without hindering or prejudicing whatever the English may erect to the north [of it]. But, considering it necessary to remove any obstacles which can cause discord, disagreement and quarrels, it seems to me preferable that you abandon Nootka and move the establishment to the north [sic] shore of the Strait of Juan de Fuca, once you have surrendered to the English the lands they claim to have acquired and purchased in the harbour of Port Cox, and they have moved to Nootka from which they claim to have been ejected by the Spanish.
9. Once Article I has been implemented, the English have no basis to claim losses and compensation as called for by Article II. Neither before nor after April 1789 have they experienced any act of violence or hostility on our part. You should not consider the detention and transfer to San Blas of the *Argonaut* and the *Princess Royal* as coming under these headings. Martínez permitted the English *Iphengenia Nubiana* to return to Macao and would have done the same with the other two ships had it not been for Colnett's attitude of resistance or hostility. He, like all his officers and crews, was generously compensated for all the losses, delays and damages they could claim. They were paid according to their rank

the same salary as the members of the Royal Navy. They were treated with kindness and granted appropriate privileges. Their ships were repaired and their cargoes stored. They were given complete freedom to return to Macao in the *Argonaut* and in the *Princess Royal* via Manila, as they could not sail together.

If, notwithstanding the above, the English seek greater compensation than they have received, you will inform me of their reasons and what they propose, and of your opinion on the matter, so that I may report to the king, who will decide what may be appropriate and with the friendly agreement of our court and that of London.

10. In order to carry out completely without any misunderstandings the correct and prompt fulfillment and detailed observance of the remaining articles of the convention before the generous surrender of the port of Nootka to the English, the transfer of our establishment to the Strait of Juan de Fuca should be done quickly. As should the survey of the coasts and lands of northern California, so as to fix for all time the boundary or dividing point between the lands which legally belong to us alone and those which are to be held jointly for the use and trade of English and Spanish subjects, in accordance with Article V of the convention.
11. The early occupation on our part of the Strait of Juan de Fuca is very important. It is also desirable that, as soon as possible, you undertake in the frigate under your command and with one of the other frigates stationed at Nootka the survey of the coasts in close combination with the two English ships coming there for the purpose.
12. As Fuca is situated at 48°30′N, I consider it to be the limit, or boundary, of our legal occupation of the northern coast of California. For this reason, I believe that the survey of the coast should be carried out as far south as San Francisco, but if you are unable to dissuade the commander of the English ships from taking part in this truly useless survey, you will carry it out together as far as San Francisco without stopping there or at any of our established settlements.
13. There will be no difficulty surveying the coasts and regions north of the Strait [of Juan de Fuca], where there is the greatest abundance of fish and amphibians and where are to be found assured and profitable opportunities for the English and the Spanish to trade with the Indians. It would not be just to allow the English to settle or trade along the coast between the Strait and San Francisco, which solely and legally belongs to us.
14. Also ours are the lands of our province of New Mexico.[1] In order to prevent the English for all time from encroaching on them, it not only

seems appropriate that the Strait be the limit or the boundary of our establishments north of California but that, as well, that from the entrance to the Strait a boundary [line] or meridian running north up to 60°N, as shown on the enclosed map, be established.

15. As far as our present establishment at Nootka is concerned, it matters nothing provided we transfer and re-establish it on the Strait in the best harbour so as to be able to observe the movements and designs of foreign ships. Fuca[2] will be our northernmost possession north of San Francisco. From this point English navigators or traders, as alleged, may not pass [to the south] or penetrate [inland]. In this way all suspicions of smuggling into Spanish establishments will be avoided and agreements may be reached on the free entry, occupation, reciprocity, use and trade between the two nations along the coasts and in the regions lying north of 48°30′N as called for by Article V of the convention.
16. Having set out in these instructions the essential particulars for your delicate mission, it is not necessary for me to mention the importance of seeking complete harmony and the most cordial relations with the commander, officers and crews of the ships of His Britannic Majesty, to be frank in all your dealings and to communicate without reserve all the information, maps and charts of [our] discoveries in order that the reports of the English commander may coincide with yours, and that any differences between the two courts may be adjusted and brought to an end. As differences have arisen over fishing, trade and navigation in the Pacific Ocean and the South Seas, the boundary line to be declared to be the dividing point between what belongs legally and solely to us and what is to be held in joint occupancy will recall and fulfill the mutual desire which led Their Catholic and Britannic Majesties to establish the most complete and most perfect and constant friendship to the reciprocal benefit of the faithful subjects of the two Crowns.

Enclosure #2, Revillagigedo's letter #56 to Floridablanca. The original text has been followed closely, but in a few places the exact wording has been paraphrased for clarity.

Appendix C

History and Description of Bodega's *Viaje*: The Official Report of the Expedition of the Limits

Bodega's journal and the accompanying maps and drawings are an important record of his mission in 1792. The Spanish archivist and historian Pilar San Pío considers it "one of the fundamental documents for understanding the most delicate chapter through which Spanish expansion on the Northwest Coast of America was passing."[1] Together with Moziño's *Noticias de Nutka*, it is the only document that gives a Spanish perspective on the Expedition of the Limits.

Bodega began to write the final manuscript of his journal for the Expedition of the Limits while waiting for Vancouver in Monterey, and he finished it en route to San Blas. On anchoring there on February 1, 1793, he forwarded it to the viceroy, who was anxious for more details about the expedition as well as for Bodega's "reflections" or assessments and recommendations.[2] As soon as Bodega y Quadra's journal and maps – and presumably the drawings as well – arrived in Mexico City from San Blas, they were copied.[3] The copies were sent off to Madrid some eight weeks later on April 12, 1793.[4]

Bodega's Report for the 1792 Expedition of the Limits

Bodega's official journal (*diario histórico*) consists of two volumes: a journal and a folio of charts and drawings. It was entitled *Viaje a la Costa N[or]O[este] ...*, and is generally referred to in this biography as his *Viaje*.[5]

Volume 1: The Journal

The narrative proper begins with his appointment as commandant of the Naval Department of San Blas and carries on to the end of his command of the Expedition of the Limits. Bodega includes brief paragraphs on politically pertinent ethnological topics such the status of the chief, social structure, religious beliefs, the native economy, and the trading partners of the Nootka. Emphasizing the peaceful nature of the Indians, he writes at length on his relations with the Nootka in general, and with Chief Maquinna in particular. Highlighting his concern over the extent of the fur trade, he records the arrival of each fur trader and comments on their activities. He recommends that Spain participate in the fur trade in order to reduce the threat it poses to Spain's sovereignty on the Pacific coast of America. He also writes about Spain's lack of naval strength in the region to compete with foreign vessels and about its inability to protect the Alta California settlements. He includes an extensive passage on the possibilities and reasons for developing Nootka as a permanent establishment.

Bodega devotes the second section of his journal to his relations with Vancouver, both personal and official, including their exchanges of hospitality. He incorporates the texts of the letters they exchanged, the originals of which he forwarded to Mexico City.

The last section of the *Viaje,* which deals with Bodega's stay in Monterey, is the thinnest part of the journal. He concentrates on his dealings with Vancouver, including the refreshments provided to his ships and the assistance extended to Broughton and Weatherhead.

A brief Spanish–Nootka dictionary provided by José Mariano Moziño and José Maldonado is appended to the journal. It includes some verbs, the months of the year, and a catalogue of flora and fauna. Also appended in tabular form are the logs of the *Santa Gertrudis* for Bodega's voyage from San Blas to Nootka and for his return voyage on the *Activa* via Neah Bay and Monterey. Each log matter-of-factly records daily the weather, the nautical miles travelled, the course sailed, and the ship's noon position.

Bodega's account has its shortcomings. Some of these are due to the haste with which it was assembled and his increasingly poor health. In this journal, he betrays some of the characteristics that can complicate the historian's task, such as too brief descriptions of important events and a brevity of expression that leaves the reader wanting more detail to better understand significant points. Thus he gives no details of the ceremonial visit to Maquinna at Tahsis.

Volume 2: The Folio

The second volume of Bodega's report is a folio that includes a number of charts, drawings of native life, and a selection of Atanásio Echeverría's drawings of Moziño's botanical and zoological specimens.[6]

Bodega put a lot of time and energy into assembling the charts for the atlas portion of the folio volume. The most important one was the revision of his third general chart, which he had prepared for the expedition. Bodega's fourth *carta general,* possibly done with the assistance of Jacinto Caamaño, Félix de Cepeda, and Gonzalo López de Haro, includes the discoveries made by Caamaño around the Queen Charlotte Islands, Vancouver's exploration of Puget Sound, and the Alcalá Galiano–Valdés circumnavigation of the newly named Quadra and Vancouver's Island. It incorporates the discoveries of some Russians and of Robert Gray, Caamaño, Alcalá Galiano, Valdés, and Vancouver up to the time of his arrival in Monterey. Spanish settlements are shown in red and those of the Russians in blue.[7]

The folio volume also contains the following charts: one of the waters around Nootka Island and a plan of the establishment; five from Caamaño's voyage in search of the supposed passage of Admiral Fonte (Bucareli Bay, Gaston, Florida Blanca, and the waters around the Queen Charlotte Islands); and two from Quimper's voyage (one of the Hawaiian Islands and one of the Puerto de Quadra, later called Discovery Bay or Port Discovery). Bodega inserted three charts copied from Vancouver, the first two being Broughton's maps of the Columbia River and Puerto Sidman, the third being Whidbey's map of Gray's Harbour. Following these are charts of various ports: San Diego, San Blas, San Francisco, Monterey, Carrasco (Barkley Sound), Acapulco, and Puerto de Claycuat (Clayoquot Sound). Bodega also included a copy of Dionisio Alcalá Galiano's map of his circumnavigation of Vancouver Island. The folio volume was embellished with three coastal profiles, one of which is of the entrance to Nootka Sound.

Echeverría's Drawings

Atanásio Echeverría was the official artist for the Expedition of the Limits. On a scientific expedition in the eighteenth century, the artist was expected to function as a photographer might today. Fidelity to detail was all-important; the artist's work was a scientific tool, not an aesthetic expression. When he returned to Mexico in February 1793, Echeverría placed his pen-and-ink-wash drawings and sketches in the hands of fellow artists at the Academy of San Carlos, as it was a common practice at that time for artists to leave their work with others to be "finished" or "improved." Echeverría resumed his position in the Royal Scientific Expedition and never returned to the academy to work on the drawings. The artists at San Carlos made at least two sets of copies of Echeverría's drawings.[8] One set was made for inclusion in the folio volume of Bodega's *Viaje*; a second set was given to the viceroy. In the process, the originals were lost.

In the folio volume of the *Viaje* there are at least four drawings of plants, three of birds, and two of fish. There are ten drawings of Nootkan people and scenes, including four monochrome portraits of Nootkan chiefs and their wives, a monochrome drawing of the interior of Maquinna's house on the occasion of the Bodega-Vancouver visit to Tahsis, and another concerning Maquinna's daughter Apenas, titled "Proclamation of the Princess Ystocoti-Tlemoc." The folio also includes three monochromes of the Nootka establishment: the first a view of the small cove that Meares occupied, the second a view of the entire cove from the establishment, and the third a plan of the establishment itself.

While we must be thankful to have at least copies of Echeverría's drawings, the "finished" drawing of a copyist can never have the accuracy or sense of place of the original, nor can it convey the artist's intentions with the same vitality. The images that have come down to us appear overly formal, even stilted. Would Echeverría, for example, when looking out across Nootka Sound from the commandant's house, have so exaggerated (as did Gabriel Gil) the profile of the mountains? Would he have made their crests jagged rather than rounded, as they actually are? Would his drawing of an upper-class Nootkan woman, gazing adoringly on her child while nursing it in its cradle, have been as idealistic as Manuel García depicted her? Echeverría's in situ drawings of Nootkan life at the time of contact would have been a particularly important legacy, as he was highly thought of by those familiar with his work. Naturalist Alexander von Humboldt praised him, and Menzies recorded in his journal that he considered Echeverría to be an "excellent draughtsman ... who as a natural history painter has great merit."[9]

Subsequent History of the 1792 Journal

At least three copies of Bodega's *Viaje* were made in the viceroy's secretariat in Mexico City.[10] The first one, together with the copies made of the charts and drawings, was taken to Spain by Cayetano Valdés and Secundino Salamanca, who were returning from the Malaspina expedition for reassignment. This set was delivered directly to Alcudia, the Minister of State, and now resides in the archives of the Spanish Ministry of Foreign Affairs in Madrid.[11] The only complete set of copies of the Echeverría drawings is also in the archives of the Spanish Ministry of Foreign Affairs in Madrid, having been forwarded by the viceroy along with Bodega's *Viaje*.[12]

A second copy of Bodega's two-volume *Viaje* would have been deposited in the Mexican archives as a matter of course. A copy of the *Viaje* was acquired some years ago by the Huntington Library in San Marino, California.[13] As the Archivo General de la Nación in Mexico does not possess a copy, it is not outside the realm of possibility that the Huntington copy was stolen from the Mexican archives in an era when security measures were notoriously lax, if not non-existent. The folio volume was not acquired with the journal.[14]

Viceroy Revillagigedo kept the third copy of Bodega's *Viaje*, complete with its folio volume of charts and drawings, for his personal use. It was later acquired, together with thirty-seven volumes of the viceroy's personal papers, by the bibliophile Irving W. Robbins of Atherton, California. He placed the collection on extended loan with the Bancroft Library at the University of California, Berkeley. This copy of the *Viaje* was bought by the Library of Congress in Washington, DC, around 1980 from H.P. Kraus of New York City.[15] The folio volume was broken up; the charts and the copies of Echeverría's drawings were sold individually and are now dispersed.[16] Twenty or so copies of Echeverría's drawings are in the collection of the Hunt Institute for Botanical Documentation at the Carnegie Mellon University in Pittsburgh.[17]

The Bodega y Quadra *Viaje* was not published until 1990, when Spanish historian Salvador Bernabeu Albert printed it with an introduction and notes, together with Bodega's journals of his 1775 and 1779 voyages, under the title *Juan Francisco de la Bodega y Quadra: El Descubrimiento del Fin del Mundo (1775-1792)*. More recently, the *Viaje* has been printed in a deluxe edition, *Nutka 1792*, by the Dirección General de Relaciones Culturales y Científicas of the Ministry of Foreign Affairs in Spain, together with eleven introductory essays, illustrations of the charts and drawings, a catalogue of the ships mentioned in the text of the journal, a compilation of relevant documents, and a bibliography. Also included are the Spanish–Nootka dictionary and the list of plants, insects, fish, vegetables, and birds compiled by Moziño and Maldonado for Bodega to append to his journal.

Appendix D
Biographical Notes

Alcalá Galiano, Dionisio Galiano was born October 8, 1760, in Cabra near Cordova. He became a specialist in cartography and hydrography. He served under Malaspina in the *Atrevida*. In the company of Cayetano Valdés of the *Mexicana,* he commanded the *Sutil* on the first circumnavigation of Vancouver Island. On his return to Spain, he worked with Malaspina to write the account of the expedition. He returned to sea after Malaspina was arrested and incarcerated. He was killed at the battle of Trafalgar, in command of his ship of the line *Bahama.*

Areche, José Antonio de Areche has been characterized as a "man of inflexible character." The extreme measures he took as the *visitador general* to Peru to increase tax revenues were universally unpopular and caused great hardship, especially among the Indians. The measures provided a spark for the rebellion of Tupac Amaru II (1780-81), the bloodiest episode experienced in Peru since Pizarro's conquest. The brutal means that Areche took to put it down, especially the manner in which its leader and his family were publicly put to death, eventually led to his recall in September 1781. Tupac Amaru's real name was José Gabriel Kunturkanki. He was the headman of a village in the southern sierra, who claimed noble Inca lineage.

Arteaga y Bazán, Ignacio de Arteaga was born of Basque parents in Aracena, Andalusia, on February 17, 1731. With both his parents being of noble lineage, he was admitted to the naval academy at Cádiz in 1747 when he was fifteen, graduating in 1754. After serving on various ships in both Spain and the Americas, he was transferred to Havana in 1766 for his first command, the sloop *Víbora.* Despite a critical assessment of his conduct – "lack of attention to his duties" – he was promoted the following year to *teniente de navío.* Returning to Spain in 1771, he ran into trouble when he tried to marry without the necessary royal and ecclesiastical permissions. When the priest discovered who he was and refused to officiate, Arteaga appealed to the ecclesiastical tribunal and became abusive, "insulting a secular member." He was thrown into the jail of the naval arsenal at La Carraca, where he remained for three years. Finally freed in 1774 in the belief that he might "be useful to the service if he corrects his ways," he was sent to San Blas, where he arrived in 1775. When Arteaga returned from commanding the 1779 voyage north, he sought and obtained a royal pardon and reinstatement of his loss of pension, but "broken health" would not allow him to go to sea again. Arteaga served as commandant of the department until his death in 1783, the same year he was promoted to *capitán de fragata.* It was his first promotion since 1767.

Ayala y de Aranza, Juan Manuel de Ayala was born in Osuna, Andalusia, on December 27, 1745, and graduated from the Real Colegio de Guardiamarinas in 1760. After serving eleven years at sea in Spanish waters, and holding the rank of *alférez de navío,* he was one of the six officers who came to Mexico with Bodega in 1775. During the 1775 expedition, he became the first to explore San Francisco Bay.

Bodega y Quadra, Alberto Magno Born in 1745, Bodega's younger brother Alberto followed their father's footsteps and became a businessman. In 1774, he was given the family home in Lima. In 1777 he was a passenger on the *Favorita,* the ship that Bodega had purchased in Peru. Whereas Bodega's other brothers followed the Spanish custom of adding their mother's family name, Mollinedo, to their father's family name, Alberto, like Juan Francisco, was known simply as Bodega y Quadra.

Bodega y Quadra Mollinedo, Joseph Antonio Born in 1737, Bodega's older brother was a student at the Colegio San Martín in 1763. Joseph Antonio studied law in Spain between 1772 and 1775. He returned to Peru and served as a priest in the Lima cathedral. What became of him later is not known.

Bodega y Quadra Mollinedo, Manuel Antonio Bodega's youngest brother, Manuel Antonio, was born in 1752. Like Juan Francisco, he manifested a more independent mind than their other siblings. He studied at the Colegio de San Martín. A brilliant student, he travelled to Spain to enter the Colegio Mayor de San Bartolomé in Salamanca. With two doctorates in law, he entered the Jesuit University of Alcalá de Henares, later the University of Madrid, where he taught until 1773. He returned to the Americas in 1785 to take up his appointment as *oidor* in the *audiencia* of Guatemala and, later, in the *audiencia* of Mexico. Returning to Spain, he was appointed first as a member of the Council of the Indies and then to the Council of State. He held a number of senior positions, including representing Peru in the Cortes, the parliament of Spain in Madrid. In 1820, when King Ferdinand VII was on the throne and the revolt of the American viceroyalties was raging, Manuel, as a member of the Council for the Pacification of America, published an important pamphlet urging more political power for *criollos.* In 1822 he served briefly as minister for overseas matters. He died in 1835.

Bodega y Quadra Mollinedo, María Josefa and María Antonia Bodega's two sisters were born in 1735 and 1737, and were the only girls in the family to survive to adulthood. They became nuns and took the veil. Little is known about them except that they lived in the Carmelite convent in the old part of Lima, and María Josefa became its abbess in 1793.

Bodega y Quadra Mollinedo, Tomás Joseph Aniceto Bodega's oldest brother was born in 1731. Tomás travelled to Spain in 1765 but returned to Lima. In 1773 he was serving as *canónigo doctoral* in the metropolitan cathedral. He later served on Lima's city council and as examiner of the Lima archbishopric, and went on to hold other senior positions in the church. He finished his career as rector of the University of San Marcos. He died in 1801.

Bucareli y Ursúa, Antonio María Bucareli was a native of Seville and related to noble families of Spain and Italy. He entered the army at an early age and rose to the rank of lieutenant general. He distinguished himself as an engineer in campaigns in Italy and Spain and as inspector general of cavalry. He then served as governor and *capitán general* in Cuba before being appointed viceroy to New Spain in 1771. Bucareli's handwriting was atrocious, but patience rewards the researcher who is willing to decipher his periodic personal letters to ministers, "for your eyes only," especially those to Julián de Arriaga, the Minister of the Indies and the Navy. Bucareli died in office in Mexico City on April 9, 1779, and was buried in the shrine of Nuestra Señora de Guadalupe.

Caamaño Moraleja, Jacinto Caamaño was born in Madrid of a noble Galician family in September 1759. He entered the navy in 1777 not as a midshipman in the Real Colegio de Guardiamarinas but as an *aventurero*, one in a class of young men who embarked on warships as cadets or unpaid trainees in the hope of being admitted to the commissioned ranks. In this he was successful, and in 1779 he began his service on various ships in Spanish waters, receiving regular promotions. Before sailing to New Spain in 1789, he was inducted into the military Order of Calatrava.

Camacho, José Early in his career, Camacho was based in Cádiz before Gálvez selected him for San Blas. He was a veteran of the San Blas corps of *pilotos*. In 1785, when seeking a promotion to *teniente de fragata* from Antonio Valdés, Camacho stated that he had already served more than thirty years in the navy. Prior to his selection to serve on the *Princesa* for the 1779 expedition, he had commanded resupply missions to San Diego, Monterey, and San Francisco. Bodega thought highly of Camacho and selected him to accompany him on his second mission to Peru in 1781-82. Viceroy Manuel Flores wanted Camacho to serve with Martínez on his 1788 voyage to Alaska, but age and poor health prevented him from doing so. Flores also considered appointing him instead of Martínez to head the expedition to occupy Nootka in 1789, but for the same reason did not. In 1793 he took the schooner *Valdez* to the Philippines and, between assignments, served as acting commandant of the department. Camacho died in Tepic on April 13, 1795.

Cañizares, José de Cañizares first served in Spanish waters as a gunner. He then attended San Telmo, the school for *pilotos*. After passing his examinations for *piloto*, he came to the Americas in the late 1760s and was attached to the staff of José de Gálvez during the latter's time as *visitador general*. He was then seconded to the mission of the Marqués de Croix for the pacification of Sonora. After that assignment, he served out of San Blas for twenty-five years "without any rest whatsoever," as Bodega wrote in 1793 when recommending him for promotion. At a later time, Bodega added that although a senior *piloto* and promoted to *alférez de navío* and then *teniente de fragata* in 1791, Cañizares's "particular services had never been adequately compensated." In support of his own petition for promotion, Cañizares said that he had served twenty-seven years at sea, attached to the San Blas department, "having suffered its bad climate, the dangers of exploration and the responsibility of twenty-seven voyages to Perú, Manila, Nootka and the establishments on the [Alta California] coast." Cañizares holds the distinction of having made the first nautical chart of San Francisco Bay while serving under Ayala in 1775. A second chart, which he made in 1776, is now in the Bancroft Library, Berkeley. Where and when Cañizares died is not known.

Choquet de Isla y Suárez de Figueroa, Diego Choquet was one of the six officers who came to Mexico with Bodega in 1774. Before going to New Spain, *alférez de fragata* Choquet served fifteen years in the Mediterranean and saw much action against the Moors. Although recruited for maritime exploration in the North Pacific, he never served on any expedition, perhaps because he proved to be a man of uncertain reliability. According to Enrique Cárdenas de la Peña, he was "in eternal conflict" with his superiors and was accused of scandalous conduct and of being a womanizer.

Colnett, James During a career in England's Royal Navy that began in 1770, Colnett proved himself an able navigator and organizer, and his rise up the ladder of commissioned ranks was steady but unremarkable. He served on the *Resolution* on James Cook's second voyage to the Pacific and then in various warships with the rank of lieutenant until 1786, when he went on half pay following the conclusion of the American War. With the Admiralty's approval, he was given command of a fur-trading expedition to the Northwest Coast between 1786 and 1788, which included the *Prince of Wales* and the *Princess Royal.* That was his first trading experience. His journal for this voyage has been published by UBC Press. His second voyage, in command of the *Argonaut* and the same *Princess Royal,* gave him much greater responsibility and led to the Nootka crisis.

Eliza y Revenga, Francisco de Eliza was born in Puerto de Santa María, Spain, possibly in 1757. Like Bodega, he graduated from the Real Colegio de Guardiamarinas in Cádiz in 1773 and saw service at sea in a number of ships in the Mediterranean area before being assigned to New Spain.

Fidalgo y Lopegarcía, Salvador Fidalgo was born to a noble Basque family in August 1756 at Seo de Urgel, Lérida, near the French border. He attended the Real Colegio de Guardiamarinas and graduated in 1775. Having demonstrated a capacity for cartographic work, he was selected to be a member of Vicente Tofiño's team employed during the 1780s in making the first atlas of Spain's ports and coastal waters. After various assignments at sea in the Mediterranean, seeing action against the British and the Portuguese, and receiving regular promotions, he served for a time as *ayudante* *mayor* to the Real Colegio de Guardiamarinas. He set out for New Spain with Bodega in 1789, just after he was promoted to *teniente de navío.*

Fitzherbert, Alleyne, Baron St. Helens His first appointments as an English diplomat were to Brussels as minister and to Paris as a member of the delegation negotiating the peace treaty with the United States. He was then appointed ambassador to Russia and later to Holland. As a reward for his successful negotiation of the Nootka Convention while English Ambassador to Spain, he was created Baron St. Helens. Later, still in Madrid, he negotiated the treaty of alliance with Spain of 1793. Mount St. Helens in Washington State was named for him by George Vancouver.

Gálvez, Jose de Born near Málaga in 1720, Gálvez studied law at the University of Salamanca and practised it in Madrid. Fluent in French, he became legal counsellor at the French embassy. He entered government service as secretary to Minister of State Jerónimo Grimaldi and quickly established a reputation for ability.

Haro, Gonzalo López de Haro was the commandant of the *San Carlos* on the Martínez-Haro expedition to the Aleutians in 1788. He was a *primer piloto habilitado* at the time of the Nootka crisis.

Hezeta y Dudagoitia, Bruno de Hezeta proved to be one of Spain's most notable sailors. Born in Bilbao in 1743 of an old Basque family, he entered the Real Colegio de Guardiamarinas in 1758. Before coming to the Americas, he served in the continuing battle against North African pirates, saw action in some ten major engagements, and was promoted to *teniente de navío* in April 1774, just before leaving for New Spain. One of the six officers who came out with Bodega in 1774, Hezeta eventually returned to Spain, where he had a successful career in a number of senior assignments, including that of commandant of the naval base at Cartagena. He rose to the rank of lieutenant general. He died in 1807.

Hijosa y Rodríguez, Francisco Hijosa was born in 1731 in the village of Medina de Río Seco, a small town 42 kilometres northwest of Valladolid. He came to Mexico in 1766 at the request of Viceroy Marqués de Croix, under whom he had served in La Coruña. De Croix appointed him treasurer and war commissary for the campaign to pacify the Pima, Seri, and Apache Indians in the province of Sonora. On its conclusion, the viceroy appointed him to San Blas to develop the port, and in this capacity he organized the construction of ships such as the packets *San Carlos* and *Príncipe* and the dispatching of the first resupply missions to California. After a brief sojourn in Mexico City, he was appointed by Viceroy Antonio Bucareli in 1773 to be the first *comisario* at San Blas, a post he held until 1780. After a brief period of service in Mexico City en route to Spain on home leave, Hijosa was yet again appointed to San Blas, and he remained there at an annual salary of three thousand pesos during the entire period of interest to us.

Manrique, Miguel Manrique was assigned to the 1775 Hezeta-Bodega expedition in command of the *San Carlos* to make the first charts of San Francisco Bay but had to be sent home when he developed signs of insanity. He was one of the six officers who came to Mexico with Bodega in 1774.

Martínez, Esteban José Martínez was a native of Seville and a graduate of the Colegio de San Telmo, the school for *pilotos*. After shipboard duty between Spain and the Americas, he arrived in San Blas in 1773. He became one of the most controversial figures in the story of Spain and the North Pacific coast when he instigated the murder of Callicum, a chief of the Mowachaht. At the time of the Nootka crisis, Martínez was *piloto primero* and *alférez de navío*.

Matute, Juan Bautista Matute commanded the *Sutil* in the failed attempt to establish a settlement in Bodega Bay in 1793. He was killed at the Battle of Trafalgar while serving on the *Santísima Trinidad*.

Menéndez Valdés, Salvador Menéndez's service record relates solely to his unsuccessful quest in 1795 for promotion, after twenty-five years of service as *primer piloto*. He came from the north of Spain and entered the navy in 1769. After teaching himself navigation, he passed the examination for *pilotín* in El Ferrol and then saw action in various ships in the American war against England. In 1780 he was transferred to Veracruz and placed in charge of the coast guard. For his good work there, he was promoted in 1789 to *primer piloto*. When the coast guard was abolished, he was transferred to San Blas. His name is sometimes spelled "Meléndez," but it never appears thus in his service file in the El Viso archive.

Mourelle de la Rua, Francisco Antonio Born in 1750 to an impoverished noble family in San Adriano de Corme, near La Coruña, Mourelle graduated from the school for *pilotos* at El Ferrol at age fifteen. After a variety of seagoing appointments, he arrived in January 1775 in Veracruz, New Spain, with the rank of *primer piloto.* He was on the same ship that brought Bodega to New Spain, and they proceeded together to San Blas, where Mourelle was the most senior *piloto* in the department of San Blas after Esteban José Martínez. Because of the abilities he demonstrated on his two expeditions with Bodega, Mourelle was promoted to ensign and then to sub-lieutenant, one of the few Spanish naval officers to be promoted from the non-commissioned ranks. He made three voyages across the Pacific, one of those in command of his own ship.

After twenty-five years of constant service at sea and because his health was weakened, Mourelle was brought by Viceroy Revillagigedo to Mexico City in 1790, to make a compendium of all the Spanish expeditions to the Pacific Northwest: those of Pérez; his own of 1775 and 1779; those of Esteban José Martínez and López de Haro in 1788 and 1789; and that of Salvador Fidalgo and Manuel Quimper in 1790. He also handled the viceroy's correspondence on naval matters and the Nootka crisis. He returned to Spain in 1794, took part in the Battle of Cape St. Vincent (1797), and eventually rose to the rank of chief of squadron (rear admiral). He died in Cádiz in 1820 and is buried in Spain's Pantheon of Illustrious Mariners just outside that city.

Noriega, Father Matías de Santa Catalina Noriega was born in 1736 near Oviedo, Spain. At the age of thirty-one, he joined the Franciscan order at the San Fernando convent in Mexico City. After returning from the voyage north with Bodega in 1779, he served at the mission of Carmel and is known to have been present at the death of Father Junípero Serra on August 28, 1784. Father Noriega returned to Mexico City at the age of fifty-three (1789) and died there in 1798.

Pantoja y Arriaga, Juan Pantoja was a graduate of the San Telmo school for *pilotos.* He was immediately appointed to the Naval Department of Callao and was one of the two *pilotines* Bodega brought with him from Lima in 1777-78. Bodega had a good opinion of him and always found him intelligent and reliable. Pantoja was promoted to *segundo piloto* on the eve of his joining the *Princesa* for the 1779 voyage, during which he would quickly show his skills as a cartographer. He also wrote well, and his journal of the expedition is one of the most interesting. On his return from this voyage, he commanded ships on resupply missions to Alta California and on mapping voyages along the southern coasts of New Spain. Eventually, he travelled to Nootka in 1791 on the *San Carlos* under Ramón Saavedra. That same year, he served with distinction on Eliza's expedition into the Strait of Juan de Fuca and Strait of Georgia. Pantoja was still in San Blas as late as 1806, battling the authorities to correct an error he claimed had been made in his pay for the time he served on the 1779 expedition. When and where he died is not known.

Quimper Benítez del Pino, Manuel Peruvian-born, he entered the Compañía de Marina in Callao and for a while served in the merchant marine. Eager to earn a commission in the Royal Navy, he left to study mathematics and navigation at the University of San Marcos, graduating in 1774. He served under Domingo Boenechea on the *Aqila* on his second expedition that same year to assert Spanish sovereignty over Tahiti. He was transferred to Spain in 1786, where he had only shore assignments before venturing to New Spain with Bodega in 1789. In 1790 he carried out the first exploration of the Strait of Juan de Fuca.

Quirós y Miranda, Fernando Bernardo Quirós was second-in-command of the Arteaga-Bodega expedition of 1779 and one of the six officers who came to Mexico with Bodega in 1774.

Revillagigedo, Juan Vicente de Güemes Pacheco de Padilla y Horcacitas, the second Conde de (sometimes spelled Revilla Gigedo) Revillagigedo was born in Havana in 1740 into a family originally from the Santander region of Spain. At the time, his father was serving as Captain General and Governor of Cuba. After residing in Mexico until he was seventeen, Juan Vicente opted for a military career, beginning in Cádiz, and then, in 1762, in Cueta. He was later sent on a mission to Panama to reorganize the militia there. Resigning from the army for family reasons and in so doing incurring the displeasure of King Carlos III, he entered private business and was appointed director of the Banco de San Carlos. On the death of Carlos III, Minister of State Floridablanca appointed him viceroy to La Plata, but when the Viceroy Manuel Antonio Flores resigned for health reasons, Revillagigedo was appointed to succeed him in Mexico City.

In the five years of his reign, from 1789 to 1794, Revillagigedo established a unique record of achievement in the domestic arena through public works, such as improvements to the sanitation, garbage collection, and street lighting of the capital. He also improved roads, reorganized the local government, and brought some order to the state finances. A popular man, he actively supported cultural institutions such as the Academia de San Carlos and created the Colegio de Minería. There was scarcely an aspect of the viceroyalty's economy and political life to which he did not make a contribution. He was frequently engaged in controversy with the church on jurisdictional matters. However, Christon Archer informs me that "Revillagigedo was a great proponent of using European Spaniards." He favoured the regular armed forces rather than the provincial militias led by European officers. When the Marqués de Branciforte assumed office in 1794, he had to rebuild the defensive forces based on the *novohispano* population.

A bachelor, Revillagigedo had prodigious energy, was intolerant of laziness and sloppiness, and in contrast to his parents was scrupulously honest.

Riobo, Father Juan Antonio García Riobo was born in Malpica, near La Coruña, in 1740. He entered the Franciscan order at twenty-two and went to Mexico in 1769. In official records, he is described as "of medium height, stout, with a thin face, and chestnut-coloured hair." After returning from the 1779 expedition, he worked for a while in various Alta California missions, returning to Mexico sometime after 1786. The date of his death is not known.

Saavedra Guiráldez y Ordónez, Ramón Saavedra was born of a noble family in April 1769 in Luga, Galicia, and attended the Real Colegio de Guardiamarinas, graduating in 1782. The red tape involved in switching assignments caused him to miss sailing with the others to San Blas on the transport ship *San Ramón* in 1774. He caught a later ship bound for Havana, where he transferred to another to reach Veracruz, and so onward.

Torres y Guerra, Alonso de Torres y Guerra, a native of Seville, was promoted to *capitán de fragata* in 1782 and given his first command, of the brigantine *Ardilla,* in 1788. Promoted in 1792 to *capitán de navío* in command of the *Santa Gertrudis,* he sailed her from Spain to Peru.

Valdés de Bazán, Antonio Arguably the ablest minister of the navy to hold the portfolio, Valdés, a native of Seville, was a career naval officer who first went to sea in the tiny navy of the Order of Malta and became *bailío* or head of that order in Spain. He attended the Real Colegio de Guardiamarinas, rose rapidly in the ranks to *jefe de escuadra,* or rear admiral, and was only thirty-nine when chosen by the king to take over naval affairs. Eventually he resigned over the Malaspina affair.

Valdés y Flores, Cayetano Valdés was born in 1767 in Seville. He was a nephew of the Minister Antonio Valdés. He served under Malaspina on the *Discubierta.* He commanded the *Mexicana* on the expedition to circumnavigate Vancouver Island. He was wounded at Trafalgar. He rose to flag rank, but his liberal views brought him trouble when the ultraconservative King

Ferdinand VII assumed the throne. In 1814 he was imprisoned. In 1820 he was released when Ferdinand VII was deposed. Caught up in the troubles of the time, he was forced to seek exile in England. In 1835 he returned to Spain to become *capitán general* at Cádiz. Valdés died in Madrid in 1839.

Appendix E

Rank Structure of the Spanish Navy

Commissioned Ranks

alférez de fragata Midshipman's title on successful graduation
alférez de navío Sub-lieutenant
teniente de fragata Equivalent of lieutenant junior grade in US Navy
teniente de navío Lieutenant
capitán de corbeta Lieutenant commander
capitán de fragata Commander
capitán de navío Captain

Flag Officers

brigadier Commodore
jefe de escuadra Rear admiral
teniente general Vice admiral
capitán general Admiral
capitán general de la armada Admiral of the fleet
capitán y director general de la armada With headquarters in Cádiz, who was also *comandante general*

Pilotos

piloto Institute-trained, not considered a full member of the *marina de* *guerra.* As a naval rank, navigator or master of a ship; does not translate directly to "pilot" in nautical terms.

primero A *piloto primero* could, at first, earn the rank of *alférez de fragata*; later, he could aspire to rank of either *teniente de fragata* or *teniente de navío.*

segundo A *piloto segundo* would be given the rank of *oficial mayor* (warrant officer); later, he could aspire to the rank of *alférez de fragata* or *alférez de navío.*

pilotín Junior *piloto*, or master's mate

práctico Essentially a coastal pilot

Seamen

contramaestre Boatswain

marinero Ordinary seaman

grumete Novice seaman

page Cabin boy

criado Officer's servant

Glossary

arroba A measure of weight, approximately 25 pounds.
aspirante On a ship, rank of cadet
audiencia Senior administrative and judicial jurisdiction, a province of the viceroyalty
auditor de guerra Naval legal adviser
aventureros A class of young men who embarked on warships as cadets or unpaid trainees hoping to be admitted to the commissioned ranks
balandra Bilander, a small, flat-bottomed vessel for use in harbours in the style developed by the Dutch
braza One fathom, or 5.48 English feet
cable A measure of distance, being one-tenth of a sea mile, 120 *brazas,* or 600 feet
carta esférica A chart drawn on Mercator's geometrical projection
carta general A chart showing ocean with coasts and islands
carta reducida A chart of a portion of coast
cédula A royal order or decree, more formal than a *real órden*
codo 18 to 22 inches
constructor Master shipbuilder; also *maestro de construcción*
contaduría Headquarters for administrative staff and storehouse for supplies
criollos Spaniards born in and residing in the Americas as opposed to the *peninsulares* born in Spain; creoles
cuartillo One pint

diario A journal or log in narrative form
dictamen Official opinion
ensenada A small bay
entrada Entry, an entrance
esmilri Small cannon
estado Ship's manifest
estero Creek or inlet
estrecho Strait
expediente A group or file of documents relating to one subject
fiscal Attorney-general; one of the personal advisers of the viceroy on financial and legal matters
flecheros Indian bowmen
flota a Nueva España Annual convoy between Spain and Veracruz
fuertes Similar to present-day usage of the term "hard currency"
grumete A novice seaman
instancia A petition
intendente The viceroy's watchdog for financial matters
intendencias Local administrative jurisdictions
junta de guerra A decision-making process used by the naval and army officers
legajo A bundle of papers or file
legua A Spanish league, being 3 nautical miles, or 3 minutes of latitude
marina de guerra The war navy
Marina Ilustrada The Enlightened Navy
meschimes Nootkan commoners
mestizos People of mixed blood
oficiales de guerra Officers of the war navy
oidor Literally, one who hears or listens; performed judicial functions within an *audiencia* but could also undertake special functions such as adjudicating commercial and taxation disputes or serving as a probate judge and inspector of ships and armies
parecer Opinion, advice, usually given in writing
peninsular An individual who was born in Spain
peón An unskilled worker
piloto Navigator, master of a ship; a specific naval rank, it does not translate directly to "pilot" in nautical terms
pita fibre Fibre made from the agave plant
plano A map of a local area such as a city or harbour
práctico Coastal pilot
promyshlenniki Russian independent fur-trade entrepreneurs

quadrante Reference to the four quadrants of compass direction, each being 90 degrees: First or NE, Second or SE, Third or SW; and Fourth or NW
quintal approximately 100 pounds
real orden An instruction
reloj de observación A device with a predetermined time setting, possibly a type of hourglass
residencia A detailed inquiry by the home government into all aspects of a viceroy's administration
sangrador Literallly, bloodletter; surgeon's mate or sick bay attendant
taise Nootkan chief
vaqueros Farmhands, especially those skilled in handling cattle
vara Measurement equivalent to 33 English inches
visitador general Inspector general

Chronology

1713

April 27 Bodega's mother, Francisca de Mollinedo de Losada, is baptized.

1728

August 22 Bodega's father, Tomás de la Bodega y Quadra, marries Francisca de Mollinedo de Losada.

1744

May 22 Juan Francisco de la Bodega y Quadra, their ninth child, is born in Lima, Peru.

1760-70

Bodega's mother dies sometime in the decade.

1761

March 16 Juan Francisco de la Bodega y Quadra is enrolled in the Colegio de San Martín in Lima.

1762

September 27 Bodega enrolls as a cadet in the Real Colegio de Guardiamarinas at Cádiz, Spain.

1765

September 21 Bodega is promoted to *alférez de fragata* and assigned to service in the Mediterranean.

1767

Bodega returns to Peru on board the *Septentrión* and is assigned to the naval squadron based at Callao, Lima.

1773

Bodega is promoted to *alférez de navío.*

September Bodega is informed of his assignment to San Blas. He spends three to four months with the hydrographer Vicente Tofiño on a special course in navigation and cartography.

1774

Bodega is promoted to *teniente de fragata.*

January 25 Juan Pérez sails on first exploration of the Pacific north of Alta California.

June 13 Bodega departs for New Spain on the store ship *Santa Rita.*

August 26 The six officers from Spain arrive in Veracruz.

October 25-December 15 They stop in Mexico City.

1775

March 7 Bodega's father is buried.

March 16 The Hezeta-Bodega expedition sails from San Blas.

November 20 The expedition returns to San Blas.
November 20-February 1776 Suffering from the rigours of the voyage, Bodega is bedridden for three months.

1776

March 16 Bodega is promoted to *teniente de navío.*

1777

March 16 Bodega arrives in Acapulco with the *piloto* Cañizares to go to Lima to purchase the *Favorita.*
Mid-June Bodega arrives in Lima.
December 19 The *Favorita* sails for San Blas with Bodega in command.

1778

February 8 The *Favorita* arrives in San Blas.

1779

February 11-12 The Arteaga-Bodega expedition sails out of San Blas in the *Princessa* and the *Favorita.*
November 21 The *Favorita* sails into her home port on November 21. The *Princesa* arrives four days later.

1780

May Bodega is promoted to *capitán de fragata.*
September Minister Gálvez sends a Royal Order to Viceroy Mayorga informing him that all further expeditions are in abeyance until the war with Britain is over. Ignacio de Arteaga replaces Bruno de Hezeta as commandant at San Blas; Arteaga is commandant of the department of San Blas until his death in 1783. Initially, Bodega is acting commandant because Arteaga takes longer to recover from their expedition.

1781

February 13 Bodega is instructed to sail for Callao to pick up quicksilver.
May 8 Bodega sails for Callao on the *Santiago.*

1782

July 16 More than a year later, Bodega sights the entrance to Callao.

1783

June 20 The *Santiago*, under Bodega's command, returns to San Blas.
December 2-20 Bodega travels from San Blas to Havana.

1785

January 14 Bodega sails for Spain.
March 2 Bodega reaches Cádiz. Soon after, he fails to gain an audience with Navy Minister Valdés.

1786

November 15 Bodega is promoted to *capitán de navío.*

1787

January 23 Bodega writes a formal letter to Minister Valdés in which he proposes an expedition to map the entire Pacific coast of the Americas. As a second option, he volunteers to return to New Spain. The letter includes a request to marry. There is no response.

1788

April 8 Bodega is inducted as a knight in the Order of Santiago.
October Bodega has an audience with Valdés.

1789

March 24 Bodega is informed of his appointment to San Blas.

August 8 After a voyage of sixty-three days from Cádiz on the *San Ramón*, the new viceroy, Revillagigedo, Bodega, and his five companions arrive in Veracruz.

October 20 Martínez sails from Nootka Sound.

Late November Martínez returns to San Blas from Nootka Sound.

December 31 Bodega takes up his post as commandant at San Blas.

1790

February 3 Eliza and his three ships leave San Blas to reopen the establishment at Nootka Sound.

Early April Eliza reaches Nootka Sound.

Juan Francisco Bodega y Marín, Bodega's son, is born this year or thereabouts.

Manuel Quimper explores the Strait of Juan de Fuca.

Salvador Fidalgo goes to the far north and surveys Prince William Sound and Cook Inlet.

October 28 The Nootka Convention between Spain and England is signed at the Escorial.

1791

Alejandro Malaspina and his scientific expedition discredit the hoax of the passage of Lorenzo Ferrer Maldonaldo at 60°N.

Francisco de Eliza and José María Narváez move through the Strait of Juan de Fuca to explore the San Juan Islands and penetrate the Strait of Georgia between Vancouver Island and the mainland.

1792

March Bodega sails for Nootka Sound to meet George Vancouver.

August Bodega greets Vancouver at Friendly Cove. Their negotiations end in stalemate.

Alcalá Galiano and Valdés complete the circumnavigation of Vancouver

Island and thereby disprove the myth of Juan de Fuca's transcontinental passage.

Jacinto Caamaño examines the waters north and east of the Queen Charlotte Islands and disproves the existence of the passage of Admiral Fonte.

November and December Bodega and Vancouver meet in Monterey.

1793

End of February Bodega returns to San Blas.

The Eliza and Martínez y Zayas expedition charts the coast south from the Strait of Juan Fuca to San Francisco. Zayas explores the mouth of the Columbia River.

October 11 Bodega travels from Tepic to Guadalajara.

November 5 Father Dávalos writes a letter from Guadalajara on Bodega's behalf.

November 13 Bodega draws up his will.

1794

March 3 Bodega adds a codicil to his will to be deposited at Guadalajara.

March 26 Bodega dies at the age of forty-nine.

Summer The Marqués de Branciforte replaces Revillagigedo as viceroy of New Spain.

1815

María Marín del Valle draws up her will and testifies that her son Juan Francisco Bodega y Quadra de Marín is a little over twenty-five years old.

1830

February 5 Juan Francisco Bodega y Marín draws up his will and testifies that he has a daughter.

Abbreviations

AGI	Archivo General de Indias, Seville
AGN	Archivo General de la Nación, Mexico City
AGS	Archivo General de Simancas, Valladolid
AHH	Archivo Histórico de Hacienda, Mexico City
AHN	Archivo Histórico Nacional, Madrid
AMAB	Archivo-Museo Don Alvaro de Bazán, El Viso del Marqués, Ciudad Real
AMN	Archivo del Museo Naval, Madrid
Bancroft	Bancroft Library, University of California at Berkeley
BCARS	British Columbia Archives, Victoria
BMAS	Ministry of Foreign Affairs, Madrid
BN	Biblioteca Nacional de Madrid
BP	Biblioteca del Palacio Real, Madrid
HL	Huntington Library, San Marino, California
PAC	Public Archives of Canada, Ottawa
RAH	Real Academia de la Historia, Madrid

Notes

Chapter 1: Beginnings

1 This figure does not include some two million unconquered Indians.
2 Located in today's Bolivia, the mountain known as El Cerro Rico (the rich hill) is still being mined.
3 Lawrence A. Clayton, "The Maritime Trade of Peru in the Seventeenth Century."
4 Frézier, *Voyage de la Mer du Sud*, p. 251.
5 Laos, *Lima*, pp. 14-15.
6 Herr, *The Eighteenth-Century Revolution in Spain.*
7 See Palacio, *España y la Mar en el Siglo de Carlos III.* Much of the information in this section is drawn from these essays and from Harbron, *Trafalgar and the Spanish Navy.*
8 Zulueta, "Trafalgar – The Spanish View."
9 New Spain included the Capitanía General of Cuba and the *audiencias* of Mexico, over which the viceroy himself presided – Guatemala (today's Central America), Santo Domingo, and the Philippines.
10 The genealogical information compiled for Bodega's *pruebas* to support his application for membership in the military Order of Santiago is to be found in AHN, Ordenes Militares, Santiago, legajo 203, expedientes 18119 and 18344. See also Ybarra y Berge, *De California á Alaska.*
11 The information on the Bodega and Quadra families comes from a number of sources: correspondence with Jorge Fernández Stoll, editor of *Revista del Instituto Peruano de Investigaciones Genealógicas;* Menchaca Careaga, *De California á Alaska*; idem, "Juan Francisco de la Bodega y Quadra y su tiempo"; Beerman, "Tomás de la Bodega y Quadra y su Testamento"; and Ortiz Sotelo, "Juan Francisco de la Bodega y Quadra, los años iniciales."
12 Zuluaga Citores, *Sebastián de la Quadra.*
13 The ancestral home remains in the family of the late Don Antonio Menchaca Careaga,

who inherited it from his father. Menchaca's mother, Doña Rosario de la Bodega, was a descendant of Juan Francisco's mother's line. Menchaca, a retired naval officer as well as a distinguished novelist and journalist, undertook an extensive restoration of the house. He also donated to the municipality of Pobeña the land for a small plaza, the centrepiece of which is a copy of a handsome bust of Bodega y Quadra that stands in Quadra Park, Victoria, BC. The latter was a gift from the Spanish government and was unveiled by Juan Carlos I in March 1984.

14 Juan de la Bodega y de la Quadra was born on May 30, 1677, and died on August 14, 1741.

15 Tomás de la Bodega y de las Llanas was born in 1701 and baptized in the parish church of San Julián de Muskiz on December 14 of that year.

16 See Appendix D, Biographical Notes, for additional information on Juan Francisco's siblings.

17 The register of births of the chapel of the sacrarium, 1744. I am grateful to the late Don Antonio Menchaca Careaga for a photocopy of this entry. The original spelling of names is maintained in this quotation. In the phonetic Spanish spelling of this time, B and V were interchangeable, as were LL and Y, G and H, and C and Z.

18 It stood on the sites of nos. 209, 213, and 217 of the Jirón Ancash.

19 The crest on the Bodega ancestral home in Muskiz has a silver tower on a golden field with black doors and windows in one quarter and three red stripes, a silver border, and eight blue crosses on a golden field in the second quarter. There is some doubt as to the authenticity of the design of the crest over the door of the Lima house. It is believed to have shown the Bodega and the Quadra crests on two equal sides divided by a vertical line. It could have been added when Bodega became a knight of the Order of Santiago in 1788.

20 The Real Colegio de Guardiamarinas was established in 1717; the naval medical college in 1748; the astronomical observatory in 1753; the Depósito Hidrográfico (later the Directorate of Hydrography) in 1770; and the school of naval engineering in 1772.

21 Equal to a junior sub-lieutenant in the Royal Canadian Navy (RCN) or a junior ensign in the US Navy.

22 Bodega's service record is in the Archivo Museo de Álvaro de Bazán, El Viso, Ciudad Real.

Chapter 2: The 1775 Voyage on the *Sonora*

1 I am grateful to Dr. Donald C. Cutter for pointing out that this was Pérez's real name and not, as is often cited, Juan José Pérez Hernández. The latter was a sergeant serving as adjutant to Governor José Antonio Roméu of California.

2 The *Santiago* (alias *Nueva Galicia*) was the first and largest ship built in San Blas. She proved to be a workhorse, serving from 1774 to 1786 until being written off as unseaworthy. She was more a merchant vessel than a warship. See Kenyon, "Naval Construction," pp. 131-39.

3 Chapman, *A History of California*, p. 270; Bobb, *The Viceregency of Antonio María Bucareli*, pp. 259-70; Servín, "The Instructions of Viceroy Bucareli to Ensign Juan Pérez."

4 Martínez's complete journal of this voyage is in the AGN, Historia 61; microfilm in the Bancroft Library.

5 These have been published in Spanish and in translation by Cutter, *The California Coast*, pp. 203-78.
6 For biographical notes on the other participants, see Beals, *Juan Pérez on the Northwest Coast*, pp. 29-33.
7 Cook terms Pérez's failure to enter Nootka Sound "a fateful omission [that] would have profound diplomatic consequences and be much lamented by Spanish officialdom." Cook, *Flood Tide of Empire*, p. 67.
8 Martínez did not mention this in his journal but made the claim later in a letter to Viceroy Flores from Nootka, July 13, 1789; AGN, Historia 65. At that time, Martínez sent his *piloto*, José María Narváez Gervete, to investigate.
9 Quoted by Christon Archer, "Seduction before Sovereignty," p. 129.
10 Another important responsibility was to supply the army during its ongoing pacification of the Indians along the northern frontier of New Spain.
11 Grimaldi to Bucareli, April 20, 1773; AGI, Indiferente General 1630.
12 Arriaga to Bucareli, San Idelfonso, August 24, 1773; AGS, Marina 37.
13 The following paragraphs are based on Bernabeu Albert's introduction to his book *Juan Francisco de la Bodega y Quadra.*
14 Bruno de Hezeta y Dudagoita's surname was variously spelled Hezeta, Heceta, Ezeta, and Eceta.
15 Arriaga to José de Rojas, from San Idelfonso, August 3, 1773; AGS, Marina 37.
16 Rojas to Arriaga, from Cartagena, August 21, 1773; AGS, Marina 37.
17 AGS, Marina 37.
18 Martín-Merás, "The Evolution of Spanish Cartography."
19 These would include the chronometer and lunar tables, improved methods of determining the variation of the compass by azimuth readings, and the astronomical clock. Tofiño to Andrés Reggio, Isla de León, September 24, 1773; AGS, Marina 37. Bernabeu, *Bodega*, quotes this letter in full, pp. 28-29.
20 Also known as *Toisón de Oro*, she displaced 196 tons.
21 Also known as the *San Antonio*, she was built in San Blas in 1768 and served in the department mainly on supply missions until 1779, when she was transferred to Cavite.
22 In the version of his journal he would later call his *Comento.*
23 Bodega, *Navegación*; Bernabeu, *Bodega*, p. 57.
24 She was also known as *Nuestra Señora de Guadalupe* and sometimes, with a touch of sarcasm, as *La Felicidad.*
25 Mourelle, "Segunda Exploración de la Costa Septentrional de California hecha en 1775."
26 Barrington, *The Voyage of the* Sonora, a translation of Mourelle's journal.
27 Fray Miguel de la Campa Cos, *A Journal of Explorations*, p. 19.
28 Bucareli to Arriaga letter #1639, December 27, 1774; AGI, Mexico 1. Bucareli to Arriaga letter #1608, November 26, 1774; AGI, Mexico 1.
29 At the end of the expedition, more appreciative of the *Sonora*'s good qualities, Bodega reflected, "It cannot be denied that the ship is solidly built, but this causes trouble, as her speed never exceeds four or five [knots] when her hold is full, and when it is not, she can make six when favoured by a very strong wind. If the waters are turbulent, she cannot even make four. I consider her incapable of sailing to the high latitudes, since there is evident danger that the honour of the individual commanding her will be jeopardized or he will be compelled to resign himself to suffering the most disastrous incidents." Bodega to Bucareli, from San Blas, November 26, 1775; AGN, Historia 324.

30 Barrington, *The Voyage of the* Sonora, pp. 18-19.
31 In a personal communication, W. Michael Mathes, an authority on Sebastian Vizcaino, states that "it is virtually certain to be the Rogue River" near Cape Sebastian, Oregon.
32 The expedition was most likely at 37°01′N.
33 Bodega, *Navegación*; Bernabeu, *Bodega*, pp. 67-68.
34 Serra, "Diario," p. 216.
35 Wagner, *Cartography of the Northwest Coast*, p. 376, says that Cabo Blanco was later named Cabo Diligencias by Bodega on his way homeward on September 27, 1775, and Cape Orford by Vancouver in April 1792.
36 At this point in his journal, Hezeta praises both Bodega and Mourelle for their "intelligence and devotion ... Not only have they been on the lookout for the most favourable sea for me to perform this dangerous manoeuvre, but they also contributed by carrying the greatest press of sail I have ever seen up to now, minimizing the very poor sailing qualities of the ship under his charge. Through his zealous vigilance he has avoided being swamped by the numerous heavy seas, currents and winds the two ships have frequently been subjected to, and which required of them, on such an extended voyage, the trouble of sailing in tow." In Beals, *For Honor and Country*, p. 62.
37 These were the Yurok Indians.
38 Hezeta's journal entry for June 11. In Beals, *For Honor and Country*.
39 Boot-topping entails cleaning off the weeds and barnacles that accumulate on a ship's hull, especially around the water line, with a mixture of tallow, sulphur or lime, and rosin.
40 The actual position is 47°03′N and 124°08′W of Greenwich.
41 Specifically, Article XV, as discussed in Servín, "The Instructions," p. 241.
42 Since Bodega and Mourelle make many of the same points, it is conceivable their reports were drafted jointly or copied one from the other. Mourelle's account is fuller and is the first manifestation of his interest in ethnology.
43 Serra, "Diario," p. 216.
44 Hezeta, in Beals, *For Honor and Country*, p. 78. This was Grenville Bay (the actual spot is clearly marked on Hezeta's chart). The massacre took place on the beach immediately south of Cape Elizabeth, given the name Punta de los Mártires by Hezeta. See Majors, "The Hezeta and Bodega Voyage of 1775."
45 A *braza*, the Spanish fathom, is approximately five and a half feet.
46 He had only eight men with him, because Mourelle and the others had gone to the *Santiago* with the longboat.
47 Hezeta, in Beals, *For Honor and Country*, p. 76. The spot where the cross was raised is marked on Hezeta's chart of the bay.
48 In his *Comento*, he says six were killed.
49 Serra, "Diario," p. 228. Campa's account is briefer and adds nothing of significance.
50 Chance, in Capoeman, *Land of the Quinault*, p. 49.
51 McBride, "Viewpoints and Visions in 1792."
52 Literally, the "ear is pointed." Landín Carrasco, *Mourelle*, p. 27, suggests that Bodega meant *puente de oreja* – that is, with the deck completely covered.
53 Bodega, *Navegación*, entry for May 21, 1775.
54 Mourelle, "Segunda Exploración."
55 Mourelle, "Extracto de Noticias," AMN, Madrid, MS 575bis. They were not that young: Mourelle was twenty-five, Bodega thirty-one.
56 Hezeta, in Beals, *For Honor and Country*, p. 33.

57 These were most likely tufted puffins (*Fratercula cirrhata*).

58 In his *Navegación*, Bodega named it San Francisco, but in his *Comento*, he calls it San Jacinto. Mourelle calls it that in his journal, and it appears thus on their charts.

59 Gilmer Bay, also on Kruzof Island.

60 The actual position is 57°18′N, 135°50′W of Greenwich. Nuestra Señora de los Remedios was a particular devotion of Bodega's.

61 These people were likely Sitka of the Tlingit nation.

62 This was too high. Assuming that Bodega made the same 20′ error he made in his sighting of Sea Lion Cove, his position would have been parallel to the entrance to the Myriad Islands and Ogden Passage at 57°38′N.

63 Mourelle, "Segunda Exploración," f. 55.

64 There is a considerable doubt as to what Bodega actually saw.

65 Port Santa Cruz is at latitude 55°16′N. The spot where the cross was raised is marked on his chart.

66 Bodega placed both Port Santa Cruz and the entrance to Bucareli Bay at this latitude, slightly too high. The entrance is in latitude 55°14′N.

67 This mention of "seven volcanoes of snow and fire" is puzzling. No volcanoes are known to have been active in the immediate region at that time.

68 Bodega called it San Carlos.

69 Bodega called it San Agustín.

70 Cape Augustine is 54°56′N.

71 Caster, "Earliest Spanish Explorations," p. 385, suggests that Bodega was referring to Cape Muzon (54°40′N), not Cape Augustine, which lies southeast of Forrester Island on the southern tip of Dall Island. If so, Pérez's earlier observation was fairly accurate, and his *entrada* would have been the Dixon Entrance. See Beals, *Juan Pérez*, p. 141.

72 Mourelle, "Segunda Exploración," f. 61.

73 Mourelle states in his *Recompiliación* that the boatswain died in San Blas after their arrival home. Landín Carrasco, *Mourelle*, p. 34.

74 The *Comento*, however, tells a different story. Bodega states that when the storm was over, he set course for Monterey on September 22 and reconnoitred the coast "without leaving any roadstead, bay or corner unrecorded, for which purpose I anchored at night so as not lose anything which might advance the distance covered."

75 Generally believed to be the Rogue River.

76 Proceeding through the narrow entrance into Tomales Bay, which he named after himself, he baptized the north point Punta del Cordón and the other Punta de Arenas, which are today Tomales Bluff and Sand Point, respectively. A third point at the entrance to the Estero Americano, which he named Punta de Murguía on his chart, has no name today.

77 See Clinton R. Edwards, "Wandering Toponyms," 253-72.

78 "Anonymous Journal," AGN, Historia 24, f. 18.

79 According to Father Campa, when the *Santiago* arrived in Monterey, thirty-six of the crew were suffering from scurvy and fourteen from "other ailments." One died as he was being taken ashore and was buried in the presidio chapel. Campa, *Journal*, August 31 and September 1.

80 Mourelle listed various illnesses that he found common to exploration missions: catarrh, rheumatic pains, diarrhea, dysentery, bleeding, scurvy, and what he called "flatulent cholic." Museo Naval, MS 331, f. 226.

81 "Anonymous Journal," AGN, Historia 24, f. 25v.
82 Hezeta, in Beals, *For Honor and Country,* p. 82.
83 Ibid., p. 88.
84 The letter goes on to strongly recommend Mourelle's promotion from *segundo piloto* to officer in the War Navy, a double progression.
85 The formal minute was forwarded by Hezeta to Bucareli, October 12, 1775, from Monterey, AGI, Estado 20.
86 Campa, *Journal.* Curiously, neither Hezeta nor Mourelle nor Bodega mention this sad event in their journals, although Bodega does so in his *Comento.*
87 See Freeman M. Tovell, "The Heceta-Bodega Voyage of 1775," pp. 57-65.
88 Hezeta, in Beals, *For Honor and Country,* p. 86.
89 Caster, "Earliest Spanish Explorations," p. 392.
90 Four years later, on Bodega's 1779 voyage, Mourelle charted the bay thoroughly.
91 Hezeta, in Beals, *For Honor and Country,* p. 72.
92 Bucareli to Arriaga, letter #2703, cited above.
93 See Wagner, "The Last Spanish Exploration."
94 Letters #2031, #2032, #2033, #2034, #2035, all dated November 26, 1775. Letters #2073, #2074 of December 27, 1775. AGN, Correspondencia de los Virreyes II; in the AHN, Madrid, Estado, legajo 2314; and AGI, Estado, legajo 20. A personal letter, Bucareli to Arriaga, is in AGI, Estado, Indiferente General, legajo 1630.
95 Bucareli to Arriaga, January 27, 1776; AGI, Estado, Indiferente General, legajo 1630.
96 Bucareli agreed with Bodega's recommendation and forwarded it to Arriaga with his support. The king approved it.
97 AGI, Estado, legajo 20.
98 Ibid.
99 Mourelle, "Segunda Exploración," in Barrington's translation, *The Voyage of the* Sonora, pp. 48-49. Although Cook had knowledge of the early Spanish voyages, it was very sketchy, and he certainly would not have had Barrington's *Miscellanies,* which was not published until 1781.
100 Bodega to Arriaga, December 22, 1775; AHN, Estado, legajo 4291.
101 Tofiño to Andrés Reggio, September 24, 1773; Archivo General de Simancas, Marina 37. Cited by Bernabeu, *Bodega,* pp. 28-29.
102 For an account of Hezeta's navigation methods, see Beals, *For Honor and Country,* pp. 103-13.
103 The principal ones are listed in Wagner's *Cartography,* #640 through #648 and #653.
104 Wagner, *Cartography,* #641, reproduced as Plate XXXIV. It is in AGN, Mapas y Planos, Mexico City. There is also a slightly larger copy in the AHN, Madrid, Carpeta de Mapas, Wagner's #671. The chart without the routes is not listed in Wagner. There are copies in AMN, Madrid, Carpeta III-B-4, and in AGN, Mapas y Planos, Mexico City, #581.
105 The map is in the US National Archives, Washington, D.C. See also Beals's article, "The Juan Pérez–Josef de Cañizares Map."
106 Bucareli to Arriaga, November 26, 1775; AGI, Estado, Indiferente General, legajo 1630.
107 Trinidad Bay, California; Grenville Bay, Washington; Sea Lion Cove, Alaska; and Bucareli Bay, Alaska.

108 Bucareli to Arriaga, letter #2073, cited above.

Chapter 3: Preparations for the 1779 Voyage

1 Agustín Albarracín, introduction to his edition of Arteaga's journal.
2 The Pérez expedition had cost 15,455 pesos; the Hezeta-Bodega expedition had cost 36,740. Chapman, *The Founding of Spanish California*, p. 242.
3 Royal Order of March 23, 1776, quoted in Bucareli's letter #2296 of June 26, 1776, to Gálvez, printed in Vol. 1 of the publications of AGN, 29, *La Administración de D. Frey Antonio María de Bucareli y Ursúa* (1936).
4 Bucareli repeated the Royal Order in his letter #2702 to Gálvez of January 27, 1777; AGN, Correspondencia de los Virreyes I, legajo 13, f. 3.
5 Quoted in Cook, *Flood Tide of Empire*, p. 91.
6 Bucareli to Gálvez, letter #2637, cited above.
7 Unless otherwise indicated, the essential facts of this voyage when at sea have been obtained from Bodega's journal, his *Viaje*. All quotations are from this journal unless otherwise indicated. See also Bodega's letter from Lima of December 9, 1777, to González de Castejón, Archivo General de Simancas, hereinafter cited as AGS, Marina 419.
8 Cañizares had sailed on the *San Carlos* in the 1775 expedition and had made the first chart of San Francisco Bay, which is now in the Bancroft Library, University of California, Berkeley.
9 The chart can be found in AGN, Californias 8, #978/205.
10 They are listed in the accounts subsequently forwarded from Lima to Mexico City; AGN, Marina 21, expediente 2, ff. 1-5.
11 Bodega to Bucareli, from Paita, in his *Viaje*, pp. 118-19.
12 Guirior was far from the ablest viceroy to govern Peru. See Sir Clements R. Markham, *A History of Peru* (Chicago: Charles H. Sergal, 1892), as reprinted in 1968, p. 189. See also Fisher, *The Last Inca Revolt*, p. 18.
13 This is the weight usually given in manifests, but Kenyon, "Naval Construction," says that she weighed 32 Moorsom tons, p. 145.
14 The vessel's owner was José Joaquin de Astolasa.
15 This was the name he had given to Sea Lion Cove, the Alaskan port at which the possession ceremony was carried out on his 1775 voyage. Later, on the *Sonora*'s safe arrival in Monterey, Bodega had carried the Virgin's image in solemn procession to the mission of San Carlos Borromeo at Carmel to give thanks for their safe return. He carried her image during the 1779 voyage.
16 Included in Bodega's journal are two drawings, the first a profile showing the *Favorita* before conversion, in the bottom left-hand corner of which is listed everything that was to be done, and the second, also a profile, showing her appearance after the conversion. In themselves, these drawings are of special importance, because they represent the only plans extant of ships either built in San Blas or that served out of San Blas. They also provide evidence of how much was done in a very short time to enable her to meet the severe winds and waters of the North Pacific.
17 See Kenyon, "Naval Construction," pp. 139-46.

18 Bodega to Bucareli, from San Blas, n/n, February 21, 1778; AGN, Californias 8, ff. 109-11v.
19 The list of passengers on the manifest, with the names of the crew, was attached to letter #481 of February 24, 1778, from Joseph Faustino Ruiz, the accountant at San Blas, to Bucareli; AGN, Marina 33, ff. 202-3v and ff. 205-7.
20 The voluminous accounts were not forwarded from Lima until March 1783, roughly five years later, and were not received in Mexico until August of that year! The costs chargeable to Mexico (excluding *reales* and *granos*) were tabulated as follows:

- Reimbursement to Bodega (of 2,000 pesos) and to Cañizares (of 1,000 pesos) for their travel expenses from Mexico City to Acapulco, and from Paita to Lima, 3,000 pesos.
- Purchase of the *Favorita*, 25,000 pesos.
- Civilian labour costs, 5,000 pesos.
- On account to the chaplain's salary and allowances to enable him to fit himself out for the expedition, 300 pesos.
- On account to Cañizares for his salary and allowances, 500 pesos.
- Supplies (e.g., timber, nails, iron work, paint, foodstuffs), 45,000 pesos.
- Miscellaneous supplies from naval stores, 17,103 pesos. In the accounts, the total cost of the frigate's conversion is stated to be 100,903 pesos, but the author's calculations make it 95,903 pesos. The cannon and other items Bodega purchased for the San Blas ships cost an additional 6,792 pesos.

21 Bodega's report consisted of a letter giving a general account of his proceedings, his *diario*, and six charts of portions of the coasts of Central America, Ecuador, and Peru as well as charts of Acapulco, Paita, and Callao. He attached the drawings of the *Favorita* before and after careening, the inventory of her equipment, and a list of the items purchased for the other ships. For good measure, he included a copy of Viceroy Guirior's decree granting exemption from the sales tax of everything acquired. The three coastal views have not been located. (Bodega to Bucareli, n/n, February 21, 1778; AGN, Californias 8, ff. 109-11v.)
22 He was also proud of the fact that he was the first to deliver a frigate from Peru. En route, he had made a number of corrections to Bellin's maps and established a route from Callao to San Blas that later ships could follow safely.
23 Bucareli to Bodega, March 18, 1778; AGN, Californias 8, f. 112.
24 Bodega to Bucareli, n/n, February 21, 1778; AGN, Californias 33, f. 3. The entire correspondence is in AGN, Californias 33.
25 Very likely Peruvian *pisco*, a strong grape brandy.
26 The Royal Order is summarized in Mayorga's letter #552 of May 31, 1780, to Gálvez; AGI, Mexico 1387.
27 AGN, Californias 33, f. 49r-v; AGN, Marina 50, f. 23r-v.
28 See his letter of November 28, 1779, to Mayorga; AGI, Mexico 1.
29 Kenyon, "Naval Construction," pp. 51-52, states that on April 20, 1778, Faustino Ruiz, the acting commissary, reported to the viceroy that she was complete except for the bottom sheathing.
30 Bucareli to Arriaga, letter #65 of December 18, 1778; AGN, Historia 63, f. 85r-v.
31 Arteaga's commission as *teniente de navío* was dated September 3, 1767, while Bodega's was March 16, 1776.

32 Quirós to Bucareli, #63 of November 27, 1778, from Guadalajara; AGN, Historia 63, f. 83r-v.

33 Bucareli to Quirós, December 9, 1778; AGN, Historia 63, f. 84r-v.

34 Letter #70 from Arteaga and Bodega to Bucareli, from Tepic, April 23, 1778; AGN, Historia 63, ff. 241-43.

35 Bodega to Bucareli, letter #29 of July 21, 1778; AGN, Historia 63, ff. 38-39v.

36 Arteaga had a total complement of ninety-eight for his ship.

37 Presumably meaning Indians and others living in New Spain.

38 Bodega's appeal may have been successful. The manifests of both ships show that each had twelve soldiers on board, but it is not clear whether they were real soldiers or seamen pressed into that duty.

39 Bernabeu, *Bodega*, p. 36.

40 Bodega to Bucareli, October 11, 1778; AGN, Provincias Internas 218, ff. 236-38.

41 Ten times approximately one hundred pounds.

42 Bucareli to Bodega, letter #302 of September 17, 1778; AGN, Historia 63, f. 40r-v.

43 The manifest is recorded in Museo Naval, MS 332.

44 And ninety-one crew of various rates and functions, for a total for the *Princesa* of ninety-eight.

45 Cañizares, after many years in the department, in Bodega's opinion had demonstrated competence and intelligence. More recently, on their voyage to Peru, Bodega noted that Cañizares had "sacrificed himself while serving under my orders" and had "acquired beneficial experience in preparing the [new] voyage." Bodega to Bucareli, letter #23 of July 21, 1778; AGN, Historia 63, ff. 47-49.

46 Ibid., ff. 51-56. The list is difficult to decipher, but it included oils for various purposes such as constipation and relief of gas, as well as sparkling waters, balms, spirits, powders, elixirs, salves, gums and herbs, vinegars, opiates, a variety of pills and powders, diuretics, salts, tinctures, ointments, and medical instruments and sponges. Also listed were a variety of syrups (including lemon, rose, peach, mint, bee's honey, juice of unripe grapes and mulberries) but no lime juice. The list was signed by Mariano Núñez Esquivel and by Gervasio Antonio Sánchez, who would serve as Martínez's surgeon on his 1779 resupply voyage.

47 His instructions to Bruno de Hezeta in 1775.

48 Bucareli to Arteaga, letter #65 of December 18, 1778; AGN, Historia 63, f. 85r-v.

49 Bucareli to Bodega, letter #66 of December 18, 1778; AGN, Historia 63, f. 86r-v.

50 The instructions Bucareli had given Pérez set out both the general purpose of the expedition and the need for reports on a wide variety of matters. Bucareli did not issue any new formal instructions for the Hezeta-Bodega expedition of 1775; instead his instructions to Hezeta were essentially amendments to his instructions to Pérez, the principal difference being that Hezeta was to explore as high as 60°N rather than 70°N. As part of his instructions for the 1779 expedition, Bucareli sent copies of his old instructions to Pérez to Arteaga and Bodega under cover of his letter of November 18, 1778.

Bucareli does not appear to have composed any formal, detailed instructions for the 1779 expedition. I have seen no other reference to them, and they are not among the numerous papers dealing with the expedition that are in AGN, Historia 63. When reporting the departure of the expedition to Minister Gálvez, Bucareli referred to "the instructions which I formulated for the previous expedition," and so it appeared to Bodega.

51 Arteaga to Bodega, December 15, 1778; AGN, Historia 63.
52 Bodega, *Navegación.*
53 Wagner, *Cartography*, #591. Two other maps were available. The first was the map printed in 1756 by Father Andrés Marcos Burriel in his publication of the Venegas manuscript, *Noticia de la California* (Wagner, *Cartography*, #585 and #587. It was printed in facsimile in vols. 1, 2, and 3 of the *Obras Californias del Padre Miguel Venegas, S.J.*, edited by W. Michael Mathes, Vivian C. Fisher, and E. Moisés Coronado, 5 vols. [1979]). In his appendix, Burriel exposed the hoax of Admiral de Fonte's apocryphal voyage. The second was the 1766 map of the French cartographer, Jacques Nicholas Bellin (Wagner, *Cartography*, #610).
54 A copy of Bodega's composite map is in AGI, Sección Mapas y Planos, Mexico 359. It is listed by Wagner in his *Cartography*, #660. The red ink has largely faded.
55 The "same point" being 58°N.
56 Bodega, *Navegación*; Bernabeu, *Bodega*, pp. 115-16.
57 Prince of Wales Island in today's Alexander Archipelago, named by the Americans in honour of the Russian tsar.
58 The *Método* is one of the few documents we have in Bodega's own hand. It is printed in Bernabeu, *Bodega*, as Appendix 1. Bernabeu, *Bodega*, p. 36, suggests that the document was drafted shortly after Bodega's return from his 1775 voyage, but internal evidence indicates that it was drafted as part of the planning for the 1779 expedition. Moreover, the treatise formed one of the attachments to Bodega's letter to Bucareli, #700 of February 11, 1779, announcing his departure.
59 Bering's Island lies in the Bering Sea, a short distance off the Kamchatka Peninsula.
60 Being 674 nautical miles.
61 The document concluded with a note stating that this course was read before a *junta* held on January 19, 1779. Some objections were raised but, in the end, there was agreement that the expedition should go ahead as proposed.
62 Bodega kept a careful record of his ship's performance on the voyage from Lima to San Blas. The *Princesa* underwent successful trials to establish her speed.
63 Kenyon, "Naval Construction," p. 193.
64 In the event of a confrontation with the British ships, Cook would have had the advantage. The Spanish ships were smaller. If the *Princesa* displaced 189 tons and the *Favorita* 193 tons, the *Resolution* displaced 462 tons and the *Discovery* 298 tons. Although the total complement of Cook's ships was lower – 181 versus 203 – his ships were more heavily armed. The *Resolution* carried twelve four-pounders, twelve swivel guns, and thirteen musquetoons, and the *Discovery* eight four-pounders, eight swivel guns, and five musquetoons.

Chapter 4: The 1779 Voyage

1 Except for Father Riobo's account, none of the documents cited in this chapter has been translated before this time.
2 It should be noted that the day began at noon when at sea and at midnight when in port.
3 Cañizares, *Diario*, entry for February 23-24, 1779.
4 A course south of them would put the ships in position to strike well to westward to gain their eventual northing.

5 Bodega, *Navegación*; Bernabeu, *Bodega*, p. 118.
6 Mourelle, *Navegación.*
7 Arteaga, *Diario.*
8 Bodega, *Navegación*; Bernabeu, *Bodega*, p. 119.
9 At this time, the expedition was due west of San Diego, longitude 32°32′ west from San Blas.
10 Bodega, *Navegación*; Bernabeu, *Bodega*, p. 120.
11 Quirós, "Diario," entry for March 22-23.
12 Ibid., entry for April 4-5.
13 Riobo, "Account," pp. 222-23.
14 Bodega, *Navegación*; Bernabeu, *Bodega*, p. 122.
15 Nuestra Señora del Rosario la Marinera was also the patron saint of Spanish sailors.
16 Riobo, "Account," p. 223. Arteaga mentions his vow but without embellishment.
17 Bodega, *Navegación*; Bernabeu, *Bodega*, p. 122.
18 Cañizares, "Diario," entry for April 28-29.
19 Most likely it was Fortaleza Bay on the north side nearest the entrance.
20 The voyage was actually eighty-two days.
21 The westernmost bay in Port Santa Cruz.
22 See Riobo, "Account," p. 223; and Pantoja, "Diario," entry for May 4. The final anchorage was the point that Camacho labelled Río de la Cruz on his chart; AGN, Mapas y Planos #3186.
23 Bodega, *Navegación*; Bernabeu, *Bodega*, p. 124. This was possibly Port San Antonio de Padua.
24 Pantoja, "Diario," entry for May 5. At the time of the 1779 expedition, the Tlingit occupied the northern half and the Haida the southern half of the Prince of Wales Island. The Indians in the Bucareli Bay area therefore would have belonged to the group today called the Kaigani Haida. See Langdon, *Native People of Alaska*, esp. Chap. 5.
25 Mourelle, *Navegación.*
26 Pantoja, "Diario," entry for May 5.
27 Camacho, "Diario," entry for May 4.
28 Bodega, *Navegación*; Bernabeu, *Bodega*, p. 125.
29 It was the first Christian religious service held on land in today's Alaska.
30 Pantoja, "Diario," entry for May 9.
31 The plan forms an extensive section of Mourelle's journal, and he is the only one to mention it.
32 Quirós, "Diario," entry for May 14-15.
33 This may have been Fortaleza Bay.
34 Bahia de la Real Armada.
35 Pantoja, "Diario," entry for May 21. Langdon suggests that these were possibly shamans' graves. See Langdon, "Efforts at Humane Engagement: Indian-Spanish Encounters in Bucareli Bay," in Stephen Haycox, James K. Barnett, and Caedmon A. Liburd, eds., *Enlightenment and Exploration in the North Pacific, 1791-1805* (Seattle and London: Cook Inlet Historical Society/University of Washington Press, 1997).
36 Bocas de Juan de Arriaga. Arriaga was Pantoja's maternal name.
37 Pantoja, "Diario," entry for June 4.
38 Quirós, "Diario," entries for June 4-5.
39 Pantoja, "Diario," entry for June 5.

40 Camacho, "Diario," entry for June 4.
41 Possibly on one of the Ladrones Islands.
42 There are at least nine different versions of the general chart: three in the Museo Naval, Madrid, MS III-E-2, and two others listed by Wagner under #662; one in the AGI, Mapas y Planos, México, #358-2 (Wagner #663); and three in the AGN-Historia 64 as part of Pantoja's "Diario" (Wagner #664); Historia 71, #247; and Californias 8, #3186 (Wagner #662). They vary in style and detail. They were likely the product of a cooperative effort under Camacho's direction, compiled when the expedition stopped in San Francisco en route home.
43 Riobo, "Account," pp. 224-25.
44 Bodega, *Navegación*; Bernabeu, *Bodega*, p. 131.
45 Camacho, "Diario," entry for June 12. Arteaga's identical comment is no doubt based on his senior *piloto*'s opinion.
46 Archer, "In Defence of the King's Domain."
47 Quirós, "Diario," entry for June 16.
48 He would later change his mind, describing native artifacts in laudatory terms.
49 The Kaigani Haida population at the time of European contact was "about eighteen hundred people." Langdon, *Native People of Alaska*, p. 72.
50 Quirós, "Diario," entry for June 5.
51 The version given here is that recorded by Arteaga, Pantoja, and Camacho.
52 None of the writers, including Bodega, speculated about how the iron, which had already been fashioned into weapons or personal adornments, had come into their hands.
53 Quirós, "Diario," entry for June 14.
54 Bodega, *Navegación*; Bernabeu, *Bodega*, p. 130.
55 Archer, "Seduction before Sovereignty," p. 135.
56 Arteaga, *Diario*, entry for May 5.
57 The children offered in trade were either prisoners of war or other disposable outcasts.
58 When Viceroy Mayorga reported the purchase of the children, José de Gálvez informed his viceregal successor, Matías de Gálvez, that when the king had learned the boy had gone to Peru, he asked that when he returned, the viceroy was to ensure that he be "well educated ... because His Majesty wants him to complete his education in Mexico." Bodega confirmed that the boy was indeed still alive, that he had been baptized in Tepic, and that he himself was his godfather. "He has never been away from my side and is always the object of my care," he wrote, adding that "he is ten to eleven years old." Bodega to Matías de Gálvez, October 1, 1783. The entire correspondence is in AGN, Californias 42, expediente 16, ff. 229-34.
59 The fate of the third sailor is not specifically mentioned in any of the journals, but Arteaga states that "all three seamen returned to their respective ships."
60 Bodega, *Navegación*. It is worth noting that none of the accounts of the voyage uses the term "deserter."
61 This is the only reference to specific punishment that the author has seen in any of Bodega's writings or the journals of other Spanish explorers.
62 Bodega, *Navegación*; Bernabeu, *Bodega*, pp. 137-38.
63 Riobo, "Account," p. 227.
64 Pantoja, "Diario," entry for May 4.
65 Ibid., entry for June 9.
66 These would appear to be the greatly prized Chilkat blankets.

67 Pantoja, "Diario," entry for June 9.
68 Aguirre, "Diario," entry for July 10-11; Cañizares, "Diario," entry for July 11-12.
69 Possibly Fairweather Ground, southwest of Lituya Bay.
70 Probably the mountain range stretching along the northern coast of Chichagof Island, across Cross Sound to Lituya Bay.
71 They were off the Fairweather Range between Cross Sound and Yakutat Bay.
72 Mount St. Elias is 18,008 feet, and Mount Orizaba in Mexico is 18,701 feet.
73 Camacho, "Diario," entry for July 15-16.
74 Father Riobo says it was named that "because it was discovered on the day dedicated to Our Lady of Mt. Carmel." Riobo, "Account," p. 227.
75 The ships were actually three leagues, or ten nautical miles, from what they thought was Cape St. Elias. Wagner, *Cartography*, p. 193.
76 These were most likely the Wingham and Kanak Islands in Controller Bay, which James Cook had also seen. J.C. Beaglehole, ed., *Journals of Captain James Cook: The Voyage of the Resolution and Discovery*, entry for May 10, 1778, p. 341.
77 Camacho, "Diario," entry for July 17-18.
78 This bare rock and pinnacle at the SW point tops off at 1,665 feet above sea level. Arteaga described it as "the same shape as the San Sebastián tower in Cádiz."
79 Mourelle, "Tercera Exploración."
80 Pantoja, "Diario," entry for July 19-20.
81 Cañizares, "Diario," entry for July 19-20.
82 By 1779, Russian fur traders were already trading in the area and had established outposts east of the Aleutians on Kodiak and Afognak Islands and on the west side of the nearby Kenai Peninsula.
83 The Russian map does indicate such a bay, but it is closed and extends only a very short distance northward.
84 Puerto de Santiago is now Port Etches. It was so named in 1787 by the English fur trader Nathaniel Portlock.
85 Riobo, "Account," p. 227.
86 The latitude of Puerto de Santiago was calculated as 60°14′N; actually, it is 60°17′N.
87 Cañizares, "Diario," entry for July 22-23; Pantoja, "Diario," entry for July 22-23.
88 Arteaga, *Diario*, entry for July 22-23.
89 Mourelle, "Tercera Exploración." as quoted in Bernabeu, *Bodega*, p. 148.
90 Bodega makes this important point casually, whereas Arteaga and Camacho recorded it more fully. Bodega, *Navegación*; Bernabeu, *Bodega*, p. 150.
91 The Pacific Yuit used the baidarka and the umiak. Langdon, *Native People*, pp. 44-45.
92 Bodega, *Navegación*; Bernabeu, *Bodega*, p. 150. Mourelle added the comment that when the Spaniards attempted to pronounce words, the natives burst out laughing.
93 Camacho, in his "Diario," entry for July 19-20, says it was red. Cañizares, in his "Diario," entry for July 22, says the colours were various.
94 Prince William Sound was inhabited by Eskimo, Tlingit, and Athapaskan people. See Langdon, *Native People*, p. 42. The throwing stick, or atlatl, combined with a short spear was their weapon of choice when hunting from their baidarkas.
95 Bodega, *Navegación*; Bernabeu, *Bodega*, p. 150.
96 Either Elizabeth Island, the Chucagh Islands, or – most likely – East Chucagh Island. These are shown on the expedition's chart of the region as the Isla de Ayala, Isla de San Angel, and the Isla de Arriaga.

97 At this rather tense moment, Arteaga had to bury the gunner Juan Rivera, who died unexpectedly the night before.
98 August 1. Bodega, *Navegación*; Bernabeu, *Bodega*, pp. 151-52.
99 The position is 59°09′N and 151°09′W of Greenwich.
100 It appears both on Gerhard Müller's map of 1754 and on the Bellin map as "Cap de St. Ermogen," in each case on the east side of the Kenai Peninsula.
101 Cape St. Hermogenes is fifty-five nautical miles due south of Elizabeth Island on Marmot Island, just off the eastern end of Afognak Island.
102 Copies of the chart are in the AGI, Mapas y Planos, México 356, and in the Museo Naval, Madrid, #3-E-7.
103 Bodega, *Navegación*; Bernabeu, *Bodega*, p. 152-53. Mount Iliamna is 10,016 feet, and the Pico de Teide on Tenerife is 12,162 feet. Mount Iliamna, seventy nautical miles east of Elizabeth Island, is an active volcano that erupted in 1778, 1867, 1876, and, most recently, in 1953.
104 Escherich conjectures that it was named for Arteaga's second-in-command, Quirós y Miranda. See Escherich, "Juan Francisco de la Bodega y Quadra," p. 101.
105 Bodega, *Navegación*; Bernabeu, *Bodega*, pp. 154-55.
106 Arteaga, *Diario*, entry for August 7-8.
107 Arteaga to Gálvez, December 5, 1779: AGI, Mexico 1.
108 Quirós, "Diario," entry for August 6.
109 Bodega, *Navegación*; Bernabeu, *Bodega*, pp. 154-55. The parentheses are Bodega's.
110 Mourelle, "Tercera Exploración," AMN MS 331.
111 Ibid., f. 137v.
112 Palou, *Historical Memoirs*, Vol. 4, p. 183.
113 Riobo, "Account," p. 229.
114 Palou, *Historical Memoirs*, Vol. 4, p. 184.
115 Bucareli died on April 9, 1779.
116 Quirós, "Diario," entry for November 17-25.
117 Bodega to Mayorga, from San Blas, letter #113, November 28, 1779; AGN, Historia 63, ff. 236-42v.
118 Ibid.
119 Bodega to Mayorga, letter #773, November 28, 1779; AGN, Historia 63, ff. 236-42v.
120 Ibid., f. 240.
121 Ibid., ff. 240v-41.
122 Mayorga to Bodega, unnumbered letter, January 16, 1780; AGN, Historia 63, ff. 252-55.
123 Mayorga to Gálvez, letter #187, December 27, 1779; AGI, Mexico 1.
124 Arteaga to Gálvez, December 5, 1779; AGI, Mexico 1.
125 The submission to Gálvez and the letter to Mayorga are both dated November 28, 1779; AGI, Papeles de Estado 20, Mexico 1.
126 Mayorga to Gálvez, letter #188, December 27, 1779; AGI, Mexico 1.
127 Gálvez to Mayorga, May 10, 1780; AGI, Mexico 1.
128 Perhaps because Mayorga had not mentioned it.
129 Gálvez to Mayorga, May 10, 1780; AGI, Mexico 1.
130 Mourelle, "Tercera Exploracíon," AMN 331, f. 139r-v.
131 Wagner, *Cartography*, p. 194.
132 Cook, *Flood Tide of Empire*, pp. 97-98.

133 Museo Naval, Madrid, A-10096-3 and 4, 1-E-9, 2-B-4, 2-B-5, 3-D-2, 3-B-13; AGN, #3210, #3187; AGI, Mapas y Planos, México, #355; Wagner, *Cartography*, #668.
134 For a detailed account of both the corrections made and the errors committed, see Wagner, *Cartography*, p. 195.
135 A list of these was attached to his letter #187 of December 27, 1779, to Gálvez; AGI, Estado 20, legajo 28.
136 The greater part of the collection is in the Museo de América in Madrid. See Cabello Carro, "The Ethnographic Collections," in Inglis, *Spain and the North Pacific Coast*, pp. 137-54. Cabello's article, "Materiales etnográficos de la Costa Noroeste de America," appears in José Luis Peset Reig, ed., *Culturas de la Costa Noroeste de América* (Madrid: Ediciones Turner, 1989), pp. 209-22.

Chapter 5: Away from the North Pacific

1 Antonio Valdés to Gonzalo de Castejón, the Minister of Finance, May 10, 1780; Royal Order of August 22, 1780; and Valdés to Gálvez, August 22, 1780; all in AGI, Estado 20, Mexico 1.
2 Bodega to Mayorga, September 16, 1780; AGN, Provincias Internas 101, f. 563r-v.
3 See Carmen Rosa Tola de Schwalb et al., *Huancavelica* (Lima: Compañia de Minas Buenaventura, 1960).
4 Mayorga's instructions to Bodega were dated Mexico City, February 13, 1781; AGN, Marina 58, f. 132r-v.
5 Bodega to Mayorga, March 16, 1781; AGN, Marina 58, f. 133. Bodega to Mayorga, March 31, 1781; AGN, Marina 58, f. 136.
6 The only officer to keep a diary was Camacho. It is in AGN, Californias 47. Most of what follows is taken from Camacho's *diario* entries for May 15-16 and 16-17. The rest of the information comes from Bodega's official correspondence before leaving San Blas, while he was in Lima, and on his return.
7 The formal record of the discussion, signed by all present, is in AGN, Marina 58, ff. 148-49.
8 Mayorga to Bodega, June 13, 1781; AGN, Marina 58, f. 146.
9 Bodega to Mayorga and to Arteaga and Trillo y Bermúdez, May 20, 1781; AGN, Marina 58, f. 145r-v and f. 147r-v respectively.
10 If Bodega kept a *diario* of this voyage, it has not been located in either the AGN, the AGI, or the Museo Naval in Madrid.
11 Bodega to Mayorga, October 5, 1781; AGN, Marina 58, f. 152r-v.
12 Camacho, *Diario*, entry for September 1-2.
13 Bodega to Mayorga, October 5, 1781, cited above.
14 Camacho, "Diario," entry for September 1, 1781.
15 Bodega to Jauregui, October 1781. Copies of this letter and subsequent correspondence exchanged between Bodega and officials in Peru are in AGN, Provincias Internas 134, ff. 449-68.
16 Bodega to Escobedo, July 30, 1782.
17 Camacho states that the *Santiago* took on board sixteen iron cannon of twenty-four pounds calibre and three of eight calibre, as well as seventeen bronze cannon of eight pounds calibre and twelve bronze of five pounds – in all, forty-eight pieces.

18 Bodega to Mayorga, June 20, 1783; AGN, Provincias Internas 134, expediente 32, ff. 449-69.
19 A brother of the minister, José de Gálvez.
20 AGN, Marina 21, expediente 2, ff. 50-57.
21 López de Toledo to Gálvez, June 20, 1783; AGN, Misiones 23.
22 Bodega to the Fiscal, August 16, 1783; AGN, Misiones 23, ff. 132-38v.
23 Matías de Gálvez to Bodega, October 2, 1783; AGN, Misiones 23.
24 Bodega to Gálvez, October 6, 1783; AGI, Guadalajara 520.
25 Unless otherwise stated, all documents in this section are to be found in Bodega's service file, Archivo Museo D. Alvaro y Bazán, Ciudad Real, El Viso.
26 Flores to Valdés, June 26, 1788; AGI, México 1517.
27 The original in his service file in the El Viso archive is in his own hand. It is undated but clearly was drafted in Havana. The eventual reply was sent to the Comandante General de la Marina in Havana, referring to his letter #129 of n/d, 1783. The Museo Naval in Madrid has a typescript copy, MS 2011.
28 Bodega to Valdés, April 26, 1785, from Cádiz.
29 Manuel de la Bodega y Mollinedo to his "dear brother" (*Amado Hermano*) Juan Francisco, Madrid, April 19, 1785; El Viso archive.
30 An *oidor* (literally, one who hears or listens) performed judicial functions within an *audiencia* but could also undertake special functions such as adjudicating commercial and taxation disputes, serving as probate judge, and acting as inspector of ships and armies. Haring, *Spanish Empire in the Americas*, notes that "*oidores*, like the viceroys and captains-general, were men of great prestige and influence in the colonies."
31 Thurman, without citing any authority, states that during these four years back in Spain, "Captain Bodega y Quadra was used primarily as a naval advisor." See "Juan Bodega y Quadra," pp. 49-63. Bodega's service record contains no documentation to support Thurman's statement or evidence that Bodega was given any special commission or appointments at this time.
32 Bodega to Gálvez, August 13, 1785, from Madrid; AGI, Guadalajara 520.
33 When the matter resurfaced shortly after Revillagigedo assumed the post of viceroy, Bodega told him he had had to make two visits to the court before this apparent blot on his record was removed. Bodega to Revillagigedo, August 27, 1790; AGN, Misiones 23, ff. 219-23.
34 AHN, Ordenes Militares, legajo 203, expediente 18119.
35 *Converso* indicated specifically someone of the Jewish or Muslim faith who had converted to Christianity.
36 This enabled him to describe himself in the preamble of the journal of his first voyage to Peru as simply "of the Order of Santiago." AGN, Californias 8, f. 116.
37 See Landín Carrasco, *Mourelle de la Rua*, p. 107.
38 At this time, because of Mourelle's poor health and his need of a lengthy period ashore to recuperate, Viceroy Revillagigedo brought him to Mexico City to make a compendium of all the Spanish voyages to the North Pacific, a task that occupied him for three years. The several volumes of this work are now in the Museo Naval, Madrid. See Landín Carrasco, *Mourelle*, pp. 114-15.
39 In his service file, there is a summary statement of his commands and commissions, "El Real Sítio del Escoríal," dated October 16, 1788.
40 The *Atlas Maritimo de España* was published in 1789.

41 The Instituto Hidrográfico in Cádiz possesses an atlas, specially prepared for Bodega on the eve of his return to New Spain, for which he selected the charts. Some of these were drafted in accordance with his instructions. What purpose he had in mind is not known, but it is conceivable he wished to establish a basis for other exploratory ventures.

42 The original in Bodega's handwriting is in his service file in the El Viso archive. Some sentences and paragraphs have been slightly altered for clarity.

43 Museo Naval, Madrid, MS 1538. *Valor* can be translated as "courage" or "bravery" as well as "worth," but the latter would be more appropriate in this context.

44 See Herr, *The Eighteenth-Century Revolution in Spain.*

45 A particular element influencing Valdés was undoubtedly the fact that he had known Malaspina for a number of years. Also, Malaspina was naval officer of the Order of Malta, of which the minister was the chief in Spain.

46 This is the date Valdés formally informed Malaspina that the king had accepted his plan.

47 Lowell Newton, "The Spanish Naval Officer Corps in the Eighteenth Century: Towards a Collective Biography," *Revista de Historia de América* 103 (January-June 1987), [n.p.].

48 In her study of Bodega's 1775 journal, Catherine Poupeney Hart suggests that he was already very conscious of his "intrinsic inferiority" as a *criollo* naval officer and of the need to counter it. Hart, "Peregrinatión por los mares del Norte."

49 Beerman, "Bruno de Hezeta." Nevertheless, Hezeta eventually rose to the rank of *teniente general.*

Chapter 6: The Nootka Crisis and the Spanish Response

1 Flores's name has been variously spelled Florez, Flóres, or even Flórez.

2 Flores to Valdés, November 24, 1788; AGN, Correspondencia de los Virreyes 19, p. 125.

3 Martínez gives the full text at the beginning of his *Diario.* AGN, Historia 65; Museo Naval, Madrid, MS 732.

4 This was a reference to the trading expedition of Robert Gray in the *Lady Washington* and John Kendrick in the *Columbia Rediviva*, which Martínez would find at Nootka.

5 Flores to Valdés, confidential letter #702 of December 23, 1788; AGN, Correspondencia de los Virreyes 19, ff. 108-15.

6 The *cédula* was dated April 14, 1789.

7 Howay, *Voyages*, pp. 84-85.

8 Martínez, *Diario*, entries for June 8, June 9, and July 5, 1789.

9 The best short but detailed account of the Nootka crisis and its consequences can be found in Cook, *Flood Tide of Empire*, pp. 146-99.

10 Martínez, *Diario*, entry for June 24.

11 From the compass coordinates Martínez gives in his account (*Diario*, entry for August 23), it appears that this took place on the sandy beach between present-day Yuquot Point and Maquinna Point.

12 For an analysis of the similarities and differences of the accounts of the two protagonists, see Howay, *The Journal of Captain James Colnett*, pp. 91-102.

13 Jose Mariano Moziño, *Noticias de Nootka*, pp. 75-76.

14 Bodega almost failed his first test as commandant soon after he arrived in San Blas.

Revillagigedo had asked him for a full report from Martínez on his treatment of Colnett and Thomas Hudson, his second-in-command. When Bodega sought an account from Martínez, Martínez refused with the explanation that he was occupied complying with a direct order from the viceroy. Bodega backed down because he had not heard anything about the direct order. In a sharp rebuke, Revillagigedo told the new commandant that he had never issued any order to Martínez nor would he give a direct order to an officer except through his immediate superior. Why, he asked, did not Bodega ask Martínez to show him the order? Martínez, for his part, received a viceregal reprimand for his "insubordination." Bodega to Revillagigedo, January 8, 1790; Revillagigedo to Bodega, January 25, 1790, and to Martínez, same date; AGN, Historia 66, ff. 112-14. The summary of "complaints" was duly drawn up and forwarded to Mexico City, but the document appears to have been lost.

15 It is in his service file and dated March 24, 1789.

16 In the opening paragraph of his report as commandant of the Expedition of the Limits.

17 Flores to Valdés, letter #686 of November 26, 1788; AGN, Correspondencia de los Virreyes I, legajo 148, ff. 148-51.

18 Flores to Valdés, letter #702 of December 23, 1788; AGN, Correspondencia de los Virreyes II, legajo 19.

19 Valdés to Flores, letter #215, April 14, 1789; AHN, Estado, legajo 4290.

20 Bodega to Valdés, August 12, 1789, in his service file in the El Viso archive.

21 Bodega to Flores, August 19, 1789; AGN, Marina 78, f. 56r-v.

22 Flores to Bodega, August 25, 1789; AGN, Marina 78, f. 58.

23 Bodega to Flores, September 2, 1789; AGN, Marina 78, f. 59.

24 Letters #702 and #703, Flores to Revillagigedo, April 14, 1789, and Revillagigedo's reply dated April 28; AHN, Estado 4289. I am grateful to the late Vivian C. Fisher, formerly of the Bancroft Library, Berkeley, for having drawn this correspondence to my attention.

25 A bilander is a small, two-masted ship with a square rig except for a lateen mainsail, designed for the coastal trade and for traversing the canals of Holland.

26 Flores's letter #1182 of August 27, 1789, to Valdés; AGN, Correspondencia de los Virreyes II, legajo 19, ff. 132-38.

27 Flores to Revillagigedo, August 27, 1789. All the correspondence on this proposed meeting will be found in AGN, Historia 65, cuaderno 8.

28 Revillagigedo to Flores, August 30, 1789.

29 Flores to Revillagigedo, September 2, 1789.

30 Revillagigedo to Flores, September 9, 1789.

31 Flores to Revillagigedo, September 16, 1789. An *abrazo*, literally "a hug," is a common Spanish salutation.

32 Revillagigedo to Flores, September 23, 1789.

33 AHN, Estado 4290, cited above.

34 Colnett's journal is an important source regarding the release of the English prisoners. Colnett's hatred of all things Spanish coloured everything he said or thought. Howay believed that Colnett's capture by the Spanish was emotionally devastating to him. Indeed, his imprisonment affected him so that soon after his arrest, he attempted suicide.

35 Revillagigedo to the commandant and commissary at San Blas, October 21, 1789; AGN, Historia 66. Howay, *The Journal of Captain James Colnett*, p. 82.

36 Colnett to Revillagigedo, undated letter clearly written shortly after his arrival in

Tepic. It begins: "I beg leave to acquaint Your Excellency of my arrival at this place with all my officers and attendants on the 31st ultimo" – that is, October. The original is in AGN, Historia 66, f. 23r-v.

37 Since Bodega's dealings with Martínez at the same time were very prickly, it is doubtful that he would have acted on Martínez's suggestions.

38 The protest is dated January 14, 1790. The original is in AGN, Historia 66, f. 16r-v. The text is also in Howay, *The Journal of Captain James Colnett,* p. 84.

39 Dated January 16. The text is in Colnett's journal, in Spanish, but is not in the AGN. The translation is in a footnote in Howay's edition.

40 Bodega to Colnett, July 8, 1790. Under the same date, Bodega informed the Viceroy and Francisco de Eliza in Nootka. These letters are in AGN, Historia 66.

41 Bodega to Revillagigedo, July 9, 1790; AGN, Historia 66, f. 18. The viceroy's detailed instructions to Bodega for the release of the ships and their crews were dated April 27, 1790, and are in AGN, Historia 66, cuaderno 7.

42 June 24.

43 Colnett to Revillagigedo, July 8, 1790; the original is in AGN, Historia 66, f. 37.

44 Howay, *The Journal of Captain James Colnett,* p. 209; AGN, Historia 66.

45 Hudson's expedition ended in tragedy, when he and all his men were drowned off Estevan Point at the entrance to Nootka Sound.

46 AHN, Estado 4290, cited above.

47 Revillagigedo to Valdés, letter #50, October 27, 1789; AGN, Correspondencia de los Virreyes II, legajo 22.

48 Revillagigedo to Valdés, confidential letter #30 of October 27, 1789; AGN, Correspondencia de los Virreyes II, legajo 22.

49 Revillagigedo to Bodega, December 7, 1789; AGN, Historia 68, f. 1; Revillagigedo to Hijosa, December 7, 1789; AGN, Historia 68, f. 2; Revillagigedo to Bodega, December 8, 1789; AGN, Historia 68, ff. 5-16.

50 Martínez's interpretation of Narváez's investigation was received with considerable skepticism. See Charles L. Stewart, "Martínez and López de Haro," pp. 179-81.

51 With the viceroy's approval, Bodega would later substitute the *San Carlos* for the *Argonauta* because of her greater carrying capacity. In another change of plans, the *Princesa Real* would be turned over to Hudson, her captain, in Nootka, because the extra cargo she could carry was needed. Revillagigedo to Bodega, December 17, 1789; AGN, Historia 68, ff. 19-21.

52 Bodega to Revillagigedo, December 23, 1789; AGN, Historia 68, ff. 24-25v.

53 Revillagigedo to Bodega, December 26, 1789; AGN, Historia 68, f. 27r-v. Bodega never lost sight of his proposal, however, and each element in it would in fact be met over time by separate expeditions. In 1790, Quimper would explore the Strait of Juan de Fuca. The survey of the coast from Bucareli Bay southward would be assigned to Caamaño in 1792, and the strengthening of the defences of the California presidios would become a personal preoccupation of Bodega at the conclusion of the Expedition of the Limits in the fall of 1792. The resupplying of Nootka would be maintained as a matter of course.

54 A confirmed *primer piloto.*

55 Literally, "pilot of routes" – that is, the officer responsible for determining the courses to be followed by the ships.

56 Bodega to Revillagigedo, December 26, 1789, from Tepic; AGN, Historia 68, ff. 30-31.

57 Martínez to Revillagigedo, December 26, 1789; AGN, Historia 68, f. 23. Some believe that Martínez was related to Flores.

58 Some were subsequently used for trade by Manuel Quimper when exploring the Strait of Juan de Fuca, thus initiating Spain's modest involvement in the fur trade.

59 *Instrucciones secretas dadas por el Comandante de San Blas ... al Teniente de Navío Don Francisco Eliza, Comandante de la Fragata Concepción ... asimismo Comandante de Nutka.* Dated February 4, 1791; AGN, Historia 69, ff. 51-59v; AMN, MS 575bis; TS in Bancroft Library, T-ZE 2:3; and printed as Document 15 in Cárdenas, *San Blas de Nayarit*, pp. 59-61. See note 107.

60 Unless otherwise indicated, the following paragraphs are based on the Alberni papers in the Henry E. Huntington Library, San Marino, California, HM 327. For Alberni's career, see Chap. 7 in Sánchez, *Spanish Bluecoats*, pp. 89-99; idem, "Pedro Alberni and the Spanish Claim to Nootka."

61 Alberni to Revillagigedo, January 22, 1790; HM 327.

62 Bodega to Revillagigedo, January 22, 1790; HM 327.

63 For the details of this incident, see Sánchez, *Spanish Bluecoats*, pp. 90-91.

64 Revillagigedo to Bodega, December 30, 1789; HM 327, f. 139.

65 Bodega to Revillagigedo, January 22, 1790; HM 327, f. 141.

66 Revillagigedo to Bodega, February 24, 1790; HM 327, f. 142.

67 Bodega to Revillagigedo, February 4, 1790; AGN, Marina 74, f. 288r-v. The total complement of the first three ships was four officers, six *pilotos*, two surgeons, two chaplains, sixty Catalonian Volunteers, and 206 seamen of all ranks and rates. On board the *Concepción* were Alberni and his second-in-command, Lieutenant Mariano Jaulia, Estéban Martínez as route pilot, and López de Haro as *primer piloto*. The latter two, because of their bitter quarrel on the 1788 expedition, were under strict orders to keep the peace and apparently managed to do so.

68 In the draft of this letter, the viceroy expressed "pleasure" instead of "sober satisfaction."

69 Bodega to Valdés, February 4, 1790; AHN, Estado, legajo 4289.

70 Alberni papers, Huntington Library, HM 327.

71 Alberni to Revillagigedo, August 12, 1791; AGN, Histórico de Hacienda 427, f. 128. The document in the file is a copy made later of the original written in Nootkan. Alberni had the substantive rank of army lieutenant colonel.

72 Alberni to Revillagigedo, July 9, 1790; Alberni papers, Huntington Library, HM 332, f. 146.

73 Sánchez, *Spanish Bluecoats*, p. 81.

74 Bodega to Eliza, April 13, 1790; AGN, Historia 68, f. 165.

75 See "Plano de la cala de los Amigos, situada en la parte occidental de la entrada de Nutka," Museo Naval, Madrid, Sig. II D(17), Higueras #1728, for both the location of the battery and the general layout of the establishment fronting the beach at Yuquot. The drawing by José Cardero (*Puerto de Nutka* in the collection of the Museo de América, which shows the battery in the summer of 1791) can be found in Sotos, *Los Pintores*, #593. A different perspective, drawn in 1792 by the surgeon Sigismund Bacstrom, who was visiting Nootka on the English fur trader *Butterworth*, can be found in Henry, *Early Maritime Artists*, pp. 117-19.

76 Eliza to Bodega, July 5, 1790; AGN, Historia 68, ff. 172-74.

77 For a graphic illustration of the progress made in a short time, see the ink and coloured wash drawing of the establishment at the time of Malaspina's visit a year later in July

1791, attributed to Felipe Bauza. Museo Naval, Madrid, MS 1723-21; reproduced in Sotos, *Los Pintores*, #591 and #601, and in Higueras, *Costa NW de America*, p. 89. There is a very similar view attributed to Fernando Brambilla in the Museo de America, Madrid, in both publications: Sotos, #592 and #602, and Higueras, pp. 90-91.

78 Bodega to Revillagigedo, #391 of June 26, 1792; Alberni papers, Huntington Library, HM 141.

79 Revillagigedo to Aranda, November 30, 1792; AHN, Estado 4289.

80 Bodega to Eliza, "Instrucciones secretas para el Teniente de Navío Don Francisco de Eliza, Commandante del Puerto de Nuca y las Fragatas Concepción y Princesa," February 4, 1791, para. 12; AGN, Historia 69.

81 Roughly translated as "Maquinna, Maquinna, Maquinna / is a great prince and friend of ours / Spain, Spain, Spain / is the friend of Maquinna and Nootka." It was sung to the tune of *El Marabú*, a popular Iberian folksong of the eighteenth century sung by Spanish sailors.

82 See Moziño, *Noticias de Nutka*, p. 79.

83 Eliza, "Costumbres de los Naturales del Puerto de San Lorenzo de Nuca, pro[puestas] para su conquista y utilidades que comprendo puede este producir," hereinafter cited as Eliza, "Costumbres," n.d.; AGN, Historia 69.

84 Pantoja's account of his participation in 1791 in the Eliza-Narváez exploration of the Strait of Juan de Fuca and Georgia Strait. Translated and edited by Wagner, *Spanish Explorations*, p. 160.

85 Saavedra to Bodega at San Blas, April 14, 1791; AGN, Historia 67. The fear that native women would be the prey of lustful sailors was constant throughout the five years the Spanish occupied Yuquot. Moziño alludes to this problem in his *Noticias*, p. 84.

86 Royal Order #305 of August 25, 1790; AGN, Reales Cédulas 146.

87 Bodega to Revillagigedo, #163 of December 18, 1790; AGN, Historia 68, ff. 174-76.

88 See, inter alia, W. Michael Mathes, "The Province of Anían and Its Strait: Myth, Reality, and Exploration of the Pacific Northwest, 1542-1792," unpublished paper given at the Vancouver Conference on Exploration and Discovery of 1992.

89 The first phase of Spanish exploration from 1774 to 1779 had been prompted by a concern over Russian incursions;. In the second phase, from 1788 to 1793, these encroachments continued to be a motive. Russian *promyshlenniki*, independent fur hunters and trappers, were extending their activities eastward from the Aleutians into Prince William Sound. Furthermore, ships from other European nations were developing trade routes across the Pacific, making a mockery of Spain's claim to a trade monopoly in the Pacific, the so-called Spanish Lake.

90 While Revillagigedo's directives to Bodega called for a major effort to survey the coast between the Strait of Juan de Fuca and Prince William Sound, Bodega's orders to Eliza specified only an examination of the immediate coastal waters.

91 Regla was at the entrance to Cook Inlet, probably on Elizabeth Island. It was named by the Arteaga-Bodega expedition in 1779 and was thought to be on the mainland.

92 See Patrick, "The Salvador Fidalgo Expedition, 1790."

93 Patrick, in her thesis, identifies them as the modern-day Port Graham and Fort St. George on the Kasilof River.

94 Patrick establishes that the places were Port Gravina, Orca Bay, and Cook's Snug Corner Cove (modern-day Port Fidalgo).

95 Eliza to Quimper, May 29, 1790; AGN, Historia 68, and AGI, Estado 43.

96 Hudson never made it. He and his small crew drowned attempting to reach Nootka from Clayoquot Sound in one of Colnett's longboats.

97 Quimper's journal is in AGN, Historia 68. For a detailed account and analysis of Quimper's exploration, see Wagner's *The Spanish Explorations*, pp. 15-25. Wagner includes his translation of the journal and reproduces López de Haro's charts of the voyage.

98 He called it Puerto de la Bodega y Quadra. When Vancouver arrived there two years later, he named it after his own ship, the *Discovery.* On modern maps it is both Port Discovery and Discovery Bay.

99 Meany, *Vancouver's Discovery of Puget Sound*, p. 307, suggests that it was named for Alonso de Haro Peralta, Archbishop of Mexico from 1772 onward and, for several months (May 8 to August 16, 1797), Viceroy of Mexico.

100 The four locations were Puerto de Revillagigedo (today's Sooke Inlet), Rada de Valdés y Bazán (Royal Roads), Puerto de Quimper (New Dungeness), and Puerto de Núñez Gaona (Neah Bay).

101 Among the locations marked on the chart of Quimper's voyage, drafted by López de Haro, are the Río Jordan (Jordan River), Puerto de San Juan ó de Narváez (Port San Juan), Puerto de Revillagigedo (Sooke Inlet), Rada de Eliza (Pedder Bay), Puerto de Valdés y Bazán (Royal Roads), and Puerto de Córdoba (Esquimalt), all on southern Vancouver Island, and Puerto de Cuadra (Discovery Bay) and Puerto de Nuñez Gaona (Neah Bay) on the north coast of modern-day Washington. The Cascade Mountains and Mount Baker are shown but not named. The original chart is in the AGI, Mapas y Planos, Mexico. Wagner lists it as #750 in his *Cartography.*

102 Floridablanca to Revillagigedo, Royal Order #116 of May 28, 1791; AGN, Reales Cédulas 149, f. 166r-v.

103 Bodega to Revillagigedo, #145 of November 19, 1790; AGN, Historia 69, cuaderno 9, f. 1.

104 Bodega to Revillagigedo, November 19, 1790; AGN, Historia 69, cuaderno 9, ff. 2-3v.

105 Revillagigedo to Bodega, December 8, 1790; AGN, Historia 69, cuaderno 9, f. 4r-v.

106 Bodega to Revillagigedo, #167 of January 1, 1791; AGN, Historia 69, cuaderno 9, f. 5r-v.

107 *Secret Instructions to Lieutenant Don Francisco de Eliza, Commandant of the Puerto de Nutca and the Frigates* Concepción *and* Princesa, February 4, 1791; AGN, Historia 67. A translation was published by Wagner in *Spanish Explorations*, pp. 137-40. See note 59.

108 Entrada de Bucareli is today's Bucareli Bay. The Estrecho de Fonte also known as the Entrada de Pérez, today's Dixon Entrance. Ezeta refers to the entrance to the Columbia River, discovered by Hezeta in 1775. Bahia de San Rafael is a bay between Clayoquot Sound and Barkley Sound, on the west coast of Vancouver Island. Bahia de Carrasco is now called Barkley Sound. Puerto de Clauycuat is today's Clayoquot Sound, Vancouver Island. Fuca is the Strait of Juan de Fuca. Elias is Mount St. Elias, Alaska.

109 Trinidad Bay, California.

110 The latter was the waterway rumoured to give access to the Great Sea of the West and believed to have been discovered in 1602-3 at latitude 43°N by the Vizcaíno expedition. It is probably the Rogue River in Oregon. Bodega to Eliza, March 12, 1791; AGN, Historia 69. There is a translation in Wagner's *Spanish Explorations*, pp. 140-41.

111 For an analysis of this expedition, see Wagner, *Spanish Explorations*, pp. 27-42. Eliza's *Extracto de la Navigación ... en el Año 1791* is in AGN, Historia 69. There is also a translation of this document in Wagner, *Spanish Explorations*, pp. 141-54.

112 Pantoja's *Extracto de la Navigación...*, in the form of a letter to a friend, is in the Museo

Naval, Madrid, MS 271. This and related documents will be also found in translation in Wagner, *Spanish Explorations*, pp. 155-200.

113 Unfortunately, Narváez's journal has been lost. See Jim McDowell, *José Narváez: The Forgotten Explorer* (Spokane, WA: n.p., 1998), about his efforts to locate it.

114 Carrasco's *Extracto de la Navigación echa con la Goleta de S.M. nombrada* Santa Saturnina ... *Año de 1791* is in AGN, Historia 44. A translation is found in Wagner, *Spanish Explorations*, pp. 200-2.

115 Wagner believed it was either the work of Narváez, assisted by Pantoja and Eliza himself, or of Carrasco. It is reproduced in Wagner's *Spanish Explorations*. In his *Cartography*, however, in which it is listed as #779, he attributes it "probably" to Carrasco.

116 That is, to the north of the Strait of Georgia.

117 Wagner, *Spanish Explorations*, p. 152.

118 Wagner #772.

119 Museo Naval, Madrid, MS 332, "Costa N.O. de América," Vol. II.

120 For a detailed account of this phase of Malaspina's expedition, see David et al., *The Malaspina Expedition*, Vol. 2, pp. 79-167. Also see Cutter, *Malaspina and Galiano*; and Robin Inglis, "Alejandro Malaspina and the Maldonaldo Myth," an unpublished paper presented at the annual meeting of the Society for the History of Discoveries, Vancouver, BC, November 1998.

121 Cutter, ed., *The Journal of Tomás de Suría*, p. 35.

122 See Sotos, *Los Pintores*, for a painting by Juan Ravenet, probably based on a drawing by Felipe Bauza, catalogue #567.

123 On modern maps it is now Disenchantment Bay. See Dolores Higueras, *Catálogo Crítico de los Documentos de la Expedición Malaspina*, Vol. II, Museo Naval, Madrid, 1987, #1722. Also in Cutter, *Malaspina and Galiano*, p. 42.

124 Letter from Malaspina to Valdés from San Blas, October 12, 1791; Museo Naval, MS 583, f. 89. This letter is translated in full in David et al., *The Malaspina Expedition*, Vol. 2, pp. 422-26.

125 The glacier on the north side of Yakutat Bay, the largest ice sheet in the world outside the polar regions, bears his name today.

Chapter 7: The Administration of San Blas de Nayarit

1 A number of places and organizations are named for this saint. Blaise was a physician and prelate, healer of people and animals, who became bishop of Sebastia, Armenia. He was tortured and beheaded in 316 AD during one of the last Roman persecutions of Christians. The tiny west coast port (not to be confused with the Caribbean coastal island) was formally named in January 1768, by order of Carlos III, in association with the founding of the Naval Department of San Blas.

2 See Miguel Mathes, "Martonchel-Puerto de Xalisco-Matanchel-Mantanchen: Ante cedentes históricos del establicimiento del puerto de San Blas, 1525-1767," in Muría, *San Blas de Nayarit*.

3 The first mission at San Diego de Alcalá in 1769 was quickly followed by San Carlos Borromeo (1770), San Antonio de Padua (1771), San Gabriel Arcángel (1771), San Luis Obispo de Tolosa (1772), San Francisco de Asís (1776), and Santa Clara de Asís (1777) and Santa Barbara (1786).

4 Chapman, "The Alta California Supply Ships," p. 184.
5 Cárdenas, *San Blas de Nayarit*, Chap. 9.
6 See the concluding paragraph of his journal of the Expedition of the Limits, 1792.
7 Inskip, "San Blas, Nayarit." Today, San Blas is about 215 miles by road from Guadalajara.
8 Kenyon, "Naval Construction and Repairs at San Blas," p. 93.
9 Trillo y Bermúdez to Bucareli, September 27, 1781; AGN, Marina 49.
10 Unsigned memorandum to Andrés Reggio, September 26, 1775; AGI, Guadalajara 514; and Bucareli to Arriaga, #1642, December 27, 1774; AGI, Guadalajara 513.
11 Bodega and Choquet to Andrés Reggio, February 13, 1775; AGI, Guadalajara 514.
12 Bucareli had undertaken the first major reorganization of the department with his *reglamento* of 1773. See Thurman, *The Naval Department of San Blas*, pp. 106-23. Concerns remained, however, and by the Royal Order of March 21, 1775 (AGN, Marina 37, expediente 1, ff. 1-3), Bucareli had to introduce further measures to increase efficiency.
13 Bodega to Bucareli, May 2, 1776; AGN, Marina 37, expediente 4, ff. 254-65.
14 See Gutiérrez, *San Blas y las Californias*, pp. 93-108.
15 In the spring of 1776, the ships were the schooner *Sonora*, the frigate *Santiago*, and the packet boats *San Carlos*, *Concepción*, and *El Príncipe*.
16 At this time, Bodega's salary as a *teniente de navío* was one hundred pesos a month.
17 Owing to the constant shortage of officers and *pilotos*, there was no opportunity for them to rest in port between voyages.
18 See Cárdenas, *San Blas*, pp. 99-110 and 158-65.
19 Novo y Colson, ed., *Viaje político-científico*, p. 126.
20 Ibid.
21 For a description of this building, see Thurman, *San Blas*, pp. 217-18.
22 Hijosa served in this capacity from 1767 to 1779 and again from 1785 to 1797. Between these dates, the position was occupied by Francisco Trillo y Bermúdez.
23 As commissary, Hijosa was responsible for the department's accounts, for its budget and customs paperwork, and for the pay packets of all civilian, army, and naval personnel. He had to ensure that the stores and other supplies required by departing ships were ordered and delivered in good time. He was responsible for all financial matters concerning the California missions and presidios and was assisted by two officials of the royal treasury. As naval commandant, Bodega was responsible for the assignment of officers and *pilotos* and for the movements of ships. He was also responsible for military discipline, the supervision of the careening and repairs of ships, new construction, the defences of the port, and the planning of all expeditions, whether to resupply the missions to Alta California or for exploration. If he were absent for any reason, the next senior officer or *piloto* would act in his place.
24 Bodega to Bucareli, May 2, 1776; AGN, Marina 37, expediente 6, f. 264. For the context in which the comment was made, see the section below on the relocation question.
25 Bodega to Revillagigedo, July 30, 1790; AGN, Californias 78.
26 Cárdenas, *San Blas*, p. 159. Unless otherwise indicated, much of the material in this section has been obtained in this indispensable work.
27 "Double salaries" referred to the doubling of the salaries of personnel serving in the South Seas in the Pacific fleet.
28 The master carpenter at San Blas, Ignacio Arteaga was no relation to *teniente de navío* Ignacio Arteaga.

29 During 1777 and 1778, the arsenal had at least 280 employees, but as a result of wartime economies in 1781, the number stood at only 77, of which only 15 were shipbuilders. Kenyon, "Naval Construction," pp. 83-87.
30 Bodega to Revillagigedo, n.n., December 23, 1789; AGN, Marina 74.
31 Cárdenas, *San Blas*, p. 166, cites a letter to the viceroy from Ramón Saavedra when the latter was acting commandant of the department, dated May 1, 1792, reporting that there were not enough officers on hand to preside over the trial of two deserters, and asking Revillagigedo for permission to apply the usual punishment to them (and to any others apprehended): a number of lashes while strapped to a cannon, depending on the circumstances of each case, as well as three months in irons and loss of salary.
32 They were José de Cañizares, Gonzalo López de Haro, Juan Kendrick, an American who had become a Roman Catholic, Juan Pantoja, Juan Carrasco, Estéban Mondófia, and José Verdía.
33 Revillagigedo to Valdés, letter #294 of March 31, 1794; AGN, Correspondencia de los Virreyes II, ff. 37-39.
34 Mayorga to Bodega, February 10, 1780; Mayorga to Gálvez, May 27, 1783; AGI, México, 1387.
35 Commanded by Lieutenant Colonel Miguel Marín del Valle, to whose daughter Bodega had become attracted, and whom he had requested permission to marry in 1787. The relationship continued. See Chapter 13.
36 Bodega to Mayorga, March 1, 1780; AGI, México 1387 and Guadalajara 517. The text can be found in Cárdenas, *San Blas*, pp. 224-26, and in Appendix 4 of Bernabeu, *Juan Francisco de la Bodega y Quadra*, pp. 252-55.
37 According to Cárdenas, *San Blas*, p. 227, approval of the formation of the battalion of militia was conveyed to Mayorga in a Royal Order of March 17, 1781; AGI, Guadalajara 517.
38 Mayorga to Bodega, August 19, 1780; AGN, Provincias Internas 101, f. 560.
39 Bodega to Mayorga, August 3, 1780; Mayorga to Bodega, August 30, 1780; AGN, Provincias Internas 101, ff. 556-57.
40 Personal communication to the author from Christon I. Archer, August 1, 1989.
41 Royal Order of March 17, 1781.
42 Mayorga to Bodega, June 27, 1780; AGN, Provincias Internas 101, ff. 454-55.
43 At this time, the army for New Spain consisted of four infantry regiments, two companies of Catalonian Volunteers, and two companies stationed in Monterey and San Blas.
44 Bodega's inventory of cannon by category and size on hand in San Blas and the ships as of February 4, 1790; AGN, Historia 68.
45 Bodega to Revillagigedo, January 14, 1790; AGN, Californias 70, ff. 164-65.
46 Bodega to Revillagigedo, April 9, 1793; AHN, legajo 4290.
47 Bodega to Revillagigedo, letter #559 of June 28, 1793; AGN, Californias 14.
48 Valdés to Bodega, June 10, 1780; AGN, Provincias Internas 101, f. 456.
49 *Pita* is, literally, "string." According to the entry in Francisco J. Santamaria's *Diccionario de Americanismos* (Mexico: Editorial Pedro Robredo, 1942), *pita* is a rope fibre produced from two *armarilídeas* plants, *agaves* and *fourcaraea*.
50 Bodega to Mayorga, March 17, 1780; AGN, Provincias Internas 101, ff. 487-526v.
51 On this point, see Cárdenas, *San Blas*, p. 110.
52 The *Concepción*, the *San Carlos*, the *Princesa*, and the *Aránzazu*. Bodega to Revillagigedo, letter #114 of August 9, 1790; AGN, Provincias Internas 4, ff. 50-52v. Hijosa's

budget, dated September 16, 1788, calling for total expenditures of 287,412 pesos, is in AGN, Provincias Internas 4, ff. 2-10.

53 The principal entries for Bodega's 1790 budget were:
Wages and salaries (total 271,610 pesos)
30,056 pesos, for naval officers,
10,407 pesos, for chaplains
5,450 pesos, for surgeons
15,966 pesos, for *pilotos*
122,363 pesos, for all non-commissioned ranks of seagoing personnel
13,995 pesos, for the army's requirements of equipment and personnel
73,373 pesos, the dockyard personnel
Supplies (total 83,000 pesos)
19,000 pesos, for tar and raw hemp
24,000 pesos, for spare canvas sails, nails, iron, and oakum
40,000 pesos, for ships' stores.

54 This document, which was signed by Bodega, Hijosa, Saavedra, José Camacho and José María Monterde, can be found in AGN, Provincias Internas 4, ff. 44-48v.

55 "Noticias de los gastos erogados en las viajes al Puerto de San Lorenzo en los quatro años desde 1789 [hast]a 1792"; AGN, Provincias Internas 4, ff. 409-36v.

56 Bodega was probably not included in the commission because he was awaiting a decision on his offer to serve on the *Sonora* as an extra officer on the Hezeta-led expedition, which was scheduled to depart in early 1775.

57 Hijosa's report, in Cárdenas, *San Blas*, citing AGI, Guadalajara 497.

58 Cárdenas, *San Blas*, summarizes the advantages and disadvantages of each alternative port and those of San Blas, pp. 93-98.

59 Arteaga to Bucareli, April 27, 1775; AGI, Guadalajara 497.

60 Costanzó to Bucareli, June 8, 1776; AGI, Guadalajara 497.

61 Following his return, Bodega attended one such meeting, held on December 4, 1775, at which he sided with those favouring a move to Chacala. Cárdenas, *San Blas*, p. 97.

62 Bucareli to Gálvez, letter #2394 of July 27, 1776; AGI, Papeles de Estado, Audiencia de Guadalajara 497.

63 Grimaldi had written that "it would be unfortunate if the port of San Blas is [further] developed if the end result is to transfer its establishment to another equally proportioned and healthier. The conservation of the [health] of the men must be the government's principal objective." Grimaldi to Bucareli, May 22, 1775; AGI, Indiferente General 1630.

64 Revillagigedo to Valdés, letter #193 of December 27, 1789; AGI, México 1530.

65 Bodega to Revillagigedo, February 20, 1790; AGI, México 437.

66 Francisco Mourelle to Revillagigedo, September 15, 1790; AGI, México 1540.

67 A courier on horseback could reach the capital from Acapulco in four to five days, whereas it took eight to ten days for one to travel to the capital from San Blas.

68 Revillagigedo to Pedro de Leréna, the Minister of Finance, under cover of his letter #230 of January 15, 1791; AGI, México 1540.

69 Letter #44 of September 1, 1791; AGN, Correspondencia de los Virreyes II, 23.

70 Revillagigedo to Alcudia (Manuel Godoy, Duque de la Alcudia), letter #162 of April 12, 1793, paragraphs 226-27; AGI, Estado 21; AGN, Correspondencia de los Virreyes, 173.

71 AGN, Marina 53, ff. 147-50v and ff. 309-20.

72 Bodega to Revillagigedo, letter #251 of July 7, 1791; AGN, Histórico de Hacienda 479, f. 38.

73 Bodega to Revillagigedo, letter #255 of July 16, 1791; AGN, Histórico de Hacienda 479, f. 38.
74 See Cutter, *Malaspina and Galiano*, p. 112; and Kendrick, *The Voyage*, p. 20.
75 Both the *Mexicana* and the *Sutil* were rigged as modified brigantines, although nominally schooners. Kendrick, *The Voyage*, p. 34. For the detailed measurements of each, see Kenyon, "Naval Construction," pp. 177-89.
76 Lamb, *The Voyage of George Vancouver*, Vol. 2, p. 593.
77 For her dimensions and characteristics, see Kenyon, "Naval Construction," pp. 191-96. In a letter to Revillagigedo dated February 10, 1792, AGN, Historia 67, f. 553, Bodega gives her weight as 270 tons, but this seems too much.
78 Revillagigedo to Valdés, letter #120 of March 31, 1792; AHN, Estado, legajo 4288, and AGN, Corresponencia de los Virreyes 168, ff. 299-302.
79 AGN, Californias 8.
80 Bodega to Mayorga, August 19, 1780; AGN, Provincias Internas 101, f. 558. He estimated the cost of making good the damage at two thousand pesos.
81 Bodega to Mayorga, September 26, 1780; AGN, Marina 44, f. 281r-v and f. 298.
82 All the documents will be found in AGN, Marina 74, expediente 20.
83 Bodega to Revillagigedo, January 8, 1790; AGN, Marina 70, ff. 365-66.
84 Revillagigedo to Bodega, February 2, 1790; AGN, Marina 70, ff. 367-68v. He sent a similar letter of the same date to commissary Hijosa.
85 Bodega to Revillagigedo, letter #22 of March 5, 1790; AGN, Marina 70, ff. 370-71.
86 Bodega to Revillagigedo, letter #79, May 20, 1790; AGN, Marina 70, f. 372.
87 Thurman, *The Naval Department of San Blas*, p. 344.
88 Revillagigedo to Antonio Valdés, letter #120 of March 31, 1792; AGN, Correspondencia de los Virreyes I, legajo 168, ff. 299-302, and AHN, Estado, legajo 4288. He sent an almost identical letter to Floridablanca, letter #84 of the same date.
89 Bodega to Revillagigedo, letter #429 of October 24, 1792, from Monterey; AGN, Historia 67, ff. 675-80v.
90 Revillagigedo to Bodega, March 24, 1792; AGN, Californias 42.
91 Revillagigedo to Antonio Valdés, letter #120 of March 31, 1792; AGN, Correspondencia de los Virreyes, legajo 168, ff. 215-18, and AHN, Estado, legajo 4288. The viceroy sent the same letter to Floridablanca (#84 of March 31, 1792), omitting his reminder of the need to replace Bastarrachea.
92 The *Princesa* continued to give good service and remained on the inventory of ships based in San Blas until at least 1810.
93 Bodega to Revillagigedo, from Monterey, letter #428 of October 24, 1792; AGN, Historia 67, ff. 575-81v.
94 Kenyon, "Naval Construction," p. 230.

Chapter 8: The Nootka Convention and the Expedition of the Limits

1 "Los extranjeros han sido siempre excluidos del comercio de nuestras Indias." Quoted by Schurz, "The Spanish Lake."
2 Flores to Valdés, letter #1182 of August 27, 1789; AGN, Correspondencia de los Virreyes II, Vol. 19.
3 Valdés to Revillagigedo, January 26, 1790; AGN, Historia 65, cuaderno 5.

4 Meares, *Authentic Copy of the Memorial.*
5 The seizures at Nootka were also the subject of a popular London "entertainment" titled *Nootka Sound, or Britain Prepar'd,* by James Byrne in May–June 1790. See "Britain Prepar'd – On the High Seas and in the London Theatre," unpublished paper by Janet R. Fireman, given at the annual meeting of the Canadian Nautical Research Society, July 1986.
6 Revillagigedo to the Conde de Campo de Alange, the Minister of War, and Pedro de Leréna, the Minister of Finance, July 27, 1790; AHN, Estado 4259. I am grateful to the late Vivian Fisher, formerly of the Bancroft Library, Berkeley, for drawing this important dispatch to my attention.
7 Floridablanca to Revillagigedo, Royal Order #305 of August 29, 1790; AGN, Reales Cédulas 146.
8 Mills, "The Real Significance of the Nootka Sound Incident."
9 Royal Order #221 consisted of twelve copies of the Nootka Convention. Floridablanca to Revillagigedo, November 27, 1790, Royal Order #182; AGN, Reales Cédulas 147, f. 304r-v; AHN, Estado 4285.
10 Floridablanca to Revillagigedo, #221, #222, #223, and #224; AGN, Reales Cédulas 147, f. 401, ff. 400-2v, f. 403r-v, and f. 404, respectively.
11 Revillagigedo to Floridablanca, #44 of September 1, 1791; AGN, Correspondencia de los Virreyes II, legajo 23.
12 Quoted in his letter #56 of October 24, 1791, to Floridablanca, under cover of which he transmitted a copy of his first instructions to Bodega y Quadra.
13 Revillagigedo to Alcudia, #162 of April 12, 1793, para. 129; AGN, Correspondencia de los Virreyes, legajo 173, and AHN, Estado 21.
14 Aranda to Revillagigedo, Royal Order of February 29, 1792; AGN, Reales Cédulas 151, ff. 197-98v.
15 Royal Order of December 11, 1790; referred to in Revillagigedo's letter #162 to Alcudia of April 12, 1793, para. 124; AGN, Correspondencia de los Virreyes, legajo 173, and AGI, Estado 21.
16 Revillagigedo to Floridablanca, #64 of November 27, 1791; AGN, Correspondencia de los Virreyes, legajo 164.
17 Revillagigedo to Valdés, #42 of March 27, 1791; AGN, Correspondencia de los Virreyes, legajo 164.
18 A copy was forwarded to Floridablanca as enclosure #2 to his letter #56 of October 29, 1791; AGN, Historia 67, and AHN, Estado 4287.
19 Revillagigedo to Floridablanca, letter #71 of January 3, 1792; AGN, Correspondencia de los Virreyes, legajo 168.
20 Although nominally a schooner , she was always referred to as such in all documentation. See Kenyon, pp. 191-96 and chap. 26.
21 See Cutter, *Malaspina and Galiano,* p. 111 and passim.
22 Not the former *North West America,* which Martínez restored.
23 Royal Order of December 11, 1790. The choice was not made on the basis of the ship's qualities. Revillagigedo described her as an "old ship, frail, slow and without adequate storage space for water and stores." Revillagigedo to Aranda #129 and to Valdés #176 of November 30, 1792; AGN, Correspondencia de los Virreyes, legajo 168, f. 254r-v.
24 Cutter, *California in 1792,* pp. 89-90.
25 Torres to Revillagigedo, November 16, 1791; AGN, Historia 67, expediente 2, ff. 188-89.

26 Bodega to Revillagigedo, November 21, 1791; AGN, Historia 67, ff. 192-93.
27 Revillagigedo to Torres, November 22, 1791; AGN, Historia 67, ff. 196-198v.
28 Revillagigedo to Valdés, letter #92 of November 27, 1791; AGN, Correspondencia de los Virreyes II, legajo 23.
29 Revillagigedo to Bodega, October 29, 1791; AGN, Historia 67. He also informed Minister Antonio Valdés in his letter #80 of the same date; AGN, Correspondencia de los Virreyes I, legajo 164, f. 306r-v.
30 Bodega to Revillagigedo, November 2, 1791; AGN, Historia 67, f. 338.
31 See Janet R. Fireman's unpublished paper, "Félix Cepeda and the North Pacific Exploration." Documents concerning him in the AGN spell his name "Zepeda."
32 See Chapter 12.
33 Bodega to Revillagigedo from Nootka, July 18, 1792; AGN, Historia 67, ff. 341-42.
34 Revillagigedo to Valdés, November 30, 1792; AGN, Correspondencia de los Virreyes I, legajo 168, f. 351.
35 Revillagigedo to Aranda, November 30, 1792; AGN, Correspondencia de los Virreyes I, legajo 168, f. 359; and AHN, Estado, legajo 4288.
36 Bodega to Revillagigedo, November 3, 1791; AGN, Historia 67, f. 382-83v.
37 Revillagigedo to the Ministers of the Treasury, November 4, 1791; AGN, Historia 67, f. 383.
38 Lavastida to Eliza, March 11, 1795; AGN, Marina 73, ff. 53-54, cited in Fireman, "The Seduction of George Vancouver," p. 438.
39 Bodega to Revillagigedo, letter #364 of February 29, 1792; AGN, Histórico de Hacienda 479, ff. 73-74v.
40 Revillagigedo to Floridablanca, letter #64 cited above.
41 Bodega to Revillagigedo, letter #311 of December 13, 1791; AGN, Historia 67, f. 254r-v.
42 These are to be found in the Museo Naval, Madrid, MS 331. Some of them are also to be found in the library of the Real Academia de la Historia, Madrid. The Huntington Library, San Marino, California, has a copy of the *Segunda Exploración*, the Hezeta–Bodega expedition of 1775, HM 161.
43 Revillagigedo to Bodega, December 22, 1791; AGN, Historia 67, f. 264r-v.
44 Close to Dixon's Port Mulgrave, explored by Malaspina in 1791.
45 Named by Bodega in 1775. Sea Lion Cove on Kruzof Island.
46 Dixon Entrance.
47 Cape Cook, at the top of Vancouver Island.
48 *Carta Reducida de la Costa Septentrional de California desde el Puerto de Acapulco hasta la Isla de Unalaska. Está construida al Meridiano de San Blas, con arreglo a las mejores Observaciones, noticias y repetidos Viages para manifestar lo que resta que examinarse, y debe ejecutar por Orden del Excm. Sr. Conde de Revillagigedo, en la Expedición de Límites, el Capitán de Navío Comandante de ella [y] del Departamento Dn. Juan Francisco de la Bodega y Quadra. Año de 1792.* Plate XXXIX and #800 in Wagner's *Cartography.*
49 Bodega to Revillagigedo, letter #337 of January 14, 1792; AGN, Historia 67.
50 See Engstrand, *Spanish Scientists in the New World.*
51 Bodega to Revillagigedo, letter #311 of December 13, 1791. Unless otherwise noted, all documents cited in this section will be found in AGN, Historia 67, expediente 12.
52 Bodega to Revillagigedo, letter #344 of January 21, 1792; AGN, Historia 67. The manifest of the *Santa Gertrudis* signed by Torres states that all told, forty-five "infantry troops" were taken on board.

53 Revillagigedo to Antonio Valdés, #105 of January 1, 1792; AGN, Correspondencia de los Virreyes, legajo 164, f. 329r-v.
54 Bodega to Revillagigedo, letter #356 of February 10, 1792; AGN, Historia 67.
55 In an unnumbered letter to Antonio Valdés of February 17, 1792, Bodega informed the minister that he intended to assign the *Aránzazu* the task of exploring the coast between the Entrada de Juan Pérez (Dixon Entrance) and the (non-existent) Rio de Martín de Aguilar in 43°N; AHN, Estado 4289.

Chapter 9: Bodega at Nootka

1 Clayoquot Sound was known to the Spanish as the Archipelago de Clayocuot or Cayuclat and to the English as Port Cox. Barkley Sound was known to the Spanish as the Archipelago de Nitinat or Archipelago de Carrasco.
2 Today many of the descendants of the Mowachaht are members of the Mowachaht-Muchalaht First Nation.
3 John Dewhirst, "Nootka Sound: A 4,000-Year Perspective," *Sound Heritage* 7, No. 2 (1978): 1-30, BC Provincial Archives; also Arima, *The West Coast People*, p. 103.
4 In Spanish documents, these names are used interchangeably to mean both the sound and the site of the establishment. The spelling varied: Nutca, Noutka, Noca, Nuca, Nootka.
5 Moziño, *Noticias de Nutka*, p. 85.
6 Ibid.
7 The fourth vessel, the frigate *Princesa*, under Salvador Fidalgo, sailed directly to Neah Bay, reaching it on May 29. See below.
8 Caamaño, *Extracto del diario*, his long entry for the month of March 1791; AGN, Historia 69.
9 Newcombe, *Menzies' Journal of Vancouver's Voyage*, p. 110. The house is shown in the wash drawing made of the establishment by Bodega's artist, Atanasio Echeverría, reworked by Gabriel Gil for inclusion in the atlas folio volume of his *Viaje;* Archivo del Ministerio de Asuntos Exteriores, Madrid, MS 146, #4. See also Henry Humphry's sketch of Friendly Cove, which was engraved for Vancouver's *Voyage.* It appears in Lamb, *The Voyage of George Vancouver*, Vol. 2, plate 31.
10 Kaplanoff, *Joseph Ingraham's Journal*, p. 213.
11 Howay, *Voyages of the* Columbia, p. 410. Any "Indians" would almost certainly have been Mexican.
12 Newcombe, *Menzies' Journal*, p. 112.
13 This was the same spot where Meares built his *North West America.*
14 Kendrick, *Voyage of the* Sutil *and* Mexicana, p. 72.
15 Bodega to Alcalá Galiano, May 25, 1792; AHN, Estado 4290.
16 Alcalá Galiano to Bodega, May 31, 1792; AHN, Estado 4290.
17 The Spanish text can be found in AHN, Estado 4287. Dobson's translation into English was attached to Vancouver's report. It was printed in the *Annual Report of the British Columbia Provincial Archives Department for 1914*, Vol. 13.
18 Ibid., Vols. 13 and 14.
19 Presumably, Wickininnish, whose village was to the south in Clayoquot Sound, where Meares had intended to build another base at what he called Port Cox.

20 The Spanish text is in AGN, Historia 65, and AHN, Estado, legajo 4287.
21 See Cook, *Flood Tide of Empire*, p. 138; and Nokes, *Almost a Hero*, p. 170.
22 Ingraham returned the compliment, declaring Bodega to be "one of the most agreeable men I ever met with." Kaplanoff, *Joseph Ingraham's Journal*, entry for August 1.
23 Ibid., pp. 214 and 227.
24 Cepeda, *Memoria*, Part 1, f. 72.
25 Translated from the Spanish. The original English text has not been located. Bodega to Revillagigedo, July 19; AHN, Estado, legajo 4288.
26 The copy that New presented to Bodega is dated May 12, 1792. The original and its enclosures in AGN, Reales Cédulas 147, #222, bear an earlier date: December 29, 1791.
27 Gray and Ingraham had not yet arrived to discuss this with Bodega.
28 Bodega to New, July 18, 1792; AHN, Estado, legajos 4287 and 4288.
29 Bodega to Floridablanca and Revillagigedo, July 18, 1792; AHN, Estado, legajos 4287 and 4288.
30 Bodega to Floridablanca and Revillagigedo, June 22, 1792; AHN, Estado, legajo 4287.
31 If Bodega was thinking here that Nootka was not worth keeping, he would later change his mind.
32 Bodega to Revillagigedo and Floridablanca, July 18, 1792; AHN, Estado, legajos 4287 and 4288.
33 Bodega to Revillagigedo, letter #389 of June 22, 1792; AGN, Historia 70, cuaderno 21.
34 Bodega to Fidalgo, June 22, 1792; AHN, Estado, legajo 4290. He had given Alcalá Galiano a similar letter for Fidalgo.
35 Torres 's instructions are in AHN, Estado, legajos 4287 and 4288.
36 Martínez had sent him in the restored *North West America* to investigate a wide opening he claimed to have seen when returning south with Pérez in 1774.
37 Tutusi was also known as Tatooche, Tatoosh, and Tootoche In his *Viaje*, Bodega refers to his brother as Tetlacu. His principal residence was Tatoosh Island at the northwestern tip of the Olympic Peninsula.
38 Revillagigedo to Floridablanca, letter #34 of March 27, 1791; AGN, Correspondencia de los Virreyes, legajo 164. Again, the reference to the north shore was an error.
39 Revillagigedo to Floridablanca, #44 of September 1, 1791; AGN, Correspondencia de los Virreyes, legajo 164.
40 Bodega to Fidalgo, February 29, 1792; AGN, Historia 67, cuaderno 15, f. 72r-v.
41 Bodega to Revillagigedo, letter #365, February 29, 1792; AGN, Historia 76, cuaderno 15, f. 70.
42 Floridablanca, who had been held responsible for the diplomatic defeat and humiliation of the Nootka Convention, had been removed from office, and the government was divided on how to adjust to the new situation on the Northwest Coast.
43 Revillagigedo to Bodega, March 7, 1792; AGN, Historia 67, cuaderno 15, f. 76.
44 Bodega to Revillagigedo, letter #385 of June 22, 1792; AGN, Historia 67, cuaderno 15.
45 A drawing by Cardero, *Vista del Establicimiento Español en el Puerto de Núñez Gaona y gran Canoa de Tetacu*, shows a panorama of the bay with the *Princesa* and the Alcalá Galliano and Valdés schooners in the foreground. On the shore, two tents are serving as shelter. Museo de América, Bauza collection, #2-269, Sotos, *Los Pintores de la Expedición Malaspina*, #633. The depiction of the canoe is almost identical to the canoe in Cardero's drawing of Tlupananulg's canoe in Friendly Cove (Sotos #593).
46 Kaplanoff, *Joseph Ingraham's Journal*, entry for September 28, 1792.

47 Howay, *Voyages of the* Columbia, p. 416.
48 Fidalgo to Bodega, July 4, 1792; AGN, Historia 67, cuaderno 15.
49 Bodega to Fidalgo, August 5, 1792; AGN, Historia 67, cuaderno 15.
50 Bodega to Revillagigedo, from Monterey, letter #427 of October 24, 1792; AGN, Historia 67, cuaderno 15, and Revillagigedo to Bodega, November 25, 1792; AGN, Historia 67, cuaderno 15.
51 Alcudia to Revillagigedo, May 8, 1793; AGN, Historia 67, cuaderno 15.
52 Bodega did not receive their written opinion, dated October 22, 1792, until much later, when they were in Monterey; AGN, Historia 67, cuaderno 15. They gave him their report orally when they returned to Nootka on August 31.
53 Revillagigedo to Bodega, letter #385 of June 22, 1792.
54 For Bodega's visit to Neah Bay in September 1792 and the gift of the barracks to Chief Tutusi (or Tatoosh) and Chief Tatlacu, see Chapter 11.
55 There is an extensive literature on the controversy the Fonte letter generated. Particular mention should be made of Williams, *The British Search for the Northwest Passage in the 18th Century;* and Wagner's "Apocryphal Voyages to the Northwest Coast of America."
56 See Cepeda, "Memoria," Part I, f. 75, Bancroft Library, Berkeley, catalogue 81/67 cp.
57 They are dated June 9; AGN, Historia 70, cuaderno 20, ff. 9-11. Revillagigedo was content to leave the instructions for Caamaño to Bodega. Cepeda was critical of those instructions, considering them too imprecise. Cepeda, "Memoria," Part I, f. 7.
58 Caamaño's journal is in AGN, Historia 71, ff. 303-92, and Provincias Internas 134.
59 Martínez Zayas was sometimes called Zayas to distinguish him from Estéban José Martínez.
60 Chart #10 in the folio volume of Bodega's *Viaje*, Spanish Ministry of Foreign Affairs, MS 146.
61 His chart is listed in Wagner's *Cartography*, #807. Bodega included a copy in his *Viaje*, chart #11.
62 Fifty-four nautical miles.
63 The family name of Minister of State Floridablanca before he was ennobled.
64 The original of Caamaño's general chart is in AGN, Mapas y Planos, and is listed in Wagner, *Cartography*, #801. It shows his route. A copy of the chart, without the route, was included in the folio volume of Bodega's *Viaje*, chart #7.
65 Wagner's translation, *Cartography*, p. 299.
66 Cepeda, "Memoria," Part 1, f. 75.
67 Chart #26 in the folio volume for Bodega's *Viaje.*
68 Unnumbered letter to Bodega of November 11, 1792; AGN, Historia 72, cuaderno 26.
69 Revillagigedo to Alcudia, letter #162 of April 12, 1793, paragraph 179; AGN, Correspondencia de los Virreyes, legajo 173; AGI, Estado 21.
70 The *Orcacitas* was the former *Adventure*, built by the American fur trader Robert Gray in Clayoquot Sound and, purchased by Bodega at Neah Bay. See Chapter 11. These latitudes encompass the coast between Nootka Sound and Prince William Sound.
71 Revillagigedo to Bodega, October 29, 1791; AGN, Historia 67, and AHN, Estado 4287.
72 Lavastida to Eliza, March 11, 1795; AGN, Marina 73, ff. 53-54, cited in Fireman, "The Seduction of George Vancouver," p. 438.
73 Lavastida to Francisco de Eliza, March 11, 1795; AGN, Marina 73, f. 92r-v.

74 Using the pretext of searching for La Pérouse, she was on an expedition trading brandy for sea otter skins.
75 Bodega to Floridablanca, June 22, 1792; AHN, Estado 4287.
76 Kaplanoff, *Joseph Ingraham's Journal*, entry for August 1.
77 Boit log, entry for July 29, printed in Howay, *Voyages of the* Columbia, p. 411.
78 Meany, "A New Vancouver Journal," pp. 221-24, 301-8, and vol. 6, pp. 50-68. Hereinafter cited as Bell, *Journal*, p. 223.
79 Lamb, *The Voyage of George Vancouver*, vol. 2, p. 661.
80 Sworn statement at San Blas, June 1, 1793; AGN, Marina 73, f. 55.
81 Meany, "A New Vancouver Journal," p. 223.
82 Kaplanoff, *Joseph Ingraham's Journal*, p. 223.
83 Ibid., p. 216.
84 Meany, "A New Vancouver Journal," p. 224.
85 Ibid., p. 225.
86 Bodega expressed the same thought in identical letters from Monterey to Revillagigedo and to Minister of State Aranda, October 24, 1792; but he added, "and the generosity with which I treated them for the honour the nation"; AHN, Estado 4287 and Estado 4288.
87 See Chapter 2.
88 Marshall, "A Political History of the Nuu-chah-nulth People," identifies (p. 342) what she calls the "Yuquot–Tahsis confederacy ... led by Chief Maquinna [who] exercised the widest political influence."
89 Articles XV and XXIII of Revillagigedo's instructions to Mourelle, printed in Wagner, *Spanish Explorations*, pp. 207-8.
90 Articles XVI and XVII of Revillagigedo's instructions to Alcalá and Valdés are printed in Kendrick, *Voyages of the* Sutil *and* Mexicana, p. 53.
91 For a detailed account of the expedition's two-week stay at Nootka, see Cutter, *Malaspina and Galiano*, pp. 71-110.
92 Andrew David et al., *The Malaspina Expedition*, vol. 2, p. 186.
93 Viana's *diario*, cited by Cutter, *Malaspina and Galiano*, p. 105.
94 Moziño, *Noticias de Nutka*, p. 80.
95 Bodega, *Viaje;* Bernabeu, *Bodega*, p. 166.
96 Kupti is today's Coopti Point, at the entrance to Tahsis Inlet. The ceremony witnessed by Bodega was described in detail by Moziño in his *Noticias de Nutka*, pp. 34-37. It was also the subject of a wash drawing by Cardero, the artist on the Alcalá Galiano–Valdés expedition, possibly based on Echeverría's drawing of the event itself. See Sotos, *Los Pintores de la Expedición Malaspina*, vol. 2, fig. 649.
97 Marshall, "Dangerous Liaisons," in Fisher and Johnston, *From Maps to Metaphors*, pp. 160-75.
98 Knowing that Moziño was preparing his own detailed account, Bodega included only the occasional paragraph on ethnological matters in his *Viaje* of 1792.
99 Bodega, *Viaje;* Bernabeu, *Bodega*, p. 177. As Maquinna came to dinner so frequently, he must have taken up residence at one of his villages closer to Yuquot, possibly Marvinas or Coopti, when not occupying one of the bedrooms in the commandant's house.
100 Ibid.
101 Marshall, "Dangerous Liaisons," p. 165.
102 Lamb, *The Voyage of George Vancouver*, Vol. 2, p. 662.

103 Inglis, "The Spanish on the North Pacific Coast," in Inglis, ed., *Spain and the North Pacific Coast,* pp. 133-36. See also "The Contact Period as Recorded by Indian Oral Traditions," edited by Barbara S. Efrat and W.J. Langlois, in *nu•tka• Captain Cook and the Spanish Explorers on the Coast,* Victoria, Provincial Archives of British Columbia(1978), pp. 54-61.
104 His former name was Cleaskinah. He had exchanged names as a token of friendship with Captain James Hanna of the *Sea Otter* in 1785-86, a practice common among some native groups of the Northwest Coast.
105 Different versions of this affair are summarized in Marshall, "Dangerous Liaisons," pp. 168-69. I follow Ingraham's version as he relates it in his journal, entry for August 8.
106 See the diagram of their relationship in Marshall, "Dangerous Liaisons," p. 168.
107 Bodega, *Viaje;* Bernabeu, *Bodega,* p. 175.
108 Most accounts say that the boy had served on the *Activa,* but Ingraham said he "belonged to Señor Caamaño's ship," the *Aránzazu.* Journal entry for September 18.
109 Bodega, *Viaje;* Bernabeu, *Bodega,* p. 197.
110 Meany, "A New Vancouver Journal," p. 308.
111 Moziño, *Noticias de Nutka,* pp. 56-57.
112 Possibly the Hesquiaht, who resided on Estevan Point at the southern entrance to Nootka Sound.
113 Kaplanoff, *Joseph Ingraham's Journal,* entry for September 18.
114 Fragment of Puget's journal in the British Museum, MS 17,548, presented by his son, W.B. Puget, in 1848, together with other of his father's papers. Transcript in Oregon Historical Society, Portland, MS 644.
115 Meany, "A New Vancouver Journal," p. 308.
116 Revillagigedo to Aranda, letter #134 of November 30, 1792, and #175 to Antonio Valdés of same date; AGN, Correspondencia de los Virreyes, legajo 168, p. 258.
117 Royal Order #162; AGN, Reales Cédulas 154, p. 209.
118 Archer, "Seduction before Sovereignty," p. 157.
119 Ibid., p. 84.
120 See Stewart, *The Adventures and Sufferings of John R. Jewitt.* This work was first published in Edinburgh in 1804.

Chapter 10: The Commissioners' Negotiations at Nootka

1 Unless otherwise indicated, all quotations are taken from Lamb, *The Voyage of George Vancouver,* 4 vols. (London: Hakluyt Society, 1984.).
2 Meany, "A New Vancouver Journal," p. 223.
3 British Columbia Archives, "Captain Vancouver's report."
4 Newcombe, *Menzie's Journal.*
5 Ibid., entry for October 2, 1792.
6 Ibid., p. 112.
7 Vancouver also recorded Bodega's invitation in his report to the Admiralty; British Columbia Archives, "Captain Vancouver's report," 1914.
8 Tovell, "Bodega y Quadra and Vancouver."
9 Vancouver was thirty-four and Bodega forty-eight. Vancouver was a "master and commander" similar to the modern naval rank of commander, and Bodega was a *capitán de návio* or four-ring captain.

10 Newcombe, *Menzies' Journal*, p. 115.
11 Bodega records it as September 3. Vancouver's dates, as mentioned above, are always one day ahead because he had not allowed for having crossed the international date line.
12 Bell says they were "armed in case of accident"; Meany, "A New Vancouver Journal," p. 303.
13 Puget, *Journal*, British Library, Add. MS 17,543; transcript in the Oregon Historical Society, Portland.
14 Newcombe, *Menzies' Journal*, p. 116.
15 Ibid., p. 117.
16 Puget says they were greeted by cries of "Wacash, wacash." He estimated the population of the village to be "at least five hundred people of all ages."
17 Bell describes the house in some detail. Meany, "A New Vancouver Journal," pp. 303-4. Moziño, in his *Noticias*, pp. 17-18, also gives a lengthy description of the house but adds a few more details.
18 "With a perfect confidence in Maquinna's professions of friendship, we left our arms in the boats with two men in each to take care of them."
19 Puget, *Journal*, British Library, Add. MS 17,543; transcript in the Oregon Historical Society, Portland.
20 Newcombe, *Menzies' Journal*, p. 117.
21 Moziño, who was present, notes that on such occasions, Maquinna would serve "up to thirty-six" dishes. Moziño, *Noticias*, p. 20.
22 Meany, "A New Vancouver Journal," p. 304.
23 Newcombe, *Menzies' Journal*, pp. 119-20.
24 Puget said the signal "was given by beating a number of small sticks on a board."
25 Lamb, *The Voyage of George Vancouver*, vol. 2, p. 671.
26 Newcombe, *Menzies' Journal*, pp. 118-19.
27 Meany, "A New Vancouver Journal," p. 304.
28 Moziño, *Noticias*, p. 16.
29 Meany, "A New Vancouver Journal," p.304.
30 Newcombe, *Menzies' Journal*, p. 119.
31 Meany, "A New Vancouver Journal," p. 305.
32 This drawing is reproduced in the atlas volume of Bodega's *Viaje*, MS 146, #27.
33 On his third and final visit to Nootka in 1794, Vancouver paid a similar visit to Maquinna. See Lamb, *The Voyage of George Vancouver*, vol. 4, pp. 1401ff.
34 Literally, "good, good," a form of salutation. Puget, *Journal*.
35 Possibly the point where the Hecate Channel enters the inlet.
36 Meany, "A New Vancouver Journal," p. 305.
37 Puget, *Journal*.
38 Vancouver says they ate "on the rocks."
39 Both names continued to appear on early Admiralty and Spanish charts, but by 1825, Hudson's Bay Company officials had shortened the name to Vancouver's Island, and by mid-century the possessive form had disappeared.
40 Bodega, *Viaje;* Bernabeu, *Bodega*, p. 201.
41 Newcombe, *Menzies' Journal*, p. 120.
42 Revillagigedo to Bodega, October 29, 1791; AGN, Historia 67.
43 "I shall most certainly quit [the Sandwich Islands] as early in the Spring as possible, my intentions being to begin my researches at their southern extremity [in] Latd.

30°No. and proceed Northward, which will ere I reach the Latitude of Nootka bring the Summer in all probability some what advanced as the examination of De Fuca's Straits &c &c will intervene in that space." I am indebted to the late Dr. W. Kaye Lamb for this quotation, which is in the PRO, C.O. 5/187, ff. 5-6.

44 Vancouver's formal instructions are reprinted in Lamb, *The Voyage of George Vancouver*, vol. 1, pp. 283-88.

45 The copy sent to Revillagigedo (AGN, Reales Cédulas 147, #222) is dated Madrid, December 25, 1790. The copy brought by Thomas New is dated May 12, 1791, six weeks before Vancouver left England, because there had been some delay in providing the duplicate either to the British Ambassador in Madrid or to the Spanish Ambassador in London or to the Admiralty.

46 The full text of the letter, dated August 29, is in Bodega's *Viaje*. The letters to Viana, Gray, and Ingraham and their replies can be found in AGN, Historia 67.

47 Excerpts from Vancouver's letters are taken from their translation into Spanish by Thomas Dobson, a midshipman on the *Daedalus*. Quotations from Bodega's letters are translated from what he wrote and recorded in his *Viaje*. See Bernabeu, *Bodega*, p. 184 passim. Bodega had sent home his interpreter, Cepeda, so Dobson performed this service for Bodega as well.

48 He was referring to Núñez Gaona, now Neah Bay.

49 Before leaving for the north, Bodega had written to the viceroy from San Blas (letter #337 of January 14, 1792) to point out that a joint survey might not be necessary, because sufficient information was provided by the charts already made of the coast and of the Strait of Juan de Fuca by Manuel Quimper in 1790 and the Eliza-Narváez expedition of 1791, together with those of the Malaspina expedition. There were some gaps to be filled in to complete the general chart, and he suggested that he would undertake to do this. In his reply, dated February 1, 1792, Revillagigedo told Bodega to do what seemed best, "as you are on the ground." AGN, Historia 67, f. 332.

50 In his memorial, Meares said he had "obtained from Wickininnish, the Chief of the district surrounding Port Cox and Port Effingham ... in consequence of considerable presents, the promise of a free and exclusive trade with the natives, and also his permission to built any storehouses, or other edifices, which he might so judge necessary." Although he never did so, the Spanish thought he had, and Port Cox was included in Floridablanca's Royal Order. Vancouver no doubt based its inclusion in his reply to Bodega on Floridablanca's understanding of the Memorial.

51 See Wagner, *Spanish Explorations in the Strait of Juan de Fuca*, p. 62. Wagner suggests that the map was obtained from an English whaler in the Bay of Paita and conjectured that it was one produced by Alexander Dalrymple, who was at the time the hydrographer of the British East India Company.

52 Bodega to Revillagigedo, "on board the frigate *Santa Gertrudis*, prepared to sail between San Blas and Piedra Blanca," letter #378, February 28, 1791; AGN, Historia 67, f. 574.

53 Revillagigedo does not appear to have considered the matter urgent. His reply to Bodega was dated March 7, 1792 (AGN, Historia 67, f. 575), and he did not report Bodega's query to Minister of State Aranda until October 10, 1792 (letter #118, AGN, Correspondencia de los Virreyes 168, f. 247). He repeated his opinion that it was clear from Article V that the boundary was yet to be agreed on and that Bodega should continue to be guided by Royal Orders and his instructions calling for the border to be determined by a joint survey of the Strait of Juan de Fuca.

54 Their report was given orally but was later confirmed in writing from Monterey. Alcalá Galiano to Bodega, October 22, 1792; AGN, Historia 67, cuaderno 15.

55 At a later time, Revillagigedo commented on Bodega's slight retreat: "Cuadra [sic] changed his mind, thinking he had exceeded his powers and considered it safer to acknowledge his error rather than continue on a course contrary to the true sense of his instructions." Revillagigedo to Alcudia, #162 of April 12, 1793, para. 268; AGN, Correspondencia de los Virreyes I, legajo 173, and AGI, Estado 21.

56 Bodega dates it September 11.

57 Bodega did not transcribe this postscript in his *Viaje*.

58 Vancouver also dated it September 11.

59 It is in his report to the Admiralty on the negotiation (PRO, C.O.5/857), which was published in the annual report of the BC Provincial Archives Department for 1914, hereafter cited as BC Archives Report, V22.

60 That is, the main portion of Yuquot, where the Spanish had erected their buildings and the cross and located their cemetery.

61 "Territories" is plural in the original of Vancouver's letter (C.O. 5/187, f. 16) and in his report of his proceedings to the Admiralty. It is also plural in the copy Bodega forwarded to the Viceroy from Monterey (AGN, Historia 70) and as Bodega recorded it in his *Viaje*. It is singular in Bodega's reply as translated to Vancouver, in Bodega's record of it in his *Viaje*, and in his letter to the viceroy from Monterey.

62 The small cove where Meares had built his hut and the *North West America*.

63 Vancouver said "one hundred yards." A *vara* was about 84 cm.

64 "But comprehending the spirit of the King, my Master, which is to establish a solid peace ... and consulting to remove obstacles which influence discord, far from thinking to continue in *this Port*, I am ready without prejudice to our legitimate rights [singular in Bodega's original letter], nor that of the *Courts better instructed resolves*, generously *to cede to England the houses, gardens, and offices which have with so much labour been constructed* [Vancouver's emphasis]."

65 In a letter to Sir Joseph Banks from Monterey of January 14, 1793. Personal communication from the late Dr. W. Kaye Lamb.

66 Meany, "A New Vancouver Journal," pp. 51-52.

67 Quoted in Harlow, *The Founding of the Second British Empire*, vol. 2, p. 479.

68 Ingraham's seventy-ton *Hope* was a brig. Quoted by Lamb, *The Voyage of George Vancouver*, vol. 2, p. 666.

69 Howell, says Ingraham, was "a gentleman belonging to the *Margaret* who came out in her to write a history of the voyage ... He assisted the Spanish commodore occasionally in negotiating the business by translating letters, etc." Ingraham, *Journal*, entry for September 11.

70 Kaplanoff, *Joseph Ingraham's Journal*, p. 235.

71 This view, with which the author agrees, was expressed in personal discussion by Dr. Donald C. Cutter.

72 See Mariñas, "El Incidente de Nutka."

73 In Tulalip Bay on Whidbey Island.

74 His reply was dated the same day.

75 Lamb, *The Voyage of George Vancouver*, vol. 1, p. 105.

76 Moziño, *Noticias*, p. 88, says that Maquinna referred to Meares as "Liar Meares" (Aita-Aita Meares).

77 He did sell muskets. Cook, *Flood Tide of Empire*, p. 138.
78 The text is in Bodega's *Viaje*; in Bernabeu, *Bodega*, pp. 205-6; and in AHN, Estado 4287.
79 Lamb, *The Voyage of George Vancouver*, vol. 2, p. 677.
80 Meany, "A New Vancouver Journal," p. 55.
81 Lamb, *The Voyage of George Vancouver*, vol. 2, p. 678.
82 To emphasize the point, Vancouver asked Henry Humphrys, one his midshipmen, to make a drawing of Yuquot to show the extent of the small bit of land Bodega had agreed to return. It is depicted between the letters A and B, and when engraved was included in Vancouver's *Voyage*, vol. 1, p. 406. It is reprinted in Lamb, *The Voyage of George Vancouver*, as plate #31 in vol. 2. Bodega also asked his artist, Atanásio Echeverría, to make a similar monochrome drawing. It is the archives of the Ministerio de Asuntos Exteriores, MS 146, #4.
83 Vancouver to Nepean, January 7, 1793, from Monterey; PRO, C.O. 5/187, ff. 75-77v. Reprinted in Lamb, *The Voyage of George Vancouver*, vol. 4, pp. 1578-81.
84 Ibid., vol. 1, pp. 108-9.
85 Harlow, *The Founding of the Second British Empire*, vol. 2, p. 462.

Chapter 11: Leaving Nootka

1 Bodega also wanted to ask Maquinna to search for the murderer of the *Activa*'s cabin boy. See Chapter 9.
2 Vancouver did not get away until October 12, 1792.
3 Lamb, *The Voyage of George Vancouver*, vol. 2, p. 678.
4 The *Adventure* was a small, thirty-four-ton sloop that had been built by Gray during the winter of 1791-92 in a small cove in Clayoquot Sound that Gray called Fort Defiance. It was built with sections and other materials brought in the *Columbia* from Boston. The actual site of Fort Defiance was discovered by Kenneth Gibson of Tofino, BC, in 1966, and subsequently confirmed by an archaeological dig conducted by the University of Victoria.
5 Log of John Boit, in F.W. Howay, *Voyages of the* Columbia, p. 416.
6 On September 23, 1792.
7 Kaplanoff, *Joseph Ingraham's Journal*, p. 239.
8 Ibid.
9 These instructions were recorded in his *Viaje*. See Bernabeu, *Bodega*, p. 208.
10 Today the Makah believe that Serrantes was murdered for having molested some of their women.
11 Although the site of the Spanish construction is known to have been by the small creek that flows into the western end of the bay, no archaeological dig has ever been carried out.
12 Boit, in Howay, *Voyages of the* Columbia, p. 487. On the other hand, Haswell, her captain, thought she was "a good sailor."
13 Bodega's papers regarding the sale, including his copy of the bill of sale and a detailed inventory of sails, cordage, and miscellaneous equipment, are in AGN, Marina 73, expediente 39.
14 Boit, in Howay, *Voyages of the* Columbia, pp. 355, 416-17.

15 Sometimes spelled Horcacitas. The Conde de Revillagigedo's full name was Juan Vicente de Güemes Pacheco de Padilla y Horcacitas.

16 The actual settlement in Monterey began in 1770 when Gaspar de Portolá established the first presidio and the Franciscans Junípero Serra and Juan Crespí opened the mission. The following year, after the site on the Estero River proved unsuitable for agriculture, Serra moved the presidio to the banks of the nearby Carmel River and named it San Carlos Borromeo de Carmelo. Monterey grew slowly. It has been estimated that by the 1790s, there were only 202 people there, both Spanish and Indian. San Francisco had even fewer: 144.

17 AGN, Reales Cédulas 151. Curiously, Bodega does not mention this point in his *Viaje.*

18 Meany, "A New Vancouver Journal," entry for November 1792.

19 All Bodega's letters to the viceroy from Monterey were sent as from the commandant of the Expedition of the Limits, not as the commandant of the San Blas department.

20 Bodega to Revillagigedo, from Monterey, n/n, October 24, 1792; AHN, Estado, legajos 4288 and 4290.

21 Witnesses disagreed on how many cannon defended the bay at this time.

22 On his chart of the bay, which he included in the folio volume of his *Viaje*, he marked *bateria* on a site about midway between the old presidio and Punto Pinos; Spanish Ministry of Foreign Affairs, MS 146, #17. This was close to the present presidio, possibly even in front of it – his chart is not at all precise.

23 Lamb, *The Voyage of George Vancouver*, vol. 2, p. 740.

24 Manby, *Journal*, p. 211.

25 Lamb, *The Voyage of George Vancouver*, vol. 2, p. 740.

26 Ibid. See also Pritchard and Spencer-Hancock, "El Castillo de Monterey."

27 As far as a place he named Point Vancouver, today Washougal. Vancouver allowed Bodega to make a copy of both Whidbey's chart of Gray's Harbour and Broughton's map of the Columbia River. They are in BMAS, MS 146, #19 and #22, respectively.

28 In his *Cartography*, Wagner conjectures it might be the estuary of the Umpqua River. The latitude of 43°56′N on the caption agrees better with Coos Bay, a little to the south.

29 In a deposition made by Salvador Menéndez, the first *piloto* of the *Activa*, in support of Bodega's attempts to obtain reimbursement for his expenses; AGN, Marina 72, f. 65.

30 Meany, "A New Vancouver Journal," entry for November 1792.

31 Manby, *Journal*, p. 208.

32 Eastwood, "Menzies' California Journal," p. 285.

33 Ibid., pp. 287-88.

34 Manby, *Journal*, p. 209.

35 Eastwood, "Menzies' California Journal," p. 283.

36 AGN, Historia 24, anonymous journal of the 1775 voyage, f. 42.

37 Eastwood, "Menzies' California Journal," p. 284.

38 Lamb, *The Voyage of George Vancouver*, vol. 2, p. 733.

39 Eastwood, "Menzies' California Journal," p. 288.

40 Revillagigedo to Valdés, November 30, 1792.

41 See Chapter 8.

42 In his instructions to Alonso de Torres y Guerra, July 18, 1792; AHN, Estado, legajo 4288.

43 Bodega to Revillagigedo, letter #408 of October 24, 1792; AGN, Historia 70, cuaderno 17, ff. 27-62. Bodega addressed a virtually identical letter to Aranda; AHN, Estado, legajo 4287.
44 Bodega to Revillagigedo, from Monterey, October 24, 1792; AHN, Estado, legajo 4288.
45 Revillagigedo, when commenting on what he called Bodega's "reflections" in a report to Aranda, warned the minister he could see no reason to retain Nootka except to be able to keep an eye on the designs of England and other foreign powers and pointed out the difficulties in sustaining an establishment so far north of Alta California. Revillagigedo to Aranda, #120 of November 30, 1792; AGN, Correspondencia de los Virreyes I, legajo 168, ff. 289-95. See Chapter 13.
46 Weatherhead, as one of the witnesses to the purchase of the *Adventure* at Neah Bay, signed its bill of sale. The fullest account of Weatherhead's story can be found in Cepeda's letter to Revillagigedo, January 8, 1793; AGN, Historia 70, cuaderno 25, f. 10.
47 The *Jenny* was a three-masted schooner of seventy-eight tons, owned by Sidenham Teast of Bristol and commanded by James Baker. See F.W. Howay, "A List of Trading Vessels," pp. 111-34.
48 Eastwood, "Menzies' California Journal," p. 113.
49 Newcombe, *Menzies' Journal*, p. 113. See also Chapter 12.
50 Bodega to Revillagigedo from Monterey, letter #417, October 24, 1792; AGN, Historia 70, cuaderno 25, f. 1.
51 Revillagigedo to Bodega, November 25, 1792; AGN, Historia 70, cuaderno 25, f. 2.
52 Revillagigedo to Bodega, November 28, 1792; AGN, Historia 70, cuaderno 25, f. 3.
53 Bodega to Revillagigedo, letter #460, February 15, 1793; AGN, Historia 70, cuaderno 25; f. 42.
54 Bodega to Revillagigedo, letter #434 from Monterey, December 30, 1792; AHN, Estado, legajo 4290, and AGN, Historia 70, cuaderno 25, f. 13.
55 Lamb, *The Voyage of George Vancouver*, vol. 2, p. 728.
56 Ibid., p. 729.
57 Bodega to Revillagigedo from Monterey, December 30, 1792; AHN, Estado 4290, and AGN, Historia 70, cuaderno 25, f. 3. Bodega's letter formed enclosure #2 to his letter #155 to Alcudia, referred to below.
58 Revillagigedo to Bodega, February 8, 1793; AGN, Historia 70, cuaderno 25, f. 17.
59 Revillagigedo to Bodega, February 8, 1793; AHN, Estado, legajo 4290. This letter and Bodega's letter were forwarded to Alcudia under cover of his letter #155 of February 18, 1793. There are copies in AGN, Historia 70, cuaderno 25, f. 15.
60 The first part of Bodega's letter #460 of February 15, dealing with Weatherhead, has been quoted above.
61 In his own journal, Vancouver states on a number of occasions that he was aware that the extra work of preparing his papers and charts for Broughton was delaying Bodega's departure. He also regretted that his lengthy stay in Monterey was delaying his own voyage.
62 Broughton spoke French, and Moziño most likely understood enough for basic conversational purposes.
63 Meany, "A New Vancouver Journal," p. 40.
64 Bodega wrote that he had instructed Sal that Vancouver should not be charged for whatever refreshments he required, adding that he would meet the costs. Menzies

confirms that Sal refused to accept payment, but he did issue a receipt. Eastwood, "Menzies' California Journal," pp. 280-81.

65 Lamb, *The Voyage of George Vancouver*, vol. 2, pp. 742-43.

66 He was later twice given two dozen lashes. Eastwood, "Menzies' California Journal," p. 289.

67 Ibid., p. 789.

68 Lamb, *The Voyage of George Vancouver*, vol. 3, p. 788.

69 Ibid., p. 789.

70 One of the *grumetes,* or cabin boys, deserted in Tahiti. Another was returned in Monterey, where he was put to work as an apprentice armourer, and the third was left at Nootka.

71 Bodega to Argüello on departing Monterey, January 12, 1793; AGN, Marina 98, f. 4.

72 For a list of what Broughton was to take, see Lamb, *The Voyage of George Vancouver*, vol. 3, p. 787, note 2. Vancouver's package included copies of nine Spanish charts, eight of them provided by Bodega and one by Alcalá Galiano. The charts are in the Admiralty's Hydrographic Office in Taunton, Somerset. See also Andrew David, "Debates and Corrections: The List of Charts and Drawings Brought Back to Britain from Monterey by Broughton in 1793," *Terrae Incognitae* 37 (2005).

73 Lamb, *The Voyage of George Vancouver*, vol. 3, p. 792.

74 Menzies wrote: "As soon as [the Spanish Officers] went on board we bore up under the brig's stern, manned ship at midnight and gave them three cheers and then parted." Eastwood, "Menzies' California Journal," entry for January 18, 1793.

75 Vancouver to Revillagigedo, from Monterey, January 13, 1793; AGN, Historia 70, ff. 18-19. This is from a translation made for the viceroy, who may have retained the original in his personal papers.

76 Lamb, *The Voyage of George Vancouver*, vol. 4, p. 1439.

77 Bodega's private correspondence has not been found.

Chapter 12: Results and Consequences of the Expedition of the Limits

1 Revillagigedo to Bodega, November 25, 1792; AHN, Estado, legajos 4288 and 4290.

2 Revillagigedo to Valdés, #20 of October 27, 1790. Revillagigedo to Valdés, November 30, 1792; AGN, Correspondencia de los Virreyes I, legajo 168, ff. 350-52.

3 Royal Order #168 of February 23, 1793, signed by Alcudia, who had just succeeded Aranda as minister of state; AGN, Reales Cédulas, Vol. 154, ff. 215-16.

4 Bodega to Alcudia, June 1, 1793; AHN, Estado, legajo 4289.

5 Revillagigedo to Aranda, #120 of November 30, 1792; AGN, Correspondencia de los Virreyes I, legajo 168, ff. 289-95. Revillagigedo to Valdés, #179 of November 30, 1792; AGN, Correspondencia de los Virreyes II, legajo 25, ff. 237v-241v.

6 Bodega's letters on this subject are dated October 24, 1792, and are to be found in AGN, Historia 70, and AHN, Estado, legajos 4287 and 4288.

7 Bodega to Revillagigedo, October 24, 1792; AHN, Estado, legajo 4288.

8 An inference drawn from Bodega's letter. Eliza's letter was not attached to it.

9 Bodega to Revillagigedo, March 14, 1791; AGN, Histórico de Hacienda, legajo 479.

10 Newcombe, *Menzies' Journal*, entry for September 4.

11 Ibid., entry for September 15.
12 Meany, "A New Vancouver Journal," pp. 305-6.
13 Ibid. p. 232, in Bell's entry for September 11, the same day the two commissioners had their first face-to-face discussion. If Ingraham made his diary entry the same day, his information seems to confirm that Bodega thought agreement had been reached. Howell, who was the historian on board the *Margaret*, kept Ingraham informed of the progress of the negotiations, since he had apparently assisted Bodega "occasionally in negotiating the business by translating letters, etc." Kaplanoff, *Joseph Ingraham's Journal*, p. 234.
14 Moziño classified it as *Lilium Kamschatkense*, describing it as a "scaly, onionlike bulb," and includes it among the "vegetables which providence appears to have provided [the Indians] in order to correct the alkaline imbalance caused by the continuous use of fish and sea food." Moziño, *Noticias*, p. 21. Engstrand also quotes Menzies's journal: "[The Indians are] searching after the Sarane or Roots of *Lilium Camschatcensa* which we knew they collect & use as food here." It is illustrated in the folio volume of Bodega's *Viaje*, Spanish Ministry of Foreign Affairs, MS 146, #35.
15 Moziño said much the same thing. Moziño, *Noticias*, pp. 4-5.
16 It is not clear which river Bodega is referring to.
17 Bodega, *Viaje;* Bernabeu, *Bodega*, pp. 175-77.
18 Bodega to Revillagigedo and Aranda, from Monterey, October 24, 1792; AHN, Estado, legajo 4288.
19 Cook, *Flood Tide of Empire*, pp. 394-95. The document, which is in the Museo Naval, Madrid, MS 575bis, ff. 133-34, appears to be the viceroy's only known, recorded reaction to Bodega's change of opinion.
20 The mouth of the Hoh River in Washington State, where some of the employees of the English fur trader, William Barkley, had been killed in 1787.
21 The mouth of the Columbia River.
22 Possibly the mouth of the Umpqua River or, by latitude, Coos Bay.
23 Either Bodega Bay or Tomales Bay.
24 The large inlet on the north coast of Nootka Island on which the establishment was located.
25 The territory of today's Nimpkish First Nation, on the northern part of Vancouver Island.
26 Barkley Sound.
27 Moziño, *Noticias*, pp. 90-93.
28 Ibid., pp. 93-95.
29 On this phase of Spain's presence on the Northwest Coast, see Archer, "Retreat from the North."
30 The Spanish text can be found, inter alia, in Appendix B of Cook, *Flood Tide of Empire*, and the English text in Manning, "Nootka Sound Controversy," pp. 469-70.
31 Article I called for the restoration of the buildings and tracts of lands that Meares had owned, to the envoy, Vancouver.
32 AGI, Estado, legajo 39(14).
33 Bodega to Revillagigedo, from Tepic, February 15, 1794; AGN, Historia 70. Quoted by Cook, *Flood Tide of Empire*, p. 415.
34 Revillagigedo to Alcudia, #224 of April 30, 1794; AGN, Correspondencia de los Virreyes I, legajo 176.

35 In September 1794. It was then that he learned of Bodega's death and recorded his most fulsome tribute to his diplomatic adversary. See Lamb, *The Voyage of George Vancouver,* vol. 4, pp. 1396-97.

36 Formerly, the ship was called the *Activa.* On returning to San Blas in early 1793, she was reconfigured from a schooner to a brigantine and called the *Activo.* Since *goleta* is feminine in Spanish and *bergantín* is masculine, the ship's name was changed to reflect its new gender..

37 Alava's detailed report of his mission can be found in his letter of April 23, 1795, to Alcudia; AHN, Estado, legajo 4290. Pearce's report to Philip Stephens, the Secretary of the Admiralty, dated from Tepic, April 25, 1795, is found in the Public Records Office, London, H.O. 28/90, and printed in Holmes's article, "Three Nootka Documents," *Oregon Historical Quarterly,* Winter 1978, pp. 397-402.

38 Unless otherwise credited, all citations are from Bodega's *Viaje.*

39 Chapman, *A History of California.*

40 Ibid., pp. 385-86.

41 Abalone shells, found in great numbers in Monterey Bay, were especially desired by the Northwest Coast Indians to adorn masks and headdresses.

42 All the above quotations are from his *Viaje;* Bernabeu, *Bodega,* pp. 182-83.

43 The latitude of the southern tip of the Alaska Panhandle.

44 Knowledge of this scheme was picked up by La Pérouse, who described Vasadre as "a young man full of intelligence and merit." The French explorer also expressed "some surprise that the Spanish ... have overlooked the value of this precious fur." J. Dunmore, *The Journal of Jean-François de Galaup de la Pérouse,* vol. 1, pp. 189, 194. See also Ogden, "The Californias in Spain's Pacific Otter Trade"; and *The California Sea Otter Trade.* For a more recent analysis, see Gibson, "Nootka and Nutria." Gibson's paper incorporates his further research on the subject, considerably revising that part devoted to Spanish participation in his 1992 book, *Otter Skins, Boston Ships, and China Goods.*

45 Martínez to Flores, from Nootka, July 24, 1789, enclosed with Revillagigedo's letter of January 12, 1790, to Antonio Valdés; AGN, Correspondencia de los Virreyes I, legajo 154, and AGI, Estado, Audiencia de México, legajo 1530.

46 Valdés to Revillagigedo, October 19, 1792; AGN, Reales Cédulas, legajo 153, f. 127.

47 Revillagigedo to Valdés, January 30, 1793; AGN, Correspondencia de los Virreyes II, legajo 26. Revillagigedo's judgment may have been coloured by animosity. He had been highly critical of Martínez's handling of the situation at Nootka that summer. Also, Martínez had vigorously objected to the viceroy's having rescinded his appointment as second-in-command of Eliza's expedition to re-establish Nootka in 1790.

48 Gibson, "Nootka and Nutria," p. 150. Details of Malaspina's ideas on the fur trade can be found in the Museo Naval in Madrid, MSS 330 and 335.

49 Gibson, "Nootka and Nutria."

50 Ibid., p. 149.

51 Revillagigedo to Aranda, letter #120 of November 30, 1792; AGN, Correspondencia de los Virreyes I, legajo 168, f. 296.

52 Bodega was aware that the intense rivalry between the British and the Americans was depleting the supply of pelts. In his *Viaje,* he wrote: "The American Gray has ruined this branch of trade by taking the pelts directly and at very low prices with the discovery of the entry to the Nuchimanes. This active trader has covered the better part of the coast ... [and] this year alone he has been able to barter for more than 300 pelts.

His example is not exceptional, because very many other nations have followed him. Thus it seems to me there is not a single point between Cape Mendocino and 52° north which they have not seen, nor a bay they have not been in nor a people with whom they have not dealt." Bodega was apparently able to separate Gray from other wide-ranging fur traders. Gray, in turn, thought highly enough of Bodega to name his son Robert John Don Quadra Gray. Bernabeu, *Bodega*, p. 182.

53 Bodega to Revillagigedo, n/n, from Monterey, October 24, 1792; AHN, Estado, legajo 4288.

54 Bodega to Revillagigedo, letter #409 of October 24, 1792 from Monterey; AGN, Historia 70.

55 Revillagigedo to Alcudia, letter #162 of April 12, 1793, paragraph 211; AGN, Correspondencia de los Virreyes I, legajo 173.

56 Revillagigedo to Aranda, letter #124 of November 30, 1792, classified "reservado"; AHN, Estado, legajo 4290.

57 On the leather jacket, or *cuera*, cavalry, equipped with lances, see René Chartrand, "The Leather Jacket Soldiers: the *Cuera* Cavalry of the American South-West," *Military Illustrated, Past and Present*, London, #53 and #54, October and November 1992.

58 Essentially, the present Mexican states of Durango and Chihauhua.

59 Alcudia to Revillagigedo, February 23, 1793, from Aranjuez; copy in AGN, Californias 9, expediente 19, f. 17.

60 Revillagigedo to Bodega, November 25, 1792. Unless otherwise indicated, all the papers on this matter are in AGN, Californias 9, cuaderno 19.

61 Bodega to Revillagigedo from San Blas, letter #446 of February 9, 1793.

62 Revillagigedo to Bodega, n/n, February 16, 1793.

63 These numbers were broken down by function: guards for the presidios, cavalry, guards for the cattle, prison guards, escorts for the missionaries, couriers, police in the village, transport of supplies, and manpower for general service.

64 Argüello's inventory included nothing more powerful than pistols, muskets, swords, and lances. He seems to have used some imagination while inventorying his arsenals; thirty being his favourite number, it being the number by which many items needed to be augmented.

65 Argüello to Revillagigedo, #101 of July 16, 1793.

66 Bodega to Revillagigedo, letter #468 of February 23, 1793, from Tepic. His very detailed estimate was broken down under headings, including materials, tools, and labour.

67 Bodega to Revillagigedo, from San Blas, letter #455 of March 9, 1793.

68 Revillagigedo to Alcudia, #215 of March 31, 1794; AGN, Correspondencia de los Virreyes I, legajo 176.

69 Revillagigedo to Bodega, March 19, 1793; AHN, Estado, legajo 4290.

70 Bodega to Revillagigedo, n/n, from Tepic, April 9, 1793; AHN, Estado, legajo 4290.

71 Eastwood, "Menzies' California Journal," p. 307.

72 Vancouver to Stephens from Karakakooa Bay, Hawaii, February 8, 1794. The text of this letter is printed in Lamb, *The Voyage of George Vancouver*, vol. 4, p. 1595.

73 The coast between Nootka Sound and Prince William Sound. Bernabeu, *Bodega*, p. 214.

74 See Chapters 6 and 8.

75 Revillagigedo to Bodega, October 29, 1791; AGN, Historia 67, and AHN, Estado, legajo 4287.

76 See Revillagigedo's letters #120 of November 30, 1792, to Aranda, AGN, Correspondencia de los Virreyes II, legajo 23; and #154 of February 18, 1793, to Alcudia, AHN, Estado, legajo 4290.

77 The viceroy's letter and the replies can be found in AGN, Historia 71, cuaderno 31.
78 Revillagigedo to Alcudia, #162, cited above, paragraph 196.
79 Revillagigedo to Alcudia, #162 of April 12, 1793; AGN, Correspondencia de los Virreyes I, legajo 173; AGI, Estado, legajo 21. Printed as appendix 17 in Cárdenas de la Peña, *San Blas de Nayarit.* This important letter is an extensive commentary on Bodega's report as commandant of the Expedition of the Limits.
80 Revillagigedo to Alcudia, letter #154 of February 18, 1793; AHN, Estado, legajo 4290.
81 Bodega to Revillagigedo, letter #439 of February 9, 1793, from San Blas; AGN, Historia 70, cuaderno 23, f. 8.
82 Bodega to Revillagigedo, letter #438 of February 9, 1793, AGN, Historia 70, f. 12.
83 Almost as an afterthought, he added that the officer in command should carefully investigate the coast between Bodega Bay and 48°N, searching for the Rio de Martín de Aguilar, which Malaspina had failed to find.
84 They were enclosed with his letter #160 of March 31, 1793, to Alcudia; AHN, Estado, legajo 4290.
85 Bodega to Revillagigedo, letter #493 of March 24, 1793; AGN, Historia 71, ff. 184-85v.
86 Revillagigedo to Alcudia, #162 of April 12, 1793, paragraphs 194 and 196.
87 Translation by Wagner in his article, "The Last Spanish Exploration of the Northwest Coast." Much of what follows regarding this expedition is based on this valuable essay, which also includes Wagner's translation of the accounts of Eliza and Zayas as well as other related documents.
88 Revillagigedo to Bodega, March 30, 1793; AGN, Historia 71, f. 186r-v.
89 Zayas's chart is listed as #821 in Wagner's *Cartography.* The copy that Bodega included in the atlas portfolio of his *Viaje,* MS 146, #22, was made from Vancouver's chart.
90 Wagner suggests this might have been about the same spot where Gray ran aground.
91 However, Wagner lists as #824 a chart that Zayas made of the bay.
92 On the confusion that has existed over the various place names of the area, see Edwards, "Wandering Toponyms."
93 Reproduced in Wagner, "The Last Spanish Exploration"; and in his *Cartography,* plate XL.
94 By November, Bodega was in Guadalajara, so ill that he drew up last his will on the 13th.
95 See Revillagigedo's letter #154 of February 18, 1793, to Alcudia. Zayas does not mention having searched for it.
96 The only known part of it was the section charted by Bodega himself in 1775, Puerto de la Bodega, to which he had given his own name. Matute's entire instructions can be found in AGN, Historia 70, cuaderno 23, ff. 27-36.
97 Matute's report was published in translation by Wagner, "The Last Spanish Exploration." There is also an anonymous summary in Museo Naval, Madrid, MS 332.

Chapter 13: Endings

1 María Marín del Valle's will is in the archives of the Audiencia of Guadalajara, in the *protocolos* of José Antonio Mallén.
2 Her three executors were her brother-in-law, Canon José Antonio Dávalos, who had been Bodega's confessor in his last days, her brother Miguel, and her priest.
3 The will is in the *protocolos* of Martín Román, vol. 3, ff. 3v-6, also in the archives of the

Audiencia de Guadalajara. I am indebted to Sr. Pedro Franco López of Guadalajara for locating the wills of María Marín and her son.

4 AGN, Reales Cédulas 142, f. 237.

5 Irving Leonard, ed., "Voyage of Amedée Frezier to South America (1712–1714)," in *Colonial Travelers in Latin America* (New York: Knopf, 1972).

6 Ignacio de Arteaga y Bazán's career was put on hold after it became known that he had formed a relationship with a Cuban woman in 1771. In 1780, Bruno de Hezeta had trouble securing a widow's pension for the woman he had married without permission.

7 Fireman, "The Strange Career of Alejandro Jordán." The relevant documents are in AGN, Californias 78, cuaderno 1, ff. 297-330, and Marina 70, expediente 6, ff. 41-52.

8 Bodega to Revillagigedo, June 25, 1791; AGN, Californias 78, f. 330r-v.

9 Revillagigedo to Valdés, #217 of April 30, 1793; AGN, Correspondencia de los Virreyes II, legajo 26, ff. 247-48.

10 Museo Naval, Madrid, MS 675.

11 Bernabeu, *Juan Francisco de la Bodega y Quadra*, p. 25. The letter is dated March 2, 1773, and is in the Archivo General de Simancas, Marina 37. Writing in Madrid, Bodega had asked for special leave to travel to Veracruz, Mexico, where his father had some business interests. The request was refused.

12 In a personal communication, Jorge Ortiz Sotelo has stated that when Juan Francisco was in Lima in 1763, he gave his father a general power of attorney, receiving at the same time an advance on his inheritance. His father's will was altered to record this advance.

13 Ortiz Sotelo, p.145.

14 Bodega to Mayorga, November 28, 1779; AGI, Estado, México 1.

15 Petition to José de Gálvez, when Bodega was in Madrid, dated August 13, 1785; AGI, Estado, Guadalajara 520.

16 Haring, *Spanish Empire in America*, p. 130 n17. Haring refers to the *fiscal* as a Crown attorney and defines the position as a "sort of royal watchdog who defended the king's interests wherever they might appear, but especially in cases affecting the exchequer, the Church, and the rights of Indians. He also tendered legal advice to the viceroy or governor in matters of administration."

17 Eastwood, "Menzies' California Journal," entry for May 20, 1793. Cited by Lamb, *The Voyage of George Vancouver*, vol. 2, p. 743.

18 The author has been unable to uncover in any of the relevant AGN *tomos* any statements about such repayments and what they amounted to.

19 In his service file in the El Viso archive.

20 Bodega to Mayorga, November 28, 1779; AGI, Estado, México 1.

21 AHN, Estado, legajo 2855; cited by Harbron, *Trafalgar and the Spanish Navy*, p. 87.

22 Bodega to José de Gálvez, letter #188 of November 28, 1779; AGI, Estado, México 1.

23 Bodega to Mayorga, November 28, 1779; AGI, Estado, México 1.

24 Bodega to Revillagigedo, from Monterey, letter #432 of October 24, 1792; AGN, Historia 70.

25 Aranda to Bodega, February 23, 1793; AHN, Estado, legajo 4287.

26 Bodega to the King of Spain, May 25, 1793; AGI, Estado, México 1.

27 Beltran to Revillagigedo, September 17, 1793; AGN, Marina 73, ff. 56-61.

28 The receipt is in AGN, Marina 73, f. 50, together with Bodega's note dated July 13, 1793, to the effect that he asked for it to be placed in the file of his debts to show that

a vessel of this size could not be built in San Blas for this amount. He had earlier obtained from Arteaga, the acting *constructor*, an estimate that to build the same vessel in San Blas would have cost 8,000 pesos.

29 Actually, the total for San Francisco was 1,680 pesos and for Monterey 5,850 pesos, or 7,830 pesos altogether.

30 Bodega to Revillagigedo, November 4, 1793; AGN, Marina 73, ff. 68-69v.

31 Gardoqui to Revillagigedo, Royal Order of June 6, 1793; AGI, Estado, Guadalajara 493.

32 Revillagigedo to Valdés, August 30, 1793; AGN, Marina 73.

33 At about this time, the viceroy would have received the nine-page undated *instancia* (memorial) from Jordán in his capacity as executor of Bodega's estate, justifiying Bodega's claims and requesting that any reimbursement be assigned to the estate.

34 Revillagigedo to Alcudia, #222 of April 30, 1794; AGN, Correspondencia de los Virreyes, legajo 176; AHN, Estado, legajo 4290; and AGI, Estado, Guadalajara 493.

35 A note to this effect from Valdés to Gardoqui, dated September 30, 1794, in AGI, Estado, Guadalajara 493, indicates that their consultation took place at that time.

36 The Royal Order was dated November 6, 1794; AGN, Marina 72, f. 100. On its receipt, Branciforte referred it to the Fiscal de la Real Hacienda for action.

37 This was not actually true. Juan Francisco's youngest brother, Manuel, then in Spain, did not die until 1835.

38 Santelier to the *fiscal*, October 18, 1799. The relevant documents are in AGN, Marina 73, ff. 110-13.

39 See Archer, "In Defence of the King's Domain."

40 Bodega to Bucareli, April 12, 1778; AGN, Provincias Internas 212, f. 244r-v. I am grateful to the late Vivian C. Fisher, formerly of the Bancroft Library, Berkeley, for drawing this document to my attention.

41 Archer cites the journal of Father Riobo, one of the chaplains on the *Princesa*, wherein he recounts that during one violent storm the medicine chest "was thrown about and the greater part of its syrups, essential oils and medicines were lost." This misfortune may possibly account for the high loss of lives on the command ship.

42 In his petition to the king from Havana, cited in note 18 above.

43 Bodega to Revillagigedo, letter #235 of June 4, 1791; AGN, Archivo Histórico de Hacienda, legajo 479, ff. 19-20.

44 Revillagigedo to Bodega, June 20, 1791; ibid., f. 3.

45 Bodega to Revillagigedo, letter #261 of August 13, 1791; AGN, Archivo Histórico de Hacienda, legajo 479, f. 34.

46 Kaplanoff, *Joseph Ingraham's Journal*, entry for August 1, 1792.

47 Menzies to Banks, from Nootka Sound, September 26, 1792; printed in Lamb, *The Voyage of George Vancouver*, vol. 4, p. 1618.

48 Bodega to Revillagigedo, letter #432 of October 24, 1792; AGN, Historia 70.

49 Bodega to Revillagigedo, from Tepic, February 15, 1793; AGN, Historia 70.

50 Bodega to Revillagigedo, letter #492 of March 24, 1793; AGN, Provincias Internas 3, f. 362.

51 Revillagigedo to Bodega, March 30, 1793; AGN, Provincias Internas 3, f. 363.

52 Bodega to Revillagigedo, letter #501 of April 9, 1793; AGN, Provincias Internas 3, f. 364r-v.

53 Revillagigedo to Bodega, April 16, 1793; AGN, Provincias Internas 3, f. 365.

54 Bodega to Hijosa, April 16, 1793; AGN, Provincias Internas 3, f. 366.

55 Bodega to Revillagigedo, from Tepic, #602 of October 11, 1793; AGN, Californias 15, expediente 1. All of the following documents will be found in this *expediente*, or file.

56 Dávalos to Revillagigedo, November 5, 1793.
57 Revillagigedo to Dávalos, November 12, 1793.
58 This is according to the statement Jordán made to the official investigating Bodega's belongings. Sr. Pedro Franco López, a professional researcher familiar with the *protocolos* in the Guadalajara archives, has been unable to find this will. He stated in a personal communication dated March 26, 1990, that "Bodega drew up a document privately which was to have been converted into a legal will before a notary, but this never came to pass." Nowhere has this author found any evidence that Bodega died of a seizure in Guadalajara, as stated by Cook and Thurman, cited above.
59 See Gutíerrez, *San Blas y las Californias*, p. 143.
60 These institutions are the Sagrario de Guadalajara, the Santuario de Nuestra Señora de Guadalupe, the Hospital de Betlemitas, and Camposanto de Belén.
61 This is according to José Gómez Moreno (1732-1800) in his "Diario curioso y Cuaderno de las Cosas memorables en México durante el Gobierno de Revillagigedo (1789-1794)," published by the Universidad Autónoma de México (1986). Item 461 reads: "En México en el Convento de San Fernando se enterró el Coronel [sic] y Comandante del Departamento de San Blas, don Juan de la Quadra [sic]." When in Mexico City in 1986, the author was unable to locate Bodega's grave, possibly because many churches and cemeteries were severely vandalized in the anticlerical disturbances of the 1860s.
62 Revillagigedo to Valdés, #286 of March 31, 1794; Bodega's service file in the El Viso archive.
63 Revillagigedo to Alcudia, March 30, 1794: AHN, Estado 4290.
64 Naish, *The Interwoven Lives of George Vancouver*, p. 321.
65 Letter from Naish to the author, November 27, 1996.
66 The viceroy's order is dated May 10, 1794. All the documents are in AGN, Historia 153, expediente 27, ff. 360-88. They were printed in the *Boletín del Archivo General de la Nación* 27, no. 2 (1956).
67 This inventory invites the intriguing question as to why Bodega's technical books and files were taken on a journey that was almost certain to end with his death.
68 Sessé was the director of the Royal Scientific Expedition to New Spain. Bodega had arranged with him to have Moziño assigned to the Expedition of the Limits.
69 A *reloj de observación* is possibly a clock with a predetermined time setting.
70 Díaz had been brought to San Blas from Peru by Bodega on the *Favorita* in 1777-78 and had served under him as chaplain on the *Favorita* during the 1779 expedition. Bodega wanted to take him to Nootka Sound on the *Activa* in 1792, but as had happened to others, his health had been "broken" on the earlier expedition and he could no longer serve at sea. The last phrase is ambiguous: Was the debt owing to Díaz or to Bodega's two servants, or perhaps even to María Marín and his natural son by her?
71 He is referred to in the documents of the investigation as "Presbítero capellán de la Real Armada."
72 The complete set of silver plate, when at the Nootka post, was sufficient to serve twenty-four.
73 The documentation on this matter is in AGN, Provincias Internas 89, expediente 34, ff. 340-58.
74 Jordán asked that his list also be forwarded to the viceroy.
75 The documents on this matter are in AGN, Californias 37, ff. 179-85v.
76 The price of the Arnold chronometer was £84; the small chronometer £47, 15 shillings,

and sixpence; the Ramsden sextant £19, 9 shillings; the artificial horizon £2, 12 shillings, and sixpence; and the shirts £78, 4 shillings, and sixpence. Broughton to Bodega, in French, from London, July 28, 1793; AGI, Estado, legajo 39.

77 This is according to Jordán in the investigation of Bodega's possessions. In the same letter, written in the most cordial terms, Broughton had expressed the hope that he and Bodega would meet again at Nootka Sound so that he could deliver everything to him personally. When Broughton returned to England, he was given command of the *Providence* on a voyage that ultimately took him to the Northwest Coast and into the southwest Pacific. His departure was much delayed, and he did not reach Nootka until March 1796, there to learn that Bodega was dead and to find that the Spanish had gone.

78 Lamb, *The Voyage of George Vancouver*, vol. 4, pp. 1396-97.

79 Ibid.

Appendix A

1 The name was changed to Cook Inlet by George Vancouver.

2 Revillagigedo's order to explore the Strait of Juan de Fuca was not repeated.

Appendix B

1 The viceroy meant Nueva España, or New Spain.

2 That is, the new establishment.

Appendix C

1 María del Pilar de San Pío de Aladrén, "El Diario de 1792 de Juan Francisco de la Bodega y Quadra," in Peset, *Culturas del Noroeste de América,* p. 291.

2 Bodega to Aranda, February 9, 1793; AHN, Estado, legajo 4289.

3 Revillagigedo to Alcudia, #154 of February 18, 1793; AGN, Historia 67.

4 Revillagigedo to Alcudia, #164 of April 12, 1793; AGN, Historia 67.

5 The full citation can be found in the Bibliography.

6 The only complete set of copies is in the Spanish Ministry of Foreign Affairs, MS 146.

7 A companion chart prepared at this time and also dedicated to the viceroy showed the routes of all the Spanish expeditions from Pérez's in 1774 to Bodega's in 1792 and is accompanied by twenty detailed sectional maps. It is the single most important testimonial of the extent to which Spanish mariners explored the waters of the Northwest Coast of America.

8 Iris Engstrand has identified the artists who completed these sketches. They are listed in footnote 77 of her edition and translation of Moziño's *Noticias de Nutka.* For the credentials of some of these artists, see Donald C. Cutter, "Early Spanish Artists on the Northwest Coast," *Pacific Northwest Quarterly,* October 1963, pp. 150-57.

9 C.F. Newcombe, ed., *Menzies' Journal of Vancouver's Voyage,* p. 128.

10 It should be noted that of the three extant copies of the *Viaje,* the ones in the Spanish

Ministry of Foreign Affairs and in the Huntington Library, are signed in Bodega's name by the copyist and certified by Antonio Bonilla, Revillagigedo's secretary. The Library of Congress copy is also signed by the copyist, but it is not certified. As it was the practice at the time for the commandant of a ship or an expedition to sign the original of his *diario*, it is possible that a fourth copy, signed personally by Bodega, existed somewhere, but if that is so, it has probably been lost forever. A careful examination of the three extant copies reveals only minor inconsequential differences, no doubt due to copyist error.

11 The copy left with the minister is MS 145.

12 *Planos geográficos y dibujos para ilustrar el Diario de D. Juan Francisco de la Bodega y Quadra*, MS 146. These have recently been reproduced in Palau et al., eds., *Nutka 1792*, together with Bodega's *Viaje*, by the Dirección General de Relaciones Culturales y Científicas of the Spanish Ministry of Foreign Affairs, 1998.

13 The Huntington Library classification is HM 141.

14 Personal communication from Mr. William P. Frank, curator of Hispanic Cartographic and Western Manuscripts, Huntington Library.

15 See Kraus's catalogue No. 144, *The American West Coast and Alaska: Original Drawings and Maps from the Expedition to Nootka Sound of Juan Francisco de la Bodega y Quadra, 1792*. Library of Congress, MS 19519. It was first offered to the National Archives of Canada, which declined to purchase it, considering the asking price of $65,000 too high. It thus lost a unique opportunity to acquire an important document of Canadian history. An informal approach by the author to the Archives of British Columbia brought the same result.

16 Of this second set of copies of Echeverría's drawings, those of four Nootka Indians and five scenes of Nootkan life were purchased by the Government of Canada's Canadian Parks Service, located in Ottawa. Charts of Nootka Sound, the Strait of Juan de Fuca, the Columbia River, and Gray's Harbour, as well as Bodega's general chart of the entire coast of 1793, were acquired by the Oregon Historical Society, Portland. The chart of San Francisco Bay was acquired by the Bancroft Library, Berkeley. I have been unable to determine the whereabouts of any of the other charts or other copies of Echeverría's drawings of fish, birds, and plants.

17 Personal communication from Dr. Iris W. Engstrand.

Bibliography

Listed below is a selection of documents, monographs, and articles that have proven valuable for the present study.

For further reference, extensive bibliographies are to be found in Warren Cook, *Flood Tide of Empire* (q.v.); in Mercedes Palau et al., ed., *Nutka 1792* (q.v.); and in Mary Gormly, "Early Culture Contact on the Northwest Coast, 1774-1795: Analysis of Spanish Source Material," *Northwest Anthropological Research Notes* 11, no. 1: 1-80 (Spring 1977).

Archival Sources

Archivo General de Indias, Seville

Section V: Audiencia de México
Section V: Audiencia de Guadalajara
Section IX: Papeles de Estado
Indiferente General
Mapas y Planos: México

Ministry of Foreign Affairs, Madrid

MSS 10, 11, 145, 146

Real Academia de la Historia, Madrid

MS 12-26-4-D-91

Biblioteca del Palacio Real, Madrid

MSS 299, 324-8, 1930

Biblioteca Nacional de Madrid

MS 19266

Archivo del Museo Naval, Madrid

MSS 126, 127, 271, 280, 317, 330, 331, 332, 335, 385, 575, 575bis, 618, 619, 622, 675, 999, 1073, 1163, 1533, 2011, 2012, 2111, 10096

Archivo Histórico Nacional, Madrid

Papeles de Estado
Ordenes Militares, Santiago

Archivo-Museo Don Alvaro de Bazán, El Viso del Marqués, Ciudad Real

Service files of Ignacio de Arteaga y Bazán, Juan Bautista de Aguirre, Juan Manuel de Ayala y de Aranza, Juan Francisco de la Bodega y Quadra, José Camacho, Jacinto Caamaño Moraleja, José de Cañizares, Félix de Cepeda y Mayo, Diego Choquet de Isla y Suárez de Figueroa, Franciso de Eliza y Rebenga, Salvador Fidalgo y Lopegarcía, Dionisio Alcalá Galiano, Gonzalo López de Haro, Bruno de Hezeta y Dudagoitia, Miguel Manrique del Lara y Bara, Juan Martínez y Zayas, Juan Bautista Matute y Corres, Salvador Menéndez, Francisco Antonio Mourelle de la Rua, José María Narváez, Juan Pantoja y Arriaga, Juan Antonio Pérez, Manuel Quimper Benítez del Pino, Ramón Saavedra y Guiraldez, Antonio Serantes, Cayetano Valdés y Flores

Archivo General de Simancas, Valladolid

Marina

Archivo Histórico de Hacienda, Mexico City

Archivo General de la Nación, Mexico City

Californias
Correspondencia de los Virreyes I
Correspondencia de los Virreyes II
Historia
Mapas y Planos
Marina
Misiones
Provincias Internas
Reales Cédulas

Bancroft Library, Berkeley

Cepeda, Félix de. "Memoria de los Viages Europeas a la Costa Noroeste de América Septentrional." Vol. 1, ff. 82-86; catalogue 81/67 cp.

The Bancroft Library also has an almost complete set of microfilms of the AGN ramos listed above.

Huntington Library, San Marino, California

HM141, HM161, HM327, HM730

British Columbia Archives, Victoria

Translation by Mary Elizabeth Daylton of various documents from the AGN (ramos Historia, Provincias Internas, Californias, Marina), relating to Spanish voyages at the end of the eighteenth century: A/A/10/M57t.
Microfilms of the above ramos

Public Archives of Canada, Ottawa

Microfilm copies of AHN legajos 4280, 4286, 4287, 4288, 4290, 4291

Diarios of the Bodega Expeditions

The Hezeta-Bodega Expedition of 1775

Bodega y Quadra, Juan Francisco de la. "Navegación hecha por don Juan Francisco de la Bodega y Quadra, Teniente de Fragata de la Real Armada y Comandante de la Goleta *Sonora* a los descubrimientos de los mares y costa septentrional de California. Año de 1775." AGN, Historia 324 (signed by Bodega and possibly in his own handwriting). Other copies: AMN, MS 622; published in *Colección de diarios y relaciones para la historia de viajes y descubrimientos,* vol. 2 (Madrid: Instituto Histórico de la Marina, 1943), 102-33; also published in Bernabeu Albert, *Juan Francisco de la Bodega y Quadra*; BP, MSS de América 622-1; RAH, 12-26-4-D91; Bancroft (hectograph copy); HL, HM 161; published as Herbert K. Beals, trans and ed., "The 1775 Journal of Juan Francisco de la Bodega y Quadra," In Herbert Beals, Roy Bridges, R.J. Campbell, Anna Savours, and Anita McConnell (eds.), *Four Travel Journals: The Americas, Antarctica, and Africa, 1775-1874* (Burlington, VT: Ashgate, Hakluyt Society. 2007).

Campa Cos, Miguel de la. "Journal of the Voyage I Made on His Majesty's Frigate Called the *Santiago* from the Harbour of San Blas for New Discovery along the Coast of Monterey as far as 50°." AGN, Historia 324. Other copies: AGI, Audiencia de Guadalajara 515; Bancroft (hectograph copy); published in John Galvin (ed.), *A Journal of Explorations: Northward along the Coast from Monterey in ... 1775* (San Francisco: John Galvin, 1964).

Hezeta, Bruno de. "Diary of the Voyage Made by First Lieutenant of the Royal Navy, Don Bruno de Hezeta, to Explore the Northern Coast of California in the year 1775." AGN, Historia 324, published in Herbert K. Beals (trans., ed.), *For Honor and Country* (Portland: Oregon Historical Society Press, 1985). Other copies: AGI, Estado 1:19; Bancroft (hectograph copy); AGI Estado 38, doc. 11; AHN, Estado 2314; AMN, MSS 127, 331, 575.

Mourelle de la Rua, Francisco Antonio. "Segunda Exploración de la Costa Septentrional de California hecha en 1775 en la Fragata *Santiago* y Goleta *Sonora* mandadas por el Teniente de Navío Don Bruno Ezeta [sic], y el de Fragata Don Juan de la Quadra [sic] desde el Puerto de San Blas hasta los 58 grados de latitud N" (handwritten copy of the original), RAH, MS 12-26-4-D-91. Other copies: HL, HM 161; AGN, Historia 324 (two copies); AMN, MSS 332 and 575 (published in Landín Carrasco, *Mourelle de la Rua: Explorador del Pacífico*, 171-215); AGI, Estado 38, doc. 5; Bancroft (hectograph copy); translation into English, *The Voyage of the* Sonora, by Daines Barrington, was originally published in 1781 as part of Barrington's *Miscellanie*, in 1920 by T.C. Russell, San Francisco, and again by Ye Galleon Press, Fairfield, Washington, in 1987 under the title *The Voyage of the* Sonora.

Sierra, Benito de la. "Diario." Library of Congress. Published in Henry R. Wagner (Introduction and notes) and A.J. Baker (trans.), "Fray Benito de la Sierra's account [*Diario*] of the Hezeta expedition to the Northwest Coast in 1775," *California Historical Society Quarterly* 9, no. 3 (Sept. 1930): 201-42.

The 1776 Voyage to Peru

Bodega y Quadra, Juan Francisco de la. "Viaje hecho a la América Meridional desde el Puerto de Sn. Diego de Acapulco y Regreso del Callao de Lima al Puerto de San Blas de Orcen del Exmo. Señor B. Frey don Antonio Bucareli y Ursúa, Virey Capitán General del Reyno de Nueva Ezpaña por Don Juan Francisco de la Bodega y Quadra del Orden de Santiago y Teniente de Navío de la Real Armada. Año de 1776." AGN, Californias 8, ff. 116-29.

The Arteaga-Bodega Expedition of 1779

Aguirre, Juan Bautista de. "Diario." AGI, Estado 39, doc. 18. Other copies: Bancroft (hectograph copy); AGN, Historia 64.

Arteaga, Ignacio de. "Diario de la navegación, que con el favor de Dios y de la Virgen de la Regla espera hacer el Teniente de Navío Don Ignacio de Arteaga, mandando la Fragata de S.M. *Nuestra Señora del Rosario*, alias la *Princesa*, desde el Puerto de San Blas que está en los 21 grados 30 minutos de latitud N. hasta los 70 de la misma especie a exploraciones de las costas septentrionales de la California, llevándole sus ordenes a la Fragata *Favorita*, mandada por el de la misma clase don Juan Francisco de la Bodega y Quadra." AGN, Historia 63. Other copies: AGI, Estado 38, doc. 13; Bancroft (hectograph copy); AMN, MSS 622, 331 (published in the series *Colección de diarios y relaciones para la historia de los viajes y descubrimientos*, Consejo Superior de Investigaciones Científicas, Instituto Histórico de la Marina, Madrid, vol. 7, 1975, ed. Agustín Albarracín and Roberto Barreiro-Meiro); AMN 575bis.

Bodega y Quadra, Juan Francisco de la. "Navegación y descubrimientos hechos de orden de S[u] M[ajestad] en la costa septentrional de California desde la latitud en que se halla el Departamento y puerto de San Blas de 21 grados, 30 minutos, hasta los 61 grados por el teniente de navío de la Real Armada don Juan Francisco de la Bodega y Quadra, del orden de Santiago y comandante de la fragata de Su Majestad *Nuestra Señora de los Remedios*, alias la *Favorita*, de 39 codos de quilla y 13 de manga, calada de popa en 14 pies y de proa en 13. Año de 1779." AMN, MSS 332, 575. Other copies: AGN, Historia 64; BN, MS 19226 (published in *Colección Chimalistac de los libros y documentos acerca de la Nueva España, notas y documentos acerca de la California 1764-1795*, vol. 5, Madrid: Instituto Histórico de Marina, 1959); AGI, Estado 38, doc. 15; Bancroft (hectograph copy); published in Bernabeu Albert, *Juan Francisco de la Bodega y Quadra*, pp. 111-58.

–. "Método de la navegación que conjeturo convendrá se observe para seguir los descubrimientos de la costa septentrional de la California, pues no obstante que por los acuerdos del diario se puede colegir, me ha parecido conveniente extraer una breve recopiliación de lo que juzgo conducente al acierto y brevedad de los viajes por evitar prolija precisión de enterarse de cuanto ha ocurrido." AGN, Historia 63, ff. 158-61v. Published in Bernabeu Albert, *Juan Francisco de la Bodega y Quadra*, appendix 1.

–. "Derrota que deberán seguir las embarcaciones destinadas a la exploración de la costa septentrional de California, formada con atención a las cartas construidas sobre los viajes de los rusos, tanto por la impresa por Monsieur Bellín en al año de 1766, como por las construidas en la Historia de Californias y otras en las Academia Imperial de Petns.burg (San Petersburgo), e igualmente bajo las noticias y práctica que adquirieron el teniente de navío don Juan Francisco de la Bodega y Quadra en la goleta de su mando en el mismo viaje de exploración del año 1776 [sic] y el alférez de fragata don Francisco Antonio Mourelle, piloto de ella; suponiendo que los rumbos que aquí se expresan son corregidos." AMN, MS 332, ff. 178-79. Published in Bernabeu Albert, *Juan Francisco de la Bodega y Quadra*, appendix 2.

Camacho, José. "Diario de Navegación que con favor de Dios y de su Santísima Madre pretende hacer el primer Piloto del número de la Real Armada Don Joseph Camacho embarcado en la Fragata de Su Majestad *Nuestra Señora del Pilar*, alias *La Princesa* desde el Puerto de San Blas que está por la Latitud norte de 21°30 y 88° y 5 al Oeste del Meridiano de Tenerife hasta los 70° de latitud de la misma especie, a fin de reconocer las Costas Septentrional de la California mandada dicha Fragata por el Teniente de Navío Don Ignacio Arteaga debajo de cuyo mando navega tembien la Fragata de Su Majestad nombrada *La Favorita* su Capitán el Teniente de Navío Don Juan Francisco de la Bodega y Quadra." AGN, Historia 64. Other copies: AGI, Estado 38, doc. 16; Bancroft (hectograph copy).

–. *Diario* of his voyage to Peru with Bodega in 1782-3. AGN, Californias 47.

Cañizares, José de. "Diario de Navegación que hizo el Alférez de Fragata graduado y Primer Piloto Dn. José de Cañizares desde el Puerto de San Blas, situado en 25 grados 30 minutos de latitud Norte a los descubrimientos de la Costa Septentrional de California en la Fragata de S.M. *Nuestra Señora de los Remedios*, alias la *Favorita* de 39 codos de quilla, y de manga 13 codos, cala de Popa 14 pies y de Proa 13 de la que es Comandante el Teniente de Navío de la Rl. Armada y Cavallero del Orden Santiago Dn. Juan Francisco de la Bodega y Quadra, en conserva de la Fragata de S.M. la *Princesa* del mando del de la misma clase Dn. Ignacio Arteaga, Comandante de la Expedición. Año de 1779." AGN, Historia 64. Other copies: AGI, Estado 38, doc. 17; Bancroft (hectograph copy).

Mourelle de la Rua, Francisco Antonio. "Navegación hecha por el Alférez de Fragata de la Real Armada Don Francisco Antonio Mourelle, destinado de segundo capitán de la Fragata *Favorita* de 40 codos de quillla, 13 de manga, calada de Popa 74 pies, 73 idem de Proa, desde el Puerto de San Blas que está en la latitud de 21 grados 30 minutos Norte, y a al Occidente de París 107 grados 6 minutos en longitud a los descubriemientos de la Costa septentrional de Californias que se estendieron hasta la altura de 61 grados 00 minutos, y al Occidente de Paris 157 40′." AGN, Californias 8. Other copies: AGN, Historia 374, typescript in Bancroft; AMN, MSS 331, 575, and 622; AMN MS 331 published in Landín Carrasco, *Mourelle de la Rua: Explorador del Pacifico*, pp. 219-69.

–. "Tercera Exploración hecha en el año de 1779 ... por Don Juan Francisco de la Bodega y Quadra" (summary manuscript of Mourelle's *Navegación*). AMN, MS 332. Also available, in another version, in the William Andrews Clark Memorial Library, University of California, Los Angeles, MS México 453-M3-R382.

Pantoja y Arriaga, Juan. "Diario de Navegación que con el Favor de Dios y de su Santísima Madre principia a hacer Juan Pantoja y Arriaga, segundo piloto de la Fragata de Su Majestad *Nuestra Señora del Rosario*, alias la *Princesa* que salió el doce de febrero de mil setecientos setenta y nueve del Puerto de San Blas ... a seguir la Exploración de las Costas Septentrionales de Californias en conserva de la Fragata de Su Majestad la *Favorita* mandada por el Teniente de Navío Don Juan Francisco de la Bodega y Quadra; siendo el Comandante de las dos el de igual clase Don Ignacio de Arteaga, y el primero Piloto de Derrota don Josef Camacho." AGN, Historia 64. Other copies: AGI, Estado 38, legajo 19; Bancroft (hectograph copy).

Quirós y Miranda, Fernando Bernardo. "Diario de la Navegacíon que con el favor de Dios espera hazer el Teniente de Navío de la Real Armada y Segundo Capitán de esta Expedición de Altura Don Fernando Bernardo Quirós y Miranda, embarcado en la Fragata *Nuestra Señora del Rosario la Marinera*; alias *La Princesa* del mando del de la misma clase Don Ignacio Arteaga, a cuyas ordenes va también la Fragata *Favorita*, mandada por el de igual clase Don Juan Francisco de Bodega y Quadra, con ordenes una y otra de llegar en Conserva á los siete [*sic*] grados de Latitud al Norte de California, y venir desde ellos reconociendo la Costa, tomando quantas posesiones se pueda." AGN, Historia 64. Other copies: AGI, Estado 38, legajo 14; Bancroft (hectograph copy).

Riobo, Juan Antonio García. "An Account of the voyage made by Father John Riobo, as Chaplain of His Majesty's Frigates *la Princesa* and *la Favorita* to discover new Lands and Seas north of the Settlements of the Ports of Monterey and of our Father, San Francisco, whose Missions are in charge of the Apostolic Missionaries of the College of San Fernando of Mexico," ed. and trans. by Walter Thornton, S.J. *Catholic Historical Review* 4 (1918-19): 222-29 (MS in University of Santa Clara, California).

Bodega y Quadra, *Comento*

Bodega y Quadra, Juan Francisco. "Comento de la Navegacíon y descubrimientos hechos en dos Viages de Orden de S.M. en la Costa Septentrional de California, desde la Latitud de 22 grados 30 minutos en que se halla el Departmento de San Blas, por D. Juan Franco. de la Bodega y Quadra del Orden de Santiago, y Capitán de Navío de la Rl. Armada." AMN, MS 618, published in the *Annuario de la Dirección de Hidrografía*, Madrid, 1865: 279-93. Other copies: typewritten translation by G.F. Barwick (1911) in BCA; AHN, Estado, legajo 4291; typescript in Bancroft.

The Expedition of the Limits, 1792

Bodega y Quadra, Juan Francisco de la. "Viaje a la Costa Noroeste de la América Septentrional por Juan Francisco de la Bodega y Quadra, del orden de Santiago, Capitán de Navio de la Real Armada y Comandante del Departamento de San Blas, en las fragatas de su mando *Santa Gertrudis, Aránzazu, Princesa* y goleta *Activa*. Año de 1792." BMAS, MSS 10, 11, 145, and MS 146. Other copies: Library of Congress MS 19519. Published in Bernabeu Albert, "Bodega y Quadra o el instante frágil," and *Nootka 1792*. English translation: HL, HN 141.

Bell, Edward. Private journal of Edward Bell, now in the Alexander Turnbull Library in Wellington, New Zealand. Extensive portions relating to Nootka and Monterey published in Meany, Edmond S., ed., "A New Vancouver Journal on the Discovery of Puget Sound by a Member of the *Chatham*'s Crew," *Washington Historical Quarterly* 5 (1914), pp. 221-24, 301-8, and 6 (1915), pp. 50-68. Republished as Edmond S. Meany, *Vancouver's Discovery of Puget Sound* (Portland: Binfords and Mort, 1957): 61-334.

Broughton, W.R. "The Journal of a Tour across the Continent of New Spain from San Blas in the Northern Pacific Ocean to La Vera Cruz in the Gulph of Mexico by Lieut. W.R. Broughton, Commander of H.M. Brig *Chatham*, in the year 1793." National Maritime Museum/Royal United Services Institute, London, NMM/RUSI/132/2.

Caamaño Moraleja, Jacinto. "Extracto del diario de las navegaciones, exploraciones y descubrimientos hechos en la América Septentrional por D. Jacinto Caamaño, teniente de navío de la Real Armada y commandante de la fragata de su Majestad nombrada *Nuestra Señora de Aránzazu* desde el puerto de San Blas de donde serio en 20 de marzo del año 1792." BMAS, MSS 10 and 11, published in the series *Colección de Diarios y Relaciones para la Historia de los Viajes y Descubrimientos* by the Consejo Superior de Investigaciones Científicas, Instituto Histórico de la Marina, Madrid, no. 7 (1975). Other copy: AGN, Provincias Internas 134, Historia 71, published as Henry R. Wagner,W.A. Newcombe (eds.), and Harold Grenfell (trans.), "The Journal of Don Jacinto Caamaño," *British Columbia Historical Quarterly* 2 (July-Oct. 1938): 189-222, 265-301.

Menzies, Archibald. Full journal. British Library, Add. MS 32641. One portion published as Eastwood, Alice, ed., "Menzies' California Journal." *California Historical Society Quarterly* 2, no. 4 (1923-24): 265-340. Another portion published as C.F. Newcombe, ed. *Menzies' Journal of Vancouver's Voyage April to October 1792* (Victoria: Archives of British Columbia, Memoir 5, 1923). A third portion published as Wallace M. Olson and John F. Thilenius, eds., *The Alaska Travel Journal of Archibald Menzies, 1793-1794* (Anchorage: University of Alaska Press, 1993).

Moziño, José Mariano. *Noticias de Nutka: An Account of Nootka Sound in 1792*. Trans. and ed. Iris H. Wilson Engstrand. First published Toronto and Seattle: McClelland and Stewart and University of Washington Press, 1970. Reprint Vancouver and Seattle: Douglas and McIntyre and University of Washington Press, 1991.

Vancouver, Captain George. "Captain Vancouver's report to the Admiralty on the negotiations with Don Juan Francisco de la Bodega y Quadra at Nootka Sound in 1792." *Papers Relating to Nootka Sound and to Captain Vancouver's Expedition*, VII, 1914, Provincial Archives Department, Victoria, BC (off print or pamphlet of text of ms V-857, Public Record Office, London, England).

Other Sources

Anderson, Bern. *The Life and Voyages of George Vancouver: Surveyor of the Sea.* Toronto: University of Toronto Press, 1960.

Archer, Christon I. "Cannibalism in the Early History of the Northwest Coast: Enduring Myths and Neglected Realities." *Canadian Historical Review* 61 (1980): 453-79.

–. "In Defense of the King's Domain: Disease Prevention and Health Care in the Spanish

Maritime Expeditions to the North Pacific, 1774-1795." *Canadian Bulletin of Medical History* 3, no. 2 (Winter 1986): 185-205.

–. "The Making of Spanish Indian Policy on the Northwest Coast." *New Mexico Historical Review* 52 (1977): 45-69.

–. "The Political and Military Context of the Spanish Advance into the North Pacific Coast." In Inglis, *Spain and the North Pacific Coast*, 1992, pp. 9-17.

–. "Retreat from the North: Spain's Withdrawal from Nootka Sound, 1793-95." *B.C. Studies* 37 (Spring 1978): 19-36.

–. "Russians, Indians and Passages: Spanish Voyages to Alaska in the Eighteenth Century." In *Exploration in Alaska: Captain Cook Commemorative Lectures*, June-November 1978: 129-43. Anchorage: Cook Inlet Historical Society, 1980.

–. "Seduction before Sovereignty: Spanish Efforts to Manipulate the Natives in Their Claims to the Northwest Coast." In Fisher and Johnston, eds., *From Maps to Metaphors*, Chap. 7.

–. "The Spanish Reaction to Cook's Third Voyage." In Fisher and Johnston, eds., *Captain James Cook and His Times*, pp. 99-119. Vancouver: UBC Press, 1979.

–. "The Transient Presence: A Reappraisal of Spanish Attitudes Towards the Northwest Coast in the Eighteenth Century." *B.C. Studies* 18 (1973): 3-32.

Arellano, Diego R. de. "La Real Academia de Caballeros Guardias Marinas de Cádiz." *Revista de Historia Naval*, Madrid, October 1940: 45-56.

Arima, E.Y. *The West Coast People: The Nootka of Vancouver Island and Cape Flattery*. British Columbia Provincial Museum, Special Publication no. 6, 1983.

Arima, Eugene, and John Dewhirst. "Nootkans of Vancouver Island." In Wayne Suttles, vol. ed., *Handbook of North American Indians*, vol. 7, *The Northwest Coast*, pp. 391-411. Washington, DC: Smithsonian Institution, 1990.

Avery, William P. "An Imposing Array: Fact or Fiction?" *Mariner's Mirror* 70, no. 1 (February 1984): [n.p.].

Barrington, Daines, trans. *The Voyage of the* Sonora. Fairfield, WA: Ye Galleon Press, 1987. [Antonio Mourelle de la Rua's 1775 journal, "Segunda Exploración," translated and first published in 1781 by Daines Barrington; translation reprinted in 1920 by T.C. Russell, San Francisco; translation reprinted in 1987 by Ye Galleon Press.]

Bartroli, Tomas. "The Malaspina Expedition at Nootka." In Inglis, *Spain and the North Pacific Coast*, pp. 85-97.

Beaglehole, John C. *The Life of Captain James Cook*. Palo Alto: Stanford University Press, 1974.

–, ed. *The Journals of Captain James Cook*. 3 vols. London: Hakluyt Society, 1967.

Beals, Herbert K. "The Juan Pérez–Josef de Cañizares Map of the Northwest Coast." *Terrae Incognitae* 27 (1995): 46-56.

–. *Juan Pérez on the Northwest Coast*. Portland: Oregon Historical Society Press, 1989.

Beerman, Eric. "A Basque Sailor at Bucareli Bay." *Alaska Journal*, Autumn 1982: 45-51.

–. "Bruno de Heceta, the First European Discoverer of the Columbia River." *Pacific Historian* 23 (1979): 103-15.

–. "Manuel Quimper: Un marino limeño en la osta oeste de Canadá." *Derroteros de la Mar del Sur* 4, no. 4 (1996): 23-30.

–. "Manuel Quimper y Bodega y Quadra: Dos limeños al servicio de la Real Armada." In Palau et al., eds., *Nutka 1792*, pp. 32-43.

–. "Tomás de la Bodega y Quadra y su Testamento." In Palau et al., eds., *Nutka 1792*, pp. 44-46.

Bernabeu Albert, Salvador. "Bodega y Quadra o el instante frágil en el Noroeste, Un retrato inacabado." In Palau et al., eds., *Nutka 1792*, pp. 20-31.

–. *Juan Francisco de la Bodega y Quadra: El Descubrimiento del Fin del Mundo (1775-1792).* Madrid: Alianza Editorial, 1990.

–. "Juan Pérez, Navegante y Descubriador de las Californias." In Peset Reig, ed., *Culturas de la costa noroeste de América.*

–. "El Tratado de Tordesillas y su repercusión en el Tratado de Límites de 1792." In Palau et al., eds., *Nutka 1792*, pp. 47-59.

Blanca Carlier, José María. "El Cuerpo de Pilotos de la Armada." *Revista de Historia Naval,* August-September 1979: 165-73.

Bobb, Bernard. *The Viceregency of Antonio María Bucareli in New Spain, 1771-1779.* Austin: University of Texas Press, 1962.

Bolton, Herbert E. *Guide to Materials for the History of the United States in the Principal Archives of Mexico.* Washington, DC: Periodicals Service Co., 1913.

British Columbia Archives. "Papers Relating to Nootka Sound and to Captain Vancouver's Expedition." *Report of the Provincial Archives for the Year Ending December 31, 1913* (1914): 11-48.

Calderón, Quijano, and José Antonio Calderón. *Los Virreyes de Nueva España, 1787-1798.* Seville: Escuela de Estudios Hispano-Americanico, 1972.

Capoeman, Pauline K., ed. *Land of the Quinault.* Taholah: Quinault Indian Nation, 1990.

Cárdenas de la Peña, Enrique. *San Blas de Nayarit.* Mexico City: Talleres de la Nación, 1968.

Carretero Collado, Leoncio. "Yuquot, Ahaminaquis, Tsaxana: The Long Road of the Mowachaht to the Future." In Palau Marisa Calés, and Araceli Sánchez, eds., *Nootka: Regreso a una historia olvidada,* pp. 197-204. Madrid: Ministerio de Asuntos Exteriores, 2000.

Caster, James G. "The Earliest Spanish Explorations to the Pacific Northwest." PhD diss., University of New Mexico, Albuquerque, 1969.

Cepeda, Félix de. "Memoria de los Viages Europeas a la Costa Noroeste de América Septentrional," vol. 1, ff. 82-86. Catalogue 81/67 cp, Bancroft Library, Berkeley, CA.

Cerezo Martínez, Ricardo, ed. *La Expedición Malaspina.* Vols. 2(a) and 2(b) (Malaspina journal); vol. 9 (Bustamante journal). Spanish Ministry of Defence, Museo Naval, Madrid, and Lunwerg Editores, 9 vols., published at intervals, 1990-99.

Chapman, Charles Edward. "The Alta California Supply Ships, 1773-1776." *Southwestern Historical Quarterly* 19 (October 1915): 184-94.

–. *Catalogue of Materials in the Archivo General de Indias for the History of the Pacific Coast and the American Southwest.* Berkeley: University of California Press, 1919.

–. "The Difficulties of Maintaining the Department of San Blas, 1775-1777." *Southwestern Historical Quarterly* 20 (April 1916): 261-70.

–. *The Founding of Spanish California: The Northwestward Expansion of New Spain, 1687-1773.* New York: Macmillan, 1916.

–. *A History of California: The Spanish Period.* New York: Macmillan, 1921.

Clayton, Lawrence A. "The Maritime Trade of Peru in the Seventeenth Century." *Mariner's Mirror,* Spring 1986: 159-77.

Cook, Warren L. *Flood Tide of Empire: Spain and the Pacific Northwest, 1543-1819.* New Haven: Yale University Press, 1973.

Cutter, Donald C. *The California Coast: A Bilingual Edition of Documents from the Sutro Collection.* Norman: University of Oklahoma Press, 1969.

–. *California in 1792: A Spanish Naval Visit.* Norman: University of Oklahoma Press, 1990.

–. "California, Training Ground for Spanish Naval Heroes." *Southern California Historical Quarterly* 39 (June 1961): 109-22.

–. "Early Spanish Artists on the Northwest Coast." *Pacific Northwest Quarterly* 54 (October 1963): 150-57.

–, ed. *The Journal of Tomás de Suría on His Voyage with Malaspina to the Northwest Coast of America in 1791.* Fairfield, WA: Ye Galleon Press, 1980.

–. *Malaspina and Galiano: Spanish Voyages to the Northwest Coast, 1791 and 1792.* Vancouver: Douglas and McIntyre, 1991.

–. "Pedro Alberni y los primeros experimentos de agricultura científica en la costa nordoeste de Pacífico." *Revista de Historia Naval* 5, no. 18 (1987): 41-55.

–, ed. *The California Coast: A Bilingual Edition of Documents from the Sutro Collection.* Norman: University of Oklahoma Press, 1969.

David, Andrew, Felipe Fernández-Armesto, Carlos Novi, and Glyndwr Williams, eds. *The Malaspina Expedition, 1789-1794: The Journal of the Voyage by Alejandro Malaspina.* Vol. 1, *Cádiz to Panama.* London: Hakluyt Society, 2001.

–. *The Malaspina Expedition, 1789-1794: The Journal of the Voyage by Alejandro Malaspina.* Vol. 2, *Panama to the Philippines.* London: Hakluyt Society, 2002.

–. *The Malaspina Expedition, 1789-1794: The Journal of the Voyage by Alejandro Malaspina.* Vol. 3, *From Manila to Cádiz.* London: Hakluyt Society, 2004.

Dunmore, J., ed. *The Journal of Jean-François de Galaup de la Pérouse 1785-1788,* 2 vols. London: Hakluyt Society, 1994 (vol. 1); 1995 (vol. 2).

Edwards, Clinton R. "Wandering Toponyms: El Puerto de la Bodega and Bodega Bay." *Pacific Historical Review* 33 (August 1964): 253-72.

Effrat, Barbara S., and W.J. Langlois. *Nu·tka: Captain Cook and The Spanish Explorers on the Coast.* Sound Heritage 7(1). Victoria: Provincial Archives of British Columbia.

Engstrand, Iris H.W. "Los naturalistas Moziño y Maldonado y sus viajes a Nueva España." In Palau et al., eds., *Nutka 1792,* pp. 98-107.

–. *Spanish Scientists in the New World.* Seattle: University of Washington Press, 1981.

Escherich, William W. "Juan Francisco de la Bodega y Quadra in America, 1774-1794." Master's thesis, University of California, Berkeley, 1947.

Fireman, Janet R. "The Seduction of George Vancouver: A Nootka Affair." *Pacific Historical Review* 56, no. 3 (August 1987): 427-43.

–. "The Strange Career of Alejandro Jordán, Naval Chaplain – or Bagman Zealot in Spanish California?" Paper presented at the annual meeting of the American Historical Association, Cincinatti, December 28, 1988.

–. "Félix de Cepeda and North Pacific Exploration." Paper presented at the sixty-ninth annual meeting of the Canadian Historical Association, Victoria, May 29, 1990.

Fisher, Lillian Estelle, *The Last Inca Revolt, 1780-1783.* Norman: University of Oklahoma Press, 1966.

Fisher, Robin, and Hugh Johnston, eds. *From Maps to Metaphors: The Pacific World of George Vancouver.* Vancouver: UBC Press, 1993.

Fisher, Vivian C., trans. and ed. *Estéban José Martínez: His Voyage in 1779 to Supply Alta California.* Bancroft Library. Berkeley and Los Angeles: University of California Press, 2002.

Frézier, Amédée-François. *Voyage de la Mer du Sud aux Côtes du Chili et du Pérou.* Thizy: Editions Utz, 1995.

Frost, Alan. "Nootka Sound and the Beginnings of Britain's Imperialism of Free Trade." In Fisher and Johnston, eds., *From Maps to Metaphors,* Chap. 6.

Gibson, James R. "A Notable Absence: The Lateness and Lameness of Russian Discovery and Exploration in the North Pacific, 1639-1803." In Fisher and Johnston, eds., *From Maps to Metaphors,* Chap. 5.

–. *Otter Skins, Boston Ships, and China Goods: The Maritime Fur Trade of the Northwest Coast, 1785-1841.* Montreal and Kingston: McGill-Queen's University Press, 1992.

Gough, Barry M. *The Northwest Coast: British Navigation, Trade, and Discoveries to 1812.* Vancouver: UBC Press, 1992.

Gunther, Erna. *Indian Life on the Northwest Coast of North America.* Chicago: University of Chicago Press, 1972.

Gutiérrez Camarena, Marcial. *San Blas y las Californias.* Mexico City: Editorial Jus, 1956.

Haring, C.H. *The Spanish Empire in America.* New York: Harcourt Brace, 1947.

Harbron, John D. *Trafalgar and the Spanish Navy.* Annapolis: Naval Institute Press, 1988.

Harlow, Vincent. *The Founding of the Second British Empire, 1763-1793.* 2 vols. London: Longmans Green, 1952.

Hart, Catherine Poupeney. "Peregrinación por los mares del Norte, o la vindicación del criollo (Juan Francisco de la Bodega y Quadra, 1775)." *Colonial Latin American Review* 11, no. 1 (2002): 109-22.

Hayes, Edmund. "Gray's Adventure Cove." *Oregon Historical Quarterly* 68, no. 2 (June 1967).

Heizer, Robert F., and John E. Mills. *The Four Ages of Tsurai: A Documentary History of the Indian Village on Trinidad Bay.* Berkeley and Los Angeles: University of California Press, 1952.

Henry, John Frazier. *Early Maritime Artists of the Pacific Northwest Coast 1741-1841.* Vancouver: Douglas and McIntyre; Seattle, University of Washington Press, 1984.

Herr, Richard. *The Eighteenth-Century Revolution in Spain.* Princeton: Princeton University Press, 1958.

Hidalgo Sereno, Jacinto. "Un Viaje de descubriemiento por la costa Pacífico norteamericano," in *Revista de Indias* 21, 1961.

Higueras, María Dolores. *Costa NW de America: Album Iconográfico de la Expedición Malaspina.* Madrid: Museo Naval, 1991.

Howay, F.W. "The Journal of Captain James Colnett, 1789." *Transactions of the Royal Society of Canada,* Section 2, 1939: 91-102.

–. "A List of Trading Vessels in the Maritime Fur Trade, 1785-1794." *Proceedings of the Royal Society of Canada,* 3rd Series, Issues 24, 25, 26, 27, 28.

–. "Some Additional Notes upon Captain Colnett and the *Princess Royal.*" *Oregon Historical Quarterly* 16 (1925): 12-22.

Howay, F.W., ed. *The Journal of Captain James Colnett aboard the* Argonaut *from April 26, 1789, to November 3, 1791.* Toronto: Champlain Society, 1940.

–. *Voyages of the* Columbia *to the Northwest Coast, 1787-1790 and 1790-1793.* Reprint of 1941 Massachusetts Historical Society edition. Portland: Oregon Historical Society, 1990.

Humboldt, Alexander von. *Political Essay on the Kingdom of New Spain.* Vol. 2. London, 1811.

Inglis, Robin. "Otras dos iniciativas: Caamaño en Alaska y Fidalgo en Núñez Gaona." In Palau et al., eds., *Nutka 1792,* pp. 108-21.

–, ed. *Spain and the North Pacific Coast: Essays in Recognition of the Bicentennial of the Malaspina Expedition, 1791-1792.* Vancouver: Vancouver Maritime Museum Society, 1992.

Inglis, Richard, and James C. Haggerty, "Cook to Jewitt: Three Decades of Change in Nootka Sound," in Bruce Trigger, T. Morantz, and Louise Dechène, eds., *Le Castor fait tout: Selected Papers of the Fifth North American Fur Trade Conference 1985* (1987), pp. 193-222.

Inskip, Edward L. "San Blas, Nayarit: An Historical and Geographic Study." *Journal of the West* 1, no. 2 (1963): [n.p.].

Instituto Histórico de la Marina. *Colección de Diarios y Relaciones para la Historia de los Viajes y Descubrimientos.* Vol. 2, 1943, Vol. 5, 1964. Vol. 7, 1975. Madrid.

Jones, Oakah. "The Spanish Settlement at Nootka Sound." Master's thesis, University of Oklahoma, Norman, 1960.

Kaplanoff, Mark D., ed. *Joseph Ingraham's Journal of the Brigantine* Hope *on a Voyage to the Northwest Coast of America, 1790-1792.* Barre: Imprint Society, 1971.

Kendrick, John. "Españoles en el Estrecho de Fuca, Última exploración Alcalá Galiano y Cayetano Valdés, 1792." In Palau et al., eds., *Nutka 1792*, pp. 86-96.

–. *The Men with Wooden Feet: The Spanish Exploration of the Pacific Northwest.* Toronto: NC Press, 1985.

–. *The Voyage of* Sutil *and* Mexicana, *1792: The Last Spanish Exploration of the Northwest Coast of America.* Spokane: Arthur H. Clark, 1991.

Kendrick, John, and Robin Inglis. *Enlightened Voyages: Malaspina and Galiano on the Northwest Coast, 1791-1792.* Exhibition of the Vancouver Maritime Museum, Vancouver: 1991.

Kenyon, Malcolm A. "Naval Construction and Repair at San Blas, 1767-1797." Master's thesis, University of New Mexico, Albuquerque, 1965. BCPA Add. MS 1063.

Krell, Dorothy, et al., eds. *The California Missions: A Pictorial History.* Menlo Park: Sunset Books/Lane Publishing, 1979.

Kuykendall, Ralph S. "James Colnett and the *Princess Royal*." *Oregon Historical Quarterly*, March 1924: 36-52.

Lamb, W. Kaye, ed. *The Voyage of George Vancouver, 1791-1795.* 4 vols. London: Hakluyt Society, 1984.

Landín Carrasco, Amancio. *Mourelle de la Rua: Explorador del Pacífico.* Madrid: Ediciones Cultura Hispanica, 1979.

Langdon, Steve J. *The Native People of Alaska.* Anchorage: Greatland Graphics, 1993.

Laos, Cipriano A. *Lima, la Ciudad de los Virreyes.* Lima: [n.p.], 1928.

López González, Pedro. *La Población de Tepic, Bajo la Organización Regional (1530-1821).* Tepic: Universidad Autónoma de Nayarit, 1984.

Majors, Harry M. "The Heceta and Bodega Voyage of 1775." *Northwest Discovery* 1, no. 3 (August 1980): 208-52.

Manby, Thomas. *Journal of the Voyages of the H.M.S.* Discovery *and* Chatham. Fairfield, WA: Ye Galleon Press, 1992.

Manning, William Ray. "The Nootka Sound Controversy." *American Historical Association Annual Report for 1904:* 279-478.

Mariñas Otero, Luis. "El Incidente de Nutka." *Revista de Indias* 27 (1967): 335-407.

Marshall, Yvonne. "Dangerous Liaisons: Maquinna, Quadra, and Vancouver in Nootka Sound, 1790-5." In Fisher and Johnston, eds., *From Maps to Metaphors*, Chap. 8.

–. "A Political History of the Nuu-Chah-Nulth People: A Case Study of the Mowachaht and Muchalaht Tribes." PhD diss., Simon Fraser University, Burnaby, BC, 1993.

Martínez, Estéban José. *Diario* of his voyage to Nootka, 1789. Vol. 6 of *Colección de Diarios y Relaciones para la Historia de los Viajes y Descubrimientos.* Ed. Roberto Barreiro-Meiro. Madrid: Instituto Histórico de la Marina, 1964.

Martín-Merás, María Luisa. "The Evolution of Spanish Cartography on the Northwest Coast of America." In Inglis, ed., *Spain and the North Pacific Coast,* pp. 18-28.

Mathes, W. Michael. "Baja California Indians in the Spanish Maritime Service, 1720-1821." *Southern California Quarterly* 62, no. 11 (Summer 1980): 113-26.

–. *Vizcaino and Spanish Expansion in the Pacific Ocean, 1580-1630.* San Francisco: California Historical Society, 1968.

McBride, Delbert J. "Viewpoints and Visions in 1792." *Columbia,* Summer 1992: 21-27.

Meares, John. *Authentic Copy of the Memorial to the Right Honourable William Wyndham Grenville, One of His Majesty's Principal Secretaries of State, by Lieutenant John Mears* [sic], *of the Royal Navy; Dated 30th April, 1790, and Presented to the House of Commons, May 13, 1790. Containing Every Particular Respecting the Capture of the Vessels in Nootka Sound.* London, 1790. Portland: Nellie B. Pipes/Metropolitan Press, 1933.

–. *Voyages made in the Years 1788 and 1789 from China to the Northwest Coast of America.* Bibliotheca Australiana, No. 22. Amsterdam: Israel, 1967.

Meany, Edmond S. *Vancouver's Discovery of Puget Sound: Portraits and Biographies of the Men Honored in the Naming of Geographic Features of Northwestern America.* Portland: Binfords and Mort, 1957.

Menchaca Careaga, Antonio. *De California á Alaska: Vida y Descubrimientos de D. Juan Francisco de la Bodega y Quadra.* Madrid: Ediciones Cultura Hispánica, 1989.

–. "Juan Francisco de la Bodega y Quadra y su tiempo." In Palau et al., eds., *Nutka 1792,* pp. 2-18.

Miller, Beatrice D. "Neah Bay: The Makah in Transition." *Pacific Northwest Quarterly* 43 (October 1952).

Mills, Lennox. "The Real Significance of the Nootka Sound Incident." *Canadian Historical Review* 6 (1925): 110-22.

Mitchell, Donald. "The Investigation of Fort Defiance," *B.C. Studies* 4 (Spring 1970) and *B.C. Studies* 6 (Winter 1972-73).

Muría, José María, ed. *San Blas de Nayarit.* Proceedings of the conference, "San Blas de Nayarit en las Exploraciónes del noroeste de América," Tepic and San Blas, September 7-8, 1992. Zapopan: El Colegio de Jalisco, 1993.

Naish, John M. "The Achievements of Captain George Vancouver: A Reassessment after 200 Years." *Mariner's Mirror* 60, no. 4 (1994): 418-30.

–. *The Interwoven Lives of George Vancouver, Archibald Menzies, Joseph Whidbey, and Peter Puget: Exploring the Pacific Northwest Coast.* Canadian Studies, vol. 17. Lewiston, NY: Edwin Mellen, 1996.

Newcombe, C.F., ed. *Menzies' Journal of Vancouver's Voyage April to October 1792.* Victoria: Archives of British Columbia, Memoir 5, 1923; British Library, Add. MS 32641.

Nokes, J.R. *Almost a Hero: The Voyages of John Meares, R.N., to China, Hawaii, and the Northwest Coast.* Seattle: Washington State University Press, 1998.

Norris, J.M. "The Policy of the British Cabinet in the Nootka Crisis." *English Historical Review* 50 (1955): 562-80.

Novo y Colson, Pedro de, ed. *Viaje político-científico alredador del Mundo por las Corbetas* Descubierta *y* Atrevida *al Mando de los capitanes de navío Don Alejandro Malaspina y Don José Bustamante y Guerra desde 1789 a 1794*. Madrid: Imprenta de la Viuda e Hijos de Abienzo, 1885.

Ogden, Adele. *The California Sea Otter Trade, 1784-1848.* Berkeley: University of California Press, 1941.

–. "The Californias in Spain's Sea Otter Fur Trade, 1775-1795." *Pacific Historical Review* 1 (1932): 444-69.

Olson, Wallace M. *Through Spanish Eyes: Spanish Voyages to Alaska, 1774-1792.* Auk Bay, AK: Heritage Research, 2002.

Ortiz Sotelo, Jorge. "Juan Francisco de la Bodega y Quadra, los años inciales." *Derroteros de la mar Sur* 14 (2006): 135-46.

O'Scanlón, Timóteo. *Diccionário Marítimo Español.* Originally printed, 1831. Reprint ed. Madrid: Museo Naval, 1974.

Palacio Atard, Vicente, ed. *España y la Mar en el Siglo de Carlos III.* Madrid: [n.p.], 1989.

Palau, Mercedes, and José Alcina Franch. "Introducción a los viajes españoles a la Costa Noroeste y Nutka." In Palau et al., eds., *Nutka 1792*, pp. 122-35.

Palau, Mercedes, and Antonio Orozco, eds. *Malaspina '92: Jornadas Internacionales, Madrid–Cadiz–La Coruña, 1992.* Cadiz: Real Academia Hispano Americana/Spanish Ministry of Foreign Affairs, 1994.

Palau, Mercedes, Freeman Tovell, Pamela Sprätz, and Robin Inglis, eds. *Nutka 1792.* Edition produced by the Dirección General de Relaciones Culturales y Científicas of the Spanish Ministry of Foreign Affairs. Madrid: Spanish Ministry of Foreign Affairs, 1998.

Palou, Fray Francisco. *Historical Memoirs of New California.* 4 vols. Ed. Herbert Bolton. Berkeley: University of California Press, 1926. Translation from the manuscript in the archives of Mexico.

Parel, Christian de. "Pitt et l'Espagne." *Revue d'histoire diplomatique* 46 (1950): 58-98.

Patrick, Elizabeth N. "The Salvador Fidalgo Expedition, 1790: The Last Spanish Exploration of the Far North Pacific Ocean." PhD diss., University of New Mexico, Albuquerque, 1981.

Paula Pavia, Francisco de. *Galeria Biográfica de los Generales de marina, jefes y personajes notables que figuraron en la misma desde 1700 a 1868.* 4 vols. Madrid: López, 1873-74.

Peset Reig, José Luis, ed. *Culturas de la costa noroeste de América.* Madrid: Ediciones Turner, 1989.

Pethick, Derek. *First Approaches to the Northwest Coast.* Vancouver: J.J. Douglas, 1975.

–. *The Nootka Connection: Europe and the Northwest Coast, 1790-1795.* Vancouver: Douglas and McIntyre, 1980.

Priestly, Herbert I. *José de Gálvez, Visitador General of New Spain.* Berkeley: University of California Press, 1916.

Prieto, Carlos. *El Oceano Pacífico: Navigantes Españoles del Siglo XVI.* Madrid: Alianza Editorial, 1975.

Pritchard, William E., and Diane Spencer-Hancock. "El Castillo de Monterey: Frontline of Defence." *California History*, Summer 1984: 230-40.

Ruby, Robert H., and John A. Brown. *A Guide to the Indian Tribes of the Pacific Northwest.* Norman: University of Oklahoma Press, 1986.

Sánchez, Joseph P. "Pedro de Alberni and the Spanish Claim to Nootka: The Catalonian Volunteers on the Northwest Coast." *Pacific Northwest Quarterly*, April 1980: 72-77.

–. *Spanish Bluecoats: The Catalonian Volunteers in Northwestern New Spain, 1767-1810*. Albuquerque: University of New Mexico Press, 1990.

Schurz, William A. "The Spanish Lake." *Hispanic American Historical Review* 5 (1922): 181-94.

Servín, Manuel P., ed. and trans. "The Instructions of Viceroy Bucareli to Ensign Juan Pérez." *California Historical Society Quarterly* 40 (September 1961): 237-48.

Soler Pascual, Emilio. "El lento declinar del Imperio español y la crisis política de Nutka." In Palau et al., eds., *Nutka 1792*, pp. 60-71.

Sotos Serrano, Carmen. *Los Pintores de la Expedición Malaspina*. 2 vols. Madrid: Real Academia de Historia, 1982.

Stewart, Charles L. "Martínez and López de Haro on the Northwest Coast, 1788-1789." PhD diss., University of California, Berkeley, 1936.

–. "Why the Spaniards Temporarily Abandoned Nootka Sound in 1792." *Canadian Historical Review*, June 1936: 168-73.

Stewart, Hilary, ed., *The Adventures and Sufferings of John R. Jewitt, Captive of Maquinna*. Vancouver: Douglas and McIntyre, 1987.

Suttles, Wayne, ed. *Handbook of North American Indians*. Vol. 7, *The Northwest Coast*. Washington: Smithsonian Institution, 1990.

Taylor, Paul S. "Spanish Seamen in the New World during the Colonial Period." *Hispanic American Historical Review* 5 (1922): 631-61.

Thurman, Michael E. "The Establishment of the Department of San Blas and Its Initial Naval Fleet," *Hispanic American Historical Review* 43, no. 1 (February 1963): 65-77.

–. "Juan Bodega y Quadra and the Spanish Retreat from Nootka 1790-1794." *Reflections of the Western Historians: Papers of the 7th Annual Conference of the Western History Association, 1967*. Tucson, 1969: 49-63.

–. *The Naval Department of San Blas: New Spain's Bastion for Alta California and Nootka, 1767-1798*. Glendale, CA: Arthur H. Clark, 1967.

Tovell, Freeman M. "Bodega y Quadra and Vancouver: A Contrast in Personalities." *Columbia*, Spring 1990: 16-21.

–. "Bodega y Quadra, the Foremost Spanish Naval Officer of the Pacific Northwest." *Resolution*, Fall 1995: 4-9, and Spring 1996: 4-8.

–. "Bodega y Quadra in Canada: An Enduring Legacy." *Derroteros de la Mar del Sur*, Lima, Peru, 1996: 85-93.

–. *Bodega y Quadra Returns to the Americas*. Burnaby: Simon Fraser University, 1990.

–. "The Career of Bodega y Quadra: A Summation of the Spanish Contribution to the Heritage of the Northwest Coast." In Inglis, ed., *Spain and the North Pacific Coast*, pp. 172-80.

–. "Chief Maquinna and Bodega y Quadra." *British Columbia Historical News* 34, no. 4 (Fall 2001): 8-14.

–. "Ending the Search for the Mythical Passage of Admiral Fonte: The 1792 Voyage of Jacinto Caamaño." *B.C. Studies*, Spring 1998: 5-26.

–. "The Heceta-Bodega Voyage of 1775: Its Significance for Spain's Presence in the Pacific Northwest." *Terrae Incognitae* 27 (1995): 57-65.

–. "Manuel Quimper's Exploration of the Strait of Juan de Fuca." *Resolution*, May 1990: 14-26.

–. "The Other Side of the Coin: The Viceroy, Bodega y Quadra, Vancouver, and the Nootka Crisis." *B.C. Studies,* May 1992: 3-29.

–. "Planning for Discovery: The Career of Bodega y Quadra." *Mains'l Haul* 36, no. 1 (Winter 2000): 23-37.

–. "Rivales y amigos, Quadra y Vancouver." In Palau et al., eds., *Nutka 1792,* pp. 72-84.

Wagner, Henry R. "Apocryphal Voyages to the Northwest Coast of America." In *Proceedings of the American Antiquarian Society,* 1931: 179-234.

–. *Cartography of the Northwest Coast of America to 1800.* 2 vols. Berkeley, 1937. Reprinted in one volume. Amsterdam: Israel, 1968.

–. "Creation of Rights of Sovereignty through Symbolic Acts." *Pacific Historical Review* 7 (1938): 297-326.

–. "The Last Spanish Exploration of the Northwest Coast and the Attempt to Colonize Bodega Bay." *California Historical Society Quarterly* 9 (December 1931): 313-45.

–. *Spanish Explorations in the Strait of Juan de Fuca.* Santa Ana: Fine Arts Press, 1933.

–. *Spanish Voyages to the Northwest Coast in the Sixteenth Century.* San Francisco: California Historical Society, 1929.

Webb, Paul. "The Naval Aspects of the Nootka Sound Crisis." *Mariner's Mirror* 61 (1975): 133-54.

Williams, Glyndwr. *The British Search for the Northwest Passage in the Eighteenth Century.* Imperial Publications Series 24. London: Royal Commonwealth Society, 1962.

Ybarra y Berge, Javier de. *De California á Alaska: Historia de un Descubrimiento.* Madrid: Instituto de Estudios Politicos, 1945.

Zuluaga Citores, Ángel. *Sebastián de la Quadra: Primer Marqués de Villarías, Secretario de Estado en el reinado de Filipe V, 1687-1766.* Editado con la colaboración de Petróleos de Norte, S.A. (Petronor) y del Ayuntamiento de Muskiz. Santander: Ediciones Tantin, 2000.

Zulueta, Julián de. "Trafalgar – The Spanish View." *Mariner's Mirror,* November 1980: 293-315.

Index

Printed and bound in Canada by Friesens

Set in Adobe Garamond by Robert Kroeger, Kroeger Enterprises

Copy editor: Matthew Kudelka

Proofreader: Desne Ahlers

Indexer: Adrian Mather